marketing research

tools & techniques

Isabelle and Jonathan, this book is dedicated to you

marketing research

tools & techniques

third edition

Nigel Bradley

OXFORD
UNIVERSITY PRESS

Great Clarendon Street, Oxford, OX2 6DP,
United Kingdom

Oxford University Press is a department of the University of Oxford. It furthers the University's objective of excellence in research, scholarship, and education by publishing worldwide. Oxford is a registered trade mark of Oxford University Press in the UK and in certain other countries

First Edition copyright 2007
Second Edition copyright 2010

Impression: 1

British Library Cataloguing in Publication Data
Data available

ISBN 978-0-19-965509-0

Printed in Italy by
L.E.G.O. S.p.A.—Lavis TN

Brief contents

Detailed contents

About the author

Copyright Chris Haydon, Alanbri

Nigel Bradley is a senior lecturer in marketing at Westminster Business School at the University of Westminster. During his time at the University, he has led modules in marketing research, digital age marketing, principles of marketing, marketing management, promotional management, and research methods for management, and has supervised student research at undergraduate, Master's, and doctorate levels.

With a Master of Science in Product Management and Marketing from Cranfield, Nigel began his career with the Burke Research Services Group, where he worked on agricultural and industrial market research studies. Following this, he joined a packaging machinery company in Italy as an OEM product manager with a particular emphasis on liaising with non-Italian partners.

On his return to the UK, Nigel became an associate director with BJM Research and Consultancy, where he helped to build a profitable research unit based on qualitative and quantitative research studies. He was later invited back to the Burke Research Services Group (now demerged under a new name—Research Services Ltd) to head the International Division, in which role he was responsible for securing significant new projects and clients, and implementing systems to increase productivity and reduce costs. Before leaving for Harrow Business School, he changed direction and moved to the media department of Research Services Ltd, where he assumed day-to-day responsibility for the National Readership Survey (NRS) and the British Business Readership Survey.

Nigel's academic research interests include green marketing, Internet marketing, media research, graphology, and 'de-marketing'.

In addition to his university teaching, Nigel is a Chartered Marketer and works as a marketing research consultant to research agencies. He is also an examiner for both the Chartered Institute of Marketing and the Market Research Society, and is a regular peer reviewer of articles for the *International Journal of Market Research*.

Nigel Bradley, 2012

Sadly, Nigel Bradley passed away as this edition was going to press. He was a valued author who will be sorely missed by all who worked with him at Oxford University Press. A tribute to Nigel can be found in the Author Information section of the title's webpage.

About the book

Market for this book

Marketing Research: Tools and Techniques has been written for university students who are taking an introductory module in marketing research as part of their business programme. The book draws on the author's years of teaching as a university lecturer and working as a market research practitioner, and endeavours to accommodate the core developments in the industry without losing its pedagogical focus.

This book has also been used extensively by students outside of the formal education system who are continuing their professional education at such institutions as the Market Research Society (MRS), the Chartered Institute of Marketing (CIM), the Communications and Marketing Foundation (CAM Foundation), and ESOMAR.

This book has been informed by both university students and practitioners. Focus groups held with undergraduates have yielded great insight into the learning needs of marketing research students and have been instrumental in guiding the preparation of this book; equally, the experiences and advice of marketing practitioners have influenced the direction of the text and formed the basis of the many rich research examples and case studies that you will see in each chapter.

Drawing throughout on the author's concept of the marketing research mix, the text is organised around the core themes of research preparation, data collection, analysis and communication of findings, and how skills and techniques are used by researchers to offer services for specific contexts.

Distinguishing features

This book contains a number of key distinguishing features that set it apart from comparable texts. Namely, it achieves the following:

- It provides a balance between the theoretical and practical sides of marketing research, thereby showing students how to 'do' market research, and encouraging them to be analytical and critical in their thinking.
- It includes real research tools and examples of poor or mishandled research practice, demonstrating what is 'unacceptable' in marketing research and not only what is exemplary.
- It offers numerous case studies and examples of marketing research in action, to help contextualise the subject and relate it to the student experience.
- It demystifies topics that have been overcomplicated in other texts and makes the world of marketing research much more accessible to newcomers to the subject.

- It bridges the gap between introductory, lower level texts and those taking a more rigorous, theoretical approach, ensuring students engage with the issues involved in marketing research while presenting material in an accessible manner.

The research environment

Market research is essential for strategic decision-making and business success. At the level of the individual, there is a need to develop skills in seeking information and understanding market issues, and to be able to assess the quality of information obtained and combine it with business instinct to make strong, strategic decisions. At the level of the company, there is a need to understand the competitive environment, to seize market opportunities where they exist, and to be more productive. The corporations with access to the right information can use their knowledge to achieve any objective; without information, the marketer depends on guesswork and intuition alone. There are many examples of product failures that might have been avoided with access to better market intelligence or through interpreting marketing research more accurately. At a national level, knowledge derived from research is essential in guiding social and business policy.

As such, *Marketing Research: Tools and Techniques* has been written with strategic decision-making in mind and driven by the combined needs of students and practitioners, in the hope that it forms an essential toolkit for business success.

The third edition

You will enjoy this third edition. It differs from previous editions in the following ways:

- All chapters have been examined and the length of box features and reading lists has been standardised to create similar-sized chapters and content.
- Careful rewriting, rather than deletion, has resulted in a saving of pages. For example, the 'short history' sections have been moved to the chapter introduction and learning outcomes have been made consistent across chapters.
- In the past few years all aspects of research have been transformed by digital developments. There has been a greater use of technology by researchers; we have seen the arrival of crowdsourcing, gamification, open data, infographics, neuroscience, MROCs, social media monitoring, and more sophisticated web analytics techniques. Every chapter has been examined and modified to accommodate such recent developments.
- Case material has been 'refreshed' and updated.
- The online research methods chapter in the second edition has been integrated into the main chapters at the most appropriate points. Similarly the previous chapter dedicated to social research has been embedded across the main text.
- A new chapter, called Web metrics, is devoted to social media monitoring and web analytics techniques.

Nigel Bradley,
Harrow, 2012.

How to use this book

Chapter guide

This chapter looks at marketing research in general and distinguishes between the terms *market* and *marketing* research. It also explains 'insight management'. By way o a description of how this industry operates across the

Chapter guide

A mini table of contents can be found at the beginning of each chapter to help guide you through the different topics you will encounter in this section of the book. This will enable you to quickly navigate your way around specific themes and issues.

Learning outcomes

By the end of this chapter, you should be able to:

Explain each stage of the research process using th as a framework

Learning outcomes

Each chapter opens with a series of learning outcomes which provide a route map through the chapter and the goals of each section, so that you know what you can expect to achieve as you progress through the chapter.

Introduction

The term 'primary data' is used to describe information purpose. Secondary data are best remembered as 'secon 'old' primary data. Good researchers start with secondary research studies.

Introduction

At the beginning of each chapter you will find an introduction offering a brief overview of the subject topic and key issues to be covered in that section of the book.

SNAPSHOT
Gamification in research

Game playing has become an important pastime for Internet users worldwide. In recent years we have seen the word 'gamification' used in business circles, it has been heavily discussed as a mechanism that can be applied to 'non-gaming' to motivate

Opening snapshots

Each opening snapshot offers a profile of an organisation from around the world and explores how that organisation has sourced and utilised market information to further its marketing strategy.

Research in focus
The National Student Sur

A researcher's job is not an easy one. Modern life seems to have affected our willingness to cooperate with interviewers. There has been a fall in response rates. The National Student Survey (the NSS)

'Research in focus' boxes

'Research in focus' boxes illustrate the everyday activities of real research agencies and client companies, and will enhance your understanding of the role that research plays in decision-making.

Common mistakes
Randomly using the term '

We come across the word 'random' in everyday speech. something on purpose'. For example, the police stop motc see whether the driver has consumed alcohol. They make street. In most cases, they are stopping people because th perform these checks at a particular time of day, in partic

'Common mistakes' boxes

'Common mistakes' boxes identify some of the most common errors made in the real world of commercial research, and will help you avoid these pitfalls during your own course of study.

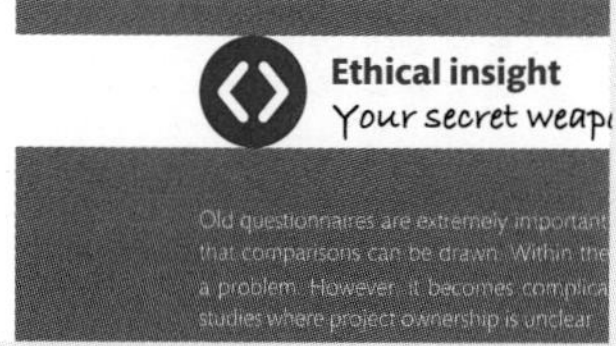

'Ethical insight' boxes

'Ethical insight' boxes present ethical considerations involved in being a market researcher, with content drawn from codes of conduct distributed by professional entities such as MRS/ESOMAR.

Chapter summary

1 Explain the purpose of qualitative research
Qualitative research involves using techniques that attempt
existence and nature of attitudes, interests, and opinions. It
may give an indication of dominant motivators. Qualitative
guidelines. It centres on words, narrative, images, and conce
There is an emphasis on understanding rather than measure

Chapter summary

At the end of every chapter you will find a summary which includes a list of numbered statements to help reiterate key points from that section.

Review questions

1 Explore the difference between the group and the depth in
2 In qualitative research, an understanding of euphemisms is
3 In what circumstances might we decide not to use qualitati
4 Researchers have been criticised for placing too much emp
5 Define these terms using examples: ethnography, semiol
theory.

Review questions

At the end of every chapter you will find a set of carefully devised review questions to help you refresh yourself on the central themes and assess your understanding of the topic.

Discussion questio

1 What would be the implications of quantifying results from
2 How could qualitative analysis research software be u
provided by dealers in the automotive market?
3 Plan a simple table to analyse data that looked into wh
particular can sizes.
4 Consult the proposal in the Market Researcher's Tooll

Discussion questions

Test your topic knowledge using the discussion questions provided at the end of each chapter. These will not only test your understanding of core concepts, but also help you to develop and improve your analytical and debating skills by prompting group discussion.

Further reading

- Gordon, W. and Langmaid, R. (1988) *Qualitative Market Re Buyer's Guide*. Aldershot, Hants: Gower.
Useful tips in the area of qualitative research reporting. C
research books that give information that can be turned
- Hague, P. and Roberts, C. (1994) *Presentation and Report W*
Written by practitioners, so there are some useful tips.

Further reading and key web links

At the end of each chapter you will find a list of suggested further reading which will direct you to key academic literature in the field to help you find out more about the issues covered within each chapter.

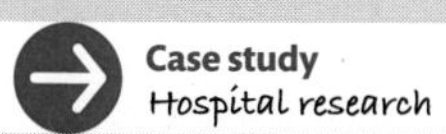

On its website, BMI Healthcare describes
itself as the UK's number one private
hospital group. It operates over 70 hospitals
and clinics across the country and is owned
by General Healthcare Group (GHG).

End-of-chapter case study

Core chapters are supplemented by a short case study that is designed to reinforce your understanding of core chapter themes through a number of real and contrived research situations.

Market researcher's toolbox

The Market researcher's toolbox can be found at the end of the book and contains a series of checklists and templates that will serve as useful models in your own marketing research.

How to use the Online Resource Centre

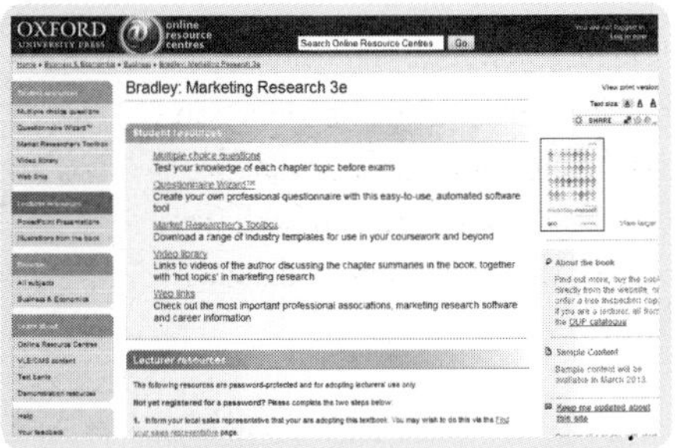

www.oxfordtextbooks.co.uk/orc/bradley3e/

For students

Question 1

Which ONE of these is NOT one of the four Ps of the original marketing m
by McCarthy in the late 1950s?

a) Product.
b) Price.
c) Publication.
d) Place.

Question 2

Which ONE of these is a technique useful in project planning?

a) SERT.
b) SPERT.

Multiple-choice questions

The best way to reinforce your understanding of marketing research is through frequent and cumulative revision. A selection of multiple-choice questions has been provided for each chapter, offering you instant feedback on your responses and cross-references to the textbook to assist you with your studies.

Questionnaire Wizard™

Download Questionnaire Wizard™

The dobney.com Questionnaire Wizard™ has been produced to simplify th
professional market research surveys. The Questionnaire Wizard™ is very
allowing you to choose your preferred type of survey and customising the qu
want to ask to suit your particular product or service.

You can output your survey in Word or in HTML format, to enable you to coll
information over the Internet, either by adding the questionnaire to your webs
attaching the form to an e-mail enabling respondents to complete the survey
return data at the push of a button.

Output can also be exported to other survey packages via the Triple S (.SSS
survey interchange, making the Questionnaire Wizard™ compatible with su
packages such as SNAP, Quantime and Bellview.

Questionnaire Wizard™

Questionnaire Wizard™ is an automated software tool created by dobney.com to simplify the creation of professional market research surveys and assist you in creating your own. Simply decide the type of questionnaire you want to carry out, enter some basic details about your product or service, and then at the click of a button you can obtain your first professional questionnaire.

Market Researcher's Toolbox

This toolbox contains a range of templates and checklists to help you in your
and in your future career as a market researcher. Click on the links below to
files in PDF format.

- Questions to ask about secondary data
- Options for primary data capture
- Considerations for qualitative group facility
- Website evaluation form
- Common screener questions
- Common rating scales
- Common classification questions

Online version of the Market researcher's toolbox

The Market researcher's toolbox that appears at the back of the book has been reproduced in electronic format on the website to provide you with immediate access to the checklists and templates that you will need throughout your course and in your future career as a market researcher.

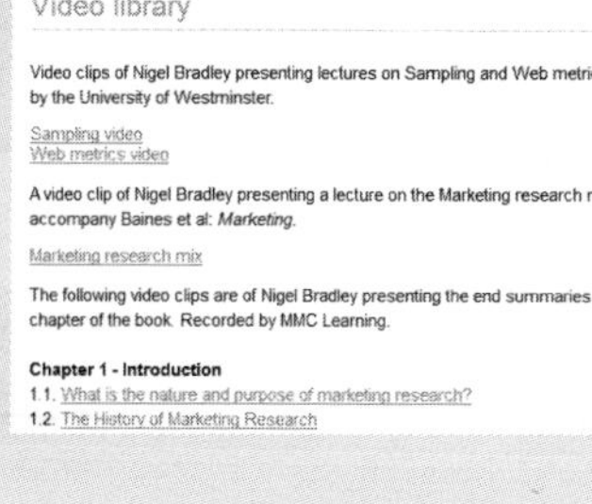

Video library

Video clips of Nigel Bradley presenting lectures on Sampling and Web metrics by the University of Westminster.

Sampling video
Web metrics video

A video clip of Nigel Bradley presenting a lecture on the Marketing research mix accompany Baines et al: *Marketing*.

Marketing research mix

The following video clips are of Nigel Bradley presenting the end summaries to chapter of the book. Recorded by MMC Learning.

Chapter 1 - Introduction
1.1. What is the nature and purpose of marketing research?
1.2. The History of Marketing Research

Links to YouTube clips of the author summarising the contents of each chapter

To reinforce your understanding of certain topics and marketing research concepts, watch these author summary clips on YouTube.

http://www.mrs.org.uk/
The Market Research Society is the professional society for UK practitioners. The contains the MRS Code of Conduct, which gives practical advice on research eth

http://www.research-live.com/
This is the official online magazine of the MRS, containing news of agencies and excellent articles on research techniques.

http://www.esomar.org/
ESOMAR is the professional society for world practitioners, with a European bias site includes a great deal of information including the ESOMAR Code of Conduct specific guidelines.

http://www.dataprotection.gov.uk/
This site explains Data Protection Legislation in a practical way. Use the menu to Data Protection Act and the Freedom of Information pages.

http://www.mrweb.com/

Web links

A series of annotated web links will point you in the direction of marketing research agencies, professional associations, directories, marketing research software, and important career information to help keep you up-to-speed with the latest developments in the field.

For registered adopters

Types of research

- Many projects concern food, drink, pharmaceutical, health and beauty produ
- Most are "ad hoc", the rest are continuou
- Face to Face quantitative is favoured in Europe whereas North America favours telephone quantitative studies.
- 80% are quantitative and 20% qualitative
- Group discussion dominates qualitative

PowerPoint slides

The author has provided a suite of customisable PowerPoint slides to assist with your lecture presentations. These are conveniently arranged by chapter theme and can also be used as handouts in class.

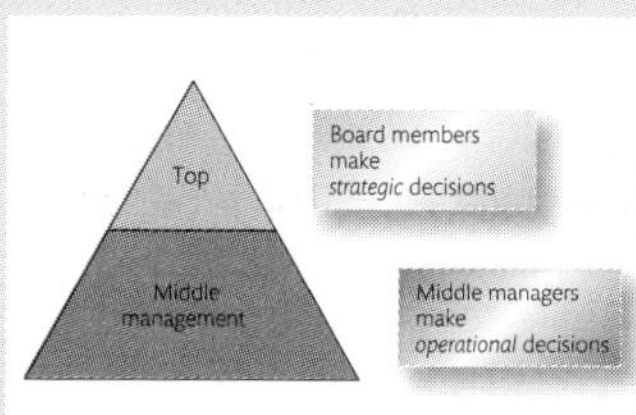

Figure 1.1 The management hierarchy

Illustrations from the book

These have been provided for your ease of use—you can insert them into your PowerPoint slides or simply show them to students on screen.

Acknowledgements

Preparation of the book has been guided by numerous educators, students, and practitioners, many of whom are named below. Sometimes, this guidance has been clear and obvious; at other times, these contributions may have been made unwittingly.

A special acknowledgement must go to my friends at the Market Research Society (MRS), the Chartered Institute of Marketing (CIM), and the CAM Foundation.

Academic publishers are extremely important to universities: they make much material available and they facilitate a great deal of peer review to ensure that books are accurate and match the needs of the marketplace. This text clearly owes much to Oxford University Press and my colleagues there.

Here are some people I wish to thank personally: Alan Wilson, Alison Bradley, Alison Rieple, Angela Adams, Anita O'Brien, Anna Zacharewicz, Ashok Ranchhod, Betty Adamou, Brian Clifton, Charles Hofacker, Charles Nixon, Chris Haydon, Clare Nash, David Lambert, David Lane, Dawn Southgate, Debrah Harding, Dennis R. Mortensen, Douglas Johnson, Elaine Clarke, Erhard Meier, Ernst Pattynama, Gerard Giminez, Gill Kelley, Greg Smith, Guy Consterdine, Helen Batley, Ian Brace, Ian Catchpole, Imran Farooq, Jackie Lynch, Jane Clayton, Jim Sterne, John Goodyear, John O'Connor, John Slevin, John Stockley, Jon Pike, Judith Kennedy, June Davies, Karen Adams, Kevin Ford, Luke Brynley-Jones, Martin Stoll, Mary Goodyear, Martin Oxley, Michael Brown, Nadia Bunten, Nicki Sneath, Pat Neviani-Aston, Paul Szwarc, Peter Chisnall, Peter Mouncey, Peter Palij, Phyllis Vangelder, Richard Bower, Richard Eldershaw, Richard Windle, Robert Kirby, Robert Tamilia, Roger Palmer, Rowland Lloyd, Sacha Cook, Seth Godwin, Shane Minett, Sharon Mire, Sophie Hartley, Stéphane Hamel, Steve Carter, and Xavier Brandt.

Very often, people move away from their employers, but the organisation itself surely deserves a mention, so here are some such organisations that have shaped the content of this book in some way: BJM, BP, Burke, BuzzBack Research, Cambridge Marketing Colleges, Chartered Institute of Marketing (CIM), Communications and Advertising Foundation (CAM), Cranfield University, ELMAR AMA, ESOMAR, Euromed Marseille, Google, IPSOS, Market Research Society (MRS), Middlesex University, Mintel, National Readership Survey Ltd, News International, Research Services Ltd (RSL), Southbank University, Taylor Nelson Sofres (TNS), The Cartoon Art Trust Museum, *The Financial Times*, *The Guardian*, *The Telegraph*, University of Derby, University of Quebec at Montreal, University of Westminster, University of Strathclyde, and Yahoo!

Part

1

Research preparation

1 Introduction to marketing research

Contents

Chapter guide

This chapter looks at marketing research in general and distinguishes between the terms *market* and *marketing* research. It also explains 'insight management'. By way of a description of how this industry operates across the world, we discover who commissions research and how much money is spent. International suppliers and trade bodies are introduced, along with the types of research and services available. There are many specialisms in this sector, so a description of jobs that exist should help you to plan your career path.

Learning outcomes

By the end of this chapter, you should be able to:

1 **Explain the nature and purpose of marketing research**

2 **Summarise the industry structure and list the different types of research service available**

3 **Show what must be considered when using research in marketing decision-making**

4 **Articulate the career opportunities available in marketing research**

Introduction

Understanding the general nature of marketing is essential before we can hope to understand market investigation. General textbooks on marketing expand on these foundations and you should have a solid grounding in these principles before proceeding with a study of marketing research. In the UK, the Chartered Institute of Marketing (CIM) defines **marketing** as *'the management process responsible for identifying, anticipating and satisfying customer requirements profitably'.* Mentioning the words 'identifying' and 'anticipating' captures the substance of market inquiry. The definition alludes to description and **forecasting**, both of which are core elements of marketing research.

Marketing research concerns inquiry into marketing; it looks at the different aspects considered when satisfying requirements. So far, we have only mentioned the term *marketing* research; it is time for a subtle difference to be introduced. There is another term, and that is ***market* research**—note the absence of the *-ing* from this word. The two terms—market research and marketing research—coexist; some academics distinguish between the two. *Market* research looks at specific marketplaces; it describes users in those markets and how much product they may use. It is an examination of what we know as **marketing metrics**—in other words, measurements taken in the marketplace. It is one part of the broad definition of 'marketing research'.

On the other hand, ***marketing* research** is the thing that assists the management function called 'marketing', it helps to fine-tune the marketing mix, and it embraces all activities that lead to meeting customer requirements. It helps to match supply with demand; it matches suppliers with customers in the broadest sense. You should accept, however, that the two terms—market research and marketing research—are often used interchangeably.

Let us turn to the 1950s, with research carried out in the area of consumer marketing for fast-moving consumer goods (FMCG). The market researcher offered information through qualitative research and also quantitative studies. The qualitative studies were typically group or single interviews and the quantitative studies were **usage and attitude studies**. In the 1960s, the **marketing information system (MKIS)** was brought to the world of management. Also, there was interest in researching **non-domestic markets**. It was sensible to apply what had been learnt in consumer markets.

In the 1970s, the concept of 'non-profit marketing' emerged. Quantitative research continued to grow. In this decade the **marketing decision support system (MDSS)** was introduced to assist executives at an individual level.

In the 1980s, cheap computer power allowed researchers to use information technology to good effect. This allowed automated data capture, first by **computer-assisted telephone interviewing (CATI)**, then by interviewers in the field with **computer-assisted personal interviewing (CAPI)**. There was an interest in researching service quality measures and **total quality management (TQM)**. Therefore, research was turning inside, towards the organisation, and some called this *internal marketing* research.

The internationalisation of research suppliers took place in the 1990s as many agencies expanded across national boundaries. Linked computer networks led to more online activities. This involved easier liaison between clients and suppliers, virtual presentations, online reporting, and also automated, online data capture, whether by **computer-assisted web interviewing (CAWI)**, by mobile (cell) phone interviewing or by other means. This was accompanied by the growing interest in researching satisfaction.

In the 2000s, technological solutions made it possible to understand customers at an individual level. **Databases** and **data mining** led to the emergence of 'insight management'. In the 2010s online activities have grown and web metrics have become important.

Table 1.1 Notable events for marketing

Years	Focus of marketing	Focus of research
1950s	Consumer marketing	Qualitative + U&A studies
1960s	Industrial marketing	MKIS, Desk research, FMCG
1970s	Non-profit and social marketing	Quantitative, MDSS
1980s	Services marketing	TQM, CATI, and CAPI
1990s	Customer relationship marketing	Satisfaction monitors
2000s	Marketing to individuals	Data mining, Insight, CAWI
2010s	Online marketing	Web metrics

Source: Adapted from Christopher *et al.* 2002. Reproduced with kind permission

SNAPSHOT
A leading bank uses research

This box describes one of the first UK banks to establish a formal market research department; in the present day many teams of people provide insight and research data. The bank employs 155,000 people across 50 countries and serves more than 48 million customers. In the UK alone around 14 million people have accounts with the bank. These segment down in various ways and two particularly interesting sectors are 580,000 small businesses and 280,000 affluent customers. Not to forget 180 medium and large sized businesses.

© istockphoto.com/kelvinjay

With this impressive set of numbers it is inevitable that the bank takes research seriously. Research is used to help the bank to assess client satisfaction, to test new products and to test promotion. It is also used to help customers and clients in their own decision-making, particularly with regard to money matters.

6

Employees benefit directly from research. The three main clusters are Investment Banking, Commercial Banking and Group Centre, employee surveys are carried out with people working in these three areas. In the 2008 survey, 91 per cent of employees expressed their views.

Compiled by Nigel Bradley 2012.

Research for the company

One definition of market research comes from the UK Market Research Society: '... *one of the most useful tools in business, any business. It is the way in which organisations find out what their customers and potential customers need, want and care about*'.

It is because of research that some lawnmowers are orange and it is the reason that most food we eat is not blue. For a member of the general public, research is the reason why adverts are memorable. Research is the reason why the battery manufacturer Duracell uses a dancing rabbit toy in promotions. It is why Ford named their motor car the Focus. It is the reason why milk is placed well inside supermarkets. Research helps to develop products, promotions, prices, and even the places used to distribute product.

Power in organisations comes from the control of knowledge and, in turn, this knowledge stems from information. Marketing research therefore equates to power. In most corporate management structures there is a hierarchy, and decision-making directly corresponds to this structure. We can envisage this as a pyramid, at the apex of which are board members, commonly known as 'top management'. This level includes the so-called C-Level executives: individuals who have the word 'chief' in their job title, these are highly influential. Below the board there are numerous individuals, known as 'middle management' and then 'lower management' (see Figure 1.1).

Important decisions about the company's future are made at board level by members of the C-Suite. These are the big decisions; they give direction to the corporate mission. The overall business objective-setting takes place here. Decisions on new locations, new products, and new markets are made at this level, not least because they have major financial implications. Therefore, we can say that board members make *strategic* decisions.

On the other hand, 'middle' managers make *operational* decisions. These are decisions concerning marketing, including how to promote, choice of media, where to distribute and who to target. They are decisions on the 'marketing mix'. They help in setting marketing objectives and also in setting communications or campaign objectives. Strategic decisions often deal with the next five, 10, or 20 years; operational decisions will usually deal with the next year, or the next few years (see Figure 1.2).

When Kellogg's decided to extend their breakfast cereal range from cornflakes to sugar-coated flakes, this was a *strategic* decision. When the decision was made to promote the product using a character called Tony the Tiger™, this was an *operational* decision.

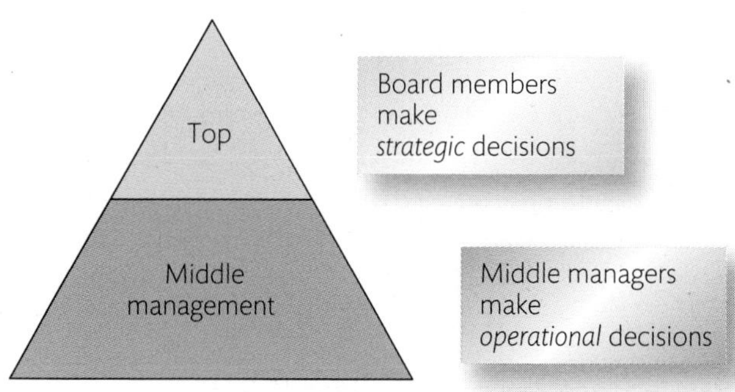

Figure 1.1 The management hierarchy

Figure 1.2 Strategic and operational decisions

Market research helps both strategic and operational decision-makers. Decision-making is a risky business and new investments can divert funds from other areas of a business. It is therefore wise to minimise risks by ensuring that the decisions are well informed. We can guess that the decision to launch a chocolate-covered cereal was made after feasibility research found that production was possible. It is also reasonable to think that market estimates were made to make sure there would be a substantial market.

Stores selling cornflakes will have had a view on the likelihood of uptake; consumer **panels** may have been asked about the concept. These are examples of research carried out to support strategic decisions. Once a decision was made, some sugar-coated flakes were probably produced and placed in homes to discover the best taste and dummy packages were probably shown at focus groups to establish reactions. Packs may have been set beside competing boxes to identify their likely impact. These are examples of research studies that can be carried out to support operational decisions.

Social research

Although marketing research has traditionally served the interests of corporations, social researchers are concerned with the interests of the respondents themselves; social welfare is of prime importance. From the respondent's viewpoint, there are great challenges in attempting to provide answers about societal issues to which they may previously have given very little consideration.

Specialisations in social research can be far more numerous than in marketing research and many disciplines are pertinent to socioeconomic research. These include: industrial relations, education, demography, statistics, economics, geography, political science, psychology, sociology, and anthropology. Social researchers benefit from having skills and a background in the particular area for which the research is being carried out, but it is important that this does not bias them in any way.

In social research, the clients are government departments or non-governmental organisations (NGOs). The latter are defined by the World Bank as '*private organisations that pursue activities to relieve suffering, promote the interests of the poor, protect the environment, provide basic social services, or undertake community development*'. NGOs include: social welfare agencies, charities (the definition may be stretched as far as consumer groups), pressure groups, and management of the mass media. Their research work results in tangible reports such as crime surveys, expenditure surveys, transport surveys, opinion polls, political polls, and other 'barometers' of opinion. In the UK, much government research goes through an organisation called the Central Office of Information (COI). As Fiona Wood, COI research director says: '*Nobody is obliged to use us. From my point of view the more departments that use us, the better, but we don't have a monopoly over research*' (Brenner 2005). To indicate the enormous amount of research that takes place, we see that the COI has a team of over 30 people working regularly with over 70 research suppliers.

Most social researchers operate on behalf of 'not for profit' (NFP) organisations. The major differences between these and entities that exist for profit revolve around differences in their objectives, target audiences, marketing mixes, and promotional activities. Although their work is not based on profit, it may be based on revenue, support, increased awareness, or non-monetary donations. For example, charities seek support, raise awareness of specific issues, or seek donations. This extends to appeals for blood or organ donation.

There are various areas in which government-supported social services act—family welfare, child welfare, youth welfare, group welfare, disaster relief, medical and psychiatric services, vocational counselling, and probation counselling services. Clearly, the objectives for research in these sectors shift from the maximisation of profit to the question of efficient provision of services, or in some cases, a changing of behaviour that may, in fact, result in a lack of consumption or a minimisation of certain behaviours. Family welfare includes such things as: marriage counselling, care before giving birth, family planning, family life, education for domestic situations, and the provision of services for older people. The area of child welfare is one of the largest areas served by the social services; it includes child health and protection, daycare, and foster care.

Many of the social services are a direct result of government policy; there are other organisations that offer similar or alternative services, and these include charities that may be permanent or may have been created temporarily, perhaps to deal with a particular disaster. They also include organisations that lobby against specific movements: for example, the political parties that are opposed to government policy. All of these organisations are potential clients for social research. Other examples are the Red Cross organisations, which exist in different countries, youth welfare institutions such as the Scouts, and similar organisations for youth welfare.

Public sector research is intended to connect policymakers with citizens; it provides those policymakers with indications of those policies that may be popular and those that are in the public interest. Citizens have several expectations from their policymakers: they expect improved service, they expect to pay a minimal cost for the services, and they expect continual cost-cutting; they also expect their opinion to be sought. From the viewpoint of the voter, research offers an opportunity to express a view outside the ballot box. This is something that we have seen in more recent years. It has been described as the 'customer-centric approach'.

As an example, research with impoverished consumers often concerns an evaluation of the social welfare system. Research may examine quality of life, discrimination, access to services, issues of justice, socioeconomic well-being, equal employment rights for disabled people, prejudice, mobility, and access to services.

Public information campaigns are those that give citizens information about activities that are important for their welfare. In the past, these have included health issues (such as AIDS), conserving resources (such as saving water), and information on rights (the importance of voting). In the same way that advertising for FMCG benefits from research results, public information campaigns can benefit from carefully designed studies.

Managing knowledge

Market intelligence

The right information does not automatically come to the person who needs it, so it is useful to look at how knowledge is managed. In the military world, sources of data are classified as 'HUMINT', 'TECHINT', and 'SIGINT'. These, respectively, refer to intelligence derived from humans, intelligence derived from technical sources, and that derived from intercepting signals. Collecting these involves questioning, using devices, and observing communications between people. Market researchers use exactly the same techniques.

A term that is commonly used in this field is 'market intelligence'. The big difference between military procedures and marketing intelligence procedures is that of transparency: the former thrives in secrecy; the latter is expected to show transparency.

Although the military definitions are subdivided further, we shall distinguish just three different types of intelligence. Montgomery and Weinberg (1979) make a valuable distinction using the terms 'defensive', 'passive', and 'offensive'. Defensive intelligence monitors the environment to avoid surprises. Passive intelligence provides benchmark data to compare with the company's own performance. Offensive intelligence identifies opportunities that would not otherwise be discovered. This is summarised in Table 1.2.

Table 1.2 Types of intelligence

Type	Description
Defensive intelligence	To avoid surprises, to monitor the environment and support any hunches of what may be happening. An alert of major changes
Passive intelligence	To provide benchmark data to compare the company's own performance and use it to evaluate objectives
Offensive intelligence	To identify opportunities that would not otherwise be discovered

Source: Reprinted with permission from *Journal of Marketing*, published by the American Marketing Association, Montgomery and Weinberg, 1979/43, pp. 41–52

On the subject of *collecting* intelligence, Montgomery and Weinberg use the term 'scanning' and further subdivide this into 'surveillance' and 'searching'. They say *surveillance* is viewing and monitoring many aspects of the environment to detect changes. In contrast, they see *search* as deliberate inquiry. So, for example, a '*signal detected by the surveillance function of scanning can lead to questions which require search to answer*'. There is empirical evidence indicating that scanning can be beneficial. It is probable that strong firms tend to use more scanning than those that are weaker.

The MKIS and the MDSS

In the 1960s, the management information system (MIS) concept was formed and this was adapted and applied to marketing; it was called the marketing information system. The abbreviation MKIS was used to make the distinction from the MIS; confusingly, many texts use the abbreviation MIS for marketing information systems.

Essentially, the MKIS is a set of procedures that have been linked to deliver information from different sources to decision-makers. It takes information from inside and outside the company. The MKIS is the link between the outside world (the marketing environment) and the decision-makers (the marketing managers) within an organisation. It is frequently shown as a diagram, as in Figure 1.3.

The elements of the MKIS are:

- Internal records
- Marketing intelligence system
- Marketing research system
- Analysis system
- Reporting system.

In the 1970s, marketing decision support systems (MDSS) were introduced to allow individual decision-makers to manipulate data. These systems give users reports that are appropriate, and relevant, to their specific needs. The MDSS should be easy to use, adaptable for different purposes, and allow the user to answer queries instantly. The user can therefore

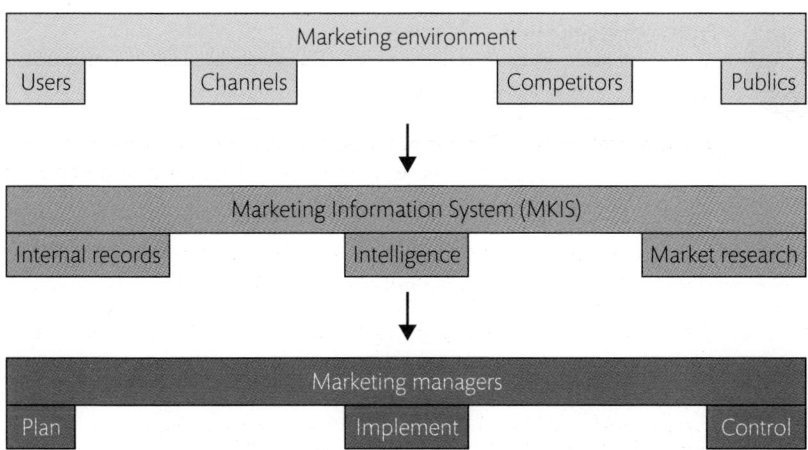

Figure 1.3 The marketing information system (MKIS)

access databases and other resources available. The MDSS can make evaluations of sales, promotions, product trends, and customer profiles, and will permit forecasts in all of these areas.

The advanced MDSS incorporates a library of mathematical models and so the user must be trained in the use of software for database mining, in **spreadsheet** use, and so on. In large companies, it is usual for executives to use some form of MDSS; indeed, recent developments in information technology mean that such information can be accessed from hand-held terminals in remote locations for even the smallest company.

Examples of MDSS models include Brandaid, Callplan, Geoline, and Mediac. Kotler (2003) describes Brandaid as '*a flexible marketing-mix model focused on consumer packaged goods*'; he describes Callplan as '*a model to help salespeople determine the number of calls to make per period*'; Geoline is '*for designing sales and service territories*'; and Mediac is '*a model to help an advertiser buy media for a year*'. A more recent software solution, which is directly applicable to the market research sector, is Research Reporter, from Australia (see http://www.researchreporter.com). This allows research buyers to create a catalogue of all research within an organisation. The tool then allows searches and retrievals to take place.

The advantages of the MDSS are cost savings in identifying waste and avoiding it, better decision-making through the availability of information and, finally, understanding customers better because the information is current and available widely. The disadvantages are that the different systems within an organisation need to be linked in some way. This can be costly and, initially, it can be disruptive. Somebody needs to analyse systems to make such links.

Academics debate whether the MDSS is part of the MIS or is a separate entity. An MIS does provide support for decision-making, but it might be argued that the MDSS is different because it incorporates decision-making models that can predict consequences and thereby minimise risk when choosing a certain solution. Another distinction is that the information system provides regular reports in an ongoing fashion, whereas the decision support system provides irregular reports, delivered when requested, but specific to the needs of the user.

In a study of over 400 UK businesses in 1991, Hirst (1994, p. 232) subdivided decision support systems into four categories:

1. **Simple query application** A data-oriented, simple query application, which extracts data from a file or a database and produces a list or report, without performing calculations on the data
2. **Report generation application** A data-oriented, report generation application, which is similar to a simple query application except that basic calculations are made on the extracted data
3. **Alternative assessment application** A model-oriented, alternative assessment application, in which the user inputs possible decisions and the system estimates the consequences of these decisions by using a simulation model
4. **Analytically assisted search application** A model-oriented, analytically assisted search application, in which the system searches the set of feasible decision alternatives and proposes the best decision.

These distinctions are useful in understanding the nature of such a system. It might be argued that the first two types are the MKIS. In the past 10 years we have seen the emergence of the Marketing Dashboard, which brings such data to the desk of marketing managers (see Chapter 15 for more on dashboards).

Research in focus
The MKIS and marketing metrics are real

Several studies have looked at the use of the MKIS in companies. One by Li *et al.* (2001) examined Fortune 500 companies to reveal their pattern in MKIS usage. The findings were compared with previous studies. In this study, marketing managers reported a decrease in the existence of MKIS in their firms. However, the study does show that many firms link marketing plans to their information resources.

The scholars say: *'Besides telephone, facsimile, and email, electronic commerce is widely adopted in these large firms. Most importantly, many marketers today are using computers and the Internet. They are more and more knowledgeable about computer technologies and actively taking part in creating computer applications to meet their own information needs'.*

This is tangible confirmation that database issues have come to the top of the agenda for the information professional. The most basic function of the database is to facilitate transactions between buyer and seller, but there are many other extra functions that derive from this. It is useful to remember that databases contain numbers and text, but can also carry static and moving images. The study also shows that research, traditionally part of the MKIS, is changing the emphasis of databases and the MKIS is being replaced by different types of support system.

On the topic of marketing metrics, Barwise and Farley (2004) looked into such measures and how they are used in 697 firms in five countries. They show that most firms 'regularly report one or more of six marketing metrics to the board'. This is evidence that research, which provides such measures, is of extreme importance. The same academics isolate two metrics as the most used: **market share**, by 79 per cent, and perceived product/service quality, by 77 per cent of informants. The study also shows that multinational subsidiaries and larger firms tend to use more metrics than others. Another difference exists between countries: Germany is an above-average user compared with Japan, which is a below-average user, but there is no difference by industry type.

The six important metrics identified by Barwise and Farley are:

1. Market share
2. Perceived product/service quality
3. Customer loyalty/retention
4. Customer/segment profitability
5. Relative price
6. Actual/potential customer segment lifetime value.

Compiled by Nigel Bradley 2012.

Sources:

Barwise, P. and Farley, J.U. (2004) Marketing metrics: status of six metrics in five countries, *European Management Journal*, June, 22(3), pp. 257–262.

Li, E.Y., McLeod, R., and Rogers, J.C. (2001) Marketing information systems in Fortune 500 companies: a longitudinal analysis of 1980, 1990, and 2000, *Information and Management*, April, (38)5, pp. 307–322.

Questions

1 Is the use of the MKIS increasing or decreasing? Why might this be?

2 Who uses marketing metrics more than other groups?

3 Identify the most important metrics and explain how they might be created. Provide full definitions for each one.

The use of marketing metrics by companies is helpful in understanding who commissions research and for what reasons. Our definition of a 'marketing metric' is a measurement that may be indicative of financial performance. There are several key marketing metrics such as market share, customer loyalty, and quality of service. Other items that have been defined as metrics are profitability of customer, customer satisfaction, duration of relationship, advertising effectiveness, sales, and repeat behaviour. Two items that are sometimes added to the list are **brand equity** and return on investment (ROI).

Customer insight

A recent development has been the emergence of new departments that carry the word 'insight' in their titles. We see 'customer insight departments', 'insight management units', 'consumer insight', and so on. This extends to the job titles of executives working in those areas.

> Now, as customer insight manager, my job is more like that of a marketing consultant. We adopt a distinct approach that aims to squeeze every drop of knowledge from projects.
>
> Markus Graw of BP Retail

One reason for this development was a realisation that the emphasis of results from individual research projects needed to be shifted to a wider understanding of the dynamics operating in the full marketplace. Another reason was the impact of information technology. Progress in technology gave way to the availability of masses of information found in databases. However, it is obvious that huge quantities of data with little meaning could not assist the marketing function; indeed, the burden created by huge quantities of paper was a major obstacle. Market researchers therefore took a new role of data mining and assimilating information from many more sources than before. These 'insight' managers were actively seeking missing parts, rather than being instructed to collect and report. This is a proactive management of knowledge, rather than simple data handling. 'Insight' is a difficult term to define. Jeremy Garlick, head of Sainsbury's Customer Insight, describes it as a penetrating discovery that unlocks value.

> It need not necessarily be new, but something we look at in a different way. It is a creative process, more of an art than a science, but crucially, it must be information that you can act upon, and make money from ... I believe that it is more than a rebranding of the function, but a fundamental difference in mindset; with insight all information meshes together.

The advantages of insight management are numerous. By making use of all existing information, there is less need to consult customers, thereby minimising unnecessary contact and costs. **Segmentation** and targeting is enhanced by drawing a full picture of the marketplace. Existing services and products can be delivered more productively and new initiatives can be developed for the marketplace. The value of individual customers can be more accurately derived from a combination of sales sources, **survey** results, and prospect databases. There is a synergy in allowing all resources to be used together.

The marketing manager must know of all of the information collected by the organisation; therefore regular MR Audits are recommended. The TOOLBOX provides a checklist of items that allow the manager to discover information that has already been collected.

Table 1.3 Distinctions between qualitative and quantitative

Qualitative	Quantitative
Words, narrative, images, concepts	Numbers
Analysis begins *during* data collection	Analysis begins after data collection
Analysis adapted to each project	Analysis guided by standard techniques
Original ways to communicate results	Standard ways to communicate results

Quantitative and qualitative research

It is almost impossible to talk about qualitative research without referring to quantitative research. Practitioners have a tendency to use word-clippings and this field is no exception; they often abbreviate the terms down to 'qual' and 'quant', so 'quallies' are people who work in qualitative research. Let us think about the two research paradigms: phenomenology and positivism. The phenomenological paradigm focuses on the subjective meaning of the subject under investigation (or phenomena). Conversely, the positivist paradigm focuses on the facts or causes of social phenomena. 'Qual' is phenomenological and 'quant' is positivist. Quantitative data can be distinguished from qualitative data by numbers: in quantitative, there are plenty of them; in qualitative, there are none.

We can distinguish qualitative from quantitative in many ways, for example qualitative research is unstructured not structured; in qualitative research, there is an emphasis on understanding rather than measurement. Qualitative research centres on words, narrative, images, and concepts, rather than on numerical values. Qualitative analysis begins during data collection, whereas, traditionally, quantitative analysis begins after data collection. Quantitative analysis is guided by standard techniques, and findings are communicated in standard ways. These differences are outlined in Table 1.3.

Ethics

Ethics concerns good practice. It is important for researchers to behave properly because, otherwise, they risk losing respondents and people to fund their work. From an ethical viewpoint, there are numerous issues that impact on the insight manager. The Market Research Society Code of Conduct and data protection legislation place specific demands on managers who wish to combine customer databases with marketing research information. If a respondent is assured of confidentiality at an interview, then personal details cannot be input into a database and be identified there. This is a contradiction that needs to be resolved.

There are also European laws to which to adhere. The laws and regulations differ by country, but, in general, they all aim to protect the privacy of an individual with particular reference to personal data. These laws require that the principles of *transparency* and *consent* are put into practice. When an individual is asked to provide personal data, it is made clear why such data is

Table 1.4 The eight principles in UK data protection legislation

Description
1 Personal data shall be processed fairly and lawfully
2 Personal data shall be obtained only for one or more specified and lawful purposes, and shall not be further processed in any manner incompatible with that purpose or those purposes
3 Personal data shall be adequate, relevant, and not excessive in relation to the purpose or purposes for which they are processed
4 Personal data shall be accurate and, where necessary, kept up to date
5 Personal data processed for any purpose or purposes shall not be kept longer than is necessary for that purpose or those purposes
6 Personal data shall be processed in accordance with the rights of data subjects under this Act
7 Appropriate technical and organisational measures shall be taken against unauthorised or unlawful processing of personal data and against accidental loss or destruction of, or damage to, personal data
8 Personal data shall not be transferred to a country or territory outside the European Economic Area (EEA), unless that country or territory ensures an adequate level of protection for the rights and freedoms of data subjects in relation to the processing of personal data

Source: http://www.informationcommissioner.gov.uk

needed and what the organisation collecting the data is using it for. This is known as the 'principle of transparency'. When an individual gives permission to gather and use personal data, agreement is secured for this and any future contact. This is known as the 'principle of consent'. In the UK, these notions are encompassed in the Data Protection Act 1998. This Act defines 'personal data' as that '*which relates to a living individual who can be identified from the data, or from the data and other information in the possession of, or likely to come into the possession of, the data controller*'. There are eight principles in UK data protection legislation. These are shown in Table 1.4.

The structure of the MR sector

There are several professional associations or 'trade bodies' that look after the interests of research suppliers, research users, and other communities. One of these is the European Society for Opinion and Market Research (ESOMAR), which brings together many agencies located worldwide. In the UK, the Market Research Society (MRS) has over 8000 members and claims to be the *'world's largest international membership organisation for professional researchers'.*

The MRS has several schemes to support professional standards. These include: giving advice to members on interpretation of the MRS Code of Conduct; and the Interviewer Identity Card Scheme, whereby over 90,000 cards are issued to interviewers working for research agencies as reassurance for respondents. MRS Freephone allows respondents to verify whether an organisation is 'bona fide'. The MRS supplies 'Thank you' leaflets to be given to respondents, again as a reassurance.

A similar pattern emerges elsewhere in the world, so, in the USA, we find the American Marketing Association (AMA), with 45,000 members. Over in France, Syntec, the French Market Research Society has 45 corporate members and the German Market Research Society (ADAM) has a similar number of corporate members. AEDOMO, the Spanish Market Research Society, has around 900 individual members. The list continues around the world.

Broadly speaking, **market research agencies** offer three types of information service. These services describe **market sizes** and are known as industrial (for numbers of production units, etc.), trade (numbers of retail outlets, etc.), and consumer (numbers of consumers, etc.). These same three groups can be researched to help in the marketing process. They can be asked about: products (size, package, and name); prices (margin, expectation, competition); promotions (reactions to adverts, source of knowledge); or place (point of sale, display impact).

Some US$29,000 million are spent each year on marketing research (ESOMAR 2011). This is a figure for the world, and using a few guidelines from various sources, we can say that there is an 80:20 pattern evident in the figures:

- 80 per cent is quantitative and 20 per cent is qualitative
- 80 per cent of qualitative money goes to focus groups
- Online data capture (around 20 per cent) is being used more than face-to-face and telephone quantitative studies.

From industry sources, we also know the methods that are most used in supplying clients with information for their decisions. Table 1.5 shows the spend on the types of research by ESOMAR members, suggesting a dominance of online, in terms of money allocated to research. This is a major change from 2000, where there was a clear dominance of face-to-face methods.

Table 1.5 World spending on quantitative research

Method	Share of spend in 2009 (%)
Online	22
Phone interviews	15
Face-to-face	12
Postal	4
Automated digital/electronic	14

Source: ESOMAR 2011

Ethical insight

Codes keep everybody happy

Researchers could be reckless. They could phone respondents at midnight, block the public highway to catch respondents, and intrude in many other ways. It is important that the marketing research process is undertaken in an ethical and professional manner. This acts as a safeguard to society in general and to the research community. Researchers must conform to the professional codes of conduct and the relevant data protection laws.

© Chris King

All professional bodies work towards ensuring that clients, employees, and the general public are fairly treated. This is done by means of continuous training, disciplinary procedures, regular meetings, and publications. There are also codes of conduct and other guidelines.

Codes of conduct that have been created by professional bodies do not constitute legal advice and should not be relied upon as such. Legal advice should be taken from a professional practitioner in relation to specific issues. However, the researcher must be aware of the laws that impact on any planned activities.

The MRS in the UK has had a self-regulatory code that has been in existence since 1954. It applies to all members of the society. The MRS says: '*Assurance that research is conducted in an ethical manner is needed to create confidence in, and to encourage cooperation among, the business community, the general public, regulators and others*'. The code goes into detail and some areas are expanded in documents called 'guidelines'. There are guidelines for research among children, Internet research, mystery customer research, qualitative research, and questionnaire design.

In 1976, the International Code of Marketing and Social Research Practice was established. This was created jointly by the International Chamber of Commerce (ICC) and ESOMAR. These codes are self-regulatory, which means that any breaches may result in membership to this body being withdrawn or suspended, and the news of such an event may be published and made known to what is actually a small community of researchers.

Many other schemes exist or have existed: for example, the Interviewer Quality Control Scheme (IQCS) is responsible for providing minimum service standards for data collection. Member companies are subject to an annual independent audit. The Market Research Quality Standards Association (MRQSA) was established to develop minimum standards for market research, data collection, and data processing. These standards have now evolved into ISO 20252.

Compiled by Nigel Bradley 2012.

Sources:

Data Protection Act 1998 (online at http://www.ico.gov.uk).
ICC/ESOMAR Code (online at http://www.esomar.org/knowledge-and-standards/codes-and-guidelines.php).
MRS Code of Conduct (online at http://www.mrs.org.uk/standards/codeconduct.htm).
Other standards online at http://www.mrs.org.uk/standards/other.htm

Questions

1 What can researchers do to upset respondents?

2 What professional bodies are mentioned above?

3 What do these professional bodies provide? And who benefits?

Common mistakes
Misunderstanding research jargon

People who are new to marketing research are bombarded with many new words and concepts. Consider these words: representative, survey, random, focus group, validity, reliability, secondary data, and significance. Many of these terms are used in common speech, but in market research, they take on a specific meaning. This is a big problem because there may be a misunderstanding between client and researcher. This is particularly important to remember if you happen to know the terms: you expect everyone else to understand, but that is not always the case! Look at these examples of what *not* to say:

'Two hundred surveys were done' (should be 200 *questionnaires*)

'A representative sample' (is this strictly true?)

'Respondents were selected randomly' (very rare, often this should read: *a convenience sample was used*)

'Secondary data were used' (often confused with *primary data*)

'Her views were significant to our understanding' (the listener may think that a statistical **significance test** was carried out).

Even the term 'market research' itself can sometimes be an example of 'clipping', a term used by linguists to mean that an existing word has been shortened to form a new word, one that is slightly quicker to say and write. So we may say 'market research' when we mean 'marketing research'. In this sector, many clippings are used and we will meet them sooner or later, so it is useful to be aware of them now. Examples include *ad* for advertisement, *info* for information, and *qual* for qualitative. It is useful to understand this device because clippings can lead to confusion: for example, 'advertising research' and '**ad hoc research**' are not the same.

The advertising business is a major originator of research projects and many advertising agencies offer market research as part of their services. Market researchers also measure audiences of television, radio, newspapers, and magazines, and these results form the basis of buying and selling advertising space.

We know that many projects concern food and drink, but other products for the human body (health and beauty, and pharmaceutical products) are extremely important.

When we examine the market research industry, we immediately come across companies that are known as 'full service'. These provide all research facilities to a client. Conversely, we can find smaller entities that provide specific services, for example, consultants, fieldwork agencies, telephone call centres and analysis bureaux. In the *Research Buyer's Guide UK & Ireland* (MRS 2012), we find over 450 full service agencies, over 200 freelance consultants, some 70 fieldwork and tabulation agencies, and 30 data preparation and analysis providers. Additionally, there are around 100 group discussion and viewing facilities available.

Jack Honomichl, a widely respected research industry observer, has been publishing reports on the top 50 research agencies worldwide for many years. Honomichl's reports are released each year. The top 10 research agencies are shown in Table 1.6, along with their revenues for global business activities and the location of the parent company. There are agencies based in

Table 1.6 Research companies worldwide

Company	Parent country	Revenue $US million
Nielsen	USA	5000
Kantar (TNS)	UK	3100
Ipsos	France	2400
IMS Health	USA	2200
GFK	Germany	1700
Symphony IRI	USA	700
Weststat Inc	USA	500
Intage Inc	Japan	400
Arbitron Inc	USA	400
NPD Group	USA	200

Source: Nigel Bradley 2012, based on data from ESOMAR and AMA

the UK, the USA, Germany, and France. Most agencies are present throughout the world, with branch offices in major cities. From this, it is clear that no one nation is dominant in the field.

International research often centres on the UK because, in common with users of the Stock Exchange, researchers see London as a bridge between Europe and the USA; this is helped by the 'special relationship' shared between the USA and the UK and the time-zone differences, which effectively make London a stepping stone to many places. There is a large number of international businesses with headquarters in the UK, which may also play a role in this.

In recent years, the situation has become more complex: we have witnessed the use of services being offered by agencies in countries where costs are significantly lower. This is known as 'outsourcing' or using 'offshore locations' and the trend is common practice in non-market research fields such as call centres. Sohoni and Mittal (2004, p. 30) identified several countries that are attractive for this, in terms of political or industrial environment and workforce skills. They identified India, Ireland, Holland, Australia, and the UK as important providers of research services.

A career in marketing research

The research industry employs many people: for example, the top 25 agencies have over 100,000 employees across the world (ESOMAR 2008). In the UK alone, there are around 500 research agencies and about 6000 people are employed full-time; there are, of course, many

Common mistakes
Confusing similar things

One problem with new concepts is that many labels are similar and we may know some of them from other sectors. Take these as examples: ABC and ABC1; NRS and MRS; Social Grade and **social class**; SIC and SOC; CAPI and CATI. They are all so similar that they may be confused.

©Nigel Bradley

ABC means the *Audit Bureau of Circulations*, whereas ABC1 are three of the six social grades. The NRS is the *National Readership Survey*, which looks at the readership of newspapers, whereas the MRS is the *Market Research Society*, a professional grouping of practitioners. SIC means the *Standard Industrial Classification*, a way to classify businesses, but SOC is the *Standard Occupational Classification*, a way to classify people. CAPI means *computer-assisted personal interviewing*, whereas CATI means *computer-assisted telephone interviewing*; both are ways to gather information from people.

more support staff. These people collect and process market information and specific job titles often reflect their roles.

In the marketing research sector, job titles differ according to whether the employer is a research agency or a user of market research. The size of organisation and style may also dictate the choice of job title. Salaries will depend on the employer, experience, and market conditions.

Graduates may enter agencies on graduate training programmes. The first post is known as a 'trainee executive'. They will then become a 'junior research executive' (JRE). The 'research executive' is responsible for specific parts of projects and is part of a team. Executives will initially check questionnaires and check the quality of results. They may also help to check reports and presentations. This task then changes into creating questionnaires, specifying tables, writing reports, and planning presentations. As responsibility increases, probably after one to two years, the title becomes 'senior research executive' (SRE) and then 'associate director' (AD) or 'group head', and, ultimately, a 'director'. The director will be on the management board and will be responsible for securing new business. This then means that s/he must be involved with client liaison and assuring that a project moves from proposal to completion successfully. Salaries increase as the employee moves through this progression.

Another acceptable way to become a research executive is to find employment in operational parts of the agency and gradually move into an executive role. The downside is a lower starting salary and the risk is that there is no assurance of progression. Many senior executives and directors entered agencies in this way and gained first-hand experience in production. Such a progression means that executives appreciate the importance of detail in each project. This, in turn, leads to being respected by their colleagues: an important ingredient for teamwork and smooth running of projects.

Table 1.7 summarises different jobs for the UK and gives a more detailed indication of 2009 salary levels derived from various sources, most notably information from MrWeb

Table 1.7 UK jobs in marketing research

Job title	Job description	Annual salary
Field interviewer	Trained to select and interview respondents using a structured questionnaire. Works from home, possibly part-time	£10,000+
Telephone interviewer	Works in-house at a research agency in a central telephone unit	£10,000+
Coder	Processes open-ended questions by developing a code frame and applying it to data	£10,000+
Spec writer	Converts questionnaires into scripts for CAPI/ CATI/CAWI. Writes table specifications for research executives	£15,000–35,000
Web analyst	Evaluates website visitor behaviour	£20,000+
Client company market research manager	Responsible for buying research from agencies. Knows the industry sector well. Has a duty to provide users with information they need	£30,000+
Research executive (agency and client)	Different levels (JRE, RE, SRE) indicate increased responsibility for specific parts of projects; may be part of a team. Will write questionnaires and analyse results. May prepare reports and presentations	£19,000–28,000
Qualitative research executive	Responsible for depth interviewing and focus group moderation. Will write reports and presentations	£25,000–50,000
Research agency project manager	Responsible for particular projects (probably several at the same time). Ensures deadlines are met and work moves through an agency smoothly	£34,000
Research agency associate director	Secures new business, then has responsibility for client liaison and projects. Actively prepares proposals, writes reports, and presents results	£40,000–50,000
Research agency director	On the management board. Secures new business, then has responsibility for client liaison and projects. May write reports and present results	£50,000+

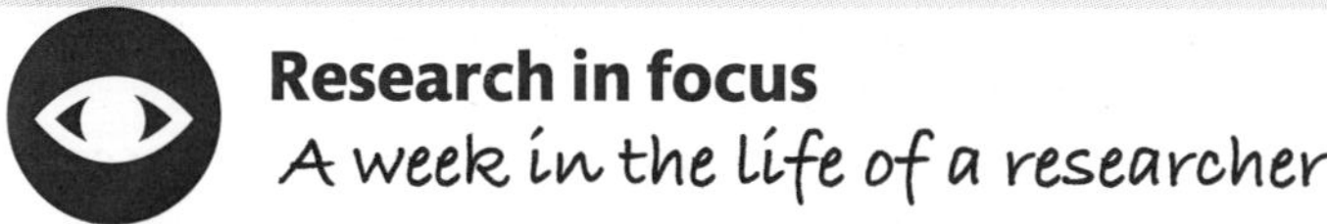

Research in focus
A week in the life of a researcher

Martin Stoll describes his life as a director in the London-based qualitative division of the international research agency Ipsos MORI. Martin is a business-to-business specialist.

I am a bit of an atypical researcher in the sense that I am more business to business than FMCG, so my typical week may be a bit more complex or a bit different as I may be doing more in-depth interviews.

This week, I did an 'extended group' on Monday night, with people who work for large companies and are all out of the office a lot and use mobile phones, PDAs, and laptops. Our client wanted to understand the needs of these mobile workers. The respondents were in a viewing facility in central London with a few of the clients watching.

Tuesday morning, I went to see a major petroleum company, as I have been coordinating a three-country study on advertising for them. The project concerned above-the-line television advertising and below-the-line posters they use on service stations. Their above-the-line campaigns are regionally coordinated, but the forecourt posters are more local. I went to their offices to run through the presentation with the client before the real one on Thursday.

Wednesday evening, I went to Birmingham to a facility and did two groups with small business people—one group was with early adopters of technology, late adopters, sole traders, and people in business that employ one to five people. That was about uses of technology.

Thursday morning, I gave the petroleum company presentation, which was with all the different people concerned. It was their people in the UK plus their ad agency and their below-the-line agency, but it was also very international and so one of the guys came in from Germany. For the IT project we had set up 10 in-depth interviews with IT managers and the first had been scheduled in Waterloo, so I hung around after the presentation and conducted my first interview in a nearby hotel café. This was with an IT manager from a travel agency with about 100+ employees.

Today, Friday, I have a telephone interview for a tyre manufacturer client, so I am speaking to one of their major customers. I have already interviewed one of his colleagues. They were meant to be face-to-face but it makes sense doing it on the telephone if it saves me going up to Edinburgh. It is a qual and quant job—we are doing the qual part and the telephone unit is doing the quant part. We are just doing the UK part of a five-country study, coordinated out of Ipsos-France. Our job is a whole series of in-depth interviews with the senior management in all the relevant organisations that sell tyres. So that is with both of the two really big chains here in the UK and a whole range of wholesalers and retailers. Then there are some car manufacturers, which also buy tyres for the replacement market.

Compiled by Nigel Bradley 2012.

Source:
Martin Stoll, interviewed by Nigel Bradley.

Questions

1. You will see that projects overlap: Martin is actually occupied with over 10 projects at any one time. What are the advantages of working in this way? What are the disadvantages from the client's viewpoint?
2. The telephone unit is doing the quantitative part of the work; Martin is doing a qualitative study for the same client. Why do you think both are necessary?
3. What are the differences in interviewing the Edinburgh respondent by phone or in person?

(http://www.mrweb.com), a website with vacancies in this field. MrWeb publishes mean salaries based on positions advertised. In addition to those listed, there are many other support roles such as fieldwork coordinators or telephone interviewing supervisors.

The term 'analyst' is often used; this implies involvement with statistics, IT, or databases. It is notable to see that a new occupational sector has emerged in the past 10 years; this is the profession called 'website analytics', and therefore web analysts occupy positions in both client companies and in consultancies offering software or support to any company with a website.

Many operational roles, specifically interviewing, draw heavily on part-time workers; these are paid on an hourly and weekly basis. The UK 2008 Annual Survey of Hours and Earnings (ASHE) shows that this group (Market Research Interviewers: SOC code 4137) earn £10 per hour (mean); it also indicates there are over 11,000 such posts. The annual salary rate is provided in Table 1.7 simply to make a comparison with the other posts.

Chapter summary

1 Explain the nature and purpose of marketing research

Marketing research assists the management function called 'marketing'; it helps to fine-tune the marketing mix and helps to match supply with demand. Decision-making carries risks and 'market' research helps both strategic and operational decision-makers to minimise risks by ensuring that the decisions are well informed.

2 Summarise the structure of the industry and list the different types of research service available

Over US$28,000 million are spent each year on marketing research, and suppliers are present throughout the world. Familiar names include Nielsen, Taylor Nelson Sofres, IMS, Kantar, GFK, and Ipsos. Full service agencies provide all research facilities to a client. Smaller entities provide specific services such as consultancy, fieldwork, telephone call centres, and computer analysis. Many advertising agencies offer market research. Professional associations such as ESOMAR and the MRS represent the interests of suppliers, users, and other communities. Researchers measure audiences of television, radio, newspapers, and magazines. Market size measurement is also carried out in three sectors: industrial, trade, and consumer. These same three groups are researched to help in the marketing process. They are asked about: products (size, package, and name), prices (margin, expectation, competition), promotions (reactions to adverts, source of knowledge), and place (point of sale, display impact). Market researchers also examine advertising effectiveness. Many projects concern food, drink, pharmaceutical, health, and beauty products. Most are ad hoc; the rest are continuous. Online data capture has increased dramatically in recent years.

3 Show what must be considered when using research in marketing decision-making

Researchers must conform to the professional codes of conduct and the relevant data protection laws. Professional body guidelines exist for: research with children, Internet research, mystery shopping, qualitative research, and questionnaire design. Legislation requires that the principles of transparency and consent are put into practice. In the UK, these notions are encompassed in the Data Protection Act 1998.

4 **Articulate the career opportunities available in marketing research**

Job titles differ according to the size and style of organisation and whether the employer is a research agency or a user of market research. Many people begin their career in operational units. Job titles include field interviewer, domestic telephone interviewer, international telephone interviewer, coder, spec writer, and sampling executive. Salaries will depend on the employer, experience, and market conditions. Graduates may enter agencies as trainee executives. This entails creating questionnaires, specifying tables, writing reports, and planning presentations. As responsibility increases, they may become directors, securing new business.

Review questions

1 Why do organisations take research seriously?

2 Explain the different phases through which study market research has passed since 1900.

3 Compare defensive intelligence with offensive intelligence.

4 What is the most important type of research used in your country?

5 Identify the main steps involved in selecting a research agency and explain each.

Discussion questions

1 Think of some examples of strategic and operational decisions made by real companies you know about. What type of research could have helped in these decisions? This is a useful exercise in a classroom because you can share your ideas and build the number of examples.

2 Name and define three important marketing metrics. How could they be measured for a company producing cuddly toys?

3 List the professional bodies that operate in marketing research and explain their major functions.

4 Consult the Glossary (p. 475). Carry out a short quiz with your class to test your existing knowledge of terms.

5 Look at a country of your choice outside the UK to discover its professional body for research and the number of members. Its website will be helpful.

6 Look at the opening Snapshot. What are the benefits of research to the bank?

Case study
Derbyshire Garage Services

Don Saltergate understands that cars are important to people because he has worked in the car repair business for many years. Originally from Sheffield, he decided to use his knowledge to form a chain of car recovery and breakdown garages across nearby areas in Derbyshire. He rents premises in six locations to offer a service to established recovery organisations such as the AA, RAC, and also to the Police. It is worth pointing out that this service is not available directly to motorists.

© Stock Up Images

Don has six recovery teams carefully positioned near the major motorways. They are available 24 hours a day to respond to calls from his three clients. The teams then find reported broken down cars, fix them at the roadside or they return them to Saltergate garages for more complicated work.

The business model is such that Don charges a retainer fee from all his clients. This allows him to pay the teams to wait. Further charges are paid for repairs either by the motorist or by the organisation, this depends on the level of membership taken out by the motorist. When teams are called out, the following information is collected: name, address, mobile and landline telephone numbers (work and home), car type, registration number, and mileage. Some of these data come from the motorist, some come from the client. All of the information is entered into a computerised database.

Compiled by Nigel Bradley 2012 (this is not based on a real company).

Questions

Saltergate Garages do not carry out annual car services or any other repairs but many motorists have requested such services. Don intends to introduce a general garage and repair service in the next few months. You are a freelance marketing consultant and Don knows that you have an up-to-date knowledge of the latest marketing developments. He is asking you to tell him what can be done to help his business. You should write memos to him for each question below.

1. Explain to Don the difference between strategic and operational marketing decisions, make it easy for him by giving examples from his business.
2. Suggest what types of research technique could help in his decision-making.
3. What ethical and legal problems may his business be facing? Particularly consider his intention to use the database of customers he has built.
4. Don has never undertaken market research, but is considering appointing a research agency. He has asked you to describe the type of people who work in research agencies.

Further reading

- ICC/ESOMAR International Code of Marketing and Social Research ESOMAR Code of Conduct and Guides (online at http://www.esomar.org).
  Also guidelines to: opinion polls; maintaining the distinctions between market research and direct marketing; customer satisfaction studies; how to commission research; interviewing children and young people; mystery shopping; tape and video-recording, and client observation of interviews and group discussions; pharmaceutical market research; conducting marketing and opinion research using the Internet.
- McDonald C. and King S. (1996) *Sampling the Universe: The Growth, Development and Influence of Market Research in Britain since 1945*. Henley-on-Thames, Oxon: NTC Publications Ltd.
  A good account of the UK market research sector.
- MRS (2012) Website page of questions and answers (online at http://www.mrs.org.uk/media/qanda.htm).
  Questions and answers about the UK market research industry.

Key web links

- The Market Research Society http://www.mrs.org.uk
- ESOMAR http://www.esomar.org
- MRWeb http://www.mrweb.com

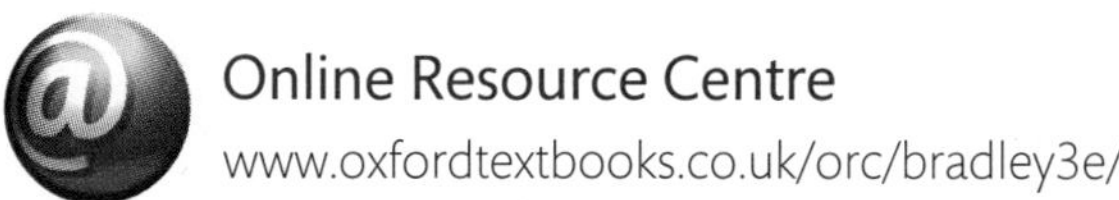

Visit the Online Resource Centre that accompanies this book to access more learning resources on this chapter topic.

References and sources

Allio, M. (2006) Metrics that matter: seven guidelines for better performance measurement, *Handbook of Business Strategy* 7(1), pp. 255–263.

Anon (2004) *Lawson Retail Insight applications help retailers strategically grow their business through customer-centric advanced analytics*, http://phx.corporate-ir.net/phoenix.zhtml?c=129966&p=irol-newsArticle&ID=483492&highlight=

Barwise, P. and Farley, J.U. (2004) Marketing metrics: status of six metrics in five countries, *European Management Journal* 22, June, pp. 257–262.

Borden, N.H. (1964) The concept of the marketing mix, *Journal of Advertising Research* 4, June, pp. 2–7.

Brenner, M. (2005) The Ministry of Research: Interview with Fiona Wood, COI Research Director, *Research*, July, pp. 22–25.

Burns, A.C. and Bush, R.F. (2003) *Marketing Research*, 4th edn. New Jersey: Prentice Hall.

Chisnall, P. (2005) *Marketing Research*. Maidenhead: McGraw Hill.

Christopher, M., Payne, A., and Ballantyre, D. (2002) *Relationship Marketing: Creating Stakeholder Value*. Oxford: Butterworth-Heinemann.

Cox, D.F. and Good, R.E. (1967) How to build a marketing information system, *Harvard Business Review*, June, pp. 145–154.

Edwards, S. (2004) What Sainsbury's wants, *MR Business*, July, p. 35.

ESOMAR (2011) *Global Market Research 2010 ESOMAR Industry report*. Amsterdam: ESOMAR, 116 pp.

Gao, Y. (2010) Measuring marketing performance: a review and a framework. *The Marketing Review* 10(1), pp. 25–40.

Hirschowitz, A. (2001) Closing the CRM loop: the 21st century marketer's challenge: transforming customer insight into customer value, *Journal of Targeting, Measurement and Analysis for Marketing*, 10, pp. 168–178.

Hirst, M. (1994) End-user computing in marketing, in Hooley, G.J. and Hussey, M.K. *Quantitative Methods in Marketing*. London: Academic Press Ltd, pp. 221–246.

Kotler, P. (1966) A design for the firm's marketing nerve center, *Business Horizons*, Fall, pp. 63–74.

Kotler, P. (2003) *Marketing Management: Analysis, Planning, Implementation, and Control*. Harlow, Essex: Pearson Higher Education.

Li, E.Y., McLeod, R., and Rogers, J.C. (2001) Marketing information systems in Fortune 500 companies: a longitudinal analysis of 1980, 1990, and 2000, *Information and Management*, April, pp. 307–322.

McCarthy, E.J. (1960) *Basic Marketing: A Managerial Approach*. Homewood, IL: Richard Irwin Inc.

McDonald, C. and Vangelder, P. (1998) *Handbook of Market and Opinion Research*, 4th edn. Amsterdam: ESOMAR.

McElhatton, N. (2004) Database mining meets market research: customer insight in stereo, *Research World*, December, pp. 20–21.

Montgomery, D.B. and Weinberg, C.B. (1979) Toward strategic intelligence systems, *Journal of Marketing*, 43, pp. 41–52.

MRS (2012) Website page of questions and answers, http://www.mrs.org.uk/media/qanda.htm

MRS (2012) *Research Buyer's Guide UK & Ireland*. London: Market Research Society.

Newport, F., Saad, L., and Moore, D. (1997) How polls are conducted, in Golay, M. and Rollyson, C.E. (eds.) *Where America Stands*. New York: John Wiley & Sons, Inc.

Research Development Foundation (1999) Business cooperation in market research, *Journal of the Market Research Society*, 41, pp. 195–225.

Rosinski, C. (2004) From data provider to leadership for growth, *Research World*, December, pp. 26–28.

Samuels, J. (2001) *Annual Study of the Market Research Industry 2000*, Amsterdam, Netherlands: ESOMAR, pp. 1–23.

Sohoni, K. and Mittal, A. (2004) More MR services outsourced to India, *Research World*, December, pp. 30–31.

Treasure, J.A.P. (1976) Ten years later, *Journal of the Market Research Society*, 18, pp. 54–63.

Wills, S. and Williams, P. (2004) Insight as a strategic asset: the opportunity and the stark reality, *International Journal of Market Research*, 46, pp. 363–410.

Zahay, D. and Griffin, A (2010) Marketing strategy selection, marketing metrics, and firm performance. *Journal of Business and Industrial Marketing* 25(2) pp. 84–93.

Planning research

Contents

Chapter guide

This chapter looks into the complex area of planning research studies and introduces a framework called 'the marketing research mix'. This new 'mix' defines the sequence of research. It reminds you to consider the purpose, population, procedure, and publication stages of any project. In practical terms, research plans are agreed between a client and supplier using two documents: the brief and the proposal. You should be able to prepare both documents and know what is good practice.

Learning outcomes

By the end of this chapter, you should be able to:

1. **Explain each stage of the research process using the 'marketing research mix' as a framework**
2. **Describe the options available to the researcher**
3. **Prepare a briefing document and a research proposal**
4. **Prepare a research proposal**

Introduction

Key aspects of the research project are communicated from a research user to a research supplier. This takes place during a face-to-face meeting, by telephone, or by means of a written brief. The research supplier will then consider the user's requirements, develop various solutions, and provide a written research proposal. Competing proposals are then evaluated and one supplier will be chosen. The winning proposal document becomes an agreement between the two parties and a guide to the research.

Planning any project requires a great deal of knowledge and coordination. It is useful to think of the complexity of a moon mission—there are thousands of activities that need to be scheduled. At a press conference in 1969, the Apollo 11 crew were asked: ***'What is the most dangerous part of the flight?'*** **The answer was simply: *'Anything we've overlooked'.* This chapter attempts to equip you with knowledge that will help you to avoid overlooking anything, and, to do this, it introduces the 'marketing research mix'.**

As far back as the 1920s, the Gantt chart was in use to show the scheduled and actual progress of projects. The inventor of this chart, Henry Laurence Gantt (1861–1919), was a mechanical engineer and realised the potential of a visual planning tool.

In the mid-1950s, two new techniques emerged to help in project planning. They were the Program Evaluation and Review Technique (PERT) and the Critical Path Method (CPM). PERT was used in the development of submarines and CPM was used to manage maintenance of an oil refinery. They were both used extensively by NASA in the American space programme and, even today, are in routine use across the world for construction and engineering projects. In the 1960s, CPM and PERT were introduced to the discipline of marketing, to speed the process of new product launches. In 1948, Culliton said that a marketing decision should be a result of something similar to a recipe. This version continued in 1953, when Neil Borden, in his American Marketing Association presidential address, coined the term 'marketing mix'. E. Jerome McCarthy, in 1960, proposed a four-P classification—Product, Price, Place, and Promotion—a classification that is still taught today. This checklist offers a useful tool to analyse the status of any marketing situation.

Table 2.1 Notable events for planning research

Year	Event
1920s	Gantt chart in use
1950s	Marketing mix born
1960s	Critical path analysis and PERT in use
1980s	Microsoft products available

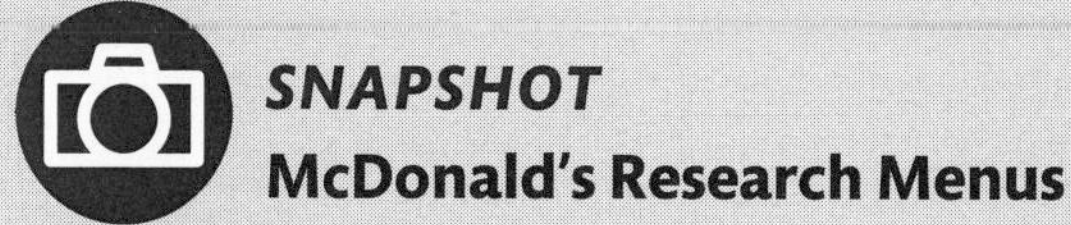

SNAPSHOT
McDonald's Research Menus

© istockphoto.com/Cienpies Design

McDonald's have built a business around burgers, french fries, and cola drinks. This offering is known throughout the world with local variations. These differences have assured success in new geographic areas. In every country the company has a different menu to meet local culture and beliefs. In some New England restaurants the McLobster is offered on a seasonal basis. The Greek burger is wrapped in pita bread. In France there is Le Croque McDo, a variant of the Croque Monsieur.

In India the Big Mac is replaced by the Maharaja Mac which is made of chicken or lamb: McDonald's India does not serve beef or pork for religious reasons. The Vegetable McCurry Pan is an original creation of McDonald's India and sells across the country.

In Hong Kong the main menu includes Shogun burger, a teriyaki pork burger, and a Rice-Fantastic, a burger with baked rice. In China there is a Chinese New Year menu, inspired by the horoscope of twelve zodiac animals. McDonald's in Japan serves Ebi Filet-O-Shrimp, a shrimp burger, and a famous green-tea flavoured milkshake.

McDonald's in Taiwan offers kao fan, baked rice which replaces buns for burgers. They also serve corn soup for side dishes or even main meals and fried chicken. Malaysia is a Muslim-majority country so the meals served in McDonald's are certified halal. McDonald's Malaysia offers a local menu of Spicy Chicken Deluxe, a marinated chicken thigh with crispy part on the outside and topped with special sauce of corn. McDonald's in Singapore also serves halal food, the main meal consisting of McArabia, a grilled spicy chicken with a herb sauce.

Test marketing allows organisations like McDonald's to offer a product in a limited way to 'test the market'. This test is often restricted to a small geographic area. If the experiment is a success then it is rolled out to other regions or if it is not deemed a success then it can be easily withdrawn and the knowledge gained will guide further new product development.

Let us take a moment to examine McDonald's research with the pizza. This is a product that has been offered and withdrawn several times over a period of several years in the USA. In the 1970s test market stores near motorways in Madison and Milwaukee offered small pizzas. In the late 1980s a large Pizza was offered in 24 stores in Indiana, and in the 1990s a family size pizza was offered in some stores in Canada. Prewitt (1991) reported a 500-unit pizza test in the USA. Feedback was rich and varied: for example in some tests Pizza Hut responded with aggressive comparative advertising and sales promotions; sometimes the costs outweighed the benefits; some customers did not like the taste. There have been other instances of the pizza being tested, but in all cases the research did not result in the dish becoming a permanent menu item in the USA or elsewhere, and interestingly McDonald's Italy does not offer any form of pizza.

Compiled by Nigel Bradley and Ozal Udaya 2012.

Sources:

Liebig, J. (2010) McDonald's—McPizza box—Pepperoni & Sausage—test market release—1987 available at http://www.flickr.com/photos/jasonliebigstuff/4443728353

McDonald's (2012) Web pages for France, China, USA, Malaysia, Singapore, India, Hong Kong.

Parasuraman, A., Grewal, D., Krishnan, R. (2006) *Marketing Research*, Cengage, p. 214.

Prewitt, M. (1991). 'McDonald's developing separate dinner menu, puts pizza test on hold'. Nation's Restaurant News (Findarticles.com). 7 October http://findarticles.com/p/articles/mi_m3190/is_n39_v25/ai_11358816/

Udaya, O. (2012) *Investigation of Multinational Companies' Business Strategies and Local Responsiveness. The case of McDonald's in Indonesia*. Dissertation for MA International Business and Management at the University of Westminster.

Zikmund, W.G., Babin, B.J. (2006) *Exploring Marketing Research*, Cengage, p. 287.

The marketing research mix

The marketing mix (see Figure 2.1) is a useful device: it can be moulded, recreated, applied, criticised, defined, adapted, adopted, but most importantly, it can be remembered. The marketing mix helps in marketing planning, and therefore is an important concept for the market researcher.

In marketing, there is the need for information, and an entire sector has been created to serve users. It may seem strange that research is not obviously part of the marketing mix. Let us return to Jerome McCarthy who, when discussing the four Ps, made this observation (1968, p. 33):

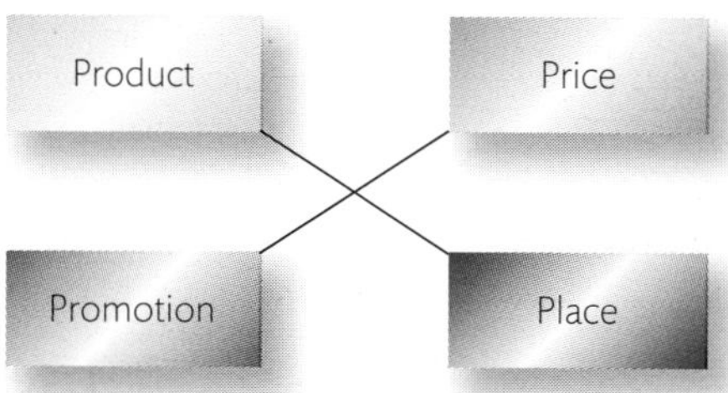

Figure 2.1 The marketing mix

The framework may appear simple enough, but the task of making choices within this framework is fairly complex. For one thing, each of the four Ps has many potential variations, thereby making the number of possible marketing mixes very large. For example, if there were 10 variations in each of the variables (10 price, 10 products, etc.) there would be 10,000 possible marketing mixes.

Marketing researchers are, for the most part, testing the marketing mix and, from this account, it is clear that the research design must adapt to accommodate these numerous variations. Let us not forget that the researcher also has many options. Sometimes, these are so numerous that we cannot consider the strengths and weaknesses of all of the many possibilities without time, resources, and debate.

Just as marketing has adopted the four Ps to help decision-making, there are ways of helping researchers to approach the complex area of designing research. In 2004, the author developed a checklist, deliberately intended to be similar to the marketing mix. It was named the *marketing research mix* (or the *MR mix*) and it also has four Ps. It was created for students, and has been used in classes with success. Unlike the marketing mix, these elements are sequential and they match the main phases that need to be followed. These four Ps are: purpose, population, procedure, and publication. Figure 2.2 shows how these stages relate to accepted research stages.

There are two obvious applications of the MR mix. The first is that the framework offers a reminder of how to structure a programme of research. If there is a need for research, this outline gives a route through designing the research and arriving at a proposal.

The second application will come after research has been conducted; the mix allows the results to be organised and questions to be asked about existing research; results can be understood and evaluated by asking the key questions about each P.

The four elements summarise the stages of the research process; they follow the sequence of research. Here is an explanation of each.

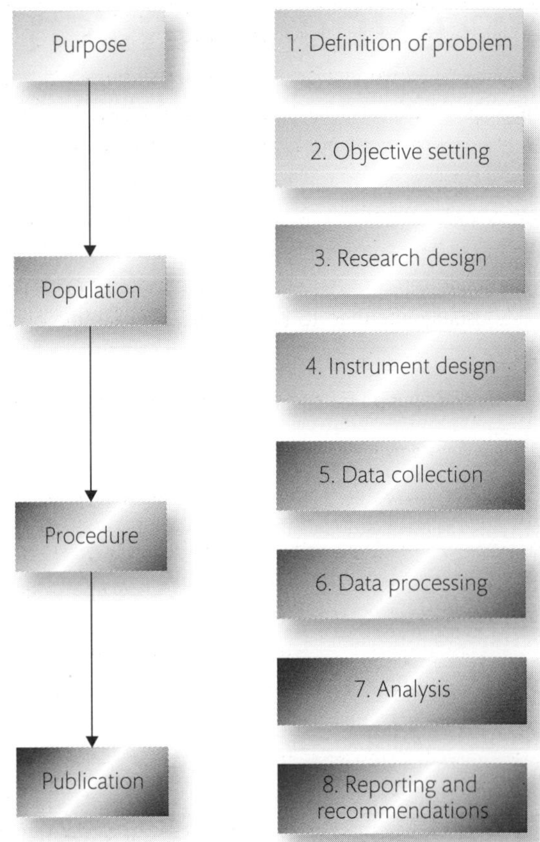

Figure 2.2 Stages of research in terms of the MR mix

Purpose

The key question is: '*Why is research being undertaken?*'. The purpose of the research is the reason why it is being done. The word 'purpose' is useful because it has rather wide coverage. It embraces the terms 'objective' and 'sub-objective'. It can be specifically defined or it can be loosely explained as a 'goal'.

The wide term also embraces studies to gather marketing intelligence, where the manager's role is to scan the environment for useful data, and when there may be no specific objective. Several concepts are found under the heading of 'purpose':

- Aims
- Objectives
- Goals
- Intention
- Hypotheses.

The last word, hypothesis (in the plural, hypotheses), is quite different from the other terms mentioned. It is an essential starting point for quantitative researchers, but takes a lesser role for qualitative researchers. Indeed, many marketers avoid it entirely and tend to use the words 'research objective' or 'aim'. The term 'hypothesis' is deeply rooted in the history of scientific thought. In considered scientific investigation, we give much time and energy to generating hypotheses, to testing hypotheses, and to rejecting hypotheses. Some people argue that we should only test one hypothesis; others say we should test several. In hypothesis testing, we create a statement, which may be true or false. This statement is best described as a 'proposition'—we propose that something may be the case. If it is right, then we accept it. If it is 'wrong', then we reject it. This is why the terms 'accept' or 'reject' are used in this area.

The first step is to formulate the **null hypothesis**, abbreviated to H0. This is a proposition that is least likely, so it is usually intended to be rejected. An example of the null hypothesis statement is as follows:

H0 'Price is not a major consideration for people who purchase cosmetics regularly.'

Another carefully constructed hypothesis is the alternative hypothesis or the H1.

H1 'Price is a major consideration for people who purchase cosmetics regularly.'

This alternative hypothesis is actually called the 'research hypothesis'. After statements like these have been created, the researcher can design a research programme to test the hypotheses.

When the results are received, they are examined against the prediction of the null hypothesis. The basic idea is to use this possible explanation and then look for data to support the explanation (or not). It is essential to spend as much time as possible on the hypothesis. It is the research question and it determines how the study is carried out; it determines the design because it defines the problem.

Hypothesis-setting can vary from a rigid set of statements for testing, to a looser, informal list of information needed to help understand the problem at hand. As a first step, the researcher is advised to take a wide view and to generate numerous hypotheses to test. Initially, it is perfectly acceptable for the wording to be raw and unrefined; it can be fine-tuned later in the process. The researcher should allow their thoughts to run freely because one idea is likely to bring other areas of relevance to mind. Indeed, overlapping or similar ideas are useful, in that the 'best' ones can be chosen and refined.

The subject of hypothesis testing has been debated heavily for many years and an excellent article on the topic by Lawrence (1982) concludes with these words: *'Practical survey researchers (realise) that, in many cases, no adequate theory exists for setting up hypotheses in advance'.* The article continues: *'Drawing one-off hypotheses out of the air offers no solution to the problem. Researchers will be guided by their own ideas, experiences, hunches'.*

A mnemonic commonly used in management is the SMART acronym. It

Table 2.2 The SMART mnemonic and varied meanings

S	Specific	Simple	Simple
M	Measurable	Measurable	Measurable
A	Achievable	Attainable	Achievable
R	Realistic	Relevant	Responsible
T	Timely	Timed	Targeted

helps us in planning: if we set a business objective, we want it to be 'Specific, Measurable, Achievable, Realistic, and Timely', summarised by the acronym SMART. We can find several variations on the wording (see Table 2.2). The fundamental idea is that any plans we have should not be vague; it should be possible to quantify them in some way so that progress can be evaluated, and it should be possible to carry them out and within a certain timeframe.

This acronym can be applied to business objectives and marketing objectives; it can even be applied to sales or communications objectives. An example of a fully articulated SMART objective is '*to increase sales by 250,000 units before December*'. However, it could be argued that SMART is not fully applicable to research objectives. Very often, research studies are **exploratory**; they are attempting to throw light on an area that needs greater understanding. There may be a clear purpose for doing research or it may be exploratory. For this reason, specific objectives and clearly formulated hypotheses may be a mistake. We might suggest that preconceptions will push the research in a specific direction. They may lead to a foregone conclusion.

SMART is extremely useful, however, and many researchers are successful when they import the idea into marketing research. It fails for qualitative research; it fails for exploratory research and indeed for any type of intelligence-gathering where the environment is constantly scanned for changes that might trigger action. Such valuable information may not be anticipated, and the SMART model is best applied to creating. Sometimes, projects are 'fact-finding' missions and the researcher strives to avoid framing preconceived ideas about the market environment.

There are mixed views on firm objectives. In the positivist world of profit-driven business, there is a reluctance to finance a project that may continue for an unknown period, which may be one week or 10 years. On the other hand, there is an understanding that human behaviour is impossible to describe in specific timeframes, using standardised tools. The tradition of deduction and induction further confirms this. If we remember that expenditure on qualitative research is substantial, this is further proof that strict objectives are, in practice, not the norm.

Much quantitative research is also 'fact-finding': most questionnaires contain questions for interest or curiosity, to follow up a hunch. In analysis of results, there is much to be said for letting the 'tables speak', for 'trawling' (see Table 2.3) through numbers to look for patterns. This is done both by machine and by the human eye.

The point is that the term 'purpose' is sufficiently loose to describe the first phase of research. It does embrace the straitjacket of the carefully worded hypothesis, but it also accommodates the other extreme of exploration—to discover patterns that do not rely on prior knowledge.

Table 2.3 The marketing research mix

Element	Coverage
Purpose	Research objective and sub-objectives, aims, hypotheses, etc.
Population	Census or sample? Considerations about the target audience, customer, or player. Users or non-users? Who is the respondent? Selection by probability or non-probability methods?
Procedure	Data capture, data processing and analysis. Desk research or primary? Qualitative or quantitative? Personal, phone, post, online? Questions, observation, or deduction? Continuous or one-off? Interviewer or interviewer-less? Research instruments: topic guide or questionnaire? Projective techniques? Video? Scanner?
Publication	Reporting and presentation. Who should know? Timing? Written report, oral presentation? Dashboard? Hard copy? Visuals?

Population

When considering the population, the key questions concern: '*Who is involved in this marketplace? Who are the players? Who should be the centre of the investigation and where are those subjects?*'. This area considers: the target audience, customer, or player; the users or non-users. In addition: '*Who is the respondent or informant? Should we contact all players or just some of them? Should we carry out a census or a sample? Should respondents be selected by probability or non-probability methods?*'.

An important concept for primary research is *sampling*. We choose to interview (or observe) people who we think will give us the information that will solve our problems. So, in choosing our research method, we need to consider both whom and how we select. This applies to qualitative research with only a few people, and quantitative research with many people.

Much emphasis in marketing research is on the end-user, but 'experts' can bridge the gap between primary and secondary data. An expert may be someone who has been in the business for many years. Aspects of the population are investigated in Chapter 5.

Procedure

When considering the procedure, the key questions are: '*How should the study be conducted? Will it be qualitative or quantitative? Will it be secondary data or primary data?*'.

Publication

Under the heading of 'Publication', the key questions are: '*Who is the audience for the results? What should be communicated? When? And how should they be communicated?*'. Research is of no use if findings are kept within the research team. Similarly, commercially sensitive

Common mistakes
Ignoring the objectives

When planning a research project, two things are likely to dominate the researcher's thinking. One of these is the subject area and the other is how to carry out the project. For example, if we are asked to investigate domestic animals, we are likely to think, by simple association, of dogs and cats, and then of all the questions we can ask about keeping these pets. The way in which we do research will also dominate our thinking: how easy is it to contact pet owners; would we speak to them when walking their dogs? In reality, we should put the topic and the method behind the objective. We cannot and should not ignore the objectives. The objectives must dictate how a study is conducted and must generate the topics for investigation.

Let us consider an example where the objectives are ignored. Here are the objectives for a study focusing on a washing powder for a segment of the elderly population that has no washing facilities at home.

Overall objective

To provide information to help in the promotion and advertising of this new washing powder.

Sub-objectives

1. To identify the number of senior citizens who use public laundrettes (or who use facilities outside their home).
2. To establish when these people do their washing the most (by day and hour).
3. To examine **attitudes** to existing washing powders.

Methodology

The method proposed is to hold three focus groups in retirement homes. This would provide individuals who are ready and willing to be interviewed.

Comment

This methodology may go some way to satisfying sub-objectives 2 and 3, but cannot possibly help with the first objective. Indeed, there are many senior citizens who are not retired, who live outside such institutions and who may well differ from their counterparts in retirement homes, which operate a rather structured day and, in many cases, take the burden of laundry away from their residents. A more appropriate methodology would involve a quantitative study; it may well begin by consulting secondary data. Questions may not even be posed to the senior citizens themselves: possibly they may be asked of public laundrette owners or relatives. It may even involve observational studies at laundrettes. It is essential to remember that the 'players' in a marketplace must be examined carefully.

The best research starts by looking at what information already exists; this is called secondary data. For example, a researcher may be confronted with a problem: promoting a product to soccer fans. It is a good idea to look at previous promotions made to this segment. Such an inspection may tell much about the use of channels, content, and style. Information technology, and specifically the

Internet, has improved the ability and speed of gathering secondary data. If secondary data does not solve the problem, then original data (primary data) can be sought. Secondary data is information that has already been collected for a different purpose than your need. The term 'desk research' is sometimes used as a synonym for secondary data and Chapter 3 develops this area. There are two basic sources: internal (within an organisation) and external (published by someone outside).

It is useful to think of different *primary methods* in these terms: we can ask people what they are doing; we can watch them or detect what they have done by counting; or we can manipulate some variables to discover the effect. This creates three categories: questioning, **observation**, and **experimentation**.

Primary data collection techniques can be subdivided into: interviewer-administered or respondent-administered; direct or indirect; or personal or impersonal. These are explored in more detail in Chapter 4 on primary data. Processing data, analysis, and interpretation are essential parts of the procedure and these are fully explored in Chapter 9. Detailed examination of the tools used in the data collection appears in Chapter 6 on **instrument** design.

information will have no competitive advantage if it is placed in the public domain. Choices need to be made on how publication takes place: *'Will a written report be created? Will tabulations be provided? Will a personal presentation take place? Who should be allowed sight of the results?'*. These areas are explored in Chapter 10.

Briefings

Successful marketing research takes place when all people involved in the commissioning of research know what is happening. Good communication is essential from start to finish. It begins when there is an initial idea to carry out research. A briefing document is therefore useful to explain what is expected from researchers. The problem faced by a client is whether to give a reduced or extended brief. Briefs can be as short as one side, or as long as 200 pages; most are around two to five pages. Typically, the layout of a research brief will follow these sections:

- Company background
- Background to the problem
- Research objectives
- Methodological preference
- Reporting expectations
- Timing
- Budget considerations.

There are more examples of briefs in Figures 2.3 and 2.4, in the Market Researcher's Toolbox, and also on the Online Resource Centre. The content of the brief is explained below each subheading.

Let us apply the MR mix framework to a well-known UK media study. The purpose of the National Readership Survey (NRS) is to provide estimates of the number and nature of the people who read Britain's newspapers and consumer magazines.

A random sample of over 37,000 individuals was selected. The population under study are those aged 15 and over in Great Britain; this was estimated at 50,239,000. Addresses are selected from the Postal Address File using a random procedure. Interviewers employed by Ipsos MORI, the research contractor for NRS, visit these addresses and individuals aged 15+ are selected for interview, also using a random procedure. The survey's response rate – those available and agreeing to complete an interview – is currently 50%. Interviews are conducted in respondents' homes. Respondents are shown mastheads of newspapers and magazines and asked which of these they have read, when they last read them, how often they read them, how copies were obtained, and time spent reading. Respondents are also asked a number of other questions for classification purposes. The average interview length is just under 30 minutes. The interviewer uses a laptop computer to conduct the interview, inputting the respondent's replies as the interview progresses. This is DS-CAPI (double-screen CAPI). All prompt material is shown to respondents on a tablet screen that is controlled by the interviewer's laptop via a radio link.

Publication of results means that there is a careful analysis; the data is weighted by sex, age, region, and social grade to ensure that the profile of the sample reflects the profile of the total population. NRS data is published as data tables on its website, and electronically through authorised computer bureaux. These bureaux have produced software that enables users to carry out a large range of different analyses of the data on their own PCs; this allows unlimited analyses.

Compiled by Nigel Bradley 2012.

Source:

http://www.nrs.co.uk with thanks to Steve Millington at the NRS.

Questions

1 Could another population (and therefore sample) be used to achieve the same objectives?

2 How could the procedure be changed to achieve the same objectives?

3 What would the implications be if the results were not published in electronic form?

Company background

This section is designed to equip a research agency with a quick understanding of the market in which the company operates. This is information of a rather historic nature; it may include a list of products or services offered with financial data. It may describe the number of outlets, whether operations are international. Clearly, sources of further information, such as websites, can be provided.

This section will draw heavily on secondary internal data; that is, it is likely to draw on information already available internally to the researcher. It will be more up to date and more relevant to the study than information that appears in the company's 'annual report'.

A good checklist for writing a brief is to consider the marketing mix. What are your products and prices? What promotional techniques are used and how are products distributed? In the case of complex offerings, it is expected that briefings explain the technical aspects of products. If there is any jargon involved, some assistance to the reader is advisable.

Background to the problem

Although the word 'problem' may imply there is something wrong, it is important to explain why it is felt that research may be of use to decision-making. This section may explain recent changes in the marketplace. It may go further than the company itself and describe the competitive situation. This section may explain past research studies that have been conducted. It may draw on secondary data to inform the researchers about the marketplace.

Research objectives

Well-articulated research objectives are essential to a good research project, although they may be extremely difficult to formulate. A client has an advantage over a research agency because the client has knowledge of both the wider business objectives and the marketing objectives. In the case of advertising or promotional research, the client will also know the promotional, creative, or communication objectives.

Therefore, it is possible that the research objectives will not be the only objectives in this section. The client may decide that business, marketing, and other tactical objectives will help the researcher to create a better proposal. It should not be assumed that all information available is given to the agency, because overinformed people can sometimes underperform; on the other hand, having a full understanding of the problem is essential.

Methodological preference

This section can be used to offer support with methodological issues. You can say what is expected in broad terms: for example, a qualitative approach. It therefore expresses what you expect the agency capabilities should be. If you expect them to have previous experience of your product area or of interviewing your target market, then it should be stated here.

The disadvantage of expressing a preferred approach is that newer or fresh methodologies may be removed from consideration. Additionally, because the client has the last word in terms of spending money, it is likely that the preferred method may be given a greater weight than one that may give superior results. In the case where a client is lacking in knowledge or experience, such a recommendation can actually be damaging. This section is therefore absent from some briefing documents, either to allow agencies to think 'freely' or because there are, sincerely, no reasonable ideas available.

Some client companies have personnel who have previously worked with a variety of agencies over many years; they may even have worked on the agency side of the relationship. It is therefore logical for them to use their experience and knowledge to propose how the research might best be done. They also have the knowledge of their own industry, so any suggestions will be well informed.

This section is a perfect opportunity to point out likely sources of sample. If customer names and addresses are held on a database, then this can be offered, or it can be made clear that this is not available for research purposes.

Reporting expectations

There are many interested parties who may be affected by research results. It is important for each audience to receive the findings from research at the right time. Reporting is therefore not limited to a simple report with 30 pages and some pictures and tables. A brief should give an indication of who might be interested in results, whether it is internal (top management, operational managers, etc.) or external (advertising or direct marketing agency, etc.).

Several report formats are available: progress reports (regular, irregular, by phone, email, Dashboards, etc.); interim reports (oral, written, face-to-face, etc.); final reports (written, as presentation software delivered via the Internet or by email); conference-style, teleconferences, video-conferencing, etc. Reporting formats may be:

- Progress reports
- Interim reports
- Final reports
- Teleconference
- Video-conference.

It should be noted that there are variations: the report and presentation may have the same deadline; sometimes a report is submitted before presentation; sometimes a presentation takes place before the report deadline; and, of course, there may be no presentation or there may be no report.

It is here that a client may point out whether a contract will be subject to strict confidentiality. All suppliers follow the industry code of conduct, which assures clients of discretion, but some clients safeguard themselves further with a precisely worded agreement on this matter. Some agreements name the individuals within an organisation who are aware of the project and who will take an active role. Some agreements have a 'deniability' clause, whereby workers must deny having worked on the project. In the aerospace field, such studies are sometimes known as 'black projects'.

Timing

Deadlines are important for all parties: they permit plans to be made and problem areas to be identified. They help to determine whether a method is feasible. Sometimes they lead to research not taking place at all. In a briefing, the client must be honest and realistic; indeed, they should make all efforts to become familiar with the timetables that operate within their own company. When are budgets set? When are products launched? What is the seasonality of this particular product? Similarly, the audiences for whom the research is intended should be considered carefully. When will they expect results? When will they be absent from work? What are the dates of public holidays? Two deadlines are important to agencies:

- Written report deadlines
- Personal (oral) presentation deadlines.

Budget considerations

A research brief should provide an indication of the amount of money available for a particular project. This amount allows an agency to eliminate certain approaches that might fall outside the spending power of their potential client. This is certainly a problem area for some clients in that they may be unfamiliar with the cost of some types of research, and may feel reluctant to show their riches or, perhaps, to show their ignorance. Budgets are sometimes expressed in terms of an upper limit or a range: for example, *'up to £10,000 is available'* or *'the project is expected to fall within £7000–£10,000'*. Hess and Lucas (2004) researched an interesting area to answer the question: *'How much marketing research should a firm do when it takes resources away from manufacturing the goods that generate revenue?'*. Some of their findings are alarming. They say that *'firms without initial knowledge of their potential customers should allocate one-third of the firm's resources to marketing research'*. This is an indication of the importance of research to corporations and a compelling argument to justify an allocation of money for research.

Figure 2.3 is an example of an extremely short 'research briefing' document. It is an example of bad practice because it is so short, it does not describe the background, and it does not explain the objectives. Furthermore, it has an unrealistic timetable. The reader must, however, realise that such documents are not uncommon and that they vary in length and in detail. In some cases, they are not even created because time pressures and good working relationships between provider and user may reduce a briefing down to a short spoken exchange by telephone or in person. It is important to stress that it is good practice to create a full written brief.

Figure 2.4 shows the same brief but in a more acceptable form. It is more acceptable because it has more content and is less likely to be misunderstood, or interpreted incorrectly. We know about the organisation now and we can go to the website for more; we have a

VERY SPECIAL EUROPEAN BODY
OUR ADDRESS
OUR DEPARTMENT
Brussels, 3rd March 2009

Pre-Testing of General Slogan for Communication Activities of the VERY SPECIAL European Union Body

Introduction

The VERY SPECIAL European Union Body now has a requirement for pre- testing of general slogans to be used for all paid-for activities in 2010 (next year).

Description

We wish to evaluate some slogans through a series of tests — in three or more member states and in three or more of the official languages of the European Union.

The contractor will be expected to organise and manage all aspects of the research. The findings of the research (synthesis, analysis, proposals — if appropriate) should be presented both orally and in report form, in either English or French.

The presentation and report should be completed by 14th April 2009.

Additional information

Francesca Garanti
Tel: 32 2123678

Email garantif@veryspecialeuropeanbody.org

Figure 2.3 An example of a poor brief

VERY SPECIAL EUROPEAN BODY
OUR ADDRESS
OUR DEPARTMENT
Brussels, 3rd March 2009

Pre-Testing of General Slogan for Communication Activities of the VERY SPECIAL European Union Body

Background to VERY SPECIAL European Union Body

Our organisation has been working since 1987 to assist European companies to operate effectively. Taxpayers fund our activities, which include representation of European companies at international trade fairs. We work closely with chambers of commerce worldwide and organise training for management in many languages. Full details may be found at our website: www.veryspecialeuropeanbody.org

Background to the problem

The VERY SPECIAL European Union Body has a requirement for pre-testing of general slogans to be used for all paid-for activities in 2010 (next year). The audiences for these activities include the people wanting to establish themselves as self-employed and wanting to create a small business. Other audiences include anyone who advises them in this task. Therefore banks, chambers of commerce, local councils, and any other group of this type should be included. Having shortlisted a number of slogans, in prior research, we wish to evaluate the potential of three we have selected as the most promising. These are:

– Plan, revise, replan: secrets of success

– Risk-takers do it with data

– Information leads to success

Versions in other European languages are currently in preparation and will be available in time for the research.

Research objectives

The overall objective is to evaluate the potential of three slogans:

– To assess how memorable each of the three slogans are among the target audiences

– To assess understanding of the slogans by the likely audiences

– To assess the likely impact of the slogans.

Methodological preference

Please consider a series of tests on a qualitative basis. This will be in three or more member states and in three or more of the off cial languages of the European Union. The contractor will be expected to organise and manage all aspects of the research. We are open to other suggestions.

Reporting expectations

We expect regular progress reports. The findings of the research (charts, interpretations, tables if appropriate) should be presented both orally and in report form, in either English or French. Location: in Belgium.

Timing

Please submit detailed timetables, taking the following into consideration:

14th April 2009	Initial thoughts should reach us
30th April 2009	Proposal deadline
30th Sept 2009	Submit final report
Early Oct 2009	Be ready to present in person in Belgium.

Budget considerations

A maximum sum of €50,000 has been allocated to this project.

Additional information

Francesca Garanti

Tel: 32 2123678

Email garantif@veryspecialeuropeanbody.org

Figure 2.4 An example of a better brief

clear understanding of the background to the issue, including the actual slogans to be tested; there is a clear indication that there will be linguistic challenges to solve. Objectives are well articulated and a methodological preference is stated; the brief stipulates a need for progress reports and an outline of timing. This all leads to the view that the client is serious, has already considered the implications of the study, and will be a good client. It is also useful to see the budget, because this will determine the methodology and may therefore impact on the objectives.

Proposals

As we have seen, the key aspects of the research project are communicated, from a research user to a research supplier, by means of a written brief. That research supplier must then consider the requirements, develop various solutions, and provide a written research proposal. This section looks closely into that research proposal, which should be prepared carefully, taking many aspects into consideration.

Typically, the proposal will include a description of each stage of the research process, ending with a timetable and a cost estimate. Successful marketing research takes place when all people involved in the commissioning of research know what is happening. Good communication is essential from start to finish. It begins when there is an initial idea to carry out research. Where money is being paid for research, the proposal will be used to select the most appropriate supplier; from the provider's point of view, it is an opportunity to 'sell' the project. In a competitive bidding situation, the document can highlight the unique skills of the research team. A proposal document is therefore essential to explain what can be expected from the research. In most countries, such proposals actually become part of the legal agreement between the two parties, so the proposal becomes a contractual obligation.

Research proposals are at least three pages and many run to between 10 and 20 pages. The length is related to the size of project: the greater the money available, the longer the proposal. Typically, the research proposal will contain these sections:

- Background
- Objectives
- Methodology
- Reporting
- Timing

- Cost
- Terms of business
- Credentials.

An example proposal can be found in the Market Researcher's Toolbox; it will be more meaningful after reading other chapters, but in general terms, the content of each section is as follows.

Background

This section is a summary and evaluation of the points made in the brief; the proposal writer may gather other facts and figures about the client and incorporate these into the document.

Objectives

This section considers the purpose stated in the brief and explains it in greater detail. It is important that the research user is assured that the supplier understands its needs exactly. The objectives may appear as simple bullet points or may be numbered. Numbers are useful in that the specific objective can be repeated throughout the proposal using the number as an identifying label. Some researchers prefer to create one overall objective and several sub-objectives.

Objectives are usually expressed using the infinitive of the verb, for example: 'to explore ...'; 'to investigate ...'; 'to establish ...'. Although it is advisable *not* to incorporate methodological notions in the objectives, an approach may be implied by the verb chosen, for example a *qualitative* research method is implied by these verbs: *To identify ... To establish ... To examine ... To describe ... To explore ... To assess ... To investigate ...*

Common wording which may lead to *quantitative* research proposals includes: *To estimate ... To measure ... To determine ... To quantify ...*

Wording which implies reworking of secondary data includes: *To analyse ... To evaluate ... To compare ...*

Poor objectives are those that lack meaning or introduce methodology, thereby making an assumption. These include such wording as: *To undertake a questionnaire ... To conduct a* sample *survey ... To research ...*

Each objective should do just one thing; not two not three, just one. It is likely that the number of objectives will be limited to 10, but will usually be less than five. It is best to avoid a long list of questions in this section. That would be the basis of the questionnaire or **topic guide** and is useful, but best kept in the methodology section. See the Toolbox for some verbs to use in objectives.

Methodology

The methodology is the key part of the proposal and is a research supplier's response to the brief. It will offer a research solution that, in turn, should supply information to solve the marketing problem.

High standards of research are expected and so the proposal writer must pay attention to validity and reliability. There must be a clear assurance that all instruments employed will

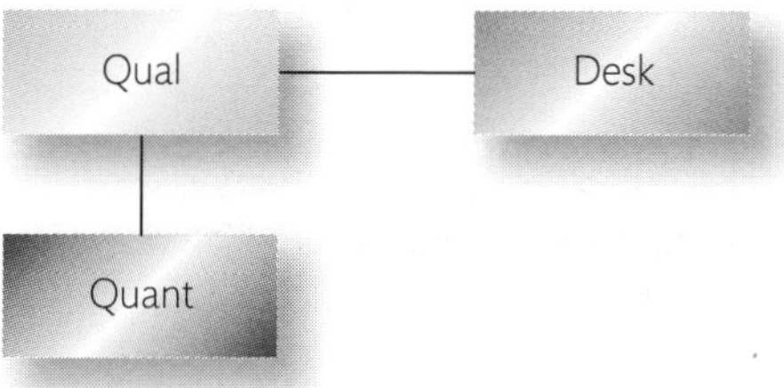

Figure 2.5 Parts of proposals

measure what is intended and that approaches can be repeated with the same outcome. Similarly, there must be assurances that ethical guidelines are being followed. This does not necessarily mean including a separate section; these considerations should be articulated in the explanations.

Methodological options and aspects of validity, reliability, and ethics are fully described throughout the textbook, so we will limit ourselves to an overview here. There are numerous methodological choices that can be used to answer a research problem and it is useful to step back and consider a project as distinct stages. We might envisage three approaches: desk research (secondary), qualitative research, and quantitative research (both primary). In Figure 2.5, the qualitative and quantitative stages take place simultaneously and provide useful information for the quantitative phase.

In the configuration in Figure 2.6, which we have called the 'traditional approach', the desk research comes first, providing information for the qualitative research, which feeds in turn into the quantitative work. Another qualitative stage is at the end of the project. An explanation for this design might be that the secondary stage discovers parameters of the population (how many people, **sampling frames**, how to contact), whereas the first qualitative stage helps to fine-tune the objectives, gives an outline of areas that need to be quantified, and discovers the vocabulary used by this group, which can be used directly in the questionnaire. The quantitative stage measures the opinions, attitudes, and behaviours that were identified in the qualitative stage. At the end of the project, the qualitative stage investigates issues that have been raised in the main fieldwork, thereby explaining the reasons for some of the numbers.

There are, of course, many variations on these designs and the illustration in Figure 2.7 summarises several combinations: Variation A is simply a project involving the use of secondary data; B has desk research and a quantitative stage; C is similar to the example above, but without a qualitative end stage. Projects D, E, and F miss any secondary phase, in which cases it would appear that it is unnecessary to seek such knowledge; it may be that the researcher is a specialist in the field and is already an expert in the background. Interestingly, F takes place without prior inquiry, which implies that the researcher has previous experience that allows construction of research instruments without reference to existing sources.

Reporting

It is important to know how information will be delivered, so proposals will indicate when and how the reporting will take place. It will show the number of reports and the type of report.

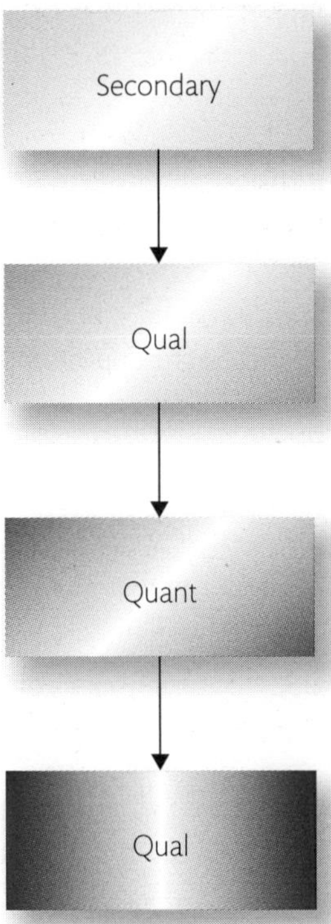

Figure 2.6 Traditional proposal structure

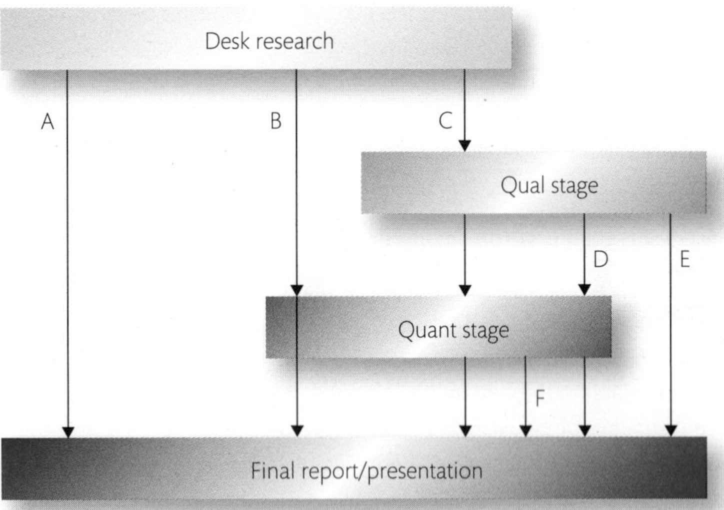

Figure 2.7 Proposal structure variations

It will also indicate the detail of personal presentation. A professional supplier of research will provide 'progress reports'. Typically, progress reports should take place regularly after any research starts, so that a researcher can explain to the client what information is being obtained and confirm that results will be delivered on time. This allows data users to prepare themselves and other managers for likely news, whether good or bad. The level, intensity, and frequency of reports are a matter of agreement because large projects will be more demanding and will need greater control. Such reports may be communicated to almost anyone in the process and may be part of a contractual obligation. When a provision for progress reporting is made, the client is assured that the research supplier appreciates that full communication between all parties must take place.

Timing

The timing section of a proposal can be the reason why a study is awarded to a competing agency. It must be realistic but, at the same time, it must satisfy the demands of the many clients who may be interested in the results. The fieldwork 'window' must be considered carefully: if respondents are being interviewed at the wrong time, then the validity and reliability of the results may be in question. For example, during summer holidays on the beach, there may be a tendency to read different magazines, perhaps more intensely. A readership study conducted with such people during that summer period may give different results than another in a different season. These principles apply to food consumption, travel, and every other activity: nature is seasonal and the weather affects our behaviour.

There are no accepted indications of how long different methods will take; it is possible to shorten activities by using more interviewers and more sampling points. Similarly, it is possible to run different activities in parallel rather than 'end to end'. Again, there can be a saving in overall time. These two approaches are known as 'sequentially phased research' and 'concurrently phased research' activities. Figure 2.8 shows the time saving made by employing concurrent phases. The timing guidelines in Table 2.4 are based on the author's experience.

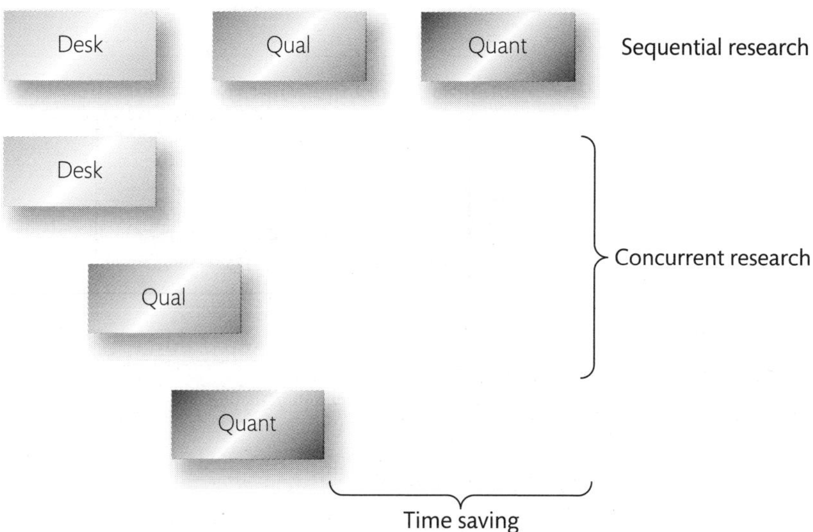

Figure 2.8 Sequential and concurrent research

Table 2.4

Timing guidelines for research

Method	Timeframe from start of fieldwork to reporting
1000 online interviews (CAWI)	Three days
1000 telephone interviews (CATI)	Seven days
1000 personal interviews (CAPI)	Two weeks
1000 telephone interviews (pen/paper)	Two weeks
1000 personal interviews (pen/paper)	One month
Three focus groups	One month

The timing will only start when the client decides to commission so using 'week numbers' rather than specific dates keeps the project flexible; a real timetable can be easily mapped onto an actual calendar when the project is near commissioning. There are two ways in which to communicate aspects of timing. One approach is a simple list of weeks and activities beside each; alternatively, the Gantt chart is an excellent way to show how activities work in parallel and overlap with each other. The first approach is shown in Table 2.5; the second, in Figure 2.9.

Critical path analysis (CPA), also known as critical path method (CPM), is extremely valuable when planning timetables for research projects. Every project is made up of different activities, each activity will have a specific time requirement, and some can take place at the same time as each other. Critical path analysis is a technique used to determine the shortest possible

Table 2.5

Traditional timing layout

Week	Activity
1–7	Desk research
8–9	Qualitative fieldwork
10	Qualitative/desk research report available
11	Quantitative questionnaire development
12	Pilot
13	Pilot debriefing
14–18	Main stage
17–23	Coding and data preparation
24	Tables produced
25	Presentation
26	Final report available

Timetable by month

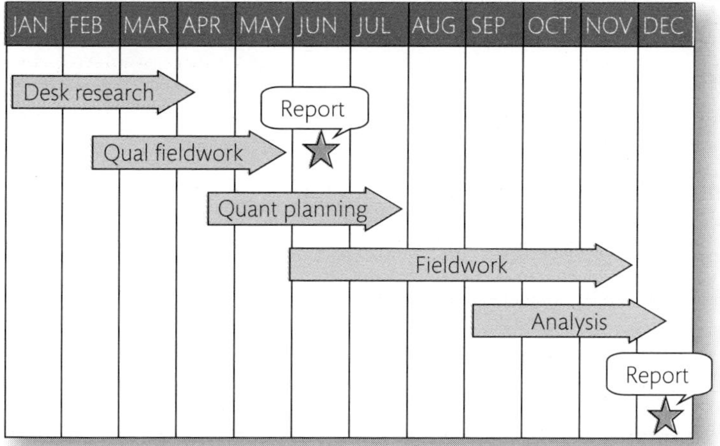

Figure 2.9 Gantt timing layout

time in which a project can take place. The technique allows the different activities to be coordinated. In its simplest form, the CPA can be created as a diagram consisting of circles connected by lines. The circles represent different tasks, some of which must be completed before the next task can start.

Table 2.6 and Figure 2.10 show how this has been applied to a simple project. The activities are listed and given a letter (A–H) and duration (in weeks). These are placed inside each circle and connections are made to the next activity.

A simple calculation can be made by viewing the activities and selecting those that will take the longest time. Planners can select the shortest times and negotiate for the longer ones to be reduced. The prerequisites for critical path scheduling to take place are:

Table 2.6 CPA applied to a research project

Activity	Duration (weeks)
A Desk research	7
B Qual stage	2
C Questionnaire writing	1
D Pilot	2
E Quant stage	4
F Prepare tables	1
G Produce tables	1
H Reporting	2

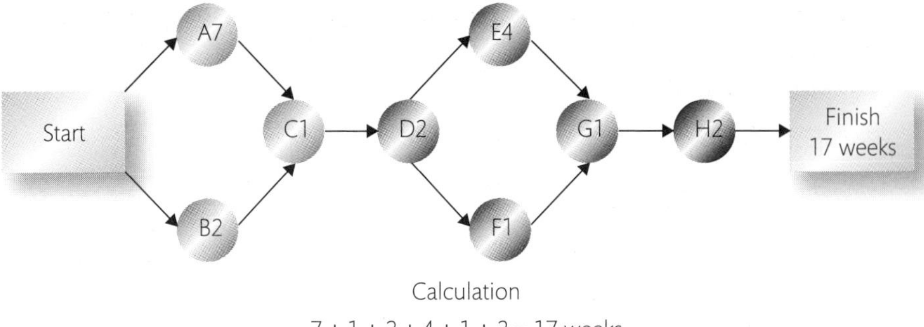

Calculation
7 + 1 + 2 + 4 + 1 + 2 = 17 weeks

Figure 2.10 CPA applied to a research project

- **Activities** It must be possible to subdivide the project into distinct activities
- **Time allocation** Each project activity can be given a time of duration. More complex versions of CPA can carry a probability of this time being achieved
- **Logic** The project activities will fit into some logical sequence. Some must be carried out before others and some may be performed in parallel
- **Resources** Each activity will need specific resources—human or material—and they can be expressed in monetary terms.

Critical path analysis allows the researcher to:

- Show the duration for a certain fee
- Show the fee for a certain time period
- Plan workloads across different projects to best use resources.

More sophisticated versions of critical path analysis include PERT (Program Evaluation and Review Technique), which applies theoretical frameworks to each table; for example the probability (optimistic or pessimistic) of completing the tasks in the time given. As a guide, the more complex the project, the more sophisticated should be the planning tool.

Cost

Typically, the fees charged are based on many considerations; some of these will be examined. The biggest problem for agencies is to anticipate what will happen on a project. In personal or telephone interviewing, an incorrect estimate of 'hit rate' by interviewers seeking users of a particular product can lead to further hours of work. A poor **response rate** on a mail survey may require a further mail-out.

Most agencies have formalised the following items into costing **forms** either on paper or online:

- Labour (director, executive, secretarial, computing/spec writing, data entry coding, other)
- Subsistence (food, lodgings)
- Location rental (facilities such as halls, group venues, etc.)
- Postal or delivery charges (outgoing, return, and reminders)

- Telephone (computer networking, communication, telephone interviewing, domestic and international)
- Travel (taxi, car, plane, train)
- Paper (questionnaires, reports, printouts)
- Overheads (depreciation on laptops, fixed hardware, electricity, etc.)
- Materials (such as CDs with questionnaires, audio recording tapes, etc.)
- Respondent **incentives**
- Sample (purchasing names and addresses)
- Translations and language checking
- Transcriptions.

The fees charged by researchers vary enormously. ESOMAR carries out a regular survey with members who are located in many countries. The studies take typical research designs and request a quotation. The results of these studies show that there are many different charging structures used. Some countries are cheaper than others; some suppliers charge more than others.

A useful guide, albeit simplified and in part based on the UK results from the ESOMAR studies, is given in Table 2.7. You may wish to use variations of this in any proposal you are required to write for study purposes.

For countries other than the UK, the rates vary: for example, the £3000 paid for a focus group in the UK might relate to £4500 in Italy, but just £1000 in Greece. The price for studies using self-completion methods is calculated using all relevant costs. If the method is postal, this should consider postage (outward, return, and reminders), paper-copying costs, labour, and so on. If incentives are given, these should be itemised (for example, £25 per person). CAWI and CAMI studies are more complicated, because they involve recovering costs of hardware and software that may be used for other purposes. The fees section of a proposal is part of the contract; therefore it must be complete and accurate. Nevertheless, any proposal will include a disclaimer of this type: *'We reserve the right to adjust the fee and date of completion in the event of subsequent alteration to the agreed specification'.*

Table 2.7 A guide to the price of research

Approach	Price
Focus group (five to eight respondents)	£3000 each
Depth interview	£750 each
Quant CAPI interview	£100 each
Quant CATI interview	£50 each
Quant CAWI interview	£35 each
Omnibus	£1000 per question
Desk research	£60 per hour

Common mistakes
Playing negotiating games

In commercial marketing research, there is much competition. This leads to 'negotiating games', whereby clients want the best deal and agencies may 'buy business' in order for contracts to be awarded.

Sometimes budgets are stated on a brief; sometimes they are not. Sometimes the stated budget is well below a real amount available. Clients sometimes argue that if a budget is given, the agency will make sure they spend it all. If budgets are not stated, agencies may argue that they may be wasting their time to create an elaborate solution to the problem. This may be fully justified if the response is that it is a good solution, but there are no funds. Another 'negotiating game' is when a client asks for several proposals, then chooses the best ideas and 'suggests' them to one of the agencies with whom that client wants to work. All of these problems can be avoided by developing honest and sincere working relationships. Asking for no more than three proposals is reasonable.

Terms of business

The terms of business include legalities and details such as ownership of materials and intellectual property. Some companies incorporate a confidentiality agreement, whereby personnel in a research supplier company agree to avoid discussing any details of a project with anyone not directly involved in the project. Some agreements contain a 'non-disclosure agreement' to reassure a client that the agency will not share or disclose any of the data provided by the client. The agreement may state that, on completion of the project, the agency must delete the customer data after a certain time period.

Credentials

The credentials are there to reassure a client that the personnel being used are capable and experienced. If previous clients have agreed for their names to be used in promotional materials, they may be mentioned in this section. Newcomers to research are often surprised by the fact that this device is used so little by researchers; advertising agencies are very active in mentioning previous clients. The main reason for avoiding mention of previous clients by researchers, however, is a desire to give prospective clients assurances of discretion. Credentials vary from two lines of mini-biography through to full résumé (CV) forms.

Selecting an agency

Research agencies are sometimes considered in the same way as advertising agencies. They both actively seek new work and in both sectors this is called making a 'pitch' for business; they will both be given a brief by the client, they will both make proposals, and they will be commissioned to carry out their jobs. During and after work, debriefs will communicate progress.

However, there are differences that sometimes leave newcomers confused. One difference concerns credentials: it is obvious if an ad agency works for a particular company—they work hard to communicate on the company's behalf. This then means that the client name can be used in the agency's own promotional materials. Generally speaking, ad agencies will not work for competing companies—there may be a conflict in commercial interest. In contrast, market research agencies pride themselves on protecting commercial secrets and this often means that client names do not appear on promotional materials. This can have a useful benefit to the agency because they can accept work from competitors simultaneously. The downside is that the usefulness of 'big name' endorsement is lost and clients need to find other ways to select agencies.

The decision to select a marketing research agency should be well considered. The prospective buyer of research will follow the steps outlined in Table 2.8. The emphasis is on finding a supplier that understands the research needs well; it should have experience in the sector or in the particular methodology anticipated. There is also the matter of personal

Table 2.8 Selecting a research agency

Step	Activity	Description
1	Internal discussions	Discussions internally about the need for research—what is the purpose? What action will be taken?
2	Create brief	The creation of a written document to outline the nature of the problem and instructions to a research agency
3	'Long list' agencies	Create a 'long list of agencies' from various sources. This will inevitably use published directories, but will also draw on the experience of colleagues and recommendations
4	Shortlist agencies	It is normal practice to brief just three agencies, so the long list needs to be reduced, keeping some in reserve in case any of the shortlisted agencies are unable to provide a proposal
5	Briefing	A briefing may be a meeting, telephone call, or just sending a briefing document by email or by post
6	Respond to queries	Agencies will now prepare a proposal, but will inevitably need clarification on specific points, usually concerning the company background and sampling
7	Receive proposals	The three proposals are received and considered
8	Reject and accept	The 'winning' agency is informed about the decision and any fine details are agreed. The proposal now forms the agreement between buyer and seller. A formal acceptance is made and this is a legally binding contract. The other agencies have invested time and energy in their proposal, so it is reasonable to give full feedback on why they were unsuccessful. Besides being good practice, you are likely to be working with them in future, so it is important to foster the relationship.

chemistry: the relationship is a partnership and if the respective teams are unable to work together the project may fail. Clearly, this becomes more important with continuous, ongoing projects. In larger organisations, a 'roster' is in place. This means that there will be a list of preferred suppliers that have been screened for suitability; the list is continually refreshed with feedback on past performance. At any of the stages, an agency may be invited to visit the prospective client in order to present its credentials.

Evaluating proposals

Having written a clear brief, it is usual to receive proposals from three different research agencies; this allows the research buyer to make a considered judgement about the final choice. It is then a matter for the 'buying team' to decide which agency to use. It is wise to create criteria specific to the project, which will embrace:

1. Resources of the agency (fieldforce, regional strengths, etc.)
2. Expertise in the sector (use of correct terminology, understanding of market)
3. Reputation (well-known references, advice from clients)
4. Understanding (originality of solutions, understanding of objectives and brief).

Although there is much simplification, the matrix in Figure 2.11 will help you to visualise the strengths and weaknesses of different proposals.

A = Misleading and poor value for money
B = Fair
C = Study is misleading
D = Good value for money.

Beyond the design and cost of research, there are other factors worthy of consideration. What quality control procedures are outlined in the proposal (for example, 'callbacks')? Are

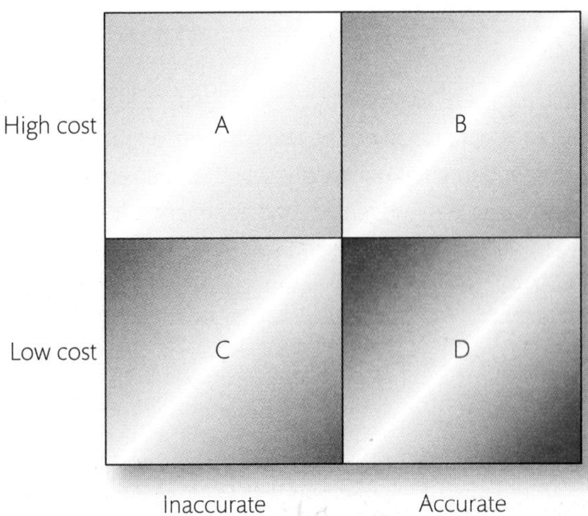

Figure 2.11 Proposal evaluation matrix

respondents recontacted to confirm that they actually participated in an interview? What measures are in place to ensure errors are minimised in the transfer of data from paper to computer? If the research team move to another project, what provision is made? Is the agency large enough to carry out all tasks? It is useful to create a checklist of items to evaluate the proposals—the checklist will vary from project to project.

Validity and reliability

Successful researchers must consider two key concepts: validity and reliability. If a study is valid, it means that it measures what we think it should measure. If it is reliable, it means that if we repeated the study, we would get the same results. Each time we come across a new study, we should ask ourselves how valid and reliable that study is. This constant 'criticism' is essential for the market researcher. Questions about validity and reliability need to be asked about every part of the study procedure: the questionnaire, the sample, the data capture method, the interviewer, etc.

Market researchers know that anything and everything they do can affect the outcome of their study. The different components of research, such as sampling, the wording of questions, the method used, and hundreds of other things, can change results.

One example might concern radio listening. A question may be created as follows: '*Q3 Yesterday, for how many hours was your radio switched on?*'. If the intention was to measure radio listening hours, the results would be incorrect. Many people leave the radio on when going shopping; they do this as a deterrent to burglars. The validity is in question here.

Consider another example: if you interview a representative sample of the nation's population every week, you can detect whether more (or less) people read a particular newspaper in comparison with another. If you decided to offer a prize draw as an incentive to do the interview, it may affect the results. It might appeal to young people, thereby increasing the sample size of youngsters, who may not be readers of that newspaper. The results may then indicate a decrease in that newspaper's readership. Here, the reliability of the study would have been affected by the incentive.

Is research really needed?

Research may not be necessary—there is always a choice *not* to listen to customers. There are many reasons why market research may not be used; there are problems with those decisions that are 'data driven'. The fundamental question is whether marketing decisions are informed by data or driven entirely by human judgement and experience. It is possible that experience can give confidence and this prior knowledge can act as a proxy for new facts. If data-driven marketing decisions are made, there are several risks: using inaccurate data, misinterpreting data, or even misusing data.

There are some other reasons why research may not be used, including:

- Study needs are misunderstood
- Proposals may not be convincing, or the overall comfort level is low
- High cost may mean the research does not fit a budget
- Low costs may evoke doubt about the seriousness of the supplier

Ethical insight
Protecting identities

Keeping the client's name and identity secret from a respondent can be useful because it can avoid any biased remarks about that company, whether they are favourable or otherwise. Additionally, it can preserve commercial sensitivity; nobody wants news of work in progress to be announced before a product is ready for market. In the past, keeping the identity of the research sponsor from the respondent was as important as keeping the identity of the respondent from the client. The right to client anonymity was, therefore, built into professional codes of conduct.

If a stranger starts to ask you questions about your opinions, you will probably want to know who is asking, and why you were chosen for interview. In the past, researchers could simply sidestep the issue. That situation has changed today because data protection laws allow you to know the source of your name and address. The Data Protection Act 1998 stipulates that individuals have the right to know who holds data on them and expects the source to be disclosed. The data controller's identity must be revealed if a respondent asks. If the name came from the customer database, that means that the data controller's identity must be revealed—and that is probably the client's name.

For that reason, the MRS Code of Conduct was modified to say that this right overrides the client's right to anonymity. If the researcher feels that this information may affect responses, the source can be revealed at the end of the interview rather than at the beginning. It is then up to the respondent to decide whether they are happy for their answers to be included on this basis.

Compiled by Nigel Bradley 2012.
Sources:
Data Protection Act 1998, http://www.ico.gov.uk
MRS Code, rules B6, B7, and B40, http://www.mrs.org.uk/standards/codeconduct.htm

Questions

1 What are the benefits of keeping the client's name secret?

2 What legal rights does the respondent have?

3 What might the role of a data controller involve?

- Timing (cannot be researched in the required time period)
- Competence (researchers with experience in the area may not exist).

Two visitor attractions in the UK were funded by National Lottery money: the Earth Centre in Doncaster and the Music Museum in Sheffield. Both failed, despite forecasts of many visitors. Whatever research method was chosen, it was unsuccessful. As an Arts Council spokesperson said: *'We expected the thousands who go to Glastonbury, to Castle Donnington, to the Isle of Wight, to go to museums, but they don't'.*

There is good reason to suggest that asking customers what they want can give misleading information (Bettman *et al.* 1998); there is evidence to show that consumer satisfaction programmes build expectations and may result in inappropriate, negative, or misleading results (Ofir and Simonson 2001). It is therefore of utmost concern that practical considerations are

Research in focus
Planning insight at BP Retail

Markus Graw of BP Retail describes the typical planning process used by the company. BP is one of the world's largest energy companies, providing its customers with fuel for transportation, energy for heat and light, retail services, and petrochemicals products for everyday items. Markus is Customer Insight Manager Europe for BP Retail M&OD (Marketing & Offer Development).

© OJO Images

My role has changed greatly over the years. In the early 1990s, I was the European research manager within BP. At that time, a client inside BP [would come] to me. I would then write a briefing, organise an agency, and oversee fieldwork; I would deliver the data back to the client and there might have been a presentation. And then it went over to the next project, exactly the same thing. Now, as customer insight manager, my job is more like a marketing consultant. We adopt a distinct approach that aims to squeeze every drop of knowledge from projects. In the period of a month, I am involved with around 35 projects.

There are three types of research. Firstly, what we call 'global projects'; continuous research like image tracking and customer satisfaction—they are standardised throughout the world. Project management for these comes from head office; we in Europe then analyse the data, use it, and inform and consult the countries using the data. The second type of projects are called 'strategic projects'. These cover certain important topics and are carried out in specific countries. For example, loyalty schemes are not set up in all countries, but where they are, we do the same research, using similar questionnaires. We use one agency throughout Europe and that is totally in my hands. Then we have 'ad hoc research' at local level, commissioned by my team members, by the responsible customer insight manager for that country, not at local level.

Compiled by Nigel Bradley 2012.

Sources:

Markus Graw, interviewed by Nigel Bradley, 2006. Reproduced with kind permission.

http://www.bp.com

Questions

1 How does the role of an insight manager differ from that of the 'old' market researcher?

2 You will see that all projects have budgets. From this account, which people in BP are likely to be involved in deciding how to spend that money?

3 BP keeps results of previous projects on an electronic database. What are the advantages for the company? What are the problems of this? What are the alternatives?

taken into account. Research can be blind, paradoxically, as Henry Ford remarked on the launch of his Model T: *'If I had asked the customer, he would have asked for a faster horse'* (Haig 2003, p. 35.) Sometimes, managers feel more confident drawing on their own experience.

All clear-minded researchers should accept the importance of the rigour of scientific enquiry. It is obvious that a sample size that is insufficient will not provide sufficient results; it is understood that using a postal questionnaire may be less efficient than using a face-to-face interview. Any responsible manager must query the basis for research and think 'outside the box'. These considerations may actually result in the research not taking place.

There are many solutions to marketing problems. Market researchers pride themselves on their ability to provide information to solve such problems and aid decision-makers. But marketing research cannot do everything; it is not the answer to all problems. Sometimes, the cost and time spent on research might not provide a value-for-money solution; it may give information, but too late. The mistake of being too ambitious can be seen in two ways: proposing a complex research project and also proposing a simple research project. A complex research project may go wrong, and a simple research project may be too ambitious because it was not necessary at all.

Therefore, to avoid any mistake, all users must ask why the research is being suggested. Is it because executives are too feeble or frightened to take responsibility for the outcome of decisions they make? There are many examples of poor reasons to do research. There are many reasons for justifying research expenditure. Think of 'brand managers' who compete against each other or who buy research to spend the entire budget in case next year's budget is cut.

As this chapter closes, you should reflect, and consider the possibility that research may not be necessary.

Chapter summary

1 Explain each stage of the research process using the marketing research mix as a framework

One way to help researchers to approach the complex area of designing research is the 'marketing research mix' (the MR mix) which, to be in line with the marketing mix, features four Ps. These elements are sequential and match the main phases that need to be followed. They are: purpose, population, procedure, publication. *Purpose* covers the objectives. The term *population* prompts the researcher to consider the target audience, customer, or player: should a census or sample be taken? *Procedures* embrace the means of capturing data, processing it, and then making analyses. These may involve desk research or using primary methods, and may be qualitative or quantitative, and in person, by phone, by post, or even online. *Publication* concerns communicating results through written reports and spoken presentation.

2 Describe the options available to the researcher

The 'traditional approach' means that desk research comes first, providing information for the qualitative research, which in turn feeds into the quantitative work. Another qualitative stage is at the end of the project. The secondary stage discovers parameters of the population; the qualitative stage then helps to fine-tune the objectives, gives an outline of areas that need to be quantified, and assists with the questionnaire. The quantitative stage measures the opinions, attitudes, and behaviours that were identified; the final qualitative stage investigates issues raised in the main fieldwork. There are variations on this design; several combinations can be found. Various aspects should be considered when selecting a research supplier. A systematic search for a supplier includes these steps: internal discussions, creation of a brief, 'long list' of agencies, shortlist of agencies, briefing, response to queries, receipt of proposals, rejecting or accepting a proposal.

Prepare a briefing document

Successful marketing research takes place when all people involved in the research know what is happening. A briefing document is there to explain what is expected from researchers. It is good practice to create a full written brief with these sections:

- Background of the company and to the problem
- Research objectives
- Methodological preference
- Reporting expectations
- Timing and budget considerations.

Prepare a research proposal

The research proposal follows a similar content list to the brief, but has a detailed description of each stage of the research process. The proposal is used to select the most appropriate supplier. In most cases, the proposal is the legal agreement between the two parties.

Review questions

1. What lessons can we draw from the past to help in planning research?
2. Compare the costs of different ways of doing research.
3. What ways of doing research are fast?
4. Why are briefs and proposals so important?
5. For what reasons may we decide not to carry out research?

Discussion questions

1. Why should the purpose of a project be debated by many people?
2. Select different combinations of research and explain how they could be used to investigate the automotive market.
3. Plan a simple proposal to determine why buyers of dog food choose particular can sizes.
4. Consult the brief in the Market Researcher's Toolbox, but do not read the corresponding proposal. Draft a possible structure for a proposal, then compare this with the one provided.
5. Read the opening Snapshot carefully. Outline a research plan that could be used for all new product test markets in the future. Be sure to include internal and external secondary data, primary data, qualitative and quantitative approaches.
6. Try to discover any brands that are being test marketed at present (ask a retailer or search the Internet).

Case study
Whiskas® Cat Food

Whiskas® meals have been satisfying cats since 1958. The brand is part of Mars Petcare and is a truly international brand well known by the distinctive purple colour and the advertising line: *'Eight out of ten owners said their cat prefers it'*. A clear segmentation is used by Whiskas®: cats are divided into kittens, adults (one or two years and above) and seniors (eight years and above). The products are divided into these three categories. Foods are available through distribution outlets as meat in cans, pouches, or as dry biscuits. Numerous ingredients and flavours are offered including chicken, turkey, duck, rabbit, beef, lamb, cheese, green beans, peas, salmon, tuna, prawns, cod, trout, sardine, herring, and whitebait.

Whiskas® spends a great deal of energy bringing valuable information to cat owners and does much of this over the Internet. The company uses visitor information to help plan promotional and business activities.

Compiled by Nigel Bradley 2012.

Sources:

http://www.whiskas.co.uk

http://www.mars.com/global/brands/petcare.aspx

Questions

1 This is a role play situation where you are acting as Whiskas® for question 1. The company website will provide information on products. Create a research brief using the information above and making any reasonable assumptions. The objective is to generate new ideas for catfoods and the research should test a new concept of inviting customers to propose their own mixtures and recipes of catfood. At the basic level the website will allow them to choose from a selection of flavours, there will also be the opportunity to propose unique recipes on a message board and this will then lead to comments from other cat owners and become a lively forum in addition to a source of new product ideas.

2 For question 2 you are now taking the role of a research agency. In response to the brief you have written, develop an outline of notes for a proposal. You should include the usual parts of the proposal. Cover the research objective/s, chosen method, and respondent profile. Pay less attention to specific aspects of methodology such as the sampling method and sample sizes, data collection, analysis, reporting, and timing. These will be covered later in the book.

3 What assurances of validity, reliability, and ethics can you provide to your client?

Further reading

- Birn, R.J. (2004) *The Effective Use of Market Research*, 4th edn. London: Kogan Page, MRS.
  Practical book on planning research with examples of good briefs and proposals.
- McCarthy, E.J. (1960) *Basic Marketing: A Managerial Approach*. Homewood, IL: Irwin.
  Classic text that started the fashion for using the marketing mix.
- McGivern, Y. (2008) *The Practice of Market Research*. Harlow, Essex: Prentice Hall.
  A practitioner textbook with a focus on social research.

Key web links

- The Research Buyer's Guide http://www.rbg.org.uk
- Free marketing research resources http://www.researchinfo.com
- Google software and applications http://www.google.com/apps

Visit the Online Resource Centre that accompanies this book to access more learning resources on this chapter topic.

References and sources

Anon. (1967) Pioneering with PERT, how to speed entry into new markets, *Business Management*, Sept, pp. 66–74.

Baskin, M. and Coburn, N. (2001) Two tribes divided by a common language? The true nature of the divide between account planners and market researchers, *International Journal of Market Research*, 43, pp. 137–169.

Bettman, J.R, Luce, M.F., and Payne, J.W. (1998) Constructive consumer choice processes, *Journal of Consumer Research*, 26, pp. 187–217.

Birn, R.J. (2004) *The Effective Use of Market Research*, 4th edn. London: Kogan Page.

Borden, N.H. (1964) The concept of the marketing mix, *Journal of Advertising Research*, 4, pp. 2–7 (available in Schwartz, G. *Science in Marketing*. New York: John Wiley & Sons, pp. 386–397).

Boruch, R.F. and Cecil, J.S. (1979) *Assuring Confidentiality of Social Research Data*. Philadelphia, PA: Pennsylvania Press.

Chapman, R.G. (1989) Problem definition in marketing research studies, *Journal of Services Marketing*, 3, pp. 51–59.

Culliton, J.W. (1948) *The Management of Marketing Costs*. Boston, MA: Harvard University.

Dimbath, M. (1968) Theory of the marketing mix, *Southern Journal of Business*, 3, pp. 21–36.

ESOMAR (2011) *Global Prices Study 2010 ESOMAR Industry report*. Amsterdam: ESOMAR, 19 pp.

Frey, A.W. (1956) *The Effective Marketing Mix: Programming for Optimum Results*. Hanover, NH: The Amos Tuck School of Business, Dartmouth College.

Glaser, B.G. (1978) *Theoretical Sensitivity: Advances in the Methodology of Grounded Theory*. Mill Valley, CA: Sociology Press.

Goodwin, T. (1997) How the new geographic systems put Boots on the right footing, *Research Plus*, May, p. 13.

Haig, M. (2003) *Brand Failures: The Truth About the 100 Biggest Branding Mistakes of All Time*. London: Kogan Page.

Hess, J.D. and Lucas, M.T. (2004) Doing the right thing or doing the thing right: allocating resources between marketing research and manufacturing, *Management Science*, 50, pp. 521–526.

Lawrence, R.J. (1982) To hypothesize or not to hypothesize? The 'correct' approach to survey research, *Journal of the Market Research Society*, 24, pp. 335–343.

McCarthy, E.J. (1968) *Basic Marketing: A Managerial Approach*. Homewood, IL: Irwin.

McGarry, E. (1950) Some functions of marketing reconsidered, in Cox, R. and Alderson, W. (eds.) *Theory in Marketing*. Chicago, IL: Richard D. Irwin, pp. 263–279.

McGarry, E. (1951) The contractual function in marketing, *Journal of Business* (of The University of Chicago), 24, pp. 96–113.

Mindak, W.A. and Fine, S. (1981) A fifth 'P': public relations, in Donnely, J.H. and George, W.R. (eds.) *Marketing of Services*. Chicago, IL: American Marketing Association, pp. 71–73.

Ofir, C. and Simonson, I. (2001) In search of negative customer feedback: the effect of expecting to evaluate on satisfaction evaluations, *Journal of Marketing Research*, 38, pp. 170–182.

Part

2

Data collection

Secondary data

Contents

Chapter guide

Secondary data should form the basis of all research projects. It allows us to refine our approach to collecting primary data and it can also answer our questions. Desk researchers should look for secondary data within the client organisation and also outside. Data are available both online and offline. Wherever the data are to be found, planning your search is essential. You will learn how to interpret published data and how to create search records.

Learning outcomes

By the end of this chapter, you should be able to:

1. **Explain the nature of secondary data**
2. **Outline the different sources of secondary data**
3. **Show the benefits and the limitations of using secondary data**
4. **List the features of a plan to carry out effective searches**

Introduction

The term 'primary data' is used to describe information that is collected for a specific purpose. **Secondary data** are best remembered as 'second-hand', because such data are 'old' primary data. Good researchers start with secondary data before designing primary research studies.

Traditionally, secondary data was found in the form of paper documents. A market researcher of the past spent hours looking for these documents at dusty desks in libraries, and, for this reason, the term 'desk research' came about, and is still used. Secondary data has various uses: it may answer the research question; it may also help to refine objectives; it may help to design primary research; it can assist in sampling; it can help to supply pre-codes for questionnaires. Desk research can be used both to enhance understanding of results and to confirm results.

It must be emphasised that desk research involves more than consulting documents; it can also mean consulting the information stored in the heads of people. Fact-finding interviews and expert interviews, with leading figures in a particular marketplace, play a major role in desk research. This is reflected in the various names used for this method of inquiry, including: fact-finding interviews, expert interviews, scoping, secondary searches, and measuring marketing metrics.

The marketer today can thank past researchers for the vast quantity of information available; they have worked tirelessly to leave their records. Where records were lost, important steps were taken to avoid this in future. One researcher was made famous for failing to leave records. For several decades at the start of the twentieth century, Sir Cyril Burt (1883–1971) carried out studies investigating various topics of great interest to psychologists. However, after his death, the findings looked suspect. Collaborators could not be found, the results he arrived at could not be replicated using similar approaches, and the data he had analysed were not available for reanalysis. This became known as the 'Burt Scandal' (see Fletcher 1991) and the major lesson that this taught the research community was to preserve raw data and make it available to other researchers. Processed data are useful, but researchers should be able to access first-hand records to replicate or extend the research. This lesson has meant that many archives are now open and that raw data sets are available for further manipulation. The ESRC Data Archive is a good example of this (see Lievesley 1993).

The evolution of storage media is important (see Table 3.1). Filing cards made from paper have long been used to store details; photographic techniques allowed masses of paper records to be reduced in size to become microfilm, or microfiche. The next step was to use electronic data transfer, which reduced documents to digital media and gave truly searchable items.

Table 3.1

Notable events for desk research

Year	Event
1910s	Filing cards
1960s	Computers available in large companies
1970s	Microfiche and microfilm became popular, many records transferred. Burt Scandal. Aggregators emerged
1980s	Electronic data transfer, World Wide Web
1990s	Internet search engines and directories introduced
2000s	Freedom of Information Act introduced to UK

SNAPSHOT
Tesco Clubcard

© Tesco Stores Limited. Reproduced with kind permission.

Every retailer has a vast amount of internal data. Sales transactions are a good example of what is known as internal secondary data. If we look carefully they can tell us a great deal, you can do this just by looking at your last sales receipt from a supermarket. We can see what particular product has been sold. We can see the price at which it was sold, we can see the time of day, the day of the week, the month and season of the year. We can see what other products were bought at the same time. We can identify whether any sales promotions, such as coupon redemptions or discount offers, were included. We can plot the location of the items in the store in order to see the likely path that was taken around the store: which aisles were used and perhaps which were avoided. We can see which checkout desk was chosen before the shopper left the store, we can discover whether a credit card or cash was used.

This information is rich and has long helped retailers to predict what stock to display and what inventory levels should be kept. As it stands, however, this information offers little insight into the shopper. In 1995 Tesco changed that with the discovery of a key to open the door to a far richer meaning to the same data.

The Tesco Clubcard gave a reason for each transaction to be related back to a specific individual and household. Shoppers were offered incentives to provide their name, address, age, sex, household profile, and more information. Those incentives included discount vouchers and special offers on things outside the store such as travel and leisure, by collecting points shoppers would continually identify themselves and link themselves to transactions. This then brings each transaction alive: it is clear why pet food is purchased as that home has a cat; babycare purchases are indicative of a new addition to the family; the occasional purchaser becomes obvious. A simple postcode can allow databases to be merged, opening up new knowledge about the occupants. As the Tesco board discussed adopting the scheme, the chairman Lord MacLaurin said *'What scares me about this is that you know more about my customers after three months than I know after 30 years'.*

Compiled by Nigel Bradley 2012.

Sources:

http://www.tesco.com/clubcard/clubcard/

Benady, D. (2007) Tesco leads the way in the loyalty program stakes, UK supermarket succeeds where so many others fall foul, *Strategic Direction*, 23(2), pp. 18–21.

Rowley, J. (2005) Building brand webs: Customer relationship management through the Tesco Clubcard loyalty scheme, *International Journal of Retail & Distribution Management*, 33(3), pp. 194–206.

The nature of secondary data

Secondary data already exists, so is likely to be less expensive than collecting information freshly. It will thus be fast to obtain and can offer a unique benefit for international studies, where barriers of distance and communication can lead to rather expensive and time-consuming data gathering.

A major limitation is that secondary data has already been collected for something other than the current research problem. Such data may not address the topic in question or may only provide part of the information expected. That information may not be accurate or it may be outdated. On the other hand, data may not actually exist, it may not have been collected and recorded, or it may be on such a new topic that it is not available outside a very small circle of people (see Figure 3.1). When the search begins or is being planned, there is no assurance that it will be a success. This uncertainty is a risk, particularly when paying someone to seek information: they cannot guarantee that hours of work will provide any results.

There are many ways of classifying data, and we will meet numerous labels in this chapter: the term, for example, refers to indexes and summaries—this is 'third-hand' data. For now, it is useful to remind ourselves of the distinction between two types of secondary data: internal and external (see Table 3.2). Internal data is generated by the organisation in question,

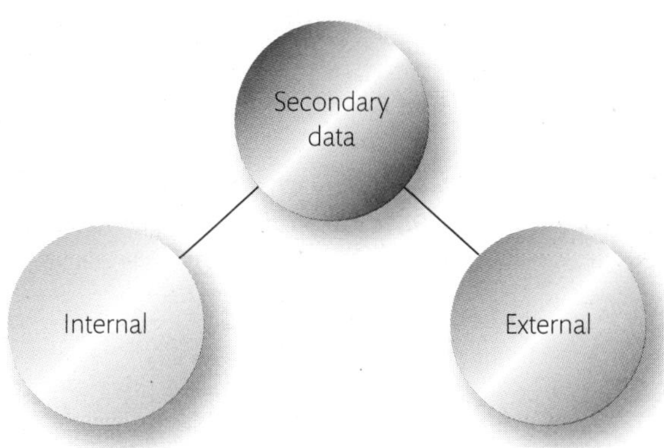

Figure 3.1 Secondary data can be internal or external to the organisation

Table 3.2 Distinctions between internal and external secondary data

Internal	External
Probably very relevant	Less likely to be relevant
May be biased (towards our company)	May be biased towards the source
Usually free	May require payment

whereas external data is more likely to be available to a wider public in the form of directories, databases, industry reports, and syndicated services.

Internal secondary data

If you work in a company, you will be surrounded by information. Here are a few examples: current and past price lists; sales force records with transactions, competitor activity; customer records with complaints, letters, comments, emails, warranty registrations, customer loyalty scheme transactions; sales by client, by geography, and by size; stock and inventory records; cost of transport; previous research studies; website visitor records.

As an employee, you have a duty to ensure that you comply with the Data Protection Act 1998 when using and controlling data. Every situation changes, but consider the following.

1. As an individual employee, do you have the authority to hand over data to someone else?
2. Does your organisation's status as data controller, according to the wording in the register, allow for transfer of information?
3. What is the information on the database? If it is individual/company details, were all of these aware when you registered their details that their information could be shared? Did you tell them? Did they consent?
4. Are any of these contacts registered with mail preference agencies?
5. How will the company use the data held?

In the past, internal data was the starting point in any research (see Figure 3.2). The idea being that there may be no need to look outside the organisation when required data could be found within. The next step was to look a little further, outside the confines of the organisation: this meant inspecting external secondary data. However, information technology has revolutionised the retrieval of data and the idea of looking at internal data first, because of ease of access, has less relevance today. It is perfectly possible that it is easier to find government data on the purchase behaviour of 2000 people than it is to find customer invoices from an accounts office in the same building (see Table 3.2).

It is worth noting that large corporations have integrated their own databases into 'intranets' and 'extranets'. This organisation of data makes it easier for information to be made available widely and quickly inside the firm. Popular search engines and information professionals have adapted their services to allow user-friendly searches of desktop computers and related networks. One such tool is Research Reporter software (see http://www.researchreporter.com), which allows large users of research to consolidate their research, so that databases of surveys are linked and are cross-searchable. Please refer back to Chapter 1 for more details on marketing decision support systems.

External secondary data

The dictionary and thesaurus are good starting points for any search of external data, not least to provide synonyms for subsequent searching. Many reference books are available, but it is worth mentioning that the UK standard dictionary is the *Oxford English* and the standard for

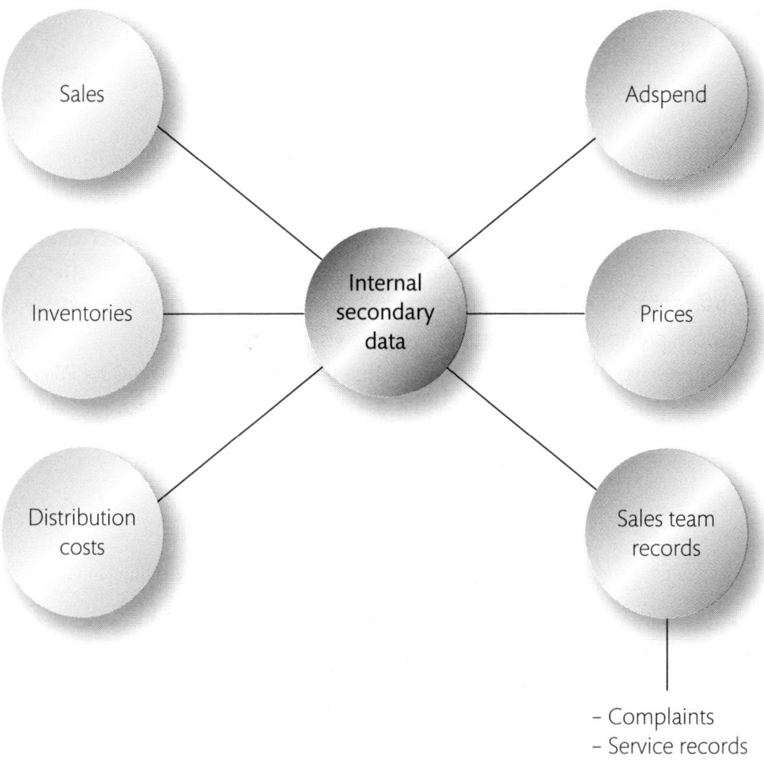

Figure 3.2 Internal data resources

the USA is *Webster's*. Similarly, any encyclopaedia can provide essential data; these are now easily available on the Internet and give knowledge along with terminology. They include the Encyclopaedia Britannica (http://www.britannica.com), and Wikipedia (http://www.wikipedia.org), available in several languages (see Figure 3.3).

The Internet

In 1965, there were final agreements, based on work by the Pentagon's Advance Research Projects Agency, to link the computers of three American universities: the Stanford Research Institute, Utah University, and the University of California. This was the start of the Internet.

In the early 1970s, computer developments promised a fast and flexible way to track down documents. The 1970s also saw the quiet arrival of firms that later took the title of 'aggregators'. These organisations combined information from various sources and made it available to customers; three such big names are now Dialog, LexisNexis, and Factiva, which were to play a big role two decades later when the Internet fully emerged.

In the 1980s, a great deal of knowledge was being shared on the Internet: for example, full-text access to newspapers, magazines, and journals started to appear. There was clearly a need to find information in an efficient way, so this was about to be created. We will look at search engines, but first, to set these into context, we will look at the Internet itself.

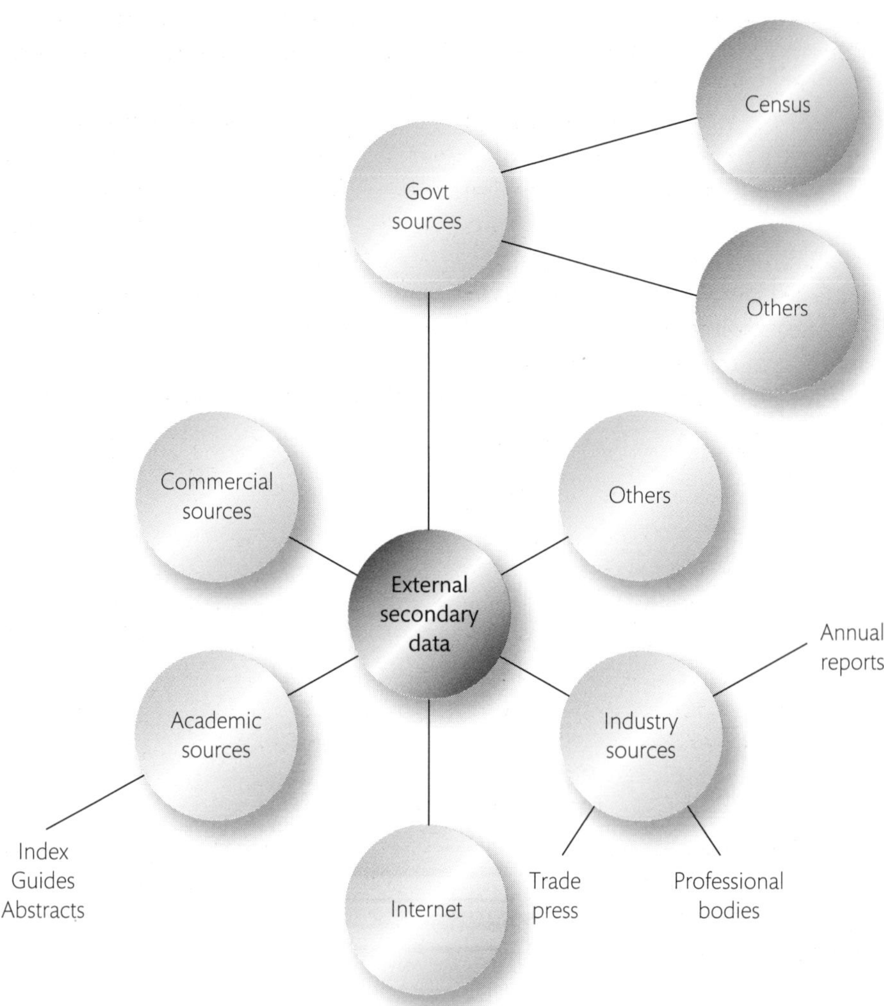

Figure 3.3 External data resources

In 1989, the World Wide Web became an integral part of the Internet as a simple method of publishing and presenting information. The web was first devised by Tim Berners-Lee, working at CERN, Europe's particle physics research centre; it was a way of linking documents. A web page is similar to an encyclopaedia page, which includes cross-references. In a book, to follow up a cross-reference, you need to find another volume, then the page number, and then the exact paragraph. The web is the same, except that it will flash up thousands of references within seconds—even if the relevant documents are on another continent. Browser software is needed to gain access to the web, and the best-known browsers are Internet Explorer and Firefox.

By 1996, over 30 million users were linked together, and the Internet, or the 'Information Superhighway', had established itself as a cheap method of making information available to the masses. The Internet performs a wide range of tasks including finding a job, finding a car, locating friends, finding book references, buying or selling any product or service, finding news, answering questions received, downloading software, searching for information, finding wanted criminals, etc. It offers the researcher a window on the world, a new avenue, a new way to access people and facts.

The very first tool used for searching on the Internet was called 'Archie'. It was created in 1990 by Alan Emtage. The program downloaded the directory listings of FTP (file transfer protocol) sites, creating a database of filenames that could be searched. The next tool used for searching the Internet was 'Veronica'. This program downloaded menu titles from Gopher servers, creating an index of plain text documents that could be searched. In 1993, Matthew Gray created the World Wide Web Wanderer. Excite was also introduced in 1993, and this engine used statistical analysis of word relationships to aid in the search process. Jerry Yang and David Filo created Yahoo in 1994. Unlike the Wanderer, which only listed each URL, Yahoo featured a description of the page content. Also in 1994, WebCrawler was introduced as the first full-text search engine; the entire text of each page was indexed for the first time. And again in 1994, Michael Mauldin created Lycos, a large search engine with relevance retrieval, prefix matching, and word proximity.

Alta Vista began in 1995 as the first search engine to allow natural language inquiries and advanced searching techniques using Boolean logic; in the same year, Metacrawler was developed by Eric Selburg. This was a novel idea whereby the search query was forwarded to several major search engines simultaneously, clearly taking advantage of the strengths and weaknesses of each. This has since been called a 'metasearch engine'. Ask Jeeves and Northern Light were both launched in 1997, as was Google. Google was created by Sergey Brin and Larry Page as a no-nonsense, quick engine, delivering very relevant answers to queries. In 1998, MSN Search and the Open Directory were also started. The Open Directory is a human-edited directory of the web, using volunteer editors.

It is fortunate that these search tools were developed because more information was soon to become available as a direct result of market demand and legislation. Market demand meant that aggregators became more important, delivering material from many sources to users, often free of charge.

We have seen much change in how materials are stored, located, retrieved, and used. From the very rigidly organised storage of documents according to the Dewey classification or other hierarchy, we are moving towards an age where data is stored as it is captured, in an apparently unorganised way, with little or no filing. Electronic searching and data capture makes sense of this and delivers the relevant information to the user.

Sources of secondary data

Government sources

Most governments in the world have statistical departments and these provide a list of publications available. Typically, such offices have general population census records and specialist censuses, for example, on agriculture, industrial output, housing, and construction.

The European Union (EU), as an institution, has extremely good resources: it has a statistical office called Eurostat, which collates figures from Member States. The idea was that decision-making and plans for European Community members should be based on reliable and comparable statistics and a coordinator was required. Therefore, in 1953, the European Community created Eurostat (see http://epp.eurostat.ec.europa.eu). Eurostat serves community institutions with information that helps them to design, manage, and evaluate EU policies. This information is also made available to public entities in Member States, to educational establishments, to companies, the media, and others. The information comes from the Member States, the United Nations, The World Bank, and the Organisation for Economic Co-operation and Development (OECD, http://www.oecd.org). Information is summarised in the *Eurostat Yearbook*, published every 12 months. It also comes from specially commissioned studies such as the Eurobarometer series. This is a continuous monitor of opinions conducted in the EU using samples of around 1000 people per country.

The UK has a statistical office and two publications: the *Annual Abstract of Statistics* and *The Guide to Official Statistics* provide excellent pointers to information. Frequently used research agencies, notably Ipsos MORI, also publish reports to access a wider readership (see http://www.ipsos-mori.com/researchpublications.aspx). The BOPCRIS service identifies relevant British official publications from the period 1688–1995 with its web-based bibliographic database (at http://www.bopcris.ac.uk). For Scotland, Scottish Executive Statistics are available (at http://www.scotland.gov.uk). Similarly, France has a statistical office called INSEE, and the Italian government office is ISTAT, and the same pattern repeats itself throughout all EU member nations. The USA has a major resource created by the Central Intelligence Agency (CIA). It is an online book that examines all countries of the world (http://www.cia.gov/cia/publications/factbook/). It provides statistics including for each population, economic overviews, transportation, government, and maps. The US Department of Commerce site at http://www.commerce.gov also offers such information, organised by industry sector.

The census and other major surveys are shown in Table 3.3. These clearly offer useful secondary data sources since the date started; this date indicates the extent of longitudinal data available for analysis. Survey sizes show the comprehensive nature of such work, but do not always show the full numbers of interviews: some studies interview all adults in a household; others interview only one. Size usually refers to that for the full cycle of the study or for a 12-month period. The survey sizes in Table 3.3 are based on recent results and have been rounded up or down to the nearest thousand.

Academic sources

The academic world also works continuously to produce new knowledge, and usually this is given free of charge and readily. In all cases, this knowledge must be organised in some way. We will see that these ways differ, but it is important to be aware of the Dewey system. The Dewey decimal classification system (DDC) is commonly used in educational libraries throughout the world. It is made up of ten categories. These are further subdivided. When seeking a book, one must be aware that class marks have more numbers after a decimal point, showing the degree of specialisation within the given subject area. Books are physically placed on bookshelves in decimal order, but because more than one book will carry the same class mark, the first three letters of the author's name is added to the end; for example: 658.0072 BRY, 658.1599 BUC, 658.3 CAR, 658.408 RES, 658.802854678 MIC, etc.

Table 3.3 Major UK social surveys

Research studies	Frequency	Started	Respondent	Survey size
Census of population	Decennial	1801	Adults	All households
Agricultural and Horticultural Census	Annual	1866	Farmers	110,000 farms
International Passenger Survey	Continuous	1970	Individuals at ports	258,000 travellers
Annual Survey of Hours and Earnings (formerly New Earnings Survey)	Annual	1998	Employees	223,000 records
Annual Business Inquiry (ABI)	Annual	1998	Company directors	78,000 businesses
Labour Force Survey	Quarterly	1979	Adults	60,000 addresses
British Crime Survey	Annual	1982	Adults	50,000 adults
Health Survey for England	Continuous	1991	Adults and children	16,000 adults
General Household Survey	Continuous	1971	Adults	13,300 adults
Expenditure and Food Survey (formerly the Family Expenditure Survey and the National Food Survey)	Continuous	1957	Household	7900 addresses
British Social Attitudes Survey	Annual	1983	Adults	3600 interviews
British Household Panel Survey	Annual	1991	Adults	5500 households
English Housing Survey	Annual	1993	Household	17,000 households

Various sources in 2012.

The Economic and Social Research Council (ESRC) is the UK's leading research funding and training agency, addressing economic and social concerns. Its intention is to provide high-quality research on issues of importance to business, the public sector, and government. There are several conditions that must be met before the ESRC provides money for research. One condition is that raw data sets are deposited with the archive and the second is that there must be some tangible output in the form of published papers, conference presentations, book chapters, etc. Because of the high budget, there is an assurance that almost 5000 researchers are actively producing new knowledge at any one time. For market researchers, this provides a massive amount of free information of high quality. Published journal articles from these projects and many more sponsors offer a great deal of information. Numerous databases contain journal articles.

Various bodies act as academic researchers. An example is the Pew Research Center, which describes itself as an independent opinion research group, serving as a forum for ideas on the media and public policy. It offers this information resource to political leaders, journalists, and scholars. All of the current survey results are made available free of charge at its website (http://www.people-press.org).

Industry sources

The commercial world has a regular output of trade periodicals. These can be identified in BRAD (see http://www.bradinsight.com). It is useful to identify five main specialist titles per sector. Once these are consulted, information will flow about that sector.

Company data are used for competitor analysis, identifying suppliers, or building profiles of potential customers. Much free data is available for UK firms from Companies House (http://www.companieshouse.gov.uk). Details available include: location addresses, date of incorporation, country of origin, status, nature of business, activities overseas. Another source of financial data is FT Interactive Data (http://www.interactivedata.com).

Annual reports are a legal requirement: the International Reporting Standards 2005 (IFRS) requires all listed European companies to report using a single set of accounting standards. This will allow investors to compare the performance of companies across the world. Also, acquired intangible assets must appear on balance sheets. This includes brands, Internet domain names, licensing agreements, trademarks, goodwill, and even customer list details. It is apparent that for the desk researcher, the annual report, easily obtained directly from the company, is an extremely valuable source.

All US public companies are required to file registration statements, periodic reports, and other forms electronically, and anyone can access and download this information for free from the US Securities and Exchange Commission at its website (at http://www.sec.gov).

Directories

Directories provide details of companies that supply or buy. They provide size in terms of the number of employees or turnover, and areas of activity. In using them, the user must become acquainted with several classifications that are used for businesses. These include the Standard Industrial Classification (SIC) and Statistical Classification of Economic Activities in the European Community (NACE). Very important directories come from Kompass (http://www.kompass.com) and from Dun & Bradstreet, such as *Who Owns Whom* and *Key British Enterprises* (http://www.dnb.co.uk). Directories that look at specific sectors can be located through guides such as Current British Directories (http://www.cbdresearch.com).

Telephone directories can inform up to a certain point. Every country has a *Yellow Pages* and *White Pages* (see http://www.infobel.com for links to every directory in the world).

Research in focus
Journals and archives

We must distinguish between secondary data consultation and secondary data reanalysis. Consulting existing sources is one thing, but we may want to reanalyse data in order to draw new conclusions. For market researchers, academic journals provide a massive amount of free information of high quality. Published journal articles from research projects offer a great deal of information. Numerous databases offer a gateway with direct links to such sources:

BIDS—Ingenta and other journals	http://www.bids.ac.uk
Emerald Library	http://www.emerald-library.com
JSTOR—Journal archive	http://www.jstor.org
Oxford University Press—Journals	http://www.oxfordjournals.org
ScienceDirect	http://www.sciencedirect.com/
Wiley Interscience	http://www.interscience.wiley.com
HighWire Press	http://www.highwire.stanford.edu

As for reanalysis, the UK is particularly well served in that http://www.data-archive.ac.uk offers quantitative data for reanalysis. On the other hand, http://www.qualidata.essex.ac.uk offers qualitative data for reanalysis. The UK Data Archive (UKDA) describes itself as a centre of '*expertise in data acquisition, preservation, dissemination and promotion*'. It claims to hold the largest collection of digital data in the social sciences and humanities in the UK. There are several thousand data sets.

Compiled by Nigel Bradley 2012.

Sources:

Lievesley, D. (1993) Role of the ESRC Data Archive in the dissemination of data for secondary analysis.

Screenshots from the UK Data Archive website have been made available with permission from the UK Data Archive at the University of Essex. For further information about the Archive and its data services, see http://www.data-archive.ac.uk

Questions

1 How can this archive help the market researcher?

2 Explain the functions of UKDA.

3 Explore websites for the other organisations mentioned above. How can these help in marketing?

Table 3.4 Professional groupings distinguished

Body	Definition
Trade unions	Represent the rights of employees
Trade associations	Represent the rights of employers
Professional bodies	Promote high quality in the sector

MacRae's Blue Book (http://www.macraesbluebook.com) is an industrial directory. These are valuable to locate companies, but also simple counts can allow the researcher to gather estimates of the numbers that exist; here, it is essential to be aware of the policy for listings. These directories are particularly good for their listings of small and medium enterprises (SME) rather than private individuals. Listings for private citizens at landlines are now incomplete, however, because we have seen a growth in mobile (cell) phone usage, and also in the choice not to appear in telephone directories (this is known as being 'ex-directory').

Individuals and companies can join professional bodies, associations, or groupings. These collective bodies exist even for the smallest sector; their main purpose is to represent interests of those concerned. It should be said that they will vary in their extent of funding, organisation, energy, size, and activities, but they are relevant to the desk researcher.

We can distinguish between trade unions, trade associations, and professional bodies (see Table 3.4). All represent the interests of members and the distinction is often blurred, but traditionally we can say that trade unions represent the 'worker' to his/her employer. Similarly, trade associations represent the company (and similar firms) within its marketplace and environment; they might lobby for government attention, for example. Professional bodies typically offer a level of competence to people employed in a specific field; they may offer qualifications and training and will most certainly keep members up to date with developments.

There are directories of these organisations such as the Directory of Associations (http://www.marketingsource.com/associations), the Directory of European Industrial & Trade Associations (http://www.cbdresearch.com), and regional versions such as the Directory of British Associations (http://www.cbdresearch.com/dba.htm). Of interest here are the British Library industry guides (http://www.bl.uk/bipc/dbandpubs/Industry%20guides/industry.html). Also the Trade Association Forum (http://www.taforum.org.uk).

A list of five of the main directories for the sector of interest is essential before contacting anyone. These will be important because they will often publish industry overviews that may be exactly the purpose of the desk research proposed.

Market research report publishers and aggregators

Several companies identify market sectors of interest and investigate existing knowledge to create an overall report on the sector; we describe these as 'market research report publishers'.

Their reports are available to anyone upon payment. The information is largely based on secondary data; compilation begins by searching news reports and consulting significant people in the market sector. Primary research may be commissioned to fill any gaps or to bring the report up to date; typically, this is done by using facilities. There are over 100 such publishers in Europe, 20 of which cover general subjects (Mort 2002a). Well-known generalists in this area are Datamonitor (360), ERC, Euromonitor (Passport GMID), Frost & Sullivan, Key Note, Mintel, BusinessMonitor (BMI), and Reuters Business Insights. On the other hand, specialist publishers concentrate efforts on specific areas such as IT, communications, or finance. Specialists include OVUM, IDATE, CIT, Forrester, Snapdata Total Research, and the Economist Intelligence Unit (EIU).

There are thousands of these so-called multiclient reports, and they can be ordered directly from the publishers. Additionally, they have been listed together in several other ways: over many years, Marketsearch has published details of 20,000 reports

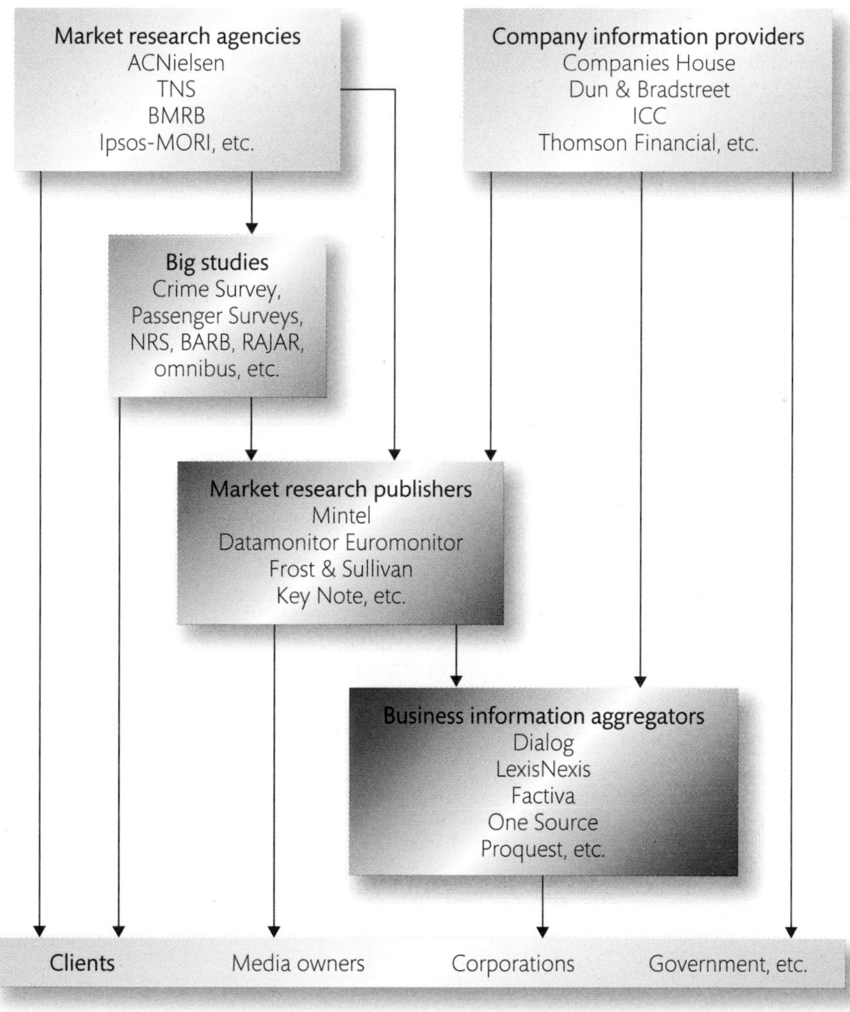

Figure 3.4 The complex desk research market

(see http://www.marketsearch-dir.com). Another database directory is Findex (http://www.csa.com/factsheets/findex-set-c.php). These are examples of tertiary data. New web-based companies have been created to act as aggregators. Two examples are marketresearch.com (350 publishers) and mindbranch.com (250 publishers). In turn, other companies, such as amazon.com, will distribute on behalf of these. It is worth saying that, although this market structure looks complex, it has resulted in lowered prices to end-users.

It is important to mention the role of aggregators. Figure 3.4 shows that these include such names as Dialog, LexNexis, Factiva, etc. These are organisations that combine information from various sources. The slight distinction with publishers is that these services are usually biased towards electronic media; sometimes they are known as online aggregators and will seek information in real time. All providers offer a service whereby email alerts can update users on new content, but this is particularly important for the aggregator.

Many databases of articles and reports are available on the basis of free trial, paid subscription, or payment according to use (so-called pay as you go). There is not a single 'host' with access to all information, which makes this field an extremely complex one, particularly for anyone other than the regular user.

Finally, there are several specialist companies that monitor media; for example, newspaper cuttings services monitor all newspapers and all magazines for the specific mention of particular companies, brands, or even products. This has been extended to radio, television and, in recent times, to the Internet. Examples of media-monitoring companies are Cision (http://www.uk.cision.com), Echo (http://www.echoResearch.com), and Prweb (http://www.prweb.com).

Competition and web activity analysis

In later chapters we address the analysis of website analytics, which emphasises analysis of an organisation's own web pages. However, there are several services that allow up-to-date comparison of competing companies. One of these is the shopping agent, which will compare specified products or services. Comparison shopping services allow products to be compared by price, delivery date, etc. Visit http://www.mysimon.com to see a shopping comparison service, or http://www.moneysupermarket.com. These are excellent ways of examining the competition. More sophisticated systems are also available, several are listed in Table 3.5. Also in the table are services that act as a monitor of web activity by individuals. We can see, for example, an increased interest in specific brands or products, and we can identify fashions as they emerge. Many devices allow the user to view information on several competitors' sites, such as daily unique visitors, comparisons by region, site visitors, and keywords used to find these sites. Complex data processing allows estimates of advertising expenditure to be made available.

Geodemographic systems

Geodemographic systems are created when general population census data is combined with other databases to create a powerful knowledge base. In the UK, this is based on postcode geography and is mainly interrogated by postcode. Customer profiles can be built and optimum locations for retail outlets can be derived. A Classification of Residential Neighbourhoods (ACORN) and MOSAIC were the pioneering systems (see their respective descriptions at http://www.caci.co.uk/acorn/ and http://www.experian.co.uk). Other geodemographic companies

Table 3.5 Competition and web activity services

Type	Description	Example
Search engine traffic	Reveals patterns across regions, categories, and time periods. Shows company ranking and relationships	http://www.google.com/trends http://www.google.com/insights/search http://www.trends.google.com/websites http://www.touchgraph.com/TGGoogleBrowser.html
Emerging fashions	Uses blog posts, twitter, and new searches to identify 'chatter' and create a view of user activity, fashions, and company popularity	http://www.twitscoop.com http://www.technorati.com http://buzzlog.yahoo.com/overall/ http://www.lycos.com http://hotsearch.aol.com http://www.attentio.com/
User-Panel Analysis	Analysis of web activity of panels of Internet users combined with other indicators	http://www.compete.com http://www.alexa.com http://www.comscore.com http://www.quantcast.com http://www.hitwise.com http://www.spyfu.com http://www.ukom.uk.net
Shopping agent	Compares prices and offerings of a specified product or service	http://www.moneysupermarket.com
Archive systems	Stores images of websites for many years, useful to monitor changing positioning and strategies of organisations	http://www.archive.org http://www.webarchive.org.uk

offer their services, but these systems can be examined at no cost at various websites such as Zoopla, which is designed for citizens to understand their local community (see http://www.zoopla.co.uk). Other systems worldwide include various versions of MOSAIC and some local services; most notably there is PRIZM in the USA. Experian produces a useful footfall index which monitors the number of shoppers by season (see http://www.footfall.com).

Major sources of external secondary data are syndicated services where data is collected and distributed to interested parties. Such services are of much use in the marketing world, so it is worth familiarising yourself with the most important ones (see Table 3.6). The service may be financed and initiated by a research supplier (e.g. TGI by BMRB) or by people who are interested (e.g. publishers finance the NRS and ask an agency to conduct the study). Most useful is the fact that the topics included are much wider than the main purpose: for example, magazine reading surveys often also look at Internet use. Because big surveys have many users, the methodologies

Table 3.6 Audience research and profile data

Name	Description
National Readership Survey (NRS)	Probability sample of the adult population. Uses CAPI to measure over 260 titles. 37,000 interviews p.a.
Broadcasters' Audience Research Board (BARB)	Continuous TV viewing information captured using meters on TV sets in over 5100 homes
Radio Joint Audience Research (RAJAR)	114,000 diaries p.a. from adults and children to measure radio listening. One-week diary to record listening every 15 minutes
UK Online Measurement (ukom.uk.net)	Continuous Performance of online media owners captured using software on user terminal sets in over 31,000 households and 4000 businesses
Footfall Index (Experian)	Created from data of people visiting over 200 retail centres and over 12,000 retail outlets in the UK

are accepted and robust, therefore trustworthy. They are long-established, so most have trend data going back for over 20 years. The data sets are large, so reanalysis and data mining are often possible. On the negative side, some information is not available for commercial reasons.

Private citizens

The individual leaves information in various places and this has become known as 'consumer-generated media' (CGM). Specifically, we might cite private web pages and blogs (web diaries). Web pages of specific interest are those that make positive or negative statements about companies, brands, or services. For example, fans of pop stars and soccer teams are very vocal and evident. Other less well-known fans exist for such areas as ceramics and sportswear. Using the 'back link' facility offered by search engines, it is possible to identify the many websites that are linked to any company's website. These can then be analysed.

Conversely, we find websites that oppose particular companies; these 'anti-corporate' sites often have the theme '*brand X sucks*'. They are easily found by adding the brand name into the URL: for example, http://www.paypalsucks.com. Clearly, these offer a different insight into a particular market sector and a potential understanding of strengths and weaknesses.

Planning desk research

The ways in which secondary data are stored are shown in Table 3.7. It is obvious that these methods feature a variety of sizes, formats, and types, but in all cases, the records must be organised in some way—or, more importantly, must be retrieved somehow. Some are still held in a rigid hierarchy following some logic—for example, the Dewey system—and books that are

Table 3.7 The ways in which secondary data are stored

Item	Content
Human memory	Information memorised by humans
Books	Info on companies, products, individuals, etc.
Journals	Academic and technical knowledge
Magnetic media	Magnetic tapes and disks
Photographic media	Microfilm, microfiche
Digital media	Offline databases stored in disks or on CD-ROM
Digital media	Online databases stored in computers, accessed through a network
Digital media	Full-text databases, includes journal articles
Statistical databases	Numerical information, often as ASCII or in spreadsheet form

large may go to an outsize section. Spreadsheets may be kept with other spreadsheets, or they may be placed under the subject heading. Or a new set of files may have been created to understand the archives available; this is known as 'tertiary data'. The term refers to indexes, citations of articles, and summaries or abstracts; in simple terms, this is 'third-hand' data.

Tertiary data should be consulted first and various publications help in this respect: for example, *Sources of Non-official UK Statistics* (Mort 2006) is one. There are also other general guides and directories of sources. A library's own cataloguing and indexing systems will assist. We must stress that the researcher can seek assistance from librarians, and should also continually refer to the 'Help' section at the top of any browser screen.

The modern trend is not to store things in a rigidly organised fashion; the emphasis is to leave the data as is, but to ensure that tertiary data is generated and that search facilities are available. This is illustrated well by Google's email service, Googlemail. Messages arrive with the user, but do not need to be deleted; they do not even need to be divided into specific folders. To retrieve any item, a simple search will locate both it and any other related items.

The MR mix framework is useful when planning desk research (see Figure 3.5). Consider the topic and use the mix as a checklist to ask questions about the *purpose* of the search and the *population* in the sector under study. Who are the players? What trade associations or professional bodies exist in this sector? List them all with approximate sizes. Will they provide information about themselves or will they be better placed to provide information about other players? Regarding *procedure*, the search for secondary data can be divided into two: identifying whether relevant data exists and then obtaining that data.

Libraries in close proximity to the desk researcher should be identified. Despite the usefulness of electronic searching, some things are easier to find in three dimensions in a public or private library. Libraries hold trade and production statistics, trade directories, market reports, country profiles, mail-order catalogues, and other items that give a real feel

Research in focus
Open data

Information available to the researcher was originally created by someone with their own resources and money; it has therefore been paid for. Some data owners realise that after their initial use, the data findings may be of little value, and so results are offered free of charge. This is sometimes as a public service or sometimes as a public relations gesture. In other cases, owners of information recognise that they have a clear asset and it would be unusual for them to give it away completely free of charge. Further sales take place in many ways; data can be bought directly from the data owner or through another company.

In the online business information segment, many free company information, government information, directory, and news sources have eroded the share taken by fee-based services in a movement that has been called 'open data'. Open data is defined as 'data that can be republished without fear of copyright restrictions'. It is particularly evident in government data sources such as that found at http://www.data.gov.uk in Britain and http://www.data.gov from the USA. These data owners are aware that they have so much valuable information that they could not possibly exploit it beyond the ways in which they already use it, and therefore invite third parties to find further uses. One commercial example is to offer smartphone apps with travel details, all derived from government transportation data.

An aggregator collects information from many different sources and might charge different rates for the content of its different databases to reflect the costs faced. Another may charge the same rate, regardless of the source, to create an easy-to-understand pricing structure for clients. Subscriptions can make some information appear to be free but a 'pay-as-you-go' option adds to the complexity. Paradoxically, this situation can mean that it is more expensive to buy directly from the company that collected the data to begin with. One thing is certain—the occasional user has reason to be confused and reluctant to invest in expensive services.

David Mort of IRN Research says: *'The free sources are often used for basic information, or used at the start of an information or research process, with more detailed content obtained from the fee-paid services'.*

Compiled by Nigel Bradley 2012.

Sources:

Mort, D. (2003) European online revenues on the rise, *Research Information* special report, http://www.researchinformation.info/special2003overview.html

Plosker, G. (2004) Making money as an aggregator, *Online*, March/April, 28(2), http://www.infotoday.com

Temperton, J. (2011) How to explore opendata. *Computer Active*, 23 June, pp. 52–53, 55.

Questions

1 Why are some data sets free or of low cost?

2 How have pricing structures changed in recent years?

3 Why are governments happy for anyone to take their data free of charge?

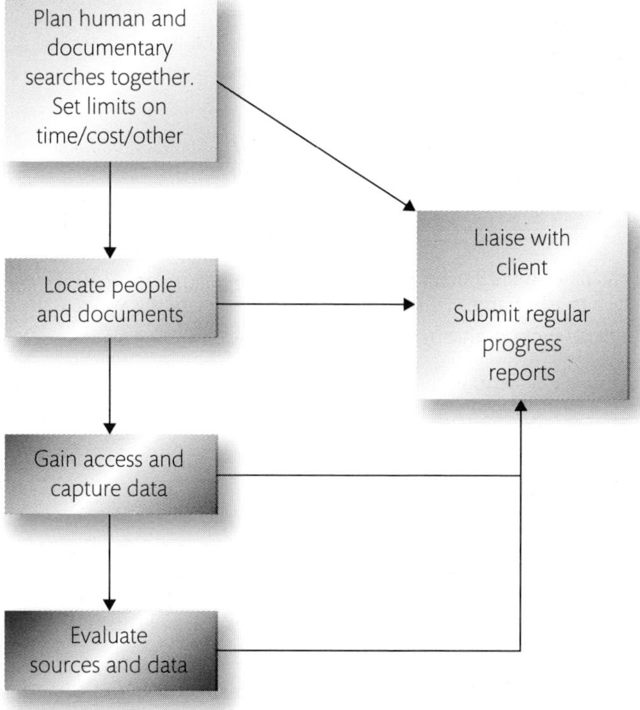

Figure 3.5 The desk research process

of a marketplace that is not possible from viewing on-screen material. There are several important libraries in each country that offer a range of services. In the UK, many such archives are in London. They include the British Library (http://www.bl.uk) and government resources such as: the Office for National Statistics Service (http://www.statistics.gov.uk), Business Link (http://www.businesslink.gov.uk), City Business Library (http://www.cityoflondon.gov.uk), and Westminster Central Reference Library (http://www.westminster.gov.uk). There are also many specialist libraries run by industry bodies, usually located at trade associations.

Two main means of location should be considered: both human searches and computer searches. Each method may complement the other and may also provide duplicate information. Researchers differ in their willingness to initiate their studies using one or the other. For example, some people prefer to avoid making contact with other people until documents have been inspected. Others prefer to ask someone to help guide them through the masses of information available. When faced with many sources of information, people employ mechanisms such as being selective, ignoring information, and also asking for help from anyone who may have carried out similar searches before.

The amount of data available from secondary sources is enormous and, as each day passes, more is added. For this reason, the desk researcher needs to set limits on the various parameters before research takes place. This is sometimes known as 'scoping' or setting the scope. There are limits that need to be set on:

- Time spent, cost expended
- Number of sources searched

- Language to use (e.g. English only)
- Geographical parameters (e.g. UK only)
- Historical parameters (e.g. one year old, up to five years old)
- Format of data (e.g. bound report, online, on disk)
- Methodology used (e.g. quant or qual).

The researcher must attempt to impose some form of sampling on the documentation available. In this case, the sample may be an indication that further investigation is needed in a particular direction. It is impossible to search for the locations of all documents and it is therefore impossible to gain access to all documents. It is feasible to divide the two activities and allocate time (and therefore cost) to each. Once the procedures begin, the time spent on identification and time spent on accessing different resources should be monitored.

Human searches

By human searches, we are referring to the idea of asking someone for directions to sources; it may be that they have the information themselves. This includes visits to general and specialist libraries. The ways to contact a human, in order of efficiency, are by email, by phone, and in person. We are not contacting the human to carry out a qualitative depth interview, or to administer a fully structured questionnaire; we are looking to glean facts or sources for other facts. The person identified will act as a 'guide' to show the way, and also to give some interesting facts. The important thing is to find the right human to ask—someone who has already had a need for the information you seek—but who would that be? A journalist? A competitor? A scholar? Does a librarian know? Find the right person and you will save hours of searching archives—that person will be your signpost. Think of the saying '*A wise man learns from experience*', and then consider this addition, '*A very wise man learns from someone else's experience*'.

Paradoxically, direct contact with individuals who have knowledge of a particular field comes from looking at published sources. Existing sources are used to identify potential contacts, and expert interviewing then permits the researcher to identify fruitful sources, thereby saving time and money. Initially, it is instinctive for us to contact known people, but the desk researcher must not be afraid to contact strangers. Indeed, Flynn (2005) found, in a study into communication, that university reference librarians are more likely to contact '*a slight pre-existing acquaintance*' when seeking assistance via email. But Flynn believes that email has made them more likely to contact unacquainted or loosely acquainted peers. The important thing is to plan human searches by identifying relevant people, then their names and contact details, before starting communications. The actual communications should not be as ambitious as a structured questionnaire nor as open as a topic guide; they should enable the 'respondent' to cooperate with ease.

Computer searches

Even when faced with the computer, it cannot be denied that human judgement comes into play by acting as a filter to reject, or to include, or even to modify, secondary data to make it useful for decision-making.

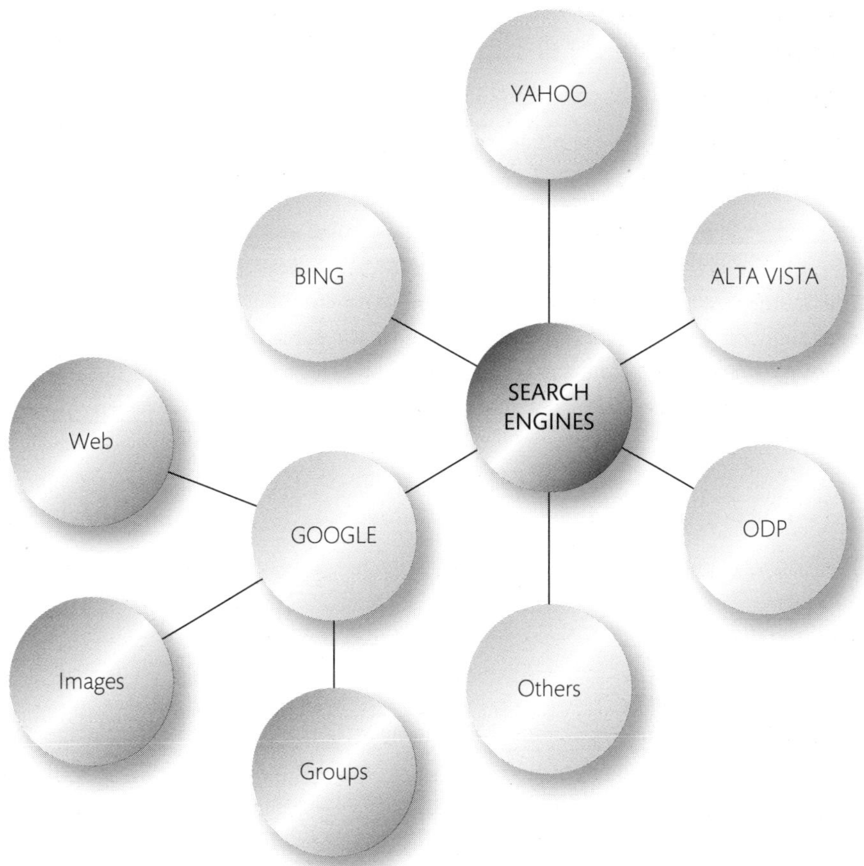

Figure 3.6 Popular search engines

The Internet is a series of 'interconnected networks' and most of the content of these networks is available as web pages or files that can be accessed using a standard browser. Desk research will inevitably start with the Internet, so it is important to be familiar with some of the devices available (see Figure 3.6).

Directories provide an ordered structure to the many websites in the world. A long standing automated example is Yahoo (http://dir.yahoo.com/). This is a logical organisation of data on the web and can be browsed or searched. The famous Open Directory is created by human editors and can be found at http://dmoz.org/. Directories are useful because they show similar services (competitors) together in context.

Search engines provide users with a service of locating and retrieving information from documents located on the Internet. Search engines can search all media, whether text, sound, or images. Search engines differ from each other, so if one does not work for a sector, the user can simply try another (see Table 3.8). The Search Engine Watch site (http://www.searchenginewatch.com) gives information on the different search engines on offer, showing their strengths.

Metasearch engines will perform a simultaneous search on several engines: for example, http://www.search.com/ or http://www.metacrawler.com.

Table 3.8 Different types of search device

Type	Description	Example
Search engine	Searches archives of images, sounds or text on a computer network	http://www.google.com
Blog search engine	Searches web-based diaries written by anyone	http://www.blogsearchengine.com http://www.google.com/blogsearch
Metasearch engines	Seeks results from several search engines simultaneously	http://www.savvysearch.com http://www.metacrawler.com

Blog search engines will search web-based diaries written by private individuals or companies: for example, http://www.blogsearchengine.com or http://www.google.com/blogsearch.

A slightly different device to the engine is an agent: the *search agent* allows users to search for information taking specific needs into account: it is a sort of intelligent search engine. This may adjust itself automatically, depending on previous actions carried out by the user, or the user can specify preferences.

Traditionally Boolean logic operators help in searching databases. Internet searches have become more user friendly and Boolean logic is largely hidden from the user. Here are a few points for users who may need these tools. The three main Boolean logic operators have three outcomes. One widens the search, one narrows the search, and the last one will exclude items. Respectively, they are the words: *or;and;not*. For example, if the words 'farmers or doctors' are inserted into a search engine query, the search engine will find documents where *either* word ('farmers' or 'doctors') appears. This will find documents that only feature the word 'doctors'. It will also find documents that only feature the word 'farmers'. If we use the word 'and' (or the sign +) with the words 'farmers' and 'doctors' and insert that into a search engine, then the engine will find documents where *both* words (farmers and doctors) appear. It will not find documents that only feature the word 'doctors'. We have effectively narrowed the search. If we use the word 'not' (or the sign –) with the words 'farmers not doctors' and insert that into a search engine, then the engine will find documents where the word 'farmers' appears, *but not* 'doctors'. It will not find documents for the word after 'not'. Again, we have effectively narrowed the search. The sign * is known as a wildcard. It can be used as a clipping. In summary, to broaden your search, use + and also – to narrow your search.

Common mistakes
Not planning

If the researcher does not set parameters, then control over the project will quickly be lost. This lack of planning results in lost time and wasted money. Furthermore, regular progress reports to the client will help to avoid wasted effort in a fruitless area.

Internet searches run the risk of using an inappropriate search engine or the wrong combination of terms. It is also important to make a distinction between two needs for desk research: we can call these 'continuous' or 'one-off' needs. Continuous needs for data are likely to be related to gathering ongoing marketing intelligence, a non-stop scanning of the environment. This continuous desk research is likely to be undertaken in-house; a client will have a manager or department dedicated to 'listening' to the marketplace for a sector in which the company already operates. The 'one-off needs' are more likely to concern sectors in which a client wishes to launch a new product, service, or even company. There is a single need for information; after that reason has gone, there will be no further need. These two purposes can have implications for the desk research plan. The continuous need will make it feasible for the researcher to set up ongoing news alerts from various sources; there will be time to implement permanent information requests and to set up more intricate delivery formats. These formats include direct delivery to intranets, availability of data at a **portal** on the user's desktop terminal, and so on. Conversely, the 'one-off' requirement points towards gleaning information quickly. This immediate need can be satisfied by human experts and by implementing temporary information requests that will cease when the project ends.

Any thesaurus will provide similar words that can be used in searches. Robot language translators can convert these into other languages (see Table 3.9).

Ask your question as a question—for example, What is biotechnology?—and place it in inverted commas (quotation marks), to become: 'What is biotechnology?'. This will search for the phrase intact, and if it appears in a page, the answer will probably be somewhere

Table 3.9 Useful resources

Language translators	Help to understand web pages published in one of the 3000 world languages
Internet directories	Provide an ordered structure to the many websites in the world
Thesauruses	Provide similar words that can be used in searches
Bookmark/favourites	Allow addresses to be stored quickly during the search process
Alert services	Offer notification that there is new content about a specific keyword or topic, e.g. Google News Alert, Amazon New Books
Aggregator	An amalgamation of a specific set of data-files, e.g. Google uses automated software to trawl 25,000 publishers and organises the results at Google News. This can then be read

nearby. Do not waste time. If a page looks interesting, bookmark it as a favourite and continue searching. If you have not succeeded after five minutes, stop and think of a different strategy. For company information, try searching on the postcode or telephone number. These are specific and will lead to specific sites.

Bookmarks/favourites allow addresses to be stored quickly during the search process. *Alert services* can notify the user if there is new content about a specific keyword or topic: for example, CNN News Alerts, Amazon New Book alerts, and so on.

Aggregators make an amalgamation of a specific set of data files: for example, Google uses automated software to trawl the news sources of 25,000 publishers and organises the results at Google News. These can then be read.

Evaluation and reverse researching

The MR mix provides a suitable framework for evaluating desk research from the viewpoints of the purpose, population, procedure, and publication.

The purpose of your search and the *purpose* of the study being examined must be both compared; they are unlikely to be the same. Are there conflicts of interest that might lead the results to be biased in a particular direction?

The population in the sector under study needs careful consideration. Who are the players of interest to you? Are they well represented by the secondary data?

The procedure originally used to collect the information must be considered. What are the limitations of this method? Have data been amalgamated at the analysis stage? If so, why? Can they be separated again? The procedure used to capture data needs to be considered carefully (see Table 3.10 for data-gathering tips). Sight of the questionnaire used is extremely important—it will help us to understand tables of numbers; this is the only place which will show the full wording; that wording must have been cut short. It is useful to discover whether *scales* were used. A 'scale' is a type of *closed question* where a continuum has been created; it is on this continuum that measured objects are located (see Chapter 6 for an in-depth discussion of scales). The researcher has a responsibility to ensure that the scale descriptors have not biased results in any direction. For example, they could have been worded to give a positive or negative view of a given firm. This is important to know when you are faced with secondary data. Similarly, clumsy description, deliberate bias, and omissions can render the secondary data untrustworthy. Questionnaire skills are not only important for writing questionnaires, they are important for reading reports and interpreting secondary data. In the automotive industry, manufacturers dismantle competitive cars to understand how they are produced; this is called 'reverse engineering'. We must carry out our own sort of '*reverse researching*' to inspect results. Table 3.11 helps in this respect.

Publication has clearly taken place, but why has the research been deemed so important to warrant diffusion to the extent that you are reading it? Who else is likely to have access?

How has it been interpreted? Is the presentation of data selective? What is missing and is it missing by intention or neglect? The analysis of secondary data will depend on the nature of

Ethical insight
Freedom of information or privacy?

More information has become available to us all as a result of legislation. In the year 2000, the Freedom of Information Act came fully into force in the UK. This act promotes greater accountability across the public sector. Public authorities include central and local government, schools and universities, the National Health Service, the police, and publicly owned companies.

These authorities are obliged to make information available through a publication scheme—a document that lists all the different types of information that are routinely made available. The scheme lists various 'classes' of information. A 'class' is a group that shares a common theme or function. Within each class, there is an indication of how to obtain and whether any access charges apply.

Personal data are not freely available: this is exempted by the acts and disclosure is governed by the Data Protection Act 1998. Other things are exempt: for example, commercially sensitive and confidential materials. This is of relevance to the desk researcher because findings of research studies carried out by many organisations will be available unless there are good reasons to refuse.

It is worth clarifying the definition of personal data—one interpretation was established by the Court of Appeal in *Durant* v *Financial Services Authority* [2003] EWCA Civ 174. This case said that personal data are '*information that affects* [a person's] *privacy, whether in his personal or family life, business or professional capacity*'.

Compiled by Nigel Bradley 2012.
Sources:
Data Protection Act 1998, http://www.ico.gov.uk; Freedom of Information Act 2000, http://www.ico.gov.uk

Questions

1. What organisations are obliged to make information available under the FOI Act?
2. What is a publication scheme?
3. What things are exempt from the FOI Act?

Table 3.10 Trouble-shooting tips at the data gathering stage

Problem	Solution
Sources unknown	Conduct expert interviews
Source known, location hidden	Use search engine
Sources not in English	Use robot translation software, then use a human to complete the translation
Sources out of date	Ask omnibus questions, make contact with opinion leaders in the sector

Common mistakes

Expecting access to data that exist

© istockphoto.com/Stuart Miles

There are many reasons why the data owner may not want to divulge further details or may not be able to help you. One reason is that storage space costs money. They may be located in buildings that are secure and not easily accessible. They may only be available on microfiche, in which case, specific apparatus must be available for viewing and data transfer. Even software and hardware have both changed over the years. On the Internet, we may find that web addresses have been changed, password protected, or entire archives have been removed. A solution to some of these problems is to use the Internet Archive's 'way back machine'. The Internet Archive is building a digital library of Internet sites and other cultural artefacts held in digital form. Like a paper library, the archive provides free access to researchers, historians, scholars, and the general public (http://www.archive.org/). Very often web addresses that are not accessible, or have been removed, can be found by typing the address into the archive search form. The UK Web Archive has been collecting UK websites since 2004 in the same way (see http://www.webarchive.org.uk).

the information found. It might already have been processed or it might be raw data (see Table 3.12). Most external secondary data have already been processed.

In reporting, it is possible to make longitudinal studies. For example, British Prime Ministers can be plotted on a graph showing their popularity during their term of government. This comparison between leaders over time, or between political parties within

Table 3.11 Things that must be considered in 'reverse researching'

Item	
Missing data	Nothing is complete, but detecting what is missing can be informative
Mistakes	Simple spelling mistakes may be indicative of a lack of attention to detail; continue checking to identify any numerical errors
Poor expression	Poor expression is a problem, especially with texts that have been produced in a language in which the original researcher is not fully fluent. The sense may have become corrupted
Deliberate bias	The initial reason for any document is to achieve some objective. This tone can sway the desk researcher
Scales	May bias the data in a specific direction

Table 3.12 Raw and processed data distinguished

Examples of raw data	Examples of processed data
Number of visitors to a store	Tables
Customer comments	List of comments classified
Sales transaction reports	Annual company report
Transcripts of conversations	Focus group reports
CCTV recordings of sales encounter	Quality assessments
Websites in other languages	Translations

a term, enables policymakers to determine the most and the least popular decisions. Long-term studies indeed show trends, but peaks and troughs can sometimes be attributed to changes in the data collection method rather than real changes. For example, the 1881 and 2001 censuses cannot be compared without accounting for basic differences. The report-writer must therefore be prepared to delve into studies far more deeply than might be anticipated.

To assess the reliability of information, it is useful to look at the source and the context. Table 3.13 shows a way to assess a particular piece of information. A score is given for these two characteristics. If the total is six or above, then the information is likely to be trustworthy; if it is five or below, then use of the data should be made with caution.

Analysis for the purposes of the current research problem inevitably means that the information may need to be reworked or combined in some way (see Figure 3.7). This

Table 3.13 Source and context appraisal

Appraisal of source (with score)	Appraisal of context
Completely reliable (5)	Confirmed elsewhere (5)
Usually reliable (4)	Probably true (4)
Fairly reliable (3)	Possibly true (3)
Not usually reliable (2)	Doubtful (2)
Unreliable (1)	Improbable (1)
Reliability cannot be judged (0)	Truth cannot be determined (0)

reworking or combining information from different sources is a form of 'data fusion': a technique that has become more sophisticated and largely automated in recent years.

For any sector, the following information should be compiled to give a complete picture:

- Six top companies
- Six important trade press titles
- Three trade associations
- Two trade directories.

A web resource created for the UK market research industry http://www.mrweb.com/sectors/ illustrates this well by giving instant links to sectors such as finance, pharmaceuticals, and many more (see Figure 3.7).

There is a distinction between synthesis and analysis that is worth stressing. 'Synthesis' is essentially description; there is little critical input apart from the decision about what to include and what to exclude. 'Analysis' implies creating an analytical framework that gives some structure that can be transferred to other evidence, to other cases. It implies the creation of a problem-solving tool. Many such tools have been adopted in the past: any matrix, a SWOT report, a PEST analysis, even the four Ps of the marketing mix.

Recording and reporting sources

In the business environment, reports are not expected to carry references to every statement made. This is primarily to remove irrelevant reading matter from reports, on the assumption that what is written is more important than who wrote it originally. This can be quite alien to the academic who is well versed in the Harvard system of referencing, whereby any new fragment of knowledge is attributed to the originator. In many ways, business reporting is more difficult for the researcher because any point may be challenged by users of the information; they will evaluate the usefulness of decision-making material in many ways, so you may well need to show the exact origin and method used to acquire the data. A second purpose for keeping detailed records is to make newer searches in a focused way and to avoid repeating abortive searches. For these reasons, it is crucial to keep good clear records.

There are two important exceptions to the attribution of sources: tables will carry a source with date and the report appendix should carry a summary of the main sources (and methods used). The 'private' records kept by the researcher should allow further detail to be provided when requested, or to extend a project beyond the initial phase. These records will be in the form of notes, photocopies, filing index cards; online searches will result in downloaded files that should also be kept in some form of system. The sources and dates of access should be recorded in all cases.

Purpose
Why was it done?
Who paid for it?
What was the problem to be solved?

Population
Who are the players in the sector?
Who was interviewed? How many?
What was the source of names?

Procedure
What data capture method was used?
What quality control was there?
Does the method make sense? What is wrong?
Is it valid and reliable?

Publication
Why was it distributed?
Who are the likely readers?
What decisions may have been made on the basis of this project?

Figure 3.7 Questions to ask about prior research

Chapter summary

1 Explain the nature of secondary data

Secondary data are best remembered as 'second-hand', because such data are 'old' primary data. This involves more than consulting documents; it also involves expert interviews with people. Internal secondary data are generated by the organisation in question, whereas external secondary data are created by agencies outside the firm. The term 'tertiary data' refers to indexes, citations to articles, and summaries or abstracts; in simple terms, these are 'third-hand' data.

2 Outline the different sources of secondary data

Internal secondary data include: sales force records, transactions, competitor activity, customer records, inventory records, cost of transport, previous research, and website visitor records. External secondary data include government output, academic knowledge, and company reports. Professional associations publish industry overviews. Market research report publishers have reports on different market sectors. Geodemographic companies produce data from the census combined with other databases. There are also 'consumer-generated media' (CGM).

3 Show the benefits and the limitations of using secondary data

Secondary data have various uses—they may answer the research question; they may also help to refine objectives, to design primary research, to assist in sampling, and to supply pre-codes for questionnaires. Secondary sources can be used in conjunction with primary research, for example, to enhance understanding of and to confirm results. Secondary data are likely to be less expensive than collecting information freshly. They are relatively easy and quick to obtain: a unique benefit for international studies. However, secondary data have already been collected for something other than the current research problem. Therefore, they may not address the topic in question or may only provide part of the information expected. The information may not be accurate or it may be outdated. Additionally, data may not actually exist, or may have restricted circulation.

4 List the features of a plan to carry out effective searches

Three approaches are likely: visits to general and specialist libraries, contacting human experts, and carrying out computer searches. For all of these, the desk researcher must set limits on time spent, cost expended, number of sources searched, language used, age of sources, format of data, and methodology used. Continuous needs for data will make it feasible for the researcher to implement permanent information requests; conversely, the occasional requirement points towards gleaning information quickly. Desk research will start with the Internet, so the user must be familiar with search tools and techniques. To assess the reliability of information found, it is useful to look at the source and its context. Use the MR mix to ascertain the original *purpose*, the *population* used, the *procedure* followed, and the reason for original *publication*. For any sector, look for the top companies, important trade press titles, trade associations, and trade directories.

Review questions

1 You interview a journalist about reports he produced two years ago on the railway sector. Is this primary or secondary data collection?

2 List the differences between internal and external secondary data. Explain whether one is better than the other and why.

3 Assess the advantages and disadvantages of using secondary data. What are the alternatives?

4 How can professional organisations be useful sources of data?

5 What are the main features of a desk research plan?

Discussion questions

1 Use the Internet to describe the market for baked beans in a particular country. You should provide market shares and brief descriptions of the major players.

2 Visit http://www.google.com You shouldn't leave the Google pages. Look at the user guide. Discover the services available and the user guides. Be sure to see Google Scholar and Google Analytics. Write a report on your findings.

3 We want to find some information about the music business in Italy. First, generate some synonyms using a thesaurus (either a real book or one built into your software). Next, translate these words from English to Italian using a language translator. Then cut and paste these words into a search engine and look at the results. Read each of the websites by selecting the word 'translate' at each result.

4 Consult the proposal in the Market Researcher's Toolbox. Draft a possible design for secondary data collection. Try to list precisely what you will do. A second task is to carry this out.

5 In the opening Snapshot, what are the advantages and disadvantages of using the Tesco Clubcard to obtain data on shopping behaviour? Why might overseas tourists need to be researched in a different way? What other 'blind spots' are there?

Further reading

- McDaniel, C. and Gates, R. (2002) *Marketing Research: The Impact of the Internet*, 5th edn. Cincinnati, OH: South Western Thomson Learning.
  Standard market research text with a good section on secondary databases and Internet searches.
- Mort, D. (2006) *Sources of Non-official UK Statistics*, 6th edn. Aldershot: Gower.
  Information of almost 900 sources from over 500 organisations, with telephone contact numbers and website addresses.

Key web links

- UK statistics http://www.statistics.gov.uk
- European statistics http://www.epp.eurostat.ec.europa.eu
- MR Web sectors http://www.mrweb.com/sectors

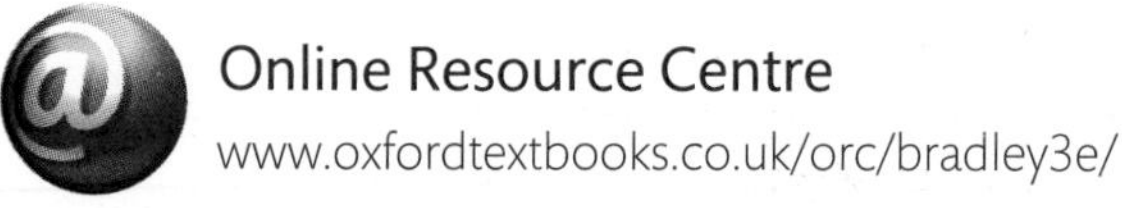

Visit the Online Resource Centre that accompanies this book to access more learning resources on this chapter topic.

Case study
Daily newspaper delivery

© Dennis MacDonald

The marketing department at the offices of a newspaper publisher were very excited. They had discovered that they could increase their market share by encouraging readers to accept home delivery of their newspaper. Some research had indicated that occasional buyers would be prepared to pay for delivery and agreed that a daily newspaper would be a '*great way to start the day*'. The research study also indicated that there was a problem, and that this related to the time of delivery. The analysis of some **open-ended questions** gave the impression that delivery was welcomed in time for breakfast, but was unwelcome after respondents had left their home to go to work.

One of the marketing executives pointed out that newspaper deliveries are traditionally made by teenagers and that there may be legislation to say that children could not begin their rounds before 7am. Or perhaps, they wondered, this was just a guideline?

The team decided that they needed more information; they needed firm information on how deliveries could be made. More importantly, they needed some indication of what the optimum time was to deliver newspapers. The seven team members decided to search secondary data to throw light on these issues; they would meet again to discuss their findings. At the next meeting, one executive was proud to report that he had found a table in a textbook, which reported two studies concerning waking in the morning. They were actually collected to help hospitals to decide what time to wake up patients, but could have offered a useful insight. They were also quite dated—one was from 1964 and the other from 1978. Both are reproduced in Table 3.14.

Executives were pleased to see the tables, but as they looked closely, they were perplexed; they wondered how such a change could have happened between 1964 and 1978. Nobody found 7am too early in 1964, but 17 per cent of people did in 1978. One executive suggested that fieldwork may have been in summer in 1964, whereas in 1978, it may have occurred during winter months, when people like to sleep longer. Another executive said that the result may have reflected the fact that we have become a much more services-based economy, where businesses open later. Another suggested that the respondents may have been older, younger, or from different occupational backgrounds. The table was raising more questions than it was answering.

Compiled by Nigel Bradley 2012.

Sources:

Cartwright, A. (1964) *Human Relations and Hospital Care*. London: Routledge & Kegan Paul.

Cartwright, A. (1983) *Health Surveys in Practice and in Potential*. London: King's Fund Publishing Office, pp. 100–110.

Gregory, J. (1978) Patients' attitudes to the hospital service: a survey carried out for the Royal Commission on the National Health Service. Research paper No. 5, London: HMSO.

Table 3.14 Waking in the morning study

Cartwright Study 1964	Proportion who found it too early (%)	Gregory Study 1978	Proportion who felt it too early (%)
Before 5am	74		
5am < 5.30am	68	5.00–5.30	67
5.30am < 6am	45	5.31–6.00	47
6am < 6.30am	24	6.01–6.30	46
6.30am < 7am	17	6.31–7.00	27
7am or later	0	After 7.00	17
All times	44	All times	43

Questions

1 List the different queries you may have about the two studies. Next to each question, write how you would find its answer.
2 The questionnaire used in 1964 was different from that used in 1978; this is evident from the table. How could this have influenced the results?
3 What value does the table have for the marketing problem?
4 In addition to the table, what other secondary data may be useful to help the marketing problem?
5 How do you rate the sources and the context (use the instructions provided in the chapter)?

References and sources

Bradley, N. (1998) An Internet tour for market research, *ESOMAR Newsbrief*, 6, pp. 12–13.

Benner, M. (2003) Milward Brown targets 'tribal' communicators, *Research*, May, p. 6

Cartwright, A. (1964) *Human Relations and Hospital Care*. London: Routledge & Kegan Paul.

Cartwright, A. (1983) *Health Surveys in Practice and in Potential*. London: King's Fund Publishing Office, pp. 100–110.

Fletcher, R. (1991) *Science, Ideology and the Media: The Cyril Burt Scandal*. New Brunswick, NJ: Transaction Publishers.

Flynn, D.A. (2005) Seeking peer assistance: use of e-mail to consult weak and latent ties, *Library & Information Science Research*, 27, pp. 73–96.

Gregory, J. (1978) Patients' attitudes to the hospital service: a survey carried out for the Royal Commission on the National Health Service. Research Paper No. 5, London: HMSO.

Lievesley, D. (1993) Role of the ESRC Data Archive in the dissemination of data for secondary analysis, *Journal of the Market Research Society*, 35, pp. 267–278.

McDaniel, C. and Gates, R. (2002) *Marketing Research: The Impact of the Internet*, 5th edn. Cincinnati, OH: Thomson Learning.

Michael, A. and Salter, B. (2003) *Marketing through Search Optimization*. Oxford: Butterworth Heinemann.

Mort, D. (2002a) European online business information market—2002 Trends, *IRN Research Brief* No. 5.

Mort, D. (2002b) Trends in market research publishing, *IRN Research Brief* No. 3.

Mort, D. (2003) European online revenues on the rise, *Research Information Special Report*, http://www.researchinformation.info/special2003 overview.html

Mort, D. (2006) *Sources of Non-official UK Statistics*, 6th edn. Aldershot: Gower.

Plosker, G. (2004) Making money as an aggregator, *Online*, March/April, 28(2), http://www.infotoday.com

Porter, Michael E. (2004) *Competitive Strategy. Techniques for Analyzing Industries and Competitors.* London: The Free Press.

Smith, D.V.L. and Fletcher, J.H. (2007) *The Art and Science of Interpreting Market Research Evidence.* Chichester, John Wiley & Sons.

Whiting, M. and Sagne, F. (2005) Windows on the world: how the study of consumers' personal web pages can provide insights to build brand strategy, ESOMAR, Innovate 2005 Conference papers, on CD-ROM, http://www.esomar.org

4 Primary data

Contents

Chapter guide

This chapter looks at data collected from the field to satisfy specific research needs. The channels used vary from face-to-face and telephone to postal delivery services and online. We discuss the different methods used to collect data and the problems posed when dealing with the measurement of human activities. Data capture may mean asking respondents to complete tasks themselves or it may involve the use of skilled interviewers. Interviewing skills are extremely important to achieve the best possible cooperation.

Learning outcomes

By the end of this chapter, you should be able to:

1. **Explain the nature of primary data**
2. **Outline the different methods used to capture data**
3. **Show the benefits and the limitations of using primary data**
4. **Explain which factors affect cooperation and how**

Introduction

One of the most challenging tasks for the researcher is collecting original information from the marketplace. There are many different methods used to collect data, so the advantages and disadvantages of these must be fully understood. Where data capture involves field interviewers, their interviewing skills are important. Where it involves using self-completion techniques, everything must be done to make the task simple for the respondent.

Political, social, economic, and technological developments have a direct influence on data capture. The channels used to convey data from the field to the researcher include face-to-face, telephone, postal delivery services, and online. Such modes of communication make it possible to carry out research, to deliver the instrument, and to retrieve records for processing and analysis.

Data capture takes time, requires methods appropriate to the purpose, will encounter opposition, and may, after much endeavour, be inaccurate.

We can find very early examples of data collection using face-to-face methods in evidence left by the Babylonians and the Chinese, who created accounts of their people for tax and military reasons. The Egyptians also needed knowledge of available manpower to plan the building of the pyramids (ONS 2001). From 5 BC, a census was held every five years across the Roman Empire. Every man in the Empire was obliged to return to his place of origin.

These were massive enterprises and relevant here because they suffered the error common to any form of inquiry today: it is not always in an individual's best interest to provide correct information.

Envisage early interviewers as we flash forward to the UK 1801 census, in which we find that leading members of the 'parish' were used to take stock. In the 1841 census, some 35,000 male enumerators were used. The selection and training of 'data collectors' is extremely important. In 1841, enumerator selection was undertaken according to these criteria: '*... he must not be infirm; he must be temperate, orderly and respectable, and such a person has to conduct himself with strict propriety ...*'.

Table 4.1 Notable events for primary data collection

Year	Event
1930s	Postal surveys
1940s	Telephone introduced
1950s	Commercial introduction of computers
1960s	Office computers available
1970s	Bar codes introduced to retailing
1980s	Personal computers launched
1990s	Email, chat groups, and message boards

For more than a decade (1886–1903), Charles Booth worked on the problem of poverty in London. He formed a team of researchers and these people carried out structured interviews with employers, employees, ministers of religion, and congregations; they also made observations and carried out unstructured investigations. The approach clearly illustrates that different methods of data capture can be used to look at a problem in different ways. The time period of 12 years also indicates that research can take a lot of time. Data are captured by the use of instruments; photography, for example, provides a unique means of observation. Today, we have moving images and digital photography, an observation opportunity that researchers have welcomed. The 'bar code' is also a relatively recent development. The device has revolutionised shopping behaviour and has made a major contribution to researchers as a means of mechanical observation.

SNAPSHOT
Neuromarketing Research

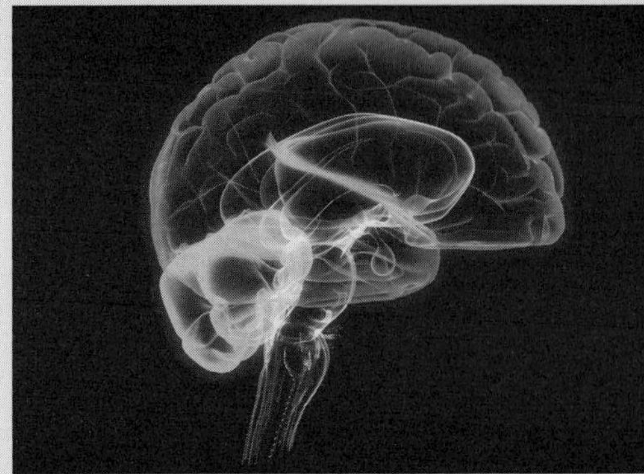
© MedicalRF.com

Our understanding of decision-making is likely to be changed somewhat with the arrival of techniques that view directly the workings of the brain. This is neuroscience and it has crept into marketing under the name of Neuromarketing.

Neuromarketing has found many applications: to test advertisements and package designs, to test store layout, to suggest the best flavours and formulations for foods and drinks. A set of specialist agencies have emerged to satisfy this demand. The names of such agencies evoke the subject area, we see companies such as NeuroFocus, Neurosense, Predictive Research International, Emsense, NeuroCompass, Neuro Insight, Innerscope, and Mindlab.

Measurement used in neuromarketing comes from science labs or medical applications. There are methods which look closely at the brain by creating images; other methods monitor reactions by physiological response, skin conductance, heart rate, respiration, and eye tracking. These are sometimes known as biofeedback methods. Sensors may be attached to the face to monitor muscles related to frowning and smiling. The apparatus used can be quite complex, for the record here are some tools employed: MEG, GSR, EEG, SST, QEEG, FMRI, MRI, PET, and CT Scanning (see the jargon buster).

The advantages of neuroscientific observation are related to the unique nature of the data capture methods. It is said that these techniques show things that answers to traditional questions cannot. Here we may be seeing a probing of the unconscious that removes any error related to interviewer or respondent, social desirability bias, satisficing and acquiescence response bias should all be eliminated. In layman's terms, we should not see any 'showing off', we should not see respondents offering the minimum needed and we should not see them agreeing with the researcher for the sake of agreeing.

The disadvantages of neuroscientific observation centre around our lack of knowledge in this area. The brain is complex and neuroscientists have much to discover. A stimulus, perhaps a view of an advert, results in a response that is registered by apparatus; however, we do not know anything about the nature of this response. Some techniques suggest that specific parts of the brain represent certain things, but science suggests that several areas of the brain are aroused by different stimuli, we therefore cannot map single actions to single zones. This in turn makes the subject more complicated and less likely to offer clear explanations. Fisher *et al* (2010) investigated the history and current state of neuromarketing and concluded 'Companies may be making premature claims about the power of neuroscience to predict consumer behavior'.

Jargon Buster

MEG = Magnetoencephalography

GSR = Galvanic skin response

EEG = Electroencephalography - skull cap with electrodes

SST = Steady state topography

QEEG = Quantified electroencephalography

fMRI = Functional magnetic resonance imaging

MRI = Magnetic resonance imaging

PET = Positron emission tomography

CT Scanning = Computerised tomography

Sources:

Bain, R. (2010) Duane Varan on standards for neuromarketing. Research Magazine. 8 October. Accessed 4 December 2010 at http://www.research-live.com/features/duane-varan-on-standards-for-neuromarketing/4003754.article

Fisher, C. E., Chin, L., Klitzman, R. (2010) Defining Neuromarketing: Practices and Professional Challenges. *Harvard Review of Psychiatry*, 18(4), July, pp. 230–237(8).

Harrison, S.A., Tong, F. (2009) Decoding reveals the contents of visual working memory in early visual areas. *Nature*, 2 April, 458(7238), pp. 632–635.

Haversmans, J. (2005) Dissecting Emotions. *Research World*, ESOMAR, June, pp. 24–26.

Gray, R. (2009) How to. ... push the brain's buy button. *The Marketer*, CIM, May, pp. 33–36.

Page, G. and Raymond, J. (2007) The truth about cognitive neuroscience. *Research World*, ESOMAR Jan, pp. 37–39.

Penn, D. (2008) Beyond neuroscience –whatever happened to neuromarketing? *Admap*, January, 490, pp. 27–29.

The nature of primary data

Primary data are 'fresh data'—the data are collected to satisfy specific requirements and therefore the procedures used follow carefully determined objectives. Methods of data capture are divided into two broad groups: questioning and observation. There are several ways to 'intercept' or gain access to respondents. This can be in person, on the phone, by post, online, or by other means. Generally speaking, the choice of approach should mimic the activity which is being measured. For example, an online method is best suited to investigate website opinions; a postal questionnaire is usefully employed to investigate direct mailshots; the telephone can be used to ask about satisfaction with telephony services, and so on. Table 4.2 summarises the advantages and disadvantages of primary data capture methods.

Once contact has been made, there are various ways to 'capture data'. We will explore a few of these. The situation can also vary:

1. In public places (for example, on the street)
2. In private places (for example, at home or at work)
3. At the interface between private and public places (at the door).

Table 4.2 Primary data capture methods: summary of advantages and disadvantages

Type	Advantage	Disadvantage
Face-to-face	Highest quality results Can use stimulus material Highest response rate	Most expensive Time-consuming Clustering will occur
Telephone	Fast Unclustered	Limited stimuli Requires skilled interviewers
Drop/Collect	Low cost Fair response rate	Can only reach respondents available
Postal	Convenient for respondents Low cost Can reach most respondents	No control over the respondent Can be slow Poor response rate
Online	Fast Low-cost Good for international	No control over the respondent Lowest response rate/device bias Gaps in coverage
Panel (all above)	Can show changes over time (advantages as method above)	High investment (disadvantages as method above)
Observation (all above)	No interviewer or interviewee bias (advantages as method above)	Ethical concerns (disadvantages as method above)

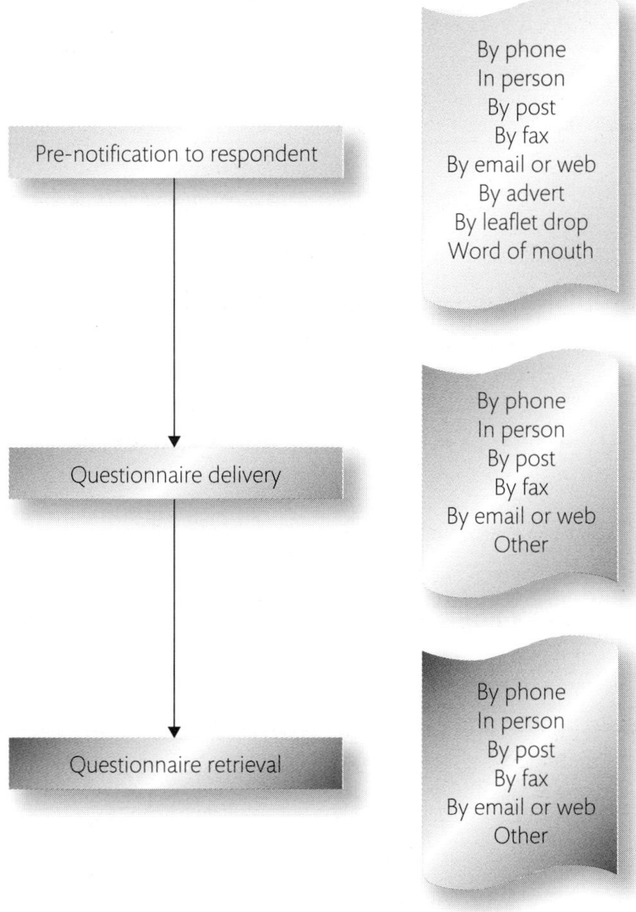

Figure 4.1 An outline of data capture methods

Figures 4.1 and 4.2 give an outline of different data capture methods. The term 'questionnaire' has been used to typify the research instrument, but we will discover that the situation is more complex than this.

These different modes of data capture have an influence on any market research study. The researcher is driven by three main constraints: the time available, the cost, and the control. Table 4.3 shows how the four different modes match to these. Clearly, the Internet is the fastest and cheapest, but it also has a major limitation of being unable to exert any control over the respondent, a weakness shared with postal methods. Although the face-to-face, personal approach is the most expensive, it does provide the research user with results of the highest possible quality.

Similarly, Table 4.4 shows some typical response rates for the main modes of interviewing. This is based on the author's experience and hides many things; it is not a definitive indication of response rates. There are many variables that intervene in any response rate calculation. The most contentious figure is for Internet response rates: practitioners who use the technique with specific populations argue that their response rates are as high as 70 per cent.

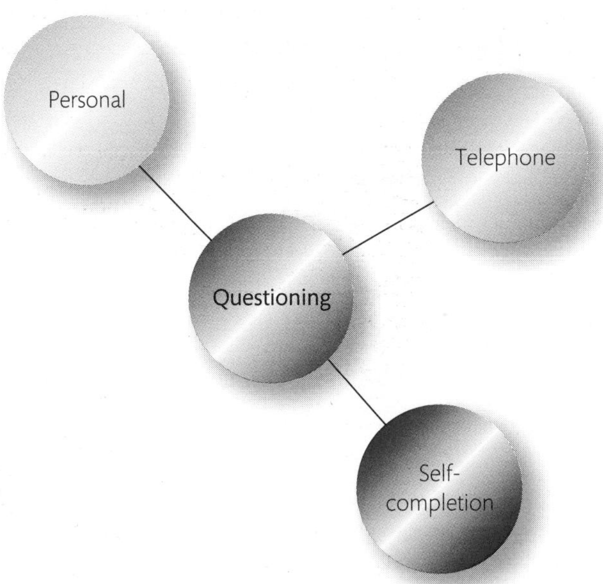

Figure 4.2 The main questioning options for data capture

Table 4.3 How methods may match up to research constraints

	Fieldwork time	Cost	Control
Personal	2–4 weeks	Very high	Very good
Telephone	1–2 weeks	High	Good
Post	3–8 weeks	Medium	Poor
Online	1–7 days	Very low	Poor

Table 4.4 'Common' response rates for the main modes of interviewing

Mode of interviewing	Common response rate (%)	Useful length
Face-to-face	60	45 mins
Drop and collect	60	Four sides
Telephone	45	20 mins
Postal	30	Four sides
Online	10	30 questions

One solution to problems created by short 'snapshot' methods of data collection is the 'panel' concept. The panel is a set of individuals who are questioned or observed, or who report over a period of time. Any changes can therefore be identified and, if necessary, investigated. All of the data capture methods can be applied to this method. The panel interview offers a unique method to assess the effectiveness of any marketing initiative; it is particularly useful to 'measure' the effectiveness of communications initiatives. The nature of the panel is explored in Chapter 8 and its applications can be seen in Chapter 14.

Interviewing

Personal interviewing

Personal interviewing is best used for respondents who need reassurance, who may not have easy access to the phone, and who may need to be guided through showcard materials. For many years, this has been the most common method of interviewing in terms of number of interviews and money paid for research. It involves trained interviewers working on location, whether in the home, on the street, or at the workplace. The advantages are those of control: it is possible to use stimulus material such as showcards or exhibits, and there is a personal touch that may allow an interview to be lengthy compared with other options. Disadvantages include the expensive nature of such a labour-intensive technique. In the long run, the process can be slow; this clearly depends on the sample size, the location, and the research instrument used.

In the 1990s, computer-assisted personal interviewing (CAPI) was introduced, offering unique benefits of speed in data collection and cost savings in processing. It was also possible to carry out routing and edit checks in the field, essentially leading to an intelligent questionnaire. Stimulus material could be stored on a laptop and could appear easily and quickly as required.

Telephone interviewing

Telephone interviewing is best used for respondents who are not readily available in person and on projects that do not have a great deal of visual stimulus material.

The telephone has passed through several phases of popularity. In 1910, there were just 122,000 telephones in the UK (Terramedia 2004). In 1912, the Post Office in the UK opened the national telephone service. We know that, in 2002 in the UK, 98 per cent of households had a telephone (ONS 2004). In an article in the 1970s, the then-president of the Market Research Society wrote: '*Personal interviewing has dominated the UK scene for many years but there are now signs that this is changing. After all, some 50 per cent of UK homes are now equipped with a telephone!*' (Treasure 1976, p. 61). The telephone became extremely important to researchers in the 1970s. In recent years, mobile phone use has increased significantly. It is estimated that, in 2006, mobile phone use accounted for one-third of all voice calls.

Telephone interviewing can be at a central location or decentralised; typically, a decentralised operation is one where trained interviewers work from home. Calls can be made

Table 4.5 Possible outcomes in telephone interviews

Contact made	No contact
Refusal by respondent	Number unobtainable
Out of quota	No answer
Ineligible	Busy
Completed	Respondent not available
Language problem	

from interviewers to respondents and this is known as 'outbound interviewing'. 'Inbound' is also possible, where respondents are given a telephone number to call, at a time convenient to themselves.

The advantages come from the speed of telephone-administered surveys: they do indeed provide quick results, and this method is generally cost-effective. The approach is particularly good at reaching neighbourhoods that may not be easily accessed by the face-to-face interviewer. Of course, this method can also be used for international work. Telephone calls can be recorded for later analysis, but remember that this needs to be made clear to respondents before the interview starts. Disadvantages concern control, which is limited, and there is little chance to show stimulus material (adverts, etc.). Indeed, other than an attractive voice and any interest the respondent may have in the topic, there is little to keep the respondent on the phone. This is illustrated well by looking at the outcome of calls. In telephone interviewing, there are several possible outcomes: contact may be made or there may be no contact. Reasons for each are shown in Table 4.5.

The calculation of the response rate percentage can change throughout the project duration. For example, if busy respondents are not recontacted, the response rate will not rise. The response rate will certainly fall if more telephone numbers are added to the sample in an attempt to increase the number of completed returns.

In the 1980s, computer-assisted telephone interviewing (CATI) came to prominence. CATI means that a questionnaire appears onscreen and the interviewer enters responses directly into the computer. This use of a computer was restricted to the manual keyboard because the first complete mouse was yet to become a standard part of computing—the first complete mouse was introduced with Apple's LISA computer.

The advantage of CATI is that it cuts out several processes, such as handwriting, moving paper, and inputting into the computer. It also allows sample management, whereby interview quotas can be monitored across the telephone unit, avoiding over- or under-sampling. In recent years, automated diallers have been introduced, whereby respondents are called by computer at a specified time. This time may be deemed convenient for interviewers and respondents, sometimes to keep an appointment. The equipment can be configured to administer a questionnaire automatically, using a prerecorded voice or to be passed to an interviewer. The Market Research Society (MRS) has guidelines on the use of such diallers, because they have caused confusion among respondents.

The final *Research in focus* at the end of this chapter brings this type of work into focus.

Interviewing skills

Clearly, telephone and personal interviewing relies heavily on the interviewer. Some have divided the needed qualities for interviewers into three: skills, attitudes, and knowledge. The skills of interviewing include listening skills, probing, and handling respondents. An interviewer needs to be well prepared, an excellent communicator, interested in people, able to work with others, able to work without close supervision, and a competent administrator. The work must be carried out without prejudice, professionally, courteously, objectively, and responsibly. Interviewers are expected to know the industry codes of conduct and data protection legislation. An interviewer is expected to have been briefed properly on the purpose and methods of the project.

We know a fair amount about different aspects of interviewing from various fields—the topics of interrogations and confessions, legal and psychological aspects, British Court of Appeal cases, and foreign cases of disputed confessions (see Gudjonsson 2003). Despite the superior control of interviewers over the data collection process, there can still be problems. By acting as a conduit for the respondent, interviewers may distort or misreport responses. This has been shown by comparing sound recordings with completed questionnaires. The effect is far greater for open-ended questions than closed questions (see Belson 1983, p. 486). It is clear that training will help in this respect, and research agencies provide regular training and project-specific briefings.

Sometimes, respondents do not answer; they may give incomplete answers or answers that are not clear. **'Probing'** is a technique used to clarify such situations; it attempts to motivate the informant to communicate more information without introducing bias into the questions or answers. Some common ways to stimulate respondents to provide more detail are: to repeat the question, to pause to motivate the respondent to speak, to repeat the respondent's answer/last word, and to ask standard (neutral) probe questions. Probing should not be confused with prompting. **Prompts** are generally showcards of brand lists (for example), which remind the respondent in order to direct him/her to answer in a particular way. Here are some neutral probe questions: '*Why do you say that? Anything else? Any others? What do you mean? Can you please explain why?*'.

Self-completion methods

Self-completion methods refer to approaches where the respondent is primarily responsible for providing responses to questions. The approach is best used for respondents who are likely to be motivated to respond and who will need little reassurance and minimal guidance: for example, people who are interested in the topic, such as their new car. The most familiar form of this is the questionnaire delivered by post.

We can also consider delivery by fax, Internet, at trade fairs, as magazine inserts and hand delivery, etc. **Comments cards**, for example, in hotels, are another option and 'diaries' are also used. For more on comments cards and diaries, see Chapter 6.

The advantage of the self-completion method is that the respondent spends his or her time in answering the questions; effectively, this is unpaid labour. There is no interviewer to expend time and money on the exercise. It is therefore a cheap option. It might also be argued that the respondent will give a more considered response without the interference or apparent pressure of an interviewer.

The disadvantages of the self-completion mode concern response quality, response rate, and the response time. There is little control over a respondent when an interviewer is not present; therefore, if a respondent does not understand something or has general queries about the research, there is not an easy way of finding out. This may lead to a poorer quality of answer, or even a lack of reply due to apathy or putting the task off until there is more time. The overall number of replies may suffer (the response or cooperation levels may be low) or replies may be received later than expected (response time suffers). By poor response rate, we are suggesting 30–40 per cent. The questionnaire must be short and simple and the number of returns can be slow. In order to overcome some of these problems, reminders can be introduced. The 'Options for primary data capture' in the Market Researcher's Toolbox list some of these options.

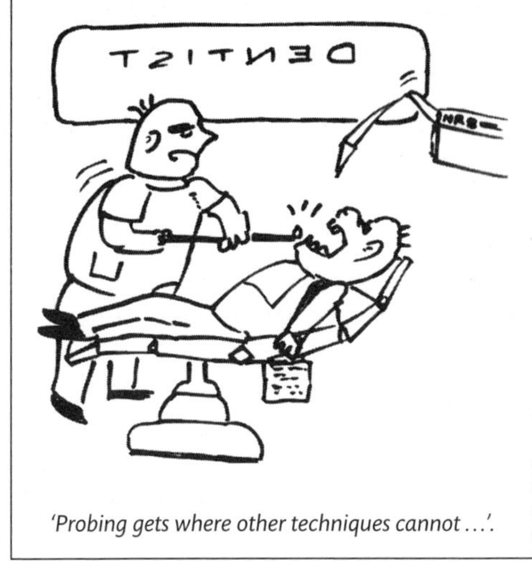

'Probing gets where other techniques cannot . . .'.

Drop and collect methods

The 'interviewer drop and interviewer collection' approach has aroused much interest in recent years. It has been called the DCS method after the words 'Drop-and-Collect Survey method' (see Brown 1987) and has been put forward as a method that can achieve higher response rates than mail questionnaires (see Ibeh *et al.* 2004).

A variation on this is for the interviewer to 'drop' the questionnaire and for it to be returned by another means. In 2001, UK census forms were returned by postal services and the information was scanned into a computer directly from the forms.

Prenotification may assist in response rate and it can be communicated in person, by post, by telephone, by advertisement, or even indirectly, by word of mouth. This then leads to many more options being available to the research designer. The 'Options for primary data capture' in the Market Researcher's Toolbox list prenotification options.

Postal methods

The postal service is an important way to deliver and return research documentation. The growth of postal services began with establishment of important routes to key destinations such as important parts of large towns. In the UK, the Royal Mail service was first made available to the public in 1635, when postage was paid by the recipient. The postcode, in the form used today, was first used in 1959 in Norwich. This was the world's first attempt to use postal address codes for sorting mail by machine. Until 1974, delivery was a fragmented affair, although efficient, and it was only in 1974 that postcodes were extended over all the UK. The postal method of delivering questionnaires probably reached its peak in the 1960s.

It is also essential to monitor progress. If there is a quota to achieve, there must be some mechanism by which to know when to stop selecting and interviewing certain people, otherwise the study is wasting the time of both respondent and researcher. In the case of a postal questionnaire, a simple graph is a useful device to keep track of receipts. This may indicate which dates are the best on which to send reminders. A good guide is to send a reminder when the graph starts a downward turn, that is when replies start to become fewer! A well-organised project allocates identity codes to all forms, so the senders of questionnaires that have already been returned are known. This allows reminders to be sent only to those people who have not replied. This saves both time and money.

Online methods

Internet questionnaires are, at present, self-completed, in that respondents use their own hands with which to respond to questions. This mainly involves the hand in conjunction with a keyboard or with a mouse. However, it must not be forgotten that it is technically possible for voice recognition software to be used to capture spoken responses and it is also possible to use handwriting recognition software to capture handwritten responses. In a similar way, it is possible for questionnaires to be 'spoken', in a way similar to telephone interviewing. With the increasing use of multimedia facilities in computing, it is also possible for an interviewer to appear 'onscreen', making the interview similar to personal interviewing methods (see Table 4.6).

In the current situation, it is the self-completion questionnaire, with words and text, which dominates the quantitative Internet research field. But this does not mean that the choices are limited. Questionnaires may be delivered as a web page, as part of an email message, or as a combination of both methods. To date, most Internet questionnaires have been computer-assisted self-completion interviews, abbreviated sometimes to CASI and other times to CASCI. Other abbreviations in use include CAWI to denote computer-assisted web interviews and CAMI to denote computer-assisted mobile phone interviewing. Note that mobile phones are also used for traditional telephone voice interviews, in addition to SMS/text message interviews and Internet research. With all modes, the intention is to return questionnaires to the sender electronically, although they may also be printed and returned offline.

The Internet is made up of numerous services. If we consider it as the 'information highway', then there are various territories, and different vehicles that can take us across those territories. Let us confine the debate to two territories: email and the World Wide Web. The two vehicles relevant here are email clients such as Microsoft Office Outlook, Hotmail, Yahoo!Mail,

Table 4.6 Modes of delivery and return for electronic data capture

Delivery	Return
Text on screen	Mouse
Interviewer voice	Keyboard
Interviewer image	Handwriting recognition software Voice (recognition software or recording)

and web browsers such as Internet Explorer, Firefox, and Chrome. These 'brand names' are not fixed—their popularity rises and falls. Some will become redundant and new names will appear, but their purposes will remain: they allow users to communicate and receive information. Internet services can be received on computers at home or in a work situation, but they can also be accessed on television sets, laptops, personal digital assistants (PDAs), and mobile phones. Email clients and web browsers can be used to receive questionnaires and also to return them to the sender. A major consideration must be the source of the sample.

Web page questionnaires can be divided into three types: the 'open-web' type, which is part of a website and 'open' to any visitor—there is no control over who visits. This type includes the 'Banner invitation'. The 'closed-web' type is closed, in that respondents are invited to visit the site to complete the questionnaire and it may be protected by a password. The third type is the 'hidden-web' type: this appears to a visitor when triggered by some mechanism. The trigger may be the date, the fact that the visitor has expressed a particular interest by viewing specific information, or it may be a simple mechanism that identifies the visitor as the tenth or twentieth, for example, when systematic sampling is being used. The 'pop-up' survey is an example of this mechanism.

Email questionnaires are of three types. The simple email is a common message, which has the appearance of a letter, with questions included in the text. The respondent simply clicks 'reply', keeping the message as a text message that s/he modifies by adding answers. These answers may be text (to open-ended questions) or s/he may be asked to simply mark 'x' after the correct answer in closed questions. It is also possible for respondents simply to delete answers that do not apply.

The email-attachment type is a questionnaire delivered as a word-processed or spreadsheet-based attachment. The respondent must 'open' the attachment and follow the instructions to complete it. It will be then 'saved' and another email to the researcher will be necessary, with the respondent remembering to re-attach the file with the answers.

The third type of email questionnaire is the email URL-embedded type. The email request for participation has a website address (a URL) mentioned in the message. For email clients that support HTML, the respondent simply links to the web page. This then evokes their web browser, presenting the reader with a web-based questionnaire.

The advantages are many. The nature of Internet interviewing is that it is not intrusive. Internet surveys are quick and easy to prepare, administer, and analyse, as well as being relatively low cost. Answers are entered directly into the software, which can mean that they are received 'live' in 'real time', and therefore give the most up-to-date information possible. The Internet makes international research feasible. The cost of researching the domestic situation does not differ from research overseas. Such research does not suffer from 'clustering',

Table 4.7 Internet questionnaires

Web page	Email
Open-web	Simple email
Closed-web	Email attachment
Hidden-web	Email URL embedded

which is a necessary feature of personal interviewing. The sample is dispersed, inasmuch as the Internet is dispersed.

We have seen that stimulus materials used in telephone interviews are very limited, whereas personal interviewers can use showcard material and technology can show respondents screens with sound and vision. Web-based surveys are able to play music and deliver rich stimulus material for careful consideration. After thoughtful construction, questionnaires on the Internet can follow an appropriate sequence and eliminate questions that are irrelevant to respondents. This is, of course, possible with both personal and telephone interviewing, but not with paper-based self-completion methods.

A disadvantage of email-related surveys is that the invitation to participate may be seen as 'spam' or an unsolicited communication. It may therefore be deleted and the overall picture will be one of a low overall response rate. In 1998, response rates of 75 per cent were common; by 2003, the number of 10 per cent was more likely (see Morrel-Samuels 2003 for more on this issue). Clearly, response rate is dictated by numerous features, but spam is one thing that has eroded cooperation levels. Computer viruses are another reason for low response rates; users are often reluctant to open attachments, fearing that a virus may be part of the package. There is also no opportunity to build a relationship with the researcher.

Web-based surveys suffer a similar threat in that pop-up advertising and the barrage of messages has tended to diminish the impact of a plea or invitation to complete a questionnaire. There are many web-based forms that are not research questionnaires. These may be forms for database building, or registration for specific services (e.g. an auction site), or may be a questionnaire with the aim of 'selling under the guise of research'. This is known as **sugging** in the world of market research. Again, these are reasons why respondents may fail to cooperate with the researcher. Another major problem of an Internet-based questionnaire, particularly where 'Windows' software is used, comes in the superior capability that the user has. Any spontaneous responses that might be expected (for example, to test an understanding of a specific issue) can quickly become overconsidered, because the user can quickly interrogate the vast knowledge of the Internet for answers.

It should be remembered that computers with an Internet connection have differing capabilities. Some machines have a continuous connection; others are only linked periodically and for specific sessions. Some machines may not be equipped for World Wide Web access; some may be limited by older, basic software. Email may be received anywhere: at home; at work; in transit. Email clients have evolved over time and many different ones are in operation. Single computer users may use different email clients and the user may operate several email accounts, some of which may themselves be based on the World Wide Web (Hotmail and Yahoo!Mail are current examples). Some email clients cannot evoke a browser; some email software configurations cannot view attachments. Spreadsheet software is not available on all machines. The Internet can be received through television receivers, and here there are also limitations.

The computer user (the human being) must also be considered. At one extreme, we have the user who is very technical, and is able to use hardware and software with ease. At the other extreme is the user who has not yet mastered the mouse. Between these, we have a variety of different people who make the job of administering online questionnaires an interesting challenge. The researcher's competence with software can also have an influence on the research quality.

The 'Checklist for Internet Studies' in the Market Researcher's Toolbox can be used as a guide to check whether your Internet approach is 'appropriate'.

Mobile phones

Mobile phones have seen massive adoption rates since the late 1970s, when the first models were made available to the general public. By 2008, almost 80 per cent of UK households had a mobile phone (ONS 2007). An example of another innovation that saw a rapid introduction is the Internet. One service, the World Wide Web, is relatively new; the first web browser was written in 1991. However, the concept was such a success that by 2008 over 1463 million users were linked together across the world (IWS 2008); in the UK, about 65 per cent of households had Internet access (ONS 2008). Both mobile telephony and the Internet play a major role in the daily life of the general population. These services are used to find information, to buy and sell, to plan careers, to be entertained, but above all they offer unique ways to communicate with other people. For the humble researcher they offer a unique way to access people for primary research. The defining characteristic of online research is that it is live, connected in real time, and there is little if any delay in transferring data from the point of collection to the point of analysis; it is usually self-completion. Such research comes under various titles: Internet research, web research, VOC (voice of customer), and CAWI (computer-assisted web interviewing). In addition to CAWI, we have CAMI (computer-assisted mobile interviewing) and ARS (audience response systems), which by our definition are all forms of online research because they involve the transmission of data across one or more networks in real time and they are self-completion.

Differences between traditional and online research

Traditional research techniques are those that were available before the widespread use of computer-assisted interviewing. These techniques are sometimes known as 'offline' and they are personal interviewing, postal interviewing, and telephone interviewing. Internet interviewing has been called the fourth research method and mobile surveys the fifth research method (Snaith 2008). Table 4.8 shows the differences between traditional and online methods. Every point of comparison can be seen in a positive and a negative way. For example, instant reporting is certainly a benefit, but at the same time it does not allow for quality control mechanisms to be put in place. In the same way we can see the cost of online being lower, which is a good point; the problem is that it is often used as an excuse to carry out 'saturation sampling', which in the longer term leads to respondent fatigue and poorer-quality responses as questionnaires are a part of everyday life.

Online research is made possible by the combination of computer networks and telecommunications systems. Arguably this could apply to CAPI with Internet connections or centralised CATI systems. Indeed off-line research may still use computers (laptops, for example) but they are, at the time of data collection, not connected; communication networks may also be used (telephone research, for example) but in a manner that is less automated.

Table 4.8 Distinctions between traditional and online research

Traditional research	Online research
Delay of data transfer from point of capture to point of analysis	Almost instant transfer of data from point of capture to point of analysis
Results reach clients via agency	Results can be delivered directly to clients
Sampling frames often from printed directories and lists	Good sample sources are often unavailable
Can reach most populations	Generally restricted to Internet/mobile phone user populations
Respondents are more likely to reveal their identities	Identities are harder to verify online
Researcher has more control over the interview situation than the respondent	Respondent has more control over the interview situation than the researcher
Daytime interviews the norm	Interviews (often called 'sessions') take place when the respondent chooses
Fieldwork period generally longer	Fieldwork period generally shorter
Results publication delayed	Results immediate, even before end of fieldwork
Respondents unlikely to view or be affected by results	If respondents view results answers may change
Cost increases as sample size increases	Large samples do not cost more than small samples

Online approaches are similar in many respects. The similarities (and differences) can be seen by mapping them against each element of the marketing research mix. The purpose, the populations, the procedures, and the publication of results all have implications for the three techniques we have chosen to examine. The purpose of a research study may rule out the choice of method. Similarly, the competence of respondents and the way they are brought to the technology can influence which 'populations' are selected and can in turn dictate the use of specific tools available. The third area of similarity (and difference) concerns the procedures and techniques used; these may be very familiar to respondents or may be completely novel. All approaches use hand-held data-entry devices to capture data. These hand-held devices include the laptop or notebook computer, the mobile phone (sometimes called the cell phone), Personal Digital Assistants (PDA), or other keypads. However, the tasks can vary from extremely easy to extremely difficult, depending on the respondent, the instructions given, and the hardware in use. At the point of publication, these techniques offer unique reporting possibilities; results can be communicated in real time. The three environments or contexts also have similarities and differences. The Internet environment has websites, pages, and search engines and directories that allow easy access. The mobile phone environment

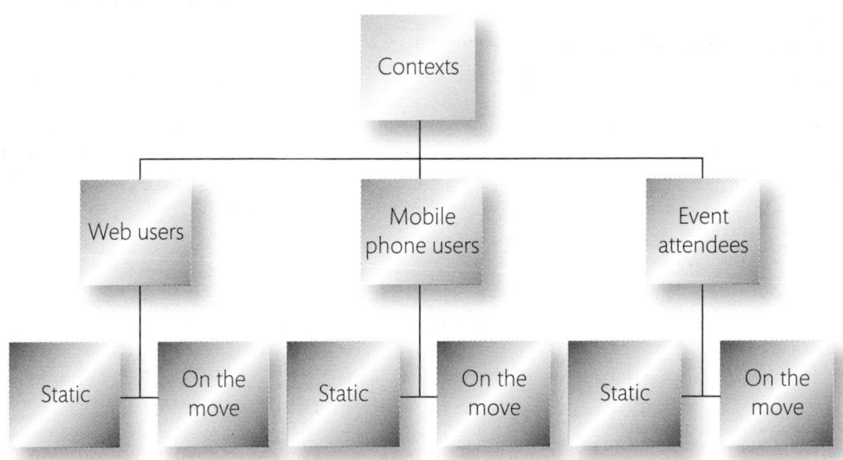

Figure 4.3 Online contexts

has mobile commerce sites and pages; it also has mobile search engines. The environment for audience response systems differs in that it is a physical world; it is an event, conference, exhibition, or similar meeting of people. Figure 4.3 shows the three contexts, highlighting the fact that they vary from having people 'fixed' or 'in transit' in these particular environments.

Purposes of online research

We know that traditional research has numerous purposes; clients were outlined in Chapter 1 as (in order of importance) food and drink, health and beauty, pharmaceuticals, public and government, media and financial. Online research is used for the same reasons but we have specific applications that are related to the medium being used. For example, web-based questionnaires are useful to test websites and mobile phones are a suitable medium to ask questions about satisfaction with a mobile phone service. Usability is the term used to describe whether hardware or software is easy to operate by intended users; therefore usability tests are the procedures used to discover whether hardware or software is easy to operate. Usability testing is not restricted to online research—indeed, traditional methods are essential to good usability tests—however, it does play a major role. Some of the main applications for online research are outlined in Table 4.9.

Audience response systems or forum voting is a quantitative technique and is becoming more common at workshops, seminars, or meetings where respondents are restricted to one room. This restriction in location is important because radio keypads are given to each person attending. The keypads may have buttons to press or a radio dial. Typically, questions will appear on a screen and the audience will be asked to 'vote'. These responses are sent to a receiver, then results are immediately collated for display to the researcher or indeed to the audience as a whole. Although the questions commonly appear on a screen, paper versions of the questionnaire can be provided. The problem with ARS is that if the sampling is done badly it will make a poor attempt at quantifying what is really a qualitative group discussion. This is neither helpful nor instructive, and can be misleading.

Table 4.9 Reasons for choosing online research

Purpose	Description example
Usability testing	To discover whether hardware or software is easy to operate. CAWI can test website usability; CAMI can test the ease of use of handset; ARS measures attitudes to a group demonstration of software
Test online promotions	To test promotions appearing in the online medium. So CAWI tests awareness of web ads; CAMI tests mobile phone ads, and ARS held at a product launch tests attitudes at that event
Test offline promotions	To test promotions appearing in a different medium. CAWI tests television adverts; CAMI tests point of sale promotions in retail outlets; and ARS tests press adverts
Recruitment	Recruiting respondents for different mode of research. CAWI used to recruit focus groups; CAMI recruiting for telephone survey; and ARS recruiting for online survey
Testing other elements	CAWI/CAMI profiling users by collecting from the marketing mix demographics; CAMI to assess mobile phone satisfaction; ARS to test satisfaction with a conference

Mobile phones can be used in the place of the handsets associated with ARS. The question responses can be easily routed to arrive and be displayed on a laptop in the same room; these can, in turn, be relayed to a large screen so that participants can see results. However, we must be aware of the problems that can occur when CAMI is used in this way (see Table 4.10). Different makes of telephones have different capabilities, and users in the same room are likely to be connected via different service providers. These differences alone can mean that text messaging will not occur simultaneously; indeed, some text messages may be stored and delivered after the event has come to an end. The nature of cellular telephony can also mean that reception can suffer so that certain phones are blocked or delays can occur in situations where call demand is high. In addition to these problems, mobile phones give an audio alert to announce the arrival of a message; when there are dozens of these alerts in one room within a matter of a few minutes, there is a great deal of disruption to the event itself.

Table 4.10 How methods may match up to research constraints

	Fieldwork time	Cost	Control
CAWI	1–5 days	Very low	Poor
CAMI (SMS)	1–5 days	Medium–high	Poor
ARS	Immediate	Low	Very good

Table 4.11 'Common' response rates for online modes of interviewing

Mode of interviewing	Common response rate	Useful length
CAWI	Opt-in 50–100% Unsolicited 10–30%	30 questions Below 50 words per screen
CAMI (SMS)	Opt-in 50–100% Unsolicited 10–30%	Five questions Below 25 words per screen
ARS	90–100%	10–30 questions Below 50 words per screen

Similarly, Table 4.11 shows some typical response rates for these modes of interviewing. This is based on the author's experience and hides many things; it is not a definitive indication of response rates. There are many variables that intervene in any response rate calculation.

Mixed-mode methodologies

Traditionally, researchers have had serious reservations about administering a questionnaire using two or more means of delivery. For example, we might send a questionnaire by post for part of the sample, but administer the same questions by telephone for another part of the sample. The reason for disapproval is that the different modes are different instruments and may give different readings. Additionally, stimulus material is best suited to certain modes.

Many evaluations of effects have been carried out (for example, Vannieuwenhuyze *et al.* 2010, Lugtig *et al.* 2011). As a result, thinking has progressed. The advantage is that this may increase participation, either by increased coverage or by increased response. In other words, a certain mode may reach respondents and also informants may refuse one type of approach but not another. The disadvantages are that there will be measurement issues as the same person may give different answers in different modes due to such things as the differing appearance of items, interviewer effects, social desirability, recall bias, acquiescence, primacy and recency effects. The National Student Survey (see *Research in focus*) is a good example of using combination methodologies to increase sample sizes.

Observation

Observation is a method of primary data collection that avoids relying on cooperation. It involves seeing, tracking, or sensing behaviour or actions in some way. Observation is an

Common mistakes
Device bias

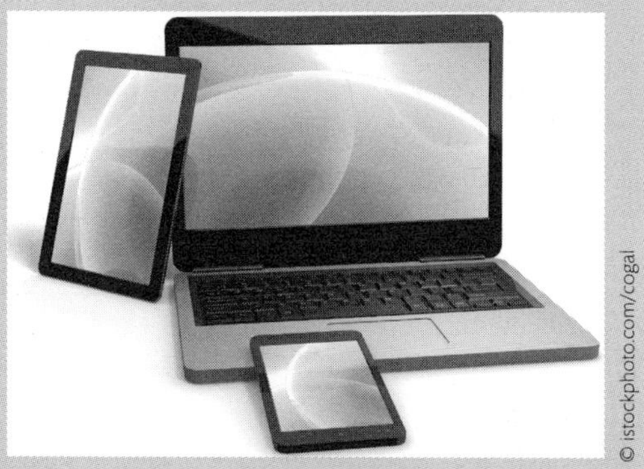
© istockphoto.com/cogal

There are many cases of researchers administering a questionnaire online then finding response rate is poor and making up the numbers with telephone interviews, face-to-face interviews or 'drop and collect'. These methods should not be mixed for the same questionnaire. The mode of collection may glean different results and we will not know if differences are real or due to the method. For example there is a difference between visual and auditive transmission of questions and scales; the *'don't know option'* may need to be hidden or disclosed for ease of administration. This is called 'mode effect' and cannot be criticised if the effect is measured in a pilot and if it is then reported or adjusted. This is the case with the NSS—it has been tested a great deal and poses no issue because the questioning is so brief.

Currently, there is a new issue being raised that is related to this mixing of methods but with a less obvious solution. It has been called *device bias.* We know that Internet questionnaires can be received on a respondent's home or work computer, this may be a fixed unit PC or a laptop or a tablet but the questionnaires may also be received on a regular cell phone or a smart phone There is evidence to suggest that the same online questionnaires answered by the same person on these different devices may differ; not because the respondent's situation is different but because each mode displays the questionnaire in a different way. For example, the smart phone often rotates a horizontal scale to become vertical, all devices modify the size of the words, some displays show more than others, and the clarity differs. Solutions to this are being investigated, one is to monitor the device used and investigate any differences, another is to only allow a questionnaire to be opened on the preferred device.

essential ingredient in marketing research. The A.C. Nielsen Company has conducted distributor audits since 1933. At first, an army of people would visit stores and count the items on shelves at the start and end of the working day. This human observation method switched to mechanical observation as technology advanced. A.C. Nielsen still offers information for food, health and beauty, confectionery, and beverages.

The process of visiting a website and scanning the contents is a form of observation. The process can be formalised by making a note of website features such as speed of download, impact, use of colour, etc. An observation form can be created for this purpose. In appearance, it is similar to a questionnaire, but is designed for the observer to 'capture' his or her observations (see the Market Researcher's Toolbox for a website evaluation form that can be adapted to your needs). The researcher can view how the Internet user behaves when looking at websites. 'Accompanied browsing' can take place both offline and online.

Observation may be covert (hidden) or overt, so the observed know. It may be mechanical, using visual or audio-recording devices. In recent years Unilever have used 'spy-toothbrushes' to record when and for how long people would clean their teeth; the toothbrushes had in-built accelerometers (Tarran 2011). The company also monitored the shower behaviour of 100 homes using a device that detected noise and temperature from pipes (Kinver 2011).

'Observing thinking inside the box'

Observation can be effective when used to identify problems; it is less associated with problem-solving research. Boote and Mathew (1999) say that observation *'may be the only method to obtain data on consumers' behaviour in certain situations'.* In recent years, the Internet has become the usual feature in homes and workplaces and the ability to 'observe' behaviour mechanically has increased.

Observation plays an indirect role in most studies. Focus group researchers rely heavily on observing how people answer questions; street interviewers observe carefully to maximise cooperation; retail interviewers take careful note of shop layout during visits. It is largely associated with the 'capture' of 'visual data', but this is a limited definition.

Observations can be carried out by human or by machine. A simple video camera recording street conversations has no researcher involved. Subsequent analysis of the recordings is, however, highly reliant on the researcher's interpretation. Observation may be contrived or natural, participant or non-participant.

There is a fine line between secondary data and observation. Website visits, for example, may be considered as machine observation that is primary data, or as internal secondary data. Whether the researcher participates in the 'observed event' leads us into the interesting topic called 'action research'. **Ethnography** is a form of participant observation and this is explored in Chapter 7.

The alternative to observation is to ask questions or to gather information in another way. The advantages are therefore inevitably related to these other options. For example, recorded observation provides an accurate record, not affected by memory problems; non-participant and mechanical observation is objective. The disadvantages are that the data collection process can take time, so may become costly; data need to be interpreted, and finally, participant observation can be subjective. Several codes of conduct cover observation techniques.

Overt observation has been favoured by qualitative researchers when investigating Fast-Moving Consumer Goods (FMCG) sales. It has become known as 'accompanied shopping'. The researcher joins the consumer on a trip to the local supermarket and observes how the decisions are made. The principle has been applied to many activities, such as:

- Retail shopping
- New product use (usability tests)
- Internet use (accompanied browsing).

Covert observation approaches include **electronic point of sale** or **electronic processing of sales**, usually known as **EPOS**. This involves the use of technology, particularly the bar code, to allow swift transactions to take place in retail outlets. The records are a powerful form of internal secondary data. In research terms, this is mechanical observation, and it is a form of hidden or covert observation.

Mechanical observation means are used to make pedestrian or vehicular counts to estimate audiences for outdoor media. As we will see, various devices are available to the researcher; they include eye equipment, voice devices, and skin equipment. Mechanical devices are also used to monitor TV, radio, and Internet audiences. Bar code readers can be used in the store, at the checkout, or at home. They can be used to understand which merchandise to stock in particular localities and, specifically, how to position products in stores.

Mechanical observation, perhaps more than human observation, evokes a fear of invasion of privacy. Invisible Internet processing, for instance, has been criticised as being an invasion of the privacy of the respondent. This may be because this data capture method has a hint of being underhand or uncensored. Many guidelines help: the ESOMAR Guidelines for Tape and Video Recording and Client Observation of Group Discussions state that respondents must be told that they will be recorded; recordings must be made anonymous by blurring faces, removing names, etc.; and human observers, more specifically clients, must abide by the same codes.

Mystery shopping

Another covert observation method is 'mystery shopping', which occurs when researchers assume the role of a potential or actual customer. The origins of mystery shopping can be traced to the early 1970s in the USA, but it has now spread worldwide. Certain aspects of the process are observed and noted by the researcher. It is usually covert because researchers monitor service performance without revealing their identity. Sometimes, a purchase is made; sometimes it is not. The technique is also called 'situation research'; mystery shoppers are also known as 'retail researchers'. The technique can be distinguished from other techniques by the fact that observers are trained (in observation techniques and the specific topic); customers or clients are not questioned; and observations are noted as soon as possible after the event.

Mystery shopping can take various forms: it might be syndicated or ad hoc; it might be qualitative or quantitative; it might be structured or unstructured. It can be self-standing or part of other research. The mode is also variable: it can be by telephone or in person; it has even been extended to the Internet, where shoppers evaluate online outlets.

Many examples of mystery shopping come from the retail sector. Typically, researchers are sent regularly to stores and numerous measurements are made. Over recent years, we have seen published examples of widespread use of the technique in the financial and retail sectors. There are examples of its use in the motor car sector. Mystery shopping has been criticised for wasting time and money in service encounters that do not result in sales and may lose other legitimate customers. Additionally, the morale of employees can be affected; there may be fear of disciplinary action or loss in wages. Finally, there may be a real loss of earnings by staff who rely on sales-related commissions or bonuses. Codes of conduct cover 'mystery shopping'. The ESOMAR (1999) Mystery Shopping Guide, for example, recommends that, if there are difficulties in following any of the guidelines, mystery shopping should not be carried out. ESOMAR states that, if mystery shopping is planned for the client's own organisation, it is

Research in focus
The National Student Survey (NSS)

A researcher's job is not an easy one. Modern life seems to have affected our willingness to cooperate with interviewers. There has been a fall in response rates. The National Student Survey (the NSS) found a creative solution to this.

© istockphoto.com/Skip Odonnell

Proposals from 25 research agencies were considered to decide who should conduct the NSS, an extremely large project worth about £2 million per year. Ipsos MORI was chosen to run the study. The NSS was piloted in 2003 and 2004, and the full-scale survey began in 2005 across all publicly funded higher education institutions in England, Wales, and Northern Ireland.

Final-year students were asked about the quality of their courses. The questionnaire probed agreement with a series of statements. Topics included teaching, assessment and feedback, academic support, organisation and management, learning resources, and personal development.

The survey was commissioned by the Higher Education Funding Council for England (HEFCE), and supported by the Higher Education Funding Council for Wales (HEFCW) and the Department for Employment and Learning, Northern Ireland (DEL). These bodies have a statutory role in ensuring that the quality of teaching in higher education is assessed, and believe that students' views should form an important part of the assessment.

The multiple attempts used to secure a high response rate are of interest; they follow a sequence that tries to catch even the busiest student. Final-year students are sent an email in February of each year; this invites them to complete the survey online. Non-respondents to the online survey are followed up with a postal questionnaire to their term-time addresses. Students who still do not respond are then followed up by telephone. In some cases, attempts are made to contact students at their 'vacation' addresses. The proposal also included the possibility of giving a small random sample of students the opportunity to complete the questionnaire by interactive voice response. This was planned to be facilitated either by supplying a Freefone number on which to record responses at any time, or by sending an SMS text message to mobile phones; on replying to the message, the student could be telephoned and connected to the service.

The project is a good example of reporting using the Internet: results are published on a purpose-built website, http://www.unistats.com. Users can filter results by university and course. In line with the MRS Code of Conduct, respondents can be identified neither directly nor indirectly, so the published information does not go down to the level of individual students; findings are based on at least 50 responses. The National Student Survey was carefully designed to help future students to choose courses and institutions.

Compiled by Nigel Bradley 2012.

Sources:

National Student Survey 2012: *Briefing for Students.*

http://www.thestudentsurvey.com and http://www.unistats.com

Questions

1 Summarise the multiple attempts used to secure a high response rate on the NSS.

2 What other data capture method could achieve the same objectives?

3 What are the advantages and disadvantages of a poster reminder?

good practice to inform staff. If mystery shopping is planned for a competing organisation, the situation is more complicated. It is recommended that, unless there is some strong technical reason to the contrary, such time should normally not exceed 10 minutes in manufacturing and retail businesses (other than automotive) and 15–20 minutes in other service industries and businesses. There are indications for mechanical observation: electronic recording should not be carried out without prior permission.

Research instruments

Chapter 6 covers questionnaire and topic guide design. That chapter equips the reader to be able to create an effective questionnaire or to determine the appropriate means to collect data. Here, we restrict ourselves to equipment and approaches used in data capture.

Photographic cameras include digital or those with traditional film. Traditional film still has a role with the single-use camera. This camera is used in ethnographic studies as a mechanical form of observation. Informants can use these 'throwaway' cameras to capture everyday occurrences. The low cost means that any losses can be absorbed. Mobile phones have in-built cameras which can also be used by respondents or researchers in the capacity of participant observers.

'Eye equipment devices' include oculometers, pupilometers, and eye movement cameras. This equipment is designed to observe eye direction and movement. It can help to discover how adverts and packaging are viewed; the sequence in which various areas of an advert or pack are viewed may be important. Pupil size may be associated with interest. A slow speed of blinking may be associated with open-mindedness. Another well-known device is the 'tachistoscope', which flashes a message in front of a respondent so quickly that it cannot be understood. It is slowed to the point at which s/he can decipher some of the message. This can be used to assess which parts of the message are stronger and which are weaker. As a result, it is used to compare different executions and to develop advertisements, pack designs, branding designs, or logos.

'Voice recording' is a well-established technique used to capture the content of the spoken word. For many years, researchers have used recorders with omnidirectional microphones. These are mainly used to record focus groups and depth interviews, but may also be used to record pilot questionnaire interviews; the recording is played back while examining the completed questionnaire. These are also used to record phone interviews, but the researcher

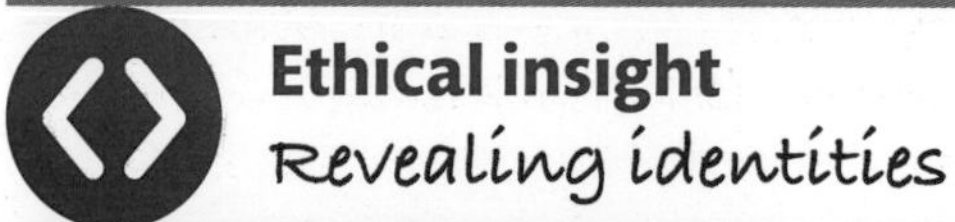

Ethical insight
Revealing identities

© istockphoto.com/narvikk

Researchers cannot research without knowing the ethical rules, but, even then, some of the rules seem to contradict each other. Before an interview, members of the Market Research Society must ensure that the name of the interviewer is given; there is an assurance that the interview will be carried out according to the MRS Code of Conduct. Respondents will also be told the general subject of the interview, the purpose of the interview, and a few other details. This obligation goes beyond the interview itself because a follow-up interview cannot be carried out if the respondent's permission was not obtained at the previous interview.

The MRS has a rule to say that respondents can be recontacted for quality control purposes; this means we can go back to respondents. As a matter of course, many respondents are recontacted to ensure the interview was actually carried out. Some agencies recontact 5 per cent; some will contact as many as 10 per cent. The 'back-checking' levels of 5–10 per cent appear as part of national and international quality standards.

However, there are some research techniques that require researchers not to introduce themselves. One of these approaches is mystery shopping. If the research is carried out for a client, but in a store belonging to one of their competitors, the MRS rules say the opposite: '*Members must ensure that their identities are not revealed*'. But there is some comfort for employees who have not been warned that a mystery shopper may appear: that small comfort is that they cannot be recorded—in other words, photographic or sound recording equipment, hidden or not, must not be used.

Compiled by Nigel Bradley 2012.

Sources:
ESOMAR's Mystery Shopping Guidelines, http://www.esomar.org. Reproduced with kind permission.
MRS Code, rules B11, B12, B21 and B43–B46, http://www.mrs.org.uk/standards/codeconduct.htm

Questions

1 List the things that an interviewer must tell a respondent before the interview.

2 What are the benefits of 'back-checking' respondents who have already been interviewed?

3 When can a researcher use a camera in mystery shopping?

runs the risk of breaking national laws if the respondent is not told that the call is being recorded. CAPI and CATI interviews, which use computers for interviewing, may be equipped with voice capture devices making a digital recording. **Automated speech recognition** (ASR) software can then be used to transfer the content into written words. There are other devices that can be used in the analysis of voices.

The basic idea with 'voice devices' is that changes in voice pitch may indicate emotion. In contrast, 'sensory devices' examine the skin. Decreases in electrical resistance of the skin come from increased perspiration, which may in turn be due to excitement or interest in a stimulus; this has been used for new product tests. One device is known as the 'psycho-galvanometer'. Another device is the 'electroencephalograph', whereby electrical frequencies of the brain are measured. Proponents of the method suggest that advertising recall and levels of attention should be detected 'at source'. Hidden observation or listening devices can be used in public places, but from an ethical viewpoint, the MRS says that signs must advise that monitoring is taking place, the purpose of the monitoring, and contact details.

'Scanning devices' read bar codes, which are a series of vertical or horizontal parallel lines. The code is read using a bar code scanner. Packaging codes identify items, prices, and manufacturer details. Scanners on electronic cash registers allow prices to be totalled and update inventory figures. When linked with loyalty cards, the devices are an extremely powerful way of mining data and identifying clusters of purchases. They can be used to understand which merchandise to stock in particular localities and, specifically, how to position products in stores. For researchers, bar code scanners can be used in three ways:

1. At the checkout, to facilitate sales and record the time, price, and quantity for analysis later
2. By auditors to analyse stock in the store
3. By researchers (or respondents themselves) at home.

The TNS Superpanel, the UK's leading continuous consumer panel, consists of 15,000 households. Data is collected twice weekly via electronic terminals in the home, with purchases being recorded via home-scanning technology (see http://superpanel.tns-global.com/superpanel/).

An 'audimeter' is a recording device attached to a television to monitor the time and channel. Different versions exist, whereby respondents are obliged to register their presence in the room. The term 'audimeter' is derived from early use with radio. The 'instantaneous audimeter' was developed to allow telephone lines to relay the information to the researcher. These are sometimes known as 'peoplemeters'.

Factors that affect cooperation

Response quality

Whether we are asking questions or making observations, there will be problems with measuring human nature. Questioning techniques are explained fully in Chapter 6 and

these offer the researcher ways to identify and to measure aspects of the human situation. However, all instruments employed share the potential problem of **instrumentation effect**. Any instability of the instrument or the mere fact that it is being used may result in an inaccurate reading. This means that, however well considered, any research study will have some defect. The good researcher tries to anticipate the best ways of minimising any problems that may affect results.

If we test the knowledge of a respondent and then repeat the test, there will be a difference in outcome. This is due to learning from the first round and this is a good example of 'instrumentation effect'. Similarly, there is a concept called **mere measurement effect**, which suggests that 'the mere measurement' of attitudes creates them, and where they exist, may change them (see Dholakia and Morwitz 2002 for more on this).

Researchers must accept that there are respondents with poor literacy skills and we also know that people do not always tell the truth. Being untruthful can be due to various things: the situation of the interview, a like or dislike for the interviewer, lack of knowledge, even simply forgetting.

The relationship with the interviewer can affect response. **Acquiescence response bias** is a form of sympathy where a respondent agrees with a proposition, rather than disagreeing. This is particularly a problem with children and the elderly, who, in an attempt to be cooperative and polite with strangers, will tend to agree before considering the full implications of a question.

Therefore, the choice of interviewer is important. A 'same sex' interviewer may be best for some topics: for example, a female for a study of breast cancer and male for a study of testicular cancer. A 'same race' interviewer may be appropriate if cultural differences affect cooperation; a 'same age' interviewer may be appropriate for some topics. Interviewers may work in pairs for such reasons and for reasons of safety.

Satisficing is relevant here. Krosnick, Narayan, and Smith (1996, p. 29) point out the relevance to the researcher when they say that informants '*shortcut the cognitive processes necessary for generating optimal answers*'. To carry out the task of answering questions efficiently, the respondent: must be fully exposed to the question, either by listening carefully or reading carefully; must understand the meaning, or at least interpret it; must recall applicable information; must process these data into something meaningful and then must be able to articulate this in a spoken or written manner, or in some cases, by non-verbal communication. Satisficing is said to occur if any of these is not carried out to the respondent's best ability or if his/her ability is not sufficient for any one part to be completed.

Satisficing can mean that a 'sufficient' answer is given when a better one might have been available.

When designing research, we must be mindful that one approach may only give one viewpoint of the issue under inspection. For that reason, researchers are advised to consider triangulating their studies. **Triangulation** means that we examine a problem from three or more viewpoints. The benefit is that there is more chance that the other approaches may identify something that was not apparent in one. This is not a case of repeating the study, but it is a case of carrying out three studies simultaneously, in a complementary way. Triangulation has been divided into various types: we can add to the data, add another investigator, add a theory, and add a different method. These interests may have arisen from concerns about response quality and response rates, which we will now examine.

Response quantity

The 'response rate' refers to the number of complete responses that have been obtained by a researcher compared with the number of eligible individuals. The response rate is always expressed as a percentage. Because the percentage will be between 0 and 100, response rates are often seen as a 'barometer' to suggest that a survey has been 'good' or 'bad', depending on how high the percentage is. This can be quite misleading, particularly when non-random sampling methods have been adopted.

Response rates vary for many reasons. Let us divide these into intrinsic factors and extrinsic factors. 'Intrinsic factors' are those that are a part of the project itself, ones that the researcher is more able to change, and extrinsic factors are exterior ones, ones that will affect response, but about which the researcher can do little (see Table 4.12).

Intrinsic factors include the interviewer. Even the most experienced and trained interviewers can introduce bias simply by interacting with people where there is a certain level of comfort. Another intrinsic factor is the sample quality: a good list of appropriate respondents is clearly superior to a poorly formatted one that contains duplicates, misspellings, and 'dead' respondents. The choice of words for use in the introduction can make or break cooperation.

Table 4.12 Intrinsic factors and extrinsic factors that affect response

Intrinsic factors	Extrinsic factors
Interviewer	Weather
Sample quality	Temporal factors (time of year, day)
Type of introduction	Interest in topic
Instrument design	Respondent profile (age, experience with surveys, personality, mood)
Motivating factors	Competing events (holidays, national events, other surveys)
Incentives	Suggers, fruggers, and duggers

The professionalism of the questionnaire or other research instrument can also affect response. Similarly, respondents can be motivated by various things: they may cooperate for altruistic reasons, or for incentives.

Conversely, 'extrinsic factors' include: the weather; the time of year or day; interest in the topic; the respondent's age, experience with surveys, personality, and mood. There may be events that compete for the respondent's attention such as holidays, national events, or other surveys. In the 1990s, interviewers were banned from the city-centre streets of Sheffield, which had extreme effects on interviewing. In 1998, this was relaxed somewhat and interviews could take place if a 'Sheffield City Badge' was worn, each of which was numbered and kept on a register.

Here we can introduce three terms specific to the market research world: the work of researchers is compromised by 'suggers', 'fruggers', and 'duggers'.

Suggers are people or firms who 'sell under the guise of research'; fruggers are people who 'fund-raise under the guise of research', and duggers are people who 'gather data under the guise of research'. These activities may be face-to-face, on the telephone, or even by post. For example, on the street, a member of the public may be approached and asked a few simple questions, but the questions will be there simply to decide if the person is a prospective customer or charity donor. Who can refuse to give money when asked: '*Do you agree that children should be given food?*'. Forms that ask lifestyle questions arrive by post or are inserted into magazines; sometimes, they come with a free pen, a prize draw, or some other incentive. If they request a donation, they are **frugging**; if they do not, they are database-building or **dugging**.

The spiral of silence

Elisabeth Noelle-Neumann developed the 'spiral of silence' concept in 1974. Her main points are these: society threatens deviant individuals with isolation; individuals experience fear of isolation continuously; this fear means that individuals assess the climate of opinion continuously; this assessment affects whether they express opinions openly or conceal them.

Let us apply this to political voting. In order to avoid isolation on favouring unpopular policies, people will look to their environment for clues about the dominant opinion; they will identify which views are gaining strength and which are in decline. If they feel that their personal views are among those in decline, they are less likely to express them openly. As a result, the views perceived to be dominant seem to gain even more ground and other possibilities decline further. These are Noelle-Neumann's own words:

> The more individuals perceive these tendencies and adapt their views accordingly, the more one faction appears to dominate and others to be on the downgrade. Thus the tendency of the one to speak up and the other to be silent starts off a spiralling process which increasingly establishes one's opinion as the prevailing one.

The spiral of silence concept therefore suggests that support for one or other political party is not recorded in opinion polls because people prefer not to admit their allegiance to an interviewer or researcher. From this, we have learnt that two important areas must be probed in addition to a question on voting intention:

1. How certain the respondent is to vote on the day
2. Whether the respondent may decide to change the vote on the day. This shows if the person is decided or undecided.

Voting certainty and indecision can then be used to filter the figures and will show how accurate the opinion poll figures are. The higher the percentage, the less certain the results are. The spiral of silence concept originated with political research, but we can see that it applies to all areas.

One technique used in monitoring opinion of political parties is the 'exit poll'. The exit poll means that voters are intercepted as they are leaving the election booth, where they have, just a few moments before, placed their vote.

If sampled properly, this method should give an accurate indication of overall voting results, before voting has ended and before the votes have been counted. It is accepted practice for the results of exit polls to be published only after voting has ended: this is because news of the survey results might affect the behaviour of those who have not voted. In some cases, people may decide not to vote; conversely, the results may motivate others to vote where they might not have done so without the survey. Effectively, the survey itself might have an impact on the voting mechanism, rather than a simple observational role.

Common mistakes
Confusing response rates

The term 'response rate' is used in both direct marketing and in marketing research. There are similarities but the two disciplines have different purposes, so there is sometimes confusion, particularly for practitioners of direct marketing.

In research, the response rate refers to how many responses have been obtained by a researcher compared with the number of eligible individuals. If we send a questionnaire with **return envelope** to 1000 people and 60 send a usable reply, then the response rate is 6 per cent. In direct marketing, the response rate is the number of immediate purchases (or sales leads) that have been generated by a campaign, compared with the total number sent out. So, if we send a persuasive letter with an order form and return envelope to 1000 people and 60 replies come back, then the response rate is 6 per cent. Those 60 replies may be valuable; they may well represent a great deal of money, so that level of response may be judged as a success. However, the market researcher will be extremely concerned with a response rate of 6 per cent to the questionnaire; quite simply, there will be no information for 94 per cent of our sample, and the views of these non-respondents may well be contrary to those of the 60 respondents. It is important to make a clear distinction between response for selling and response for researching. A good response rate for a direct mail campaign is usually a very poor response rate for the market researcher.

Research in focus
A peek into the life of an interviewer

Chris Garvey describes life as a telephone interviewer in a top UK full-service research agency. Chris is based at the Ipsos MORI CATI centre in Harrow and deals with respondents based in the UK.

Credit: Ipsos MORI

Interview quality controller

Training is an important part of this job. We are given initial induction training, which ensures that we know and obey the Market Research Society's Code of Conduct during our telephone interviewing. We are also listened to internally by monitors to make sure we are following our training. This ensures quality of interviews and also protects the respondent. When a new project starts, a briefing is given to all interviewers. This is very useful as it tells us the purpose of the project, background information, and allows us to go through a test interview. When the project goes 'live' we are ready to make calls.

In telephone interviewing nowadays, there is no manual dialling; numbers are called automatically either through random digit dialling or by direct sampling. When a connection is made, most people are cooperative when you explain how you are not trying to sell them anything, but just trying to get their valued opinion. Yes, respondents vary enormously, as do people in life. I have interviewed people from 18 to 90 years' old.

Our work is organised around respondents. We have people to contact at work, then others who are at home. For that reason, we have two shifts, there are 'business shifts', from 9.00 am to 5.30 pm, and there are what we call 'consumer shifts', from 2.45 pm to 9.00 pm. We can also work during the day on Saturdays and Sundays. We can choose hours to suit our own situation.

This week, on the business shift, I worked on a project where we were calling up companies to contact their IT managers. This is to get their views and opinions on IT brand awareness and advertising. This is often difficult as they are busy people, and each interview can take up to 30 minutes. However, we are given specialist business-calling techniques; these show us how best to do this and we feel a sense of achievement when we get the interview.

On the consumer shift, I am working on a project for a telephone service supplier, where we call customers directly to get their opinions on the service they receive. It covers reception, prices, tariffs, customer service, etc. As you see, the projects are very varied: one day I can be interviewing an elderly lady in Newcastle about which food her cat prefers, the next day I can be interviewing an 18-year-old student about their opinions of their university course. The centre also carries out European and worldwide projects so there are telephone interviewers from many other countries. That makes this an exciting environment in which to work.

Compiled by Nigel Bradley 2012.

Source:
Information provided by Christopher Garvey; edited by Nigel Bradley; reproduced with kind permission of Robert Kirby, Ipsos, March 2006.

Questions

1 List the different points at which Christopher receives training and supervision.

2 Why do you think the research agency chose to interview IT managers by telephone rather than online?

3 What do you think are the main motivators for telephone interviewers?

Chapter summary

1 **Explain the nature of primary data**

Primary data are "fresh data" - they are collected to satisfy specific requirements and therefore the procedures used follow carefully determined objectives. Methods of data capture are divided into two broad groups: questioning and observation. Under these headings there are many subdivisions. Face-to-face methods have been used for many years. The postal method probably reached acceptance in the 1960s, whereas the telephone became important from the 1970s. In the late 1990s Internet-related services were used. Observation is an essential part of research and regular audits have taken place since the 1930s. This switched from human counting to mechanical observation as technology advanced. Another approach, 'mystery shopping', using participant observation, can be traced back to the early 1970s.

2 **Outline the different methods used to capture data**

There are several ways to gain access to respondents: face-to-face, by telephone, by post, online, or by other means. Once contact has been made, there are various ways to capture data. A variation of these methods of data collection is the panel, a set of individuals that reports its experiences over a period of time. All of the data capture methods can be made into panels. Observation is a method of primary data collection that involves seeing, tracking, or sensing behaviour or actions in some way. It may be hidden or the observed may know. It may be mechanical using visual or audio-recording devices. This approach can be effective when used to identify problems. Mystery shopping and accompanied shopping are forms of observation.

3 **Show the benefits and limitations of using primary data**

The different modes of data capture have an influence on any market research study. The researcher is driven by three main constraints: the time available, money available, and the control that can be achieved. The Internet is the fastest and cheapest way, but researchers are unable to exert any control over the respondent, a weakness shared with postal methods. The face-to-face approach is the most expensive, but it can provide results of the highest possible quality. In terms of response rate, we can suggest these as a guide: personal–60 per cent; telephone–45 per cent; postal–30 per cent; Internet modes–10 per cent. In panels, any changes over time can be identified and, if necessary, investigated. Mystery shopping offers a unique way to see service from the customer's viewpoint, but has been criticised for wasting time and money in service encounters that do not result in sales and may lose other legitimate customers.

Explain which factors affect cooperation and how they do this

Inaccurate measurement can be due to: the instrument, the situation of the interview, the interviewer, lack of knowledge, even forgetting. There are several names for such problems, such as 'mere measurement effect', 'acquiescence response bias', and 'satisficing'. Both 'response quality' and 'response quantity' are affected by intrinsic factors and extrinsic factors. Intrinsic factors are part of the project itself, ones that the researcher is more able to change; extrinsic factors are ones that will affect response, but about which the researcher can do little. Everything affects response: sample quality, the choice of words used, the instrument, incentives. The work of researchers is also compromised by other activities that are mistaken for research; these activities are often referred to as sugging, dugging, and frugging.

Review questions

1 Why should control be one of the most important considerations for the researcher?

2 What lessons can we draw from the past to help in collecting data?

3 Assess the advantages and disadvantages of using mobile phone interviews to investigate car driving.

4 Why is it so important to consider existing respondent knowledge when deciding on the best data capture method?

5 For what reasons may we decide to reject mystery shopping when we carry out research?

Discussion questions

1 Evaluate the ways used to capture data from tourists passing through Britain on their European tour.

2 Explore the ways to capture data that can be used by small companies with limited research money. What problems are associated with this approach?

3 How can in-store methods be used to understand who buys dog food? Evaluate the good and bad points of this approach.

4 Consult the proposal in the Market Researcher's Toolbox. With your knowledge of primary data, draft a possible design for different data capture techniques than those proposed. Try to improve on the design.

5 Look at the opening Snapshot on neuromarketing research. What advice would you give to a company wishing to use this technique? Outline the likely procedure that might be used to test a press advertisement.

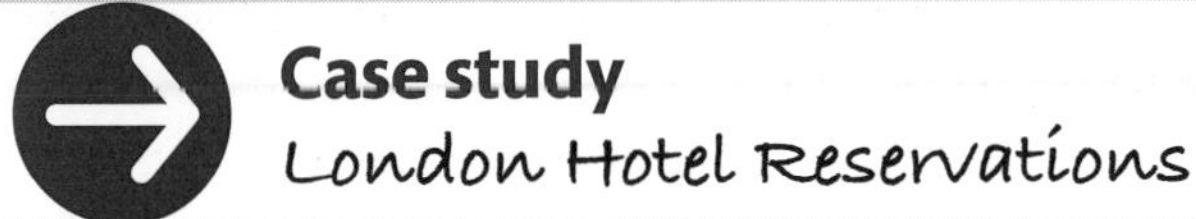

Case study
London Hotel Reservations

Nick Dudman understands how hotel reservations are made because he has worked in the hotel business in London for many years. In 2000, he decided to use his knowledge to form his own business. He had seen how easy it was to use the World Wide Web and so created a website. He created a successful operation whereby anyone could book a hotel in London using his website. The business model was such that Nick negotiated with several hotels and agreed to feature them on his website. People needing a hotel in London would simply reserve a room using the website; confirmation of booking would be made by email, but no money would change hands until checkout. Nick received a percentage of any bookings made in this way through his agency; he sent an invoice to all hotels each month, to include all bookings made in the preceding period. The idea worked well and generated a fair amount of money, so, last January, he decided to launch an extension to his business. The new venture incorporated a sophisticated database; this could keep records of customers and automatically send accounts to hotels. The new system also had a link to several hotels at which direct reservations could be made. This meant that Nick did not have to intervene personally.

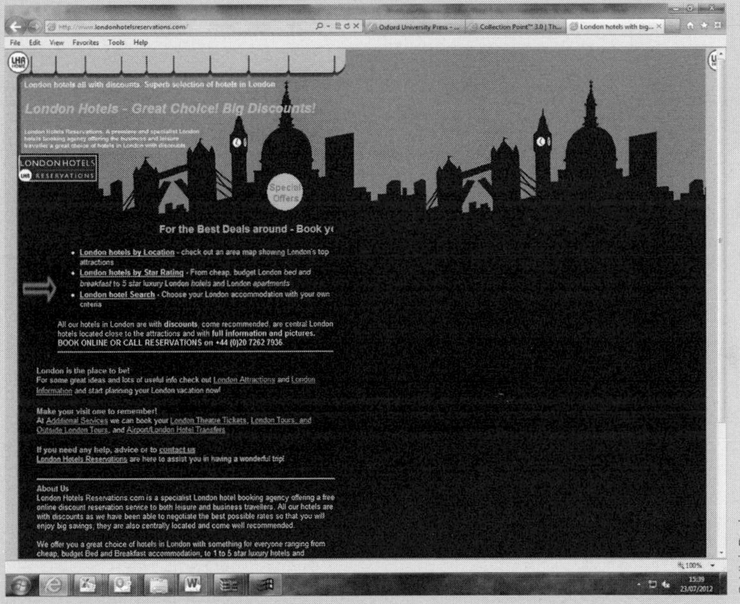

© Nick Dudman

Compiled by Nigel Bradley 2009.

Source:
Interviews with Nick Dudman; http://londonhotelsreservations.com. Reproduced with kind permission.

Questions

1 Nick is asking you to tell him how research might help his existing business. You should write memos to him for each question.

2 Explain to Nick what different ways of capturing data can be used for his business.

3 He has heard about mystery shopping and comments cards in hotels. What are the advantages and disadvantages of these approaches?

4 In your opinion, which data capture method would be most helpful? Consider particularly the new venture.

Further reading

- Bryman, A. and Bell, E. (2003) *Business Research Methods*. Oxford: Oxford University Press.
  A very thorough textbook with sound examples and descriptions of research design.
- Gudjonsson, G.H. (2003) *The Psychology of Interrogations and Confessions: A Handbook*. Chichester: John Wiley & Sons.
  A text for criminologists, with much to learn for marketing.
- Jones, S. (ed.) (1999) *Doing Internet Research: Critical Issues and Methods for Examining the Net*. London: Sage.
  An early book (with various authors) giving practical assistance on Internet researching.

Key web links

- NRS Response Rate History http://www.nrs.co.uk/sample.html
- National Student Survey http://www.thestudentsurvey.com/faqs/faqs_1.html
- Google Analytics http://www.google.com/analytics

Online Resource Centre
www.oxfordtextbooks.co.uk/orc/bradley3e/

Visit the Online Resource Centre that accompanies this book to access more learning resources on this chapter topic.

References and sources

Adam, S. and McDonald, H. (2003) Online versus postal data collection methods: an examination of issues and a comparison of results, *Australasian Journal of Market Research*, 11, pp. 3–9.

Belson, W. (1983) The accuracy of interviewer reporting of respondent replies to open ended and to fully structured questions, *MRS 26th Annual Conference papers*, 15–18 March, pp. 479–505.

Boote, J. and Mathew, A. (1999) Saying is one thing; doing is another; the role of observation in marketing research, *Qualitative Marketing Research: An International Journal*, 2. pp. 15–21.

Brown, S. (1987) Drop and collect surveys: a neglected research technique? *Marketing Intelligence and Planning*, 5, pp. 19–23.

Cook, C., Heath, F., and Thomson, R. (2000) A meta-analysis of response rates in web- or Internet-based surveys, *Educational & Psychological Measurement*, 60, pp. 821–826.

Crawford, S., Couper, M., and Lamias, M. (2001) Web surveys: perception of burden, *Social Science Computer Review*, 19, pp. 146–162.

Dholakia, U.M. and Morwitz, V.G. (2002) The scope and persistence of mere-measurement effects: evidence from a field study of customer satisfaction measurement, *Journal of Consumer Research*, 29, pp. 159–167.

Groves-Hill, J. and Poulton, M. (1997) *Are you being served? Mystery shopper research and its effects upon the UK retailing sector*, ESOMAR Retailing Research Conference paper, Madrid, November.

Gudjonsson, G.H. (2003) *The Psychology of Interrogations and Confessions: A Handbook*. Chichester: John Wiley & Sons.

Hillier, J. and Dawson, J. (1995) Competitor mystery shopping: methodological considerations and implications for the MRS Code of Conduct, *Journal of the Market Research Society*, 37, pp. 417–427.

Ibeh, K., Brock, J.K-U., and Yu, J.Z. (2004) The drop and collect survey among industrial populations: theory and empirical evidence, *Industrial Marketing Management*, 33, pp. 155–165.

IWS Internet World Stats (2008) Internet Usage Statistics. Accessed 6 September 2012 http://www.internetworldstats.com

Jones, S. (ed.) (1999) *Doing Internet Research: Critical Issues and Methods for Examining the Net.* London: Sage.

Kinver, M. (2011) People's showering habits revealed in survey. BBC News November 22. Accessed at http://www.bbc.co.uk/news/science-environment-15836433

Krosnick, J., Narayan, S., and Smith, W. (1996) Satisficing in surveys: initial evidence, *New Directions in Evaluation: Advances in Survey Research*, 70, pp. 29–44.

Lugtig, P., Lensvelt-Mulders, G.J.L.M., Frerichs, R., and Greven, A. (2011) Estimating nonresponse bias and mode effects in a mixed-mode survey, *IJMR* 53(5), pp. 669–686.

McDonald, H. and Adam, S. (2003) A comparison of online and postal data collection methods in marketing research, *Marketing Intelligence and Planning*, 21, pp. 85–95.

Millward Brown (2008) *Top 100 Most Powerful World Brands 2008*, http://www.millwardbrown.com/Sites/optimor/Media/Pdfs/en/BrandZ/BrandZ-2008-Report.pdf

Morrel-Samuels, P. (2003) Web surveys' hidden hazards, *Havard Business Review*, 16–18 July.

National Student Survey (2005) *Briefing for Students' Unions*, http://www.thestudentsurvey.com and http://www.unistats.com

Noelle- Neumann, E. (1974) The spiral of silence: a theory of public opinion, *Journal of Communication*, 24, pp. 43–51.

ONS (2001) *200 Years of the Census*. London: Office for National Statistics.

ONS (2004) *Living in Britain*. London: Office for National Statistics. No. 31, Results from the 2002 General Household Survey, http://www.statistics.gov.uk/downloads/theme_compendia/lib2002.pdf

ONS (2007) *Focus on the Digital Age*. Palgrave Macmillan, Basingstoke. Accessed 6 September 2012 as a PDF at http://www.ons.gov.uk

ONS (2008) *Internet Access*. Estimates derived from the 2008 National Statistics Omnibus survey. Accessed 6 September 2012 as a PDF at http://www.ons.gov.uk

Oshima, V. (2003) Research: anytime, anywhere: mobile research in Japan. *Research World* 11(1), 20–21 January.

Pincott, G. and Branthwaite, A. (2000) Nothing new under the sun? *International Journal of Market Research*, 42, pp. 137–155.

Rodriguez, E. (2003) Google Product Development/Management Process. Notes of a presentation on 8 January 2003 to Silicon Valley Product Management Association by Google Product Manager Manssa Mayer, http://www.evelynrodriguez.typepad.com/crossroads_dispatches/files/GoogleProductDevProcess.pdf

Rogelberg, S.G., Gwenith, G.F., Douglas, C.M., Milton, D.H., and Michael, H. (2001) Attitudes toward surveys: development of a measure and its relationship to respondent behavior, *Organizational Research Methods*, 4, pp. 3–25.

Schwarz, N., Strack, F., Hippler, H., and Bishop, G. (1991) The impact of administration mode on response effects in survey measurement, *Applied Cognitive Psychology*, 5, pp.193–212.

Shannon, D. and Bradshaw, C. (2002) A comparison of response rate, speed and costs of mail and electronic surveys, *Journal of Experimental Education*, 70, p. 179.

Snaith, T. (2008) *Mobile Research: The 5th Methodology*. OnePoint Surveys White Paper, May 2008.

Stafford, M.R. and Stafford, T.F. (1993) Participant observation and the pursuit of truth: methodological and ethical considerations, *Journal of the Market Research Society*, 35, pp. 63–76.

Tarran, B. (2011) *Unilever and the tale of the spy toothbrush*. Research 2011 conference blog, http://www.research-live.com/unilever-and-the-tale-of-the-spy-toothbrush/4004848.blog

Terramedia (2004) Chronomedia 1910, http://www.terramedia.co.uk/Chronomedia/years/1910htm

Treasure, J. (1976) Ten years later, *Journal of the Market Research Society*, 18 (April), pp. 54–63.

Vannieuwenhuyze, J., Loosveldt, G. and Molenberghs, G. (2010) A Method for Evaluating Mode Effects in Mixed-mode Surveys. *Public Opinion Quarterly*, 74(5), pp. 1027–1045

Vise, D. A. (2005) *The Google Story*. London: Pan Books.

Yun, G. and Trumbo, C. (2000) Comparative response to a survey executed by post, e-mail, and Web form, *Journal of Computer-Mediated Communication*, 6, http://jcmc.indiana.edu

5 Sampling

Contents

Chapter guide

Sampling means taking one or more examples from which to learn something new. This chapter examines the purposes and procedures of sampling. The sources of the sample are discussed, with a detailed examination of techniques for telephone, face-to-face, and self-completion research. We learn the differences between probability and non-probability methods. Quota sampling is of great importance to market research, so this area is emphasised. You will understand how sample sizes can be determined, both for qualitative and quantitative research.

Learning outcomes

By the end of this chapter, you should be able to:

1. **Explain the stages of sampling**
2. **Describe the different types of sample source**
3. **Show the benefits and the limitations of sampling approaches**
4. **Explain how sample size is determined**
5. **Articulate how qualitative sampling differs from quantitative sampling**

Introduction

There is a similarity between the terms 'example' and 'sample'. This similarity is no coincidence because these words share a common root. If we take part of a bigger thing, we have an example of something—we have a sample. 'Sampling' is the process of taking parts from a defined population in order to examine these parts, usually with the aim of making judgements about the parts of the population that have not been investigated. The major advantage of this approach is that it usually involves less cost and time than looking at every member of the population. The major disadvantage is that the process cannot summarise every characteristic in that given population. Sometimes, a survey will have a shortfall in the number of respondent data available for analysis from specific groups. The most popular procedure to correct these 'errors' is to employ weighting. Weighting ensures that the sample is balanced, usually in terms of sex, age, social grade, and region.

Many people see sampling as a magic trick. By using sampling, the researcher is able to amaze and surprise in providing results that have large implications for society. You may hear people ask the question: '*How can they know that three million people nationwide watched that soap opera on TV? Nobody asked me, and I saw it!*'.

In the British Isles, a detailed inventory of land and property was completed in 1086—it is known as the 'Domesday Book'. Regular census-taking began in 1790 in the USA and in 1801 in Britain. The important thing about the census is that it is an account of every member of the population.

Francis Galton (1822-1911) is well known for many things—one of these is his study of heredity, and part of this was his studies of twins (see Table 5.1). In 1875, Galton located twins by asking people for referrals (Galton 1883, p. 156).

In the 1930s, sampling took centre stage for many reasons. Jerzy Neyman (1894-1981) laid the basis of probability methods and developed a theory of survey sampling. George Gallup (1901-1984) completed a PhD thesis at the University of Iowa in 1928. Following this, he went on to establish research institutes, which used the famous 'Gallup poll' technique. The term, Gallup poll, is now firmly embedded in the dictionary and marked the introduction of probability sampling to the world of commercial research.

In 1939, Renesis Likert (1903-1981) was appointed director of the Division of Program Surveys in the Bureau of Agricultural Economics of the US Department of Agriculture in Washington, DC. The US Department of Agriculture had established the Division of Program Surveys to provide a means by which farmers and other citizens could communicate their experiences with federal programmes. Likert, along with others, collaborated to develop a method for sampling households and individuals based on the identification and listing of small units of land. The selection developed by this team was another contribution to probability sampling (Campbell 1988).

Table 5.1

Notable events for sampling

Year	Event
440 BC	A Persian king estimated his army size by sampling (according to Herodotus)
1870s	Francis Galton used snowball sampling to locate twins
1930s	Neyman laid the basis of probability sampling. Gallup popularised it to examine readership and voting intentions
1960s	A section called Yellow Pages was published in the Brighton telephone directory, UK
1970s	Sampling use in animal behaviour
1990s	Poll Tax left the Electoral Register incomplete

In 1961, Leo A. Goodman suggested a formal use for a technique called 'snowball sampling'. Since the 1960s, this procedure has been implemented by researchers in many different spheres, most commonly, in qualitative research.

SNAPSHOT
RAJAR

© Getty images/Joos Mind

RAJAR is a continuous survey of radio-listening conducted among individuals living in households in the UK. To accommodate the various demands of the hundreds of clients, the sample size is large. Radio-listening **diaries** are completed each week by 3000 different and carefully selected respondents aged 4+ years, living in private households. At the end of each week, the diaries are collected and returned to the research company, where they are electronically scanned and checked. Once these data have been processed, they are published and made available, in print or electronically via the Internet, every three months. An extremely elaborate sampling and analysis method is used. In 2001, the procedure was described as follows. First, addresses are preselected from the Postcode Address File; second, they are divided into assignments that give a suitable workload for an individual interviewer. Typically, a weekly assignment has 150 addresses, and 15 diaries must be placed.

There are various constraints, which mean that the 15 diaries cannot be placed at the first addresses contacted. These constraints include when placed (Friday pm, Saturday, Sunday, and other constraints); how placed (a detailed face-to-face briefing takes place with each respondent); where placed (at geographically dispersed points, inside the home, etc.); finally, with whom placed (quotas, exclusions, etc.).

Each interviewer is carefully briefed to ensure that diaries are placed as far apart as possible, but within the addresses given. This is done in order to avoid errors associated with clustered samples. To ensure that this policy is adopted, every fourth address is marked as a 'priority address'. This means that interviewers must contact these addresses first. Furthermore, they must make two attempts to contact respondents at the priority households before going to non-priority addresses. Having successfully contacted a 'responsible adult' at the household, the interviewer has a set of quotas that are derived from government population profiles of the local area. They embrace: age (15–24 years, 25–64 years, 65+ years); gender (male, female); working (hours worked); household size (number of adults). When the required individuals have been identified, they must be willing to complete the diary over the next seven days.

Compiled by Nigel Bradley 2012.

RAJAR web page:

http://www.rajar.co.uk Reproduced with kind permission.

Purposes of sampling

To understand sampling, it is useful to think of blood samples. When a doctor takes a blood sample, we can see how our own body is operating. We do not need to see all the blood. Similarly, if we taste a sample of wine, we get an indication of the rest of the wine, without actually drinking it all. The blood and wine examples are useful because they show clearly that the sampling technique may go wrong. It may miss something: there may indeed be some wine that is not quite right. Similarly, the human body may develop something after the sample has been taken. These problems (and more) also apply to sampling when it is used in marketing research.

The alternative to taking a sample is to interview (or observe) everybody in the chosen population. The market researcher may decide to take a census when there are good reasons: for example, the National Student Survey attempts to interview all final-year students in universities, and this allows subsequent students to interrogate the data set to make appropriate choices about their future place of study. This approach is called a census; so we can undertake a census or take a sample.

The key to taking a 'good' sample is to know enough about the universe to select the right numbers and types of people. However, this may be more complicated than it first appears; if we are trying to find out about a universe, it is clear that we do not know everything about it. Think of foxes living in the wild across the country. Foxes do not need to register their births (or deaths) and they are not listed in phone directories; there is no database that lists all living foxes. We might, however, capture several hundred to examine their health—but how will we know whether our fox sample is representative? We can thank statisticians for their work on estimating the total numbers of unseen species. Essentially, sightings are recorded and geographic areas are noted. Calculations on frequency of sighting within an area lead to estimates of the total population. Changes in the numbers of sightings indicate increases or decreases in population size. It is an extended version of the estimation of the number of grains of sand on a beach: you simply count the grains within a square inch then multiply that up to the size of the entire beach. The simple idea is that known facts are combined with observations to create estimates of the whole. It is this principle that will be used to calculate the population of businessmen, the population of users of lawnmowers, and so on.

Fortunately, we do know a great deal about populations, thanks to the way our civilisations work. A census is a complete 'view' of the population and most governments carry out a census every 10 years. This gives a full picture; however, a great deal of money, labour, and time are required.

In stark contrast, by taking a sample, the work can be done relatively quickly; in some cases, a project can be finished in less than a day.

This distinction and the discussion about the sample allow us to see the topic from many different angles. They show that we should not restrict our thinking of sampling to statistics. We can derive an overall definition of sample such as *'a relatively small part of a whole, which can tell us about that whole'*.

Let us move closer to marketing research. Here, we use the term 'population'; in the wide sense, this means the adults and children who make up the nation's population, but we also use the term to cover specific groups of interest, for example, the populations of farmers, employees, doctors, and so forth. It is from the population of interest that a sample is drawn. Adding to the definition, we can say that a sample is 'a relatively small part of a *population*, which can tell us about the whole *population*'.

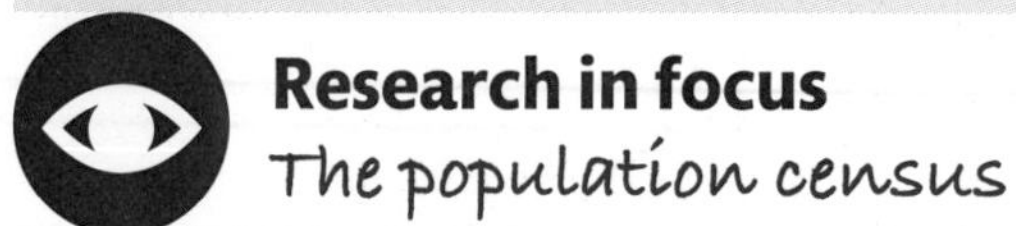

Research in focus
The population census

The general population census is an account of every member of the population. We have very early examples from the Babylonians and the Chinese, who created accounts of their people for tax and military reasons. The Egyptians also needed knowledge of available manpower to plan the building of the pyramids (ONS 2001). From 5 BC, a census was held every five years across the Roman Empire. In order to eliminate errors due to mobility, every man in the Empire was obliged to return to his place of origin.

© istockphoto.com/Ian Jeffery

In the British Isles, a detailed inventory of land and property was completed in 1086, known as the Domesday Book, and this was the result of several years of work. There are other examples of early census studies: 1666 (Quebec), 1703 (Iceland), 1749 (Sweden). In the 1700s, the census was resisted in the USA and Britain for various reasons: one was a fear that a census *'might incur the wrath of God'*; another was that foreign enemies would be able to detect weaknesses or *'individual liberty would be impaired'*. Despite these objections, regular census-taking began in 1790 in the USA, and in 1801 in Britain.

Because the census is an account of every member of the population, it relies on cooperation from the public. Resistance is usually overcome by explaining that statistics will mask individual identities. Refusal to complete the UK 2001 census was met by an offer of prosecution and a fine of up to £1000. Indeed, 38 people were prosecuted and fined in the 2001 UK census; one person was imprisoned for refusing to pay the fine.

The disadvantage of the census is that a great deal of skilled manpower is required. Leading members of the 'parish' were used to take the UK 1801 census and, in 1841, some 35,000 male enumerators were used. The US 1880 census used 31,382 interviewers and the 1960 US census required 160,000 enumerators. For the 2011 census in the UK, 37,000 people were employed and 3 million reminder letters were posted. A large budget is needed and it can take a long time to complete: in the 2001 UK census, the programme plan was for 13 years (1993–2006) and the cost was estimated to be £254 million. The cost of the 2011 census was estimated to reach £480 million, the increase down to inflation and an extra 3.5 million people to count, mainly immigrants.

Compiled by Nigel Bradley 2012.

Sources:

HMSO (2010) *The 2001 Census of Population*, www.ons.gov.uk/ons/guide-method/census/census-2001/index.html

Mouncey, P. (2011) 2011 Census: a CGG Seminar. *IJMRS* 53(5), pp. 569–570.

Office for National Statistics (2001) *200 Years of the Census*. London: ONS, http://www.ons.gov.uk/ons/guide-method/census/2011/census-history/200-years-of-the-census/index.html

Questions

1 Why do most nations carry out a census regularly?

2 Who benefits from census results?

3 Besides prosecution in a law court, what steps could be taken to encourage participation?

Sampling does not always select 'people' to be questioned; sometimes, 'situations' or 'locations' are sampled. In observational research, ethnography, and action research, it is probable that neither situations nor people can be predicted, that new situations will introduce themselves, and that people will enter and exit from the research project. Additionally, some research naturally moves to new locations. We may take a sample of speech to illustrate points made in a qualitative study; in secondary data analysis, we may sample certain documents, but not all. Therefore sampling must relate back to the purpose of the study. We may be sampling:

- People (as individuals or as groups)
- Time (in terms of minutes or days)
- Places (public or private)
- Behaviour (in terms of individual events or states)
- Items (documents in archives).

Time sampling can offer some useful data, but the disadvantages can be that the period sampled is not 'representative' of the full behaviours. Sampling called 'behaviour' above can be usefully classified ad lib sampling, focal sampling, all-occurrence sampling, and scan sampling. We can thank Altmann (1974) for these distinctions.

1. **Ad libitum sampling** A record is made of as much information as possible. This attempts to monitor all activities. Such observations will always be biased by the behaviours, individuals, or situations that most attract the observer's attention. It is costly and time-consuming; it can be used as a qualitative phase or to plan a study.
2. **Focal sampling** All occurrences of specified actions of one individual are recorded during a certain time period, often 60 minutes. The advantage is that unbiased data can answer numerous questions.
3. **All-occurrence sampling** The observer focuses on a particular behaviour, rather than a particular individual. For example, we might count the number of requests for information coming to a helpdesk in a supermarket. This can give a quantitative measure of the rate of occurrence of behaviour.
4. **Instantaneous or scan sampling** A subject's activities are recorded at predetermined instances, such as every 45 seconds. It is a 'sample of states' and is used to study the percentage of time spent in a certain activity. If the behaviours of all members of a group are surveyed within a short period of time, we call it scan sampling.

Social classification

Social classification or grading is a useful indicator of predisposition to consume specific products and services. At the most basic level, we might use age, sex, and terminal education age (TEA).

The attempt will be to find divisions in a society that are not likely to change and that can indeed be identified. Classifications then become more complex as we incorporate other aspects such as educational attainment, occupation, family stage, social standing, and income. These classifications are a combination of objective and subjective measurements. Despite any problems with the validity and reliability of such measures, they are useful because there are correlations with aspects that are less apparent, but important for marketing. For example, clothing, fashion, shopping, leisure, saving, and spending are similar for specific groups in society.

In the UK, there are several established systems that are associated with government surveys: socioeconomic groupings (SEG), social class, standard occupational classification (SOC), and other variants. A newer classification, called socioeconomic class (SEC), was released in 1998 and validated on the Labour Force Survey (see Rose and O'Reilly 1997; Rose 1998). This offers a division into 14 groups using over 350 occupations: these 14 groups can be collapsed to nine, eight, five, and three categories; the government has adopted the version with eight divisions. It is based on the premise that there are three types of people in the workforce: employers, self-employed workers, and employees. Furthermore, there are two types of relationship: the labour contract and the service relationship. The labour contract is short-term: the contract is easily ended and so there is a low level of job security. Conversely, the service relationship is longer-term, with greater job security and will feature various 'packages' such as pension and health schemes; this is a trust relationship. One benefit is that it can be converted to the 'old' social class. The structure is shown in Figure 5.1.

Of particular note in the UK is 'social grade'—not actually a government classification. This divides the population into groups denoted with letters and numbers: A, B, C1, C2, D, and E. Working definitions are shown in Table 5.2. This classification dates back to before the Second World War and was developed in conjunction with early readership media surveys. It is based on occupation and is used widely by the market research industry in the UK. However, it is specific to the UK and does not appear elsewhere in the same form.

Inevitably, the focus of research will be on the target audience as defined by the objectives of the marketing plan. Target audiences are often defined in terms of social grade, sex, age, and region. These are clear demographics also used in marketing research because they distinguish behaviour. In turn media planners use market research audience surveys to choose the best

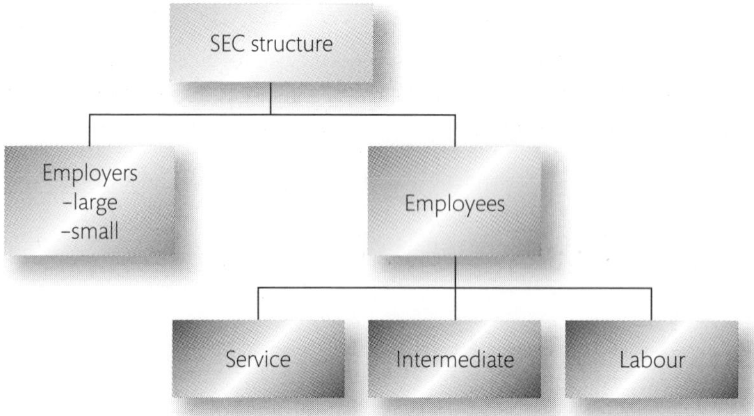

Figure 5.1 SEC structure

Table 5.2 Working definitions of the UK social grade system

Grade	Definition	Description
A	Upper middle class	Higher managerial, administrative, or professional
B	Middle class	Intermediate managerial, administrative, or professional
C1	Lower middle class	Supervisory or clerical and junior managerial, administrative, or professional
C2	Skilled working class	Skilled manual workers
D	Working class	Semi- and unskilled manual workers
E	Lowest levels of subsistence	State pensioners or widows, casual, or lowest grade workers

mix of vehicles to carry the advertising. It is important to say that such audiences may *not* be users, or likely users, of the product or service in question. In some cases, the buyer does not use the product, but decides on its purchase and actually buys it. There are also other audiences, such as shareholders or associated companies, who will benefit from knowledge about a product or service in their own decision-making. Some generic audiences are shareholders, users, buyers, and gatekeepers.

The challenge for the researcher is to select the target, but also to ensure that the procedures used are appropriate to the target audience, and that the actual sample selected is sufficiently coherent and articulate to be able to voice its knowledge and perceptions. In many cases, this might mean replicating the recruitment procedure used on audience measurement surveys. This may mean investigating the screening procedures and instruments used on the major studies; this way, the sample matches the intended target precisely.

Choices of sample size should be guided by the planned task. In idea generation, the sample is less important than the usefulness of the ideas being generated. In testing the effectiveness of an advert, a split sample of matched respondents may be required. This way, there must be similar profiles that ensure that two different sets of results can be compared, that is results obtained from people who have been exposed to two different treatments (ad executions).

Populations involved in social research

Marketing researchers deal mainly with consumers of Fast-Moving Consumer Goods (FMCG), people who are within their target market. Conversely, social researchers question people from all walks of life: the unemployed, the old, the inarticulate, and the disabled. Our social and welfare services look to provide disadvantaged, distressed, or vulnerable people with support. Social research has no buyers, but audiences may be numerous. Audiences may receive or need services; they may even act as a resource, perhaps as volunteers; they may be managers of such resources. Respondents may be drug addicts, carers, manual workers, scientists, voters, etc.

Table 5.3 categorises typical populations that are central to social research studies; we see that institutions such as public authorities, hospitals, and utilities may be used. In common with B2B research, these organisations have complex hierarchies and decision-making units, so respondents can span many people, from council members, department heads, and purchasing managers to administrative staff. The stakeholders and players involved in non-profit organisations—perhaps volunteers or potential donors—are also used. Members of the professions—lawyers, solicitors, doctors, and architects—will be extremely important to certain projects. This is also the case with opinion leaders, such as journalists, politicians, shareholders, and activists in pressure groups. Finally, the largest group of all is the general public. Members of the public are the recipients of most social services. As a consequence, household members, whether they are families or sharers, will all be central to studies.

Specific members of the public may become the focus, and each of the subgroups will need careful definition. For example, let us look at one definition of disabled people. The Disability Discrimination Act 1995 defines disability as '*a physical or mental impairment which has a substantial and long-term adverse effect on a person's ability to carry out normal day-to-day activities*'. Long-term is usually seen as 12 months or more in this context. Clear definition of the population of interest must be created at the outset.

Most marketing research examines consumers and how they process information, make decisions, and consume products. In social research, minority groups may be interviewed for the opposite reasons; such individuals are disadvantaged or vulnerable to many forces in society. For research, these groups often require a modification in sampling and collecting data. Such groups may be a minority because of their race, belief, income level, or behaviour.

Table 5.3 Typical populations for social research

Population type	Examples of typical respondents
Public authorities, hospitals, utilities	Council members, department heads, purchasing managers, administrative staff
Non-profit organisations, charities	Volunteers, potential donors
Professionals	Lawyers, solicitors, doctors, architects
Opinion leaders	Journalists, politicians, shareholders, activists in pressure groups
Members of the public	Families, household members, institutions. Specific groups, e.g. disabled people and carers

The stages of sampling

Before proceeding with fieldwork, we need to define our population and the source of the sample; we need to decide how to take a sample and we need to decide on the sample size. These are the basic elements involved in selecting a sample.

The first step is to examine the purpose of the study to decide what degree of precision is required. After this, we must define the population. We must decide a suitable source for the population members; this is the 'sampling frame'. Having done that, we determine the sampling procedure, to be clear how the members are selected or recruited; this may be by probability or non-probability methods. Sampling may be done in the office by researchers or in the field by interviewers; these two approaches are called 'preselected sampling' and 'field sampling', respectively. The sample size is generally agreed before undertaking fieldwork, although in a few projects, the sample size may be determined after it has started. This is explored further later in this chapter. After fieldwork, any sampling errors will be identified and corrected at the publication stage.

Sampling frames

The 'sampling frame' is an important part of sampling (see Table 5.4). As shown in Figure 5.2, it should mirror the population of interest in summary form. It should include summary information of key features of all units in the population of interest. It is the basis by which respondents are selected: people, telephone numbers, or addresses are sampled from a frame. It might be a tangible list such as a phone directory or it might just be a set of instructions; it may take the form of geographic maps, to divide sample by region, or even at street level.

Remember the '-ing'; it is sometimes written as 'sample frame'; to be pedantic, this is incorrect because it is the frame from which sampling happens. If we imagine books on a bookshelf against a wall, it is the shelf from which we take down volumes; it is the place from

Table 5.4

The stages of sampling
1. Examine the objective of the study—purpose
2. Define the people of interest—population
3. Find suitable source for the population members
4. Decide on the sampling type and approach—procedure
5. Decide on the sample size
6. Proceed with the fieldwork
7. Correct sampling errors ready for reporting—publication

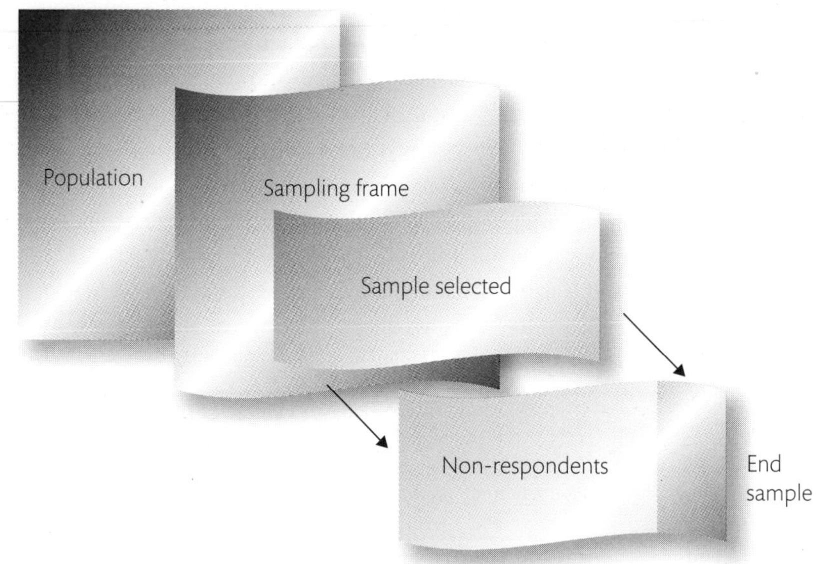

Figure 5.2 From the population to the end sample

which sampling occurs. Sampling frames must be up to date, complete, affordable, and easy to use, in the sense that they can be manipulated and transferred into other media. They should be easily exported into software such as spreadsheets (e.g. Excel), databases (e.g. Access), or word processing programs (e.g. Word).

The identification of a useful sampling frame can be time-consuming, and where one needs to be created, this can be a project in itself (see Figure 5.3). Any source used must be checked for duplicates. In the case of preselected samples, the duplicates must be removed before fieldwork takes place in a process known as 'de-duplication'. Where sampling takes place in the field, duplicate interviews must be avoided by careful record keeping.

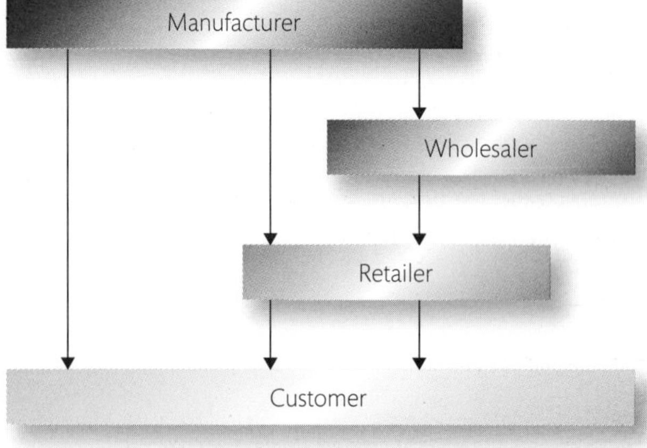

Figure 5.3 Sampling frames: sources of sample

Poor sampling frames are 'old, incomplete, and inappropriate'. Typically, bad frames are made up of databases with individuals who have volunteered themselves or have been selected based on criteria that do not match the purpose of the project in question.

Table 5.5 lists different sources available to the researcher, and a few of these sources will be described. If several are merged together, then a very powerful sampling frame can be created; this merging process can make (for example) sampling using the Postcode Address File (PAF) feasible for the telephone. Some providers of these services may offer their product already merged with other databases.

The Electoral Register

Until 1990, the main source of general population samples in the UK was the Electoral Register (ER). This lists all those eligible to vote, so is useful for sampling because it is expected to be

Table 5.5 Sample sources and suitability to different methods

Source suitability for surveys using . . .	**Telephone interviews**	**Personal**	**Post**	**Online**
The Electoral Register			Yes	Yes
Postcode Address File			Yes	Yes
Random digit dialling		Yes		
Telephone directories		Yes	Yes	Yes
Announcements	Yes	Yes	Yes	Yes
Email directories				Yes
Subscriber/members records	Yes	Yes	Yes	Yes
Customer records	Yes	Yes	Yes	Yes
Interest group members				Yes
Registration forms				Yes
Snowballing		Yes		
Invitations (e.g. banners)				Yes
Hypertext links				Yes
Printed directories	Yes		Yes	
Pop-up surveys				Yes
Harvested addresses				Yes
Website directories				Yes

complete. The Register includes all British, Northern Irish, Commonwealth, and Irish Republic citizens who are aged 18 or over, or who will become 18 during the life of the Register. The Register is compiled in October of each year and comes into effect in February, remaining in effect for 12 months.

From a practical angle, it is not essential to visit local town halls to have access to the electoral roll; records can be searched by directory services such as http://www.192.com. Of particular interest is that searches on this website can be made on relationships—particularly interesting if de-duplication is necessary.

This Register is made up of individuals, so is useful for sampling people, rather than addresses. It is possible to use the ER to sample households, but it is worth noting that, if no registration form is returned, the same information as the previous year is often left unamended. This can create inaccuracy. If it is used to sample addresses, then selection must be done carefully, for example, by using only the first entry for any one address (this is known as 'firsting'). Alternatively, weighting should take place after collection; this is described further in Chapter 9 on analysis. A disadvantage is that there are reasons why people fail to register. This happened during the introduction of Poll Tax and there are cases where people prefer not to register (and lose their vote) simply to avoid the arrival of junk mail (because this register can be purchased by direct marketers).

From Autumn 2002, an 'opt-out' facility was offered; this means that people listed can opt out of making their names available for mailing. In 2003, 21 per cent of people took this option; the percentage rose to 26 per cent in 2004 and then to 32 per cent in 2005. Clearly, the rise is disturbing for sampling and it is important to decide who has opted out, and whether the reason is relevant to the specific subject under study.

In April 1990, the Poll Tax was introduced. This meant that a tax was due from each person aged 18 years or over, and one way the government could identify people was through the ER. Here is an extract from one of many leaflets produced during the movement against the 'community charge' or Poll Tax.

> The most important thing to do now is to ensure that your name and address are not added to any local or national government lists, e.g. the Electoral Register. In the event of a census being carried out, refuse to give any information. If possible, remove snoopers from your area by force. Sabotage, industrial action and refusal by those asked to administer the system are also important possible forms of resistance.

As a result of such resistance, up to 18 million people refused to pay Poll Tax, and one way to avoid this was not to register for voting. This left the Register incomplete, and the Postcode Address File became the sample source of choice.

Postcode Address File

The postcode is an extremely powerful tool in sampling. Royal Mail uses the postcode to plan the way it sorts, transports, and delivers mail in the UK. There are 124 postcode areas in the UK.

A postcode is divided into two parts: the first part shows the destination area of the letter, and the second part guides the letter from the final sorting office to its delivery point. For example, a code might be DE55 6JT. The first part has letters to denote the postal area and then numbers for the post town or district. For example, DE55 is a delivery area of Derby. The second half of the code has a number, to indicate the sector or locality, and then two letters for the unit—often a street—which may have 14 to 100 delivery points. 6JT is a detached house in a village in Derbyshire, some distance from Derby.

The Postcode Address File (PAF) is extremely useful for sampling addresses. It is a database of around 28 million postcodes. The database is divided into two parts on the basis of the delivery point count: the 'large user file' is for delivery points with an average of 25 or more items of mail delivered per day, and the 'small user file' for the remainder. This distinction is useful because it helps to distinguish between domestic and non-domestic addresses. The small user file does contain a number of commercial and industrial properties, but these can be excluded during the fieldwork process. The PAF can be accessed on the Royal Mail website at http://www.royalmail.com.

Telephone directories

Telephone directories fall into two categories—*White Pages*, listing individuals at domestic addresses, and *Yellow Pages*, which list businesses at their normal place of work. Sometimes, business directories are not yellow, but for our purposes, this definition is useful. Although traditionally these are published as hard-copy books, they can be delivered once a year electronically, with the most up-to-date version in a form that can be quickly manipulated. All world types are collected together at http://www.infobel.com/teldir/.

White Pages is the well-known telephone book with lists of land-line phone numbers and it is a cheap sample source. Directories can also be used for surveys that do not use the telephone. In an electronic form, it is easy to manipulate and usually offers a name, address, and, of course, a telephone number. Major problems are that some households are unlisted, or are listed by mistake—a result of different things that include: the fact that the person has a land-line but has opted to be 'ex-directory', the person only uses a mobile/cell phone, the telephone has been disconnected, or a telephone was installed after the listing was made.

Yellow Pages are designed for buyers to locate sellers efficiently. For the UK, 1966 is the milestone year when the General Post Office first published a classified section called 'Yellow Pages' in the Brighton telephone directory. The disadvantage with some providers is that not all businesses may be listed. For example, lecturers have no need to list themselves, but plumbers do because they are selling their services to the public. Additionally, newer businesses, which are usually small, may be absent. Therefore, the supplier should be asked about criteria for inclusion.

In the UK, Yell.com offers *Yellow Pages* business phone numbers, along with other details such as: business type (Standard Industrial Classification, SIC), financial indicators (such as turnover, profitability, year end, net worth), number of employees, whether head office or branch, and named functions (such as sales director). *MacRae's Blue Book* is the industrial directory of Yell.com (see http://www.macraesbluebook.com).

Customer records

Customer records, or client lists, are another source, possibly provided as a subset of a customer database. Here, an ethical dilemma can emerge for the research agency: respondents may demand to know where their name came from. The Market Research Society (MRS) Code of Conduct gives the client a right to anonymity but the Data Protection Act 1998 states that individuals have a right to know who holds data on them. In this case, the respondent must be told the source, so the client identity will be revealed. This clearly needs to be explained to the client at the proposal stage.

A related problem can emerge if the client would like to receive information to bring its list up to date: it has a duty under the Data Protection Act to keep these lists accurate and up to date. In the MRS Code, respondents are assured of their anonymity and this can be compromised, directly or indirectly, by providing feedback to a client on the integrity of a list. This needs to be outlined at the proposal stage, and one solution is to secure respondent permission to relay changes to the client.

One of the principles of the Data Protection Act is that 'Personal data shall be obtained only for one or more specified and lawful purposes and shall not be processed in any manner incompatible with that purpose or those purposes'. Here there may also be problems. These issues need to be established at the proposal stage of research.

For example, a provider of gas may have a big database of domestic customers. It is kept in order to send invoices to customers, and they have been told that this is the reason. If that gas company decided to diversify and offer financial services, such as a credit card, it may see the customer list as an asset, a good way to target and reach specific targets using a direct mail campaign. If the customers were told the purpose of the records were for invoicing, then this campaign could not take place. The researcher must similarly be aware that customers may not have agreed to their names being used for research purposes. This is known as client surreptitious sampling: '*the use of customer lists that have been collected by the client without the consent of the individual*' (MRS 2012).

Other sources

Other sources include: 'membership lists' for associations, trade bodies, and similar organisations; 'subscribers' to Internet interest groups; and subscribers to magazines and journals. Information from 'list brokers', who serve the direct marketing industry very efficiently, can be a useful alternative to the options already described. These lists are largely based on magazine subscriber details and specially developed groups of interest from various sources; these are generally a last consideration because the nature of their construction is often poorly documented. The MRS (2012) describes this as surreptitious sampling: '*.... the purchase of bulk email addresses from sources that have not provided verifiable documentation on the validity of the collected data*'.

Geodemographic companies also offer various services in relation to their classifications (such as ACORN and MOSAIC). These services are based on information from various sources, and are generally extremely powerful if used correctly. A great deal of data is sourced for these geodemographic systems: over half come from the latest census; the rest from such things as the electoral roll, credit databases, house price data, county court judgements, and government research.

Finally there are numerous sources of sample for online research; these are described in Table 5.5.

Sampling procedures

The science of statistics and knowledge of the nature of probability has brought useful design notions to the study of sampling. There are two research designs: 'probability' (also known as random) and 'non-probability' (also known as non-random), see Figure 5.4.

A major advantage of the random sampling method is that we can see the levels of cooperation, so we can calculate non-response; we can then apply tests to see how accurate our results are at the analysis stage. In non-random approaches we are less sure of accuracy because the levels of non-cooperation are mixed together with many other things. One of these things is the researcher's decision-making on who should be included and who should be excluded from the study. Another problem with random sampling is that it takes control away from the field interviewer; this can lead to field staff feeling extremely demoralised. This, in turn, can lead to a decrease in productivity as refusal rates increase by slow progress associated with seeking respondents who are not available. Therefore, interviewers working with random sampling need to be well trained and to exert good discipline. There is a threat to the method if pay structures are linked to the number of interviews achieved. This then calls for higher paid staff, adding to the criticism that this is an expensive approach.

Numerous probability techniques can be derived from the combinations of aspects of the random technique. Add to this the fact that it is possible to create hybrids by using non-probability techniques and it is clear that there are a high number of options. It is useful to visualise a rainbow with the word 'random' at one end and 'non-random' at the other. Along the rainbow are different types of sample; it is not exactly a continuum, because they do not have a special place, but it is useful to visualise the complex nature of sampling.

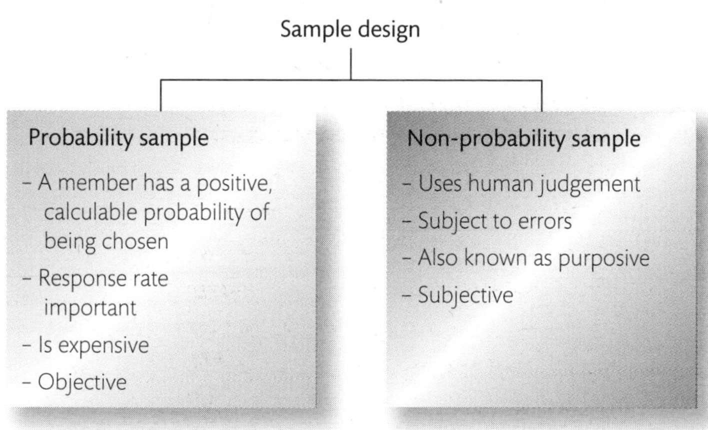

Figure 5.4 Distinctions between probability and non-probability sampling

Probability methods

Under the title of probability methods, we find different techniques that have the word 'random' integrated into the title. Indeed, random sampling is also given the term 'probability' sampling. It is because the items being selected have a known probability of being selected. We know how likely it is that something will be selected in a random sampling. It is, therefore, far from haphazard. There are several probability methods: for example, simple random, systematic, stratified random, and cluster sampling.

With 'simple random sampling' (SRS), there is a known and equal probability of any element being selected. If random sampling is carried out with a small sample size, the composition of the sample is often very different from that of the population. This does not mean that random sampling should not be considered, because mathematical procedures can be applied to correct for this. To understand this defect, you should envisage a map of any nation of your choice. Consider where most people live (think of the cities and large towns). Now imagine 100 dots placed over the country at random. You can guess that they may fall evenly across those largest towns or they may fall mostly in one city. This is the risk you run with a random sample: the sample may be random, but it may not be representative (if the numbers are low). A favoured option is to modify this slightly by creating strata and sampling from these in a random way; this is called 'stratified sampling'.

In 'systematic random sampling', a starting point is determined at random. Next, elements are taken from the sampling frame at equal, predetermined, intervals. The number of 'gaps' is decided by calculations that consider the desired sample size and the total number of elements available in the sampling frame. For example, we might take the fifth or the sixth respondent or another number. If we replace the sample number by the letter '*n*', it is clear why this is commonly referred to as taking the '*n*th' element. This is sometimes known as 'periodic sampling'.

Often a sample of adults is needed when in the field. The interviewer might interview the first person to answer the door, or the first person to volunteer themselves from within the household. This would give a sample of people who select themselves: it is unlikely to be representative; indeed, it is likely to be skewed towards older people and the unemployed. To overcome this, the Kish grid has been used for many years (see Kish 1965). The selection procedure is as follows:

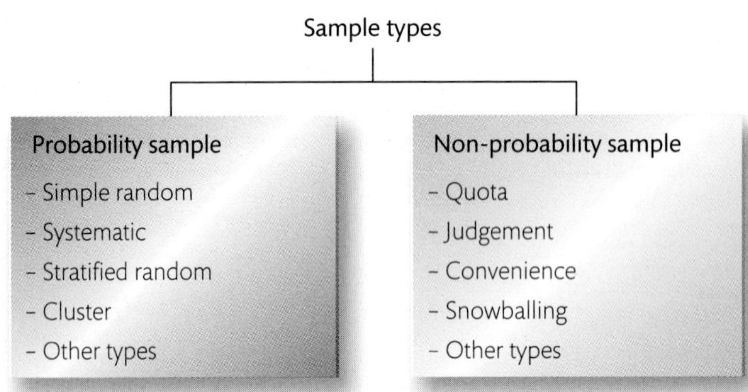

Figure 5.5 Types of probability and non-probability sample

1. At the household, list all persons aged 15 and over. List them in alphabetical order (by surname, then initials)
2. Select one of these from a Kish selection grid (see Table 5.6). For example, at the sixth household (Address 6), we may find there are five people, so we will interview the person we have designated as number three.

'Random route sampling' is also known as 'random walk'. The field interviewer starts at a specified point, which is randomly chosen, and calls on the households that fall at set intervals. Although this has good face validity and has the benefits of random sampling, critics argue that, because of unknown elements of the universe, it has more errors than **quota sampling** and is more expensive than preselected random samples. The benefit is that it allows sampling to take place where sample lists are poor or do not exist. For example, where recent building work changes the appearance or location of some households, the system can be useful in that it accommodates change.

With 'stratified random sampling', there are two stages. At the first one, the researcher divides the population into subgroups, known as 'strata'. Elements are selected from each stratum by a random procedure. This type of sampling means that the sample matches the population for the variables by which it has been stratified. This is very similar to quota sampling (see below) in that the most used variables are age, sex, and social grade. The difference is that objective, random selection is used, rather than the subjective decision of the research team and the interviewer's judgement of who to intercept.

In 'cluster sampling', a two-step probability sampling technique is used. The target population is first divided into mutually exclusive and collectively exhaustive subpopulations called 'clusters', and then a random sample of clusters is selected, based on a probability

Table 5.6 Kish selection grid

Address	Number of people in household					
	1	**2**	**3**	**4**	**5**	**6 or more**
1	1	2	1	4	3	5
2	1	1	2	1	4	6
3	1	2	3	2	5	1
4	1	1	1	3	1	2
5	1	2	2	4	2	3
6	1	1	3	1	3	4
7	1	2	1	2	4	5
8	1	1	2	3	5	6
9	1	2	3	4	1	1

Common mistakes
Randomly using the term 'random'

We come across the word 'random' in everyday speech. One meaning is akin to 'choosing something on purpose'. For example, the police stop motorists to take 'random breath tests' to see whether the driver has consumed alcohol. They make 'random searches' of people in the street. In most cases, they are stopping people because they suspect them to be guilty. They perform these checks at a particular time of day, in particular areas, and they target particular people. This is not random for marketing researchers; it is a 'judgement' sample.

A second use in everyday speech conveys the notion that if we 'pick anything or anyone', then it is random. If I have an apple tree and offer my friends some apples, and I ask them to choose some 'at random', they are likely to take those that they can reach, those that are nearest to them. For a marketing researcher, this is a 'convenience' sample.

sampling technique such as SRS. For each cluster taken, all the elements are included in the sample or a sample of elements is drawn following probability theory. The advantage of cluster sampling is that there is a cost saving over SRS. Furthermore, the greater the clustering, the greater the cost saving. It is cheaper to choose 100 locations and pay 100 interviewers to administer 10 questionnaires each than it is to choose 1000 locations and pay 1000 interviewers to administer one questionnaire each. The disadvantage of this approach is that more clustering may lead to higher sampling error. In other words, the clustered approach may not give a true picture: we know that similar people spend time together and we may not be representing diversity. Harris (1977) outlined the relationship between cost and sampling error; with substantial information available, he was able to show that less clustering reduces sampling error, but increases costs. There is a direct link between the two.

A domestic, residential sample can be generated for a telephone survey using 'random digit dialling' (RDD). In the UK, this involves selecting 10- or 11-digit numbers at random, as these are the national standard. The first digits are taken from the published list of prefix numbers, which relate to locations in the country. These first digits are randomly selected. The last four digits are generated entirely at random. The resulting numbers are then dialled. Business numbers are screened out, and any numbers not in use are eliminated, to leave residential numbers. For telephone sampling, RDD has the potential to provide a true probability sample, which is representative of the land-line population. Another interesting variation of this is the 'number plus one' technique, typically used in conjunction with omnibus surveys. An existing omnibus survey will have created a representative sample of the population, and during fieldwork, it will have collected the telephone numbers of respondents. Because telephone numbers are allocated by locality, and because different neighbourhoods have residents who are similar, we can take the telephone number and simply change the final digit, by adding one. The result should be a representative sample that mirrors the first study. This technique relies on the way land-line telephone numbers are allocated to domestic addresses, so is not useful with mobile phone numbers or business addresses.

Research in focus
Eurobarometer

Eurobarometer 76 covered over 30 countries or territories. TNS Opinion & Social carried out this wave of the Eurobarometer, for the European Commission, Directorate-General for Communication, 'Research and Speechwriting'. Fieldwork was 5–20 November 2011.

The Eurobarometer covered residents in each of the Member States aged 15 years and over. It also included the five candidate countries (Croatia, Turkey, the former Yugoslav Republic of Macedonia, Iceland, and Montenegro) and the Turkish Cypriot community. In these countries, the survey covers the national population of citizens of the respective nationalities and the population of citizens of all the EU Member States that are residents in those countries and have a sufficient command of one of the respective national language(s) to answer the questionnaire.

The sample design applied was multistage and random (probability). In each country, a number of sampling points were drawn, with probability proportional to population size (for a total coverage of the country) and to population density. The sampling points were drawn systematically from each of the 'administrative regional units', after stratification by individual unit and type of area. They thus represent the whole territory of the countries surveyed, according to the Eurostat NUTS II (or equivalent) and according to the distribution of the resident population of the respective nationalities, in terms of metropolitan, urban, and rural areas. In each of the selected sampling points, a starting address was drawn, at random. Further addresses (every *n*th address) were selected by standard 'random route' procedures, from the initial address. In each household, the respondent was drawn, at random (following the 'closest birthday rule'). All interviews were conducted face-to-face in people's homes and in the appropriate national language. Computer-assisted personal interviewing (CAPI) was used where this technique was available.

In each country, the sample is around 1000 persons, except for smaller States, which are around 500. For each country, the table shows the population and the sample achieved. The universe description was derived from Eurostat population data or from national statistics offices.

Compiled by Nigel Bradley 2012.

Sources:
Online at http://ec.europa.eu/public_opinion/archives/eb/eb76/eb76_en.htm © European Union, 1995-2012.

Questions

1 Was the sampling procedure non-random?

2 Why is the sample size for Latvia the same as that in Denmark?

3 Explain the 'closest birthday rule'.

Table 5.7 Country and population

Country	Population 15+ years	Interviews
Turkish Cypriot Community	143,226	500
Iceland	252,277	500
Malta	335,476	500

Table 5.7 Country and population (Continued)

Country	Population 15+ years	Interviews
Luxembourg	404,907	498
Montenegro	492,265	1008
Rep of Cyprus	651,400	504
Estonia	916,000	1003
Latvia	1,448,719	1009
Former Yugoslav Rep of Macedonia	1,678,404	1056
Slovenia	1,748,308	1017
Lithuania	2,849,359	1026
Ireland	3,375,399	1015
Croatia	3,749,400	1000
Finland	4,412,321	1002
Denmark	4,533,420	1009
Slovakia	4,549,954	1000
Bulgaria	6,584,957	1003
Austria	6,973,277	1001
Sweden	7,723,931	1022
Portugal	8,080,915	1,002
Hungary	8,320,614	1021
Greece	8,693,566	1000
Belgium	8,866,411	1028
Czech Rep	8,987,635	1002
Netherlands	13,288,200	1005
Romania	18,246,731	1011
Poland	32,306,436	1000
Spain	39,035,867	1004
France	47,620,942	1031
United Kingdom	51,081,866	1312
Italy	51,252,247	1031

Table 5.7 Country and population (Continued)

Country	Population 15+ years	Interviews
Turkey	52,728,513	1001
Germany	64,545,601	1538
TOTAL	469,946,984	31,659

Non-probability methods

Non-probability methods rely heavily on human judgement. There are several non-random methods: for example, quota, judgement, convenience, and snowballing.

Although quota sampling methods are often seen to be 'faulty' from an academic viewpoint, 'quota sampling' is the most used method in the market research sector in the UK. A subjective decision is made by the researcher to divide the population into useful groups, often based on known divisions from census data. Typically, for consumer studies, these are age, sex, and social grade. Other possible quotas include region, household size, whether a potential, past, or present customer, and purchase history. These segments, groupings or 'cells' are then examined and the researcher decides how many should be contacted.

It is a form of stratified sampling in which the selection of sample members within each stratum is made, but rather than these elements being selected in a random way, the selection is non-random. The quota decided by the main researcher is then 'filled' during fieldwork. Interviewers will then screen people for age, sex, and social grade. On the telephone, it is necessary to ask such questions to ensure a respondent matches the quota. In a face-to-face interview, this might take place by 'sight screening': although this can be very productive, it does highlight the fact that interviewers will only interact with likely respondents. Therefore, the calculation of response rates for these groups becomes meaningless.

The most contentious part of quota sampling is the use of social grade; social grade is not easily evident in the field. Interviewers are trained to ask a series of questions to classify someone as A, B, C1, C2, D, or E, but this takes time and can be off-putting to a stranger who may be required to cooperate further. In postal surveys, it is impossible for a person to be selected on social grade, but a questionnaire may collect sufficient details to derive a suitable category. Sometimes, these are collapsed together, so we may seek three groups: AB, C, and DE. In other words, this is: A together with B, C1 together with C2, and D together with E. A common grouping is ABC1. This early grouping at the data collection stage can actually hinder analysis if specific segments cannot be ungrouped or if there is insufficient representation within a group.

Quota sampling further divides down into 'interlocking' and 'non-interlocking'. In Tables 5.8 and 5.9, one sample selection is interlocking and the other is non-interlocking. They are the same in that we have set the end sample to be 400 interviews with 200 men and 200 women; they are different in the level of detail.

Interlocking is the most difficult for the interviewer because, when the strata are linked, respondents are more difficult to locate, especially at the end of the assignment. Non-interlocking is not so difficult because, when strata are unconnected, the job is quite simple. Interlocking is likely to give a more representative sample because there is more control (see Table 5.9). The people recruited may be a better match to the population. Conversely, non-interlocking is likely to be less representative because the sample is likely to be made up of the most cooperative people.

'Judgement sampling' means that the researcher or fieldworker makes a decision about who might best help in the study. This is a judgement of the most appropriate set of respondents. It may be based on formal indicators, such as the experience in the sector, or less objective indicators, such as 'looking like they are employed in the sector'. An interesting form of judgement sampling is to look at the names listed in a sampling source to identify minority groups. Himmelfarb *et al.* (1983) examined the usefulness of this technique to identify American Jews. Furthermore, they speculated how the selection compared with generally available demographic indicators. In summary, they suggested that the technique was worthwhile.

The 'convenience sample' uses respondents who are easily or conveniently available. This method has the advantage of time and cost savings, but it does recruit respondents who may not be appropriate to the study purpose. If an interviewer stands on a street and speaks to anyone who walks nearby and who does not ignore her or him, then this is a convenience sample. Many newcomers to marketing research erroneously consider this to be random sampling.

Table 5.8 Non-interlocking quotas

Sex	**Sample needed**
Men	200
Women	200
Total	400
Social grade	
AB	100
C1	100
C2	100
DE	100
Total	400

With 'snowball sampling', the principle is straightforward: the sample is generated from the people who are initially contacted. These initial contacts are asked if they know people with particular characteristics, and, in turn, these people are recruited for the specific research. There are other ways of describing snowball sampling. For example, the term 'network sampling' has been used. Similarly, the term 'reputational sample' was used in a study that relied on the reputation of individuals for identification in a study of Mexican immigrants in the USA (Reyes 1997).

We might argue that quantitative quota samples may, in part, be recruited by snowballing. This is particularly the case where quotas are set. An interviewer may ask for referrals to fill the quota. This is a time-saving activity and is snowballing under another name. There are, of course,

Table 5.9 Interlocking quota sample

Social grade	Total	Men	Women
AB	100	50	50
C1	100	50	50
C2	100	50	50
DE	100	50	50
Total	400	200	200

some disadvantages with snowballing. It inevitably relies on the memory or knowledge of respondents. People vary enormously in their abilities: for example, some do not know their neighbours; some do not know the geography of their neighbourhood; some only have vague recollections of other people; some do not know when people move in or out; some people are reluctant to give information. Snowballing can be used in conjunction with any other sampling method: for example, to locate groups that are underrepresented. Commonly, these will include minority groups, but also young people, who are less cooperative than older people.

Street sampling is common.
Credit: Nigel Bradley

Snowballing has a special contribution to make in social research. It can be used for minority groups or to redress any imbalance in samples obtained by other means. For example, accessible sampling frames do not exist for drug-takers, patients of specific illnesses, illegal immigrants, etc. It is worth commenting that the use of snowball sampling can be problematic for several reasons, ranging from respondent negativity towards certain groups and negativity to the survey, to negativity towards the researcher. This may be due to a sense that the study appears to discriminate in favour of groups other than that of the respondent, or perhaps because of a perceived prejudice against the minority held by the respondent. Snowballing is particularly pertinent when interviewing people with differing origins.

Populations involved in online research

There are many ways to monitor online behaviour and levels of Internet traffic; various aspects of the website analytics industry have been described throughout the book. Most of these involve mechanical observation and cannot explain motivations. It is therefore important that questioning techniques are also used. These questioning techniques have been called the 'Voice of Customer' or VOC. This name is useful because it draws a clear distinction between web analytics implemented to track computer use and questions posed to real people; however, it is a misnomer in that web users go beyond customers. Web users include business partners, distribution personnel, other staff members, shareholders, competitors, and many other stakeholders.

Online techniques are often used because they offer access to respondents who may not be as easily available through traditional research approaches. For example, young people who have a high likelihood of not participating in any research have a particularly high penetration of cell phones. Similarly, business people who are well protected by gatekeepers, answerphones, and other barriers, have a high penetration of Internet access. There are other groups who have a specific interest in, or rely heavily on, these technologies. Let us cite professional sectors, which include IT managers and related occupations. Also, anyone involved in the educational sector has a greater than average use of email and the World Wide Web; this is because universities were important to the diffusion of the Internet.

It is essential to understand the population under study and the researcher must examine published data to discover how representative the chosen group is. One way to do this is to consult the ICT Development Index (IDI), previously known as the DOI (see ITU 2011).

Web users 'on the move' may use laptops with WIFI, they may use smart phones, and of course they may use the mobile phone itself. Public users may use Internet cafes, terminals in libraries, kiosks, or similar.

With online research there is a big risk that a respondent cannot be identified; the online environment allows and encourages users to hide their real name and anything that might identify them (see Figure 5.6). This can be a problem because, without knowing the identity, we can receive multiple returns from the same person; we can annoy people by sending blanket reminders. The date of birth (DOB) is a useful question that allows us to

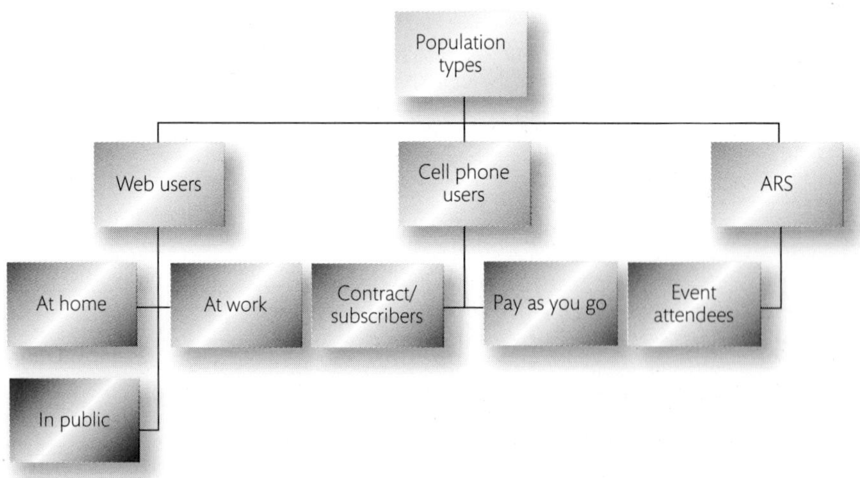

Figure 5.6 Online population

identify multiple returns but also allows us to identify minors. Minors are subject to special measures (see the MRS/ESOMAR guidelines for online research and Researching Young People) and so must be identified early in a survey, even if the survey is not intended for young people. The postcode is another unique identifier that can help de-duplicate multiple responses.

As with other methods of research, respondent selection for online surveys requires a certain amount of creativity and careful thinking. There are numerous sampling solutions. Table 5.10 gives a few ideas and indicates which sources have been associated with the three main approaches of computer-assisted mobile interviewing (CAMI), computer-assisted web interviewing (CAWI), and audience response systems (ARS).

At this point it is worth mentioning 'river sampling'. The idea with this is that respondents are chosen from the constant arrival of online users, akin to taking fish from a

Table 5.10 Sample sources for online surveys (*** = most common)

Sample sources/examples	Selection for CAMI	Selection for CAWI	Selection for ARS
Announcements on sales receipts	***	*	
Poster signage at point of sale/experience	***		
Announcements on packaging	**	*	
Sales staff referral	*		**
Flyers/handouts	*	*	**
Big screen	*		***
Directories		*	
Email announcements and invitations	*	***	*
Records of subscribers/members/customers	*	*	
Interest group members	*	***	*
Registration forms	**	***	*
Snowballing	**	*	
Invitation banners	*	***	
Hypertext links/link from another web page		***	*
Printed directories	*	*	
Pop-up (triggered by visits, times, dates, or day)		***	*
Email addresses harvested from websites		**	

flowing river, rather than choosing them from a database that (akin to a lake) can become stagnant, poorly refreshed and over-used. In practical online terms, river sampling takes the form of intercepting respondents by interstitials, banners, pop-ups, and website visitor invitations.

The composition of invitations and reminder, whether by email or text message, largely follows the best practice found in regular postal survey cover letters in that they should

- Be short and have a clear 'call to action'
- Explain the topic and reason for contacting them
- Assure confidentiality
- Give an estimate of the time needed.

The difference with an email or text message is that the sender's name, the subject line, or the content that appears in a preview pane can mean the difference between opening or deleting an invitation. Inboxes and mobile phone displays are full of messages competing for attention.

Recruitment from web pages is another skill that needs to be developed by the researcher. Good and suitable design can lead to large samples from the sample of interest. Conversely, poor design can lead to a self-selected sample that is skewed in one particular direction. The following pictures taken from real websites gives examples of how respondents can be recruited using hypertext links.

Starting via web pages

Please help us serve you better by taking our user survey

Basic invitation link from web page (to all visitors)

Invitation to take a survey as a small tab at the bottom right of a web page

Invitation pop-up, gives choice of YES/NO (may be to all visitors but can be triggered by something)

Win £50 in 1 minute

To assist us with our continuing improvement of the website and a chance to win £50 in a monthly prize draw, please complete our short survey.

Yes please **No thanks**

(Survey will start upon leaving website.)

One example of an invitation pop-up gives choice of YES/NO, the questionnaire is not immediate, but permission is obtained (may be to all visitors but can be triggered by something)

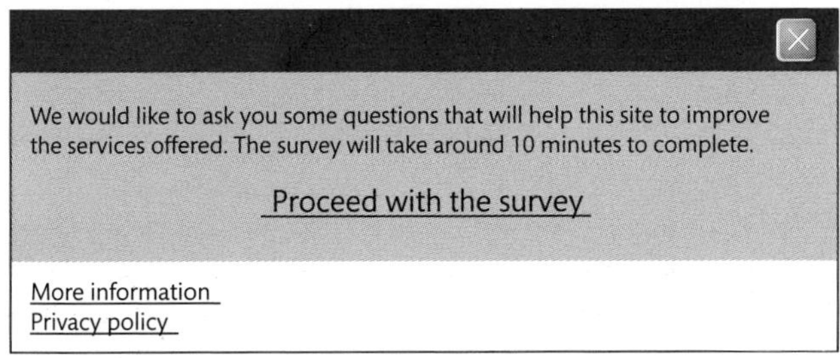

A further example of an invitation as a pop-up window, does not give choice of YES/NO, but this is implied by the hyperlink (representing YES) and the CLOSE buttons at the top right (representing NO).

Qualitative recruitment

In this section, we concentrate on focus groups and depth interviews. With these approaches, researchers need to adopt a viewpoint that is very different from that used in quantitative studies. This means being open-minded, using lateral thinking, and even creative thinking. Non-probability methods of sampling are used in qualitative research, so a great deal of human judgement is used to decide which people and situations will provide the best opportunities for decision-making material. In most cases, a quota sample is employed, arrived at by the researcher in collaboration with the client.

People and situations are chosen to satisfy the research objective. The profiles of subjects must fit the topic, so, for example, people may be chosen because they behave in a particular way—they may consume a particular product. Alternatively, they may *not* consume a particular product. A typical quota includes sex, age, social grade, and something related to the topic under study, perhaps awareness or usage.

A quota is predetermined by a researcher for each focus group and for the set of depth interviews. In practice, recruiters, rather than a moderator or interviewer, will locate such people and invite them to a venue at a particular time and place. Moderators are rarely involved in recruitment because the two skills of recruitment and moderation are seen as quite distinct. Additionally, commercial pressures mean that the moderator's highly paid skills are best used for posing questions rather than persuading the respondent to cooperate.

The recruitment procedure may be done using a screener questionnaire or simply using the needed criteria. In interviewer training for 'quantitative' research, it is emphasised that questionnaire wording should be followed precisely: question order cannot be changed and each word of each question should be read in a neutral voice. In 'qualitative' recruitment, fieldworkers report that this structured approach, using a screener questionnaire designed to be read word by word, inhibits them. They prefer to use it as a guide and to complete the form after securing cooperation. This needs to be outlined clearly in instructions to recruiters; otherwise, the rigid approach may lead to poor recruitment.

Respondents may be located by interception in public places, from lists, by referral or snowballing, or by other means. The important principle is to fill the quotas. The various ways in which such quotas are achieved are by intercepting users in transit or waiting, for example, in car parks, at schools, in queues. Alternatively, people known to interviewers may be asked to assist in identifying friends and family with a view to recruiting them.

Quota samples ensure that certain demographic characteristics, deemed appropriate by the researcher, are apparent in the sample. This is not to say that the sample is representative of the population as a whole. Focus group results are not intended to be subjected to quantitative weighting: results can never suggest that a certain percentage of the population shares a certain view. The choice of sample changes from project to project and, within the *same* project, the composition of each group will change, if only by different geographic location. Inevitably, the selection will depend on many things:

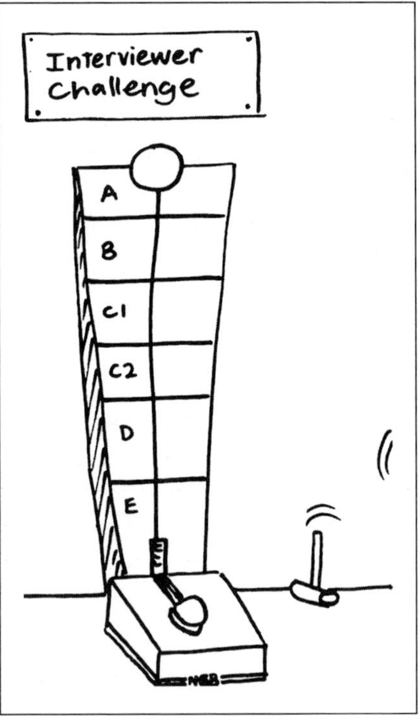

- Aim of the study
- Money available
- Time available
- Respondent locations
- Ease of contacting respondents
- Client judgement.

Usually, individual groups are made up of similar participants to encourage positive discussion. For example, we expect ABC1 females to be more likely to discuss their food preparation in greater detail with other ABC1 females, rather than with C2DE men. Practitioners with many years of recruiting experience will confirm that similar respondents will indeed debate more actively, and, as a result, many groups in the UK are recruited using these criteria:

- Age
- Sex
- Geographic area
- Social grade (ABC1, C2DE)
- Life stage
- Characteristics relevant to product.

Common mistakes
Misusing the word 'representative'

The term 'representative' is often used in discussions concerning sampling, but not all samples are representative of the whole population. Qualitative samples are never representative: they are too small and this is not the reason for qualitative enquiry. The group may be 'typical'; it may contain people we expect to look 'average' or 'normal', who can illustrate a specific issue. Respondents interviewed may have 'similar' profiles and this will be done in order to probe deeply into the topic. 'Quantitative' samples are also drawn to examine extremes within a population. We may deliberately look for non-users, or users of above-average quantities; samples may be selected to understand minorities. The end sample may well be a good mirror, or representation, of these groups, but not of the overall population. It is worth adding that some newcomers to the field use the terms 'random' and 'representative' interchangeably; this is not the right thing to do! These notions are not helped by the fact that we might want to ensure that minority groups are in our sample; here, we refer to minority groups in a political sense—we want the 'small man' to be represented somehow. Take care when using the words 'representative' and 'representation'.

© Nigel Bradley

Although similar respondents are often used in a single group, this can change for the second or third group in the project. Also, we can go against the 'similarity' rule and have 'conflict groups' with people who are at the extremes: for example, very heavy beer drinkers or non-drinkers. A 'typical' sample would be people who, in the judgement of the researcher, resemble the majority of people in that population: for example, average age or average drinker.

Sample size determination

A common question in research is: '*How many people should we interview?*'. This is a simple question with a complex answer. The sample size for any study depends on:

- The required precision of the study (the purpose)
- The size and nature of the people under study (the population)
- The time, budget, and resources available (the procedural aspects)
- The importance of the results (publishing aspects).

The sample size is generally agreed before undertaking fieldwork, although in some projects, the sample size may be determined after it has started. There may be several reasons for this: first, the early part of fieldwork may have been designed to estimate the universe and

Ethical insight
Qualitative recruitment

Many groups in the UK recruit to standard criteria—social grade, age, sex—then also attitudinal criteria. This is a systematic way to find the right respondents, but, behind the scenes, clients express concerns over other aspects of focus group respondents.

Over many years, standards of good recruitment for focus groups have been established by professional bodies such as the MRS (Robson 1979). These standards include such things as ensuring that: respondents do not know each other; they are 'inexperienced' in focus groups; and they do not know the subject before the group. Similarly, recruitment criteria such as the quota should be met and recruiters should not know respondents. There are various explanations for this: two friends may dominate or withdraw and people may behave artificially; or if respondents have previous experience with such research, they may intimidate other participants and give well-rehearsed answers and reactions. Without the agreed types of people, the group will not function as expected. If recruiters know respondents, there is a risk that they will overuse the same respondents. These 'rules' are generally adopted (Rose *et al.* 1996), but sometimes this may not be possible. For example, there are some fields that have very few protagonists; agriculture is one sector that is so small that it is almost impossible for respondents not to know someone else in the room of a focus group held locally. In recent years, these issues have continued to be of concern (see Parker and Francis 2003).

Compiled by Nigel Bradley 2012.

Sources:

Parker, K. and Francis, E. (2003) *Tonight Matthew I'm going to be . . .* MRS Conference 2003 paper (online at http://www.warc.com).
Robson, S. (1979) *Recruitment standards in qualitative research*, Report of MRS Working Party.
Rose, J. *et al.* (1996) Qualitative recruitment, *Journal of the Market Research Society*, April, 38(2), pp. 135-143.
Stoll, M., Ipsos research, UK.

Questions

1 Why is the industry concerned about qualitative recruitment?

2 What standards have been agreed for recruitment?

3 Why are these standards broken for some sectors? Suggest five sectors where the standards may be a problem.

therefore give information to calculate an optimum sample size; second, fieldwork may yield early results that can be used and the study can end early; conversely, there may be a need to seek more views and therefore increase the number of respondents.

Qualitative versus quantitative research

In qualitative research, sample size is far more subjective than in quantitative approaches; it is also complex. In theory, qualitative sample sizes should *not* be fixed firmly at the start of the project. The overriding idea is that new cases should be selected until the data bring nothing new. In practice, a methodological compromise is made and most proposals set a certain

Table 5.11 Qualitative sample sizes

Qualitative studies	Size (people)
Five groups with readers	Eight at each
Depths with newsagents	Ten

number of groups and depths (see Chapter 7). This then allows budgets to be controlled and timetables to be developed. As a guide to typical sizes, it is useful to refer to recent studies; Table 5.11 shows the sample sizes used for a study of newspaper delivery.

In quantitative research, the main ways of deciding on sample size are: by calculation, by using 'accepted' industry standards, by budget (time or money available), and by 'building' analysis cells.

The optimum sample size can be determined by a series of calculations. The 'calculation method' implies that the sample will be selected by probability means. It takes account of the population size and the expected accuracy of results. In theory, this is the best way to arrive at a sample size; in practice, it is only used with government or cross-industry studies. For very large populations, the size of the sample is entirely independent of the size of the population. We can discover what the UK population thinks by posing questions to a sample of just 1000; we can know what the US population thinks also by taking a sample of just 1000. Remember there are 60 million people in the UK and over 290 million in the USA. For newcomers, this can be a surprise: the common misconception is that the sample should be taken in proportion to the population. The important thing is how homogeneous the population is, rather than its full size. To make this point, let us say that if one million people were exactly the same as each other, we would only need to take a sample of one person. Similarly, if there were 200 very different people, we would need to interview all 200.

There are two main formulae: one is used for studies that involve the estimation of the average (mean) value in a population; the second is used for studies that involve proportions. The formulae change, depending on the type of probability method used. This book does not give details of the formulae used in sample size estimation. The reader is advised to consult statistical texts and to search the Internet, where 'sample size estimation software' can be found relatively easily: for example, http://www.surveysystem.com/sscalc.htm (Creative Research Systems 2009) and Lenth (2009).

The use of 'accepted' industry standards is more common than we might imagine. At some point, people working in a specific field have drawn conclusions from studies using a certain sample size. When repeat studies seem to be stable, then there is no reason to increase sample sizes. This method is also used 'as a proxy' for non-probability methods (where calculations cannot take place); it is as if a 'past' probability sample composition is replicated for a non-probability sample. Rather than performing calculations, the researcher seeks comparable studies and examines the methodology. As a guide to such standards, look at the following sizes used in some recent UK studies (Table 5.12). Remember that the detailed composition of each sample is not reproduced.

Many sample sizes for research studies are decided by researchers on what is feasible within time or money available: these are 'budget' limitations (see Table 5.13). The final method of

Table 5.12 Quantitative sample sizes

Surveys	Size (people)
UK National Readership Research Survey	36,000 p.a.
Omnibus Survey	1000
FMCG usage study	500
Product test in-home	200

'building' analysis cells is associated with non-probability methods. Consider the final results, and then think backwards. If you want precise results, you need a large sample; if you are happy with 'indicative' data, then you can get away with a smaller sample. You are likely to provide table breakdowns on some standard demographics: male and female, for example. It is reasonable to think that percentages will be applied. A percentage is based on 100, so a minimum of 100 people might be chosen. The sample size can be built up in this way. We may assume that we want to see cross-analyses of the standard demographics (sex, age, region, social grade) and perhaps of other aspects important to the subject area (high, low, or medium consumption; high or low awareness). If we accept that an analysis cell should have a minimum of 100 people, then the sample will be at least 600 (there are six social grades) and even higher if the other cells are not satisfied by this selection. In part, this relies on forecasting likely incidence; in part, it is based on known characteristics of the marketplace. Some practitioners say there should be a minimum of 50 in a cell; others say 100. In fact, these choices are based on their own experiences and knowledge of the marketplace in question.

Table 5.13 Summary of sample size determination approaches

Method	Comment
Calculation	The 'ideal'. For quantitative studies, based on probability, common in large studies
'Accepted' industry standards	Past experience can identify 'safe' sizes, unknowingly
Money available	Common reason for using quotas
Time available	A very poor reason, and a good reason to cancel research
Building analysis cells	Commonly used, particularly in non-consumer studies
Researcher's judgement	The best method for qualitative research
Combination of above	Commonly used for both quantitative and qualitative commercial research

Chapter summary

1 Explain the stages of sampling

The first step is to examine the 'purpose' of the study to decide what degree of precision is required. After this, we must define the 'population' and decide a suitable sampling frame. We next determine the 'procedure': how the sampling takes place. The procedure may use probability or non-probability methods. Probability methods include simple random, systematic, stratified random, and cluster sampling. Non-probability methods include quota, judgement, convenience, and snowballing sampling. The combinations mean we have a vast number of options. The sample size is generally agreed before undertaking fieldwork, but, in some projects, it may be determined after it has started. Any sampling shortfalls should be identified and corrected at the 'publication' stage.

2 Describe the different types of sample source

The sampling frame should include summary information of key features of all units in the population of interest. Sampling frames must be 'up to date', 'complete', 'affordable', and 'easy to use' and sources must be checked for duplicates. Poor frames are 'old', 'incomplete', and 'inappropriate'. Common sources include: the Electoral Register, the Postcode Address File, telephone directories, subscriber/membership records, and customer records.

3 Show the benefits and the limitations of sampling approaches

Sampling involves less cost and time than looking at every member of the population. The major disadvantage is that the process cannot summarise every characteristic in that given population; it may also suffer when there is a shortfall in data available for analysis from specific groups. Weighting is used to correct this, but it can affect the results. With random sampling, we can see the levels of cooperation and calculate non-response; this tells us how accurate our results are at the analysis stage; however, it is expensive. Non-random approaches are cheaper but we are less sure of accuracy as the levels of non-cooperation are mixed together with many other things.

4 Explain how sample size is determined

The sample size for any study depends on the required precision; the size and nature of the 'population' under study. 'Procedural' aspects such as time, budget, and resources available will dictate the size, as will 'publishing' aspects, in terms of importance placed on the results by the audience. The main ways of deciding on sample size are: by calculation, by using 'accepted' industry standards, by budget (time or money available), and by 'building' analysis cells. The calculation method takes account of the population size and the expected accuracy of results. In theory, this is the best way to arrive at a sample size; in practice, other methods are used. Many sample sizes for research studies are decided on the basis of what is feasible within time or money available. The sample size is often built up from the minimum numbers expected in each analysis cell.

5 Articulate how qualitative sampling differs from quantitative sampling

Non-probability methods of sampling are used in qualitative research, so a great deal of human judgement is used to decide which people and situations will provide the best opportunities for obtaining useful material. In most cases, a quota sample is used based on sex, age, social grade, and something related to the topic under study. The sample is unlikely to be representative of the population as a whole. Usually, individual focus groups are made up of similar participants to encourage positive discussion. This composition can change for the next groups. In qualitative research, sample size is also far more subjective. In theory, qualitative sample sizes should not be fixed firmly at the start of the project. The overriding idea is that new cases should be selected until the data brings nothing new. In practice, a methodological compromise is made and most proposals will set a certain number of groups and depths. This then allows budgets to be controlled and timetables to be developed.

Review questions

1 What lessons can we draw from the past to help in sampling?
2 How can sample size be determined?
3 What is a population? What is a sample? What is a survey?
4 What are the differences between simple random sampling and systematic random sampling?
5 Why is knowledge about the universe so important before sampling?

Discussion questions

1 Why should the sample be debated at all stages of a project?
2 What sampling frames are available to investigate the automotive market?
3 Plan a sample to determine why buyers of dog food choose particular can sizes.
4 Consult the proposal in the Market Researcher's Toolbox. Draft a possible design for sampling; try to improve on the sampling details provided.
5 Read the opening Snapshot carefully. Both random and non-random methods are used. Describe these and suggest why this was an appropriate solution. Suggest other possible sampling approaches that could be used to monitor radio listening.

Further reading

- Kish, L. (1965) *Survey Sampling*. New York: Wiley & Sons.
  A classic text on the subject, which has formed the basis of much thinking on probability sampling.
- Moser, C.A. and Kalton, G. (1971) *Survey Methods in Social Investigation*, 2nd edn. London: Heinemann Educational Books.
  Another text that has forged thinking and gives full explanation of statistical methods.
- National Statistics (2006) The NS-SEC self-coded method (online at http://www.ons.gov.uk search for SEC classifications).
  Information on applying the five-class self-completion version of the UK government Socio Economic Classification.

Case study
Fantasia Kingdom

© istockphoto.com/Jon patton

Fantasia Kingdom is located in the English countryside in the Peak District. For many years, it has attracted thousands of visitors to its theme park attractions. The attractions include a 'haunted house' with ghost train, two water rides, several big dipper rides, an ice rink for shows, several train rides, and much more. Massive car parks allow thousands of visitors to arrive, either by car or by coach. Several restaurants and eating stations ensure that visitors are well fed during the day.

A more recent initiative is a hotel, which allows visitors to spread their fun over two days; the major benefit is to arrive at the park early, thereby avoiding queues for the most popular rides. Fantasia Kingdom staff work very closely with well-known brand names, which have seen that sponsorship can offer mutual benefits. Five sponsors provide substantial amounts of product free or at a discount. The return is brand exposure or exclusive sale or use of their products on the complex. The five are:

- an ice-cream seller
- a soft drinks company
- a film and single-use camera supplier
- a chocolate and confectionery company
- a car manufacturer.

All of these companies value feedback from customers and Fantasia Kingdom has agreed to provide market research information as part of the sponsorship.

One project that provides most feedback is called 'Fantasia exit interviews'. Every day, one of the Fantasia staff members is positioned near the exit (there is only one exit). He or she is instructed to let nine people walk by and to approach the tenth person. If that person agrees, an interview takes place. If there is a refusal, this is respected and nine more people are allowed past before approaching the tenth.

Interviewing does not start until 4pm of each day and continues until the park has closed. The number of interviewers does not change each day, despite the fact that there are 'peak' and 'off-peak' periods. The park is open every day of the year, even on Christmas Day. It needs to be said that weather conditions vary and, on some days, more people leave before 4pm than on other days.

The interviewer team changes throughout the year and regular training takes place. In the last 12 months, over 200 different staff members were able to conduct the interview. This is necessary because staff need breaks between 4pm and final closing at 9pm; also, there is a high turnover of staff. When the visitor is stopped, the questions are as follows:

1 How many rides did you go on?

2 Were there any rides you couldn't get on for any reason? Which and why?

3 What did you think of the queue times?

4 What did you think of catering?

5 Overall, how satisfied were you with your visit?

All of these questions are closed, in the form of satisfaction scales, and the name of the visitor is not asked.

Every quarter, the sponsors are invited to a day at Fantasia Kingdom. Their representatives are able to inspect the park and see how their sponsorship is put into practice. They can make suggestions. They also have a meeting where the results of the 'Fantasia exit interviews' are presented.

The soft drinks firm representative is new to the meeting and is not happy that the 'exit' interviews are conducted by Fantasia staff. He feels that a professional research agency should be used.

Compiled by Nigel Bradley 2012.

Questions

1 What reasons would the soft drinks representative give for being unhappy with the interviews? Consider the data capture and preparation of results.

2 Should interviews take place before 4pm?

3 If every third visitor were to be sampled, what effect would this have? Consider congestion, cooperation, and representativeness.

Key web links

- Postcode Address File http://www.royalmail.com/paf
- Sample Size Calculator Device http://www.surveysystem.com/sscalc.htm
- UK Census http://www.statistics.gov.uk/census

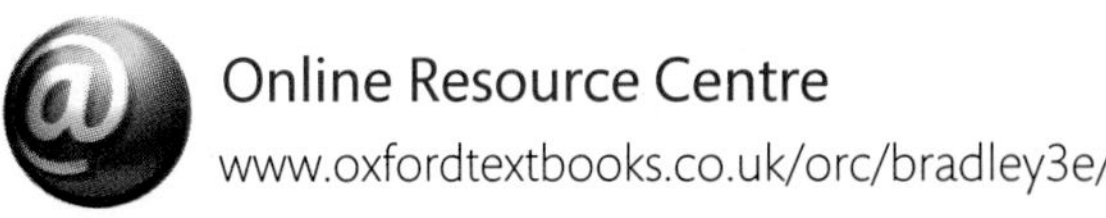

Visit the Online Resource Centre that accompanies this book to access more learning resources on this chapter topic.

References and sources

Altmann, J. (1974) Observational study of behavior: sampling methods, *Behaviour*, 49, pp. 227–267.

Bradley, N. (1999) Sampling for Internet surveys: an examination of respondent selection for Internet research, *Journal of the Market Research Society*, 41, pp. 387–395.

Campbell, A. (ed.) (1988) *International Encyclopedia of the Social Sciences: Biographical Supplement*. New York: The Free Press.

Creative Research Systems (2009) Sample size calculator (Computer software), http://www.surveysystem.com/sscalc.htm

Elwyn, G., Edwards, A., Mowle, S., Wensing, M., Wilkinson, C., Kinnersley, P., and Grol, R. (2001) Measuring the involvement of patients in shared decision-making: a systematic review of instruments, *Patient Education and Counselling*, 43, pp. 5–22.

Faugier, J. and Sargeant, M. (1997) Sampling hard to reach populations, *Journal of Advanced Nursing*, 26, pp. 790–797.

Gallup, G. (1928) *A New Technique for Objective Methods for Measuring Reader Interest in Newspapers*, Ph.D. thesis, University of Iowa.

Galton F. (1883) *Inquiries into Human Faculty*. Macmillan, http://www.mugu.com/galton/books/

Goodman, L.A. (1961) Snowball sampling, *Annuals of Mathematical Statistics*, 32, pp. 148–170.

Harris, P. (1977, reprinted 1997) The effect of clustering on costs and sampling errors, *The Journal of the Market Research Society*, 39, January (Special edition: Milestones in market research), pp. 39–51.

Himmelfarb, H.S., Loar, R.M., and Mott, S.H. (1983) Sampling by ethnic surnames: the case of American Jews, *Public Opinion Quarterly*, 47, pp. 247–261.

HMSO (2012) *The 2011 census of population*, http://www.ons.gov.uk/ons/guide-method/census/2011/the-2011-census/index.html

Hughes, A.O., Fenton, S., Hine, C.E., Pilgrim, S., and Tibbs, N. (1995) Strategies for sampling black and ethnic minority populations, *Journal of Public Health Medicine*, 17, pp. 187–192.

ITU (2011) Measuring the Information Society 2011. International Telecommunication Union, Geneva, Switzerland, http://www.itu.int/net/pressoffice/backgrounders/general/pdf/5.pdf

Kaplan, C.D., Korf, D., and Sterk, C. (1987) Temporal and social contexts of heroin-using populations: an illustration of the snowball sampling technique, *The Journal of Nervous and Mental Disease*, 175, pp. 566–574.

Kish, L. (1965) *Survey Sampling*. New York: Wiley & Sons.

Lenth, R.V. (2011) Java Applets for power and sample size (computer software). Online at www.stat.uiowa.edu/ ~ rlenth/Power

Lenth, R.V. (2012) Java Applets for power and sample size (computer software), http://homepage.stat.uiowa.edu/ ~ rlenth/Power/ accessed on 6 September 2012.

Lopes, C.S., Rodrigues, L.C., and Sichieri, R. (1996) The lack of selection bias in a snowball sampled case-control study on drug abuse, *International Journal of Epidemiology*, 25, pp. 1267–1270.

McDonald, C. and King, S. (1996) *Sampling the Universe: The Growth, Development and Influence of Market Research in Britain since 1945*. Henley-on-Thames, Oxon: NTC Publications Ltd.

McIntosh, A.R. and Davies, R.J. (1970) The sampling of non-domestic populations, Reprinted (1996) *Journal of the Market Research Society*, 38, p. 4.

Moser, C.A. and Kalton, G. (1971) *Survey Methods in Social Investigation*, 2nd edn. London: Heinemann Educational Books.

MRS (2012) *Online Research Guidelines*. London: MRS. Online at http://www.mrs.org.uk/standards/internet.htm Accessed 6 September 2012.

National Statistics (2006) The NS-SEC self-coded method, http://www.ons.gov.uk search for SEC classifications.

ONS (2001) *200 Years of the Census*. London: Office for National Statistics.

ONS (2002) *Census 2001 Review and Evaluation*, www.statistics.gov.uk/census2001/pdfs/noncompliancees.pdf

Parker, K. and Francis, E. (2003) Tonight Matthew I'm going to be . . . MRS Conference 2003 Paper 5. Online at www.warc.com

Reyes, B.I. (1997) *Dynamics of Immigration: Return Migration to Western Mexico*. San Francisco, CA: Public Policy Institute of California. Online at www.ppic.org/content/pubs/report/r_197brr.pdf

Robson, S. (1979) *Recruitment Standards in Qualitative Research*. Report of MRS Working Party.

Rose, D. (1998) *ESRC Revision of Govt Social Classification*. London: HMSO Stationery Office.

Rose, D. and O'Reilly, K. (eds.) (1997) *Constructing Classes: Towards a New Social Classification for the UK*. Swindon: ONS/ESRC.

Rose, J. *et al.* (1996) Qualitative Recruitment, *Journal of the Market Research Society*, April 38(2), pp. 135–143.

Thompson, S.K. (1997) Adaptive sampling in behavioural surveys, *NIDA Research Monograph*, 167, pp. 296–319.

Questionnaires and topic guides

Contents

Chapter guide

All research needs to have instruments of some sort. An important tool in quantitative research is the structured questionnaire, so this chapter helps you to design a questionnaire that is 'fit for purpose'. To do this, we learn about open and closed questions, projective techniques, and scales. For qualitative researchers, the 'topic guide' is important and again guidance is given. The chapter concludes with an account of questionnaire variants: the diary and the observation form.

Learning outcomes

By the end of this chapter, you should be able to:

1. **Explain the purposes of questionnaires and topic guides**
2. **List the supporting materials used by researchers**
3. **Explain the nature of projective techniques, questions, and scales**
4. **Create a questionnaire and topic guide**

Introduction

Investigating what is going on in the human mind is not an easy task and it offers unique challenges. There are really only two options for 'mind-reading'—we can tap into the mind of a consumer by posing questions or we can measure the human condition with equipment. Nobody has yet developed telepathy to the point where it can help in marketing! Over the years, questionnaires and measuring devices have evolved, and these now give numerous choices to the researcher. Researchers are advised to look at existing questionnaires in order to see examples of good and poor practice. We need to ensure that our chosen instrument does what we expect it to do and that it will do that job consistently. If it is not 'fit for purpose', the client must feel confident to reject it and it must be rewritten. We will examine specific aspects of questionnaires and topic guides. This knowledge will allow anyone performing quality checks to make informed judgements about the suitability of these instruments.

To trace the origins of questioning techniques, we need to go back at least 400 years before Christ, to the Greeks who, we might say, were the first people in recorded history to be users of the open-ended question. Over time, these techniques have evolved to give us a form called the 'questionnaire'. The 'questionnaire era' can be traced back to the 1920s and 1930s (see Table 6.1). In 1939, the director of the Division of Program Surveys in the Bureau of Agricultural Economics of the US Department of Agriculture in Washington felt that better methods could be used. The standard practice for government agencies at that time was to use a form that specified broad areas of information required; interviewers used different approaches. That division adopted formal questionnaires that interviewers were instructed to follow without deviation. That director was Renesis Likert (1903–1981) and he was prepared to stand by this decision. He had actually written a dissertation on the measurement of attitudes in the 1930s. After this, standard procedures were implemented across other government agencies. Another outcome of this work was the creation of a widely used scale that now carries his name (the **Likert scale**).

Table 6.1

Notable events for questionnaires

Year	Event
1900s	Early questionnaires in use
1930s	Postal surveys
1940s	Projective techniques introduced to consumer research (Dichter)
1970s	Personal computers launched
1980s	CATI introduced
1990s	CAPI Introduced
2000s	CASI techniques for online data capture

SNAPSHOT
Google asks questions

Google is now a household name. Although it offers secondary data to everyone on the planet, primary data are paramount to Google's success. The company began as a graduate school research project.

Marketing research looks to the marketplace, and the company soon saw the benefits in its early years of operation. A first-user study was held at Stanford University, with the enticing incentive of a free pizza to the 16 students who came in response to a flyer. To quote from David A. Vise (2005: 78), *'Google was looking to recruit an engineer to analyze, test, and improve the layout of the search engine's Web site'.* After reviewing several candidates, the decision was made to recruit someone with a master's degree in computer science who had also studied linguistics and psychology. In an early test 16 people were invited to the firm's premises, with two people per computer to be observed by four people from the company. This was to ensure that the testers spoke to each other, rather than to the corporation. A simple task was given: to answer the question 'Which country won the most gold medals in the 1994 Olympics?'. The subsequent reactions and comments of the users were important factors that have shaped Google's home page to this day. Research continues, the Google Blog (2010) described the testing for Google Instant: *'we ran through a sequence of prototypes, usability studies (testing with people from the community), dogfooding (testing with Google employees) and search experiments (testing with a small percentage of Google users)'.*

Compiled by Nigel Bradley 2012.

Sources:

Google (2010) Google Instant, behind the scenes. Google blog. September 9, http://googleblog.blogspot.com/2010/09/google-instant-behind-scenes.html

Google (2012) Google Research, http://research.google.com/about.html

Rodriguez, E. (2003) Google Product Development/Management Process. Notes of a presentation on Jan 8, 2003 to Silicon Valley Product Management Association by Google Product Manager Marissa Mayer, http://www.evelynrodriguez.typepad.com/crossroads_dispatches/files/GoogleProductDevProcess.pdf

Vise, D.A. (2005) *The Google Story*. London: Pan Books.

Purposes of questionnaires and topic guides

In quantitative research, an obvious research tool is the questionnaire. Qualitative research takes a less structured approach. Newcomers to research see this as unstructured: there appears to be little direction—the researcher seems to just go with the flow of conversation. This is not, in fact, the case: qualitative research requires the interviewer to drive the research; otherwise, the conversation might easily turn to television and sport—the two most popular topics of conversation. Qualitative researchers have their own set of research tools.

The **topic guide** is a qualitative research instrument which provides an area agreed between the researcher and client; it determines the ground to be explored. It is sometimes known as a **discussion guide** or an interview **schedule**. It is a short document used to agree the areas for discussion, containing carefully chosen areas. Its purpose is to assist in the investigation of a specific subject. Topic guides are written for focus groups and for depth interviews, but, paradoxically, they should rarely be referred to during debate; the process of producing one helps the researcher to learn the topic. Knowing the guide allows eye contact to be maintained; recall of each item should act as a trigger, to elicit responses. Leading questions are allowed in order to bring out replies. It is unusual for this guide to be longer than five pages; indeed, many are no longer than two sides.

The questionnaire is a valuable instrument for the quantitative researcher. It is commonly employed with sample surveys and this close association often leads students to refer, incorrectly, to the questionnaire as a 'survey'. It is also known as an interview form, or schedule. Questionnaires are primarily designed to be answered by a person who is known as a respondent or informant. Such forms may be used in interviewing, but a variant is also used in observational research, to make a record of observations. A questionnaire can be defined as *'two or more questions containing carefully chosen vocabulary. Its purpose is to assist in the investigation of a specific subject'.* It is a formalised set of questions for obtaining information from respondents. Table 6.2 distinguishes these tools.

Questionnaires and topic guides are used to identify and then to collect data. There are three skills that we should master in relation to such devices:

- Being able to recognise an efficient instrument
- Being able to develop an efficient instrument
- Being able to evaluate reports by understanding the efficiency of the research instruments used.

Such capabilities are important for both clients and researchers. It is reasonable to stop a project if the instrument is not 'fit for purpose'. The principles and problems of question design also apply to the design of diaries and observation forms. The third skill involves some backward thinking. The report reader must attempt to guess, visualise, and deduce what data collection instruments were used to arrive at the data available (this has been called 'reverse researching' in Chapter 3). This will permit the user to give more or less emphasis to results, depending on the faith he or she has in the efficiency of the data collection method.

The questionnaire is the interface between the researcher and respondent, but it is also the link between the client and the researcher. It represents the way in which the researcher

Table 6.2 Distinction between questionnaires and topic guides

Questionnaires	Topic guides
Associated with quantitative studies	Associated with qualitative studies
Questionnaire length is fixed. The session length is determined by the questionnaire	Length is not fixed; the time spent is variable and depends on the respondent rather than the instrument.
Standard ways are used to collect information, e.g. neutral questions, scales, showcards	'Original' ways are found to collect information, e.g. projective techniques, demonstration
Questions should be posed in order, but filters may mean the questions asked vary	The order of questions is driven by the situation, nature of answers, and the respondent situation
Question wording is carefully formulated before the session and should not be modified	Question wording during the session likely to be modified
Answers are recorded on the questionnaire either by pen or via a keyboard	Answers not recorded on the topic guide, usually visual or audio data capture
Well-worded questions	Bullet points and checklists

has translated the client's needs into a method of data capture. For the research to be efficient, the data instrument must also be efficient. The client can take a passive role and accept the researcher's tools or he or she can take an active role in checking and suggesting improvements. The successful researcher will always seek such approval and input. At each stage in this process, it is useful to bear in mind that the researcher must:

- Address the objectives
- Be able to analyse the information
- Consider the respondent's situation.

Questionnaires and topic guides must always relate to the study aims. Everyone is sometimes tempted to write a questionnaire (or topic guide) that includes questions about interesting, but irrelevant, topics. The fault with many instruments is that they have little relevance to the objectives of the study. Sometimes, exploratory studies do need to ask wide questions, but these should be clearly identified, and will probably be open-ended in nature. A common mistake, therefore, is forgetting the objectives.

Respondent abilities

Carefully developed materials are important because respondent abilities differ. The issue of knowledge and recall is a complex one and the process by which information is remembered has implications for the researcher. A respondent must:

- Understand what is required
- Be able to cooperate
- Be willing to cooperate.

Factors that make respondents forget include 'retroactive inhibition'—new information inhibits recall of previously memorised information. There is also 'proactive inhibition', whereby previously memorised information inhibits the memorisation of new things. Emotional factors also have an impact: positive emotion can help; negative emotion can inhibit. Psychoanalysts refer to 'repression', where respondents might avoid the recall of information that has unpleasant associations. The human memory is such that there is competition between similar events and, over time, forgetting increases as these different memories conflict with each other. This is known as 'interference theory'.

Another problem has been called the **telescoping effect**. This relates to remembering something from the distant past. To be more precise, it involves remembering an event as occurring more recently than it actually did. In questions of recall over a set period, it can lead to overclaims, because events that happened earlier than the required period are included. Research does confirm the notion that 'time flies when you are having fun'; it has been shown that after boring tasks, individuals think the task has taken longer than when they have completed tasks they enjoy (Coull *et al.* 2004). This has an implication if we are asking respondents to recall the last time they did something: the nature of the activities before the reporting period can affect the estimates given.

There are many reasons why responses may not be accurate. These include: *guilt*—a smoker may not admit to their habit; *social norms*—toothpaste use may be exaggerated; *low interest*—toilet paper use is not something that motivates a respondent (Menneer 1978).

'Stimulus material' is used to assist respondents when being interviewed. Such exhibits may be showcards, audio snippets, advertising jingles, photos, pictures, scales, lists, etc. They will help to 'prompt' respondents into recall. Too many showcards can be counterproductive. There are arguments that favour pictorial representation over verbal descriptions (Loosschilder *et al.* 1995, p. 32) and evidence to show that validity of respondent judgement increases with the realism of pictorial representations (Loosschilder and Ortt 1994). Problems with telephone surveys can be overcome by reading lists or sending material by mail, fax, or directly to a computer screen.

Supporting materials

The research instrument, whether a questionnaire or topic guide, is only one part of a data collection package that should include materials to help in the selecting and questioning of respondents, aids such as showcards, pictures, and some reward offered for cooperating. Examples of these are shown throughout this book.

A booklet of several pages should be created for all studies; this is known as the **interviewer instructions (or manual)**. An equivalent set of instructions should be created for the qualitative researcher. This explains how to select respondents and how to conduct the interviewing. It is particularly useful in settling queries that would otherwise clutter up the main research instruments. It often includes a summary of the particular market sector, for example a glossary of terms, along with a list of what to do and what not to do. It will include details of sampling, reminders, and likely problems.

A **quota sheet** is commonly issued to interviewers in order to keep a record of sampling progress and to assist in identifying appropriate respondents to complete the assignment.

The **recruitment questionnaire** contains very few questions; just the essential elements of the sample profile to allow correct recruitment. Often, this short questionnaire is the first part of the main questionnaire, whether by design or by being attached later.

Cover letters and cover emails are essential with self-completion questionnaires: they introduce, provide assurance, and they should motivate. They should be designed carefully, have just a few carefully chosen words, and be from a real person. With an email, the subject line must be chosen carefully; with a real letter, a signature increases the response rate. The formula for success for such messages is to include:

- A plea for help
- The topic of the study
- Reassurances
- How to do it (Instructions)
- Time needed
- How they will benefit.

Pre-notification letters may also be considered as a way of securing cooperation before receiving a phone or personal call.

An **'incentive'** is any device used to encourage respondents to answer or comply with a researcher's requests. Respondent underperformance (satisficing) can be reduced by careful motivation of the respondent, and also by eliminating difficulties from the research task; this might mean that an incentive of some sort may be considered. The researcher's dilemma is to decide whether the incentive brings about a biased type of cooperation and whether it is ethically correct.

Typical examples of incentives are a summary report or some other feedback of results. A pen is of low cost and is also practical because it forms the means with which to fill in a questionnaire. There may also be entries into competitions and prize draws. Money may be offered (or sent with a mail questionnaire); related to this is a gift (such as food or drink). Charity donations are a popular incentive because they appeal to the goodwill of the respondent and are likely to have no influence on the answers given (for a list of charities, see http://www.charitychoice.co.uk/categorysearch.htm). There are several studies on the usefulness of incentives for response rate. Church (1993) carried out a meta-analysis in this area and found that non-monetary incentives may increase response rate by over 7 per cent.

One would expect that the presence of a 'return envelope' should increase response rates for self-completion questionnaires. This simple device might have postage paid (or not) and, if it does, might carry a postage stamp, be freepost, or be prepaid. Each one can affect success of a postal survey. There is a belief that real postage stamps lead to a greater response. This seems to be because respondents see the stamp as money and are less likely to throw it away; in comparison, a freepost or pre-paid envelope is worthless.

Projective techniques

We can also elicit opinions and underlying feelings using various **projective techniques**. These offer a way of finding out about people through the use of association and allow respondents to express themselves in different ways. Ernest Dichter (1907–1991) is credited for introducing projective techniques to consumer research in the period 1940–1960 (DePaulo 1990, p. 4).

Projective techniques enable the informant to communicate things to the researcher. For this reason, they are sometimes known as 'enabling' techniques. They offer an alternative to direct questions, and allow us to open the respondent's mind to any topic in a very unique way.

Such techniques are often associated with qualitative research, but they can also be employed in quantitative studies, usually in the form of well-worded open-ended questions. Qualitative studies usually allow respondents to take time in considering responses and the researcher can spend more time eliciting responses.

Association

Several techniques that use 'free association' may be used. The procedure consists of eliciting words or some other reaction. Several stimuli may be used; they may be visual such as words on pictures, or even sounds.

'Word reaction' or word association involves presenting a list of words to the respondent; often these are read out. For example, the words may have been chosen as possible vocabulary to be used in future advertising. The respondent then reacts with his or her own word, which he or she may write down or say aloud. Any words that spring to mind for several respondents can then be analysed to discover whether there is a negative or positive impact on any planned campaign.

Association techniques can be used in both qualitative and quantitative research.

In picture association, a number of photos may be shown, typically from magazines, and respondents will be asked to relate them to the product or service being studied.

The inkblot test, popularised by Rorschach and Holtzman, is another form of picture association. Such tests involve previously created symmetrical 'ink pictures' being shown to respondents who, in turn, describe what they may signify. This technique has not been used to a great extent in marketing research.

Completion tasks

Several techniques require informants to provide information in order to complete various exercises. These exercises have been started and are clearly unfinished: for example, a sentence, or a longer set of phrases made into a short story. The completion may also be diagrammatic, in the form of a cartoon. Cartoon completion tasks typically feature one or more people and the caption from the speech or thought bubble is missing. The situation is likely to represent the topic of the study: for example, two characters may be looking at a product package. The respondent simply tries to guess what is being said, or thought.

In sentence completion, respondents are invited to complete a phrase. For example, *'I like my favourite brand of Cola because ...'* will result in some interesting reactions that can be subjected to further discussion. The procedure is carried out rapidly. This tempo helps to avoid overconsideration by the respondent and researchers argue that it uncovers thoughts respondents have, but are unable to articulate when questioned in traditional ways.

Completion tasks can be applied in a quantitative context. By example, to create a list of the dimensions of brand choice, Cowling (1973) showed that quantitative studies can be as effective as depth interviews. He used the following non-directive question on hundreds of respondents: *'What comes into your mind when you think about buying ...?'*.

Story completion differs from 'sentence completion' because respondents are encouraged to take time to consider how a story might continue. They may be invited to spend time to consider the opening paragraphs of a story and use visual aids to finish it. In a sales encounter, there may be an expectation that is not fulfilled by the service provider; such scenarios can identify steps that help match supply with desired demand. The thematic apperception test (TAT) involves showing photos and asking about each picture. It was developed by Christiana D. Morgan and Henry A. Murray.

Analogy

Analogy embraces various techniques: symbolic analogy, obituary, role-playing, personification, third person test, brand personalities, indirect questions and metaphor (see Table 6.3). The Oxford English Dictionary definition of 'metaphor' is useful here:

> A figure of speech in which a name or descriptive word or phrase is transferred to an object or action different from, but analogous to, that to which it is literally applicable; an instance of this, a metaphorical expression.

We can also draw a distinction between direct and indirect questions. We might ask a question directly, for example: *'Did you buy a loaf of bread yesterday?'*. Alternatively, we might ask an indirect question such as: *'Did your best friend take drugs yesterday?'*. The indirect method is high-risk because the respondent may not know the answer, but it does allow the probing of difficult subjects (such as drugs, personal issues) without asking the person concerned.

Respondent effort

Storytelling requires respondents to share small accounts about any experiences that are broadly related to an issue. The technique was used by Kimberly-Clark to help in the introduction of Huggies Pull-ups training pants, and by an outdoor-sports clothing company, to collect stories of extreme adventures for direct use in marketing (Leiber 1997). This technique is particularly popular with respondents because people like to hear stories: they

A collection of projective techniques

Association	
Word association	Image response, picture association
Completion tasks	
Sentence completion	Thematic apperception test
Story completion	Cartoon completion
Picture completion	Rosenzweig's Picture-Frustration Test, picture interpretation
Analogy	
Analogy	Symbolic analogy
Obituary	Role-playing
Personification	Third person test
Brand personalities	Indirect questions
Metaphor	Job interview
Techniques that require respondent effort	
Future scenario	Construction tasks
Fantasy	Psychodrama
Psycho-drawing	Brand mapping
Creative writing	Gaming
Guided dreams	Collage
Photo sorts	Pictured aspirations technique (PAT)
Storytelling	Photo and tale method
Postcard writing	Letter writing
Role-play	Friendly Martian
Protocol analysis	Network pictures
Graphology	

generally have a beginning, middle, and end, so they leave the storyteller and listener with a sense of accomplishment. Such stories may be amusing and therefore allow respondents to feel at ease, particularly in a group situation. The problem may be that there is a grey line between reality and fantasy, so respondents may exaggerate for effect.

A variation on storytelling, which is likely to be based on the past, is to use photographs or magazine cuttings. These can become a collage, which communicates something about the product under study. After the session, the collage remains and allows these unique expressions of opinion to be communicated to clients.

Postcard writing is another technique similar to storytelling, and can be very powerful. For example, postcards might be distributed to a group with the instruction: *'Write a postcard to the Prime Minister to say what he should do about the country'.* The person might instead be a supplier of foods, a manager, a subordinate, etc. The small space forces the respondent to think clearly and express views succinctly, and the cards become useful at analysis and presentation stages.

The 'photo and tale' method is a further variation of the storytelling technique. Here, respondents may be involved in the creation of photographs, which are then collected together into a form of collage with an accompanying story. This involves less emphasis on the past. The future can be probed by something that has been called **protocol analysis** (see Burns and Bush 2000, p. 252).

In 'protocol interviews', the respondent is asked to envisage a decision-making process. They might, for example, consider the purchase of a named item such as soap or a car. The respondent is required to go through the phases of the buying decision. This is the 'protocol' or account of the transaction. As an individual record, this is interesting, but compared with similar ones from other people this gives a valuable insight.

In the **pictured aspirations technique (PAT)**, several photographs are shown to the informant, and these are sorted to communicate aspirations (or hopes).

Brand mapping involves several steps. The first is to establish what features of a product offering are important to respondents; a full list of features is created and shown to respondents. The second step is to identify just two of the features that are important. These two features are now examined and, for each one, labels are created to establish a 'continuum'. For example, if price is chosen, we might have low price and high price as dimensions. This is done for the second feature and the two dimensions are put together as a large cross in front of respondents. Brand names will now be placed into this map; they are plotted to show their positions in the mind of respondents. Dimensions can be established qualitatively and measured accurately, in a quantitative way. Actually, a qualitative examination can provide good indications of the likely outcome of quantification.

The friendly Martian technique is popular. Here we imagine a person from Mars has come to Earth and we are acting as a friend. Everything we take for granted must be explained, so different situations are posed and respondents must explain them to the friendly Martian.

The shopping list typically presents respondents with two lists, identical but for one item, perhaps two competing brands. Respondents are asked to describe the two shoppers thereby giving an indication of what the brands mean to respondents.

Network pictures are visual representations of people involved in buying decisions, often used in business to business research. Any handwritten output can be subject to graphological analysis, for more on this refer to Bradley (2011).

Open-ended questions

The open-ended question can usefully be employed in both qualitative and quantitative research. The open question is exactly that—respondents can reply 'openly', in their own words. Those replies may be captured **verbatim** as handwriting (by the respondent or the interviewer), or as a script typewritten by the respondent or interviewer. In both cases, respondents use their own language.

Open-ended questions have the advantages of providing full answers and exploring issues that are new to the researcher. The open question often elicits responses of items or ideas overlooked by the researcher; it uncovers themes that were not expected. The disadvantages include misinterpretation and slow speed of asking and analysis. There can be problems in coding results—it is time-consuming and needs a great deal of skill.

The respondent is not given an option of possible answers. Indeed, the researcher may not have any indication about the possible answers to such a question. Three powerful open-ended questions that can be used for most topics concern what is good, what is bad, and what changes could take place. So, for example, we might ask these key questions in relation to a motor car: '*What do you like about your car? What do you dislike about your car? What improvements could be made to your car?*'.

These open-ended questions might be part of a self-completion questionnaire or of an interviewer-administered one. The researcher should be aware that these different techniques might elicit differing responses, either in length or nature.

In the example in Figure 6.1, space has been provided for the answer. Only three lines are provided. The space available is a cue to the person recording the answer. It may imply that a long answer is expected, or a short space may elicit one-word answers. One-word responses can be misleading: for example, the word 'speed' may imply fast or slow; the word 'price' can imply the correct price or a cheap price. Conversely, long, complete sentences may slow the interview process and cause questions to be answered badly later on.

The space available to each open-ended question manifests itself in various forms. For example, in a telephone interview it might be the time left for a respondent to reply; in a personal interview, the body language of the interviewer may be suggestive that time is short and that answers should be brief. On an Internet questionnaire, the 'box' available in which the

Q.1 What do you like about your car?

____

____

____

Q.2 What do you dislike about your car?

____

____

____

Q.3 What improvements could be made to your car?

____

____

____

Figure 6.1 Three open-ended questions

Common mistakes
Using yes/no questions

Respondents hate monotony. Good questionnaires use a variety of techniques to help answer the research question. Simple 'yes/no' questions will inevitably give poor data, but are easy to transform into a scale. The scale adds interest and will help to collect data that are rich in content and also can be subject to different types of analysis. On the other hand, a questionnaire full of closed questions may not give solutions to problems; some open-ended questions should be used. Three key open-ended questions (or variations adapted to the subject) can be used in any questionnaire: What is good? What is bad? What improvements might be made?

Generally speaking, open-ended questions within structured questionnaire forms are a valuable tool: they allow unknown areas to be probed effectively and included in the data collection. The disadvantage is that analysis can be time-consuming and inconclusive. Researchers are advised to attempt to investigate the areas and try to 'close' them, to provide pre-coded answers. Pre-codes allow analysis to take place efficiently. However, some research tasks mean that the researcher cannot anticipate likely replies; there may be no clear hypotheses ready and open-ended questions are extremely valuable. A good tip for self-completion questionnaires is to leave a full back page free and invite 'other comments' from respondents. This large space is a small gesture, but is rewarded with most interesting feedback.

respondent can type may be small or large, or may even expand to the amount of words used in the reply.

There is another aspect to open-ended questions that deserves consideration: the position of the open-ended question can affect the content of responses. This can be illustrated using the car example. It is possible that the preceding part of the questionnaire has covered such issues as seat comfort, engine efficiency, speed of service, reliability, and colours used, among other features. These aspects are clearly 'top of mind' for respondents because they have been under careful consideration just moments before the open-ended questions. It is therefore not surprising that these very features may be mentioned in the open-ended replies.

Closed questions

Closed questions have answers that are already determined. Wherever possible, answers to questions should be coded on the questionnaire to facilitate analysis; this is called pre-coding. Closed questions are ones from which the researcher feels able to anticipate the types of answer that may result from a given question. They can be disclosed to the respondent or they may not be given.

Closed questions that are disclosed may be spoken (e.g. in a phone interview), they may be made visible as a showcard (in a personal interview), they may be shown onscreen (for a web-based interview) or on a printed questionnaire (for a self-completion interview).

Ambiguous example 1
Are the recycling centres few and far? Yes or No?
This is asking two questions: firstly, 'Do you think there are too few centres?' and also, 'Are the centres far away?' It also assumes that the respondent has some knowledge.

Ambiguous example 2
Do you recycle or not? Yes 1
No 2

This is ambiguous because it asks two questions; additionally, the person may have recycled in the past but not now, and so the truth in the results will be hard to decipher.

Figure 6.2 Two examples of ambiguous questions

When pre-codes are not disclosed a question appears open-ended from the respondent's viewpoint, but it is not. Pre-codes will be examined and answers will be chosen by an interviewer. Answers may not be disclosed if they would be time-consuming to read or because the answer is obvious. Some questions lend themselves to being 'undisclosed'. For example, if a question asks, '*Did you travel by train yesterday?*', the answer will certainly be '*Yes*' or '*No*'. This is known as a 'dichotomous' question because it has two possible answers.

The advantages of closed questions are that they are fast to administer and easy to analyse. The disadvantages include the fact that, to develop the correct options, there needs to be a pilot survey, and error is inevitable when thoughts are summarised as single words. The designer should not use leading questions and must avoid ambiguous or double-barrelled questions (see Figure 6.2).

In designing interviewer-administered questionnaires it is important to decide whether to give the instructions SHOW CARD or READ OUT or DO NOT READ. If this is unclear some interviewers will read and others will not, and it will be impossible to know whether different answers are due to the method or are real differences in the marketplace.

The various types of closed question include administering 'lists' and 'scales'.

Lists

There is evidence to show that respondents may answer with early statements on any list. This is called **order effect** or **position bias**. Order effect can come into play if a particular question comes early or late in a questionnaire and it has also been found within a specific question. For example, with the benefit of a split sample, Benton and Daly (1991) reported that the overall quality of services in a local government survey were rated more favourably when the question was asked *before* questions on 12 specific services. Conversely, Barnes *et al.* (1995) found no order effect when the product ratings were made in a different order.

Rotation is a method used either to measure or to diminish the effect of order bias. Typically, lists of items will be 'rotated' during interviews, meaning that they may be shown (or spoken) in the given order for some of the interviews and in reverse order for others. The researcher can rotate the order of the questions so that the effect of order bias is dissipated across the results.

Some researchers argue for 'random' rotations, but these do not allow us to measure the effect of position. Others say that the rotations should be known, so that the effect can be measured and adjustments made in the analysis phase. Two typical rotations are:

- Reading a list of items in one order (forward) with the first respondent, then from the last item (backwards) for the next respondent, etc.
- Starting the list at item one for the first person, item two for the second, and so on.

To help interviewers to distinguish between rotations, different coloured paper is often used.

Scales

The 'scale' is a type of closed question. Scaling involves creating a continuum on which measured objects are located. The researcher must ensure that the scale descriptors do not bias results in any direction. For example, they might be worded in a way that gives a positive or negative view of a given brand.

Do not 'reinvent the wheel' by creating wording for scales; it is not useful to make up new ones on the spot. Look at the scales in Figure 6.3, which were made up by students in an exam. These are *not* good scales. Those in Table 6.4 show the range of those in common use.

Scales can be horizontal or vertical; they can be changed from words to numbers, or to pictures. Scales can have a neutral point or 'escape option', or respondents can be forced

Silly scale 1
Q How often do you recycle your household waste?

Never

Randomly

Often

Everyday

Always

Silly scale 2
Q Do you think this song is:

Really cool

Wicked

OK

Useless?

Silly scale 3
Q What do you think of the product?

No idea

Know very little about it

Excellent idea

Don't care about it

Figure 6.3 Some silly scales

Table 6.4 Itemised rating scales

Scale	Features	Example
Simple itemised rating scale	Limited number of ordered and labelled categories	Purchase intent, quality, frequency
Likert	Degree of agreement on a 1 (strongly disagree) to 5 (strongly agree) scale	Measuring attitudes
Semantic differential	Five- or seven-point scale with bipolar labels	Brand, product, and company images

to make a firm judgement about a topic. Research shows that the use (or exclusion) of this neutral point can affect replies (Nowlis *et al.* 2002). However, Nowlis *et al.* (p. 332) raise the question: '*Which of the two scales is likely to best reflect the underlying attitudes?*'. Other researchers offer the answer: for example, O'Muircheartaigh *et al.* (2000) evaluated data from the 1992 Eurobarometer survey and concluded that '*middle alternatives should be included in order to maximise data quality*'. Without the neutral point, they discovered acquiescence response bias.

Many scales have been developed for marketing applications and you are advised to consult existing scales and adapt them to your purposes. Table 6.4 shows three important categories of scale.

In the 1930s, the Likert scale was introduced. This 'summated rating scale' is associated with the American, Renesis Likert, and it takes his name. It is the type of question that asks: '*How much do you agree/disagree?*'. This is a rating scale used to measure the strength of agreement towards one or more clearly worded statements. The major advantage is that it is free from bias; scales used before this appeared to take a position—respondents may have felt constrained to share the value simply because the question was being asked. Likert scales helped avoid this by giving the respondent the opportunity to take other stances (see Table 6.5).

Likert scales are ordinal, but are commonly used with interval procedures, where there are five or seven categories. The midpoint of the scale is reserved to reflect an undecided position. Responses are tabulated and each attitudinal statement can be compared. The scale is rather simple (as shown in Table 6.6), but there are slight modifications in the wording and the last example, it might be argued, holds more in common with the **semantic differential scale**.

Osgood *et al.* (1957) developed the 'semantic differential scale'. This is a scale designed to measure the 'semantic space' of interpersonal experience. Respondents do not make an evaluation using numbers, nor do they read labels for individual rating points. Instead of numbers or words, they identify the 'position' of their answer on a line, or space between two descriptions. It was designed to measure the 'semantic space' of interpersonal experience.

Table 6.5 Simple itemised rating scales in common use

Excellent	Very true
Good	Somewhat true
Fair	Not very true
Poor	Not at all true
Very good	Definitely yes
Fairly good	Probably yes
Neither good nor bad	Probably no
Not very good	Definitely no
Not good at all	
Very important	Very different
Fairly important	Somewhat different
Neutral	Slightly different
Not so important	Not at all different
Not at all important	
Very interested	Extremely unique
Somewhat interested	Very unique
Not very interested	Somewhat unique, slightly unique
Uncertain	Not at all unique

The original **Osgood scale** was a series of seven-point bipolar rating scales. Bipolar adjectives anchor the beginning and end of the scale (e.g. good/bad, new/old). The mean or median is used to compare a product profile with competing products. It is widely seen to provide interval data, but critics say it is only ordinal because the weights are arbitrary.

The steps in questionnaire design

The procedures involved in questionnaire development apply to mail, telephone, personal, and computer-assisted interviews, but the mechanics for each differ. The stages of creating a questionnaire can be divided into distinct phases. Eight steps are as follows:

Table 6.6 Different Likert scale wordings

Different Likert scale wordings
Strongly disagree
Somewhat disagree
Undecided
Somewhat agree
Strongly agree
Strongly agree
Agree
Undecided
Disagree
Strongly disagree
Strongly agree
Agree
Neither agree nor disagree
Disagree
Strongly disagree

1. Formulate hypotheses
2. Choose collection method
3. List topics
4. Plan analysis
5. Draw a diagram
6. Lay out the form
7. Approve and pilot the form
8. Fine-tune the form.

Each of these steps will be examined more closely. It is important for the reader to bear in mind the fact that the steps may not always be followed in sequence. Indeed, the experienced researcher may create a questionnaire and use it immediately, thereby skipping all phases.

Step 1 Formulate hypotheses

Hypothesis-setting can vary from creation of a rigid set of statements to that of an informal list of questions needed to help understand the problem at hand. At this first step in

Common mistakes
One questionnaire for all purposes

The method of implementing a chosen questionnaire will dictate its style. A personal interview is rich: it benefits from the advantage of being able to show a respondent stimulus material. It can use showcards, packaging, and other materials. Over the telephone, there can be no visual stimulus material and possible answers need to be spoken clearly. A questionnaire that is delivered by post lacks control—stimuli are visible when the respondent opens the package. The online questionnaire offers many solutions but has no personal contact. These different questionnaires are like different rulers; they are measuring in a different way. If a study moves from one mode to another (for example, personal interview to telephone), there may be some changes in answers. These may be changes that are not real in the marketplace, but are simply a result of the way in which questions are posed. The mistake is, therefore, in thinking that the same questionnaire will suit all modes of data capture.

questionnaire design, the researcher is best advised to take a wide view and to generate numerous hypotheses to test. At this stage, it is perfectly acceptable for the wording to be raw and unrefined; it can be fine-tuned later in the process. For questionnaire development, an understanding of hypothesis wording can help in developing powerful questionnaires and the reader is advised to develop a full understanding of hypothesis-setting (see Chapter 2).

Step 2 Choose collection method

The choice of 'collection method' must take into consideration costs, timing, and sampling. It must also embrace the efficacy of the data capture options (personal, phone, self-completion) and mode (language, by computer, etc.). It should include decisions on incentives, interviewer briefing, and instructions. These areas are covered in Chapter 4 and are worth revisiting now. It must be stressed that the choice of data collection method dictates the appearance of the questionnaire, so design can progress only once this has been decided.

Step 3 List topics

The process of listing the topics forms the basis of the questionnaire. At this point, it is important to be fully aware of the different types of question available to the researcher.

Step 4 Plan analysis

It is a good idea to plan how the collected data will be processed at an early stage in questionnaire development. This simple step ensures that the questionnaire covers the necessary subject area. If more than 50 questionnaires are likely to need analysing, formal tabulations will be employed. At this stage, the researcher can usefully draw up a series of

Hypothesis to test

Question	H1	H2	H3	H4	H5	H6	H7
Q1			x	x			
Q2		x					
Q3	x	x			x	x	
Q4			x				
Q5							
Q6		x		x			
Q7					x		
Q8							x
Q9							x

Figure 6.4 How questions link to hypotheses

'blank' tables that show the major breakdowns and side-headings that will help to explore the aims of the study.

Consideration needs to be paid to the method by which the collected data are processed before the analysis can take place. Areas of specific concern will be whether the data will be input manually or by some other means (such as automatic scanning). The matter of 'coding' also needs to be considered.

If numerous hypotheses (or objectives) have been written, then the researcher may consider sketching out a grid showing how these hypotheses and the questions relate to each other. This is demonstrated in Figure 6.4 and identifies which questions support which hypotheses.

Step 5 Draw a diagram

A useful tool for planning questionnaires, topic guides, or any other instrument, is the diagram. Some researchers (see Brace 2004) feel comfortable using the flow chart as a planning tool, where a diagram shows the key pathway for the respondent answers. An example flow chart is shown in Figure 6.5.

An alternative is to use a radial diagram, sometimes known as a 'radial map'. Both the flow chart and the radial diagram offer a useful solution to planning a questionnaire document. We will examine the radial diagram.

Radial diagrams are sometimes known as 'cognitive nodes' or 'mind maps'. The mind map is associated with Tony Buzan who, in the 1960s, saw the usefulness of the technique. It is the visual representation of reality, where the facts or ideas are organised according to the impulses of the individual author, rather than in traditional or logical ways. The radial map is an effective planning tool because it allows the overall questionnaire to be viewed on one page. An advantage of this approach is that the order of questions in each section can be changed easily before writing the final questionnaire. Similarly, questions can be switched from one section to another, or entire sections can be moved.

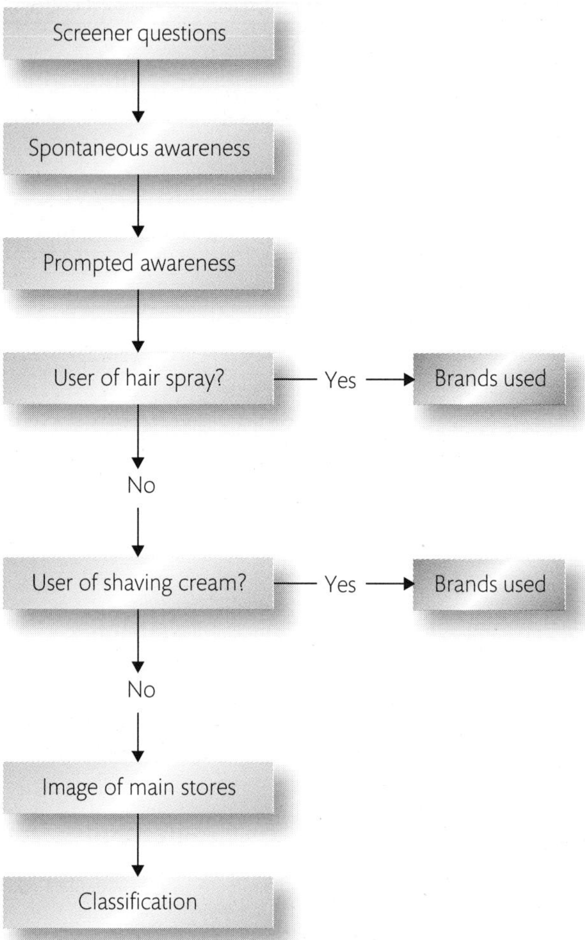

Figure 6.5 Flow chart example

Radial diagrams are easily created by hand; Microsoft Word software can also create them. Simply go to the 'Insert' menu, then to the 'Diagram entry', and select the term (radial diagram). Specialist software called 'Mind Manager' is also available at http://www.mindjet.com.

Here is a simplified example:

- First create six sections and in a clockwise direction, starting at the position of one o'clock, call them A, B, C, D, E, and F.

Section A will always be a screener (or introduction) and section F, a classification (see Figure 6.6).

Screener questions

Questionnaires must be introduced carefully to the respondent to ensure a high response rate. For self-administered questionnaires, this should take the form of a covering letter; for

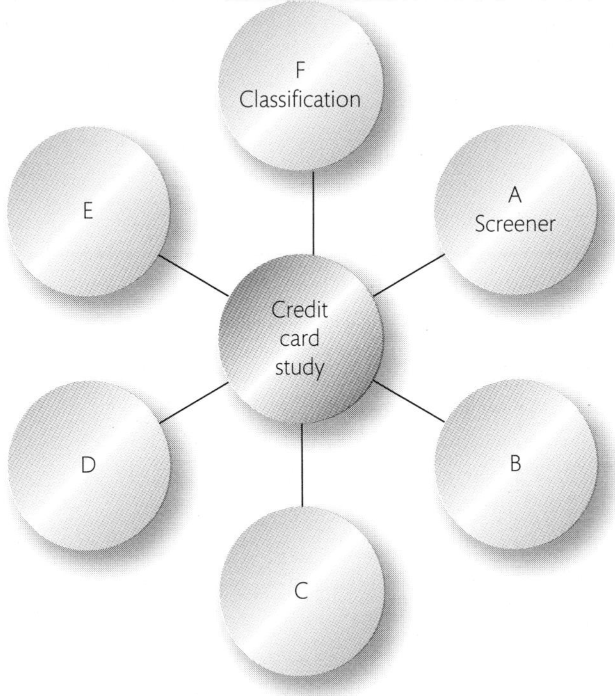

Figure 6.6 Radial diagram 1: Credit card study

interviewer-administered questions, this will be done by the interviewer following a script that is printed at the start of the questionnaire.

The introduction must explain who the researcher is and the topic of the study. Some mechanism must select the correct informant. Perhaps only users of a particular type of product or service are wanted. The introduction must be persuasive and it must qualify the respondent as someone who belongs in the sample.

Ethics comment

On web-based surveys, a *privacy statement* must be available so that respondents can see it. Extra windows can be used to explain why you want answers to specific questions such as those on income or other sensitive issues.

Poor instruments suffer if they have no form of filtering or **screener questions** at the start. No respondent should be interviewed if they are not needed. Similarly, the introduction should be neutral; it should not lead respondents towards a particular viewpoint and should be clear and simple. There is evidence to show that participation, and therefore response rate, is affected by the way questions are introduced; this is called the 'framing explanation' (see Gaskell *et al.* 1995).

An **exclusion screener** may be incorporated at this point. This is a question posed to determine if the informant, family, or friends work in specific occupations. An example might be: '*Do you or do any members of your family or close friends work in: advertising, marketing, journalism and market research?*'. If the answer is 'Yes', then the interview will not take place.

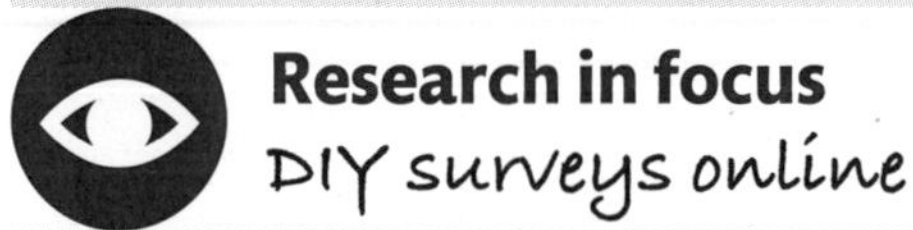

Research in focus

DIY surveys online

© istockphoto.com/German

When considering whether to carry out primary research, a company has two options: it can stay in-house or go to an outside agency. From the 1980s, several large multinationals were so confident in their ability to do their own research that they recruited their own interviewers and sold any spare capacity – ICI Paints was one. There are many reasons not to do research in-house: for example, respondents may be biased, people may not trust results and some companies have a policy to prohibit staff carrying out their own research. The in-house teams seem to have dissolved, but in the 1990s, DIY survey software arrived.

DIY survey software allows the researcher to create questionnaires using an easy template; effectively, this is a 'questionnaire wizard'. Email addresses belonging to customers or prospects can then be inserted into the software. At the touch of a button, email messages go to hundreds of respondents simultaneously. The recipient can link to the questionnaire from the message. This is an online survey and easily administered via the Internet. Many packages also allow immediate analysis of results; visual displays of data can be produced instantly.

Many of these services are free of charge, and the rest are certainly affordable. We now see that companies, large and small, are turning to this approach to conduct research. Reader's Digest supplies reading matter, music and financial services, and is a big user of research; the company sees 'DIY research' as an integral part of its business. Product managers in many companies, hard-pressed for results, will turn to DIY survey software. Suppliers tell us that their clients are household names such as Nike, Visa, Domino's Pizza and Gillette.

If you have a Google account you can produce a questionnaire online. Go to Google Docs and click on NEW. Then select FORMS from the drop down box. Here are a few commercial providers of these services along with their websites; most have free trials and instant demonstrations. As one claims, *'you can begin creating online surveys in minutes'*.

Advanced Survey	http://www.advancedsurvey.com/
CreateSurvey	http://www.createsurvey.com
Google Docs	http://docs.google.com
KwikSurveys	http://www.kwiksurveys.com
Make Survey	http://www.makesurvey.net
Market Sight	http://www.marketsight.com
Poll Daddy	http://www.polldaddy.com
Qualtrics	http://www.qualtrics.com
Survey Garden	http://www.surveygarden.com
Survey Gizmo	http://www.surveygizmo.com

Survey Professionals	http://www.surveypro.com
SurveyMonkey	http://www.surveymonkey.com/
ThesisTools	http://www.thesistools.nl
Vovici	http://www.vovici.com/personal.aspx
Web Surveys	http://web-online-surveys.com
Wufoo	http://www.wufoo.com/
Wysu Forms	http://www.wysuforms-en.com/
ZipSurvey™	http://www.zipsurvey.com
Zoomerang	http://www.zoomerang.com

Compiled by Nigel Bradley 2012.

Source:
Heeg, R. (2006) Do it yourself: are quick and cheap surveys harming the industry? *Research World*, February, pp. 14–16.

Questions

1 Why do you think traditional research agencies are now offering online solutions?

2 What quality control problems may be associated with using DIY services?

3 Visit some of the websites and try the demos or 'take the tour'. What are your impressions?

4 What are the alternatives to this software?

5 Can you use such services in your work?

Other occupations related to the topic under study may be added to this list. The idea behind this is to avoid news of this project reaching competitors and also to avoid answers that might not be typical of the target audience.

You should explain the likely interview length, describe the interview topic, and give respondents the right *not* to answer a specific question. Table 6.7 specifies some ways of encouraging respondents to answer different types of questionnaire.

Table 6.7 Tips to encourage respondent cooperation

Type	Tip
Online questionnaire	Use hyperlinks to help your respondent
Postal questionnaire	Use a cover letter and enclose a return envelope
Drop-and-collect questionnaire	Use a collection box
Personal questionnaire	Alert respondents beforehand
Telephone questionnaire	Agree a convenient time to phone back

Classification questions

The last section of the questionnaire is related to the first because it seeks information about the individual and their home or work. You may find that you move some information from the start of the form to the end (and vice versa). The introduction will help in selecting the correct respondent. This last part helps to confirm that the sampling was successful. It is also a method for identifying differences of key results in response between subgroups such as sex and age. It almost always includes demographics about the household, that is aspects such as family size and income. Some questions may have been used in the introduction to screen people.

Demographics or 'classifiers' are needed for analysis. Standard demographics include age, sex, and social grade. Non-standard demographics are common to all studies, but less well used, for example cars in household, ethnicity. Other demographics are specific to the topic under study, for example lapsed users, number of years subscriber. Finally, we can combine items. These can only be created after data collection by dissecting and adding items together, for example females who are AB with two cars—'sagacity' groups are a known example. It is the researcher's task to choose the classifications that promise the most meaningful tabulations. From a marketing point of view, they are the first process in segmenting the market.

Asking **classification questions** about a respondent's age, sex, occupation, or income can result in several reactions. Respondents may feel suspicious about the research, may refuse to participate, or may not tell the truth. For this reason, they are known as 'sensitive' questions. The questionnaire writer must be aware of these and should position demographic questions in such a way that any of these reactions are minimised. If most of these questions are at the end, the effects will be minor. At that point, it is likely that the respondent will feel comfortable with the research. If not, there are no subsequent questions, so there will be no negative effect from refusal or lying.

An example of deliberately giving wrong information was evident from the UK census: women were encouraged to be honest about their age in the 1951 census because previous results carried some inaccuracies. There was a suggestion that women had adjusted their age upwards if they had married young and down if they had married later in life.

Asking about family members also falls into this category of question. There are many reasons why respondents may provide the *wrong* replies. These include: pretending someone is in the house for security or tax reasons, the desire to have children, a wish to *disown* misbehaving children, sincerely underestimating how long members are at home, etc.

Educational qualifications have changed over time: A levels have not always been with us (and may disappear); perceptions of quality of university degrees vary and therefore questions may be difficult to create. We can talk of terminal education age (TEA), which may help analysis, or we can be specific about respondents.

- Second, add section titles (see Figure 6.7). A good tip is to use the study objectives to divide up sections.
- Third, add screener information from sampling design and jot in rough ideas of questions to ask (see Figure 6.8). These are based on the objectives.

The main body consists of questions that cover information needed to solve the marketing problem. It will make the best use of scales. The topics include facts, opinions and attitudes, motives, and possible future behaviour. Factual questions include ownership, buying behaviour, and media exposure. Questions may measure opinions and attitudes about products, firms, and advertising. There is also the measurement of motives and intentions. The positioning of the

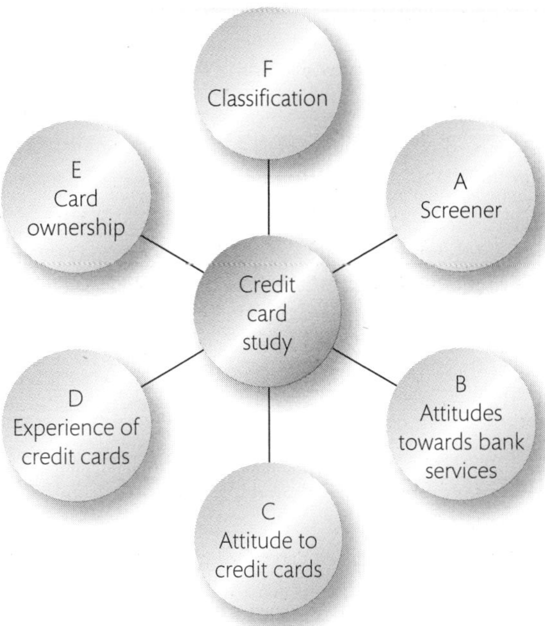

Figure 6.7 Radial diagram 2: Credit card study

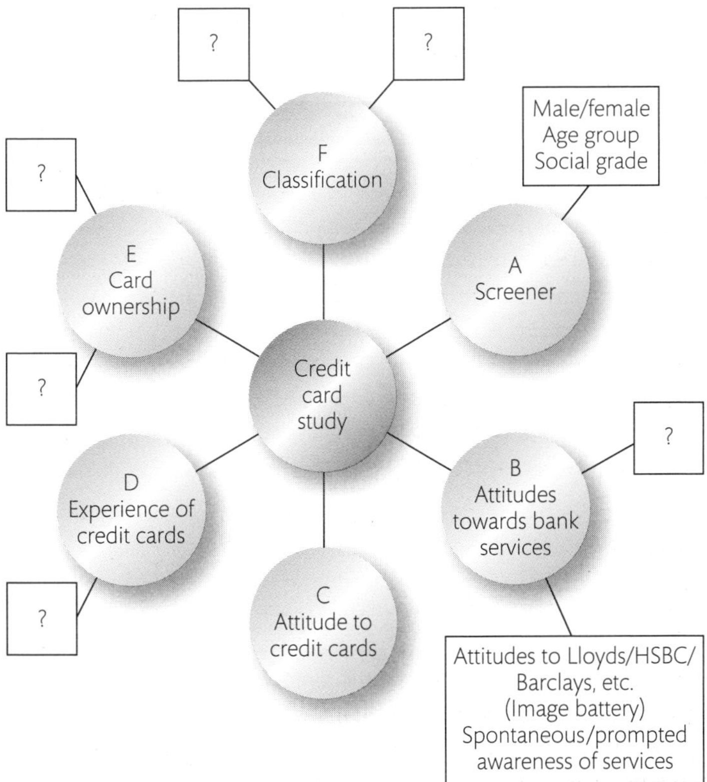

Figure 6.8 Radial diagram 3: Credit card study

questions must be examined carefully to help recall, but also to avoid bias caused by position. For this reason, some scales and sections may be varied (or rotated) from interview to interview.

A way to minimise the number of irrelevant questions posed to a respondent is to use filters. The respondent can be 'routed' to a suitable question. The technique can be used in all types of questionnaire; the computer-assisted personal interviewing (CAPI)/computer-assisted telephone interviewing (CATI)/computer-assisted self-completion interviewing (CASI) solutions allow it to be most sophisticated, whereas the postal questionnaire needs to keep it simple (for example, '*if yes, go to Q5*'). There are two benefits: one is timing, the other is minimising respondent irritation. Both contribute to a higher response rate.

Step 6 Lay out the form

Write out the questionnaire (or topics) in a linear way. Start new sections on new pages to allow related questions to be viewed together easily.

The progression of any interview should be fluent; there should be a good flow. The step of laying out the questionnaire form involves a careful wording of each question and a thoughtful choice of the sequence used. At this stage, the researcher needs to be aware of the questions and words that the chosen respondent will find neutral; there are also issues that may cause some type of reaction.

Some words may cause informants to react positively or negatively and the researcher must anticipate what these are. This understanding can allow the researcher to order the questions in such a way that respondents cooperate fully.

Integrity questions help to check the consistency of both respondent and fieldworker. Two such devices can be incorporated into questionnaires to assist with validity and reliability: **sleeper questions** and **cheater questions**. The sleeper question is one that is used to decide whether a respondent is giving incorrect answers (either by guessing or misleading). Conversely, the cheater question is embedded in a questionnaire to detect interviewers who may not be following the required procedures (either deliberately or through negligence).

The physical appearance of the questionnaire is important. In self-completion questionnaires the colour chosen for the questionnaire may affect whether a questionnaire is completed and returned. The effect is not fully understood; it appears to be linked to impact and visibility among other papers on the respondent's desk. A questionnaire printed on yellow paper is hard to lose under a busy desk, and this may lead to a greater level of cooperation. Response rate improvement is the main reason why colours other than white are chosen. Fox *et al.* (1988) put the increased response rate at 2 per cent. Additionally, the researcher can use typeface size, colour, and font to good effect. Conversely, a form that appears complicated can be damaging to response rates.

Colour can also be used to help the interviewer, both on paper or onscreen. For example, if there are different sections to a questionnaire, colour coding can help the interviewer to navigate the materials. If a similar questionnaire is used for different respondent types, then one type might be allocated to yellow, another to pink, etc.

For CATI, CAPI, and computer-assisted web interviewing (CAWI) questionnaires it is likely that professional web page designers may be involved or that so-called DIY software is used. In both these cases the researcher must be cautious, as the software solution may compromise the original intention. Pay particular attention to routes and filters.

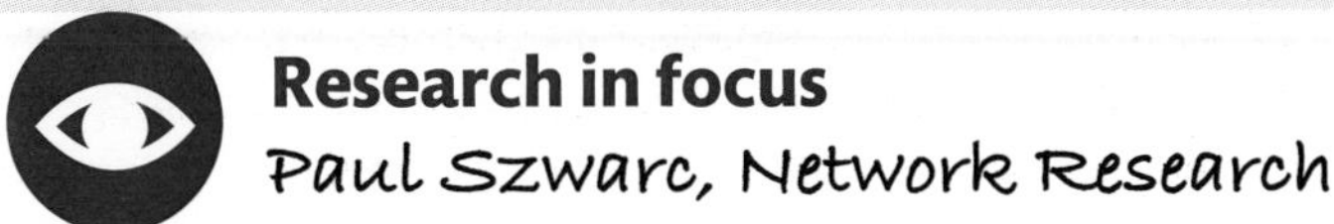

Paul Szwarc from Network Research has the following to say about questionnaires.

A client will say what they want to have covered in their survey. You will convert it into a questionnaire, into language that the consumer will understand. You send it back to the client. You say *'here is the questionnaire we are proposing'*, and because it hasn't got any of their jargon in it, they say that they don't understand what we are doing...

To give you an example, the client might talk about 'distribution channels', whereas a customer would talk about 'access channels'. The customer takes the stance: *'I want to talk to this company by telephone or writing'*. So the questionnaire is written as ways of accessing the company; the company are looking at it as ways they might be distributing their products and services.

Compiled by Nigel Bradley 2012.

Source:
Paul Szwarc, interviewed by Nigel Bradley July 2003.

Step 7 Approve and pilot the form

It is at Step 7 that the researcher should seek full approval from the client. With pen and paper questionnaires (sometimes known as PAPI) this does not pose a problem; they are self-explanatory. However, with computer-assisted questionnaires (CAPI, CATI, and CAWI) the way a questionnaire works may be unclear because the working is hidden inside the software. It does need to be clear—one solution is to create the questionnaire as a respondent would see it but then have a column on the right to explain what happens to the software. This type of instruction is needed when communicating with web designers anyway.

Before a questionnaire is used in the *real* survey, it should be tested well; this is called a 'pilot test' or a 'pretest'. Respondents in a pilot test should be similar to those that will be included

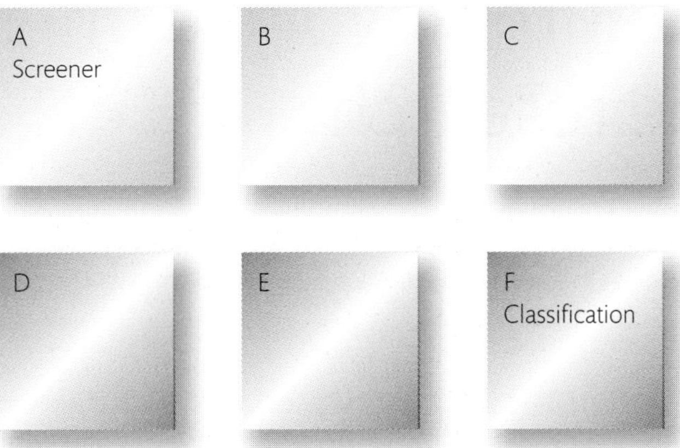

Figure 6.9 Laying out the form

in the actual study. They are likely to be familiar with the topic. The test may be informal, involving trying out the draft on friends, or formal, involving using hundreds of interviewees; this depends on the importance of the study. It is always good advice for the research team to be part of the pilot interviews, if only as an interviewer.

There are distinct phases to the pilot. First of all, the researcher will conduct the interview. Second, another interview will take place with the same respondent to discuss what he or she was thinking, intending, or understanding. Finally, when all pilots are conducted, a debrief meeting will be held with the research team. Further piloting may be necessary. An alternative method is to ask a respondent to 'speak his/her mind' during the interview; this 'thinking aloud' can help to capture the reaction at the moment a question is asked because it may be forgotten later.

Sometimes notes are taken or a debrief questionnaire form is created; sometimes researchers find that tape recording of pilot interviews is useful for later analysis and debate within the research team. Typical issues are: Do respondents understand the questions? Does the routing work? Does the wording need changing? Do the pre-codes cover the real situation?

Piloting is the best way to see whether a questionnaire is working as expected. The pilot test may also test the sampling procedures, fieldforce, and other resources.

Step 8 Fine-tune the form

The questionnaire should now be ready for use in the field. Interviewers should carry out 'dummy interviews'. These are intended to make them familiar with the questionnaire and are part of their training. They are not included in the analysis and there will be no feedback to the researcher, therefore dummy interviews are not pilot interviews. At this point, it is worth considering who is the rightful owner of the questionnaire. The ICC/ESOMAR Code of Conduct states that the questionnaire is the property of the client, if that client has paid for it to be developed.

The Market Researcher's Toolbox 'Checklist for questionnaires' can be used as a guide to check whether your questionnaire is 'fit for purpose'. After honestly answering each question carefully, inspect why you answer 'No' for some questions.

Procedures involved in online research

Computer-assisted web interviewing is simply a questionnaire that appears as a set of web pages to be answered by Internet users. Computer-assisted web interviewing questionnaires require extremely careful design. Here we have unique features which are described in Table 6.8.

Progress indicators

Respondents should be told the length of time a questionnaire will take (in minutes) at the outset. This is a calculation that should be made from pilots of the questionnaire. Online

Table 6.8 Essential features of the web questionnaire

Feature	Description and example
Invitations	Email or pop-up window Carefully composed email with hyperlink or pop-up window. See examples in the section above called *Populations and sampling*
Filtering, routing and piping	The ability to skip questions. Screening questions. Filters change the route through the questionnaire to meet a respondent's profile. To select the correct language simple selection at the top of the first screen changes the questionnaire language. Not visible to respondents but routes MUST be documented so other researchers and clients understand the questionnaire. [DE | EN | ES | FR | IT | NL | PT]
Progress indicators	Page numbers, percentages, visual progress bars. Page 2 of 5 or 10% complete (see examples in the text below) [70% completed]
Forward button	A click takes the respondent to the next question. Some survey software avoids this option
Radio buttons	Circular, only one can be selected (single code) Yes or No Likert scale Should not be preset because respondents may not respond [Are you a member of any other airlines' frequent flyer schemes? ○ Yes ○ No]
Check boxes	Square, several can be selected (multi-code). Newspapers read Should not be preset because respondents may not respond
Reminder emails	Sent if the first invitation to participate did not work. A common mistake is to send this to all people, it is easy but lazy. This is irritating to respondents who have already replied and in total has a cumulative effect to erode goodwill towards online surveys.

questionnaires allow the average time taken to be calculated after each interview is completed, therefore the latest average can be inserted into the invitation or introduction. Furthermore, it is good practice to give an indication of the progress during the interview itself and progress bars allow this to be done easily and effectively. Most survey software offers the facility. The best progress bars do not clutter the page and give respondents the information at a glance. Progress bars can be positioned at the top or bottom of the page. The advantage at the top of the page is that it can encourage the respondent to attempt this new question in the knowledge that the task is nearly complete. The following example bars show different approaches, moving from the most basic to the examples with greater precision.

PROGRESS

Basic progress bar (no percentages, has page numbers)

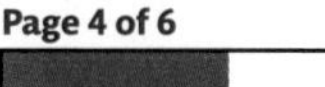

Basic progress bar (no percentages, has page numbers)

0% 100%

Basic progress bar turns round the 'barber shop' effect (has percentage numbers at extremes)

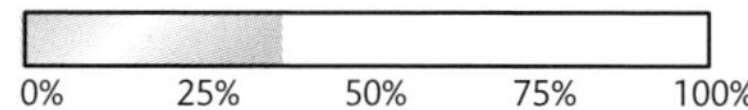

Static progress bar with percentage and with numbers that imply precision

89%

Static progress bar with percentage and with precise numbers

Progress:

Static progress bar with no percentages, no precise numbers but 'bits' that show the position (Note how the colour is dark and turns to pale)

More advanced features of web questionnaires include those outlined in Table 6.9.

Computer-assisted mobile interviewing (CAMI) is a lesser known approach and is simply a series of questions that appear as several consecutive text messages on a mobile phone to be answered by cell phone users. These responses are sent to a researcher, then another question is immediately sent. As replies are received, results are collated for display to the researcher and client in the form of a dashboard. In terms of design, CAMI poses greater challenges than CAWI because the text message does not allow much space or creativity. Where a CAWI screen should not exceed 50 words,

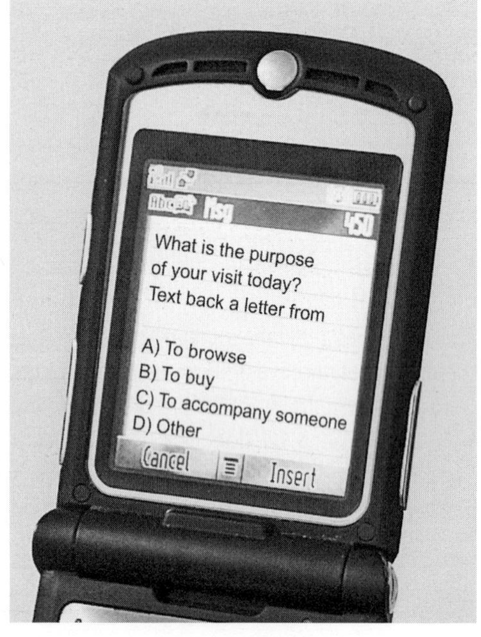

Table 6.9

Optional features of the web questionnaire

Feature	Description and example
Back button	A click allows respondent to see last question. Not recommended on any questionnaire. May be seen when the respondent must return to change a previous question (discovered through automatic edits or discovered through piloting)
Drop-down menu	Hidden text is revealed; only one item can be selected (single code). Your country. Should not be preset because respondents may not respond **Which country/region/territory are you in right now?** --Please select-- --Please select-- UK Ireland Other European country (excluding the UK and Ireland) USA Canada South & Central America Australia & New Zealand India Middle East Asia (excluding India) Africa Other
Free text input	Open-ended answer to accept words and numbers. A maximum number of characters can be specified. Improvements to the brand. Word clouds can be created from the answers If you would like to add any other comments on your journey experience with British Airways, please type in the space below, and we will forward them for you. ☐ No comment
Number box	Open-ended to accept numbers only. A minimum and maximum number of characters can be specified. Year of birth
Slider bar	Visual scale to capture respondent answer between two extremes (single code). Semantic differential scale; estimates of percentage Place your cursor over the branch to display the frequency Your local branch 3 Local/regional events 3 CM National Events – e.g. Annual National Conference Very dissatisfied

Table 6.9 Optional features of the web questionnaire (Continued)

Feature	Description and example
Repositioning effects	The sequence of lists can be changed into forward or reverse order. This can allow order effect to be measured. The sequence can become random to 'dilute' order effect. Adjectives to describe your attitude towards your supermarket
Grid	Tabular answer space incorporating any of the features above. Stating if product used (radio button), then brand used (drop-down menu), then satisfaction level (slider bar). Grids can lead to incomplete questionnaires if seen as a complex task

a CAMI screen should not exceed 25 words. The picture below shows the typical screen that faces the mobile phone respondent.

The topic guide (for qualitative studies)

Consider two types of topic guide: one is highly structured, with rough timings for each section and very specific questions; the second guide is merely a checklist of agreed areas. The most structured one is the closest to the quantitative questionnaire. The steps of topic guide design are:

1. **Examine the research question.** Poor topic guides do nothing more than repeat the research question in different words; good guides examine the issues from many angles.
2. **List topics of interest.** Avoiding questions on the respondent's personal situation is wrong because this can bear on the problem and will assist in subsequent analysis. Good discussion guides include checklists of most items likely to emerge. They include background questions (age, family, etc.), but also directly ask about the area of investigation; context can be important for any problem. This 'halo' or 'indirect' aspect can be alien to goal-oriented researchers who have mastered questionnaire writing.
3. **Develop a list of relevant ideas and create a list of relevant vocabulary.** You may need to consult experts and secondary data.
4. **Decide on projective/elicitation techniques.** Any projective or elicitation techniques, such as stimulus material, should be mentioned and fully explained on the discussion guide. These are likely to draw out different responses and clients should be aware of their use. They might be as simple as a poster, or as sophisticated as a TV advert.
5. **Lay out the guide.** Good topic guides follow some logic—this logical progression should help the researcher to memorise the subject areas. Unlike the questionnaire, the form

Ethical insight
Your secret weapon may not be so secret

Old questionnaires are extremely important. A study can be repeated using the same wording so that comparisons can be drawn. Within the same organisation, this does not usually give rise to a problem. However, it becomes complicated when dealing with **multiclient studies** and for studies where project ownership is unclear.

If you know the name of the research agency, you can ask them for the questionnaire, but they may tell you that it is the property of their client. Indeed, the ICC/ESOMAR Code of Marketing and Social Research Practice states that the questionnaire is the property of the client, if that client has paid for it to be developed (item 21c). If the project was initiated by the agency, the questionnaire may belong to that agency.

If we look at the MRS Code, rule B50, we see that MRS members *'must comply with reasonable requests to make available to anyone the technical information necessary to assess the validity of any published findings from a research project'*. This has implications about the use of results. If they are intended to be communicated widely, even just in part, then you must be prepared to show questionnaires and other instruments from behind the scenes.

A curious problem arises if a Freedom of Information request is made for information about research conducted by public authorities. Such a request may bring research instruments and results into the public domain even though they were not intended for the public. This is an interesting dilemma.

This moves us into copyright laws, which are extremely complicated. Here, a suitably qualified legal advisor should be consulted.

In discussing 'old questionnaires', we must make it clear that actual completed questionnaires contain personal data that cannot be shared with anyone. If the respondent has not consented for their data to be shared, doing so would be a breach of the Data Protection Act 1998.

Compiled by Nigel Bradley 2012.

Sources:
ESOMAR Code, rule 21c, http://www.esomar.org
MRS Code, rules B14 and B50, http://www.mrs.org.uk/standards/codeconduct.htm

Questions

1 What are the uses of old questionnaires and who owns them?

2 Why might someone not want others to see their questionnaire?

3 Why do some people want others to see their questionnaires?

does not need to be complete; it can contain bullet points and look 'unfinished'. It is an aide-memoire for the researcher and will not be seen by the respondent. The structure will have introduction, discussion, and closure sections. The introduction section is the opening part of the interview; the discussion section comprises the main part of the interview; the closure section brings the interview to a close.

Quasi-questionnaires

There are other instruments that are questionnaires or topic guides in a slightly different format. These include comments cards, diaries, and observation forms. We have called these 'quasi-questionnaires' because they are almost questionnaires.

Suggestion cards

Suggestion cards or comments cards are left on hotel beds or in the reception areas of service organisations, on restaurant tables, sometimes inserted with a mailing (perhaps an invoice; see Figures 6.10 and 6.11). On the face of it, comments cards are used to monitor satisfaction, but the scales are often poorly planned and the usefulness of such devices is dubious. They tend to be completed by a self-selected sample of people who for some reason decide to cooperate. They may have very positive or very negative views. Perhaps the major benefit, however, is that a consumer feels that the hotel is responsive to customer needs and is trying to build a relationship (see McDaniel and Gates 2001, pp. 285–286).

The diary

A diary is an autobiographical record that can be used in both qualitative and quantitative research. The word 'diary' has its origins with the Latin word for day ('*dies*'), which helps us to remember that the diary records something on a daily basis. Most diaries are created for each of the seven days of the week.

We're Listening!

Do you have a complaint or suggestion?

Date Time

Location

Was your stay:

Very good Good Fair Poor Very poor

Why?

Your name
& contact details

Please leave this card at reception

Figure 6.10 Suggestion card ('We're listening!')

RESTAURANT REVIEW

"We are committed to providing hot fresh food with fast efficient friendly service in clean and pleasant surroundings"

Please take a minute to review our restaurant and tell us how we measure up to the above statement. When you've completed this form, please place it in the comment box. Thanks for helping us to improve our service.

PLEASE TICK	VERY GOOD	GOOD	FAIR	POOR	VERY POOR
SERVICE	☺	☺	😐	☹	☹
FOOD	☺	☺	😐	☹	☹
STAFF COURTESY	☺	☺	😐	☹	☹
CLEANLINESS	☺	☺	😐	☹	☹
VALUE FOR MONEY	☺	☺	😐	☹	☹

DATE OF VISIT________________ **TIME OF VISIT**________________

COMMENTS

*How can we serve you better in the future?*________________

*What would make you return more frequently?*________________

What additional facilities would you like to see at this restaurant in the future?

Please write here any further comments or suggestions you may have (especially if you feel strongly about any of the above subjects).

How often do you visit our Restaurants?

Daily ☐
Weekly ☐
Monthly ☐
Infrequently ☐

Please tick

Male ☐
Female ☐
Age Group
12–15 ☐
16–24 ☐
25–34 ☐
35+ ☐

Please speak to the Restaurant Manager if you wish to discuss your comments further, or alternatively call CUSTOMER SERVICES on * *********

Figure 6.11 Restaurant review card

In qualitative research, a diary may cover as little as a day; some may go on for years. They usually take the form of open-ended accounts of events and feelings. This is in contrast to quantitative diaries, where the emphasis is on recording behaviour rather than the feelings of the individual.

In quantitative marketing research, most diaries cover seven days, often in periods of one hour or less. After the seven days, the task is complete. Research results are then analysed for each day. In a quantitative context, where numerous respondents are sampled over a full year, results might be made available that relate to every day of the year. The results can be amalgamated to show activity by the week, month, quarter, or full year. Such diaries are preprinted and allow respondents to give a simple tick or mark with a pen.

If designed properly, the diary will avoid any errors resulting from forgetting or confusing facts. The so-called telescoping effect is avoided. The diary is particularly useful in panel research because, after initial instruction, the respondent will need little or no further assistance in the task. Another advantage comes from the solitary nature of the exercise; without another person present, respondents are able to express themselves and admit their behaviour, however embarrassing. Diaries are often returned to the researcher by post, which reinforces confidentiality. The diary is usually designed to be portable and so stands a good chance of being completed soon after an event, thereby contributing to its accuracy.

There are several disadvantages to the diary. First, the diary relies on the commitment of the writer—not everyone is able or willing to complete one. The researcher has very little control over the respondent and so the physical design of the diary and the instructions must motivate. Some incentive may be offered. In the case of household diaries, where one person records on behalf of others, there may be problems of misreporting; there may also be gaps in information. The nominated respondent may be unaware of some activities conducted by other household members.

Sometimes, the early days of a respondent's reporting are not consistent with the behaviour of that respondent and the records may therefore be invalid. Depending on the study, a decision may be made to reject these early readings. Conversely, attrition may be a problem; respondents may reach a point where they are tired of the tasks required to fill in the diary. This may lead to poor records and gaps. This may also result in 'dropout', whereby a certain number of respondents do not submit their diaries at all. Clearly, this may pose problems for representation, and needs to be considered from the outset. Incentives are often used to combat dropout.

Keeping a diary can affect behaviour. It is inevitable that the diary-keeper will reflect on the information that has been collected. As an example, this reflection may lead the respondent to reduce consumption. The change in consumption may then be shown in the diary, but it would not have occurred if the diary had not been used.

Sometimes respondents are recruited as part of a panel, and cooperation may be continuous. Nevertheless, it is usual for 'rest periods' to be built into the study. If long-term diaries are created, design must be modified to accommodate new situations. New products or new ways of packaging a product may be introduced. Therefore, the diary must be open to modification. Modification can affect results and a form of 'pilot' is recommended. In common with the self-completion questionnaire, the designer of the diary must consider: length, size, colour, and spacing.

Technology has allowed us to create electronic versions of the diary; the 'blog' is a good example. Portability is so essential to the diary. Helping with portability we have seen the emergence of the smartphone, the PDA, the notebook; even smaller is a wristwatch device, which can help monitor respondent behaviour.

The applications of the diary in marketing research include those that assist in product placement, shopping behaviour, travel monitoring, and media exposure.

Observation forms

The structure of the observation form is similar to that of the diary and the self-completion questionnaire. The difference is that observation forms are primarily designed to be answered by a researcher rather than by a respondent or informant. The form is there to make a record of observations.

Observation forms must make it clear who and what is to be recorded. It is useful for the research objective to be evident, so that incidental, but relevant, events are recorded. In structured observation, 'closed' questions will predominate, whereas a less structured approach (for example, in qualitative research) will tend to include open-ended questions.

The researcher must remember that the form is in the field. Therefore, practicalities such as size, ease of use, discretion, and weather must be considered.

The example in Figure 6.12 is a manual register of people and vehicles entering various petrol stations in the UK. Quantitative analysis can be made by hour, day, location, and people. There is nowhere to record the possible reasons for entering; petrol stations provide many services besides fuel. The large space for entries is there to accommodate 'tally marks', which become five-bar gates. You will note that the observer counts people for a few minutes, then vehicles for the next few minutes. This is to provide variety and to minimise observer error. The task requires concentration, so a rest period is built in too.

Chapter summary

1 Explain the purposes of questionnaires and topic guides

Carefully developed materials are important because respondent abilities differ. The issue of knowledge and recall is a complex one and the process by which information is remembered has implications for the researcher. Factors that make respondents forget include retroactive inhibition, proactive inhibition, and emotional factors. Repression can lead respondents to avoid the recall of information with unpleasant associations. These aspects and others have implications.

2 List the supporting materials used by researchers

In quantitative research, an obvious research tool is the questionnaire. The topic guide is a qualitative research instrument. There are variations on the questionnaire and topic guide, which include comments cards, diaries, and observation forms. Supporting materials include interviewer instructions, sampling sheets, recruitment questionnaires, cover letters, incentives, and return envelopes. Stimulus material is used to assist respondents when being interviewed. Such exhibits may be showcards, audio snippets, advertising jingles, photos, pictures, scales, lists, etc.

3 Explain the nature of projective techniques, questions and scales

Projective techniques offer a way of finding out about people through the use of association and allowing respondents to express themselves in different ways. Such techniques are often used with qualitative research, but they can also be employed in quantitative studies in the form of well-worded open-ended questions. Techniques include association, completion tasks, analogy, and techniques that require respondent effort. There are many types of questions, the open-ended and closed question being the most evident. Behind these headings we find leading questions, integrity questions, double-barrelled questions, probing questions, ones that reveal possible answers, others that do not. Scales are a sophisticated form of closed question whereby respondents are able to offer a degree of attitude or opinion rather than a simple yes and no.

J. 2870 BODY COUNTS

DAY	( )
Wednesday....	1
Thursday........	2
Friday............	3
Saturday.........	4
Sunday...........	5
Monday..........	6
Tuesday..........	7

SHIFT	( )
8 – 2.30pm..........	1
2.30 – 9pm..........	2
Date: / /	

	( )
Tewkesbury.........	1
Chippenham........	2
Reading................	3
Oxford...................	4
Milton Keynes......	5
Malvern.................	6

INT. NAME: ______________________ No ☐ • ☐☐☐☐

TIME	WHAT TO COUNT	NUMBER
8.00 – 8.04	Bodies entering	
8.04 – 8.08	Vehicles entering	
8.08 – 8.12	Bodies entering	
8.12 – 8.16	Vehicles entering	
8.16 – 8.20	Bodies entering	
8.20 – 8.24	Vehicles entering	
8.24 – 8.28	Bodies entering	
8.28 – 8.32	Vehicles entering	
8.32 – 8.36	Bodies entering	
8.36 – 8.40	Vehicles entering	
8.40 – 8.44	Bodies entering	
8.44 – 8.48	Vehicles entering	
12 MINUTES BREAK		
9.00 – 9.04	Bodies entering	
9.04 – 9.08	Vehicles entering	
9.08 – 9.12	Bodies entering	
9.12 – 9.16	Vehicles entering	
9.16 – 9.20	Bodies entering	
9.20 – 9.24	Vehicles entering	
9.24 –9.28	Bodies entering	
9.28 – 9.32	Vehicles entering	
9.32 – 9.36	Bodies entering	
9.36 – 9.40	Vehicles entering	
9.40 – 9.44	Bodies entering	
9.44 – 9.48	Vehicles entering	

Figure 6.12 Observation form

4 Create a questionnaire and topic guide

The preparation of questionnaires and topic guides is related: both should be planned carefully and follow a sequence that is logical from the respondent's point of view. Similarly, objectives are fully covered in both and projective techniques can be used for either. Both should feature some form of screener and introduction, the main questions and also classification questions (often at the end). Beyond this there are important differences: in the questionnaire, each word must be written (and delivered) extremely carefully; scales may be used and the questionnaire should be piloted. Topic guide questions may be modified at the interview and the document takes the form of bullet points. Questionnaires may be used face-to-face, on the telephone, or as self-completion methods, and this choice changes their design and appearance. A useful tool for planning questionnaires, topic guides, or any other instrument is the diagram. Both the flow chart and the radial diagram offer a useful way to plan. They allow the overall instrument to be viewed on one page and the order and content of questions can easily be changed before writing the final document. The best advice about design is to answer many questionnaires, to collect examples, and then to take any opportunity to practise writing questionnaires and topic guides.

Review questions

1 What three skills should researchers master in relation to questionnaires?
2 Define retroactive inhibition.
3 Why are interviewer instructions important?
4 What are projective techniques and how can they be used by quantitative researchers?
5 Why is piloting important for questionnaires but not for the topic guide?
6 Why are scales so important?
7 Create a simple questionnaire to determine why buyers of soup choose particular can sizes.

Discussion questions

1 For what reasons may we decide not to use a questionnaire?
2 Start a collection of questionnaires. Attempt to find these types: postal, personal, telephone, Internet. Evaluate the ones you collect.
3 Why might we decide to use projective techniques with focus groups, but not in depth interviews?
4 Is it sensible to use a structured questionnaire in a focus group? Assess the implications.
5 Consult the proposal in the Market Researcher's Toolbox. Draft a possible questionnaire and topic guide following the objectives and specifications given.
6 Look at the opening Snapshot on Google. What advice would you give to Google about allowing respondents to talk to each other? What are the advantages and disadvantages of inviting them to Google premises to explain their views and show their computer use behaviour? What alternatives are there to lab usability tests of this type? Evaluate these against the test described.

Further reading

- Brace, I. (2004) *Questionnaire Design: How to Plan, Structure and Write Survey Material for Effective Market Research*. London: Kogan Page.
  A practitioner writes from experience about questionnaire design. This is current and very useful when creating new forms. Includes a CD to help the process.
- Edwards, P., Roberts, I., Clarke, E., DiGuiseppi, C., Pratap, S., Wentz, R., and Kwan, I. (2002) Increasing response rates to postal questionnaires: systematic review, *BMJ* vol 324, 18 May, http://www.pubmedcentral.nih.gov/picrender.fcgi?artid=111107&blobtype=pdf
  A review of over 250 studies to identify the 'secret' of increasing response rates.
- MRS (2006) *Questionnaire Design Guidelines*. London: Market Research Society.
  The industry trade body explains what to do and what not to do; this publication integrates the code of conduct.
- Oppenheim, A.N. (1992) *Questionnaire Design, Interviewing and Attitude Measurement*. London: Pinter.
  Classic text on instrument design that has been used for decades to teach questionnaire design.

Key web links

- Survey Question Bank http://www.surveynet.ac.uk
- SurveyMonkey http://www.surveymonkey.com

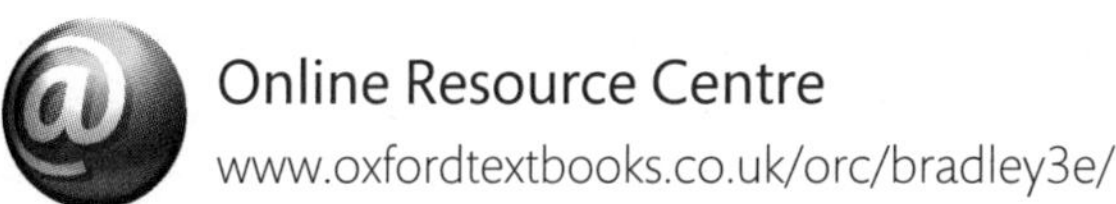

Visit the Online Resource Centre that accompanies this book to access more learning resources on this chapter topic.

Case study
East Anglian Air Ambulance

Research for Success
PO Box 205
HARROW
HA1 1ZU

Please help us today

Dear Mr/Mrs/etc. (name inserted from database)

The East Anglian Air Ambulance is a 365-day-a-year life-saving charity and serves Bedfordshire, Cambridgeshire, Norfolk, and Suffolk. We are independent of government funding and are entirely dependent upon fund-raising and contributions to keep the two air ambulances flying and provide advanced medical equipment.

We are reviewing our website to make sure you, as one of our valued supporters, find it useful. We have asked an independent research consultancy called 'Research for Success' to help us.

Please take just 12 minutes to complete the attached questionnaire, then return it in the prepaid addressed envelope supplied. There is no need to access this website to answer the questions.

Your feedback is of vital importance to us. Please help.

The questionnaire follows the Market Research Society code of conduct. Your answers are confidential to the research team, and the information you supply will only be used for the purpose stated above and not shared with third parties.

We need you today. You may need us tomorrow.

Yours sincerely,

Signature

Vivien Winders

Marketing and Communications Manager

East Anglian Air Ambulance

Your support enables the EAAA to continue the life-saving service. Your time and/or money makes a real difference. Please tick the following box/es which apply to how you support the charity.

Volunteer your time	☐	Corporate sponsors	☐
Donate—frequently/one-off	☐	Lottery member	☐

If none of the above please tick this box and go to Q14. ☐

Your computer usage

1. Do you have access to a computer and the Internet? (please tick) Yes ☐ No ☐
   If you answer 'no' please refer to the 'you've finished' section at the bottom of the questionnaire.
2. How often do you access the Internet? (please tick one answer)

Every day	☐	More than twice a week	☐	Weekly	☐
Fortnightly	☐	Monthly	☐	Rarely	☐

3. How often do you access the EAAA site?

Every day	☐	More than twice a week	☐	Weekly	☐
Fortnightly	☐	Monthly	☐	Rarely	☐
Never	☐	(If you answered 'never' please go to question 10.)			

Your opinions of the East Anglian Air Ambulance website

4. If you have accessed the EAAA website, which pages/areas did you refer to? (You can tick more than one box.)

Latest news	☐	Lottery news	☐	Forthcoming events	☐
About us	☐	Helping us	☐	Shops and merchandise	☐
Corporate sponsorship	☐	Other	☐	Please specify ____________	

5. When you accessed the pages did they provide the answers you were looking for? Yes ☐ No ☐
   If you answered 'no' please briefly explain the reasons for your answer.
   ____
   ____
   ____
   ____
   ____
   ____
   ____
   ____
6. Did you find the EAAA website easy to navigate? Yes ☐ No ☐
   If you answered 'no' please state an example of how you found it difficult.
   ____
   ____
   ____
   ____
   ____
   ____
   _____
7. Please use the scale to answer your opinions to the following: (1 = very poor 5 = excellent)

	1	2	3	4	5
a. Do you find the website exciting?	☐	☐	☐	☐	☐
b. Layout easy to follow?	☐	☐	☐	☐	☐
c. Use of photographs good?	☐	☐	☐	☐	☐
d. Language is easily understood?	☐	☐	☐	☐	☐
e. Consistent look throughout website?	☐	☐	☐	☐	☐
f. Easy to navigate?	☐	☐	☐	☐	☐
g. Information up to date?	☐	☐	☐	☐	☐
h. Overall opinion of the website?	☐	☐	☐	☐	☐

8. Please name a charity which you believe would score higher when using the scale above. ______________

9. Please name another charity that you feel strongly about. ______________

10. For your answer in question 9, please complete the following question; use the scale below to answer your opinions to the following: (1 = very poor 5 = excellent)

	1	2	3	4	5
a. Do you find the website exciting?	☐	☐	☐	☐	☐
b. Layout easy to follow?	☐	☐	☐	☐	☐
c. Use of photographs good?	☐	☐	☐	☐	☐
d. Language is easily understood?	☐	☐	☐	☐	☐
e. Consistent look throughout website?	☐	☐	☐	☐	☐
f. Easy to navigate?	☐	☐	☐	☐	☐
g. Information up to date?	☐	☐	☐	☐	☐
h. Overall opinion of the website?	☐	☐	☐	☐	☐
i. How do you believe the EAAA website compares?	☐	☐	☐	☐	☐

11. Briefly describe what would encourage you to use the website more.

____
____
____
____
____
____
____
____
____
____

12. Would you use the following if offered on our website? (More than one box can be ticked.)
    a. Online buying of merchandise Yes ☐ No ☐
    b. Online donating Yes ☐ No ☐

13. Did you consult the website to help answer this questionnaire? (You did not need to visit the site but it is helpful for us to know.) Yes ☐ No ☐

About you

This information helps us to analyse the data collected.

Name: ______________

Postcode: ______________

Occupation: ______________

Are you Female ☐ Male ☐?

Age at last birthday: ____________ years

If you would like to receive the results of the research please tick here. ☐

14. Please use the space below to make any additional comments on the East Anglian Air Ambulance service.

____
____

You've finished the questionnaire! Thank you for your time.

Please insert your questionnaire into the supplied envelope.

If you have any questions please contact the Marketing Department on (t)01284 762338, (e-mail) marketing@eaaa.org.uk

Research for Success, http://www.researchforsuccess.com has been authorised to carry out this research on behalf of the EAAA. If you want to contact Research for Success please quote the reference J5456 and BT01.

Case compiled by Nigel Bradley 2012

With thanks to Viv Winders at East Anglian Air Ambulance. Reproduced with kind permission.

Questions

1. Critically evaluate the questionnaire and this postal research design. You may want to consult the operational guidelines at the end of the toolbox section.
2. A cover letter has been produced, but no reminder letter/s; create a suitable reminder letter.
3. There are some objectives that are not answered. Which are they and how could they be addressed? List the many types of design that might be used for this project. Show the benefits and the limitations of each approach. How would the questions change if it was face-to-face?
4. An extension to the research project is proposed. The aim is to discover what non-supporters think of the website. Focus groups are planned. Write a topic guide and instructions for the moderator. The guide and instructions will be used in a focus group with non-supporters. Include projective techniques in the guide, with a full explanation of how to use them in the instructions.

References and sources

Albaum, G. (1997) The Likert scale revisited, *Journal of the Market Research Society*, 39, pp. 331–348.

Barnes, J.H., Banahan, B.F., and Fish, K.E. (1995) The response effect of question order in computer-administered questioning in the social science, *Social Science Computer Review*, 13, pp. 47–53.

Bearden, W.O. and Netemeyer, R.G. (1999) *Handbook of Marketing Scales*, 2nd edn. Thousand Oaks, CA: Sage.

Benton, E.J. and Daly, J.L. (1991) A question order effect in a local government survey, *Public Opinion Quarterly*, 55, pp. 640–642.

Boddy, C. (2005) Projective techniques in market research: valueless subjectivity or insightful reality? *International Journal of Market Research*, 47, pp. 239–254.

Brace, I. (2004) *Questionnaire Design: How to Plan, Structure and Write Survey Material for Effective Market Research*. London: Kogan Page.

Bradley N. (2011) Graphology: A Tool for Marketing? *The Marketing Review* 11(2), pp. 103–115.

Burns, A.C. and Bush, R.F. (2000) *Marketing Research*, 3rd edn. New Jersey: Prentice Hall.

Campbell, A. (ed.) (1988) *International Encyclopedia of the Social Sciences*. New York: The Free Press, Biographical Supplement.

Church, A. (1993) Incentives in mail surveys: a meta-analysis, *Public Opinion Quarterly*, 57, pp. 62–79.

Coull, J., Vidal, F., Nazarian, B., and Macar, F. (2004) Functional anatomy of the attentional modulation of time estimation, *Science*, 303, pp. 1506–1508.

Cowling, A.B. (1973) Use of elicitation technique for producing dimension of brand choice. *Annual Conference of the Market Research Society papers*, pp. 139–156.

DePaulo, P.J. (1990) View from the front: an interview with Ernest Dichter, Ph.D., *The Communicator* (the Newsletter of the Society for Consumer Psychology), 25, pp. 4–9.

Fox, R.J., Crask, M., and Kim, J. (1988) Mail survey response rate, *Public Opinion Quarterly*, 52, pp. 467–491.

Gaskell, G.D., Wright, D.B., and O'Muircheartaigh, C. (1995) Context effects in the measurement of attitudes: a comparison of the consistency and framing explanations, *British Journal of Social Psychology*, 34, pp. 383–393.

Leiber, R.B. (1997) Storytelling: a new way to get close to your customer, *Fortune*, 3 February 1997.

Likert, R. (1932) *A Technique for the Measurement of Attitudes*. New York: McGraw-Hill.

Loosschilder, G.H. and Ortt, J.R. (1994) The effect of the realism of product representations on the validity of consumer evaluations. ESOMAR Congress papers, pp. 353–377.

Loosschilder, G.H., Rosbergen, E., Vriens, M., and Wittink, D.E. (1995) Pictorial stimuli in conjoint analysis, *Journal of the Market Research Society*, 37, pp. 17–34.

McDaniel, C. and Gates, R. (2001) *Marketing Research Essentials*, 3rd edn. Cincinnati, OH: South Western College Publishing Thomson Learning.

Menneer, P. (1978) Retrospective data in survey research, *Journal of the Market Research Society*, 20, pp. 182–195.

Nowlis, S.M., Kahn, B.E., and Dhar, R. (2002) Coping with ambivalence: the effect of removing a neutral option on consumer attitude and preference judgments, *Journal of Consumer Research*, 29, pp. 319–334.

O'Muircheartaigh, C., Krosnick, J.A., and Helic, A. (2000) Middle alternatives, acquiescence, and the quality of questionnaire data. Working paper of the Harris School, University of Chicago, http://www.harrisschool.uchicago.edu/pdf/wp_01_3.pdf

Osgood, C., Suci, G., and Tannenbaum, P. (1957) *The Measurement of Meaning*. Urbana, IL: University of Illinois Press.

Searles, J.S., Helzer, J.E., and Walter, D.E. (2000) Comparison of drinking patterns measured by daily reports and timeline followback, *Psychology of Addictive Behaviors*, 14, pp. 277–286.

7 Qualitative research

Contents

Chapter guide

This chapter defines one of the two main branches of inquiry. Qualitative research helps us to go to the key motivation behind behaviour, so we explore a few of the different methods employed. Focus groups and depth interviews are of extreme importance to qualitative market researchers, so these two techniques are emphasised. You are given an understanding of the Delphi method, ethnography, semiotics, and grounded theory. There is detailed examination of both the spoken word and body language, which will help you to start to interpret group dynamics.

Learning outcomes

By the end of this chapter, you should be able to:

1. **Explain the purpose of qualitative research**
2. **Describe the different approaches to qualitative research**
3. **Show the benefits of different approaches to qualitative research**
4. **Show the limitations of different approaches to qualitative research**

Introduction

'Qualitative research' involves using techniques that attempt to gain an understanding of the existence of attitudes and opinions. It then goes on to assess the breadth and depth of those attitudes. Qualitative research studies do not measure the 'amount' of emotion or opinion, but they may give an indication of the dominant feelings. Rather than measurement tools associated with quantitative methods, the use of discussion, observation, and projective methods are used to elicit responses.

Let us begin in the 1930s, with Paul Lazarsfeld and Robert Merton, who used the term 'focused interviewing'. The focused interview involved asking questions of a single individual in a quiet, private setting. Merton further developed these interviewing techniques and coined the term 'focus group' in 1946. This is the reason why groups are similar to the 'focus interview', now more commonly called 'depth interview' or simply 'depths'.

'Action research' has its roots in the work of Kurt Lewin in the early 1950s. The researcher participates in the 'observed event' and may even affect the course of events by taking action. In the late 1950s, the Delphi forecasting method was developed at the Rand Corporation. Unlike other qualitative approaches, it uses a carefully designed questionnaire. The research involves several stages whereby the questionnaire is modified.

In the 1960s Ernest Dichter's 'motivational research' emerged. Dichter did much to integrate psychoanalysis into marketing (see Stern 2004). In 1965, Tuckman identified key stages in the group process—forming, storming, norming, and performing—which could be applied directly to the researcher's focus group.

By the 1970s, group discussions were fully accepted in marketing research, but it was not until the 1980s that academics and government had fully adopted these techniques.

In the 1980s, tools used in anthropology, linguistics, and sociology found their way into commercial research. These tools included ethnography and semiotics.

In recent years, computerised analysis has changed qualitative research. The use of Internet techniques have been successfully employed by practitioners. Still today mainstream qualitative marketing research is associated with two techniques: focus groups and depth interviews. Table 7.1 summarises a few notable events for qualitative research.

Table 7.1 Notable events for qualitative research

Period	Event
1940s	Merton's *focused interviewing* techniques
1950s	Delphi technique predicted the first space satellite would be launched
1960s	Dichter introduced 'motivation research'
1970s	*Focus group* discussions fully accepted in marketing research
1980s	Widespread use of focus groups by academics and government
1990s	Ethnography and semiotics in use
2000s	Depths/groups by email, chat groups, message boards, SMS
2010s	Social media leads to a renewed interest in text analysis

SNAPSHOT
BMW New Product Development

© BMW (UK) Limited. Reproduced with kind permission

New products are important to all organisations, but they carry many risks. A part of the skill of marketing managers is to identify risks and where possible suggest how they can be minimised or even eliminated.

In the years up to and after 2000 the motor industry worldwide had seen sales success in two sectors: the SUV and the MPV markets. SUV means Sports Utility Vehicles and MPV means multi-purpose vehicles. Precise definitions of these terms are not easy to arrive at, but it can be said that these models are bigger and more robust than regular family cars. The SUV is often four wheel drive but there is an emphasis on comfort; the MPV is sometimes associated with the 'people carrier', a small family bus.

At this time BMW prided itself as the only manufacturer to focus solely on the premium segments of the car market, and it did not want to jeopardise this position by introducing an SUV or MPV or a combined model, if it was perceived to be outside their image.

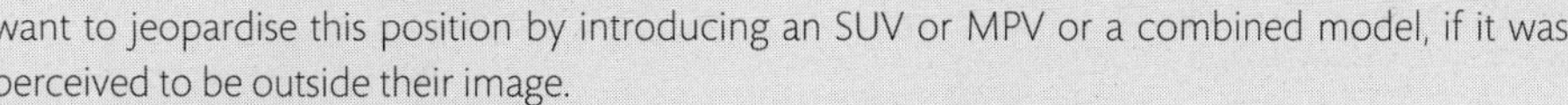

A research programme was designed that was qualitative and then moved onto a quantitative study. Respondents were screened so that interviews took place with people prepared to spend a minimum amount on their next car, were potential 'premium car' buyers, and would not reject an SUV or MPV. Focus groups helped to understand the 'underlying thinking' of the target market with regards to a concept that was discussed but had not yet been fully finalised. The qualitative stage highlighted the language used by respondents, it tested the use of a grid to be used in the quantitative phase and allowed the next phase to be designed with confidence. The focus groups helped to investigate and answer some of the research objectives, but also provided the means for other parts of the study to answer specific questions by going to 1000 respondents.

Compiled by Nigel Bradley 2012.

Sources:

Ellinghaus, U., Suntook, F. and Strange, P. (2004) Market Research for a new car concept. An example from the BMW Group. In the book Fellows, D.S. (ed) (2004) *Excellence in International Research 2004*, Amsterdam, Netherlands: ESOMAR, pp. 209–228.

BMW web pages:

http://www.bmwgroup.com

http://www.bmw.com

Depth interviews

Depth interviews (often called 'depths') are one-to-one conversations that do not use questionnaires. The structure must address the aims of the research, but is largely dictated by the situation, the researcher, and the willingness of the respondent to cooperate. The researcher and respondent are alone, so there is no pressure from group members; on the downside, an absence of other people can mean that there are fewer stimuli to trigger questions and answers. The interviewer therefore needs to adapt his or her skills to this situation.

Such interviews can probe sensitive issues and respondents can answer in their own time, in their own way. The technique is 'mobile', so it can take place where the respondent spends time; this may be at home, at the place of work, or even in transit. Most interviews are sound-recorded for later analysis.

There are variations on the depth interview and various names are used for this type of interview. They are not always synonyms and some writers will defend specific names with definitions.

The names used include:

- In-depth interview
- Depth interview
- Depth
- One-to-one
- Focused interview
- Unstructured interview
- Feminist interview
- Ethnographic interview
- Phenomenological interview
- Creative interview.

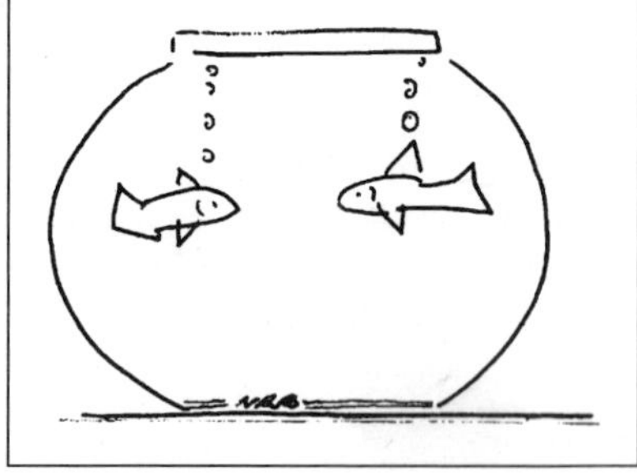

DEPTH INTERVIEW

In some cases, it is useful to meet two respondents together; they may have joint responsibility for household purchases. An example of this is a couple, a family, or unrelated people sharing a living area. These are called 'paired interviews', 'dyads', or 'friendship pairs'. Such sessions have similarities with group discussions, but differ in that respondents often join and leave during the interview. Depth interviews usually take place face-to-face, but some practitioners carry out depths by telephone, by video conference, or even by email.

Focus groups

A great deal of market research money is spent on focus groups. We hear about them daily in the news because they are a favourite tool used to shape government policy. A 'focus group' or 'group discussion' is a conversation between several people sitting together, usually in a circle. One person acts as a moderator, starts the debate, and intervenes periodically to keep the session on the desired topic. This person will close the discussion when s/he deems the time to be right. Behind the scenes, there is a lot of preparation and a lot of knowledge involved, that of both the researcher and the respondent. The researcher has prepared carefully and the respondent comes prepared with a lifetime of experience.

Like the depth interview, groups are generally carried out in a personal, face-to-face manner, but there are variations. These include: groups as phone conference calls, groups as videoconference sessions, groups on chat groups, and groups by email.

There are also variations in running the group. These include:

- No moderator, respondents given the task, no-one responsible
- Two moderators (joint moderation, perhaps taking two viewpoints)
- Respondent moderation, for part or all of the group
- Undercover respondents, to deliberately direct conversation.

Interviewer skills

A moderator should be a good listener, well organised, and be a quick learner. A good memory for names is also useful. The words people choose may be used to show solidarity with ideas held by other group members; they may also be used to exclude people. These are things that the moderator must be aware of and use to his/her advantage. Body language can also act as a cue to further questioning. Moderators must therefore try to be conscious of gestures.

In group situations, respondents can be faced with a situation where they may want to speak, but someone is already speaking. They have several options: they might wait for a pause; they might interrupt the speaker; they might simply give up. The result of interruption is that there will be an overlapping dialogue or the first speaker's communication will be truncated. Both pose problems for transcription and subsequent interpretation of the group discussion.

Highly skilled speakers use several strategies to become the main speaker. Here are three strategies identified by Jefferson (1973): adding an extra few words to the prior speaker's sentence; anticipating the sense and finishing a sentence before the prior speaker is able to do so, which is effectively hijacking the sentence; and finishing a sentence before the prior speaker is able to do so, but changing its sense.

In turn, the moderator must develop ways to deal with respondents, specifically those who are dominating the situation. The participants who are shy must be reassured; those who are negative must also be dealt with in the situation. Table 7.2 shows some moderator strategies.

The moderator will be the person analysing the data, and one of the concepts worth becoming familiar with is **bracketing**. We all come to a problem with prior knowledge: sometimes we need to put that aside (or put it in brackets) in order to probe for other information, and so that there will be less influence on the results. For the origins of bracketing, see Husserl (1931).

An extremely powerful tool is silence. At least once in a group the moderator should pose or imply a question and then pause. If an answer is not forthcoming respondents must be allowed to 'break the silence'. This mere act can help to identify the nature of participants: it can indicate who in the room is dominant, who is polite, who is shy, who is bored, who is destructive, and what links have been forged, along with many other things. This means that the moderator needs to maintain a concentrated and close observation of all group members. This is sometimes known as the *probe and five second pause technique*.

Table 7.2 Moderator strategies for respondent types

Respondent type	Strategy
Timid	Explains that there are no right or wrong answers
Saboteur	Suppresses or ejects the saboteur
Rambler	Continually reminds of the topic
Leader	Uses the leader to encourage others to speak
Defensive	Gives reassurance that other people share such views
Mob	A request for silence forces thought or conversation

The topic guide

In quantitative research, an obvious tool is the questionnaire. Qualitative research takes a more unstructured approach but must have guidelines in order to explore the research question. The 'topic guide' or 'discussion guide' is one such instrument and it provides an agreed area that should be explored. The items should act as a trigger, to elicit responses. Leading questions are allowed for these purposes.

Good guides include checklists of most items related to the subject. They include background questions (age, family, etc.), but also ask directly about the area of investigation; context can be important for any problem. This 'halo' or 'indirect' aspect can be alien to goal-oriented researchers who have mastered the writing of questionnaires. Good guides follow some logic—although this linkage may not be the order used in the field interview, it does help memorisation of the subject area.

Topic guides list the areas that should be covered in interview situations; they may contain questions, but the documents are not fully structured questionnaires. When any item is present at the interview, it is a distraction for those present; worse still, it may become the centre of attention. Furthermore, reading questions from a sheet prevents eye contact; it also stops the researcher from observing the dynamics of the situation. Even the briefest moment of distraction can allow group members to initiate discreet communications and networks, and this is one step towards losing control. If a researcher follows the topic guide too closely, it will imply that the same sequence should be followed at each session. Again, this is inappropriate because the best way to 'see into the mind' of the respondent is to use his or her own words, in the most appropriate order for that issue.

As an alternative to asking questions, the moderator can use elicitation and projective techniques to help draw out different responses. They can be as simple as a typed showcard sheet, or as sophisticated as a TV advert. They involve sentence completion, word association, thematic apperception tests, cartoon tests, brand obituary, and photosorts. Topic guides will mention projective techniques. See Chapter 6 for more on projective techniques in the context of writing topic guides. Table 7.3 highlights some of the differences between focus groups and depths.

Table 7.3 Summary of differences between focus groups and depths

Focus groups	Depth interviews
Usually take place face-to-face, less effective by telephone, by video conference or online	Effective by telephone, sometimes carried out by email. Can be extended to paired interviews or friendship pairs
The group processes of forming, storming, norming, and performing are an extremely useful framework for moderators	Will be paced to suit the individual respondent. The depth interview allows probing without pressure from other people; respondents can answer in their own time, in their own way
Can be carried out with a moderator or respondents can 'solve' the task themselves	Researcher must control fully
Length is fixed; the time spent is agreed and is less likely to be extended or shortened	The time spent is variable and depends on the respondent. Question wording during the session is likely to be modified more than a group
Fixed location means that a greater range of stimuli can be organised e.g. large products, projective techniques requiring materials.	The technique is 'mobile' so it can take place where the respondent spends time; at home, at the place of work or even in transit. This 'mobile' nature can restrict stimuli possible, but can draw on items in the respondent's normal environment
Respondents themselves will trigger debate and probe unexpected areas	The questions are driven by the respondent situation
More difficult to organise than depths.	Will be organised at a time and place to suit the individual respondent
Client observation becomes more likely. Video/sound recording easier	Usually audio data capture, observers may have a more negative impact than groups

The Delphi technique

The Delphi technique was developed at the Rand Corporation, in the late 1950s, as a forecasting method. Unlike many qualitative techniques, it uses a carefully designed questionnaire that is circulated to a panel of experts—a panel composed of individuals selected using various criteria specified by the researcher. Respondents are not told the identities of other people on the panel. The research involves several stages or rounds as shown in Table 7.4.

This can continue until the researcher finds it appropriate to stop. The Delphi idea combines the benefits of individual and group interviews, and allows the researcher to take the position of 'facilitator', towards the common aim of uncovering a result from what may be a complicated situation.

Table 7.4 Delphi technique stages

Stage 1	Experts identified
Stage 2	Experts contacted and asked to cooperate
Stage 3	Questionnaires sent to panellists by post
Stage 4	Replies analysed and recirculated stating the main results. People with views outside of the 'main' opinions are asked to give reasons (they may be ignorant or may have exclusive information). All are asked to reconsider answers
Stage 5	New analyses are made and recirculated, with the reasons for extreme views. Again, all are asked to reconsider

There have been many variations on this approach and Delphi has been used for reasons other than general innovation forecasting, which was the initial intention of the Rand Corporation. We have seen it applied to the market research industry, to new product development, even to personnel selection issues. The Internet offers an excellent way to administer the technique and a Delphi programme was developed by J. Scott Armstrong. This was funded in part by the International Institute of Forecasters and is freely available for use at http://armstrong.wharton.upenn.edu/delphi2/.

For more information on Delphi, see a summary in the original works by Brown (1968) or Dalkey *et al.* (1969).

Observation research

Observation is a technique that is often overlooked or considered to be time-consuming, but in recent years, with ethnography and action research, the technique has become extremely powerful.

Ethnography

Ethnography is a descriptive technique. It describes behaviour in a natural setting and is made possible by participant observation: the researcher becomes part of the community under study. The approach has its origins in anthropology and it refers to a practice in which researchers spend long periods living within a culture in order to study it. Ethnography has been integrated into qualitative research and personnel spend hours, days, or weeks with participants in areas of their everyday lives. During these interactions, observations are being made. This is distinguished from interviewing because it means that longer durations of time are spent with respondents. Additionally, the interview location is often outside the respondent's normal environment, whereas the ethnographer enters into the respondent's world.

There are many ways of conducting ethnographic studies: they may be intrusive or nonintrusive; they may be short term or long term; they may study the consumer or be of a nonconsumer nature; they may be fully participant or less participant; and they may go deep into the situation (deep) or simply be an overall view (shallow). For these reasons, we have seen a new term emerge—'quasi ethnography'—which takes us away from the purist form of becoming a full member of the culture being studied.

Ethnography is therefore an extreme form of participant observation whereby the researcher spends time with the subjects who are under investigation. It involves seeing the world through the eyes of the subjects under study.

Stages of ethnography

From a practical viewpoint, we can visualise ethnography as a series of stages.

1. **Decision on location.** The researcher must consider the objectives and decide on the cultural group and physical location in which ethnographic research should take place.
2. **Decision on team composition.** It is unusual for an ethnographer to work totally in isolation, so a team of several researchers must be created. These can be distinguished as 'backup' and 'front-line'; the front-line researcher or researchers will be fully immersed in the culture and so there must be careful justifications for the choices made. It should be noted that it is unreasonable to expect researchers to make major changes to their personality, lifestyle, and attitudes before entering a location. Following is a list of questions that can be asked to help in decisions about team composition:
   - Can the researcher communicate in the language of the target?
   - Does the researcher have empathy?
   - Will the researcher match the destination in terms of personality?
   - Will the researcher match the destination in terms of dress?
   - Will the researcher match the destination in terms of lifestyle?
   - Can the researcher absorb experiences and then stand aside to articulate these experiences?
   - Are several people necessary? Should they have different characteristics?
   - Will the researcher be an ally to the group under study?
   - Will the researcher be a threat to the group under study?
   - What equipment is needed (video cameras, sound recording, diaries, etc.)?
3. **Entry-point analysis.** There are various ways to enter into a particular culture and these should be listed. The listed items will typically include the identities (and sometimes names) of people who may assist in introducing the researcher into the culture; these people are sometimes known as **gatekeepers**.
4. **Arrival and full immersion.** The researcher or team must arrive at the desired cultural destination and quickly become immersed in the culture chosen. S/he or they must be exposed to all experiences and stimuli that are evident at the chosen locations. This implies full involvement in everyday life, whether by the preparation and eating of food or arranging other aspects of life. This arrival may be a gradual process or it may be abrupt.

5. **Identification of informants.** A systematic way to carry out ethnographic research is for the researcher to identify informants from 'within'. This stage draws on the objectives and needs to set these elements against the resources that have been discovered while in full immersion. Informants can help to interpret the situations that arise and can help the ethnographer to gain further access. For example, when looking into the use of paints, the ethnographer can observe how a house is decorated. But an informant can go further and explain why woodwork was prepared in a particular way before decoration; the informant can also indicate the source of that knowledge and where to discover more information. Note that the term 'informant' is used rather than 'respondent'. This emphasises a desire to be informed rather than seek answers to pre-defined questions.
6. **Data gathered and reported.** There are no set ways involved in capturing data, but such analysis must be linked to the research objectives. Some ethnographers prefer to analyse and report during their time in the field. When transforming experiences to words, the researcher can draw on the stimuli available in the chosen environment. Often this data capture takes the form of a 'field diary', an open-ended account of experiences that tells the story. Physical evidence of the experience can also be useful for analysis later. Such evidence will again be relevant to the objectives, but this is not necessary: for example, a sales receipt may be useful to show a cluster of other items purchased alongside a product under investigation. Physical evidence can include travel tickets, receipts, labels, packaging, magazines, tools and implements, sound recordings, photographs, and so on. These are often called 'artefacts' or 'ephemera' and their importance may not be clear until the researcher has left the field.
7. **Departure from the field.** Once the information is safely 'captured' and artefacts are secured, then the operative should leave the field. There are many ways to close the relationship that has been created between researcher and informant, but in a market research context, the researcher has a duty to the public, to the respondent, to the client, and to other researchers, so this farewell should be appropriate and without friction.

Netnography

Netnography is ethnography but applied to the Internet environment. It is therefore a qualitative online method associated with a researcher called Robert Kozinets, who introduced it into academic research. The technique has subsequently been used by commercial researchers (see Kozinets 1999 and 2002). We have met the stages of ethnography and these are adapted to the online environment as follows.

Stages of netnography

1. **Decision on location.** For this stage, appropriate online communities must be identified. This means using search engines to identify online forums such as virtual groups, lists, and chat rooms. Kozinets recommends online communities with higher numbers of postings. He found that groups with larger numbers of single message posters and those with more detailed messages will give richer outputs.

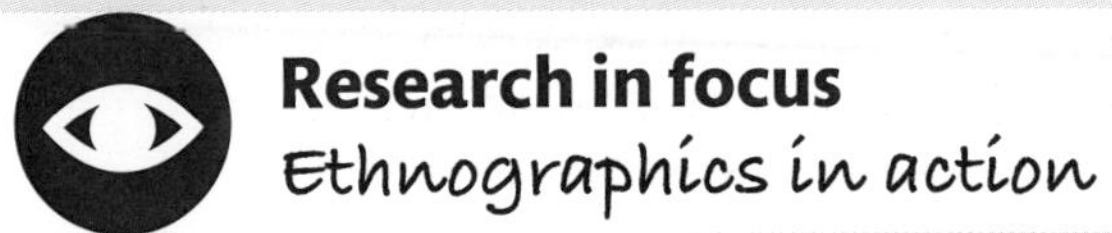

Research in focus
Ethnographics in action

A real sense of ethnographic research is conveyed well by Nancy MacDonald, who switched from anthropology to market research: *'I spent three years in the field conducting ethnographic research with illegal graffiti writers in the UK and the USA. At the other end of the spectrum, I spent three days shopping for tea with housewives in High Barnet'.* In the UK, a dynamic marketing agency called ?WHATIF! described their unique way of interpreting the world: *'Over the last few years we've been to breakfast with a different family every day of the week'.*

It is astonishing to find that 'path-breaking' ethnography has been welcomed by companies with a track record of using traditional marketing research: Ericsson, Kimberley Clark, and S.C. Johnson have all used ethnographic research. More recently, there is evidence to show that it has been used by the Intel Corporation, Gap, MSN/Microsoft, J.C. Penney Co., Unilever Home and Personal Care, and Hewlett Packard. All of these were featured at the Market Research Event in November 2005 and are just a few names to have crept into the public eye.

An indication of how corporations use the technique is exemplified by Nestlé, the *'biggest food-producing company in the world'* (Vladimirova and Petrin 2001). The methodology was in three stages. Stage one was a first visit to homes in Russia—a diary was left at homes for one week. Stage two was a second visit to homes to collect the diary, and a decision was made to prepare a dish of food for a third visit. The stage three visits involved the in-home preparation of the agreed dish. The cooking process was video-taped and the housewife was interviewed during the preparation. Almost 50 depth interviews were carried out during this third stage. The study provided much food for thought! One finding was that cooking has become stable: each housewife has a set repertoire of ingredients that are used in different combinations and the attitude during cooking is 'automatic', in that dishes are prepared while watching TV or preparing the next day's meal. These are aspects that are difficult to detect from traditional interviews outside the home. Ekaterina Vladimirova, marketing research officer for Nestlé Food LLC, points out one disadvantage of ethnography as *'the necessity to learn in the process, which means that every minute of observation and discussion needs to be instantly interpreted and processed by the researcher. For many experienced moderators this task was so stressful that only a few days could restore them to their "normal" state'.*

Compiled by Nigel Bradley 2012.

Sources:

MacDonald, N. (2003) People watching, *Research*, July, p. 28.

http://www.iirusa.com

http://www.pointforward.com

Vladimirova, E. and Petrin, K. (2001) Russia: pyramid on the kitchen table: how an ethnographic study of culinary habits helped develop a unified marketing approach, *Qualitative Research*, Budapest: ESOMAR, pp. 289–297.

Waymire, G. (2002) *Ethnography*, Silicon Valley American Marketing Association paper, 18 September.

?WHATIF!(2002) *Sticky Wisdom: How to Start a Creative Revolution at Work.* Oxford: Capstone.

Questions

1 From the information above, what do you detect that ethnography can offer that other methods cannot?

2 From the evidence above, what are the disadvantages of ethnography as opposed to other methods?

2. **Decision on team composition.** It is unusual for a netnographer to work totally in isolation, so a team may be created. Here three qualities are essential: knowledge of technology, an ability to adapt to the linguistic conventions used by the particular forum, and a broad knowledge of the topic under investigation. Depending on the study it is probable that shift-work will be necessary; availability online is not a simple question of a daytime job.
3. **Entry-point analysis.** There are various ways to enter into a particular forum and these should be examined carefully; it is essential to gain access past the 'gatekeepers'. Often this is a simple case of completing a registration form or asking a moderator's permission to become part of the group.
4. **Arrival and full immersion.** The researchers must become immersed in the chosen forum. This arrival is likely to be a gradual process as the netnographer becomes a 'lurker' before fully becoming part of the group.
5. **Identification of informants.** In the same way that traditional ethnographic researchers quickly identify participants who will provide fruitful data, the netnographer must do the same. Kozinets has identified some people frequently found in online communities. In his opinion, insiders and devotees offer the best source of information.

    - Insiders are strongly linked to the group and to the consumption activity and tend to be long-term participants
    - Devotees have strong consumption interests but few links to the group
    - Tourists pose few questions rather than carry out deep debate; they are not major participants; may become devotees and insiders
    - Minglers have strong links but little interest in the activity, again of interest because they may become devotees and insiders

6. **Data gathered and reported.** Netnography offers two sources of data. The first is the communication between group members; in the case of most online research there is a major advantage in that most communications are written; there are, of course, groups where the spoken word is made possible by the use of telephony over the Internet. The second source of data comes from self-memos and reports prepared by the team of netnographers. This is the equivalent of the traditional ethnographer's field diary. Other evidence referred to in conversations such as screen shots, web sites, video clips, and similar are used in analysis.
7. **Departure from the field.** Once the information is safely 'captured' and artefacts are secured, then the researcher should leave the group.

Action research

Another variant form of observation is known as 'action research'; here, the researcher participates in the 'observed event' and may even affect the course of events by taking action. At the same time, the researcher distances him/herself from the respondent. The researcher is responsible for the research plan, and the subject is expected to conform to the demands made. Typically, action research will follow a series of cycles, whereby there is a plan, an action takes place and is observed, a reflection takes place and the plan is revised, action takes place, and so on. Translated into market research, we can see that this approach can be (and has been) adapted directly to new product development. The researcher becomes involved in the research by becoming a user; additionally, users can be recruited to become researchers. Action research has its roots in the work of Kurt Lewin (1952).

Grounded theory

'Grounded theory' is associated with work by Glaser and Strauss (1967), which was continued by Strauss and Corbin (1998). The idea is that the researcher has a broad area of investigation and will collect information, which is then analysed very carefully. The procedure means that the information is inspected and the researcher will base an explanation on the findings: the theory is 'grounded' in the data. The alternative is to start with a series of specific questions or hypotheses.

The specific procedures involved have been called: open coding, axial coding, and selective coding.

'Open coding' means giving labels to similar parts of the raw data. Usually, these labels will be the words used in the literature, terms decided by the researcher or, most interestingly, any vocabulary used by the subjects of the research. These have been called '*in vivo*' codes. This initial procedure will highlight relevant issues and narrow the study to a scope that can be managed.

'Axial coding' is the next step and this means that relationships are sought between the categories of data that have come from open coding. A hierarchy is then arranged and sub-categories are identified. The next step is to return to the data and confirm that these relationships do indeed exist.

'Selective coding' is the subsequent phase; it involves choosing a single category, which is designated as the core category. The other categories are related to this central category and grounded theory is then completed. The overall explanation (or theory) stems from this central category.

The grounded theory approach has been criticised as time-consuming and intensive; there is also a possibility that little of significance may be derived from the data. A major advantage is that it avoids creating a preconceived idea of the outcome, and forces the researcher to keep an open mind.

Verbal communication

An appreciation of 'discourse analysis' is essential for the qualitative researcher. It is important for the analysis stage, but also during the planning of a research project and the data collection stage. In simple terms, respondents must be selected to provide the required information, but if they are incapable of expression in a particular situation (for example, a group), another method must be used (for example, a depth interview or the use of intermediaries). Poor selection of respondents from a linguistic viewpoint can lead to insult, condescension, or indifference, which may not coincide with the research objectives.

Common mistakes
Taking answers at face value

It is tempting to give an order to information uncovered in qualitative research. For example, we may be examining satisfaction. Qualitative research is perfectly capable of generating a list of aspects that drive satisfaction. For example, in the purchase of televisions we may identify the following five 'drivers of satisfaction': quality of picture, price paid, size of screen, portability, and colour. It is easy, and a good idea, to ask respondents to create an order of importance for these, but that order will change from depth to depth and from group to group. The question and answer is valuable because it is a further way of probing the positive and negative aspects of these drivers.

The linguistic options open to the respondent's community are important to the researcher. In English, there are several degrees of formality. These use different sets of vocabulary, but also have varied grammatical construction, dialect, and modification of voice.

In British English, we are all aware of the fact that there are many ways of speaking; we can distinguish between the most formal way of speaking, known as 'received pronunciation' or RP, and 'Standard English'. Standard English is a way of speaking used by people from different backgrounds; it is a neutral way to communicate with each other. It is a way for them to converse without showing weaknesses or strengths of their own background. If they do not use Standard English, it might be indicative of many things, and the researcher may need to investigate these. Certainly, in a focus group situation, the researcher must be fully aware of individual differences.

'*I will buy this product*' may be a prediction: the speaker may be forecasting his/her behaviour; it may be a promise; or it may have been said to satisfy the interviewer and anyone else who may be listening. If the words are in the context of negativity, it may be a complete untruth, even a dishonest statement. The researcher needs to be aware of many aspects of language during the evaluation of respondent output. Let us examine just three of these: euphemism, hyperbole, and metaphor.

Euphemism

Words chosen by a respondent go beyond the functional meaning and can take the form of 'euphemism'. It may indicate a reluctance to be frank or a desire to use discretion. Euphemisms describe the way things are named, but they go further than single words. They can be apparent in phrases. Euphemisms can also be present in non-verbal behaviour: for example, the pauses or the speed of speech or the combination of hand and eye movement, can all indicate euphemisms; even silence, in response to a question, can be an indication of euphemism.

There are several aspects to euphemism; let us look at 'litotes'. A litote allows a strong statement to be communicated to avoid immediate reaction; it does this by saying the opposite, but with a negative. For example, '*a car not as large as I expected*' or '*a company that has never had a reputation for good customer satisfaction*'.

'Understatement' is another feature of euphemism. This is something said that is well below the reality of a situation. Again, this can prevent a potentially explosive situation, but still allows communication: for example, a life-threatening situation may be described in an understated way as a 'problem'. A well-known use of this was during the Apollo 13 flight to the moon: '*Houston, we have a problem.*' Other understatement words we commonly find in marketing include terms such as 'awkward', 'issue', 'flexible', 'adjustment', even 'care'.

'Inexact communication' is another characteristic of euphemism. If we are approximate or are vague, then there is a fog of confusion. It may be the case that inexact communication is found in areas that are sensitive to respondents. If we think of everyday life, we hear the word 'thing' to mean penis; we hear the term 'got done' to mean 'was caught cheating'; we know the term 'adult content' often means pornography. This is evident in marketing contexts in many ways: '*I must get a new computer*' rather than '*I must buy a new computer*' may indicate that the word 'buy' is being avoided because the person hasn't enough money or is reluctant to spend it in this way.

'Impressive communication' is yet another form of euphemism. Here, technical terms, 'big words' or other rather impressive expressions are used. Occupations are a fertile ground for identifying impressive titles. The words 'operative' and 'engineer' are two favourites: for example, 'cleaning operative' (for cleaner) or 'sales engineer' (for salesperson). The never-ending search for unique selling propositions (USPs) involves names and an advantage may be gained over the competition by using a new term. In time, such jargon may disappear or become a part of everyday language. 'Learning resource' for textbook or 'interpersonal communication device' for telephone, are just two examples. New technology has heralded the arrival of thousands of terms. One thing is certain, the researcher may hear respondents use these terms, and the reason may require investigation, but it is important to recognise them.

Hyperbole

Hyperbole is an exaggerated manner of expression: it is not always intended for the words to be taken at face value, but what is said should convey extravagance or grandeur. Examples of the hyperbole include: 'bestseller', 'classic', 'masterpiece', and 'new'. These words turn the ordinary into something magical. Small-sized products are often described as 'regular' or 'standard'. Therefore medium often becomes 'large' and large becomes 'extra large', 'extra-extra large', 'jumbo', or 'family'. Cheap becomes 'economy' and small becomes 'compact'. In the field of pricing, cheap and expensive are hard terms both for the buyer and seller, so they become 'low cost', 'budget', 'economy', 'great value'. At the other extreme, 'deluxe version' or 'prestigious', 'gracious', ignoring price references at all, or referring to the product as, for example, 'outstanding' or 'sought after' may be evident. The term 'used' may also be avoided, so it has become 'nearly new', 'pre-owned', or 'previously owned'. The word 'classic' or 'rare' may be used. The researcher needs to recognise hyperbole because respondents may use such terms or may be affected by the use of such terms by the researcher, advertiser, or even other respondents.

Metaphor

Finally, the metaphor is a figure of speech where something is used to mean another thing. For example, a respondent may say s/he feels '*under fire by advertising messages*' or feels '*under attack from assaults by other sellers*'. The respondent is using military metaphors and these are

Common mistakes
Leading respondents

There are many ways to tease out information from respondents; one way is to elicit answers by provoking people, even by criticising them. This must be done in a gentle way because threatening, abusive or insulting words are likely to cause alarm or distress (the Criminal Justice and Public Order Act 1994 states that this is an offence). We can go to the other extreme and make respondents feel at ease, to make them feel comfortable, so it is easy for them to express their points. The problem here is that all of this can amount to leading respondents in one direction and answers may be flavoured by the mood of the moment. This is a problem for inexperienced researchers, and for clients who observe the process and take it at face value. The experienced moderator will, however, take these factors into account when analysing the data.

worth probing further; there may be an underlying feeling that the consumer feels opposed to the supplier rather than a partner in its business. Respondents can use metaphors that are completely confusing to anyone not understanding their intention. On the other hand, the subconscious trail left by the respondent can be very indicative; this has been the subject of much academic interest. Most recently, Zaltman (2003) dedicated an entire book to the subject, called *How Customers Think: Essential Insights into the Mind of the Market*.

Table 7.5 shows other things to watch for in respondents.

Non-verbal communication

Non-verbal communication is another important feature of all qualitative research, particularly for focus groups and depth interviews. The successful researcher will use knowledge of body language to interpret answers, but also will use it in eliciting responses; it is another way to ask

Table 7.5 Things to watch for in respondents

Irony	Using words to express the opposite of what is meant
Sarcasm	Making bitter remarks about the product, customers or even the research process
Humour	Bringing about a situation whereby anyone might smile or laugh
Wit	Intellectual use of humour by combining ideas or expressions
Freudian slips	Using one idea or word instead of another, or making an omission. Not intended for irony or sarcasm or humour, but may show such urges

Table 7.6 Common behaviour in interview situations

Hand	Finger raised, fists clenched, finger tapping
Voice	Stuttering, hesitation, speed of speech
Mouth	Yawning, tightened lips, lifeless (silent), poised
Posture	Sitting up, slouching back or forward, stiffening, turning away or towards
Eyes	Blinking rate, eye contact, looking away, vacant look, staring into space, lowering eyes, looking at time/door
Nose	Expelling air
Face	Blushing

questions. The subject area is fascinating and many popular psychology books are available on the topic—notably those of the famous anthropologist and zoologist Desmond Morris (2002). The knowledge has been applied to different situations: for example, Pease and Pease (2004) used the approach in training sales personnel.

There are no single meanings for specific non-verbal communications. Touching the nose may mean the person is lying, but it may also indicate a physical reason for scratching the nose. All people who tell lies do not touch their noses as they go through the act. There is no straightforward link; instead, different behaviours collaborate, so we can take a cluster of individual signals and start to suggest an explanation. They might result from emotion, personality traits, and attitudes. To understand more, we need to look at all of these things.

The first stage is to recognise common behaviour, regardless of any explanation. Table 7.6 shows some common behaviours found in interview situations. At any moment, we can see several of these, and it is the gradual repetition or evolution of them that needs to be observed and remembered. It is then that the researcher can decide whether to take action.

Gabbott and Hogg (2001) reviewed the literature on non-verbal communication and divided the subject into these four areas: proxemics, kinesics, oculesics, and vocalics (see Table 7.7).

Table 7.7 Four aspects of non-verbal communication

Proxemics	The use of space, the proximity
Kinesics	Movement and body posture
Oculesics	Eye behaviour, gaze, eye movements
Vocalics	Tone, intonation, and other features of the voice

After Gabbott and Hogg 2001.

'Proxemics' is the use of space or the proximity.

'Kinesics' relates to movement and body posture: yawning, tightening the lips, sitting up, slouching, stiffening, turning away or towards, finger raising, fists clenching, finger tapping.

'Oculesics' concerns eye behaviour, the gaze, and eye movements. People change the number of blinks per minute; they may look away, have a vacant look, stare into space, lower their eyes, or look at objects such as the door or a clock. Eye contact boosts activity in the brain's ventral striatum. This is said to be linked with the expectation of a reward.

'Vocalics' refers to the tone, intonation, and other features of the voice. Stuttering, hesitation, and speed of speech all fall into this category.

Silence is not an obvious part of this list and it has received relatively little attention by marketing academics. Instinctively, we would place silence into the vocalics category, but it has significant implications for the others. Kurzon (1998) distinguishes between intentional and unintentional silence: the former is a refusal to answer and the latter is an inability to answer.

It is useful to distinguish between the individual and the group. A group consists of several individuals who all have their own lives; they express themselves in unique ways—some can articulate themselves well, others less so. Some use gestures more than others. At a group level, there is also an overall body language in play. We will first examine body language of the individual, and then body language of the group as a whole.

Body language in the individual

Body language of the individual is important in depth interviewing, but also in group discussions. It is useful to say that a respondent can show more defensive signals in a depth interview than in a group. This is probably because s/he can hide behind the 'shield' of others in a group situation.

Defensiveness is shown by gestures that 'protect' the person from attack. Defence mechanisms were identified by psychoanalysts to describe devices used by the individual to avoid danger. There is no widely agreed list of mechanisms, but some different ones are: projection (e.g. allocating blame elsewhere), rationalisation (justifying something by giving a plausible explanation), regression (reverting to a younger age), or identification (associating closely with others in reference groups). In a non-verbal sense, these vulnerabilities can be detected as shown in Table 7.8.

The five things that can be attacked are the senses—touch, sight, hearing, smell, and taste. When faced with attack, we tend to adopt one of the defence mechanisms. We can say that the individual under attack will guard those senses. By placing the hands over the ears, s/he will be saving the eardrums from bursting if there is a high decibel noise; if there is something that is not loud, but perhaps disgusting, that same gesture of blocking the ears with the hands is used. This same mechanism is also used when the person is hearing something s/he does not like. However, the hands rarely reach the ears, so we have an unfinished gesture, but the moderator does recognise the thought (as if by mind-reading). In a similar way, the nose and the eyes are blocked from undesirable smells or sights, but in a controlled situation, the gestures will be incomplete.

Table 7.8 Defence mechanism manifestation

Defence mechanism	How shown
Projection	Deliberate and decisive tone, hand and arm gestures away from the body
Rationalisation	Taking calm approach, measured movements, gestures of empathy and understanding
Regression	Becoming child-like, seeking reassurance, becoming more dependent, agreeable, limbs closer to person
Identification	Mirroring gestures of the interviewer or other people in vicinity, 'chameleon-like' gestures

Faced with an uncomfortable situation, a person can choose to leave it. In an interview situation, this can mean a complete departure from the room, or causing the interviewer to be ejected. Before that point, there are several warning signs: for example, taking phone calls, accepting interruptions, leaving the situation to do something important, going to the toilet, etc.

Before reaching any of these points, it is necessary to position the body of the respondent in a way that will allow them access to an exit, such as the door. The researcher can then detect 'exit predisposition' by looking at the feet; feet generally point towards the door if a person is considering leaving: if the feet move nervously, there may be ambivalence.

Credit: Nigel Bradley

Negative body language: defensiveness

Body language in the group

Non-verbal communication changes throughout the period of the interview. In a group discussion, for example, the body language will be consistent with the point of the discussion. Gordon and Langmaid (1988) match body language with the group process steps of forming, storming, norming, performing, and mourning: for example, at the 'norming' stage they say that '*body language settles, becomes more peaceful and calm. There is more mirroring of each other's language, posture and gesture. Proffering of cigarettes, sharing of spoons, agreeing on the weather, moving up to allow more space to another*'. These are small acts that show a group has formed.

This situation is quite dangerous for the researcher, who may (or may not) have been accepted by the group as a member. This situation of harmony can be equivalent to a leading question. Depending on the topic, we might now receive an inaccurate reaction. To use a simplistic example, there may be interest expressed in a new product because group members want to reinforce their agreement with each other. In idiomatic terms, they 'go with the flow', so the moderator must identify this from body language, and use verbal language (real words) to ensure that respondents do not agree for the (temporary) reason that they feel at ease with other group members.

An opposite situation is where body language is suggesting that norming has not been achieved, and group members are demonstrating a lack of interest. Here, individual body languages will not show mirroring; there will be many things happening in the room. There may be unpleasant silences, resistance to cooperation, closed legs, folded arms, lack of eye contact, pairs developing with the group, people leaving for the bathroom, several conversations emerging. Here, the moderator uses body language to understand that there is a big problem. It takes a very experienced moderator to turn this situation into one that can be productive. In this state, the respondents are again likely to give inaccurate reactions. In this case, the reactions to a new product may be more of an expression of the respondents' discomfort with their present situation. If respondents want to leave, they may try to give quick replies to bring the session to a close quickly. If they want to 'entertain' themselves before they leave, they may decide to start asking questions themselves, to see what becomes of the session.

The body language of the group as a whole can be described as 'positive' or 'negative', as we have seen above, and there are grades between. Furthermore, the levels of negativity and positivity will change throughout the session.

Another important aspect of body language in the group is that of subgroups. Within any group of five to ten people, there will be those who share certain characteristics and have more links than other group members. This leads to subgroupings within the main group, often indicated by the use of space. A proximity zone that equates to an arm's length is intimate; this zone expands in relation to the mental distance an individual wants to have. The people involved can be identified by interpreting their body language. It is important to do this because those groups run the risk of agreeing (or disagreeing) simply to build their ties. This open expression of unity can, in turn, sway other members; it can create different factions. This is not totally undesirable, but it is the moderator's job to recognise it in order to guide questioning and also to interpret the information received.

'Mirroring' is the term used to describe similar body language. People who form subgroups will often use similar body language. They may sit with limbs in similar positions; their eyes may move to the speaker at the same speed; they may quickly adopt similar ways of sipping their drink. Moderators will detect that the respondents notice what other members of their 'subgroup' are doing: they may yawn together, begin to speak at the same time and, most telling, they will smile at each other and their eye contact with each other is better than that with anyone else.

Ethical insight
Can anyone watch my focus group?

It is useful to see a focus group in action: we can see real people talking about live issues; the information is exciting and unpredictable. But should we watch this rather personal event, and, perhaps more importantly, is it right to do so?

When someone is watching a focus group, the respondents may feel intimidated, they may limit their contributions or, worse still, say nothing. To get round this, the nation is full of observation rooms. Viewers look through large viewing windows, which take the appearance of a mirror facing the respondents. These facilities make it possible for a focus group to be viewed. Technology has taken us one step further and we can place video cameras with the respondents, or behind the mirror. Clients can take a DVD home to watch as they wish. Martin Stoll, Ipsos-MORI, says: '*There is a trend to use a lot more video clips. So instead of a quote from somebody you put a clip up, a 30-second clip of a person saying this is what happened. This is called "voxpops", it is a very small snippet*'. Filming also allows images of that same group to be relayed to another room or to another building in real time; this is known as 'video streaming'. A more recent development is to use webcam technology and give a password to clients so that they can view a group on the Internet by what is called 'web streaming'. This can clearly even be used in another country, so a client in the USA can watch a group in the UK as it happens.

One Market Research Society FAQ states: '*Video clips from group discussions can be shown to clients as long as written permission has been given by each respondent in the groups before the video recording begins. The agency should at the same time obtain written assurance from the client that the use of such video clips would be limited to the use specified to respondents*'.

But is it reasonable to watch these rather personal scenes? The MRS Code, rule B15, says: '*If there is to be any recording, monitoring or observation during an interview, respondents must be informed about this both at recruitment and at the beginning of the interview*'. Respondents should have enough information from the outset to make a decision whether or not to withdraw; similarly, they can avoid saying anything they may regret later. Because webcam viewing has the potential for a wide audience, the MRS suggests that the research agency contract should be modified. The contract should tell their client that all viewing should be conducted in such a way that no one outside the project team can view the research.

And here is the dilemma: some countries neither have such rules, nor do they enforce them. At the most extreme, with the help of the Internet, anyone may watch my focus group.

Compiled by Nigel Bradley 2012.

Sources:

Brenner, M. (ed.) (2006) Finding and hiring a viewing facility, *Research Decisions*, March.
MRS Code, rule B15, B34, and B42, http://www.mrs.org.uk/standards/codeconduct.htm. Reproduced with kind permission.

Questions

1. Why would a client want to see a focus group?
2. Why would a respondent not want other people to see the group?
3. What are the risks of using modern technology in qualitative research?

Table 7.9 Materials available for semiotic analysis

Articles in the press	Typeface associated with the company
Competitor press releases	Promotional output
Colours used in a communication	Packaging
Odours associated with the product	Brochures
Company names	Style of the offering
Brand names	Reputation
Transcripts of groups	Retail outlet 'feel'
Past questionnaires	Web pages
TV programmes	Posters
Radio programmes	Adverts
Body language (e.g. service staff)	News reports
Photographs and images	
Ephemera	

Semiotics

'**Semiotics**' is the study of communication through the careful analysis of signs. 'Signs' are signals embedded in some interchange between individuals; they may be intentional or not, they may be obvious or hidden and they may be perceived through any of the human senses. The approach was derived from structural linguistics and is particularly useful to the analysis of advertising, packaging, and other material where symbols are present.

Semiotics is associated with Ferdinand de Saussure (1857–1913) and Charles Sanders Peirce (1839–1914). More recently, these names have dominated the debate: Roland Barthes (1915–1980) and the Italian popular writer Umberto Eco. In the past, the word 'semiology', a term apparently coined by Saussure, was in use; nowadays, the term semiotics is in widespread use.

Analysis can take place using items that are easily available to the general public, because these are the communications directed towards potential customers. It is worthwhile considering the types of items that are used in semiotics: they are often found in language, whether spoken or written; they may be visual devices or symbols. Table 7.9 lists some of the types of materials available for analysis; this is not exhaustive, but rather evocative, to prompt the reader to consider anything that might impinge on the topic under study. Some materials are tangible and clearly associated with the client company, and may therefore be easy to obtain; others may need to be 'discovered' by undergoing the consumer experience, directly or by analysis of previous research. The procedure searches the obvious for something that is hidden.

Signs are extremely diverse. Some signs are 'dormant', and only uncovered when there is some stimulus to bring them out; some signs are 'lapsed', in that they were important one day but are now outdated; some signs are 'current' and worth investigation. Interestingly, some signs can be identified, but have specific meanings in different circumstances; this gives them a 'chameleon-like' nature.

Very different stimuli create a new reality in the mind of the target audience, and it is this reality that is being discovered. The alternative to semiotics is to ask respondents for their opinion, and this is still possible as a support or as a supplement to the semiotic form of inquiry. The strength of semiotics lies in the fact that respondents cannot always articulate their view within the framework of a short interview session. Semiotic analysis allows detailed and lengthy analysis of situations in an isolated manner.

From a practical viewpoint, we can visualise semiotic analysis as a series of stages.

1. **Thinking stage** Here the researcher must consider the objectives, possibly with the client and other researchers. This discussion and exploration will permit the research to be focused in a specific direction.
2. **Listing of materials** Materials should be listed; these will be pertinent to the topic and to the objectives. These are intended to be 'current' signs that are meaningful to the target audience. This listing may be extremely long, and will be culled later in the process. Despite the long list, this is a worthwhile exercise, because new ideas will be generated during the process, and it is not possible to see whether the sign is 'lapsed' or 'chameleon-like'. Additionally, some signs will be 'emergent'; this means that they have no significance at present, but are likely to have importance in the near future. There are different 'semiotic modes' such as written, spoken, non-verbal, etc. It is useful to be aware of the nature of signs, but there is a problem with imposing such categories early in the study: the researcher may miss meaning by seeking order. The semiotic practitioner will attempt to begin in an open-minded way, unconstrained by classification. This stage is therefore concerned with the assembly of seemingly unrelated materials.
3. **Exposure to materials** The research team must be exposed to some or all of the materials listed. In some cases, this will be a physical collection of items; in other cases, it may mean undergoing the consumer experience in order to generate a non-tangible sign. As a general rule, it is valuable to create a library of materials from the outset. This will be used for analysis and demonstration when reporting the findings.
4. **Identification of absent materials** One useful way to interpret these materials is to consider what is absent—in other words, to discover what is missing. Television adverts may be missing because you were unable to obtain them, rather than because they do not exist. If they do not exist, this may be significant: it may mean something to the target market. For example, it may indicate that the brand does not waste money, or it may mean quite the opposite, perhaps that the brand is not well established.
5. **Interpretation** There are no set methods of analysis. Some semioticians are extremely systematic and will list each item with a meaning; others will take an overall view and a more holistic approach. The aim here is to see relationships between materials, and the best way to do this is to look for contradictions or differences in the items. The idea is not to look at the frequency of occurrence of different signs (this is the domain of 'content analysis'), but at the meanings they provide to the people of interest. There follows a list of questions that can be asked to facilitate interpretation of materials available for analysis; again this is not exhaustive, but rather evocative. Questions must be related to the objective of the study.

- Does the code have single or multiple meaning?
- What assumptions are needed to see the meaning?
- Does it link closely to the target?
- Is it formal or informal?
- Does the arrangement in space have meaning?
- Is the code specific to the medium?
- Are there secret messages, or metaphors?
- Do codes work with each other or do they work against each other?
- Is there any confusion for the target?
- Is the sign open to interpretation?
- Are different people likely to see different things?
- What are the reasons for a particular meaning being communicated?
- What does the communication tell us about the communicator?
- What does the communication tell us about the target?
- What does the communication tell us about the communicator's view of the target?
- What does the communication tell us about how the communicator wishes to be seen?

6. **Reporting** It is not easy to report the findings of semiotic analysis, because it is not easy to articulate experiences and feelings. However, the skill of the semiotics practitioner is in doing exactly that: communicating the meaning of multiple messages that are directed towards a person, who is the target of communications. Chapter 10 goes further into reporting, but in the context of semiotics it should be emphasised that face-to-face presentation is particularly valuable. The semiotic practitioner must also reproduce and preserve materials for further scrutiny. At the least, some examples should appear in the main findings, to illustrate points made, and then a more extensive set can appear in appendices to the final report.

Critical evaluation of semiotics

A major reservation about using semiotics is its reputation for being 'academic and obscure' (Harvey and Evans 2001). Because the semiotic procedure cannot examine all materials from the past and present, the researcher is necessarily being selective in what is used for analysis. It is not known whether these materials convey the same meaning to the target audience as they do to the researcher. This is a sound reason for criticism of the technique, which can be counterargued by suggesting that the researcher is applying 'empathy' and can therefore stand back from the situation.

Additionally, the researcher is able to fill any gaps with likely meaning gleaned from similar studies and sectors. This is a specific strength of semiotic analysis: a semiotic expert experienced in one industrial sector can inform another. A major criticism concerns subjectivity: we might accuse the researcher of taking materials and simply giving impressions and interpretations, rather than applying scientific approaches that are objective, reliable, and valid. Conversely, if

Research in focus
Semiotics for beginners—beers, buses, and business

Semiotics can be applied to drinks, transportation, and control solutions. Let us look at beers, buses, and business-to-business applications.

Semiotic analysis was used to look at competitor advertising by Guinness. The objective was to provide Guinness marketers with an understanding of competitive positioning. The researchers sourced beer brand advertising from Cameroon, Germany, Malaysia, Spain, the UK, and the USA, and this was analysed by experts in each of these markets. Harvey and Evans (2001) explained that '*after reviewing the ads, the semiologists mapped out the codes characteristic of their market, then analysed advertising for the major brands in terms of the overall profile of codes deployed or broken—residual (dated ad styles and conventions), dominant (middle-of-the-road for today), or emergent (dynamic, innovative)*'. The process was straightforward, fast, and cost-effective and is updated by Guinness personnel using the most recent TV and print ads. The output gave a clear understanding of what positioning consumers will have for any brand that could be considered competitive.

Lawes (2002) described how she did semiotic analysis on transportation, to investigate what discourages the use of the bus. She explained how this began with a first stage, which '*drew on every resource we could think of: songs, jokes, TV entertainment, things in the news, personal experiences*'. The results allowed the clients to know what prejudices exist and to understand which ones their advertising agency might be able to change. Clearly, this is valuable fodder for the creative advertising field.

In a business-to-business context, Nicks (2003) described how Ipsos UK helped Norgren to redefine its brand. Norgren is a leading supplier of motion and fluid control solutions. The items analysed, semiotically, were materials drawn from the UK, Germany, and the USA. They were corporate brochures, websites, and the trade press. A major observation was that the colour blue was used by the major brands '*alongside strong, masculine fonts. People and products seldom mix and products are displayed in precise photographic detail; companies are "big" and talk about their origins and their products, rather than relationships*'. This formed the basis for an appraisal of the brand positioning and a platform for change.

Compiled by Nigel Bradley 2012.

Sources:

Harvey, M. and Evans, M. (2001) Semiotics: a window into competitor advertising, *ADMAP*, June, pp. 36–39.

Lawes, R. (2002) De-mystifying semiotics: some key questions answered, *Journal of the Market Research Society*, 44, pp. 251–264.

Nicks, G. (2003) Liquid assets, *Research*, May, pp. 36–37.

Questions

1 List the materials we know were used in each of these studies. Also list both those that might have been helpful and those that might not. Why are some more helpful than others, and how is this decided?

2 Is semiotics better suited to FMCG (Guinness) or B2B (Norgren)?

3 From the evidence, which signs do you think are 'chameleon signs' for any of the cases mentioned?

semiotics are able to uncover 'emergent signs', it may be one of the few ways of predicting the future; this area therefore may predict fashions by providing informed speculation. If used in conjunction with other approaches (groups and depths), then it can offer an extremely powerful sounding board.

Chapter summary

1 Explain the purpose of qualitative research

Qualitative research involves using techniques that attempt to gain an understanding of the existence and nature of attitudes, interests, and opinions. It does not measure the 'amount', but it may give an indication of dominant motivators. Qualitative research is unstructured, but does have guidelines. It centres on words, narrative, images, and concepts rather than on numerical values. There is an emphasis on understanding rather than measurement. The researcher must interpret verbal and non-verbal communications.

2 Describe the different types of qualitative research

Discussion, observation, and projective methods are used. Sessions can be individual, in pairs, or as groups. In a group discussion a moderator will direct conversation. These interviews best take place in person, but may be carried out by telephone, or online. The Delphi technique uses a carefully designed questionnaire that is circulated to selected experts; there are several rounds that result in a forecast. In 'grounded theory', collected information is inspected and the researcher will 'ground' explanations in the data. Ethnography and action research is participant observation. Semiotics is the study of communication by careful analysis of signs.

3 Show the benefits of different approaches to qualitative research

A major advantage of grounded theory is that it avoids creating a preconceived idea of the outcome, and forces the researcher to keep an open mind. On the other hand, in all qualitative projects, the researcher is able to fill any gaps with likely meaning gleaned from similar studies and sectors. The depth interview allows probing without pressure from other people; respondents can answer in their own time, in their own way. The technique is 'mobile', so it can take place where the respondent spends time; this may be at home, at the place of work, or even in transit. The Delphi approach is powerful in forecasting innovations; it can also be applied to anticipate the future of market sectors. Because semiotics is able to uncover 'emergent signs', it may be one of the few ways of predicting the future; this area therefore may predict fashions by providing informed speculation.

4 Show the limitations of qualitative research

There is always a risk that little of significance may come from qualitative data. This is especially true for grounded theory. Is it objective, reliable, and valid? It is seen to be too subjective, so qualitative researchers need highly developed interpersonal skills that combine empathy with analytical ability. Without this, respondents may be led in one direction. Semiotics researchers must be selective in choice of material.

Review questions

1 Explore the difference between the group and the depth interviews.

2 In qualitative research, an understanding of euphemisms is important. Why?

3 In what circumstances might we decide not to use qualitative research?

4 Researchers have been criticised for placing too much emphasis on body language. Why?

5 Define these terms using examples: ethnography, semiology, Delphi, depths, grounded theory.

Discussion questions

1 Justify the decision to remove a moderator from the focus group. Explain the implications for respondents.

2 Investigate the contribution of Dichter and Lazarsfeld to qualitative research.

3 Ask family and friends if they have attended a focus group. Ask them to explain the topic and how they felt about the technique. Did they think it was useful to the researcher?

4 How can qualitative research mislead the researcher?

5 Plan an ethnographic study to investigate the use of perfumes.

6 In the opening Snapshot, why was the target market chosen to be the sample? What other people could the researchers have included? Give reasons for your answers.

Further reading

- Darlington, Y. and Scott, D. (2002) *Qualitative Research in Practice: Stories from the Field*. Crows Nest, Sydney: Allen & Unwin.
  A very useful summary of experience from the field.
- Denzin, N.K. and Lincoln, Y.S. (2000) *Handbook of Qualitative Research*. London: Sage.
  An extremely thorough, almost encyclopaedic, tome with theoretical and practical assistance.
- Gordon, W. and Langmaid, R. (1988) *Qualitative Market Research: A Practitioner's and Buyer's Guide*. Aldershot, Hants: Gower.
  A very practical manual to assist the researcher in carrying out depth interviews and focus group discussions. Some useful tips on projective techniques and the use of caption completion.
- Mariampolski, H. (1999) The power of ethnography, *Journal of the Market Research Society*, 41, pp. 75–86.
  An extremely well written account of ethnography.

Case study
Testing a weedkiller advert

An agrochemical producer had booked advertising space in several farming publications for their herbicide called 'Basta!' and approached a research agency with a request to test three possible executions of the intended advertisement, there was a desire to find one single version to use. It was agreed to carry out three focus groups in the UK, two in East Anglia, another in Hampshire; there would be eight respondents at each group all of whom already use the weedkiller brand 'Basta!'. Farmers had varying farm sizes: the smallest 40 acres, the largest 1600 acres. All were growing Winter Wheat and most Winter Barley. Spring Wheat and Spring Barley were also cultivated.

©istockphoto.com/Dave White

Discussion guidelines were produced by the research agency and agreed with the client and ad agency. The ad agency provided large colour mock ups of the proposed adverts. The client and advertising agency were invited to all sessions, which were held in large meeting rooms of public houses. Pubs were chosen as convenient to reach, with catering and ample parking.

The objective was to ensure that the visuals were suitable for the target audience and portrayed the brand properly. The first group took place in Norwich and immediately problems were identified with the ads. One showed a healthy wheat field with 'Basta!' apparently responsible; however, there was one single red poppy at the side of the field that the ad agency had used as a device to attract the viewer's attention. Farmers argued that this showed 'Basta!' did not work. The second execution had pictures of weeds that would be eliminated by the herbicide: Chickweed, Cleavers and Mayweed. Farmers criticised these because the plants looked too healthy, a good weedkiller should be associated with wilting weeds, not strong upstanding ones.

The client, ad agency, and researchers held a late night meeting after the farmers had gone home, which meant that the next two focus groups were rescheduled in order for the artwork to be modified. The discussion guide was also changed and new artwork was introduced. In order to explore issues with the three new executions in a balanced way, the order in which they were shown to respondents varied. There was nothing 'scientific' about this, it simply meant that discussion time would not be concentrated on one specific visual. There were less objections at the next two groups, in fact useful suggestions were gathered that helped the adverts. All moderation was carried out by the researchers without interruption from the client and ad agency viewers. At the end of the second group the representative from the ad agency was invited to ask anything that might have been missed. To the shock of the researchers he asked the eight attendees to give a show of hands to vote on the best visual. This question was repeated at the final group. There was no clear 'winner'.

After careful analysis of notes and sound recordings, the researchers presented their results to a debrief meeting at the ad agency. Minor modifications were used and all three advertisements were used in the campaign. The results of the 'vote' were not part of the debrief.

Compiled by Nigel Bradley 2012.

Questions

1. Critically evaluate the research design. The study could have been done in other ways. What are they? Make a comparison between the possible approaches. Why were depth interviews not used?
2. What are the reasons why non-users of the brand are often excluded from such research?
3. Why was the researcher shocked when the ad agency asked for a vote to identify the 'best' visual?
4. The ad agency asked for transcripts of the groups to be provided. The researchers refused to provide them, what reasons do you think they gave for this?

Key web links

- Association for Qualitative Research http://www.aqr.org.uk
- Viewing Facilities Association http://www.viewing.org.uk
- Market Research World (MRW) http://www.marketresearchworld.net

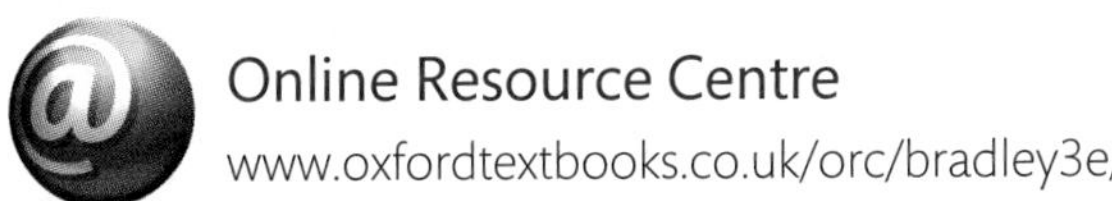

Visit the Online Resource Centre that accompanies this book to access more learning resources on this chapter topic.

References and sources

Bienner, M. (ed.) (2006) Finding and hiring a viewing facility, *Research Decisions*, March.

Brown, B.B. (1968) *Delphi Process: A Methodology used for Elicitation of Opinions of Experts*. Santa Monica, CA: The Rand Corporation.

Clarke, B. and Saunders, M. (1997) There's trouble in classes for lads who wear glasses, *Research Plus*, November, p. 7.

Coulthard, M. (1977) *An Introduction to Discourse Analysis*. Harlow, Essex: Longman.

Dalkey, N., Brown, B., and Cochran, S. (1969) *The Delphi Method*. Santa Monica, CA: Rand Corporation, http://www.rand.org/publications/classics/delphi3.pdf

Elliot, R. and Jankel-Elliot, N. (2003) Using ethnology in strategic consumer research: qualitative market research, *An International Journal*, 6, pp. 215–223.

Floch, J-M. (2001) *Semiotics, Marketing and Communication beneath the Signs: The Strategies*. New York: Palgrave Macmillan.

Flores, L., Moskowitz, H., and Maier, A. (2004) From 'weak signals' to successful product development, *Excellence in International Research*, Netherlands: ESOMAR, pp. 97–124.

Gabbott, M. and Hogg, G. (2001) The role of non-verbal communication in service encounters: a conceptual framework, *Journal of Marketing Management*, 17, pp. 5–26.

Glaser, B.G. and Strauss, A.L. (1967) *The Discovery of Grounded Theory*. Chicago, IL: Aldine Publishing Company.

Gordon, W. (2000) *Goodthinking: A Guide to Qualitative Research*. London: ADMAP Publications.

Gordon, W. and Langmaid, R. (1988) *Qualitative Market Research: A Practitioner's and Buyer's Guide*. Aldershot, Hants: Gouler.

Greenbaum, T.L. (1998) *The Handbook for Focus Group Research*, 2nd edn. Thousand Oaks, CA: Sage Publications.

Harvey, M. and Evans, M. (2001) Semiotics: a window into competitor advertising, *ADMAP*, June, pp. 36–39.

Husserl, E., trans. Boyce Gibson, W.R. (1931) *Ideas: General Introduction to Pure Phenomenology*. London: George Allen & Unwin Ltd.

Jefferson, G. (1973) A case of precision timing in ordinary conversation: overlapped tag-positioned address terms in closing sequences, *Semiotica*, 9, pp. 47–96.

Kaushik, M. and Sen, A. (1990) Semiotics and qualitative research, *Journal of the Market Research Society*, 32, pp. 227–242.

Kozinets, R.V. (1999) E-Tribalized Marketing? The Strategic Implications of Virtual Communities of Consumption, *European Management Journal*, 17(3), pp. 252–264.

Kozinets, R.V. (2002) The Field behind the Screen: Using Netnography for Marketing Research in Online Communities, *Journal of Marketing Research*, XXXIX, pp. 61–72.

Krueger, R.A. and Casey, M.A. (2000) *Focus Groups: A Practical Guide for Applied Research*. 3rd edn. Thousand Oaks, CA: Sage Publications.

Kurzon, D. (1998) *Discourse of Silence*. Amsterdam: John Benjamins.

Lawes, R. (2002) De-mystifying semiotics: some key questions answered, *Journal of the Market Research Society*, 44, pp. 251–264.

Lewin, K. (1952) *Field Theory in Social Science*. London: Tavistock.

MacDonald, N. (2003) People watching, *Research*, July, p. 8.

Mariampolski, H. (1997) Solving the problems of observational research: field tactics in corporate ethnography. ESOMAR Conference papers, Lisbon, July, http://www.warc.com

Merton, R.K., Fiske, M. and Kendall, P.L. (1956, reprinted 1990) *The Focused Interview*. New York: The Free Press.

Morris, D. (2002) *Peoplewatching*. London: Vintage.

MRS (2006) *Qualitative Research Guidelines*, http://www.mrs.org.uk/standards/qual.htm

Nicks, G. (2003) Liquid assets, *Research*, May, pp. 36–37.

Pease, A. and Pease, B. (2004) *The Definitive Book of Body Language*. London: Orion Publishing Co.

Stern, B.B. (2004) The importance of being ernest: commemorating Dichter's contribution to advertising research, *Journal of Advertising Research*, June, pp. 165–169.

Strauss, A.L. and Corbin, J. (1998) *Basics of Qualitative Research*, 2nd edn. Newbury Park, CA: Sage.

Taylor, D. (1997) An MR boost helps Disneyland Paris take off into profit, *Research Plus*, June, p. 6.

Tuckman, B.W. (1965) Developmental sequences in small groups, *Psychological Bulletin*, 63, pp. 384–399.

Tuckman, B.W. and Jensen, M.A.C. (1977) Stages of small group development revisited, *Group and Organizational Studies*, 2, pp. 419–427.

Valentine, V. (2002) Repositioning research: a new MR language model, *Journal of the Market Research Society*, 44, pp. 163–192.

Vladimirova, E. and Petrin, K. (2001) Russia: pyramid on the kitchen table, how an ethnographic study of culinary habits helped develop a unified marketing approach, *Qualitative Research*, Budapest: ESOMAR, pp. 289–297.

Waymise, G. (2002) *Ethnography*, Silicon Valley American Marketing Association paper, 18 September.

?WHATIF (2002) *Sticky Wisdom: How to Start a Creative Revolution at Work*. Oxford: Capstone.

Zaltman, G. (2003) *How Customers Think: Essential Insights into the Mind of the Market*: Harvard, MA: Harvard Business School Press.

8 Quantitative research

Contents

Chapter guide

A great deal of marketing research money goes into quantitative research projects aimed at evaluating different elements of the marketing mix. In decision-making, managers like to have hard figures, and quantitative research offers precisely that. This chapter examines some regularly used approaches such as experimentation, hall tests, panels, and the omnibus. This is a field that has been revolutionised by the use of computers, so you are given guidance on databases, data marts, and data warehouses. Finally, we look at the role of software in data mining.

Learning outcomes

By the end of this chapter, you should be able to:

1. **Explain the purpose of quantitative research**
2. **Describe the different approaches to quantitative research**
3. **Show the benefits of different approaches to quantitative research**
4. **Show the limitations of different approaches to quantitative research**

Introduction

Quantitative research is everything concerning numbers and statistics. One major reason for this branch of research is the creation of meaningful **segmentation**, which brings us back to the original meaning of statistics, which concern providing information for government about the nation, about the *state*—it gives an account of the population. Quantitative research goes beyond basic profile **demographics**; it gives accounts of usage and attitudes. In order to make measurements, we use various measures of dispersion: when we know how a data set is distributed, we can learn much.

There are several ways to measure the variability of the data. Typically, we look at the mean score—the arithmetic average—then at the standard deviation—which provides an average distance for each element from the mean. Several other measures are also important. Here, it is useful to distinguish between four types of data: nominal data, ordinal data, interval data, and ratio data. 'Nominal data' gives a name to an item, so there is a limited amount that can be done at analysis. 'Ordinal data' creates an order, so that the relative position is evident. 'Interval' and 'ratio data' include indications of *distance* between items and so there is a greater possibility to apply statistics such as means and standard deviations. We can classify **scales** as comparative and non-comparative. Comparative scales involve the direct comparison of stimulus objects.

Comparative scale data must be interpreted in relative terms and have only ordinal or rank order properties. In non-comparative scales, each object is scaled independently of the others in the stimulus set, so the data are interval or ratio scaled. These scales are favoured in market research because so much more can be done with them. Chapter 6 on questionnaire design looked further into scales and the scale remains a key part of the quantitative toolbox.

The word 'statistics' refers to numbers related to 'the state' such as births and deaths. In 1834, the Royal Statistical Society was founded to use *'figures and tabular exhibitions to illustrate the conditions and prospects of society'*. Members used tools invented many years earlier: the slide rule (John Napier in 1617) and mechanical calculator (Wilhelm Schickard in 1623).

In the 1930s, retail panels were established in the USA by A.C. Nielsen Company (see Table 8.1). During the Second World War, the first UK consumer panel was operated by the agency, BMRB, for the Ministry of Food to assist in planning food rations (Buck 1982). The next credible panel was undertaken in 1950 by Attwood Statistics Ltd. Using the little-known technique of random sampling to recruit 2000 homes, the venture was successful because of the commitment by Fast-Moving Consumer Goods (FMCG) companies, notably Unilever. Such was the success that Attwood extended the concept to Holland, Germany, France, Italy, Austria, Belgium, and Denmark. In turn, local agencies in those countries responded to Attwood with similar panels, ensuring that the methodology became a solid part of quantitative research.

Another one of the quantitative researcher's tools is 'experimentation' and this has also been used since the 1950s; it was first applied to mail-order catalogue selling. In the 1960s and 1970s, field experiments in the form of **test marketing** were extremely popular. At that time, terrestrial television divided the nation into broadcast regions, which were used either as experimental or control groups. This was particularly useful for new product launches.

Table 8.1 Notable events for quantitative research

Period	Event
1600s	Key instruments invented (the slide rule and mechanical calculator)
1830s	Royal Statistical Society founded
1930s	Retail panels established by A.C. Nielsen
1950s	Commercial computers, experimentation
1960s	TV test marketing emerges
1970s	Cheap electronic calculators
1980s	Electronic spreadsheets, geodemographics, databases
1990s	Powerful data mining feasible on most computers

The 1990s saw the arrival of satellite, cable, and Internet broadcasting. These developments meant that the distinctions between geographic zones became more complicated, so experimentation had to adapt. Databases offered a fertile ground for testing new ideas; the outcome of variable manipulation could be detected easily. Data analysis techniques were refined as spreadsheet and data-mining software applications became commonplace.

Novel products also emerged in the field of segmentation. In the mid-1970s, the geographer Richard Webber categorised deprived areas of Liverpool. He revolutionised research when his attentions switched to commercial classifications. Webber established ACORN, and then went on to create a competing product called MOSAIC.

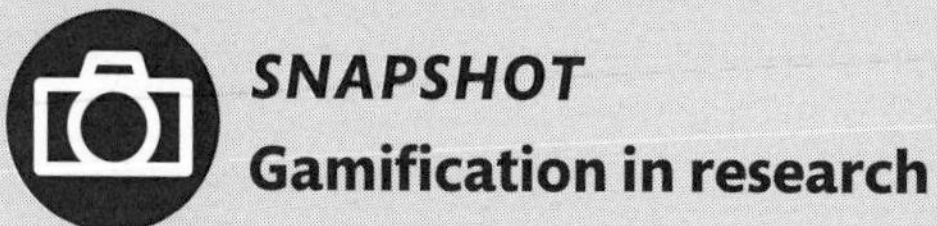

SNAPSHOT
Gamification in research

© istockphoto.com/TommL

Game playing has become an important pastime for Internet users worldwide. In recent years we have seen the word 'gamification' used in business circles, it has been heavily discussed as a mechanism that can be applied to 'non-gaming' to motivate people in carrying out tasks. It is the use of game design techniques to enhance non-game contexts. We all know how addictive online games can be; we see the satisfaction in reaching the next 'level', we have the joy of receiving rewards—or the jolt of disappointment when we are so close.

There are two extremes for using gamification in research (Ewing 2011), one called *hard gamification*, whereby a radical change is made to the research task so that games are created that have research tasks embedded, almost invisible to the user. *Soft gamification* is at the other extreme, and here the regular business of creating surveys takes place but adding the secrets of gaming success to enhance engagement. Leedy and Royle (2011) have identified seven gameplay aspects that can be of potential use to studies: 1. sense of achievement; 2. rewards given to mark arrival; 3. status is important so ranking against others can encourage panel participation; 4. group pressure can attract other informants; 5. ownership holds appeal; 6. real-time feedback can motivate; and 7. group collaboration can push individual engagement.

So what can we place in the market researcher's toolbox from gaming? Interestingly much of this is in common with projective techniques: impactful visuals, storytelling, feedback, interactivity, entertainment, the use of play, leader boards, progress indicators, virtual currency (points mean prizes!), challenges between people, surprises (sub-games), sets of rules, and the use of larger than life characters.

The advantages of gamification of research include the ability to engage people and to encourage informants to perform what were previously seen as boring tasks. Gaming should be fun, and that is why enthusiasts such as Betty Adamou make it fun by introducing a new vocabulary: *Playspondents*™ who will be found in the *PlayspondentPlayhouse*™. Gamification should increase cooperation and quality of responses; it should motivate to achieve the tasks which have been specified. Importantly it has the ability to attract hard to find respondents: teenagers and young adults.

The disadvantages of gamification of research include the need for specialist skills required to produce a credible vehicle; personnel need to be artistic, have writing skills and of course be technically competent. Without the right balance it is possible to create unrealistic expectations for participants, tasks need to have the correct balance of making chores relatively easy but at the same time be challenging. This all requires different and more extensive testing than that to which the regular researcher is accustomed. In the final analysis we must ask whether findings from the 'fun' are valid and reliable.

Compiled by Nigel Bradley 2012.

Sources:
Adamou, B. (2011) The Future of Research Through Gaming. CASRO Online Conference March 2011 in Las Vegas transcript available at http://rwconnect.esomar.org/2011/04/13/the-future-of-research-through-gaming/

Ewing, T. (2011) State Of Play: Four Types Of Research Gamification. Blog, Nov 28 available at http://blackbeardblog.tumblr.com/post/13452542524/state-of-play-four-types-of-research-gamification

Leedy E. and Ruyle E. (2011) Game the system, *Research*, December, pp. 28–29.

Research Through Gaming web page: http://www.researchthroughgaming.com

Some applications

Using numbers, the quantitative researcher looks at customers, whether they are past, present, or potential. Quantitative methods are able to test variants of the marketing mix. Table 8.2 shows how different elements of the mix can be measured, with some examples of sources. Clearly, these will change, depending on the firm and product sector. These methods will be explored further in this chapter and elsewhere.

Brands and brand equity

Brands are big business. We have seen many consultancies that have grown on the basis that corporations equate good branding with increased market share, and advisers reap rewards. Perhaps as a consequence, academic literature on branding has become very popular in recent years. The market researcher has a toolbox that allows the marketer not only to create brands, but also to diagnose any problems. Such research can give information to help fix things that go wrong.

Jean-Noël Kapferer (2001) implies that research is an essential tool in taking brands forward. Leslie De Chernatony (2001) also confirms the role of marketing research in 'building brands'. It might be argued that for a complex subject—which branding is—research does not fit easily into a box. One term that emerged from all of this activity was 'brand equity'. In response to interest in the topic, the Market Research Society convened a seminar in 1998 where different views on the subject of brand equity were discussed. We can find many definitions of brand equity: for example, there are nine in Keller (1998), but Feldwick (2002) prefers to focus on three different senses, which he describes. Furthermore, he explains their measurement. In summary, these three are: values of the brand as an asset (to the company); measures of consumers' attachment to a brand; the **beliefs** the consumer has about the brand.

Interbrand is a firm that has expertise of branding, and its measures for brand equity are shown in Figure 8.1. They are divided into four: financial-related, market-related, consumer-related, and a legal analysis. Together, these are a good description of the brand in tangible terms. These are explored by quantitative researchers.

Experimentation

'Experimentation' is a research design that is used to change some things, but not others. The effects of this 'deliberate manipulation of variables' can be detected by questioning or observational methods. Typically, experimentation compares several possible versions of the marketing mix to decide the most effective way to market specific products; it may therefore apply to price, place, product, or promotion. For example, if we were to change a shop's layout to see the effect before and after alterations, we would either need to observe a changed effect or we would need to detect it by asking questions. It should not be forgotten that observation encompasses mechanical observation, so we might examine transactions that have been recorded by the reading of bar codes throughout the period.

Table 8.2 How quantitative research measures elements of the marketing mix

Element	Methods
Product	
Sales	Internal secondary
Sales by segment	Internal secondary/primary data
Market share	Primary data
New products	Hall tests, sales force, complaints, experiments
Claims on warranty	Data mining
Repairs	Channel surveys/panels
Repeat purchase	Data mining, panels
Place	
Channel cost	Data mining
Channel volume	Data mining
Channel growth/new stores	Geographic information systems (GIS)
Delivery time	Surveys, panels
Stock levels	Geographic information systems (GIS)
Price	
Profit margins	Databases
Discount levels	Surveys with non-customers
Price by segment	Surveys, panels
Price comparisons	Surveys, omnibus
Promotions	
Cost per contact	Data mining
Media coverage	Audience surveys
Sales per call	Data mining
Awareness levels	Omnibus, panels, surveys
Enquiries generated	Data mining
Effectiveness	Experiments, data mining

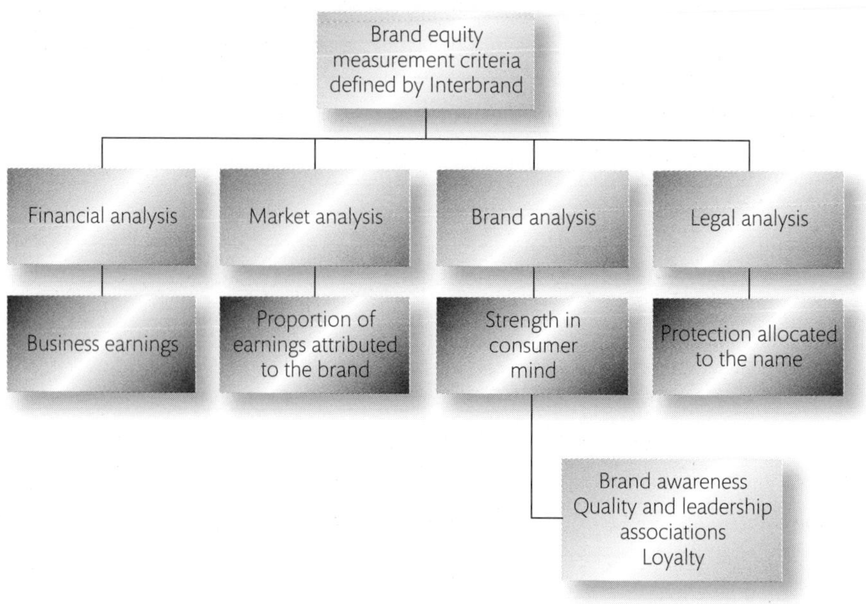

Figure 8.1 Brand equity measurement according to Interbrand

Variables come in many forms: independent variables—ones that we can change; dependent variables, where we would expect to see a change; or extraneous variables, which may change outcomes, but which we do not manipulate. As an example, consider a juice seller. If the seller were to reduce the price of the orange juice sold, price is the independent variable. We would expect to see a change in the number of bottles sold (so the sales figure is the dependent variable). However, if a new competitor juice were to be launched, this would be an extraneous variable.

Figure 8.2 simplifies the idea that variables affect marketing outcomes. We see that marketing stimuli (in the form of the marketing mix) can be varied. Environmental variables, such as political, economic, social, and technological effects cannot be controlled, but will affect the outcome. We cannot control the weather, but we can control our prices.

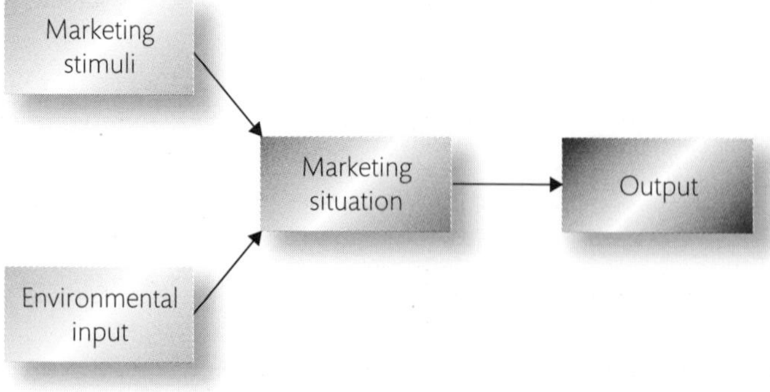

Figure 8.2 Variables that affect marketing

In recent years, experimentation has been particularly powerful in the field of direct marketing: first of all with mail order and, more recently, with online transactions. Experimentation can be qualitative, but definitive results come from hard numbers; only the quantitative approach can examine causal influences. Therefore, in recent years, quantitative experiments have been favoured.

In principle, the idea is to show **causality**, to provide an explanation of the *only* reason why something happens. Compare this with correlation, which simply shows association. Old people die in cold weather every year but weather may not be the cause of death. There may be a variable that affects old people (such as lack of money to heat the home). The problem in marketing is that many variables are in action, so the relationship between cause and effect is unclear: it is only 'probable'.

Before we assume causality, three conditions need to be satisfied:

1. **Concomitant variation**—this shows correlation between the variables, which vary together in a predictable way
2. **Time order**—the effect is observed after the event, not before
3. **Elimination of other factors**—other possible causes.

Unfortunately, even if these are satisfied, this does not necessarily prove causality—but there will be a good case.

Experimental designs

Many combinations of experiment are possible. Sometimes, the distinction is made between true experiments, quasi-experiments, and action research. In the 'true experiment', the researcher has the most control; this diminishes in 'quasi-experiments' and is almost absent in 'action research'. However, all types share the characteristic that the researcher makes a direct intervention that is then measured in some way. It is probably fair to say that most market research experiments are quasi-experiments.

'Control groups' are a feature of experimental designs. These do not receive treatment, but they are 'tested' after changes have been made. Because the control group is matched to the experimental group, if there are similar changes, they cannot be attributed to the variables that have been altered.

We can therefore have a design called the 'after-only with control', which means that observations or questioning take place after the change, and a control sample is used to see the differences. Control groups are not always used in research and this is for several reasons: one is the time taken to construct a larger study, and another is the difficulty of shielding such groups from treatments. Less powerful than the 'after-only *with* control' is the 'after-only *without* control' design: this means that observations or questioning take place after the change, but there is no control sample; any differences must be inferred from the results. Another design that can take place without the control is the 'before-after' design, whereby observations are taken before a change is implemented and also afterwards; changes are therefore apparent.

Other types are the 'times series', 'cross-sectional', 'randomised block', 'Latin square', and 'factorial' designs (see Figure 8.3).

1. After-only without control
2. After-only with control
3. Before-after
4. Cross-sectional
5. Randomised block
6. Randomised block
7. Latin square
8. Factorial design

Figure 8.3 Experimental designs

Sources of bias

There are at least three potential sources of bias that can arise in an experiment.

1. **Subject bias** In simple terms, if someone is the subject of a test, they may react in a different way than if the test was not there. The famous 'Hawthorne effect' (described fully by Roethlisberger and Dickson 1939) is a suitable label for this.
2. **Measurement changes** People may withdraw from the experiment (this is called 'experimental mortality') or the instrumentation may change during the process.
3. **Changes to people involved** Unforeseen events can affect the subjects. These may be things that affect their lives, whether physically, mentally, or emotionally. These, in turn, become 'extraneous variables'.

Besides these sources of bias, the disadvantages concern the following.

- **Expense** Some managers prefer to put research money into some marketing activity that will lead to extra revenue. Experiments can be the most expensive form of research and the customised nature makes shared studies undesirable.
- **Time** Long-term effects, by definition, do not give instant information. New product launches need quick feedback and experiments, and have long set-up time frames.
- **Competence** Well-designed and conducted experiments demand excellence in theory and practice. These qualities are available, but in great demand.
- **Secrecy** If a product launch is delayed by testing, then competitors can take a lead in the marketplace.

There are various problems with all experiments and these are known as 'experimental errors'. Nine types have been identified, as shown in Figure 8.4. It is normal to explain to respondents what the experiment was about and what the process involved. It may also involve asking the respondent to explain any suggestions they have in interpretation. This two-way debrief helps to conform to the code of ethics, but can also enhance the richness of results.

Market tests

'In-home **placement tests**' are a useful way to gather similar information—still quantitatively—but on a smaller scale than that of an entire field region. Here, respondents are asked to try

1. Pre-measurement
2. Maturation
3. History
4. Instrumentation
5. Selection
6. Mortality
7. Interaction
8. Reactive error
9. Measurement timing

Figure 8.4 Experimental errors

out products in the normal way in which the product would be used. With some techniques, products are used in view of the researcher; in placement tests, they are used in private. For example, a new form of breakfast cereal might be given to a household to be used alongside, or as a substitute for, an existing cereal. The advantage of an in-home placement is that errors associated with an artificial situation are avoided.

Similarly, 'store tests' can be carried out. These allow consumers to be observed or questioned before and after some change—perhaps of shelf positions or package design. The measurement may be a simple question of detecting a change in footfall, that is the numbers of shoppers who visit the store, or a complex association with purchase clusters. This then enters the field of artificial situations or what are known as 'laboratory experiments', among which are test centres and **hall tests**.

'Test centres' are premises built for the purposes of testing. Some of the larger supermarkets actually have 'dummy stores', where manufacturers are invited to carry out tests of their packaging. Shoppers are invited to make purchases in a 'normal way' and become respondents. These are large supermarkets, but the retailers benefit from the investment because it helps to build a close relationship with their suppliers and it offers a facility suitable for training their own staff.

Hall tests

The idea of a hall test (or **central location test**) is to show respondents stimulus material in a secure, sheltered, and private environment. The name derives from the fact that the UK has hundreds of village halls and church halls that are available for hire by research agencies. These locations are widespread; they offer a useful, low-cost option for researchers; and are reassuring to respondents because they are situated within their own communities.

The hall test is used to present materials to respondents that would be too large or too heavy to transport to the home or which may be unsuitable to show in the street. Food and drink are obvious products for such tests because they require specific conditions for preparation and presentation. The correct temperature is likely to be an issue. So, for example, hall tests typically test packaging, new products, and advertising. These items are usually at a sensitive stage in their development and so the closed hall offers a suitable location in which to maintain secrecy. For example, M&M Mars, a division of Mars Inc., regularly uses these types of interviews to test confectionery, such as variations on the Mars Bar and Milky Way (see O'Rourke 2000).

Over the years, church halls and village halls have taken on an image of dusty and cold environments, which can affect opinions expressed by informants. Perhaps as a result of this possible negative effect on cooperation levels and response quality, a new set of venues has emerged. These are the hotel and public house (pub); both venues have rooms for hire and offer a warmer, more welcoming option. They also offer the possibility of preparing foods for taste tests. Problems can arise when unwanted guests gravitate towards the rented room, or respondents are distracted into other rooms, particularly if there is a delay in entering the viewing facility.

A variation of the hall test is the **clinic**. It is common for car manufacturers to hold 'car clinics', whereby a prototype car, sometimes a clay model, is brought to the venue—sometimes alongside existing cars, sometimes with competing models. Respondents are asked to view and then comment. Clinics have been extended to other vehicles and products, so there are now 'lorry clinics', 'tractor clinics', 'mobile phone clinics', 'washing machine clinics', 'fridge clinics', and so on.

Most hall tests are quantitative, and use a structured questionnaire. The method lends itself to securing responses from large numbers of people who have a limited amount of time available. Qualitative research is possible using such a research design, but is less likely because respondents spend less time than would be suitable for a depth interview.

A major issue to consider with such central location interviewing is the type of sample that will result. Interestingly, some centres do not permit market research interviewers, deemed as an unnecessary nuisance. A given location can only intercept people within a limited range: for example, of less than five minutes by foot. Therefore, the research will be limited to the type of people who are mobile at the specific time of day chosen for fieldwork. This is a classic convenience sample, although quotas may be applied. Respondents tend to be self-selecting because they will choose to be stopped or choose to go to the venue. In the case of shopping areas, this will probably bias the sample towards medium or heavy shoppers. This can be overcome to a small extent by boosting the sample with other respondents recruited by another means (email, phone, in person) and giving appointments at the venue. This booster can affect the sample composition negatively, however, in that these individuals will have had longer to consider the interview and may therefore behave differently.

A further disadvantage is that this environment is artificial. Where consumption is tested—for example, eating, drinking, or trying a product—it is important to acknowledge that this is being done outside the normal environment.

Hall tests are almost the same as **mall intercepts**, mostly found in North America. Interviewers work entirely at shopping centres (known as 'shopping malls' in the USA). They are located at entrances or at a central point, so respondents can be intercepted and invited to a special room or venue within the centre. This offers the advantage of limiting expenses associated with both interviewer and interviewee.

In the USA, they are extremely important and estimates suggest that they account for about one-third of all personal interviews (McDaniel and Gates 2002, p.173), assisted by the fact that around 500 malls have permanent facilities belonging to research agencies. This popularity is said to be due to the expense of in-home and executive interviews, which has forced researchers to seek a viable alternative (Bush and Hair 1985). Certain research agencies, actually with their own offices situated in malls, have negotiated exclusive interview rights for their mall. This has two implications: first, not all locations are available; second, research costs may be inflated, because work in that mall must be subcontracted to a specific agency.

Another variation of this method is the **theatre test** or **cinema test**, whereby a cinema (or theatre) is hired and a film or television programme is shown, along with advertisements. Any of these three—the film, TV programme, or advertisement—may be tested. Several things distinguish a hall test from a theatre test: for example, the fact that the latter is pre-recruited, and respondents often complete a questionnaire themselves with minimal intervention from interviewers. Bush *et al.* (1991) investigated differences between using an interviewer or respondent to complete questionnaires in mall intercept surveys and concluded that for non-complex questionnaires, self-completion can be achieved at lower cost. Therefore, even within this research design, many variations are possible.

Another difference is that the hall test requires a great deal of design: a floor plan can help advance planning of positions for viewing; the flow of respondents through the facility must be carefully organised; such factors as lighting, heating, noise, smells, etc. need to be carefully controlled or noted.

Yet another variation of the hall test is the **van test**, where a caravan or motorised caravan is parked in a suitable area. Respondents are recruited in a similar way to the 'fixed' hall and invited inside the 'mobile' facility to view products and answer questions. This approach can rectify any sample deficiencies associated with a specific location.

As we have seen, hall tests are a quantitative technique, but a qualitative dimension is often added by conducting mini-depths with respondents who have already completed the quantitative questionnaire. This adds more detail and explanation to some of the responses that will later be tabulated.

A useful aspect of the hall test concerns observation. Respondents are inevitably asked to give their opinion about different, often competing, products. This gives a unique opportunity to observe how they approach each product: how they handle it, what they look at first of all, how they open it, how they use it, etc. These can be assessed in a structured or unstructured way, and observation can take place at the same time as questioning occurs.

Typically, tests are carried out over a two- to three-day period, with two to five recruiters situated outside the venue, who bring respondents inside the facility. The interview may continue with the same interviewer or another who is stationed within the location. Hall tests often result in a sample size of 100–200 respondents.

Panels

The term 'panel' refers to a set of individuals who are questioned or observed or who report over a period of time. This must not be confused with a focus group—panel members do not meet: they are interviewed separately and in a quantitative way. The research instrument may be a questionnaire, observation form, diary, or some mechanical means of data capture.

The approach means that quantification is possible and this then can act as a longitudinal measure of changes. Such quantification can lead to elaborate analysis to determine cause and effect. Much panel research is archived and therefore becomes a rich source for secondary data searches. Any changes at the micro- and macro-levels can be identified and investigated further. There are two approaches: the end-user can be part of the panel, or some agent throughout the distribution network can form a panel. These are respectively known as the 'consumer panel' and the 'retail panel'.

The advantages of the panel approach are clear in that opinion can be tracked over time and any changes can be detected. These reactions can also be related to key events, whether the event is a product launch, a product withdrawal, a scare story, an industrial strike, or a wider activity such as a political event. Because respondents have been recruited carefully, and know they will be contacted again, cooperation levels are generally good. Certainly, the response rate is better than that of an unsolicited approach by telephone or in the street; this, in turn, leads to cost-savings. Another small point is that a panel often identifies minority behaviours and therefore provides respondents that should be investigated further. The alternative would be to screen many people to find such groups.

The disadvantages of panels concern the respondent. Some argue that anyone who agrees to be on a panel, to promise willingly a long-term commitment, will have a strong opinion or be 'different' in some way. There is also a possibility that respondents will be conditioned by the task and demonstrate learned behaviour; they may be tempted to work from knowledge and memory rather than to monitor their real activities. Respondents are prone to fatigue, particularly if the task loads are heavy. Respondent fatigue has two major effects: one is that answers may be provided without thought (stock responses); the other that there will be dropout or panel erosion where further cooperation ceases. Any dropout means that panellists must be replaced, something that has been referred to as 'churn'. Dropout may mean that the data must be weighted. Both churn and weighting will have an impact on the results, timing, and costs.

There are two designs of interest: the 'continuous panel' and the 'interval panel'. The continuous panel features constant measurement and recording of data. The interval panel refers to a situation where reporting is less constant and, in some cases, the intervals between reporting are irregular.

Recruitment and maintenance can be difficult, so panel administration has become a skill in itself. The key to good panel management is to be continuously active: to recruit regularly, to keep the panel's interest, to monitor, and to provide incentives. A certain amount of 'churn' will occur, so a method of replacement needs to be in place from the outset. Sample size needs to be such that it can accommodate dropout and allow meaningful analysis. Incentives need to be considered carefully, that is whether to use a gift or regular communication such as a newsletter or a point-collection device. The use of incentives to secure cooperation and to keep panel members can be expensive and, if ill-considered, they can be ineffective.

Looking at the panel as a longitudinal monitor, we must be aware that techniques and providers will change over time. This type of research has changed in line with technology, so panels have moved from pen-and-paper records of purchases and visual observation of waste packages towards electronic data capture.

To quote two practitioners: '*Since 1977, there has been a change of benchmark methods in many grocery panels, from* dustbin *and* diary techniques *to in-home scanning of bar-coded packs*' (Buck and Jephcott 1997, p. 21). One argument says that changing the mode of data capture can have a detrimental effect on data quality; another states that some respondents prefer, or are better suited to, certain modes of reporting. For example, office workers may find Internet reporting more convenient than manual workers.

Some practitioners refer to 'contractor effect': this means that results change if a new agency takes over a large contract. The changes cannot be attributed to a change in method if the research instruments and panel profiles remain constant. An agency's own panel may not be responsible for differences, but the different procedures, the different incentives, the different treatment, and the different type of contact lead to subtle differences in findings. The differences in results have been referred to as the 'seam effect' and much effort has been put into making the data sets look 'seamless' (for example, Rips *et al.* 2003 propose a model based on respondent ability to remember).

Omnibus

Omnibus surveys are quantitative studies and are made possible by small monetary outlay from several clients. Research agencies initiate, design, and manage omnibuses. Clients provide one or more questions and, of course, payment. In this way, data-gathering costs are offset and divided. Well-designed omnibus surveys allow each participant to have its own unique set of findings. There are those that question general consumers, including children; they may investigate products for the workplace, for the home—even motorists may be the theme of the study.

The disadvantage is the risk that one set of questions might be affected by other sets. To ensure that this is not a problem, survey managers try to avoid accepting questions covering similar topics; they position personal and sensitive questions at the end and restrict the average interview length. These precautions minimise the risk of respondent fatigue and also mean that fewer topics will be covered. This means that clients cannot have all the space they might want. The client does not know what other questions are—these are confidential, so it is impossible for the client to judge their effect.

The omnibus is, therefore, not a substitute for custom-designed market research, but should be seen as an essential part of the marketing budget, a provision for expected and unexpected events. Any unexpected observations in home markets can be investigated—for example, a sudden fall in sales or reduction in market share—and the researcher is well placed to monitor changes over time. Its other key function is as a tracking device: 'matched' samples can be provided week on week.

Omnibus surveys are available 'off the shelf' in most countries of the world, which offers the benefit of being able to inspect international markets very quickly. Some business surveys exist and, where a particular market is not covered, research agencies will consider creating one. Most large omnibus surveys are listed in the ESOMAR directory and on web directories for marketing research.

Most omnibus surveys are carried out face-to-face or by telephone. There are examples of self-completion omnibus, carried out either delivered by regular post or, more recently, via the Internet. Self-completion studies are not favoured for omnibuses because of a slow turnaround; additionally, the questions are less likely to be kept confidential. Research agencies assure clients that any indication about their specific questions will not be revealed to anyone else—interviewers work with a code of conduct and respondents are usually 'screened out' if

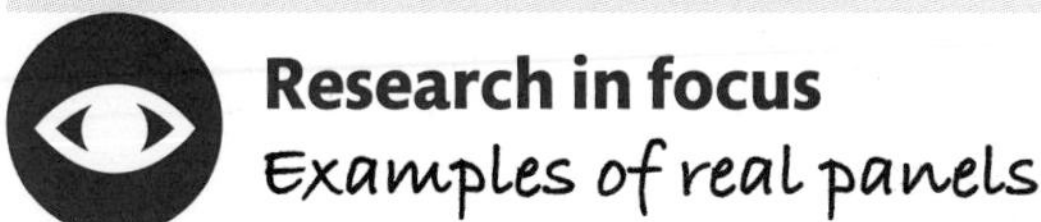

Research in focus
Examples of real panels

British Household Panel Study—carried out by the Institute for Social and Economic Research (ISER). A questionnaire is used by an interviewer on this annual survey with each adult (16+) member of a nationally representative sample of more than 5000 households, making a total of approximately 10,000 individual interviews. These households are revisited, which provides longitudinal information on social and economic change at individual and household levels in Britain. It provides information on household organisation, employment, accommodation, tenancy, income and wealth, housing, health, socioeconomic values, residential mobility, marital and relationship history, social support, and individual and household demographics.

A.C. Nielsen Homescan—launched in 1989, this panel uses in-home bar-code scanners to collect data. It has over 10,000 GB households. Homescan is regionally and demographically balanced to represent the household population and captures consumer package goods purchases brought back into the home, including variable weight and non-bar-coded fresh products. It acts as a highly effective market-tracking vehicle and consumer diagnostics tool, providing insights into buying behaviour.

TNS Superpanel—has 15,000 households, demographically and regionally balanced to offer a representative picture of the GB marketplace. It has been in operation since 1991. Data are collected twice weekly, using electronic terminals in the home, with purchases recorded using homescanning technology. A large amount of information about consumer purchasing behaviour is available on the panel.

Smaller panels also exist to serve the specific needs of individual clients. In 2005, Research Now developed an online panel of new and expectant mothers using Bounty's database. This comprises over 5000 people. A continuous viewer panel was created for a television company, in 2004, by the research agency Skopos. The GMTV online panel has about 3000 members and claims a response rate for re-interviewing of over 60 per cent. The panel serves sales and programming needs, so has been used for pre- and post-awareness studies; it has asked omnibus-style specific questions such as: '*How long do you spend on makeup in the morning?*'.

Compiled by Nigel Bradley 2012.

Sources:

Aitken, L. (2005) Net evidence, *Research in Business*, September, pp.10–13.

http://superpanel.tns-global.com/superpanel/

http://www.acnielsen.co.uk/products/cps_homescan.shtml

http://www.esds.ac.uk/longitudinal/access/bhps/

they (or close relatives) work in marketing or specified fields. Self-completion cannot provide such protection, so the method has historically been less popular with clients and agencies.

Omnibus surveys may take place weekly, monthly, or at other regular intervals. The research institute decides the frequency. It is likely to decide this based on its forecast of whether it can sell enough questions to justify expenditure on the fieldwork. The UK's first daily omnibus was launched in 2002; in 2005, an 'omnitaxi' service was launched, whereby the timing is decided by the client. This flexibility has been made possible by Internet data capture methods. The

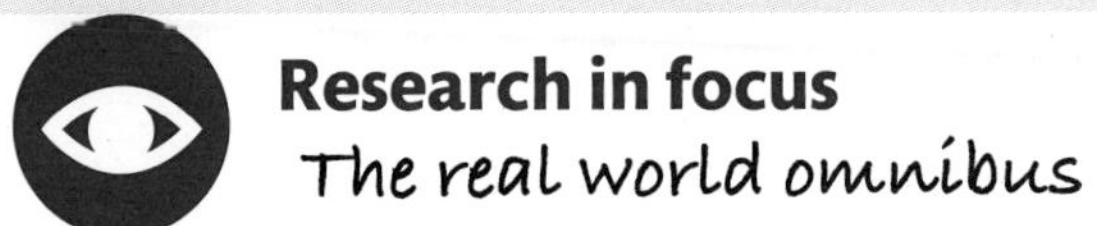

Research in focus
The real world omnibus

Omnibus services look at many subjects and respondents: there are services on children, old people, motorists and more. Directories such as the ESOMAR guide or Mr Web compare many of these services. To show the specialist nature of the omnibus, let us cite an agency called Beaufort, which conducts the Welsh Omnibus Survey, and the Omnibus Survey of Welsh Speakers and, in 2001, it launched CWMNIBUS, a CATI omnibus of Welsh SME businesses. These regular surveys provide a fast and cost-effective means of obtaining robust information from representative samples of both the public and businesses in Wales.

Omnibus Express has the honour of being the UK's first daily omnibus service. It was launched by My Voice Europe in June 2002. Five hundred adults are selected from an Internet panel of 100,000 members worldwide. Questions start at £285 if submitted by 10am; daily answers arrive by 5pm.

GFK e-Interquest gives access to general practitioners (GPs), specialists, and opticians in the UK, Germany, France, Spain, Italy, the USA, Canada, Brazil, Japan, and China—with additional countries available. Through six different surveys each month, the omnibus uses the Internet or telephone. Users can choose the sample size, whether 50, 75, or 100 doctors per country.

The Ipsos Capibus™ Service is a nationally and regionally representative sample of 2000 adults in the UK. All interviews are carried out in-home by Ipsos interviewers, using CAPI (computer-assisted personal interviewing). It is carried out every week of the year. The same methodology and service is available in France, Germany, Spain, and Italy.

Ipsos MORI has a school-based omnibus study to explore the views, experiences, and aspirations of a sample of around 2500 young people, aged 11–16 in around 125 schools. The sample is designed to be representative of all those secondary and middle schools in the state sector. A teacher's omnibus interviews 900–1000 maintained primary and secondary school teachers across England and Wales.

Omnitaxi was launched in the UK, France, Germany, Italy, and Spain in 2005 by Research Now. It allows clients access to a target sample of 500, 1000, or 2000 people and the results are supplied within 48 hours of supplying the questionnaire. The agency emphasises the idea of a taxi rather than a bus: '*The concept of the Omnitaxi is that it goes to who you want, when you want, where you want*'.

Compiled by Nigel Bradley 2012.

Sources:

http://www.beaufortresearch.co.uk/index.php/site/omnibussurveys/omnibus_surveys/

http://www.capibus.co.uk

http://www.gfknop.com/customresearch-uk/expertise/omnibus/index.en.html

http://www.ipsos-mori.com/omnibusservices.aspx

http://www.mrweb.com/omni

http://www.myvoice.co.uk

http://www.researchnow.co.uk

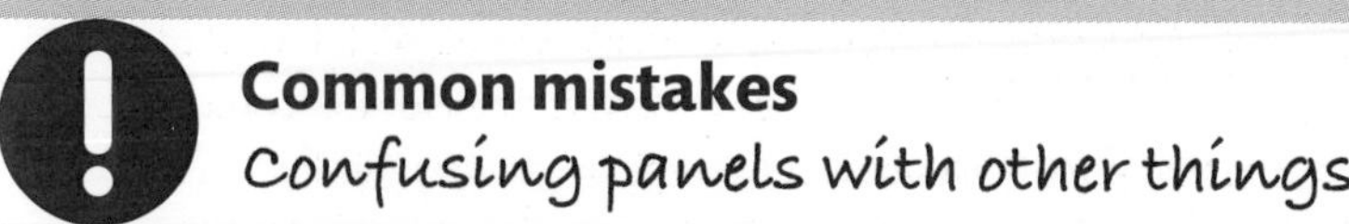

Common mistakes
Confusing panels with other things

Newcomers to research are introduced to many terms that may be confused with each other and with techniques in other fields. The research 'panel' is sometimes mistaken for such diverse things as focus groups, interviews for personnel recruitment, and the omnibus.

The term 'panel' is used on television or radio: a panel of experts offer their own judgements on a particular issue on a news documentary programme, or they may be part of a game show. Sometimes, the qualitative focus group is given the name of panel, perhaps because of the implications that expert judgement will be offered. In human resource management, some job candidates are interviewed by several people at one session: the candidate is face-to-face with an interview panel. None of these is the meaning of a quantitative research panel.

A research panel is a set of individuals who are questioned or observed, or who report over a period of time. It has a longitudinal implication because the process is repeated with those same individuals; it also implies quantitative research. There are similarities with the omnibus: both are quantitative and both usually are representative of the population. Indeed, a panel may be used for an omnibus and an omnibus may be used to recruit a panel; the difference is that the omnibus generally recruits fresh respondents each time, whereas the panel keeps respondents as long as they are willing to cooperate. In recent years, we have witnessed the introduction of a new term: the 'access panel'. This refers to a general 'pool' of people who have agreed to be available for questioning in the future. Essentially, they have promised cooperation in the same way that regular panel members promise their time. However, the use of their time is unpredictable and the topics of the study may well change each time, making the panel similar to the omnibus.

nature of the omnibus can also dictate the timing: general population omnibus surveys, for example, may run every week because there is a constant demand. In contrast, omnibus studies that focus on specific targets, for example, beer drinkers, may only run according to irregular demand.

Within the general structure of the omnibus questionnaire, the research agency will ask basic classification questions. Typically, these will embrace such areas as the respondent's age, sex, social grade, geographic region, income, and other demographic details. Beyond this, the question topics will vary dramatically, depending on the needs of clients involved in that particular survey.

Crowdsourcing research

Crowdsourcing is one of the newest additions to the market researcher's toolbox, therefore let us look into the subject and how it can be of value.

It is useful to think of the term outsourcing; this is a management technique whereby a company pays outsiders to provide services rather than using employees within the organisation.

Crowdsourcing is a variant of outsourcing that seeks the skills, knowledge, and time of people who are not normally associated with offering a commercial service. The crowd is consulted en masse and volunteers provide a service sometimes free of charge, sometimes paid for.

Software has been developed to help in crowdsourcing. Names include Livework, Crowdtap, Crowdflower and Do My Stuff. One example is provided by Amazon and is called "Mechanical Turk". A simple website page appeals to the crowd to make their services available, another appeal is to those in need of the resource.

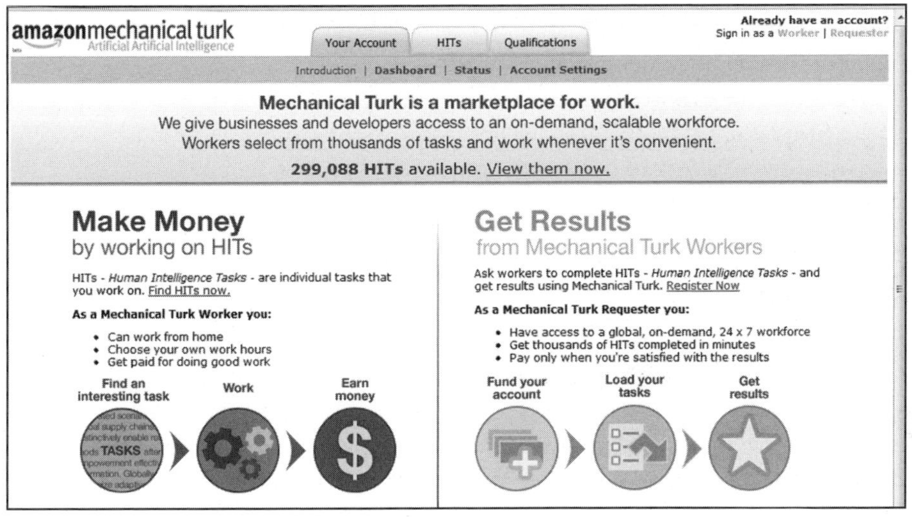

The ease of contacting thousands of people across the Internet has made crowdsourcing a feasible method. At the click of a button we can make an open call and create real physical change in the world.

Examples of work have been to provide specific home photos, podcasts and videos, to write book chapters, to label images for easy recall by search engines, to design t-shirts, to look up addresses for direct mailing.

In the sphere of marketing research, crowdsourcing allows us to tap into the knowledge that exists in the marketplace. We have seen it used by Ford (your ideas), Dell (Ideastorm), and Lego (Cuusoo). Here are some examples of the applications:

- Generating new product names
- Comparing package designs
- Advertising concept testing
- Providing product reviews
- Assessing satisfaction
- Analysis of search terms to identify trends and forecast.

What are the advantages and disadvantages? Well the advantages include speed, low cost, and matching the needs of the customer by direct collaboration. On the down side we can cite a possible lack of understanding of the profiles of collaborators, workloads can easily become large and there may be a loss of control, and finally there are ethical issues of paying workers below agreed fair wages.

Databases

Database issues have come to the top of the agenda for the information professional. The development of cheap information processing gave rise to the availability of masses of information found in databases. It is obvious that huge quantities of data with little meaning cannot assist the marketing function, so several proprietary database software packages are available to marketers. These include familiar names such as Microsoft Access, FoxPro, Filemaker Pro, Corel Paradox, and Lotus Approach. The sophistication of databases and data mining has now led to the emergence of 'insight management'.

Let us define the database as a collection of data on individuals or organisations, which is structured in a way that allows data to be reorganised to provide meaningful information. The database is more likely to be in electronic rather than hard-copy form, and will be updated on a regular basis. The modern database can be accessed quickly through computers. The limitations of databases are that they do not give motives for behaviour and are always historical; they focus on existing or lapsed customers and not on potential customers.

The most basic function of the database is to assist in the transactions between the supplier and the buyer, but there are many other extra functions that derive from this. It is useful to remember that databases contain numbers and text, but can also carry static and moving images. Customer data are generated both internally, within the organisation, and also externally, by other bodies. Internal sources include accounts, complaints, transactions, and warranty cards. External sources include the census, list brokers, directories, credit reference data, and even market research information. There are various types of customer data: behavioural data, volunteered data, and attributed data.

'Behavioural data' are evident from observation, whether by machine or human; this embraces transactions captured electronically on bar codes. 'Volunteered data' are given by individuals. The Data Protection and Data Privacy Acts generally impose transparency and consent as a condition of accepting this information. Interestingly, several studies show that, when information is requested, people may volunteer the requested data, but it may not be true. 'Attributed data' are derived by extrapolation or interpolation. Where data can be inferred from other sources, this is then attributed to the record.

These three data sets can indicate FRAC profiles: the frequency of use, the recency of use, the amount of use, and the category of product being used. Such key indicators are extremely valuable in interpreting customer databases.

Research studies carried out may be seen as a good way to enhance information on a database. However, the research industry codes of conduct state that the direct or indirect identification of respondents who have participated in research should not be possible. Future cooperation is at risk if respondent confidence is eroded. The way to overcome this problem is to ask permission from respondents or to ensure that any inclusions into a database are made at a summary level, whereby data are partly aggregated and not provided at a personal level. For example, we might go to a higher level of postcode, rather than a precise area.

We must continually remind ourselves that there is a need for a clear distinction between marketing research and the creation of databases for direct marketing purposes. Marketing research must have transparency, respondents must be assured of confidentiality, and data gathered for research purposes must not be used to 'sell' to the respondents.

Sometimes we see that some activities use research as an entry point to open a dialogue with a person: when companies sell under the guise of research, we call this activity 'sugging'. When charity workers carry out fundraising under the guise of research, it is called 'frugging'. Typically, the dialogue begins with: '*Could you please spare a moment to answer a questionnaire?*'. The creation of databases for direct marketing purposes may also mean that questionnaires are used to collect data for direct marketing. If individuals are misled into believing that the purpose is for research, rather than building a tool for direct selling, this is sometimes known as 'dugging'—database building under the guise of research.

These methods are similar to research because they use a questionnaire as a starting point. But they are different, so caution needs to be exercised in using the data. These data sets should not be combined with research unless adjustments are made or limitations are observed; the knowledge has been created in a different way.

Figure 8.5a and 8.5b shows the general procedures involved in creating and keeping a database. The phases move from definition of the functions through to maintaining the database. We must define the requirements, identify information sources, select the hardware, and then select the software, even creating new applications. The database is then filled with entries and this is maintained.

Although the development phases are clear and act as a good theoretical basis, in practice, the real situation is more complicated. This is because several concepts such as the **data mart**, the **data warehouse**, and data mining are rather complex. Let us look at these in more detail.

Data marts, warehouses, and mining

The 'data mart' is a collection of subject areas based on the needs of a given department. We may find a data mart for the finance department, one for marketing, one for personnel, and so on. It is a system that is created piecemeal, in a decentralised way. The relevant departments are responsible for the choice of hardware and software for their own data marts. Each department decides what its data mart should include and exclude. It will solve short-term issues and is therefore unlikely to contain much historical information. There are two kinds of data mart: independent and dependent. An 'independent' data mart is one based on active systems: data arrive directly from other applications or activities within the company. This means that the independent data mart may be unstable and less planned. On the other hand, a 'dependent' data mart is built on information provided from a larger source called a data warehouse and is probably well planned.

The 'data warehouse' is an extremely large database with a store of transactional data that allows the researcher to make useful analyses. It is usually built and owned by a business unit with central responsibility, such as the IT department. Warehouses are organised by subject

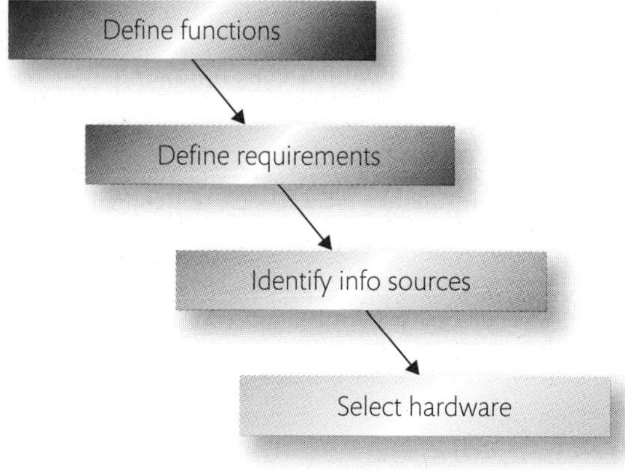

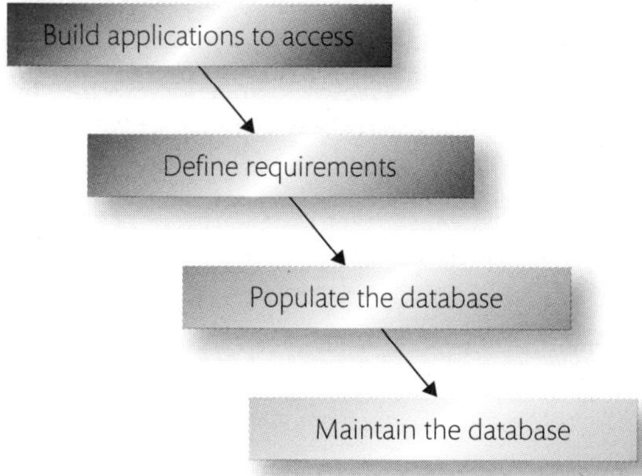

Figure 8.5 a and b The general procedures involved in creating a database

areas, which may not be the same as the departments found in the corporation. Therefore, the data warehouse is centralised and belongs to the organisation rather than to a specific department. Data warehouses contain more detail than data marts, which tend to summarise items. The term used for this is 'granular', because the information is in a very raw form. The data warehouse also contains much historical data.

It is argued by some that several data marts added together become a 'data warehouse'; this is disputed by others who consider the warehouse to be well planned and more powerful. The users of the marts are different from the types of user found in the data warehouse. Users of marts are sometimes called 'farmers' because they 'harvest' data; users of warehouses are known as 'explorers', because they concentrate on overriding ideas. If a data warehouse is not built in a planned way, there is likely to be information that is collected, but not used: inconsistent data that cannot be fused between one data mart and the next. The idea that a data mart can be turned into a data warehouse when it reaches a certain size, or that data marts can be integrated together, is no more valid than saying that a bicycle can grow into a lorry.

'Data mining' is the procedure that selects and manipulates large amounts of data to uncover previously unknown relationships and patterns. There are various levels at which the database can operate. The simple query application of the database extracts data and produces a report, without performing calculations on the data. The next level is when basic calculations are made on the extracted data. Higher levels apply knowledge from outside to information within the database, in order to perform calculations or to test ideas. Here, it is useful to say that relationships found in the data mart may differ from those found in the data warehouse. Furthermore, the types of query satisfied by the data mart are quite different from those queries found in the data warehouse. Databases can be analysed for key indicators such as geographical spread, frequency of purchases, volume of purchases, rates of retention of customers, profitability, and price sensitivity.

Data mining uses models and the process refines the information gathered from its operating procedures. O'Connor *et al.* (2004) grouped the more popular techniques into the following types: inductive reasoning, artificial neural networks, data visualisation, and memory-based reasoning.

'Inductive reasoning' starts with specific facts and uses reasoning to derive an explanation. 'Artificial neural networks' allow the computer to learn solutions by recognising familiar patterns. 'Data visualisation' is the display of data in a form that is meaningful: for example, maps with overlaid layers of information. Finally, 'memory-based reasoning' compares database features against records previously stored in the computer's memory.

Spreadsheets and survey software

The 'spreadsheet' is a worksheet with cells that can be filled with numbers to perform simple calculations. There have been interesting developments in this field in recent years. For over a century, we have had 'ledger paper': large pieces of paper divided into small squares. This paper unfolded and could be filled with numbers that could all be added to create a total. Looking up and across the columns and rows, the information would make sense. Historically, this worksheet or 'spreadsheet' was not easy to use, physically it was uncomfortable, and in terms of space, it was impossible to go very far into any calculations: they were limited by the size of the paper. Mistakes were possible and rather cumbersome to correct, but there was nothing better. This was soon to change with the advance of technology, and the ledger was to go onscreen.

Dan Bricklin, a 28-year-old master's student at Harvard Business School, wrote the first spreadsheet program with his colleague Bob Frankston. It was called VisiCalc and was for the Apple II computer. It went on sale in October 1979. The modern-day evolution of this is the Microsoft product called Excel, which is used widely, not least by market researchers.

Questionnaire data can be input directly into a spreadsheet or can be imported. The spreadsheet should be prepared so that each respondent is allocated to each row. The columns are used for each code within a question. In Excel, the pivot table feature is used for this operation. The pivot table in the data menu can be used to generate summary tables of means, standard deviations, counts, etc.

Ethical insight
Using MR to update database

The Data Protection Act 1998 stipulates that: '*Personal data shall be accurate and, where necessary, kept up to date*'. This means that data controllers are obliged to update their customer databases. If market research is taking place, surely this is a good opportunity to refresh the database.

© istockphoto.com/Onur kocamaz

We can turn to the Market Research Society to shed light on this area. The MRS answer is simple and concise: it says that this is not market research. Indeed, it points out that survey research means that only a small part of a database would be chosen for sampling, so the full database is not being updated. However, it is possible to change the whole approach and extend the work to contact the full database. It should be made clear to respondents that this is a mixed-purpose exercise called 'market research *and* database building'. The MRS Code of Conduct now has separate regulations concerning the use of research techniques for non-research purposes.

These regulations are quite radical in that they allow respondents' names and address details to be given to clients to use for profiling purposes. This is a research purpose, so it is acceptable with the consent of the respondent. If used for non-research purposes, however, it would be unacceptable. The general rule is that personal data can only be used for the purposes for which it was collected and for which respondents have consented. Accountancy, canvassing political support, prosecution of offenders (including the use of CCTV), debt administration, education, pastoral care, and private investigation are a few purposes for which personal data are collected.

Finally, it is not acceptable to ask additional questions for non-research purposes at the end of a market research survey. On the other hand, '*if respondents request individual complaints or unresolved issues to be passed back to a client, members must comply with that request*' (MRS rule B10).

Compiled by Nigel Bradley 2009.

Sources:

Data Protection Act 1998, http://www.ico.gov.uk.

MRS Code, rule B48, http://www.mrs.org.uk/standards/codeconduct.htm

Questions

1. What is the difference between accuracy and being up to date?
2. What proportion of a database is likely to be sampled?
3. Explain some purposes for which personal data may be collected.

Common mistakes
Misunderstanding survey software settings

Survey software settings differ from vendor to vendor, but the researcher has a responsibility to understand and use settings properly to avoid problems. For example, they should be configured to prevent people from completing more than one questionnaire. Similarly, the study may be affected if someone forwards a link to the questionnaire to ineligible, but well-meaning respondents. Radio buttons, check boxes, and drop-down menus can be preset with answers for respondent convenience, but this is dangerous. We need to positively know if the question is answered or not. Some respondents will abort a questionnaire; some settings allow the questionnaire to be resumed another time. Some respondents provide ill-considered responses or partial answers. At the analysis stage these answers may mislead or the sample numbers and composition for these questions may differ substantially from the respondents to other questions. The researcher must decide whether to keep or edit these partial answers; software familiarity is again vital.

Sources:

Goldwater, E. (1999) Using Excel for statistical data analysis, http://people.umass.edu/evagold/excel.html

McDaniel, C. and Gates, R. (2002) *Marketing Research: The Impact of the Internet*. Cincinnati, OH: South-Western Thomson Learning, p. 484.

Sounderpandian, J. (1999) *Market Research Using Microsoft Excel*. Cincinnati, OH: South-Western College Publishing.

There is an interest in the use of Excel (and other spreadsheets) by market research agencies and their clients as opposed to survey software such as SPSS and SAS, not least because newly purchased computers often arrive with Excel already loaded.

Indeed, Excel is becoming more sophisticated and is able to perform some of the tasks of survey software, and because users are acquainted with Excel, there is evidence to suggest that it is becoming more widespread (see Table 8.3). There is a likelihood that it will progress and evolve into an even more powerful tool. At present, criticisms of Excel concern: the way missing values are handled (inconsistently); the fact that data needs to be reorganised each time an analysis is made; the fact that many analyses can only be done on one column at a time; the fact that output is poorly labelled. Other critics say that there is no record of how an analysis was accomplished.

Some people see Excel as a convenient method for data entry, with rows representing each respondent and columns for the questionnaire answer codes. At this point, Excel can be used for simple tasks such as descriptive statistics and perhaps correlation, but anything more complicated should be carried out with a statistical package. All supported statistical packages can read Excel files, so this is a feasible way to use both tools (see Table 8.4).

In 2007, Google made widely available a spreadsheet it had been developing behind the scenes. This was significant because a year later, in 2008, it introduced a feature called 'forms' into the spreadsheet; in the words of Google (2008) '*Create a form in a Google Docs spreadsheet and send it out to anyone with an email address*'. Effectively this is a way to create a web page questionnaire and announce it via email and to have results collated. If you have a Google

Table 8.3 Uses of software for market research

Application	Spreadsheets (Excel, Quattro Pro, Lotus 1-2-3)	Databases (Access etc.)	Survey software (SPSS, SAS, SNAP, SYSTAT, MINITAB)
Project costing	***		*
Significance tests	*		***
Questionnaire design	*	**	***
Data entry	***	***	* or ***
Questionnaire analysis	**	**	***
Sampling administration	*	***	* or ***
Chart drawing	*		***
Multivariate analysis	*	* or ***	***
Easy reanalysis	*	*	***

* = adequate, ** = good, *** = very good

account you can produce a questionnaire online. Go to Google Docs and click on NEW. Then select FORMS from the drop-down box. Adobe systems also have a useful form capability and this can be used by any respondent with Adobe Reader; the capabilities are being developed, but they allow onscreen completion and printing.

Chapter summary

1 Explain the purpose of quantitative research

Quantitative research tests variants of the marketing mix using numbers and statistics. It creates meaningful segmentation and measures brand equity, usage, and attitudes. The mean and the standard deviation are important. Nominal, ordinal, interval, and ratio data are all important ways to detect differences. Comparative scales make direct comparisons, whereas in non-comparative scales, each object is scaled independently of the others. Interval and ratio scales are favoured because so much can be done with them. Longitudinal studies can identify and monitor changes over time.

Describe the different approaches to quantitative research

In 'experimentation', the researcher makes a direct intervention, which is then measured in some way. These tests are used in-home, in stores, or in test centres. Central location tests or 'hall tests' show material to respondents in a secure and private environment; variations include the clinic, the 'mall intercept', the 'theatre test' or 'cinema test', and the 'van test'. A 'panel' is a set of individuals questioned or observed over a period of time. There are two types: the consumer panel and the retail panel. In a 'continuous' panel the same questions are posed to the same individuals regularly; in the 'interval' panel content may change or gaps between fieldwork may be irregular. In omnibus surveys clients ask their own questions on a survey run by research agencies.

Table 8.4 Quantitative approaches: summary of advantages and disadvantages

Type	Advantage	Disadvantage
In-home placement	Normal usage, in private Convenient for respondents	Most expensive Time-consuming
Store tests	Non-intrusive	Self-selecting sample Buyers may not be users
Central location - Test centres - Hall test - Mall intercept	Artificial environment Cheaper than in-home Good for bulky, confidential materials	Clustering will occur Unsuitable for certain products
Panel	Can show changes over time Provides rich data Cost-effective over long periods	High investment Long-term commitment Panellists are different Respondent fatigue Panel erosion Need to replace
Omnibus	Cheap and easy to use Available worldwide	Data integrity concerns, questions may affect each other
Customer Databases	Powerful source of data Can identify changes Allows segmentation and profiling Can assist Customer Relationship Management (CRM)	Historical Do not show reasons for behaviour

Show the benefits of different approaches to quantitative research

The hall test can be used for bulky or confidential stimuli; they are low-cost. The mall intercept limits expenses associated with in-home work. The panel allows opinions to be tracked over time and avoids response rate problems; panel data is a rich source for secondary data. Omnibus surveys are available in most countries of the world and offer an extremely low cost for researchers.

Show the limitations of different approaches to quantitative research

There are several problems that can arise in experimentation that include subject bias, measurement changes, expense, time taken, and design competence. Central location interviewing is unsuitable for certain products and will be limited to those people available at specific times. Panellists are different: they will be conditioned; respondent fatigue may cause stock responses and panel erosion. In the omnibus, one set of questions might affect other sets. The client does not know what other questions are—they are confidential, so it is impossible to judge their effect. In most quantitative work data will need weighting—that procedure will also impact results.

Review questions

1 Explain the difference between the hall test and the placement test.

2 In quantitative research, an understanding of the average is important. Why?

3 In what circumstances might we decide not to use quantitative research?

4 Explore the advantages and disadvantages of panel research.

5 Define these terms using examples: data mart, data mining, survey software, and spreadsheets.

Discussion questions

1 What would be the implications of testing several variables in an experiment at the same time?

2 Create a list of 20 terms used in experimentation. Try to create definitions that you all understand.

3 Investigate the contribution of the Royal Statistical Society to quantitative research.

4 Ask family and friends what they think of opinion polls published in the newspapers. Ask them to explain the topic and how they feel about the technique. What are their criticisms and what do they like?

5 How can quantitative research mislead the researcher?

6 Plan an experiment to investigate the preference for perfumes.

7 In the opening Snapshot, how and why is quantitative research used?

Further reading

- Hofacker, C.F. (2001) *Internet Marketing*. New York: Wiley.

  Web experiments, involving page and banner ad studies, are examined over several pages.

- Mercer, A. (1991) *Implementable Marketing Research*. Hemel Hempstead: Prentice Hall.

  Case studies based on the author's experience. They explore experiments on branded goods (confectionery, cigarettes), in addition to undifferentiated goods (shrubs).

- The Office of National Statistics, http://www.statistics.gov.uk

  The main provider of statistics—a useful source of data for the student to use and manipulate.

- Stone, M., Bond, A. and Foss, B. (2004) *Consumer Insight: How to Use Data and Market Research to Get Closer to your Customer*. London: Kogan Page.

  An excellent explanation of the operational side of databases and their relationship to marketing research, with some excellent case study examples. The primary author is an academic and consultant with IBM.

Case study
Hospital research

On its website, BMI Healthcare describes itself as the UK's number one private hospital group. It operates over 70 hospitals and clinics across the country and is owned by General Healthcare Group (GHG). Treatments and services are provided in over 100 areas of medicine: from cardiology to neurosurgery; from urology to gastro-enterology; from cosmetic to general surgery. Each year the BMI Healthcare facilities deal with over a million outpatient visits and over a quarter of a million inpatient procedures. Over 6000 consultants work at BMI hospitals, served by some 9000 employees who include specialists, nursing staff, caterers, and accommodation personnel.

The decision to use a private hospital can be rather complex, it can depend on the medical need, the prospective patient's location, the method of funding. Some patients pay from their own money, others are insured with such organisations as BUPA; the state may pay through the National Health Service (NHS). This is a complex situation and one where marketing research has an important role to play to make sense of the overall service provided by these many people. BMI Healthcare employ the research agency Howard Warwick & Associates to conduct a continuous Patient Satisfaction Survey, this uses a questionnaire at the locations of treatment.

The research agency firmly believes these studies are important, their view is clear: '*We know that satisfied patients recover more quickly and that patients who remain anxious, in pain or upset with any part of their care will take longer to recover*'.

The questionnaire is an attractive single sheet of paper folded four times with an invitation to complete from the Managing Director of BMI Healthcare. Distribution happens in several ways: every room has an information pack and a copy is there, each nurse station desk has a display with copies, it is given with discharge papers and staff will encourage completion. There are always pens available as each room has a telephone with pen and notepad.

There are 65 closed questions and nine open ended questions. There is a simple formula: easy to use tick boxes using the same 5-point scale throughout: Excellent, Very Good, Good, Fair, Poor. There are sections on Arrival, Consultants, Nursing Care, Accommodation, Catering and Going Home. Each section has open-ended questions asking how that area can be improved. Key Performance Indicator (KPI) questions come at the end of each section as an Overall Impression Rating. Another KPI is on recommendation: "Would you recommend this hospital to your family and friends?" Yes definitely, Yes Probably, No. There is an Overall Rating of the Quality of Care.

Once completed, the questionnaire can be returned in one of several ways. If it is finished on the premises before departure it can be put into a purpose-built box nearby exit areas. These boxes are emptied at intervals and sent to the research agency. Additionally the form design has an address panel with a pre-paid postage facility (freepost), so it can be dropped into any letterbox outside the hospital.

On arrival at the research agency handwritten comments are examined for anything urgent and copies of the verbatim are immediately sent to the hospitals in question for action.

Within BMI results are disseminated at all levels, they are used to motivate, they are used in meetings to review progress. All personnel in different departments see results, whether they be from catering or nursing. BMI Healthcare say: 'we surveyed 69.332 inpatients/daycase patients during the period January - December 2011 and 99% of those surveyed rated their Overall Quality of Care as either good, very good or excellent. Furthermore, 90% would definitely recommend the hospital to their family and friends'.

Information derived from this survey is also used to reassure investors. The 2008/09 annual report of the General Healthcare Group reported the satisfaction of overall quality figures of the NHS with BMI Healthcare. The NHS figure was 75.6%, that for BMI was 98.4%. Prospective users of BMI's hospitals also benefit from the study as the web pages relating to each location carry relevant results. Below are the results of the satisfaction survey for patients who have received treatment at one of the hospitals.

BMI Bishops Wood Hospital

- BMI Bishops Wood Hospital
- About the hospital
- How to find us
- Hospital services
- Our consultants
- Treatments
- Make an enquiry
- NHS patients
- Patients satisfaction
- Quality of care
- News & events
- Find another hospital
- Self-Pay prices and information
- Same sex declaration

We are proud of our patient care and work hard to make each patient's time with us as pleasant as possible. Our patient satisfaction survey is an important indicator of how well we achieve this and we monitor the results very closely.

The graphs below show the % of patients rating each area as either good, very good or excellent. The results are based on a survey of 982 inpatients / daycase patients who completed a questionnaire during the period January - December 2011.

The results were compiled by an independent agency (Howard Warwick Associates Ltd) on our behalf.

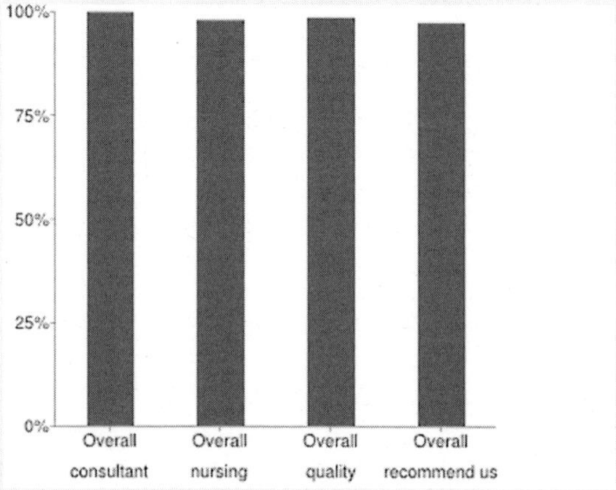

Compiled by Nigel Bradley 2012.

Sources:

Online at http://www.bmihealthcare.co.uk

Online at http://www.generalhealthcare.co.uk

Online at http://www.howardwarwick.co.uk

Annual Reports: http://www.apax.com/media/49338/General%20Healthcare%20Group%20Annual%20Report%202008-09.pdf

http://www.apax.com/media/159676/General%20Healthcare%20Group%20Annual%20Report%202009-10.pdf.pdf

Questions

1 How is research used by BMI Healthcare? What is the purpose?

2 Who benefits from the patient satisfaction survey research? Detail the different audiences.

3 Critically evaluate the sampling used for the patient satisfaction survey.

4 Critically evaluate the data collection procedures used.

Key web links

- Omnibus directory http://www.mrweb.com/omni
- Google Docs http://www.docs.google.com
- ACORN http://www.caci.co.uk/acorn

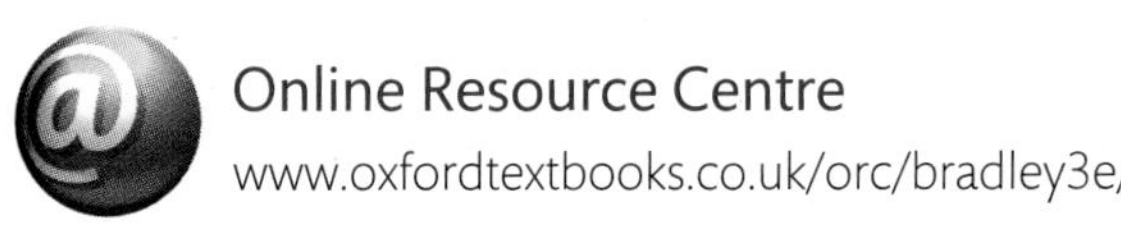

Visit the Online Resource Centre that accompanies this book to access more learning resources on this chapter topic.

References and sources

Aitken, L. (2005) Net evidence, *Research in Business*, September, pp. 10–13.

Amazon's Mechanical Turk web page, http://www.mturk.com

Buck, S. (1982) Consumer panels in the UK: past present and future. *MRS Conference papers*, 16–19 March, pp. 43–54.

Buck, S.F. and Jephcott, J. St. (1997) Conditioning and bias in consumer panels: some new results, *Journal of the Market Research Society*, 39 (Special edition: Milestones in market research), pp. 21–38.

Bush, A.J. and Hair, J.F. (1985) An assessment of the mall intercept as a data collect method, *Journal of Marketing Research*, May, pp. 158–167.

Bush, A.J., Bush, R.F., and Chen, H.C.K. (1991) Method of administration effects in mall intercept interviews, *Journal of the Market Research Society*, 33, pp. 309–319.

Chakrapani, C. (2004) *Statistics in Market Research*. London: Arnold.

Ching, W-K., Ng, M.K., and Wong, L-K. (2004) Hidden Markov models and their applications to customer relationship management, *IMA Journal of Management Mathematics*, 15, pp. 13–24.

Crowdflower web page, http://crowdflower.com/

Crowdtap web page, http://crowdtap.com/

Curwin, J. and Slater, R. (2004) *Quantitative Methods: A Short Course*. London: Thomson Learning.

De Chernatony, L. (2001) *From Brand Vision to Brand Revaluation: Strategically Building and Sustaining Brands*. Oxford: Butterworth Heinemann.

Dell Ideastorm, http://www.ideastorm.com/

Do My Stuff web page, http://www.domystuff.com/

Feldwick, P. (2002) *What is Brand Equity Anyway?* Oxford: World Advertising Research Centre.

Ford Your Ideas web page, http://social.ford.com/your-ideas/

Gabor, A. (1977) *Pricing: Principles and Practices*. London: Heinemann Educational Books.

Goldwater, E. (1999) Using excel for statistical data analysis, http://www.unix.oit.umass.edu/~evagold/excel.html

Google (2008) *Stop Sharing Spreadsheets, Start sharing Information*, http://www.googledocs.blogspot.com/2008/02/ stop-sharing-spreadsheets-start.html

Heeg, R. (2006) Do it yourself: are quick and cheap surveys harming the industry? *Research World*, February, pp. 14–16, http://www.Free-Online-Surveys.com

Hoad, T.F. (ed.) (1986) *Concise Oxford Dictionary of English Etymology*. Oxford: Oxford University Press.

Kapferer, J-N. (2001) *[Re] Inventing the Brand: Can Top Brands Survive the New Market Realities?* London: Kogan Page.

Keller, K.L. (1998) *Building Measuring and Managing Brand Equity*. New York: Prentice Hall.

Latham, J. (1997) A database segmentation approach to customer retention, CIM Northwest Branch Meeting Paper, 13 November.

Lego Cuusoo web page, http://lego.cuusoo.com/

Livework web page, http://www.livework.co.uk/

Lusher, A. (1999) Hospital poll sent to dead patients, *Telegraph*, 15 April, p. 13.

McDaniel, C. and Gates, R. (2002) *Marketing Research: The Impact of the Internet*. Cincinnati, OH: South Western Thomson Learning.

Melvin, A. (2006) Council tax summons for dead woman, *Harrow Times*, 9 February, p. 1.

Mitchell, C.G.B. and Lawson, S. (1998) *The Great British Motorist*. Automobile Association, http://www.theaa.com/staticdocs/pdf/aboutaa/gb_motorist_text.pdf

O'Connor, J. Galvin, E., and Evans, M. (2004) *Electronic Marketing: Theory and Practice for the 21st* Century, 3rd edn. Harlow, Essex: FT Prentice Hall.

O'Rourke, K. (2000) New Milky Way seizes the night, *Drug Store News* 22, p. 212.

Pitre, C. (2011) Why Marketers Should Invest in Crowdsourced Research. 18 January, http://mashable.com/2011/01/18/marketers-crowdsourced-research/

Rips, L., Conrad, F., and Fricker, S.S. (2003) Straightening the seam effect in panel surveys, *Public Opinion Quarterly*, 67, pp. 522–555.

Rodger, L.W. (1984) *Statistics for Marketing*. Maidenhead: McGraw Hill.

Roethlisberger, F.J. and Dickson, W.J. (1939) *Management and the Worker*. Cambridge, MA: Harvard University Press.

Schlackman, W. and Chittenden, D. (1988) Packaging research, in Worcester, R.M. and Downham, J. (eds.) *Consumer Market Research Handbook*. Amsterdam: Elsevier Press, pp. 513–536.

Sounderpandian, J. (1999) *Market Research Using Microsoft Excel*. Cincinnati, OH: South Western College Publishing.

Spencer, C. (2005) How did market research help corral public support and bring the 2012 Olympics to London? *Research*, August, pp. 24–27.

Stuart, M. (2003) *An Introduction to Statistical Analysis for Business and Industry: A Problem Solving Approach*. London: Arnold.

Tarran, B. (2011) Lego makes crowd-sourcing platform global. *Research*, 7 October, http://www.research-live.com/news/news-headlines/lego-makes-crowd-sourcing-platform-global/4006168.article

Welsh, M. (2000) A Lowe Partners presentation to the Hungarian Direct Marketing Association, http://www.dmsz.net/ie/welsh.htm

Part 3

Analysis and communication

9 Analysis

Contents

Chapter guide

Analysis means that we spot something useful in what we have seen. In this chapter, a distinction is made between qualitative and quantitative data analysis. Transcripts and computer software are features of qualitative analysis; on the other hand, quantitative processes imply preparation, checking, editing, and coding. The coding of open-ended questions is examined in some detail. The chapter covers measures of dispersion, averages, and significance testing. Univariate, bivariate, and multivariate analyses are explained, as are procedures for tabulation weighting and grossing.

Learning outcomes

By the end of this chapter, you should be able to:

1. **Explain the purpose of analysis**
2. **Explain the nature of qualitative analysis**
3. **Explain the nature of quantitative analysis**
4. **Describe ways to assess the accuracy of results**

Introduction

Analysis concerns the identification of meaningful patterns in data. If we look at sales of products from supermarkets and take the outside temperature into account, we see some fascinating relationships. When there is a sudden cold spell, we see that there is an increase in sales of 'comfort foods' such as root vegetables and soups. Such analysis has a practical use: the layout of stores can be modified and stock can be ordered according to weather forecasts.

There are many ways to analyse data, but all of these cannot be applied in all cases. If data have been collected in a certain way, using certain instruments, then any analysis will be limited by those constraints. Quantitative studies can take full advantage of statistical techniques in attempting to analyse data. Such studies embrace univariate, bivariate, and multivariate analysis. There is also a useful tool to assess accuracy, known as significance testing. Qualitative researchers have different challenges. An eating metaphor is a good way to visualise this issue. Consider the preparation of food—we cannot make a fruit dessert without fruit.

Additionally, the researcher must be alert to the danger of collecting too much information. There is a risk of being unable to see the essential facts when there are so many facts available. Back in the kitchen, we might forget to cook the potatoes if other colourful and attractive ingredients distract us.

Back in 1888 the US Census Bureau held a competition to avoid the massive manual sorting exercise needed for census forms. The winner was a statistician called Herman Hollerith (1860–1929). He developed a system that allowed data to be encoded on cards through a series of punched holes.

The Hollerith system made an enormous contribution: analysis of the US 1890 census was completed extremely quickly with less manpower than previous surveys. The system was then used for the 1891 census in Canada, Norway, and Austria, and for the 1911 census in the UK. Hollerith founded the Tabulating Machine Company in 1896 and this ultimately became the International Business Machines Corporation, now known as IBM (see Russo 1997).

©istockphoto.com/Massimiliano Fabrizi

Table 9.1 Notable events for analysis

Year	Event
1890s	Hollerith punch cards used in 1890 US census
1900s	Galton and Pearson initiate correlation and regression
1930s	The nomogram was introduced
1980s	Direct data entry
1990s	Spreadsheets introduced
2000s	Data mining became feasible

With the arrival of more complex devices, the punched card was read by machine and the computer held a record of the readings. These readings became known as 'hole counts'. These hole counts needed to be checked and any anomalies corrected. The unchecked version took the name of 'dirty hole counts'—there was dirt blocking the holes; the checked versions were 'clean hole counts'. In today's speech, we talk of clean data and dirty data. The top line of the row data tables gave a summary total of the many pages. This is why we use the term 'top-line data'.

In the 1980s, punch cards were replaced by the direct entry of responses into computers via the keyboard. The vocabulary has remained, but it is useful to remember its origins.

The researcher needs to make sense of the output after data processing and we have learnt a great deal over the years. Francis Galton (1822–1911) took a keen interest in all measurement methods and is said to have 'invented' statistical correlation and regression. It took Karl Pearson (1857–1936) to work on the formulas for correlation and these take his name as the 'Pearson product-moment correlation coefficient'. Significance testing shows how 'accurate' sampled results may be and various tools have been created. In 1939 Joseph Zubin introduced the nomogram. This simple picture of three scales parallel to each other, helps the reader to find values from a formula.

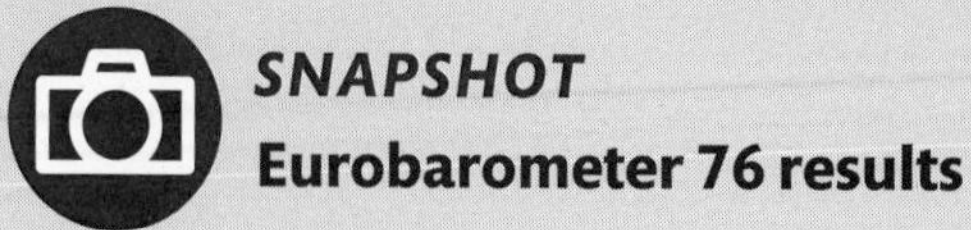

SNAPSHOT
Eurobarometer 76 results

The Eurobarometer is a survey that investigates attitudes to Europe.

Eurobarometer 76 covered over 30 countries or territories. TNS Opinion & Social carried out this wave of the Eurobarometer for the European Commission, Directorate-General for Communication, 'Research and Speechwriting'. Fieldwork was carried out in November 2011.

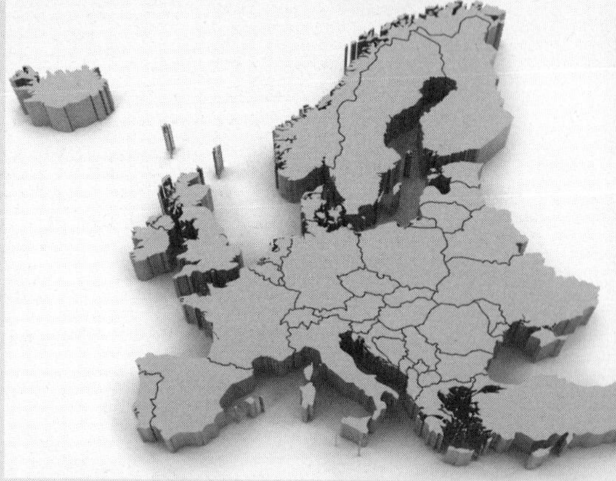

© istockphoto.com/German

The report addresses the climate of opinion: current satisfaction, expectations, and concerns of EU citizens; how European citizens view membership of the EU; the EU's image; confidence expressed in the Commission and the European Parliament; support for a European constitution; support for future enlargement; evaluation of the common foreign and security policy; evaluation of European democracy; support for the euro; and the EU's budget.

This Eurobarometer showed that European citizens are critical in their analysis of the EU. By way of example, let us look at the results for selected countries in Table 9.2 for question A11, which was: '*In general does the European Union conjure up for you a very positive, fairly positive, neutral, fairly negative or very negative image?*'. We will compare results with the same question posed some five years earlier.

In order to interpret the results, the technical side of the study must be considered. The survey covers the population of the respective nationalities resident in each of the Member States and aged 15 years and over. All interviews were conducted face-to-face in people's homes and in the appropriate national language. CAPI (computer-assisted personal interview) was used in those countries where this technique was available. For each country, a comparison between the sample and the universe was carried out. The universe description was derived from Eurostat population data or from national statistics offices. For all countries surveyed, a national weighting procedure, using marginal and intercellular weighting, was carried out based on this universe description. In all countries, gender, age, region, and size of locality were introduced in the iteration procedure. For international weighting (i.e. EU averages), TNS Opinion & Social applied the official population figures as provided by Eurostat or national statistic offices.

The report stated that the results are estimations, the accuracy of which, everything being equal, rests on the sample size and the observed percentage. With samples of about 1000 interviews, the real percentages vary within the following confidence limits:

Observed percentages

10% or 90%	± 1.9 points
20% or 80%	± 2.5 points
30% or 70%	± 2.7 points
40% or 60%	± 3.0 points
50%	± 3.1 points

Compiled by Nigel Bradley 2012.

Sources:

http://ec.europa.eu/public_opinion/archives/eb/eb76/eb76_en.htm

http://ec.europa.eu/public_opinion/archives/eb/eb63/eb63_en.htm

Respondents answering 'positive' to Eurobarometer 76 question A11: 'In general does the European Union conjure up for you a very positive, fairly positive, neutral, fairly negative or very negative image?' (n = c1000 per country). Compared with Eurobarometer 63.4 QA10

Country	Spring 2005 (%)	Winter 2011 (%)	Diff
Sweden	34	31	–3
Denmark	35	32	–3
Austria	30	25	–5
Netherlands	38	31	–7
Finland	30	22	–8
Poland	51	42	–9
Estonia	38	29	–9
Germany	42	30	–12
Hungary	43	31	–12
Slovakia	46	34	–12
United Kingdom	28	13	–15
France	49	32	–17
Slovenia	57	40	–17
Czech Rep	43	26	–17
Romania	66	49	–17
Lithuania	49	31	–18
Latvia	40	21	–19
Italy	63	42	–21
Belgium	56	31	–25
Greece	54	28	–26
Portugal	56	26	–30
Ireland	68	37	–31
Spain	57	26	–31

Analysis of qualitative data

A unique characteristic of qualitative research is that analysis actually begins before data collection ends. If we take a research project with five group discussions, analysis begins within the first minutes of the first group and continues until the last minutes of the final group. Unlike the structured questionnaire, the focus group agenda requires that the moderator opens up areas of investigation and probes them until they yield nothing new. In qualitative approaches, the project is modified as it progresses.

Questions may therefore be formulated at the interview in response to points made by respondents. In practical terms, you may be faced with notes from groups and depth interviews; you may have sound tape recordings, videos, and perhaps transcripts. Transcripts take the appearance of typed-out versions of conversations. Historically, researchers would take a pair of scissors and cut them up, making little piles for each subject that emerged.

These isolated bits of information could then be subjected to tabular or matrix analysis. This does not mean statistical tabulations, but one of words and quotes. The best way to do this is to take an extremely large piece of paper (poster size) and to divide it into cells. Table 9.3 is an extract from an analysis of numerous depths carried out to investigate chocolate-buying behaviour. The respondents are shown on the left with some basic demographic data; the themes are chosen by the researcher as ones that are likely to be meaningful.

For report writing this matrix is used as an aide-memoire; it allows comments to be extracted and dominant themes to be seen; it may also show the links between items.

In simplistic terms, qualitative data are analysed by:

1. Data reduction to organise and develop categories
2. Displaying the data to create text, charts, flow diagrams, matrices
3. Drawing conclusions to describe patterns and give explanations.

Several terms are used to describe different types of qualitative analysis. These include 'thematic analysis', 'radial diagrams', 'laddering' techniques, 'explanation building', and the

Table 9.3 Tabular analysis of depths on chocolate

Respondent	Price	Taste	Sales staff	Ads
1 High user, female, 32 years (C2)	'cheap chocolate tastes bad'	Brand X Melts in the mouth	'not important'	'use sex and fantasy, which I like'
2 Low user, male 45 years (B)	No comment	No comment	Irrelevant—buy self-service	I like the one with the girl
3 Female, med user, (D)	'Swiss choc is dear'	Varies from brand to brand	'friendly'	Are a waste of money
4 School girl 13 years	'Price doesn't enter my mind'	Most important	–	Can't think of any

'gestalt' approach. Despite the rather elaborate names, these methods simply assist the researcher to make sense of a great deal of data and to answer the research problem. In some cases, researchers may do 'follow-ups' by consulting participants and use their transcripts to probe further into what was really meant. This is a form of **triangulation** and it is done to confirm findings.

Dolan and Ayland (2001) made a comparison of three approaches to the analysis of qualitative data. These were: 1. holistic; 2. cut and paste; 3. computer-assisted. The study favours the 'cut and paste' approach.

There are important differences between analysis of depth interviews and groups: the results of individual interviews place different demands on the researcher. Careful recording and complete transcription may be easier for solus interviews than for groups, but the bridges between themes are often clearer to see in group discussions.

Typically, a client will be debriefed during fieldwork (the client will probably be at some or all of the groups to receive feedback) and an agreement may be made to modify the approach. This may mean excluding or including questions or stimulus materials, and perhaps even replacing a certain profile of respondent with another.

During fieldwork, most moderators take notes and write short memos for their own use. This is evidence of early analysis of this complex data set. After the data have been collected, the researcher is left with recordings and notes. Along with memories of the sessions and any stimulus materials used, the task of making sense of the research can be progressed.

Transcripts

Some researchers may organise transcripts for each group and depth interview. Across the nation, there are dozens of homeworkers with headphones who listen carefully to recorded interviews. Word by word, utterance by utterance, they create typewritten pages of the conversations.

These transcripts do not come cheap and so they are not always requested by clients. For some researchers, they are essential, to ensure that detail is not lost, to act as a ready reminder, or as a basis for a 'cut and paste' method of analysis. It is, however, commonly agreed that transcripts can be dangerous. People do not talk in a way that can easily be transformed into written script.

Just think of the key emotions (sometimes called the 'big six'): fear, anger, happiness, sadness, surprise, and disgust. These are normally lost in a simple transcript of the spoken word. Similarly, timing, interruption, overlapped speech, body language, and intonation are all lost. Someone who speaks sarcastically about an intention may be taken literally if a transcript were to be used alone.

For some clients, transcriptions represent a way of checking the quality of the researchers they have employed and an opportunity for seeing the result of the research in its unprocessed form. If a client insists on seeing transcripts, then the researcher is advised to add a 'health warning' with each interview and the identity of the respondent must not be evident.

Having said that, a transcript should 'speak for itself': sentences should be left unfinished, illogical utterances should be left. The transcript can be a strong reminder of the original interview and can convey its sense to people who were not there. Transcripts show several things: who asks to speak, who takes the floor, who concedes, who succeeds. They show dominant thoughts, controversial positions, and so on.

Common mistakes
Making counts

It is often tempting, at focus group discussions, to ask for respondents to show a hand to count up answers to various questions. Taking a hand count is wrong because the question has been posed in a different way to all respondents. Sometimes, the context 'leads' the respondent to answer in one way; group pressure can also lead a respondent to show a hand or not. The sample will not have been selected in a way that draws any great conclusions from this vote.

© Radius Images

A good way to see group pressure in action is to ask a question and notice that people look at each other before raising a hand. Those hands will rise at different speeds, suggesting that some people are more convinced than others. This mistake can also be extended to analysis, whereby notes and recordings are inspected to make guesses and estimates of likely numbers. It can go as far as the report and presentation: if pie charts and bar charts, with numbers, appear in a qualitative project, questions need to be asked. Perhaps this happens because some clients like to see hard facts (such as numbers) and see this as a tangible outcome of what they see as a pleasant chat with their customers.

The true value of this form of inquiry is to look at the breadth and depth of opinion and feeling. Quantitative research will provide the hard numbers; qualitative should not.

Psathas and Anderson (1990, pp. 80–84) state that these types of information can be made available in transcripts: words as spoken; sounds as uttered; inaudible or incomprehensible noises; spaces and silences; overlapped speech and sounds, pace, stresses and volume. The task ahead is one of reducing these data to a form that makes sense. That process can involve words and pictures, but rarely numbers.

Themes are discovered from the information and overriding explanations are suggested. This is called 'thematic analysis', and Aronson (1994) gives a good account:

> When gathering sub-themes to obtain a comprehensive view of the information, it is easy to see a pattern emerging. When patterns emerge it is best to obtain feedback from the informants about them. This can be done as the interview is taking place or by asking the informants to give feedback from the transcribed conversations.

This approach of checking the 'pattern' ensures that the project is reliable, in the scientific sense of 'reliability', as opposed to the layman definition of 'you can rely or depend on it'. Although this might take place in academia, in the practitioner's world, time constraints are less likely to permit further access to respondents.

Analysis follows the specific research questions. Several styles can be found among different researchers:

- Selecting examples to illustrate points made
- Implying importance because words or comments were repeated numerous times
- Systematic coding to discover links
- A global (or gestalt) look at the groups, avoiding paying too much attention to the detail.

Researchers are advised to start analysis as soon as possible, whether by simple reflection within the first minutes of the first session or in considered introspection. Researchers are also advised to finish analysis as soon as possible after fieldwork ends; if it is left for too long, the memory can suffer and events totally unrelated to the interviews may affect recall. There is much to be said for continuing to reflect: sleep researchers have discovered that mental processing can assist in making new discoveries in data (Wagner *et al.* 2004).

Radial diagrams

The use of qualitative methods in marketing research relies heavily on the individual researcher's experience and capabilities. At one extreme, some researchers rigidly follow a discussion guide that has previously been agreed by their client; at the other extreme, researchers will rely entirely on an imaginary structure, or on creating a structure by probing techniques. Some researchers will make contemporaneous notes during an interview; others will rely entirely on memory or on recordings.

There are advantages and disadvantages of the different methods: from transcripts to notes made from recordings; from gestalt interpretation to the combing of the detail. In contrast to these methods, 'radial diagrams' (also known as cognitive nodes, spider diagrams, and mind mapping) can be a useful and invaluable tool in interview administration and subsequent analysis.

Tony Buzan trademarked the technique under the name of Mind-Mapping™ and popularised it. He has several books and training courses on the subject. His view is that most knowledge we pass on is linear—we write lines of words—but that this opposes the natural state of the world. Furthermore, he argues that memory and thought can easily be portrayed in diagrammatic form. As a starting point, maps are created on a single page with lines linking ideas, spanning outwards from a central point.

Computer analysis of qualitative data

In recent years, software has been developed for qualitative researchers. At their most basic, these programs take transcripts and notes and seek patterns in order to make analyses. This effectively makes use of all methods open to the human analyst.

Speech recognition software is also available and is able to create written transcripts of conversations. These can be combined with researcher notes and observations.

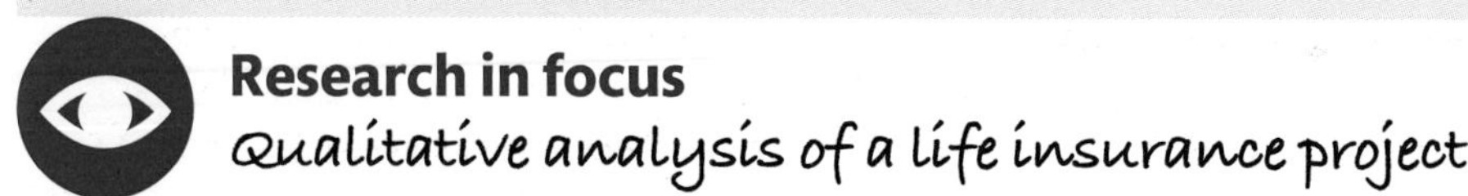

Research in focus
Qualitative analysis of a life insurance project

You know whilst being aware that he gets his whack, that there's a commission involved in this but I think it just was easier to be honest.

Do you think that you're satisfied with the products that you've got? Are you satisfied with the products you've got?
Yes I guess so but then we've never had to make a claim on anything so I think you never really assess how good they are until you actually need some . . . you know in terms of administration and getting things through the post when you're supposed to be getting and speed of the way the policies were set up then no I've got no problems.

What you've outlined is the life insurance relating to a mortgage, is it an endowment mortgage? Is that the sort of mortgage that you have?
No it's not an endowment mortgage, we did it on Chris's pension so it's a pension mortgage.

So it's actually running as life insurance as well to make sure that the lender gets the money back basically in the event of somebody dying?
Yes.

Do you know of any other types of life insurance that take risk?
No. You mean in terms of the sort of policy? I mean you can take out life insurance at any point, it doesn't have to be attached to a mortgage. As I say I don't know if whether it's our age or we just didn't think about it, it's never really been something that we thought about outside the context of the mortgage, although once we started talking about the remortgage, I think we were both concerned to bump up the life insurance cover and maybe it's something that we'll think about more seriously when and if we have kids.

You see that's another thing that I've seen come across as well is that there is a trigger that makes people more insurance aware. What would that trigger have been for you then, because something happened last Autumn didn't it basically?
It was the remortgage so basically I was . . . instead of having a joint mortgage we were going to have two mortgages each in our own name, so I actually had to take out life insurance for the remortgage. As it happened the remortgage didn't go through but the life insurance was already underway and I just decided to go ahead with it and partly of course because it was linked to the critical illness which I think is one of these short term things isn't it and I guess that's probably more important to me at the moment than life insurance.

And is that because you've been exposed to people confronted with . . . ?
Not it hasn't actually, it was something ridiculous that set me off with it because Chris rides a bike and wouldn't wear a helmet and I remember we started having these conversations where I'd say 'Will you wear your bloody helmet? What happens if you fall off your bike and you end up disabled?' and then it was at about the time I guess that there was lot more discussion in the media and papers and stuff about critical illness because I'm not sure how long these policies have gone on but they're not that recent and it just seemed sensible to do. You know it's quite a scary thing and especially I suppose that there's less you can rely on from the State and so I guess it's covering us in that so I think critical illness is more important than the life cover to be honest.

While you're still alive?
Yes. Exactly.

SUE, 14TH AUGUST

Figure 9.1 Interview transcript

The figures show three examples of analysis from a real project on life insurance. You can see the 'discussion guide' used for this project in the Market Researcher's Toolbox. The key questions were how and why people buy life insurance; then, more specifically, why people choose specific policies.

Figure 9.1 is one page taken from 50 transcribed from part of a single interview, for a respondent called Sue, on 14 August. We see that cycling (without a helmet) by her partner prompted Sue to look into life insurance. The transcript shows the wealth of information available, but the problem comes with dissecting the numerous points and reorganising the information. This transcript has been corrected twice.

Figure 9.2 shows a timeline analysis of involvement with life insurance. This concerns a female respondent in her 80s, who took out a policy in her 40s to cover funeral expenses for her mother, who died some 20 years later.

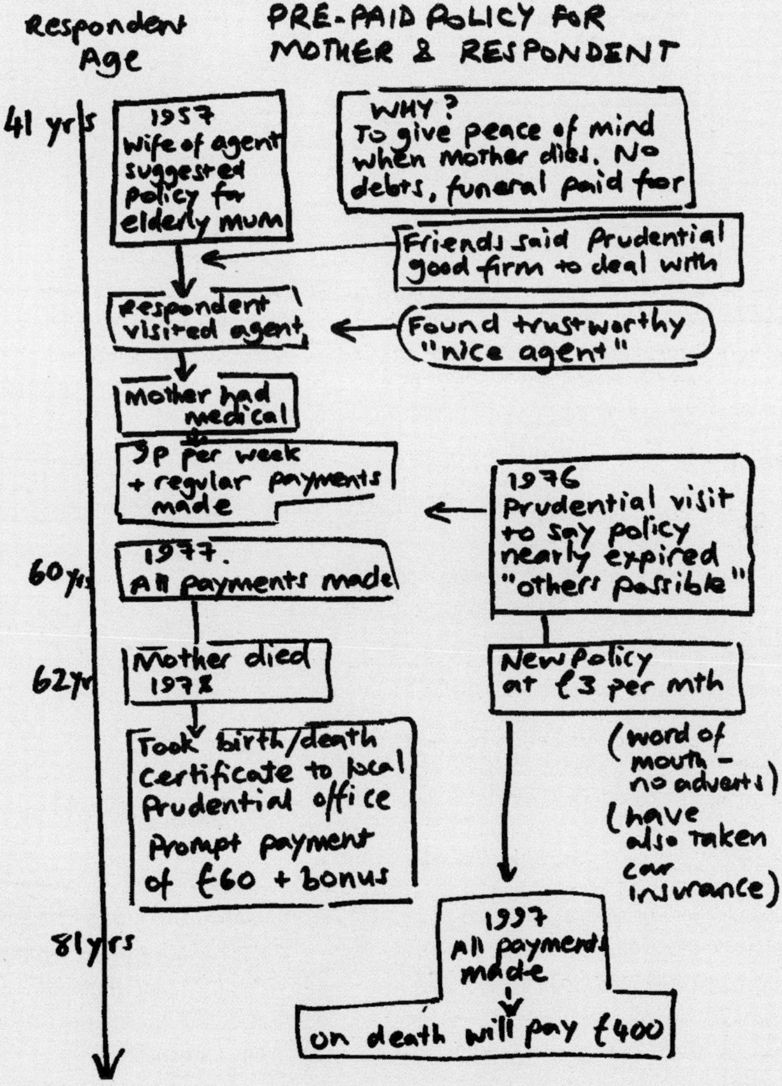

Figure 9.2 Timeline analysis

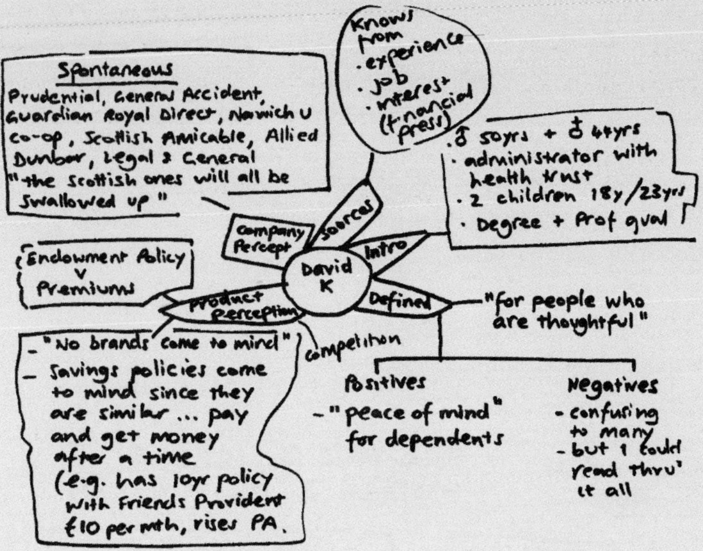

Figure 9.3 Summary mind map of interview

Radial diagrams (cognitive-nodes or mind maps) were used during the interviews for this project and in subsequent analysis that took place in the office.

Figure 9.3 shows a summary mind map of a depth interview with David K, a 50-year-old. David sees life insurance as giving 'peace of mind', but it is confusing. The source of this respondent's knowledge is his job in personnel and his own interest in reading the financial press.

Compiled by Nigel Bradley 2009.

Questions

1 Identify idiomatic phrases and explain how they can help or hinder understanding of meaning.

2 Which parts of the transcript (or elsewhere) show that the respondent was not listening to the interviewer? Which parts of the interviews do not make sense?

3 Which questions show that the interviewer is using prior knowledge (information analysed from earlier interviews) in the data collection?

4 Create a mind map from the transcript. What are the good and bad points about mind map analysis?

5 What are the good and bad points about the timeline style of analysis?

Different software programs can make analysis of such documents to create categories and a database that can be interrogated in many ways. The various advantages are that: they can find concealed data, reanalysis is easy, and report-writing is made more efficient. The disadvantages concern data preparation time, the fact that output quality depends on the input quality, and that the software available varies in capability and quality.

Traditional qualitative research practitioners have hesitated to welcome this innovation with open arms. Such software has received more positive attention from practitioners of online focus groups, possibly because they use 'chatroom'-type software where participants type their messages, which effectively creates instant transcripts. There are benefits in that the software finds concealed patterns, different attempts at analysis are fast, and reporting is made easier. All of this is possible because the material is already in text form. The resistance from traditional researchers may be related to the time taken to input data, loss of control by researchers, and the barrier of learning about the software. The final criticism from practitioners is that it is easy to misconstrue meanings by using systematic analysis: the human being is capable of detecting subtle nuances in expression.

Analysis of quantitative data

Consider a study of restaurant diners: the team of researchers, by the end of the study, has become a team of experts. They can now give their clients different levels of service, from the most basic to the most 'de luxe':

1. Raw data—questionnaires
2. Processed data—tables
3. Analytical report—a commentary on the tables
4. Interpretative report—a commentary, but with the researcher's own views added.

The quantitative researcher must edit raw data; these data are then coded and finally input into a computer. If computer-assisted data capture is being used, these processes may happen simultaneously.

Editing

'Editing' ensures that answers are complete, accurate, and suitable for further processing. Questionnaires are inspected to identify questions that are answered incorrectly or not answered at all. This is sometimes called 'cleaning' the data, but it is just one 'cleaning session'—if the preliminary tables look 'dirty', they too will be cleaned. Tables are inspected to ensure that there are no obvious irregularities; this is known as 'sense checking'. The researcher can do various things with any identified problems:

- Deduce the answer by inspecting other answers from the same respondent
- Deduce the answer by inspecting answers from other respondents
- Return to the respondent and ask the question again
- Discard or reject the entire data record for the given respondent
- Do nothing and leave the data 'dirty'.

Coding

'Coding' is the name given to the procedure whereby complex descriptions are broken into simpler meanings and are allocated a code, usually a number. Closed questions are generally pre-coded. This means that numbers have already been allocated to the possible answers. These may have been allocated after a pilot study, or because the codes are clearly defined (e.g. brand names). Most closed questions include the 'other' category in which other answers appear; these responses need to be inspected and coded.

When informants are allowed to answer a question in their own words—expressing their views freely and without further direction by an interviewer—this is known as an ' open-ended question'. Open-ended questions generate answers that may not have been anticipated, making them similar to the 'other' category.

In an interview that is administered by an interviewer—for example, face-to-face or by telephone—the answers will be written down (or typed) verbatim. In a self-completion interview, the respondent will express views using familiar language.

It is not entirely true to say that the respondent is free to answer such questions. There are various factors that will influence the length, quality, and content of response. The length might be determined by the space available to record comments, and also by the real and perceived time available. Similarly, the quality depends on such factors as the time allowed for the question to be considered, the integrity of the interview situation, and the respondent's interest in the topic. The content of responses is also affected by time aspects, but by the position of the question in the interview: preceding concepts can actually 'lead' the informant towards a specific thought and answer.

Verbatim answers need to be categorised after interviews have taken place. This categorisation is commonly described as coding, because numerical codes are applied to commonly occurring word combinations. This allows questionnaires to be analysed by computer and quantities of response to be measured.

Coding open-ended questions is a time-consuming activity and, where pre-codes can be created before questionnaires are administered, this is preferable. The researcher needs to make sense of open-ended questions. This involves a considered process of extracting and classifying key concepts, as follows:

1. A number of answers are written out (often on 50 questionnaires)
2. Answers that occur frequently are noted (using five-bar tally gates)
3. Code frames or 'codebooks' are created
4. The 'code frame' is used to allocate code numbers to each answer
5. The code numbers are put into the computer for further analysis.

Data entry

Data which have been collected need to be input. This involves reading each code and manually typing the number into some form of matrix. This can be quite a tedious task because the process is repetitive; each key depression involves one of ten numbers. Mistakes are inevitable, so some form of checking needs to be in place. The best form of quality control is to repeat the process completely and to compare the two data sets. This is called 'verification'. It may take place on as few as 20 per cent of all records or as many as 100 per cent.

More recently, recognition software has meant that scanned documents will be read automatically without human intervention. Again, there needs to be some form of quality control. Such programs can make mistakes if handwriting appears in the wrong place or irregular marks are taken for responses. Quality checks for scanners mean regular cleaning, changing parts, and simply running 'blank' forms to make sure scanner settings are accurate.

Computer-assisted data collection techniques (CAPI, CATI, CASI) skip this phase, but in these cases, it is critical to ensure that the original scripts (or programs) are accurate and well-considered before fieldwork starts. An incorrect route or filter can be damaging to the study.

Tabulation

Most quantitative marketing research is conducted using basic tables. A table consists of a side heading and a top heading (also called a 'top banner' or 'breakdown'). The main body of the table contains numbers. Table 9.4 is an example of a quantitative table, simplified in that it only shows percentages.

It is a good idea to produce dummy tables before collecting any data (see Table 9.5). These dummies (sometimes called 'empty shells') have everything except the numbers. Because they are created before data collection, it is best to sketch them out before writing a questionnaire; this then helps to avoid missing questions.

Many tables also carry means, standard deviations, and a predetermined 'significance' number. It is important to make decisions on the base, side headings and breakdowns, the percentages and weighting.

- **The base** On what is the table based? Who goes into the table? It might be 'all respondents' or some group, usually selected from the classification questions.

Table 9.4 Reasons for choosing brand X final table

	Total	Sex		Region			
		Male	Female	North	South	West	East
Base	400	200	200	100	100	100	100
	%	%	%	%	%	%	%
All	100	100	100	100	100	100	100
Easily available	5	2	3	1	1	2	1
Recommended	7	–	7	3	1	1	2
Prefer the taste	5	1	4	1	2	1	1
Like the colour	2	2	2	1	1	1	–
Other							

Table 9.5 Reasons for choosing brand X dummy table

	Total	Sex		Region			
		Male	Female	North	South	West	East
Base							
All							
Easily available							
Recommended							
Prefer the taste							
Like the colour							
Other							

- **Side headings and breakdowns** Scales may be collapsed, ranges may be summarised or converted into means.
- **Percentages and absolute numbers** Are real numbers kept beside the percentages? Are both column and row percentages used?
- **Weighting** Should data on the tables be weighted? Should another set of 'unweighted' tables be provided? The cell weighting method may be used or rim weighting might be employed, or tables might show results from both.

For the users and producers of research data, standard demographics (or classification questions) are useful because they provide a known point of reference. In questionnaire design, researchers should include specific demographic measures. Practitioners have tended to standardise how these are reported on tables. Table 9.6 shows how the different labels might appear. The number of subdivisions is kept deliberately small: for example, social grade is often reduced from six to four categories, age to just six, income to just three. This is to ensure that each cell has sufficient sample size to draw meaningful conclusions from these basic building blocks of analysis.

Non-standard demographics

More 'classifiers' may be needed for specific studies. These may be:

- Items common to all studies, but less used, such as household composition, interests
- Items relevant to the topic under study, such as past users, number of friends in a similar position
- Combined items—these can only be created after data collection by amalgamating items. Such an example is to create a label of CD males with two cars.

The researcher must choose classifications that are likely to provide meaningful tabulations. Indeed, from a marketer's point of view, this is the first process in segmenting the market.

Research in focus
Automated open-ended coding

The procedure of sorting open-ended questions and categorising answers needs skill and meaning can be lost. McDonald (1973) proposed a way to preserve the rich data. By drawing on the work of Noam Chomsky, he developed a computer program for 'linguistic coding'. Since then, there have been various other attempts to automate the process. An early UK program was the 'OpenCode' system that was used successfully in the agency called BJM. This identified frequently occurring (recurring) words and needed human intervention to confirm whether the meanings were similar.

Current offerings on the market include Ascribe™ Coding from the USA and Verbastat from SPSS. SPSS claims that large market research organisations such as NFO Research and Harris Interactive use its product. Such software gives researchers a big commercial advantage: SPSS argues that NFO reduced labour by 25 per cent. In the USA, in 2004, SPSS Inc. made its 'SPSS Text Analysis for Surveys' available. The company says it can distinguish between positive and negative open-ended responses.

With these computerised systems, all open-ended answers are input into the computer, which is beneficial because it allows the coding procedure to take place using every single word, thereby providing a better quality codebook. Another major benefit is that, after results are presented, it is easy to recall full verbatims, which explain summary codes. On the downside, the process of inputting data can be time-consuming and labour-intensive.

The number of web-based surveys has increased in recent years and many open-ended questions are answered in typed form, so input labour is not such an issue. This increase in uncoded verbatims has generated renewed interest in automated coding, so researchers are attempting to fine-tune software to meet this demand. Research is pointing to the use of fuzzy logic and neuro-linguistic programming as ways of taking the burden from the human and giving it to the machine. A current development is Decooda which is a 100 per cent automated natural coding process. Text analytics allow these results to be scored on sentiment, emotion and context.

Compiled by Nigel Bradley 2012.

Sources:

Anon (2011) $20k innovation prize for Decooda. *Research*, December, p. 8.

Holder, M. and Johnson, D. (1984) OpenCode: what we have learned from the recession, *37th ESOMAR Congress paper*, Rome, 2–6 September.

McDonald, C. (1973) Linguistic coding – a new solution to an old problem, *Journal of the Market Research Society*, 15, pp. 163–181.

Macer, T. (2004) Textual analysis, *Research*, August, p. 37.

http://www.spss.com/verbastat/

http://www.languagelogic.net/

Questions

1. What can computer open-ended analysis do that other methods cannot?
2. What are the disadvantages of these computerised approaches in comparison with other methods?
3. What is fuzzy logic and what is neuro-linguistic programming? How can these be integrated into this specialism?

Table 9.6 Standard demographics

Demographic	Usual labels
Sex	Male, female
Age	18–24, 25–34, 35–44, 45–54, 55–64, 65+
Terminal education age (TEA)	15 or under, 16, 17–18, 19+, still studying
Employment status	Full-time, part-time, not working
Income	Ranges vary, often around the average annual income at the time of study
Household size	1–2, 3–4, 5+
Occupation (social grade)	Used to compute social grade AB, C1, C2, DE
Region	TV areas, sales regions, country regions

In recent years, we have seen a revival of **data dredging**, a term used by Selvin and Stuart in 1966. This refers to approaches used to analyse data when specific hypotheses have not been created. The two authors said that the most common type under this subheading is 'hunting'. Here, every variable is cross-analysed against every other variable in the study. This leads to numerous tables, and the researcher seeks (or 'hunts') for patterns. Since 1966, this procedure has been made far easier by more powerful computers, and analysing many variables (multivariate analysis) has become relatively straightforward. If simple approaches cannot provide meaningful patterns, it is reasonable to see whether advanced data analysis techniques can help.

Weighting

'Weighting' is used to ensure that the sample is balanced, usually in terms of sex, age, region, and perhaps, social grade: for example, if a sample is selected and there are fewer men than in the population, the results can be adjusted. Weighting is a way of calibrating the survey: we are 'reascribing' respondents to ensure balance. The advantage is that it corrects some of the error that may have arisen during the fieldwork. A disadvantage with weighting is that it reduces the effective sample size. Another problem is that the procedure affects variables not covered by the weighting criteria.

In the case of mall intercept surveys, weighting is commonly used to 'correct' the problems associated with interviewing heavy users of a particular shopping mall. The respondent replies are weighted by the number of visits made to the mall in a set amount of time (this approach was proposed by Sudman 1980).

There are two main types of weighting: cell-weighting and rim-weighting. In 'cell-weighting', variables form a matrix of target cells. These variables are usually sex, age, and region. The weight is then calculated for each cell in order to achieve that cell's target. In 'rim-weighting', each variable is looked at one by one. For example, region may be weighted first, the variables are kept and the second variable is used, and so on. Each time a new set of weights is derived, it will be automatically repeated until the best fit is achieved.

Weighting should not be confused with 'grossing up'. Grossing simply means that figures are multiplied up to the population level to show how many hundreds (or thousands) of people behave in a particular way as opposed to a percentage of those people.

Two other concepts of relevance are the design effect and the weighting effect. The 'design effect' has been labelled as 'Deff'. It is the ratio of the variance associated with a particular sampling method compared with a simple random sample. If the Deff is less than one, a smaller sample is needed. If the Deff is over one, a larger sample is needed; some quotas have carried design effects of five or more. Estimation of design effects is not considered in this book.

The 'weighting effect' (or Neff) is the value of the sample size that should be used when calculating standard errors in preference to the unweighted sample size.

There are several problems associated with such adjustments: they may '*affect variables that are not covered by the weighting criteria*' and weighting '*increases the variances of estimates from the sample*', or, put another way, reduces the effective sample size (McDonald and Monkman 1995, pp. 21 and 110). This is undesirable for any survey because extra cost may be incurred to increase the sample size, or severe corrective weights employed may lead to an increased sampling error.

Most industry guidelines require that weighted and unweighted base figures are shown alongside tables—they should also be included in presentations. This allows the reader to calculate standard errors, or in simple terms, to give an indication of how good the results are.

Identifying meaningful patterns in data

There are easy ways to analyse data and there are complex ways. Table 9.7 shows some techniques for the analysis of quantitative data. These techniques have been divided into univariate techniques, bivariate techniques, and multivariate techniques.

To illustrate this, it is useful to look at university students. 'Univariate' analysis takes just one variable; it gives frequency counts. It may use single summary statistics such as the mean: for example, the average age of students is 20 years.

'Bivariate' analysis takes two variables at a time and inspects the pattern between them. A simple table with a side heading and a breakdown is an example of a bivariate technique. 'Correlation' is the measure of the nature and the strength of association between two

Table 9.7 Univariate, bivariate, and multivariate techniques

Univariate techniques	Summary statistics, frequency counts, graphical techniques
Bivariate techniques	Two-variable, correlation, correspondence, exponential smoothing, cross-tabulation
Multivariate techniques	Discriminant analysis, factor analysis, log-linear analysis, multiple regression, AID, cluster analysis, conjoint analysis, MDS

variables: for example, age crossed against the subject studied—at one university, there may be 150 marketing students aged 18 years.

'Multivariate' analysis takes three or more variables at a time and inspects the pattern between them: for example, age crossed against the subject studied, crossed against geographic location, crossed against family income, crossed against sex—at one university, there may be 150 marketing students aged 18 years and who are female, living locally, and coming from families with above-average income.

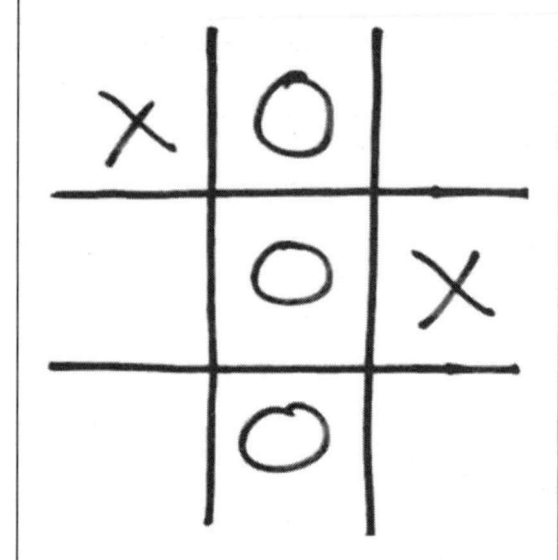

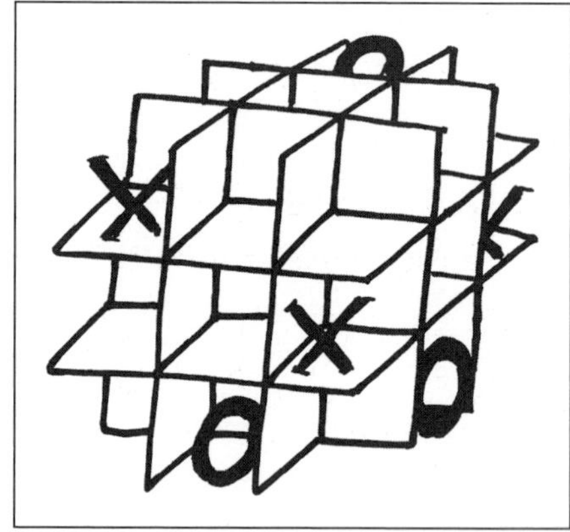

To explain the differences between bivariate and multivariate techniques, consider the simple pen-and-paper game of 'noughts and crosses' (see diagrams). This is played on a piece of paper with a simple grid; a player must consider the columns and rows when marking a square. In this traditional game, two aspects (the column and row) must be considered. If we now imagine a three-dimensional noughts and crosses game, a third dimension has been introduced: in addition to rows and columns, we now have depth. The game is more complicated because the player must go around the shape to see the best place to place a mark, and still then it may be difficult to see. This is analogous trivariate analysis; add another aspect and we can picture a more complex shape; yet another and we would be incapable of playing the game.

This multivariate analysis is almost impossible to carry out without the use of computers or some other calculation device. The human mind is not able to envisage the 'meaningful pattern'.

There is no doubt that people are confused by complex methodologies; there is no need to use sophisticated techniques when basic procedures will do. In any project, an audience needs to understand easily.

Simple cross-tabulation techniques are more often used by research agencies than others.

Multivariate data techniques can be classified into two categories: interdependence techniques and dependence techniques (see Table 9.8). The word 'dependence' refers to whether variables have been designated as dependent on other variables.

We will look at brief definitions for a few multivariate analysis techniques: regression, analysis of variance, factor analysis, discriminant analysis, cluster analysis, and CHAID.

Regression is used to analyse associative relationships between a ' metric-dependent variable' and one or more 'independent variables'.

Analysis of variance (ANOVA) is used to examine the differences among means. It is a statistical technique that is used with two or more populations.

Table 9.8 Multivariate data analysis techniques

Interdependence techniques	Dependence techniques
Factor analysis	Discriminant analysis
Cluster analysis	Conjoint analysis
Multidimensional scaling	

Factor analysis is a term used to describe a set of procedures used to reduce and summarise data. It does not distinguish dependent from independent variables and so seeks to identify the factors underlying any relationships. The method aims to discover simple patterns. It does this by grouping the variables and reducing them to a small set of factors, hence the name 'factor analysis'. It is impossible to measure or observe these factors directly. A 'factor loading' shows how close an indicator is to the factor. It signifies the degree to which each variable correlates with a factor:

- Very high factor loading (>0.6) The variable describes the factor very well
- High factor loading (>0.3) The variable describes the factor well
- Low loading (<0.3) Should be ignored.

A positive loading shows a positive relationship of the variable with the factor, whereas a negative loading shows an inverse relationship of the variable with the factor. Finally, 'rotated' factor analysis arranges the indicators so that each loads highly on just one factor.

Discriminant analysis is used when the dependent variable is categorical and the independent variables are interval.

Cluster analysis is a term that describes a set of techniques used to put items into groups. These groups contain items that, within a group, are similar—but one group will differ from another. Other names for this are 'classification analysis' or 'numerical taxonomy'.

CHAID is another term likely to be encountered; it stands for 'chi-square automatic interaction detection', and is a way to study the relationship between a dependent variable and a series of predictor variables. It selects a set of predictors and their interactions that optimally predict the dependent measure. The developed model is a classification tree that shows how major 'types' predict a dependent variable. It is particularly used to identify different customer segments hidden inside a customer database.

Data fusion

'Data fusion' techniques were established in the 1980s and have been the subject of much debate since. Data fusion involves merging data from two studies. Various 'hooks' are used to match respondents. These hooks (or bridge variables) are typically: demographics, media habits, consumption, lifestyles, and attitudes.

The two samples are called the 'donor' and 'recipient' samples. Software inspects all of the data available and identifies the best matches for each respondent in the donor survey.

The advantages of data fusion include the fact that it allows shorter questionnaires, so there is less pressure on respondents. Additionally, the method can provide answers to questions that were not posed to all respondents. There are a few disadvantages, which mean that the underlying procedure is complicated and treated with suspicion, not least because the statistical margin of data error is unknown. Data ownership may not be clear and the fusion means that all common variables should be perfectly matched.

There are several negative remarks made about data fusion, which make it easy to remember the technique: for example, it has the potential to create a set of men who use female sanitary towels or a set of cat owners who regularly buy dog food!

It is likely that data fusion will become more and more popular because IT has opened the way to generating, storing, and making available much more information than ever before. Most of these data sets can be merged or 'fused'. This might be seen as a method of 'data capture' and the fact that it can provide answers makes this a unique analysis tool.

Accuracy of results

A common and important question in research is: '*How good are the results?*'. This is a simple question with a complex answer. The accuracy of studies depends on the information people give and the procedures used. In studies where sampling is used, there are two considerations that can account for variations in results: sampling error and non-sampling error.

'Sampling error' is a difference between the characteristics of the sample and the population as a whole. It is the difference between the value shown in the sample and the value found in the real population. It is, indeed, an error in the sampling, but it goes beyond this; it is not a mistake, but it is a real fact of life. If we select a sample, we must miss out some people. The error may be that the sample is the 'wrong size' or we have omitted the 'wrong people'. Sampling error occurs with random samples and also with non-random samples. However, it can only be measured in surveys that use random samples.

In contrast, 'non-sampling error' results only from the way observations are made. It may relate to the sampling frame ('sampling frame error') or the process ('interviewer error', 'respondent error', 'data input error', etc.). All of these errors may lead to a survey that is *not* representative of the population it is intended to represent. We have divided these into 'respondent' and 'researcher' errors in Figure 9.4.

Let us start with respondent errors. We have used the label 'response bias' for one type of respondent error. This is error that comes from problems that originate with respondents. For example, respondents may be found to be telling things that are not true (lying), they may agree with cues that originate with the researcher (acquiescence response bias), they may express themselves in a way that projects a particular image for themselves (social desirability bias), they may take an extreme position for some reason (extremity bias), or there may be genuine problems of memory (poor recall). See Chapter 4 for more information on some of these aspects.

Another type of respondent error has been called 'non-response bias'. This is where the researcher has little control and relates to the respondent's presence or absence during the fieldwork period. Respondents or their 'spokesperson' may decline to cooperate (refusals); they may be on holiday or elsewhere (away); or there may be an inability to gain access to them, which means that there is scant information (no contact). Another aspect is that, although

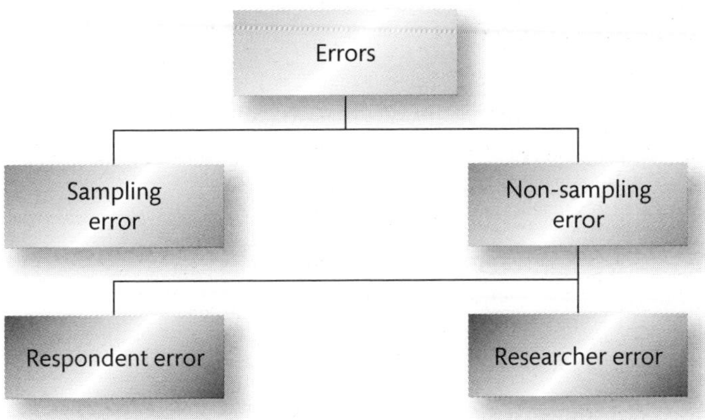

Figure 9.4 The family of errors

eligible, some respondents may be more enthusiastic than others and there may be a bias called 'self-selection'.

Researcher errors may be associated with fieldworkers or the research team. 'Fieldworker bias' may involve outright fabrication of responses (cheating), or it may be a more subtle aspect, whereby the personality or physical presence and appearance of the fieldworker may affect the results (interviewer bias). Genuine mistakes may be made in the field when an incorrect respondent is recruited (sample selection errors), and, of course, there are possibilities of other problems emanating from the fieldworker (interviewer mistakes).

Researcher errors that are associated with the research team include inaccurately transferring recorded responses from paper into a computer (data input errors), poor wording used in questions, or the mechanism for registering them may be defective (instrument errors). Finally, the source of the sample may not cover the target population, or there may be duplicates or other defects (sampling frame errors).

The accuracy of studies depends on how people give information and the procedures used. Some variations in results can be explained by sampling error and non-sampling error (see Figure 9.5). These errors should be prevented or minimised at the planning stage by training, quality control, timing the fieldwork, pilots and supervision—but at the analysis stage, they must be identified and taken into account. Then, significance testing will allow us to be cautious about the results.

Significance testing

Let us examine significance broadly. Consider the verb 'to signify', which is another way of expressing 'the notion of meaning'. With significance, we are asking whether something is meaningful; to be meaningful, something needs to be useful and be indicative of something.

The word 'significance' is often used loosely by newcomers to research, and indeed by established personnel. It is a powerful word that, when used in business meetings, can stir quite a few emotions. The simple question *'Are these results significant?'* can strike fear into the most experienced researcher. The reason for this is the fact that the person posing the question

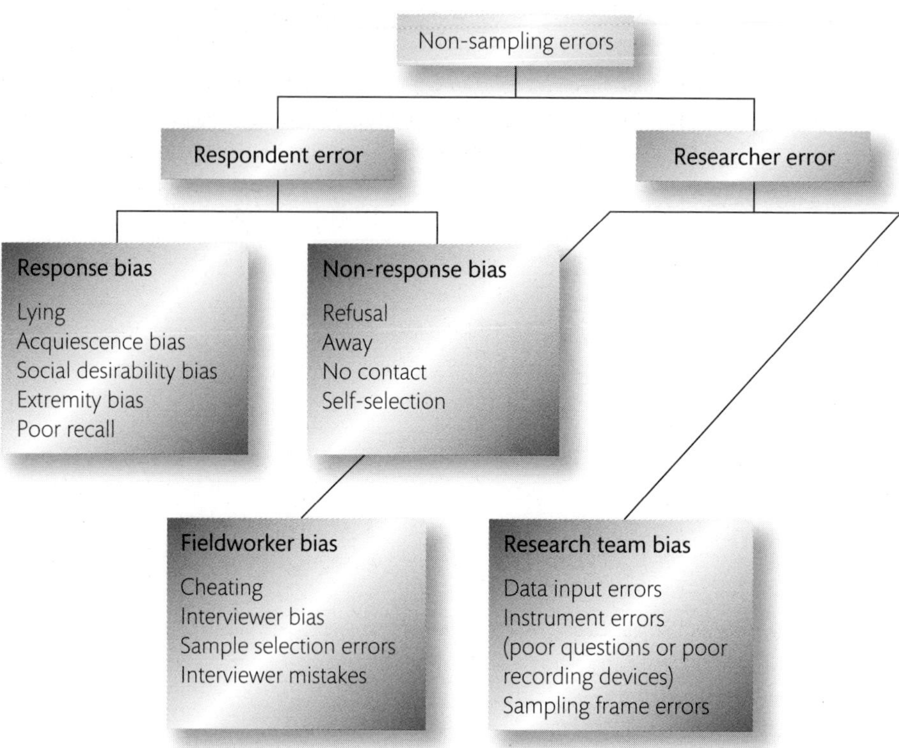

Figure 9.5 Non- sampling errors

may, unknowingly, be shedding doubt on the whole research. It is a little like asking a chef whether there is too much salt in the food. For many people, understanding can be confused by the many meanings of the word, but they will know that it is important to research.

As with other words such as 'scientific', 'representative', 'random', 'survey', etc., there is a real possibility of misunderstandings. We might, at this point, introduce different types of significance. We will consider 'statistical significance', but there is also something called 'practical significance' (Churchill 2001, p. 635), sometimes known as 'commercial significance' (for example, by Alt and Brighton 1981, p. 210). Practical and commercial significance indicates that the manager may need to take action and that decisions must be made to make changes. This may coincide with statistical significance or it may not.

We can talk about the significance of findings in qualitative research. We can decide whether an utterance by a respondent is worth taking to a client for action. But it is unusual to 'test the significance' of qualitative results.

Quantitative research is the area where 'significance testing' is valuable. In statistics, it is useful to think of significance as meaning 'probably true', rather than 'important'. It is here that the hypothesis, which has been carefully formulated at the planning stage, is tested. One way in which we might accept or reject the hypothesis is to see whether there is a 'significant difference' between the findings from the sample we have selected, and what the findings would have been if we had carried out a census.

It is important to accept that there are many tests and there are many assumptions. Most of the tests and assumptions are based on random sampling, but many practitioners employ them for studies that have used non-random sampling. This may be because no suitable equivalent is available (see Kent 1999, pp. 200–203).

This concept is difficult to visualise: there are so many aspects. In simple terms, we have results in front of us, but they are partial. We need to decide how accurate they are, and significance testing is the key to doing this. Here are some examples.

In 1991, a newspaper was read by 9 per cent of the UK adult population. In 2001, the readership figure was 19.7 per cent. We know that there is a difference that might have an impact on the work of newsagents, printers, etc. So, the figures are certainly different, but from another viewpoint they may not be statistically different. The 'true' result for 1991 may have been as low as 8.6 per cent or as high as 9.4 per cent. Similarly, in 2001, the 19.7 per cent may have been 19.1 per cent or 20.1 per cent. The two results are significantly different, so there was an increase in readership.

We know, from survey results, that 9 per cent of females are reported to be left-handed, but 11 per cent of males are left-handed. We know that the people interviewed were definitely different, but does this indicate that more men are really left-handed? If we do a significance test, we find that the figure for males may be 10–12 per cent, and for females, it may be 8–10 per cent. If they are, in reality, both 10 per cent, then there is no difference between men and women (Bradley 1992).

These two examples illustrate that there are two possible outcomes when testing has been completed:

- Not significant
- Significant.

To take this one step further, we can specify how accurate our significance test is. This becomes a more complicated issue and true statisticians will be critical of the way in which market researchers simplify the process. The procedure should involve specifying three things: the degree of confidence, the power, and the size of the effect it is necessary to detect. It is the case that market researchers simply specify the degree of confidence (Churchill 2001, p. 635). Moreover, the confidence level is not usually selected according to the study in question. There are two confidence levels that have been adopted *'as implicit industry standards'* (Alt and Brighton 1981, p. 210). These are 5 per cent (0.05) and 1 per cent (0.01). If we take the 1 per cent level, this means that there is only one chance in 100 that the hypothesis will be rejected, so we can be 99 per cent confident.

Significance testing allows us to make the statement that a result is 'statistically significant' or 'not statistically significant'. A result is said to be significant where it seems unlikely to have come about only as a consequence of sampling error. We may want to obtain the confidence limits for a percentage.

Is a reported percentage of 25 likely to be plus or minus 3 per cent? Perhaps it might be plus or minus 15 per cent? We may want to look at:

- Differences between answers in the same sample
- Differences between answers in two different samples.

The choice of statistical test is assisted by 'tree diagrams'. By following a series of routes such as *'How many groups?'* and *'Are the variables ordinal?'*, the choice of test is reached. The researcher then needs to take the collected data and make the appropriate calculations.

There is a well-known statistical significance test called the 'chi-square test'. This measures whether differences in cross-tabulated data are statistically significant. As we know, tables are commonly used, so much use is made of the chi-square test.

There are several aids available with which to assess significance:

- **'Ready reckoners' or ' look-up tables'** These are small tables that can be consulted and allow one to read off the values that are already worked out
- **The nomogram** A diagram to find values from a formula. There are three scales parallel to each other. A straight edge is laid between two of the scales. The result is found at the point of intersection on the other scale
- **Automatic significance testing** This is added to tables as an extra label or notation to show how significant particular figures are
- **Online or offline software devices** Software packages include buttons to make assessments when tables have been created. There are also websites with online calculators (see http://www.surveysystem.com/sscalc.htm).

Users of research must avoid drawing conclusions that are not supported by the data.

Data storage

Data files are the way in which we store data, where we find it. Before it is 'filed', it must be in a format that is known and useful, otherwise any future consultation will be impossible. One important aspect of stored data is whether it is 'multipunched' or not. This term and others go back to Hollerith's cards. Each column and row was given a number and the holes were registered. If one column had more than two holes, it was called 'multipunch'. We will look at ASCII, IBM Column Binary, CSV Files, and ITE Fiche, paying particular attention to the aspect of multipunch.

ASCII is an acronym of American Standard Code for Information Interchange. In ASCII, there can be no multipunched data, so the input data needs to accommodate separate columns for each. IBM Column Binary is perhaps the most practical of the data files. Each data position contains 12 binary codes (1 to 9, 0, -, &.) and these can be multipunched. CSV files is an acronym of 'comma-separated variable files'; here, information is separated by commas. They can be easily read on spreadsheets such as Excel. Finally, the ITE Fiche is used to keep electronic table files instead of having paper copies. They take up less space than normal tables. An ITE browser views them.

These descriptions highlight a problem, particularly for international research: software vendors and users have not created software that connects easily. The same questionnaire may be written several times in different countries using different software. The result is that errors in conversion can affect a project quality. An organisation called OpenSurvey was created to promote the concept of open standards in survey software.

Ethical insight

Is the truth out there?

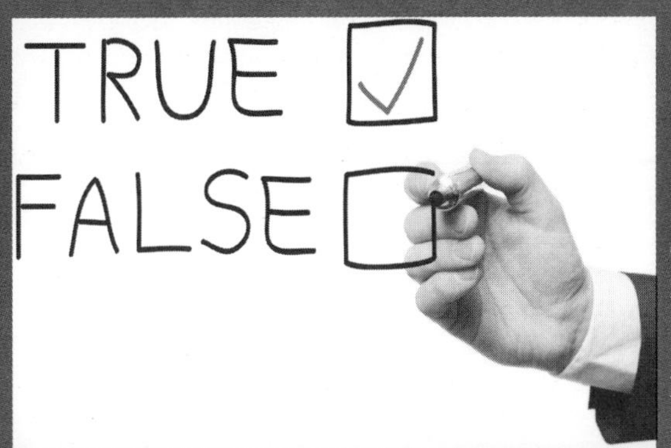

© istockphoto.com/Mats Persson

As human beings, we are capable of 'jumping to conclusions'. Indeed, many consultants are paid to do exactly that, based on a minimal amount of evidence; they have experience instead. This is perfectly acceptable at the point of final decision-making and, to some extent, it is expected from qualitative researchers. But surely clients have a right to know what is 'truth' and what is conjecture? Surely market researchers have a duty to make it clear when they are speculating?

Codes of conduct do cover this in various ways: for example, The Royal Statistical Society Code of Conduct, item 6, states that its fellows *'should not allow any misleading summary of data to be issued in their name'*. Again, in its words: *'A statistical analysis may need to be amplified by a description of the way the data were selected, and the way any apparently erroneous data were corrected or rejected'*. The Society also draws an important distinction between reporting from the data and giving views: *'Opinions based on general knowledge or belief should be clearly distinguished from opinions derived from the statistical analyses being reported'*.

The Social Research Association has a similar stance in its ethical guidelines. It says that social researchers *'have a responsibility to maintain high scientific standards in the methods employed in the collection and analysis of data and the impartial assessment and dissemination of findings'*.

This is everything to do with validity—are we measuring what we think we are measuring? Interestingly, the Market Research Society rules actually use the term 'validity' in several places. Because the nuance of wording is crucial, those references are reproduced here exactly as they appear in the code:

B50 *Members must comply with reasonable requests to make available to anyone the technical information necessary to assess the validity of any published findings from a research project.*

B53 *Members must provide clients with sufficient technical details to enable clients to assess the validity of results of research projects carried out on their behalf.*

B54 *Members must ensure that data tables include sufficient technical information to enable reasonable interpretation of the validity of the results.*

B55 *Members must ensure that reports include sufficient information to enable reasonable interpretation of the validity of the results.*

Compiled by Nigel Bradley 2012.

Sources:
MRS Code, rules B50–B52, http://www.mrs.org.uk/standards/codeconduct.htm
The Royal Statistical Society Code of Conduct, rule 6, http://www.rss.org.uk
The Social Research Association, http://the-sra.org.uk/sra_resources/research-ethics/ethics-guidelines/

Questions

1 In the text above, identify where the following words are used: scientific, validity, reasonable. What do these terms mean?

2 Should qualitative and quantitative research have the same guidelines?

3 Examine the differences between MRS rules B54 and B55 and apply this to a real project.

Chapter summary

1 **Explain the purpose of analysis**

Analysis allows the meaningful patterns to be identified. There are many ways to analyse data, but if data have been collected in a certain way, using certain instruments, then analysis will be limited by those constraints. Quantitative studies can take full advantage of statistical techniques in attempting to analyse data; qualitative researchers have different challenges. Additionally, the researcher must be alert to the danger of collecting too much information. There is a risk of missing the essential points when there are too many facts available.

2 **Explain the nature of qualitative analysis**

In qualitative research, analysis begins before data collection ends and the project is modified as it progresses. Notes, audio recordings, videos, and transcripts are analysed by: data reduction, displaying the data, and drawing conclusions. Different types of qualitative analysis include thematic analysis, radial diagrams, laddering techniques, explanation building, and the gestalt approach. Radial diagrams can be a useful and invaluable tool in interview administration and subsequent analysis. Qualitative analysis software can mean long data preparation time but programs find concealed data; reanalysis is easy and report-writing is extremely efficient. Researchers are advised to finish analysis as soon as possible after fieldwork ends.

3 **Explain the nature of quantitative analysis**

Coded data are input into a computer manually or scanned. Tables are then produced. Cell or rim-weighting is used to ensure that the sample is balanced. Grossing means that figures are multiplied up to the population levels. Bivariate analysis takes two variables at a time and inspects the pattern between them and correlation is the measure of the nature and the strength of association between two variables. Multivariate analysis takes three or more variables at a time and inspects the pattern between them. Regression is used to analyse associative relationships. Other techniques of relevance include analysis of variance (ANOVA), factor analysis, discriminant analysis, cluster analysis, CHAID, and data fusion.

4 **Describe ways to assess the accuracy of results**

The accuracy of results depends on many aspects. Sampling error and non-sampling error account for variations. Non-sampling error may relate to the sampling frame or the process of data capture. Significance testing shows if there is a meaningful difference between the findings from the sample selected, and what the findings would have been if we had carried out a census. Tests and

Common mistakes
Confusing usership with usage

When faced with information about the use of products and services, the user of data will meet two distinct terms: 'usership' and 'usage'. The newcomer to this sector often confuses the two metrics. 'Usership' is an indication of the number of people who use the product in a given period. 'Usage' refers to the amount of product used in the period or the speed (or rate) of consumption.

assumptions are based on random sampling, but many practitioners use them with studies that have used non-random sampling. There are several aids available to assess significance: ready reckoners, nomograms, and software devices.

Review questions

1. What lessons can we draw from the past to help in analysis today?
2. In the analysis of qualitative research, transcripts are sometimes not used. Why is this the case?
3. What are the main features of quantitative tables?
4. What are the differences between bivariate and multivariate analysis?
5. Define these terms using examples: correlation, regression, the punch card, radial diagrams.

Discussion questions

1. What would be the implications of quantifying results from qualitative depths or groups?
2. How could qualitative analysis research software be used to investigate the service provided by dealers in the automotive market?
3. Plan a simple table to analyse data that looked into why buyers of dog food choose particular can sizes.
4. Consult the proposal in the Market Researcher's Toolbox. With your knowledge of analysis, discuss the ways in which you would analyse data collected according to the proposal.
5. Read the opening Snapshot carefully. Which five countries seem to have respondents who are most positive? And which five seem least positive? Apply the confidence limits to the latest figures and decide whether the order might change.

Case study
Open-ended questions analysis

© istockphoto.com/Scott Thomas

London is a centre of excellence for many reasons; and many people choose the city for their studies. In order to help with promotional activities, Harrow Business School, part of the University of Westminster, decided to ask existing students about their reasons for coming to the University. The study was undertaken during classes, using a convenience sample. This study provides us with a good illustration of the procedure that is employed when coding open-ended questions in quantitative research. In this project, 100 students were asked three open-ended questions as follows:

1. *Why have you chosen to study in Great Britain?*
2. *Why have you chosen to study in London?*
3. *Why have you chosen to study at this university?*

The students were a mix of: overseas and home students; males and females; first, second, third, and fourth years. Question 2 is used for our example: *'Why have you chosen to study in London?'*.

Step 1 involved making a list of responses for a substantial number of questionnaires. A rule of thumb is for 50 replies to be listed, but the number depends on the repetition or diversity of response that is encountered. An extract from the full list of 100 replies follows. You will see that people use different words to express the same thing. For example: *'I reside here/I live here'* or *'it's home/close to home'*. Also note that two or more answers can come from one respondent. For example: *'I live here and it is interesting'*.

- Because I reside in London
- I live in London
- Many more resources readily available compared to other cities
- I think it is more lovely
- (It) is a great city with lots of different things to do and to see that I couldn't do in my own city
- (It) is a great place to be, good experience, loads to do and to see
- Because I like this city and there are lots of interesting things to do
- Within Britain, I wanted to live in a big capital
- My university in Spain chose this university for me
- I live in London
- The general social life, etc.
- My family and friends are here, it's home, it's familiar, it's interesting and modern, up to date
- Close to home.

Step 2 involved a careful inspection of the listing to identify common patterns. This gave a list that is more compact and five-bar gates were made to give an indication of important themes. These were not counted; they were used to make decisions about whether to eliminate, merge, or reorder categories.

- More resources/lively/good social life/a lot to do/more to do/interesting ||
- I reside in London/live in London/close to home/family ~~||||~~ ~~||||~~
- A city/a capital |
- Exchange/reciprocal agreement gave no choice, ||| etc.

Step 3 involved revision of the listing to confirm the common patterns. This gave a similar list, but now numbers are allocated to each. These are codes that were written onto the questionnaire and then entered into the computer when all information was input:

1. I reside in London/live in London/close to home/family
2. Exchange/reciprocal agreement gave no choice
3. More resources/lively/good social life/a lot to do/more to do/interesting
4. A city/a capital, etc.

Questions

1 What are the benefits of analysing open-ended questions for quantitative research as shown above?

2 What are the limitations of analysing open-ended questions for quantitative research as shown above? (Please consider qualitative data in your answer.)

3 In what ways can we assess the accuracy of results that come from open-ended questions? Suggest further research for the example above.

Further reading

- Birn, R.J. (ed.) (2002) *The International Handbook of Market Research Techniques*. London: Kogan Page.
  A very full account of research analysis from a practitioner viewpoint.
- Chakrapani, C. (2004) *Statistics in Market Research*. London: Arnold.
  A very full account of research analysis with a particular strength in multivariate analysis.
- Harris, P. (1978) Statistics and significance testing, in Worcester, R.M. and Downham, J. (eds.) *Consumer Market Research Handbook*. Wokingham: van Nostrand Reinhold.
  Perhaps the best account of significance testing for market research. See look-up tables on pp. 308–310.
- Riley, J. (1990) *Getting the Most from Your Data*. Bristol: Technical & Educational Services Ltd.
  A practical guide to analysis of qualitative data.

Key web links

- Software Reviews http://www.meaning.uk.com
- NVIVO software http://www.qsrinternational.com
- Text Analysis Software http://www.provalisresearch.com

Online Resource Centre

www.oxfordtextbooks.co.uk/orc/bradley3e/

Visit the Online Resource Centre that accompanies this book to access more learning resources on this chapter topic.

References and sources

Alt, M. and Brighton, M. (1981) Analysing data: or telling stories? *Journal of the Market Research Society*, 23, pp. 209–219.

Aronson, J. (1994) A pragmatic view of thematic analysis, *The Qualitative Report*, 2, http://www.nova.edu/ssss/QR/BackIssues/QR2-1/aronson.html

Baker, M.J. (1991) *Research for Marketing*. London: Macmillan Education Ltd.

Birn, R.J. (ed.) (2002) *The International Handbook of Market Research Techniques*. London: Kogan Page.

Bradley, N.R. (1992) British survey of left-handedness, *The Graphologist*, 10, pp. 176–182.

Chakrapani, C. (2004) *Statistics in Market Research*. London: Arnold.

Churchill, G.A. (2001) *Basic Marketing Research*. Orlando, FL: Harcourt.

Conway, S. (1982) The weighting game. *MRS Society 25th Annual Conference papers*, pp. 193–207.

Diamantopoulos, A. and Schlegelmilch, B.B. (1997) *Taking the Fear out of Data Analysis*. London: Dryden Press.

Dolan, A. and Ayland, C. (2001) Analysis on trial, *International Journal of Market Research*, 43, pp. 377–389.

Harris, P. (1978) Statistics and significance testing, in Worcester, R.M. and Downham, J. (eds.) *Consumer Market Research Handbook*. Wokingham: van Nostrand Reinhold.

Holder, M. and Johnson, D. (1984) OpenCode: what we have learned from the recession, *37th ESOMAR Congress papers*, Rome, 2–6 September.

Johnson, D. (1989) Openended warfare: cybernetic nirvana or information graveyard? *Journal of the Market Research Society*, 31, pp. 331–361.

Kent, R. (1999) *Marketing Research: Measurement, Method and Application*. London: Thomson Business Press.

Kent, R. (2007) *Marketing Research: Measurement, Method and Applications in Europe*. Andover: Cengage.

Macer, T. (2004) Textual analysis, *Research*, August, p. 37.

McDonald, C. (1973) Linguistic coding—a new solution to an old problem, *Journal of the Market Research Society*, 15, pp. 163–181.

McDonald, C. and Monkman, M. (eds.) (1995) *Guide to Media Research*. London: Media Research Group.

McQueen, R. and Knussen, C. (2002) *Research Methods for Social Science: An Introduction*. Harlow, Essex: Prentice Hall.

Monkman, M. (2002) *Maths In Media Research*. London: Media Research Group.

Psathas, G. and Anderson, T. (1990) The 'practices' of transcription in conversation analysis, *Semiotica*, 78, pp. 75–99.

Riley, J. (1990) *Getting the Most From Your Data.* Bristol. Technical & Educational Services Ltd.

Russo, M. (1997) *Herman Hollerith: The World's First Statistical Engineer.* New York: University of Rochester, http://www.history.rochester.edu/steam/hollerith/

Selvin, H.C. and Stuart, A. (1966) Data-dredging procedures in survey analysis, *The American Statistician*, 20, pp. 2–23.

Sounderpandian, J. (1999) *Market Research Using Microsoft Excel.* Cincinnati, OH: South Western College Publishing.

Sudman, S. (1980) Improving the quality of shopping center sampling, *Journal of Marketing Research*, 17 November, pp. 423–431.

ten Have, P. (1999) *Doing Conversation Analysis: A Practical Guide.* London: Sage.

Thompson M. *et al.* (2007) *This is not just Advertising, This is Your M&S Advertising.*

Wagner, U., Gais, S., Haider, H., Verleger, R., and Born, J. (2004) Sleep inspires insight, *Nature*, 427, pp. 352–355.

Wyndham, R. and Goosey, R. (1997) It is time we started using statistics! *Marketing and Research Today*, November, pp. 244–253.

Zubin, J. (1939) Nomographs for determining the significance of the differences between the frequencies of events in two contrasted series or groups, *Journal of the American Statistical Association*, 34, pp. 539–544.

10 Reporting and presentation

Contents

Chapter guide

Reporting can be the key to the credibility of a research project, so this chapter examines the skills involved in communicating findings. This includes an explanation of different visual displays of data and what is expected from writers of research reports. It is important to use a style that is appropriate to the situation. In recent years, the Internet has been used to communicate the results produced by market researchers, so there is information on this new channel.

Learning outcomes

By the end of this chapter, you should be able to:

1 **Explain the purpose of reports and presentations**

2 **Show the main aspects of report-writing**

3 **Show the main aspects of personal presentations**

Introduction

The results of a research project are of great importance. If these findings are communicated badly, the credibility of the project, no matter how professionally carried out, will be in question. We are now concerned with publication: publicising or communicating research findings to the appropriate audiences. This final part of the research depends on the ways by which information can be delivered to the right people. Decisions will be taken, based on the results of research, so the pertinent information should be available in a suitable form that does not detract from the sense. If information is missing, it may be appropriate to point out the gaps in knowledge; if information is ambivalent, the researcher must be well prepared to assist in clarification. Reporting skills are as important as any other skills employed in marketing research.

The ways in which we can summarise or illustrate data have advanced, and the communication channels have changed in many ways. These changes have had an impact on the market researcher. The Royal Society (founded 1660) and the Royal Statistical Society (founded 1834) were important meeting places for people who initiated the various tools that help to communicate complex data sets.

William Playfair (1759–1823) lived in Scotland and was elected fellow of the Royal Society in 1807 (see Table 10.1). He invented the most common graphical forms, such as the bar chart, the scatterplot, and the line plots. Another significant figure was John Venn (1834–1923), who introduced the famous Venn diagrams around 1880; he was elected a Fellow of the Royal Society three years later. For more information on this fascinating area, see the comprehensive article by Friendly and Denis (2004).

In the late nineteenth century, David Gestetner had created the first stencil duplicator, which enabled in-house, multi-copy document reproduction; in the 1960s and 1970s, such equipment became extremely popular. This coincided with the arrival of the electric typewriter, and the telex was now in common use, which was particularly important in allowing the researcher to communicate progress and top-line results. In the 1980s, photocopiers were in greater use, as was the facsimile machine, again an important way to communicate results quickly. The postal service and courier services were still used to deliver larger reports and full findings.

The 1980s also saw the arrival of word-processing software and presentation software, both of which, along with email, had a direct influence on bettering communication of research findings. Additionally, they have blurred the difference between the written report and the personal presentation. Reports and presentations have largely been combined as a result of the arrival of electronic data file transfer, permitting large documents to be delivered by email and other Internet services.

Notable events for reporting

Year	Event
1800s	Playfair creates visual data display methods
1960s	Postal service and courier services deliver reports
1970s	Telex, duplication by Gestetner
1980s	Fax machines, photocopiers in greater use, word processors
1990s	Email delivers reports, PowerPoint presentation software
2000s	Web-based reporting, multimedia presentations, dashboards
2010s	Interactive software, word clouds, infographics

SNAPSHOT
Computer bureaux

© istockphoto.com/ Lise Gagne

Some marketing research projects have so many end-users and generate so much information that it is almost impossible for one company to deliver the results efficiently. The sponsors of such research are aware of this problem and have authorised special companies, called computer bureaux, to carry out this function of delivery. These companies receive raw data from research companies and insert it into their specific software applications. The findings are then delivered to customers with 'value added'. Electronic delivery of results has become extremely important, but hard-copy reports still have a place. This happens for TV, radio, and newspaper audience research. Delivery is quite complicated because complex pricing and charging structures are in place.

By way of example, let us take a brief glimpse at MediaTel Ltd, which was launched in 1981. MediaTel is owned by its directors and managers, and gives independent analysis. It describes itself as: *'The UK's largest single-source of media intelligence: the essential planning and research tool for all media professionals. The current client list is over 140 companies, including 29 of the top 30 media agencies, plus major media owners, research companies, industry bodies and investment banks'*. The services offered include planning data across press, TV, radio, cinema, online, outdoor, ambient, SMS, and direct mail.

MediaTel operates *'an online updating system, whereby publishers can amend their data at any time. New information is then immediately cross-checked by our data team before it goes live'*. Its system incorporates a geographic mapping system, whereby users can *'map media coverage areas for regional newspapers and radio stations, and build in cinema locations and retail outlets (via retail locations). [They] can select towns, regions or postcodes, or create drivetime areas. Maps can include overlays and can be downloaded to PowerPoint if required'*.

Clearly, personnel are important and MediaTel has a knowledgeable team, familiar with the data and the industry. An alert service keeps users immediately informed of new data added to the system. There is also simple transfer of data to other applications for reports and client presentations.

Compiled by Nigel Bradley 2012.

Sources:

http://www.barb.co.uk/about/registeredBureaux?_s=4

http://www.nrs.co.uk/subscribe.html

http://www.rajar.co.uk/content.php?page=how_to_subscribe_licenced_bureaux

MediaTel web page: http://www.mediatelgroup.co.uk

The purposes of reports and presentations

There are many different readers of research reports and these audiences all have very different expectations. Stephen Few (2012) identified five purposes for the display of quantitative information which we can extend to all reports and presentations, they are:

1. Lookup – to refer to the information
2. Narrative – to tell the story which will inform, explain and persuade
3. Monitoring – to maintain an ongoing awareness of the situation
4. Exploratory analysis – to uncover 'hidden' facts, to make sense of data
5. Prediction – to forecast what might happen in specified situations.

Reporting must be personalised; writing and presentation style must be customised and adapted to the user (see Table 10.2).

At one extreme, there is the general public. There are many reasons why research is reported to the 'mass consumer'. It may be a government report that has been commissioned to be in the public interest, concerning health, welfare, transport, and so on; it may be a consumer report. Consumer watchdog reports are of much interest to the man on the street; *Which?* magazine and similar bodies have made the population able to appreciate research findings. Editors of newspapers regularly commission research because it provides useful editorial comment, so the results may become part of an article in a newspaper. The research agency may report directly to the public on web pages, by email, or by post. This is because it is now common to offer a short summary report to a respondent as a gesture of goodwill, an incentive, or a thank you for cooperating in the research. Research findings may appear as part

Table 10.2 Common ways to disseminate findings

Audience	Spoken delivery (presentation)	Written delivery (report)
General public	Television or radio broadcast, auditorium presentation, conference, CD-ROM, DVD, podcasts, online video	Newspaper article Short 'incentive' report (by post, email, web page) As part of an advert
Business manager/ top managers	Face-to-face, virtual, video conference, webinar	PowerPoint show Handouts and notes
Marketing managers	Face-to-face, PowerPoint, conference calls	PowerPoint show Handouts and notes
Marketing research managers	Face-to-face, PowerPoint	Full technical report Internet or intranet-based reporting Dashboard reports

of a promotional campaign, appealing to the consumer's need to know that this is indeed a best-seller (e.g. '*nine out of ten cats prefer...*').

Then there are smaller audiences, such as managers, who are anxious to receive a report in order to make instant decisions. Additionally, there are managers who will benefit from the information much later, when the report is consulted as secondary data in the future.

A typical marketing team will be made up of several people, each of whom will contribute their own knowledge to the report. Each team member will find something different in reports; furthermore, the researcher's tone and style will also imply a specific outcome. A good research project should: answer the brief, have a clear structure, and provide interpretation and conclusions. It should make recommendations in a concise way, perhaps using visuals. A clear executive summary is essential.

Research reports should lead to a 'go' or a 'no-go' decision. The biggest problem is indecision. It is worth considering three simple aspects of decision-making from research reports: a decision to go ahead, a decision not to proceed, indecision—not knowing what to do. We can transfer these three states to any marketing problem. By way of example, let us consider a new product launch. Research may be employed to help decision-makers to decide whether to go ahead with the launch or not. There is therefore an expectation that results will provide clear guidance. In many cases, findings will indeed provide support both for and against the new product.

Indecision can lead marketing teams to waste time, and in product launches, time can be crucial. Indecision can lead to poor teamwork, when some individuals are marginalised; energy will be lost or directed towards unproductive activities. Both time and energy loss has a monetary impact. A frequent outcome of indecision is to seek more information, and suppliers of research data will happily accommodate such requests. However, the cycle can be continuous, so, at a certain point, a firm decision needs to be taken. When that decision has been taken, it may prove to have been correct or it may have proven the wrong decision. Doing nothing through indecision is most certainly the wrong decision.

There are different levels at which a report can be written. At the first level, it can simply relate facts, or reproduce them. The second level will involve making some interpretation of these facts and some recommendations. A third level will go beyond the data, possibly by incorporating knowledge found elsewhere, and will speculate or make predictions about what a future state may be. This third level is true consultancy, where the researcher is almost acting as a decision-making partner. This level of reporting requires confidence and intuition (see Smith 2003 for an excellent discussion of the nature of intuition and the use in research analysis). These levels are outlined in Table 10.3.

Table 10.3 Different report contents

Level 1	**Level 2**	**Level 3**
Reportage	Interpretation	Speculation
Fact	Recommendations	Forecasting by empathy

Q What would the respondent think if we modified . . . ?

Q How resolute is the respondent on this point?

Q How much of this do you (as researcher) attribute to novelty effect?

Q What is the respondent thinking when buying the product?

Q What is the repondent thinking when using the product?

Figure 10.1 Questions to ask report writers

The best guidance for the report-writer is to present the facts in as neutral a way as possible. If the client has requested recommendations, then these should be clearly marked as such. These interpretations are signposts, they are judgements, and they are made by the report-writer on the basis of working closely with the data. The decision-making team knows the background; members can reject these viewpoints or accept them.

The report-writer is in a unique position, and the decision-makers can use that writer in some valuable ways. Once the report has been completed, the report-writer can be invited to answer some speculative questions. Such questions might be: '*What might respondents say if the product were to be modified in this way?*'. This assumes that the researcher has built up a lot of knowledge of the marketplace, and knows the respondent's thought processes. This is a short cut to seeking more information by further research. It is a way for researchers to deliver more value and for decision-makers to be decisive. A few other questions are outlined in Figure 10.1.

Planning

Lack of planning is extremely obvious in any report or presentation. Unplanned work demonstrates a lack of harmony; ideas are missed or added carelessly. There is an imbalance between coverage of the objectives; some are extremely long, others are too short. Poor planning will lead to digression.

It is useful to structure any report or presentation by envisaging a story (consider a fairytale). There will be a beginning ('once upon a time'), a middle ('something interesting happened'), and an ending ('everybody lived happily ever after'). The report, or story should have a flow; there is an expectation that the researcher (the storyteller) will entertain the reader and audience. This is not to say that the written report is written as a best-seller, or that the presentation becomes a stand-up comedy, but the elements of interest should be the same.

We all apply our own methods to planning. Consider two researchers: one has received training as a journalist and the other has a background in advertising. Imagine that there has been an event: someone has run onto a soccer pitch completely nude. This has implications for public relations, and the market researcher has been asked to report to a board.

The journalist (now market researcher) plans by thinking of a bar conversation. The journalist envisages two friends discussing the event; the first friend was at the football match. The story unfolds gradually and the journalist tries to anticipate what question the second friend will ask, what expectations she will have. Where was it? How many people saw it? What

Research in focus
Misreporting crimes

© istockphoto.com/NREY

On Thursday 11 December 2008, the then Prime Minister, Gordon Brown launched an anti-knife campaign in the midst of a big media turnout. In this flurry of excitement he announced that there had been a big fall in stabbings. He said that there was a *17 per cent fall in serious injuries and deaths in knife-crime hotspots*. This statement quite clearly contains no time period and no obvious location; yet it is very specific—17 per cent bestows an air of accuracy, and the source is impeccable. A press release stated '*the number of teenagers admitted to hospital for knife or sharp instrument wounding in nine ... police force areas fell by 27 per cent according to new figures published today*'.

By Saturday, the UK newspapers had changed the emphasis from a fight on knife crime to an attack on the Prime Minister. Headlines on December 13 included '*Knife figures were "dodgy"*' and '*Brown is accused of spin over knife crime*'. These attacks originated with Sir Michael Scholar, who, as head of the independent UK Statistics Authority, criticised the government for the '*premature, irregular, and selective*' release of information. He added that thorough checking had yet to take place. What is interesting is that Scholar has a duty to do this, regardless of whether the figures were correct or not. A 'safety reporting valve' is built into Section 8 of the Statistics and Registration Service Act 2007. This law forces the Board to '*monitor the production and publication of official statistics*' and to '*report any concerns it has about the quality of any official statistics, good practice in relation to any official statistics, or the comprehensiveness of any official statistics, to the person responsible for those statistics*'. By 15 December, the Home Secretary, Jacqui Smith, said '*I am sorry that we were, I think, too quick off the mark with the publication of one number in relation to the progress that had been made in tackling knife crime*'. This is a safety valve that should be seen as good practice for all companies.

Compiled by Nigel Bradley 2012.

Sources:

Porter, A. (2008) Brown is accused of spin over knife crime. *Daily Telegraph*, 13 December, p. 15.

UK Statistics Authority (2009) Knife crime statistics—a review against the Code of Practice, http://www.statisticsauthority.gov.uk/assessment/monitoring/monitoring-briefs/knife-crime-statistics--a-review-against-the-code-of-practice.pdf

Wilson, G. (2008) Knife figures were 'dodgy'. *The Sun*, 13 December, p. 2.

Questions

1 Why do decision-makers sometimes want to report research findings early?

2 Summarise the research that might have been carried out to produce the figures. In your opinion, was it sufficient? What other research could have assisted?

3 What lessons are there for reporting?

did the players do? What did the referee do? Why did it happen? When was it? How did it all end? This 'anticipation of questions' creates a suitable structure and sequence to report the event; it keeps the interest of the reader and ends in the way expected. The two friends and the bar will not appear in the report, but they provide a suitable method with which to create a structure.

The advertiser (now market researcher) creates a storyboard, commonly used in television advertising planning. She takes a piece of paper and divides it into nine rectangles (three simple lines drawn horizontally and three more vertically). She sketches an outline: in the first box is a title page, in the second, an agenda (or set of objectives), the next slide is marked as 'Introduction' and the last slide is marked 'Conclusion'. Gradually, words are put into these slides to tell the story. The advantage here is that everything is in view: with a single glance, the entire story can be seen. If it cannot be reduced to nine 'images', then further pages can be added. This can be directly converted into a slide show and forms the basis of a written report.

All presentations embrace these two approaches to some extent; the personality and the style of the researcher inevitably add flavour. The important thing is to plan fully.

It is useful to consider the report and presentation together, but it is also valuable to see what distinguishes them. Many researchers initially create an oral presentation; they then share this with the clients and, at a later stage, build this information into a full report. This order has come about for several reasons. One reason is the time constraint placed on research: as soon as information is available, decision-makers want to make decisions—the spoken presentation of 'top-line results' is a way to satisfy this demand. Another reason is that the report can delve deeper into issues of interest to the audience.

It is inevitable that questions and methods will be modified throughout a research project. This is why we collect secondary data and why we conduct pilot studies.

However, we have an expectation that the reason for carrying out research will not change. We hope that the objectives will stay the same from start to finish. In academic research, this is often the case. In the world of dynamic business situations, however, things change. During the course of a project, there may be many changes: competitor products may seem to appear from nowhere; business decisions may be made that make the content of the research more, or less, important; there may be a shift in emphasis whereby some previously minor issue now becomes paramount.

All of this is extremely disconcerting, particularly to personnel from a research agency who visit the company to present a report of the study but are unaware of the change in interest, emphasis, or even objective of the study. In most cases, researchers can modify the results to address areas of concern, but they cannot do this if the new emphasis is unknown. The solution is, of course, to keep in touch, to watch the goalposts move and to change play accordingly.

Report structure

There are some principles that apply to written output. The first must be to adapt the report length and style to the type of audience. It is no good using technical jargon for a reader who cannot, and does not need to, understand it. Similarly, punctuation is important in report-writing. In 2003, an unlikely book became a best-seller; it was a book that was an open lament, a yearning that we might all improve the way we express ourselves. Why was the book written?

In searching the book, we find the reason early (Truss 2003, p. 4): *'It does matter that there's no question mark on a direct question. It is appalling ignorance'.* In the world of research, we are attempting to build the belief that the information we provide is valuable and accurate. To use a marketing metaphor, we have an unwritten understanding that the package may be considered indicative of the content.

In the large market research agency, a quality control mechanism has been created whereby a senior executive or director will write the report and a junior will carry out proofreading and other quality controls. At a certain point, as part of this training, the junior will attempt to write a report, which is then checked by the senior. This transition is one where report-writing quality can suffer and a client must be aware of the team working on the project, and must be sensitive to any problems.

There is no 'average' length of report. This is something agreed between client and researcher. Short reports are extremely useful because they focus the mind on key issues. A short report is certainly the starting point, because it can be expanded and developed. There is no definitive length of time required to write reports, but Hague and Jackson (1996, p. 181) suggest that two to four days should be sufficient, after analysis.

Typical sections of any research report include a title page, a contents list, an executive summary, an introduction, the objectives of the study, and the findings and conclusions. An appendix will include methodological information that will have been mentioned in the introduction.

The presentation is very similar. Typical sections include a title page, an agenda (the equivalent of the report contents list), an executive summary, an introduction, the objectives of the study, and the findings and conclusions. The similarities are made evident in Table 10.4.

There are numerous examples of research reports on the Internet, easily found with search engines. One example of a large study on the London congestion charge has responses

Table 10.4 Similarities between reports and presentations

Sections of a report document	Sections of a presentation
Title page	Title of study
Contents list	Agenda
Executive summary	Executive summary
Introduction	Introduction
Objectives	Objectives
Findings	Findings
Conclusions	Conclusions
Appendix: Methodology	Emergency slides

from over 100,000 people. The final report can be found at http://www.tfl.gov.uk/roadusers/congestioncharging/6722.aspx. It is sufficient to look at the 24 pages called 'Contents and Executive Summary', but you may wish to view the full document of 152 pages.

The following is a description of the key parts of a standard report and presentation. The two approaches are considered together.

- **Title page** This might seem petty, but some of the most professional researchers forget the detail of a 'title page', which is there to help with archiving and quick retrieval of reports in the future. The title page should include: a date, the name of the study (either a coded name such as 'Project Green' or a description), for whom it was prepared, and by whom it was prepared. Postal addresses on the front cover are useful. Most research is confidential, so this identifying device allows the most junior executive to distinguish different reports from each other without having to read further. Many research agencies allocate a 'job number' to projects, which is also a useful identifier, and this can appear on the cover.
- **Contents page** Again, it might seem petty to mention a 'contents page' for a report, but when forgotten or badly produced, it makes it extremely difficult to navigate a large document. The mere act of creating a contents page forces the author to read the text and to create page numbers. A report without page numbers can be extremely confusing for the user. The same principles apply to a presentation, where an agenda acts as a signpost; it gives an impression of length and also of content. It is worth noting that word-processing software can produce content lists automatically. These are useful, but will need careful checking.
- **Executive summary** This is a summary and evaluation of the points made in the report. It usually appears as the first part of the report and presentation. This position allows the reader of the report to know its full contents without reading the full set of findings. This is clearly a benefit to executives who are faced with numerous tasks. The 'executive summary' should be created after the report has been written; it is basically taken from the content of the report. Once it is removed, the report should stand as a self-contained unit. In a presentation, this section is generally 'spoken' first of all; busy executives (usually top managers) can then leave the room knowing the important parts. They will leave the finer detail to the remaining audience, members of which are likely to be working more closely with the projects.
- **Introduction** This will explain the background to the project. The written version will go into more detail than that used at a presentation. The spoken 'introduction' should attempt to motivate listeners, to encourage them to take a great interest in the project. The written 'introduction' should do the same, but give a more detailed rationale for the research.
- **Objectives** This tackles the research 'objectives' and clarifies the reason for the study. At a presentation, the listener will keep the objectives in mind and will gather all of the results together to set against these aims. In these report, the objectives are explained in greater detail.
- **Methodology** The methodology is a key part of the report, but must be secondary to the results, so any mention within the main body of the report should be restricted. There is an expectation that the following details should be known to the reader: approach (phone, face-to-face, postal, etc.), sample size, number of sampling points, and dates of fieldwork. Indeed, even the shortest newspaper articles are likely to include these details.

- **Findings** The findings are the results. A good subdivision of the content is to use the objectives as headings; this gives categories of interest to the client and gives an approximate division of time and space in order to plan dissemination of the results. Quantitative studies will inevitably offer numerical findings, with appropriate visual displays (bar charts, pie charts, etc.). The main body will feature important highlights; any lengthy tables will appear in the appendix or in separately bound volumes. Qualitative reports focus more on words and concepts; visual representations will be used to explain meaning via diagrams, cartoons, and photographs. The appendix (or other volumes) may carry full transcripts of interviews. Specific guidance is provided below, but it is worth considering that key pages may be copied for separate distribution. A final check with this in mind will help to ensure that all parts are self-explanatory. Specifically, a footer built into the report can carry a job number, project title, date, and page number.

- **Conclusions and recommendations** Here, the research must be clearly matched back to the objectives and a response for each one should appear. Recommendations may be made if the researcher is sufficiently familiar with the marketing problem. Such recommendations may not be welcomed, so it is an area that needs to be carefully discussed with clients.

  Sometimes researchers choose to add a section on 'Limitations'. It is a good idea to say what problems there were, how this affected the findings, and what the research was not able to do. Typically, this section will use budgetary constraints or time limitations to explain why the research did not go further. This brings us back to validity and reliability.

- **Appendix** The 'appendix' of a report will include more on the methodology, which should be explained. Although it was the means to the end, a description of the method allows the reader to assess how well the project was done; this is particularly the case for sampling—the source and selection should be outlined fully. The appendix should also include any field materials relevant to the study: the questionnaire, the topic guide, the observation form, and any cover letters to respondents. They are included to help the reader to understand the study, but also may be used to repeat the study in future. The appendix also includes a timing section: if respondents were interviewed at the 'wrong' time, then the validity and reliability of the results may be in question. Some researchers include significant correspondence between researcher and client in the appendix. This may be for legal reasons, to show what was purchased and what was delivered, or it may be a simple case of putting the research into context and explaining the rationale. Quantitative report-writers use the appendix to reproduce full tabulations (these may also go into different volumes). The appendix may also include details of response rates, geographical coverage, weighting schemes, and statistical guidance with such things as nomograms or tables of statistical significance. Glossaries of terms, whether research or concerning a specialist area, may also be given in this section. If the research involved desk research, it may be appropriate to list sources used: websites, book titles, periodicals, directories, or even library addresses.

- **Emergency slides** In any presentation, there will always be a 'Question time'. Everyone needs to have some backup visuals: these are the presenter's equivalent of the appendix supporting a report. At a presentation, there will be several questions, and they can usually be anticipated. Therefore, some 'emergency slides' can be created to answer such questions. The queries will inevitably concern the method, so some detailed slides on the approach should be ready in case they are required. The careful presenter will arrange information and use a delivery style that encourages an audience to ask specific questions; this is useful because it makes the session look professional.

Qualitative reporting

Qualitative reports most often deal with what people say. Traditionally, spoken words are included in reports within quotation marks; it may be helpful to indent them and put them into italic font. The choice of quotation must be made to support the points the writer is making. It may be an example of an overall statement; it may be one of several sub-categories to the statement; it may be an example of an exception.

The person who made the comment will also be identified, but not by name. Some characteristic will be found that is relevant to the context. This identifying caption is likely to change throughout the report. For example, the same respondent may be identified as any one of the following, depending on the point being made:

- Standard Life policyholder
- Respondent living in the Midlands
- Person who uses Halifax Financial Services
- A reader of the *Daily Telegraph*
- Former salesman.

The important thing is to choose the correct label to make the point. Qualitative reports can use such quotations and labels to tell the 'story'. However, quotes are best used as examples to illustrate a point being made in the main commentary. An extract from the report might be as follows:

> There is evidence to suggest that the presence of a dependant has an influence in attitudes to life insurance policies. The absence of a dependant may be an obstacle to purchasing this product. This was found both directly and indirectly in the focus groups and depths. For example: '...life insurance shows that you care about your children' (father of five children in Derbyshire).

Although the written word can exemplify the views of respondents, sound and vision can also be very effective. The low cost of digital data capture now makes it easy and feasible to capture responses that can be viewed by research users. The term **vox pop** is used to refer to such methods; the term was derived from the Latin phrase *vox populi*, meaning 'voice of the people'. The technique is commonly applied to small sound or vision clips of an individual making a specific point. The vox pop therefore gives a qualitative indication of public opinion. To see examples of vox pops on the web, point your browser to http://www.voxpops.co.uk then select 'Watch the Vox Pops Show Reel'. Caution does need to be exercised because there are code of conduct issues to consider.

There are many problems involved at the reporting stage of projects. An example was made evident by academics who accused the UK government of misleading the public on the effectiveness of its anti-crime reforms. This involved the distortion of research results at the reporting stage. The Home Office spends around £20 million on research each year. *'Through various manipulations of the data, the Home Office method does what it can to capitalise on chance, producing much more favourable findings overall'*, said Professor Tim Hope of Keele University's criminology department (Secker 2006).

Word clouds

Word clouds are visual representations of the vocabulary used by people in response to some stimulus. The visual display gives greater prominence to words that occur most frequently in the text provided. There are variations, for example, rather than words, phrases may be chosen; importance may judged by something other than frequency, such as how early the word occurs in the text or how unusual the word is compared with common speech. Additionally colour may be used as a variable to stress importance or to maintain interest and thereby ensure that readers spend more time on the issue. Word clouds, also known as Tag Clouds can be traced back to the 1990s but have increased in popularity as a tool to bring some structure to consumer generated content on the media. They are commonly seen to provide a real time description of 'chatter' from blogs, microblogs (such as twitter), online communities (such as Facebook), and feedback comments. They may be an analysis of open-ended questions from a questionnaire, transcripts from depth interviews or focus groups may be used. They therefore offer viable alternatives to qualitative analysis and coding open-ended questions (both described in Chapter 9). Word clouds may be applied to vocabulary used during participation in web forums and to interpret websites of similar corporations or specific themes. This means that they offer unique assistance to semiotic analysis (described in Chapter 7). Word clouds can be created for two or more different groups, for example UK and US respondents, and a visual comparison made. The advantage is that precise quantification is avoided, yet dominant positions can be identified, the disadvantage is that word cloud interpretation is extremely subjective. The word cloud in Figure 10.2 was generated from 7000 words on the subject of online research.

Quantitative reporting

The quantitative researcher inevitably deals with numbers that may have one or more decimal places. It is tempting to keep these numbers in that form, but there are several disadvantages. One problem is that a number that has several digits after the decimal place appears to be accurate. As research is likely to be based on sample surveys, this degree of accuracy will not always be the case. A second disadvantage of keeping the full, long number is that the user of the research will be distracted by the content.

In many instances, it is advised to keep decimal places in full tabulations, but to bring other figures, in interpretative reports or presentations, to whole numbers, whether they are units

Figure 10.2 Word cloud generated on http://www.wordle.net

or percentages. This rounding procedure is simple and allows for quicker communication of research findings. Readers interested in the exact source can consult tabulations. Consequently, tables that are reproduced in summary form in reports, or presentation tables, may have totals that do not sum exactly to 100 per cent. This is called 'rounding error'.

Visual display of data

The 'visual display of data' is of major importance in marketing research. The techniques available allow the researcher to convey complex information in a meaningful way. Visual displays can describe and explain situations; they may also imply a future outcome. Patterns and trends may be discernible. Visual displays are also useful to make comparisons. Bar charts, pie charts, and other methods are generally associated with quantitative data, but non-numerical information, such as that derived from qualitative research, can also be communicated using diagrammatic representations. Jacques Bertin (1983) identified seven important visual variables: position, form, orientation, colour, texture, value, and size.

An essential feature of any visual display is that the audience's attention should be focused on one main point. Any of these seven variables can achieve this end; ideally, they should all work together. It is possible to distinguish between two-dimensional and three-dimensional displays, but also static and dynamic displays.

Two-dimensional displays are those displays that do not appear to come away from the paper (or screen). Three-dimensional displays, in contrast, appear to protrude from the display, thereby implying contours, height, or other protrusions. Traditionally, displays have been static, but with the arrival of computer technology, dynamic and moving displays have become more common. It is now possible to 'build' a display, effectively adding features as the viewer watches. Dynamic displays may be two- or three-dimensional. In three dimensions—the use of sound, colour, and other tools—the display can have strong impact.

The displays can be categorised as 'curved' or 'angular' in appearance; it might be argued that curves are aesthetically more appealing. Table 10.5 illustrates which charts give a message that is simple and those that communicate complex messages. This is largely dictated by the number of data points or items that are being communicated.

Sometimes, the words 'chart' and 'graph' are used interchangeably. The charts can all be adapted for qualitative and quantitative research results, and for all types it is recommended that your sample size is noted with the title.

Common mistakes
Mistrusting numbers

© istockphoto.com/ Nikolaas Boden

Figures can cause some problems in reporting. There is an unwritten policy with numbers. If you are discussing one, two, three, four, five, six, seven, eight, nine, ten, you can use letters; when you go over ten (e.g. 123, 5076), you should use numbers. There are some exceptions such as 50 per cent and 3 per cent or pp. 1–13. When you read articles and books, observe carefully what conventions are used. Avoid writing 'the sample size was one thousand and thirteen' or saying '3 respondents denied this': it is cumbersome and doesn't help the reader.

Reports must highlight specific results and use them to explain a particular viewpoint. The report-writer always tries to put words around such figures, if only to introduce them to the reader. Beware of the impact that small adjectives can have on the overall communication. By way of example, consider the figure of 8% (often written as 8 per cent). It is important to be aware of the effect that small connecting words can have. Look at the effect of the adjectives below:

Eight per cent of 'high earners' cycle.
There are some 136,000 'high earners' who cycle.
As many as 8 per cent of 'high earners' cycle.
Incredibly, 8 per cent of 'high earners' cycle.
It is no surprise that 8 per cent of 'high earners' cycle.
Only 8 per cent of 'high earners' cycle.

Two more expressions that cause confusion are 'less' and 'fewer'; they are not interchangeable. We use 'less' before singular nouns and 'fewer' when nouns can be counted. Look at the following examples:

- *56 per cent less respondents visited the store* (this is wrong)
- *56 per cent fewer respondents visited the store* (this is correct)
- *56 per cent less sugar was sold* (this is correct)
- *56 per cent fewer sugar was sold* (this is wrong).

Several visual displays will be considered briefly in this section. They include the bar chart, the pie chart, the line graph, the scatterplot, the doughnut, and Venn diagrams.

Bar charts (see Figure 10.3) may be vertical (column) or horizontal (bar chart). They are used to compare items.

The pie chart is generally used for percentages (see Figure 10.4). It is commonly agreed that if the pie chart has more than six segments, the viewer will find it hard to make sense of the information; therefore a final category called 'others' may need to be created. Some tabulations have items with percentages that, when added together, total more or less than 100 per cent. This information cannot be used in pie charts, as the chart relies on mutually exclusive segments.

Table 10.5 Visual display items classified

	Simple message (few data points)	Complex message (many data points)
Curved	Pie charts	Polar chart
	Cartoons	Doughnut chart
	Thought bubbles	Venn diagrams
	Speech bubbles	Chernov faces
Angular	Bar graph	Line charts
	Text in bullet points	Stacked bar chart
		Quotations

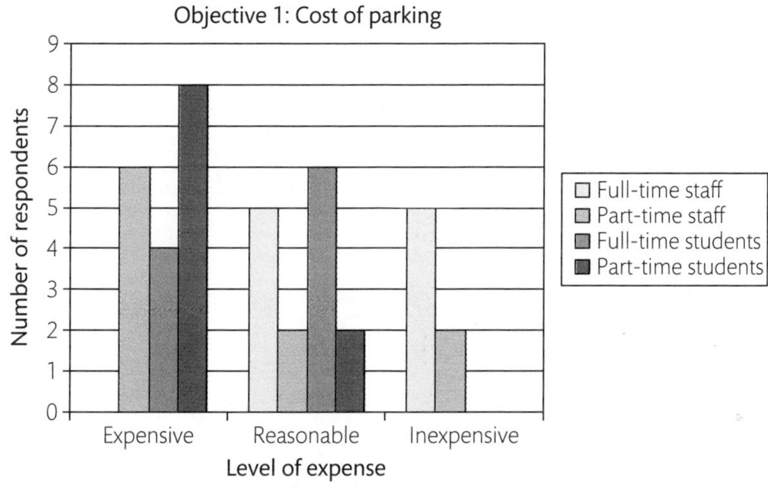

Figure 10.3 The bar chart

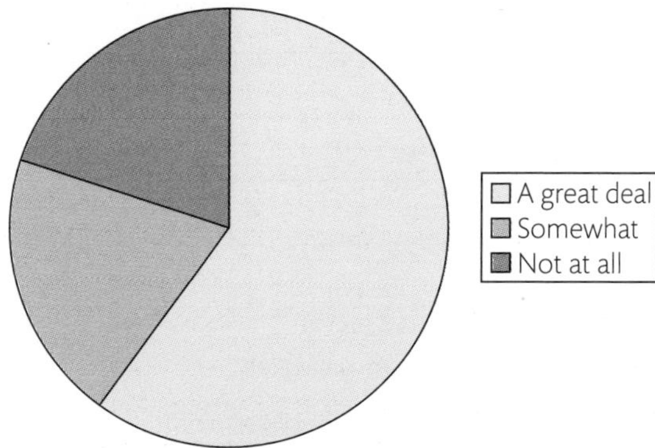

Figure 10.4 The pie chart

There are several options for the person constructing the pie chart. It might use two, three, four, five, or six segments; an 'exploded' segment might be employed to highlight items. There may be percentages beside each segment or they may be absent. Segments may use colour or use black and white shading.

Line graphs (see Figure 10.5) are useful to show relationship between items, particularly over time: the most common horizontal axis is time. Data points are connected by lines, which make it easy for the observer to spot anomalies worth investigating. The lines also suggest the trends for the next period, which effectively converts a forecasting calculation into a visual representation.

The scatterplot (Figure 10.6) is an extremely useful way of visualising relationships, or correlations between variables.

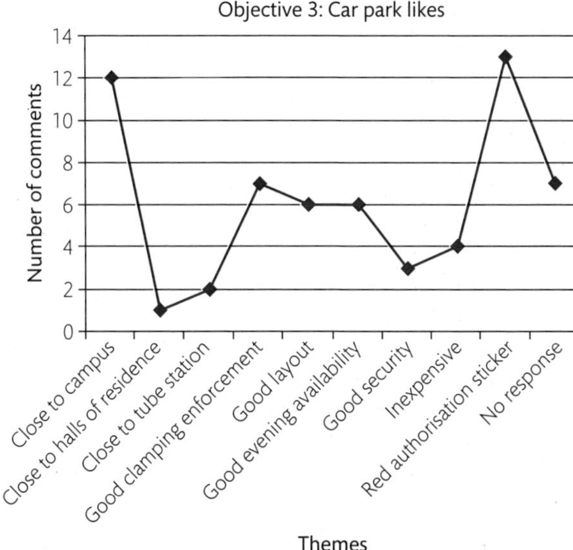

Figure 10.5 Line graphs

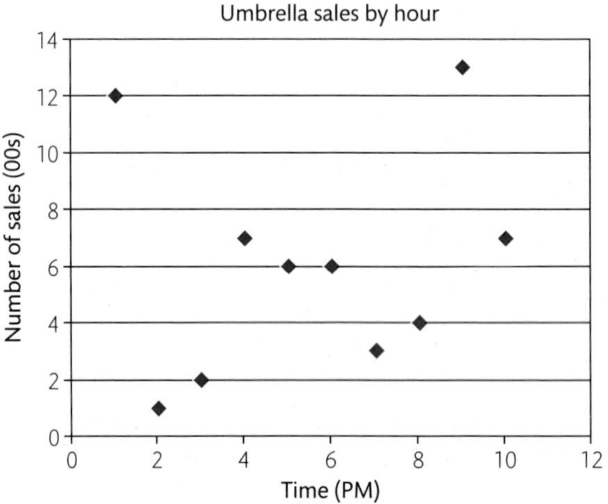

Figure 10.6 The scatterplot

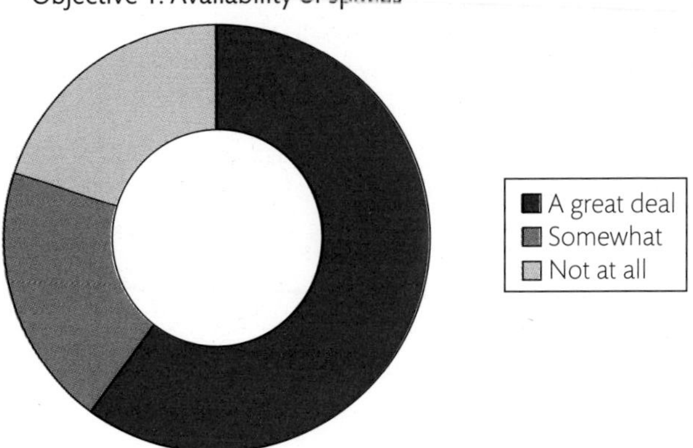

Figure 10.7 The doughnut

The doughnut is a variation of the pie chart (see Figure 10.7). Some doughnuts have an inner and outer ring, which are useful to show different things, for example last year compared with this year.

The Venn diagram consists of two or more circles that intersect or overlap. They are used to show the common nature of two different sets of data. In qualitative research, they can indicate ideas that people have in common; in quantitative research, numbers can be attached to show the sizes concerned. Indeed, the size of the circles can indicate magnitude and captions can provide numbers. The classic Venn diagram has eight regions: seven inside the diagram and one outside, with this last one being an empty set. The charts can show association and help to indicate a possible cause or influence of certain aspects of the data set. Priorities can be conveyed and the observer can focus on important aspects. It can help to prioritise efforts in one area. The Venn diagram in Figure 10.8 can be used (for example) to help to explain differences and similarities of different behaviours.

Some scales or projective techniques used in data collection lend themselves to being used directly to present results. These are visuals based on the research instrument. If we were to

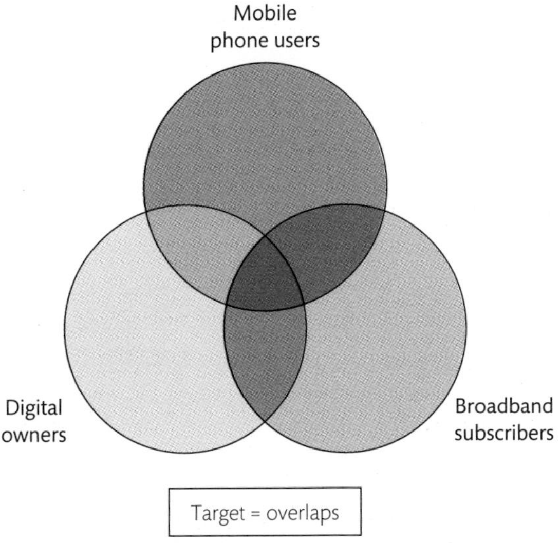

Figure 10.8 The Venn diagram

take the 'semantic differential display' as an example, we might use averages and join them together for different brands.

A visual display can draw attention to the main point but it can also lead attention to less important issues. This may be done by accident or design.

Concealed or absent data People may be misled if important results are left out. The sample size is important and should appear on each display.

Changing scales When the scale of something is modified it is possible to make it look *better* or *worse* than it really is. These are sometimes known as 'goosed-up graphics'. Skilful manipulation of axes may be used to enhance or suppress differences. A variation on this is the 'rubber band scale', where a scale is changed partway through an axis. If the axis values are small and difficult to see, the audience may not suspect the data.

Poor comparisons Comparisons between products, brands, and companies are extremely useful. However, the data need to be compared on an equal basis, in the correct context. A graph showing a decline in sales in a particular period may mask the fact that the previous and following periods showed growth. Pie charts should have no more than six segments; the viewer finds it hard to see differences where there are more.

Images

A possible alternative to words and numbers is to use images or 'clipart'. With some thinking, any set of numbers or piece of text can be turned into an image. Images may become effective metaphors and humour can be incorporated. Clipart was invented by Microsoft; it literally means a piece of art that can be cut (or 'clipped') from one thing and attached ('clipped') to another. That other thing might be a report or a presentation. Microsoft makes clipart available with most of their products and other galleries of clipart are available for use; many of these sources are in the public domain and therefore not protected by copyright. Clipart can be found through any search engine using the keyword 'clipart'. It is also possible to create clipart for a specific purpose: for example, to incorporate a brand name or logo.

There are, however, several problems associated with clipart: images may be inappropriate for the purposes required, images may be misleading, images may be too well-known or there may be too many of them, or images may be confusing, not least because of contradictory colours.

Infographics

The infographic is a visual representation of knowledge, identifiable for the numerous messages that are communicated by both words and pictures. The device has been with us for many years, often seen under the name of pictogram, but it has seen a recent revival, perhaps for two reasons. Firstly, we might see the renewed interest being due to the arrival of software that makes production relatively easy. Secondly, we have seen a surge in data available: there is now a massive amount of information that must be synthesised and understood.

The modern infographic is often a long stretched 'skyscraper' form, that lends itself to a web page where the message can be gradually revealed as one scrolls down the page (see Figures 10.9 and 10.10).

The advantage is that it communicates complex data sets relatively clearly, the main criticism is that the reader can be confused by the multiple images and messages. However, good design and long preparation periods can resolve any disadvantages.

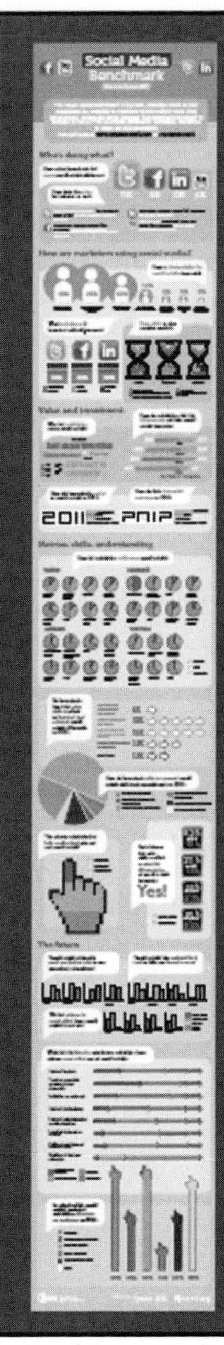

Figure 10.9 Infographic by the Chartered Institute of Marketing available at http://www.smbenchmark.com/wp-content/uploads/2012/02/SMB-W1-infographic-WEB.pdf Reproduced with kind permission of The Chartered Institute of Marketing, please visit www.smbenchmark.com for more information on the survey

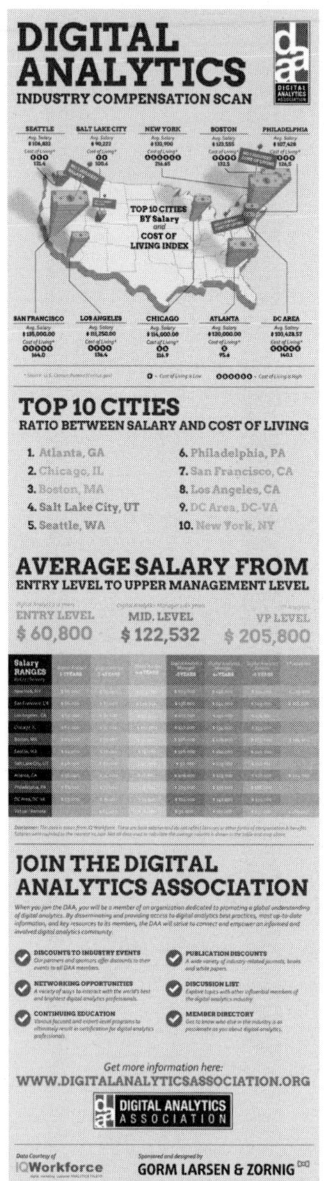

Figure 10.10 Infographic by the Digital Analytics Association available at http://www.digitalanalyticsassociation.org/?page=industrycompensation Credit: Digital Analytics Association)

Presentations

The presenter who is able to captivate an audience can make people believe the data. One way to do this at the start of a presentation is sometimes known as the **Wall Street approach.** *The Wall Street Journal* has been essential reading for business workers for decades, and its style of writing has been adapted to suit people with little time. There are two ways of writing a news article: one is to develop the story and end with a climax—what actually happened; the other is to use the Wall Street approach—to give a full summary of the situation in very few words, then to explain more and more. The Wall Street approach means that an editor can reduce the size of an article to fit the available space by chopping from the bottom upwards. In presentations, this technique is useful, because it also allows a presentation to end at any point; if it is of sufficient interest it might also be extended. The executive summary helps to do this: it summarises the main points in one short way, it gives the headline, and it communicates everything. This is also known as the 'inverted pyramid' technique: most of the content comes first, then tails off to the end. The alternative is the 'pyramid', where the story gradually unfolds and the main points are delivered towards the end.

A common technique useful in presentations is the PASS mnemonic. The letters represent: Purpose - Audience - Style - Structure. These letters allow the presenter to be reminded constantly: to return to the aims of the session (the purpose); to consider the importance and needs of the people there (the audience); to adopt the correct dress, verbal and non-verbal language (the style); and to keep the content within a reasonable timeframe (the structure).

There are many aspects of presentations that are often overlooked, but they help to make a presentation successful. For example: interaction with audience before, during, or after presentation; handshakes; humour; dress and appearance; small talk; and assessing an audience by their clothing, expressions, and body language.

Tools

Let us suggest that you should be able to stand up and speak on a new topic for 20 minutes with no aids. All experienced presenters are able to do this. Why? Because it is easy: the mind is not distracted by a large screen, pens, or charts; there are no colours, moving images, or noises. Visual aids make the presenter's job more difficult; nevertheless, such aids can enhance a session in a meaningful, exciting way. Variety in presentations is a good thing; mannerisms (repeating 'you see', 'okay', 'you know') are bad. Some useful things to remember are: keep the content of each slide at 14 lines maximum; employ a font size that can be seen at the back of a hall; and avoid capital letters for more than five words together. Have a backup plan. What if the projector fails? What if your co-speaker does not attend? Table 10.6 shows the tools typically available for use in presentations; not included are items such as a paper agenda, handouts, or other notes, and the 'pointer' stick, which may be a stick or a torch that projects light onto a screen.

The software product that has been branded with the name PowerPoint by Microsoft has become the chosen presentation software for most people (see Figure 10.11). This is best learnt onscreen, using the software's own tutorial. PowerPoint has found its way into all aspects of business: presentations, meetings, web pages, and even email. It is extremely easy to use and it is useful; it provides animated slide shows. The 'Notes' section allows users to add substantial amounts of commentary to slides and these can be used as prompts during a presentation or simply left for reference at a later date.

The resource is so powerful that it is hard to find any disadvantages. However, there are indications that people are a bit tired of it. The slide shows are predictable and the clipart illustrations have been used time and time again. There are other software packages available. One is MindManager, which is not a slide show (see Figure 10.12). It encourages collaboration between the presenter and audience; it results in a 'mind map' created by everyone in the room. It keeps the 'big picture' in view. In recent years we have seen the arrival of 'interactive

Table 10.6 Presentation tools available in order of complexity

Tool	Description
Flip chart	Flip chart pens
Blackboard	Chalk
Whiteboard	Whiteboard pens
Interactive whiteboard	Whiteboard pens
Large screen	Overhead with overhead projector transparency
Large screen	PowerPoint projector and laptop with software, e.g. MindManager, PowerPoint
Large screen	Visualiser to project documents or items from desk to screen
Video walls	

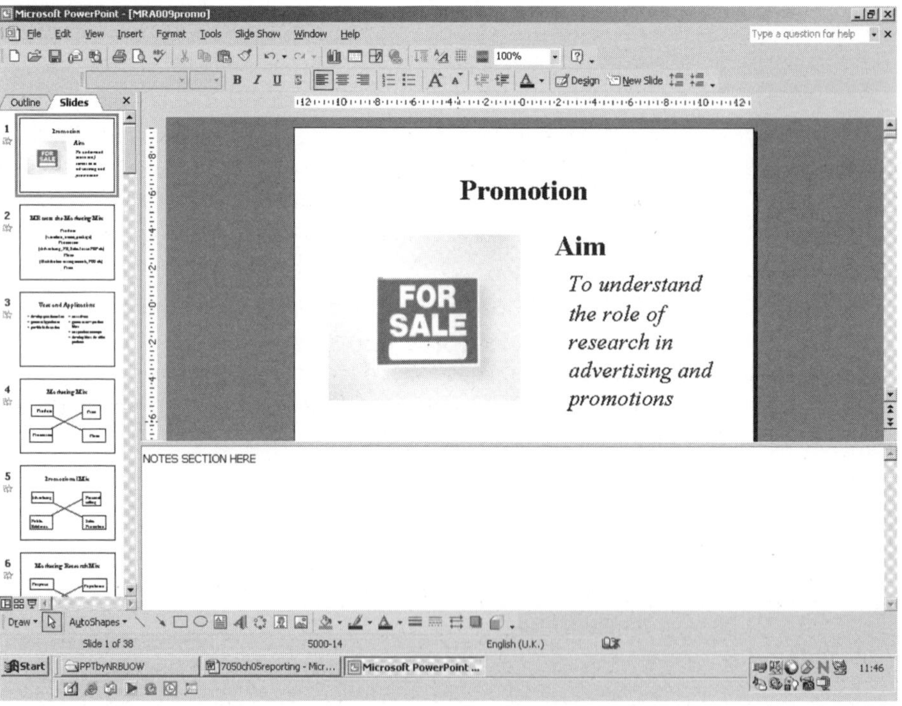

Figure 10.11 PowerPoint

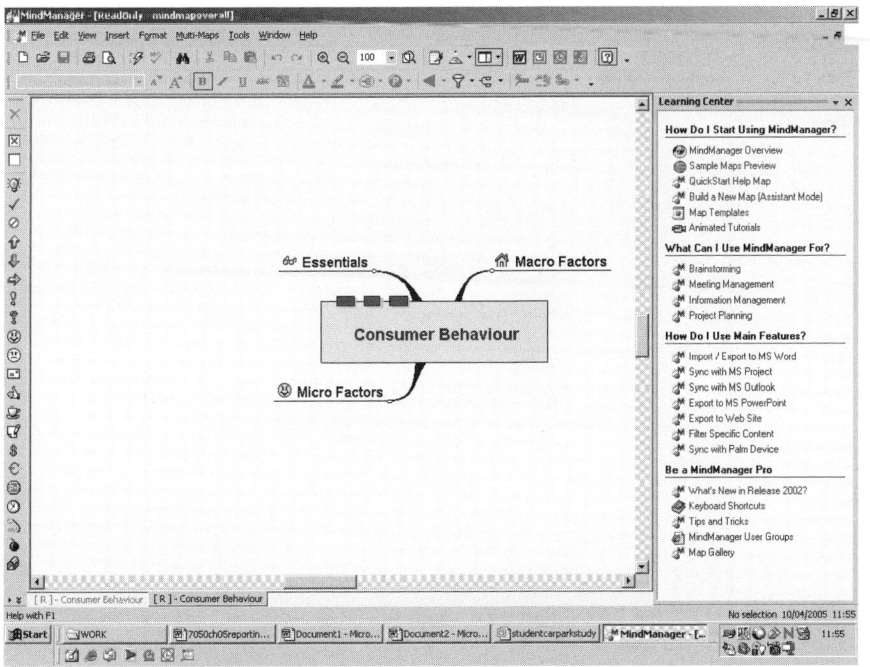

Figure 10.12 MindManager software for mind maps

software' such as Tableau Public (see http://www.tableausoftware.com/public) whereby the user can drill down into any element of a display see Figure 10.13)

A visualiser, sometimes known as a document camera, can display documents or objects onto a screen, television, projector, or monitor. Documents such as newspapers, magazines, or maps can be placed underneath the visualiser so that they are displayed onscreen. This allows the user to display small objects such as packaging, or promotional materials that overhead projectors and PowerPoint projection cannot do without suitable preparation. This permits the presenter to show materials that have been created only a few minutes before a presentation.

Good timekeeping is essential for the presenter; an audience might be dissatisfied if they must miss a next meeting or leave the room before the end. Besides the overall length, the timings within the session are equally important. Good presenters rely on timing, and part of this is revealing information gradually, when the time is right. Presentation software has a 'build' facility; with flip charts, simply fold a piece of paper upwards and gradually unroll.

Audience understanding

Empathy is an important ingredient for good personal presentations. In any gathering, there will be people who have different reasons for attendance. Although we would hope that most people are there because they want to hear the results and go on to make decisions, there are other motives. Some people attend presentations to be made aware of the results, but intend to take no specific action afterwards; others are there to report to absent colleagues; some feel duty-bound to be there for some internal political reason.

Faced with such differing motives, the presenter needs to adopt a strategy to satisfy all demands. Alan Wilson (2006) listed six useful points under the title of 'the audience's thinking

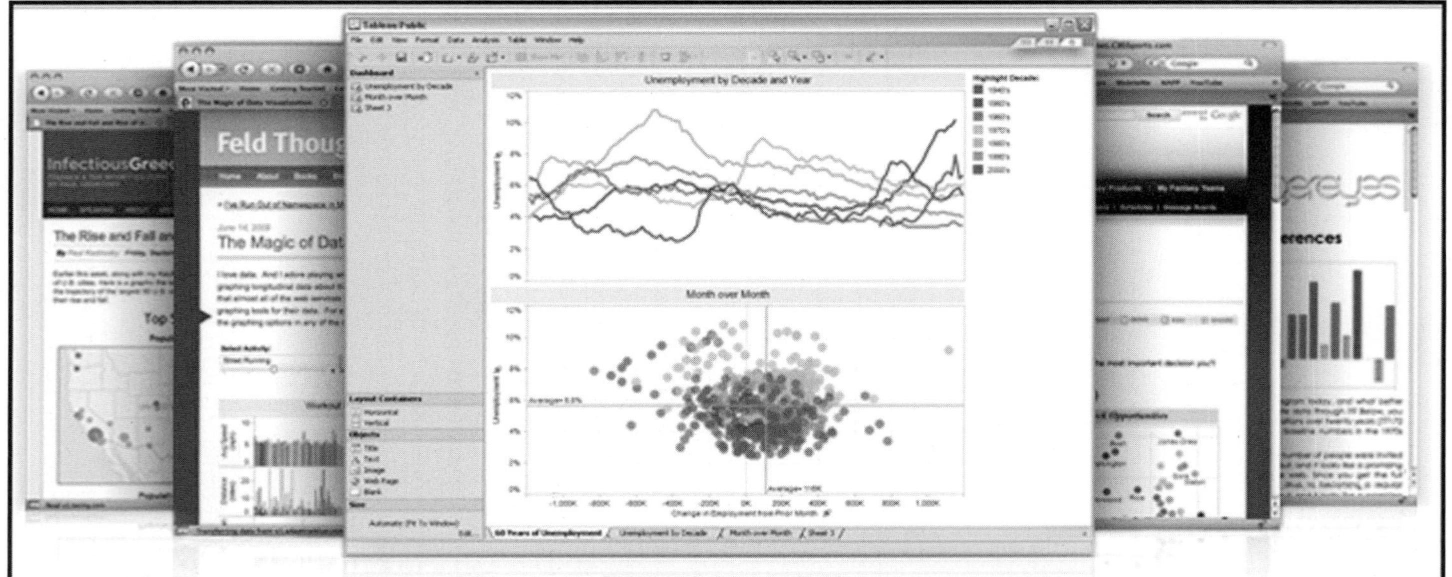

Figure 10.13 Tableau Public Interactive software. Source: http://www.tableausoftware.com/public/download © Tableau Software, Inc. Reproduced with kind permission.

sequence'. These points are really a way of describing how to show empathy with an audience, by putting yourself in the position of an audience member:

1. Respect my importance
2. Consider my needs
3. Demonstrate how your information helps me
4. Explain the detail that underpins your information
5. Remind me of the key points
6. Suggest what I do now.

Each meeting will have a mood. There is general agreement on the so-called big six emotions (see Cornelius 1996):

1. Fear
2. Anger
3. Happiness
4. Sadness
5. Surprise
6. Disgust.

This is a useful framework. You can describe the 'event' as one of these. You can also look at individuals in your audience and use the checklist. It is worth learning the six because they can also be used to good effect in qualitative research. Recognise the mood and recognise who will influence other people. The audience can be a problem: some people may arrive late or chat. You need to develop strategies to get the session started: move your audience closer. It seems that a closer audience can help to overcome problems such as: dry throat, forgetting your script, negative reaction, or hecklers. It is useful to remember that the speaker can manipulate an audience; the presenter can both lose and hold an audience's attention. All presentations must finish, so it is the presenter's job to close the session on time and ensure that people depart with a sense of achievement. It is possible to encourage people to clap (or applaud) at a certain moment. This is a device used in theatres every day; it is called the 'claptrap'. The way to bring about applause, or to delay it, involves careful timing of content and requires careful voice intonation. Additionally, the speaker must make use of body language and must carefully choose their words.

Appropriate style

The style adopted by the person making a presentation should be appropriate to the situation. This does not mean that there is a standard formula, nor does it mean that the style should 'mirror' the audience. A client may dress casually, but this is not usually expected of the presenter. Style goes beyond that of dress to that of communication. A client may use expletives, but again this is not something usually expected from a presenter. The style of the presentation should never be such that it makes things sound more complicated than they really are. Consider, for example, *'our new product launch will sunset any other launches'* or *'there is a baggage of issues; this needs to be unpacked'*. These are novel ways to say that *'the new product launch will be the best'* or that *'there are problems that need to be resolved'*. Or consider, *'the ball's in our court now'* and *'the buck stops here'*. They may work in some situations where

Common mistakes
Reading the presentation

Reading the presentation prohibits eye contact and does not allow you to project your voice in the direction of the audience. Eye contact is just one small tool in the presentation toolbox, but it is an important one. Time and time again, it has been shown that eye contact is important. Eye contact boosts activity in the brain's ventral striatum and this is said to be linked with the expectation of a reward. Instead of reading from a screen or from a written page, reminders should be used to prompt recall. Things that can help include: keeping the agenda or the report contents page visible, having adverts in view, using notes cards, and simple memorising. When you break eye contact, your audience will be distracted and may converse. It is possible to give the impression of keeping eye contact with a large room full of people by scanning the audience constantly. Presenters who wear spectacles can do this very effectively as the audience cannot precisely see their eyes. When you have spent hours preparing your presentation, give a thought to the politician Winston Churchill, who is said to have spent one hour of preparation time on every minute of his delivered speeches. Although such preparation time is unlikely to be available for a business presentation, it does serve to remind us that impact is best achieved by well-controlled sessions. As Cicero declared: *'There is only one kind of perfect orator: the one whose speech instructs, delights and moves the mind of the audience'*.

Martin Stoll of Ipsos Research, UK, makes these comments: *'In regard to PowerPoint, it does slightly depend on who the audience is; on a one-to-one, you would feel like a bit of a twit standing up with a PowerPoint projector, so you just talk them through it'*.

'There is the question of historic record … The more demanding big clients will say that they want a report and all of the details, because when you come back to someone's PowerPoint a year later, you need to know what it means. It depends how organised you are; I have been to presentations where they have got the PowerPoint and then a complete set of notes underneath.'

the audience likes soundbites and motivating, exciting language, but with certain audiences, they will be seen as juvenile and they will erode the credibility of the data. You might think of other expressions or tones that give an impression that the researcher is flippant or patronising.

Onscreen reporting

The Internet and local networks now mean that reports can be made available to multiple users simultaneously. Dashboard displays allow key performance indicators to be communicated in real time.

Report-writing has changed as a result of these innovations. We know that, when faced with something onscreen or in paper form, people read information differently. The onscreen reader is more likely to scroll downwards or to move rapidly forwards and backwards. Signposting is important for both, but takes on a different meaning for reading on a screen. The printed report is more likely to be read like a novel, whereas the onscreen report will be scanned and skimmed. The inverted pyramid (or Wall Street) approaches described earlier are more appropriate for onscreen reporting.

The onscreen report will work better with short sentences and with regular repetition of key concepts. Headings and titles may communicate key points before they unfold in the subsequent communication; the onscreen report is likely to be more similar to a tabloid newspaper style than it is to an academic textbook. It is useful to consider the idea of tempo or rhythm: the reader adopts a time or a pace of reading for printed matter and onscreen material. This pace may be slow, medium, or fast: it is likely to be faster on the screen simply because the mouse and keyboard can turn pages quicker than the hand; this must be considered carefully when producing final reports.

The checklists in the Market Researcher's Toolbox can be used to evaluate your report and presentations. After honestly answering each question carefully, inspect why you answer 'No' for some questions.

Dashboard reporting

Dashboard reports are visual displays of performance information, usually from multiple sources, that appear on a single computer screen. The term is well known because it is used to describe the console found in every motor vehicle. In the same way that we can monitor the functions of our car at a glance, the marketing manager is in the 'driving seat' and is able to see his situation. Instead of a speedometer, petrol gauge, light monitor etc,. the marketing manager can choose any key performance indicator (KPI) that will help in the evaluation of progress towards objectives.

Whereas traditional presentation methods are primarily for an attending audience and the hard copy report may also have several readers, the dashboard is intended for one person. Table 10.7 shows a few differences between traditional and dashboard reporting. The dashboard is the tangible output and visual component of the marketing decision support system (MDSS as described in Chapter 1). This assists business executives at an individual level. Other terms are used to describe this application; therefore we find the term 'portal', derived from the Latin for gate or doorway. Here we can envision a door that opens to sources of information outside the organisation. For many software providers the digital dashboard is seen as just one of several types of portal. For marketing research we can distinguish different types of dashboard

1. **The real-time dashboard**, where results from surveys and web traffic activity can be viewed in real time and updates take place in real time
2. **The monitor dashboard**, or control panel, which acts as snapshot of recent events.

The dashboard must be customised for the user, and software providers offer numerous facilities (widgets) to do this. Paradoxically the vast number of facilities means that sometimes design is actually compromised. There are several steps necessary for effective dashboard design.

1. Selecting correct metrics

It is important to identify the Key Performance Indicators (KPIs) that apply to the business and the user of the data. Measurements of marketing outcomes collated from online and offline computer systems or paper-based records. These are usually expressed as units, averages and percentages. Typical metrics include sales, complaints, comments, and enquiries. Also numbers of website visitors, footfall, orders by type, revenue and store sales. Additionally these will include market share, user numbers, usage, demographics, customer satisfaction, campaign effectiveness, competitive activity, PR activity, news alerts, promotional success, and time series data.

Research in focus
Chocolate dashboards

Daniel Young, Insight Manager at Thorntons ('Britain's leading high street chocolatier'), describes his use of dashboards. *'Their use was essentially borne out of a recognition that there is no "one size fits all" approach to communicating customer insight. There are times when a detailed deck of charts is completely necessary, but increasingly I was finding key stakeholders asking me to review the detail on their behalf and produce topline summaries instead. ... It's all too easy for an organisation to view consumer-based metrics as being the "soft measures", nice to have, but inferior to the "hard" metrics such as sales, retention rates, etc. In such a situation, the consumer insight function can become quickly marginalised. However, by creating a one-page summary that presents all of these metrics together, it helps to cement them in key stakeholders' minds as being equally important, equally easy to access, and equally open to influence.'*

© Jack Sullivan

'Our current dashboard contains overall sales figures, average transaction value, transaction volumes, customer advocacy, and customer ratings on a number of key image statements. The customer measures come from our brand tracker. In previous organisations I've also used retention rates, % of calls answered, and average call handling time, to name just a few. ... These are circulated widely – when everyone from the chief exec down to individual product managers is seeing the same metrics, it makes them very hard to ignore. And as it's only one page, it's quick and easy to digest, and to keep in the back of your notebook. Of course, every measure on the dashboard is just the tip of its own iceberg. There's a whole report behind each of those figures – but we only share that information with people who need it. The dashboard is not intended to tell everyone everything. It's intended to tell everyone just enough to see the "big picture".'

Compiled by Nigel Bradley 2012.

Sources:

Daniel Young interviewed by Nigel Bradley November 2008.

See http://www.thorntons.co.uk

2. Selecting correct visual displays
Some features are shown in Table 10.8.

3. Arranging the metrics in a meaningful way
The incorporation of targets, forecasts, norms, and competition allow us to make sense of the data.

4. Ensuring that important details are emphasised
Design must consider "sensory memory" – for example a scroll down the page or a switch to another page will not be beneficial because the dashboard must communicate data immediately, at a glance.

5. Installing 'alerts' to indicate changes that may require attention.

Table 10.7 The differences between traditional and dashboard reporting

Traditional reporting	Dashboard reporting
Hard copy, static	Onscreen, dynamic, constantly changing
Created at one moment in time	Continuous transfer of data
Simplified, attempts to reduce information. Uncluttered appearance	More complex, attempts to communicate multiple information sources simultaneously. Cluttered appearance
Designed for audiences of several people	Assists business executives at an individual level
Customised for the marketing group	Customised to the individual
Generally created from one study	Generally created from several studies and other data sources

Table 10.8 Features of the dashboard

Feature	Description and examples
Bullet graphs	Similar to progress bar but has 3 features. Invented by Few (see Few 2012, pp. 128–129)
Tickertape news	Small phrases or sentences that move across the screen continuously
Comparisons	With competition, with past activity
Lists	Top five competitors, top five stores
Alerts	Flickering light or other features. Faster flickers attract more attention. Announce changes that may mean intervention is needed Red light for urgency, amber for impending problem
Dials	Similar to car speedometers or thermometers. Criticised for looking good (other features are usually more useful)

Ethical insight
Destroying and keeping records

When research projects come to an end, what happens to materials, such as the thousands of questionnaires and all of the reports? Here, we enter an area of ethics, because researchers have various duties. How should documents be stored? And for how long should they be kept?

First of all, data must be kept safely. The Data Protection Act 1998 states: '*Appropriate technical and organisational measures shall be taken against unauthorised or unlawful processing of personal data and against accidental loss or destruction of, or damage to, personal data*'. If it is stored in another country, we must remember that the Data Protection Act 1998 states: '*Personal data shall not be transferred to a country or territory outside the European Economic Area, unless that country or territory ensures an adequate level of protection for the rights and freedoms of data subjects in relation to the processing of personal data*'.

The MRS reinforces these aspects with rule B62: '*Members must take reasonable steps to ensure that all hard copy and electronic lists containing personal data are held securely in accordance with the relevant data retention policies and/or contractual obligations*'. This goes beyond the immediate research team, as rule B63 points out: '*Members must take reasonable steps to ensure that all parties involved in the research are aware of their obligations regarding security of data*'.

The law in most countries states that citizens have the right of access, modification, rectification, and suppression of information concerning themselves; this is usually by a simple written request to the holder of records. In the UK, this is explicit in the Data Protection Act. As citizens, we can approach any organisation to ask what personal data they have that concerns us.

There is a problem for marketing research in doing this. Most data sets are merged. If we consider a tape recording of a group discussion, it is impossible to extract comments on one respondent. In the process, the privacy of another respondent will be compromised. A questionnaire loaded and recorded to a laptop is also part of a data set, perhaps with a dozen other records from other respondents. This may exist in duplicate when data files are backed up. It would involve a massive administrative task to locate records. The MRS (2003) states that '*the rights of data subjects to request access to personal data held about them does not apply once any personal identifiers have been removed from the data*'. So it is a good idea to remove such things as name, email address, and telephone number as soon as possible.

At some point, the report and working documents are destroyed by the client and the researcher. The ICC/ESOMAR Code states that primary data records should be kept for one year and secondary records for two years. The MRS says that disposal should be mentioned in the contract between the research supplier and the client.

Compiled by Nigel Bradley 2012.

Sources:

MRS Code, rules B49–B61, http://www.mrs.org.uk/standards/codeconduct.htm
MRS (2002) *Data Protection Categories*.
MRS (2003) *The Data Protection Act 1998 and Market Research: Guidance for MRS Members*.

Questions

1 Can respondents and clients view a tape of a focus group they attended?

2 Why is it best for record destruction to be supervised and records kept?

3 What is MRS rule B62? What might this mean in a real agency?

Chapter summary

1 **Explain the purpose of reports and presentations**

Few (2012) identified five purposes that we can extend to all reports and presentations, they are: lookup, narrative, monitoring, exploratory analysis, and prediction. Reporting allows the researcher to select the most important results and to communicate them effectively. The display of data in visual form allows the researcher to convey complex information in a meaningful way. If findings are communicated badly, the credibility of the project, no matter how professionally carried out, will be in question. The important thing is to plan fully; poor planning will lead to digression—lack of planning is extremely obvious. There are three outcomes from communicating findings: a decision to go ahead, a decision not to proceed, and indecision. Indecision is most certainly the wrong outcome and probably due to deficient reporting.

2 **Show the main aspects of report-writing**

Reporting style must satisfy different users. At the first level, it might simply relate facts, or reproduce them. At the second level it will make some interpretation of these facts. A third level will go beyond the data, incorporating knowledge found elsewhere, and speculating. A report has: a title page, a contents list, an executive summary, an introduction, research objectives, and the findings and conclusions. An appendix will carry methodological information. Qualitative reports often use spoken words within quotation marks. The quantitative researcher inevitably deals with numbers and can help the reader to absorb data quickly by using visual displays. Onscreen reading makes new demands on report-writers as content is scanned and skimmed. Video, sound clips, and dashboards have moved reporting away from text.

3 **Show the main aspects of personal presentations**

A good presenter can captivate an audience. The style adopted should be appropriate to the situation. Visuals include the large screen, the flip chart, blackboard, whiteboard, interactive whiteboard, and video walls. Displays include pie charts, cartoons, doughnut charts, Venn diagrams, bar graphs, text in bullet points, line charts, stacked bar charts, quotations, and clipart. PowerPoint is popular because it is easy to use, provides animated slide shows, and the 'Notes' section provides a fuller explanation. Other software packages are available that encourage collaboration and data-sharing.

Review questions

1. What contribution did Playfair and Florence Nightingale make to our knowledge of statistics?
2. What are the benefits of planning report-writing?
3. What are the main sections of a typical report?
4. What can a presenter do to ensure that a presentation session is valuable to everybody?
5. What are the differences and similarities between the reporting of qualitative and quantitative findings?

Discussion questions

1 What would be the implications of providing a client with raw data (transcripts and computer tables) and with nothing else?

2 In regard to PowerPoint, why do some commentators think that the written report is a thing of the past? Identify some up-to-date developments.

3 Create six charts of different types, based on data from newspaper surveys. Now modify these to show how they can be redrawn to mislead the reader.

4 How can a written report mislead the client?

5 Consult the proposal in the Market Researcher's Toolbox. Draft all possible questions that someone at the presentations may ask.

6 Plan a PowerPoint presentation based on any one of the case studies in this book.

7 In the opening Snapshot, what services do computer bureaux offer? Why do you think these services are offered? Give reasons for your answers.

Further reading

- Gordon, W. and Langmaid, R. (1988) *Qualitative Market Research: A Practitioner's and Buyer's Guide*. Aldershot, Hants: Gower.
  Useful tips in the area of qualitative research reporting. One of the few qualitative research books that give information that can be turned to use immediately.
- Hague, P. and Roberts, C. (1994) *Presentation and Report Writing*. London: Kogan Page.
  Written by practitioners, so there are some useful tips.
- Smith, D.V.L. and Fletcher J.H. (2004) *The Art and Science of Interpreting Market Research Evidence*. Chichester: John Wiley & Sons Ltd.
  The 'best' book on the specific area of reporting in marketing research.

Key web links

- Marketing Charts http://www.marketingcharts.com
- Plain English Campaign http://www.plainenglish.co.uk
- Google Docs http://www.docs.google.com

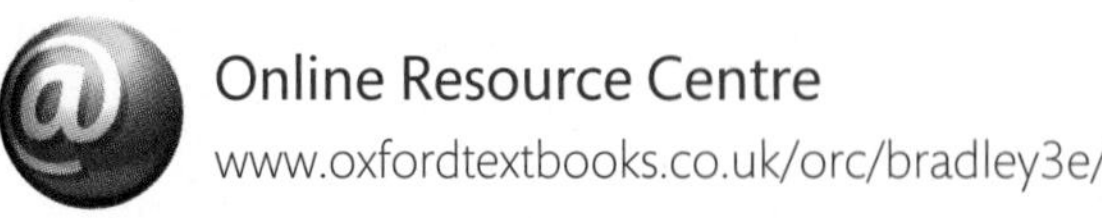

Visit the Online Resource Centre that accompanies this book to access more learning resources on this chapter topic.

Case study
Passcarte

Passcarte is an established credit card with a large client base worldwide. It is well recognised by consumers. Five thousand restaurants in the UK accept Passcarte. The management of Passcarte has received some complaints from cardholders, who are clearly dissatisfied. It would appear that some restaurants, when presented with Passcarte by a customer, are then suggesting that the customer pay in cash, rather than use Passcarte. This may be because Passcarte charges the restaurant 5 per cent on each transaction and restaurateurs may be avoiding this charge. It may also be that some waiters want to discourage the use of a credit card because some restaurants may retain the service charge when it has been included on a credit card bill. The complaints came at the busy Christmas period.

The research department at Passcarte decide to carry out a study to find out whether this practice of asking for cash is common, to investigate the reasons, and to explore means by which it may be stopped.

Five test interviews were carried out by telephone and the responses were used to develop a questionnaire. This was undertaken in March because this is a less busy period. The questionnaire developed is shown below. The researchers could not immediately access the exact addresses of all of the restaurants because these are kept by another department, so they asked around the office for names of restaurants to contact. This generated a list of 250 restaurants. The researchers then used Yellow Pages to find the telephone numbers of these 250 restaurants. Each telephone interview took 20 minutes. The whole process resulted in exactly 100 telephone interviews.

The questionnaire and top-line results are copied and given as a handout (as follows). At a meeting, the research manager announces that the results are good news for Passcarte because they show that the 100 respondents were in very good restaurants with high turnovers and not one of the restaurants refused the credit card and asked for cash.

Compiled by Nigel Bradley 2012.

Passcarte Ltd **Telephone questionnaire on restaurants**

Hello, my name is ____ calling from Passcarte. Please may I speak to the manager?

(Repeat introduction and confirm restaurant manager is your respondent.)

I am calling to ask a few questions about your attitude to Passcarte cards. This should take only five minutes of your time.

Q.1 First, may I ask whether you consider your restaurant to be a large, medium, or small restaurant?

Large	[ ]	*1*
Medium	[ ]	*2*
Small	[ ]	*3*

Q.2 Which of the following forms of payment do you accept? (Read list.)

Cash	[ ]	*1*
Credit cards	[ ]	*2*
Charge cards	[ ]	*3*

Vouchers [ ] *4*

Others [ ] *9*

Specify ....

Q.3 Which form of payment do you prefer? (Write answer.)

....

....

Q.4 If a customer asks whether you accept Passcarte, what is your reply? (Code answer; do not read list.)

Yes, we accept Passcarte [ ] *1*

No, we don't accept Passcarte [ ] *2*

We prefer cash [ ] *3*

Q.5 Do you accept Passcarte?

Yes [ ] *1*

No [ ] *2*

Q.6 What do you like about Passcarte? (Write answer.)

....

....

Q.7 What do you dislike about Passcarte? (Write answer.)

....

....

Q.8 What improvements could we, Passcarte, make to our service? (Write answer.)

....

....

Q.9 Where is your restaurant? (Code answer to our sales region.)

North [ ] *1*

South [ ] *2*

East [ ] *3*

West [ ] *4*

Q.10 How many staff do you employ full-time and part-time?

	Full-time	Part-time
1	[ ]	[ ]
2–4	[ ]	[ ]
5–9	[ ]	[ ]
10 +	[ ]	[ ]

Q.11 Do you like Passcarte?

Yes [ ] *1*

No [ ] *2*

Q.12 How often do you personally take the customer's payment

Always [ ] *1*

Sometimes [ ] *2*

Rarely [ ] *3*

Never [ ] *4*

About the service we offer you

Please indicate your response to the following questions by stating the number that represents the statement that best describes your views.

I strongly agree with the statement	*1*
I agree with the statement	*2*
I am uncertain about the statement	*3*
I disagree with the statement	*4*
I strongly disagree with the statement	*5*

Q.13 Passcarte always informs us of the details of stolen cards. (Circle response code.)

1 2 3 4 5

Q.14 Passcarte is prompt in responding to our telephone calls to check card security.

1 2 3 4 5

Q.15 Passcarte's charge of 5 per cent on each transaction is reasonable in relation to that of other companies.

1 2 3 4 5

Q.16 Passcarte meets the needs of my restaurant.

1 2 3 4 5

Thank you for your help.

Passcarte Ltd results

Q.1 Restaurant size

Large	20%
Medium	40%
Small	40%

Q.2 Forms of payment accepted

Cash	100%
Credit cards	90%
Charge cards	10%
Vouchers	5%
Others	0%

Q.3 Which form of payment do you prefer?

Cash	70%
Credit cards	50%

Q.4 If a customer asks whether you accept Passcarte, what is your reply?

Yes, we accept Passcarte	100%
No, we don't accept Passcarte	0%
We prefer cash	0%

Q.5 Do you accept Passcarte?

Yes	100%
No	0%

Q.6 What do you like about Passcarte?
Good image/low charges/well advertised/others.

Q.7 What do you dislike about Passcarte?
Nothing.

Q.8 What improvements could we, Passcarte, make to our service?
More regular calls/nothing.

Q.9 *Where is your restaurant?*

North	5%
South	80%
East	10%
West	5%

Q.10 *Staff employed*

	Full-time	Part-time
1	10%	5%
2–4	20%	5%
5–9	20%	10%
10 +	50%	80%

Q.11 *Do you like Passcarte?*

Yes	100%
No	0%

Q.12 *How often does the respondent personally take the customer's payment*

Always	0%
Sometimes	10%
Rarely	80%
Never	10%

Q.13 *Passcarte always informs us of the details of stolen cards.*

I strongly agree with the statement	5%
I agree with the statement	75%
I am uncertain about the statement	5%
I disagree with the statement	5%
I strongly disagree with the statement	10%

Q.14 *Passcarte is prompt in responding to our telephone calls to check card security.*

I strongly agree with the statement	80%
I agree with the statement	5%
I am uncertain about the statement	5%
I disagree with the statement	0%
I strongly disagree with the statement	10%

Q.15 *Passcarte's charge of 5 per cent on each transaction is reasonable in relation to that of other companies.*

I strongly agree with the statement	0%
I agree with the statement	75%
I am uncertain about the statement	5%
I disagree with the statement	5%
I strongly disagree with the statement	15%

Q.16 *Passcarte meets the needs of my restaurant.*

I strongly agree with the statement	5%
I agree with the statement	80%
I am uncertain about the statement	5%
I disagree with the statement	5%
I strongly disagree with the statement	5%

Compiled by Nigel Bradley 2009.

Questions

1 Create 10–20 presentation slides to summarise the research project.

2 What objections do you think will be raised at the presentation by your audience?

3 List the different types of visual display that might have been used for the results. Explain the benefits and the limitations of these approaches.

4 What is wrong with the research?

References and sources

Becker, H. (1986) *Writing for Social Scientists*. Chicago, IL: University of Chicago Press.

Bertin, J. (1983) *Semiology of Graphics*. Madison, WI: University of Wisconsin Press.

Bonnett, A. (2001) *How To Argue*. Harlow, Essex: Prentice Hall.

Cornelius, R. (1996) *The Science of Emotion*. New Jersey: Prentice Hall.

Ehrenberg, A.S.C. (1982) Writing technical papers or reports, *The American Statistician*, 36, pp. 87–96.

Few, S (2012) Use-based Types of Quantitative Display. Visual Business Intelligence Newsletter. *Perceptual Edge*, Jan–March, pp. 4.

Friendly, M. and Denis, D.J. (2004) *Milestones in the history of thematic cartography, statistical graphics and data visualisation*, http://www.math.yorku.ca/SCS/Gallery/milestone/

Gordon, W. and Langmaid, R. (1988) *Qualitative Market Research: A Practitioner's and Buyer's Guide*. Aldershot, Hants: Gower.

Hague, P. and Roberts, C. (1994) *Presentation and Report Writing*. London: Kogan Page.

Hague P. and Jackson P. (1996), *Market Research: A Guide to Planning, Methodology and Evaluation*, London: Kogan Page.

Hague, P., Hague, N., and Morgan, C-A. (2004) *Market Research in Practice*. London: Kogan Page.

Haig, M. (2003) *Brand Failures: The Truth About the 100 Biggest Branding Mistakes of All Time*. London: Kogan Page.

McCarthy, P. and Hatcher, C. (2002) *Presentation Skills: The Essential Guide for Students*. London: Sage Publications.

Morris, R. (1998) *The Right Way to Write*. London: Judy Piatkus.

MRS (1998) *Qualitative Research Guidelines*, new edition, September, http://www.mrs.org.uk/standards/qual.htm

Porter, A. (2008) Brown is accused of spin over knife crime, *Daily Telegraph*, 13 December, p. 15.

Sampson, E. (2003) *Creative Business Presentations: Inventive Ideas for Making an Instant Impact*. London: Kogan Page.

Secker, M. (2006) Home Office accused of distorting crime research to support political agenda, *Research*, March, p. 11.

Smith, D.V.L. (2003) *Factoring 'Intuition' into the Analysis of Market Research Evidence*. The Hague, Netherlands: ESOMAR Congress.

Smith, D.V.L. and Fletcher J.H. (2004) *The Art and Science of Interpreting Market Research Evidence*. Chichester: John Wiley & Sons Ltd.

Truss, L. (2003) *Eats, Shoots & Leaves: The Zero Tolerance Approach to Punctuation*. London: Profile Books.

UK Statistics Authority (2009) Knife crime statistics—a review against the Code of Practice, http://www.statisticsauthority.gov.uk/assessment/monitoring/monitoring-briefs/knife-crime-statistics-a-review-against-the-code-of-practice.pdf

Ward, T. (2003) At the mercy of anodyne lecturers, *The Guardian*, 20 May, http://www.education.guardian.co.uk

Wilson, A. (2006) *Marketing Research: An Integrated Approach*. Harlow, Essex: Prentice Hall.

Wilson, G. (2008) Knife figures were 'dodgy'. *The Sun*, 13 December, p. 2.

Part 4

Marketing research contexts

11 Business-to-business research

Contents

Chapter guide

This chapter looks at research into 'non-consumer' sectors. Such research comes under various titles such as 'business-to-business', 'industrial', 'trade', and 'retail'. The chapter examines industry structures, different classes of product, and the elements of 'organisational buying behaviour'. We come to appreciate the importance of satisfaction, quality, image, and employee satisfaction studies. We highlight the differences of this research with that used in the fast-moving consumer goods (FMCG) sector and describe the techniques used in measurement.

Learning outcomes

By the end of this chapter, you should be able to:

1. **List the differences between FMCG research and business-to-business research**
2. **Explain the purposes of business-to-business research**
3. **Describe the populations involved in business-to-business research**
4. **Explain the procedures used in business-to-business research**
5. **Show what must be considered at the publication stage of business-to-business research**

Introduction

The word 'business' covers many activities relating to occupations and transactions: it considers the offerings made from one private organisation to another in industry, commerce, and the professions. In recent years, we have seen a set of descriptors that summarise these activities; these include 'B2B' to denote the words business-to-business. Business-to-business research concerns investigating the part played by people who deliver or receive products and services on behalf of their employer. There is also 'industrial research', 'trade research', and 'retail research'. It is worth pointing out the descriptor 'B2C', which means business-to-consumer. The consumer marketplace is also sometimes known as the fast-moving consumer goods (FMCG) sector and this sector brings a never-ending stream of revenue to manufacturers. There is also 'C2C', meaning consumer-to-consumer, where private individuals sell products and services to other private individuals (the term 'P2P', or peer-to-peer, is sometimes apt for such situations). We find also 'B2G', which refers to business-to-government, where businesses concentrate their efforts on supplying government services.

Differences between FMCG research and B2B research

Standard research techniques, based on marketing FMCG, are used in the B2B sector. For many years, it has been recognised that business research might benefit from the application of the already-tried-and-tested consumer research techniques that had been developed (see, for example, McIntosh and Davies 1970). However, there are subtle differences: for example, in a business context, desk research is far more important in the B2B sector than it is for FMCG. Projects must follow the etiquette of the specific marketplace and respect respondent behaviour in a different way. Table 11.1 summarises some key differences between the two sectors. Sampling frames are often found in directories and are complete. Privacy laws allow the creation and use of client databases without further permission because they do not contain personal data. Among business respondents, there is good penetration of the Internet, so online

Summary of differences between B2B and FMCG research

B2B marketing research	FMCG marketing research
Sampling frames often from directories, and are complete	Sampling frames are often incomplete
Privacy laws allow creation and use of client database without further permission	Privacy laws only allow creation and use of client database with specific considerations
Good penetration of Internet, so online research is a viable option	Incomplete penetration of Internet in domestic communities, so online research not always a viable option
Daytime telephone interviews the norm	Evening/weekend telephoning the norm
Gatekeepers cause difficulties for cooperation levels	Less likelihood that gatekeepers will cause difficulties
Cold calls less acceptable for personal interviews	Cold calls more likely for personal interviews
Few off-the-shelf segmentations available; likely to emerge from research	More off-the-shelf segmentations available (e.g. TGI)
Segmentation likely to be based on monetary bases	Segmentation likely to be based on multivariate analyses (e.g. geodemographics)
Consumption is financed by the employer	Consumption is financed by the individual
Consumption is related to the employer's activities	Consumption is related to the individual's activities

research is often a viable option. There is a greater stress on making advance appointments with respondents, which can affect the time spent or the method chosen; daytime telephone interviews are the norm, compared with the domestic population, where evening and weekend work yields better results. Businesses have more gatekeepers that can cause difficulties. Segmentation is likely to be based on monetary bases. Consumption of the product in question is financed by the B2B employer and is related to the employer's activities. Conversely, in FMCG sectors, consumption is financed by the individual and is related to the individual's activities.

Purposes of B2B research

Many things are examined in the business sector. Market structure and size can be established for most activities. B2B research looks at aspects of the relationship between the manufacturer and the retailer. Satisfaction, quality, and image are all the focus of research. Competitive analysis is another activity that preoccupies many managers in this field.

Image and reputation are important. The *Dictionary of Market Research* gives this definition for 'image':

> 'People's perceptions or impressions of a product, service, company, person, etc., however these may have been formed, and however much they may reflect reality. Image research sets out to discover perceived strengths and weaknesses, relative to the images of competitors or of an ideal, which may then be exploited or repaired as appropriate'.

The concept of 'image' is important to any corporation: if the image of that company is good, it follows that customers will employ the company or use its products and services; employees are likely to perform better and the sector will be attractive to new customers and new employees. Conversely, if its image is poor, the company will have greater difficulty in finding clients or new employees and existing employees may suffer and feel demoralised.

It has been argued that a recognisable image and a favourable reputation are linked to success. This may be external, that is, related to the marketplace, or it may be internal, related to the act of supplying services to that marketplace. For example, a company may be successful because it has a good image and consequently customers decide to buy its products. Several authors have explored the external effects of image (see Gray and Balmer 1998). Success that is related to the internal aspects of supplying a service is evident in employees who are motivated. This motivation and commitment may, in part, be related to the reputation of their company: they are proud to work for an organisation with a good name. The motivational aspect of 'organisational identification' has also been explored widely by researchers (for example, see Siegel and Sisaye 1997).

Aspects of the distribution relationship are also measured and tested: for example, communications promotions for the trade, brochures, rebates, or discount policy, point of sale (POS) effectiveness, usefulness of industrial or trade fairs and exhibitions. Formal information gathering for 'satisfaction' is evident in this sector and techniques developed in the FMCG area have been imported and play an important role. One particular area is the use of customer relationship management (CRM) programmes, which require research to monitor the service levels delivered to customers.

Employee satisfaction studies are one facet of relationship research. These sometimes take the politically correct name of 'colleague opinion survey'. The aim is often to bring about motivation by knowing the results, but also by knowing that employers are responsive; the mere existence of such a survey is evidence of a 'caring' employer. Microsoft regularly has surveys on working conditions: one survey covers its 55,000 employees across the world (*Expansion*, September 2004, 689, p. 160).

Populations involved in B2B research

A great deal of progress has been made in the field of business sampling. We must cite work carried out by Deming (1960), McIntosh and Davies (1970), and Macfarlane (2002), all of whom appreciated similarities with 'domestic' populations, but identified important differences. Research for B2B differs from research used in the B2C sector in various ways. In business markets, the number of buyers is greatly reduced, yet their total purchases are greater. There are fewer 'players', so this effectively creates a small community of people who often know each other; this is far from the case in mass markets. For the researcher, this can be a problem because specific people are of most interest, which has led to 'over-sampling' or 'over-researching' of particular groups. We therefore see a differing response rate, where some groups are more cooperative than others. Incentives may help in this regard. Typical respondents in this field are shown in Table 11.2.

In small companies, there is a notorious difficulty in identifying one set of entrepreneurs: these are the owners and managers in micro-, small-, and medium-sized enterprises (SMEs). They may be individuals working from home, the so-called small office home office (SOHO) sector. All of these are of interest to banks and investors because they are companies of the future; knowing about them can offer an opportunity to establish a relationship from their beginnings. In total, they also offer a lucrative niche. Unfortunately, because many are newly established, or have limited means to make their existence known, they are not easily evident to researchers.

In the larger companies, we see challenges for sampling that do not exist with consumers in the general population, or in the small business arena; this concerns the **decision-making**

Table 11.2 Typical business-to-business populations

Business type	Examples of typical respondents
Companies	CEO, board members, department heads, IT department managers, purchasing managers, executives, administrative staff
Retail outlets	Owners, managers, buyers, after-sales service managers, sales staff
Professionals	Lawyers, solicitors, doctors, architects, pharmacists
Opinion leaders	Journalists, politicians, shareholders, activists in pressure groups

unit (DMU). Although one definition of the population is likely to be the number of companies in a specific marketplace, we must acknowledge that there is a wider population if we account for the full number of decision-makers. Furthermore, there will be several in each 'establishment' or location, which may increase the population substantially.

Decision-making units are made up of various people; typically, these are categorised as the user, the influencer, the decider, the buyer, and the gatekeeper. Their various roles are indicated in Table 11.3.

The role and importance of each DMU member changes depending on the company size, the sector, and the specific needs. The identity of the members often changes depending on the nature of the purchase. Additionally, the nature of purchases has an impact: some purchases are complex; some are simple. The purchase may be seen as a 'new buy' because it is a first-time purchase; it might be a 'modified rebuy', meaning that it was purchased before and the specification is changed slightly, or it might be a 'straight rebuy', where the specification does not alter at all. The decision about who to interview must be carefully analysed by taking into account the likely DMU, as derived from the nature of the purchase, before planning primary data collection.

The 80:20 rule is commonly applied to B2B sampling. If 20 per cent of the companies account for 80 per cent of the purchases, then it is logical to concentrate on that 20 per cent. This leads us to taking judgement samples and to dramatically over-sampling the 'important groups'. Furthermore, because B2B populations can be carefully examined, quota sampling is favoured because it offers the opportunity to apply weights at the analysis stage. This means that a judgement can be made, taking into account specific characteristics of the marketplace. Quotas may be set for any of the organisational 'demographics'. Typically, these are some aspect of size—employees, turnover, consumption, hectares farmed, patients served, and so on—or the role played by the individual—job title, DMU role, and so on. Money is a good common denominator for most firms. A very common quota method is to divide buyers into different groups according to the monetary amount spent with the company or with competitors. This is particularly surprising in some cases where we might expect the number

Table 11.3 Decision-making unit (DMU) members

DMU member	Description
The user	Person who consumes or uses the product or service
The influencer	Sometimes a specialist who provides other DMU members with guidance on the use or purchase of the product or service
The decider	The final decision-maker who can veto the purchase decision, often a department head
The buyer	The person involved with the tactical decisions of the purchase, often called the procurement manager Inevitably deals with financial aspects
The gatekeeper	Controls the flow of information from the seller to members of the DMU within the organisation

of units to be a better indicator of client differences. But it can be understood when we see that there are 'hidden' incomes when providing any service. For example, in a company selling gas, gas consumption may not be used because there may be rental charges on containers. For a car manufacturer, the number of vehicles purchased may not be useful because it may hide rental or lease agreements and will certainly mask the spare parts market.

There are many classifications that place companies into sectors, sometimes using a logical hierarchy, other times with less meaning, created for convenience. The best known of these is the Standard Industrial Classification (SIC). It is worth saying that there are different SICs available—a US version and a UK or European version. The latter is known as NACE ('Nomenclature statistique des activités économiques dans la Communauté Européenne'—Statistical classification of economic activities in the European Community). These codes have changed over the years.

Sampling frames, in the form of trade directories, are often surprisingly complete for many business sectors. This is in stark contrast to the FMCG sector, where sampling frames suffer from opt-out by individuals wishing to avoid unsolicited approaches from marketers, or other factors that lead to gaps in coverage. List owners and list brokers form an important part of the B2B sampling toolbox. Although list selling is primarily for direct marketing purposes, the lists offer ready-made sampling frames for the B2B market researcher. In this sector, with a few exceptions, privacy laws allow the creation and use of client databases without further permission from respondents; this is because the private individual is not the subject of interest. The in-house database must be considered before looking outside; it is likely to contain many years of experience from sales personnel, and should reflect the precise marketplace of interest. The next consideration will be to detect representative people and firms that do not appear on the list: lapsed buyers, dissatisfied customers, or non-customers.

© Nigel Bradley

Procedures involved in B2B research

A look at the development of marketing highlights the type of procedures that are the subject of non-consumer research approaches. After the Second World War, in the 1950s, production of goods was rather basic and the emphasis was on selling products available rather than using a marketing orientation. In line with this approach, research was basic, so it focused on secondary sources and expert interviews. By the 1960s, different disciplines had started to be defined as important marketplaces: agriculture, construction, service industries—all of their suppliers developed branded products. There was a lucrative market for office equipment, such as copiers and typewriters, and for office consumables, such as stationery and printed matter. Licensing production was found to be an extremely effective way of increasing production for all areas. Here, research was particularly useful in the identification of distributors and dealers; it was important to make estimates of market size and the type of players, and to investigate market shares. Besides the continuing use of desk research, techniques developed for the consumer markets were gradually being introduced.

In the 1970s, a new sector based on technological developments emerged; this led to a shift in attention to microchip production and the assembly of components for electronic products, not least computers. At the same time, a variant of licensing, known as 'franchising', was being applied to service industries in a big way. For the researcher, this meant further work in the evaluation of distributors and potential partners, not only to screen suitability, but also to assess their performance. Quantitative research of a primary nature therefore became extremely important and became a permanent addition to the secondary data capabilities that had traditionally been in place. In the 1980s, marketing in the services sector had become a well-established discipline, so much so that service quality measures and satisfaction monitors of different types were implemented. Total quality management (TQM) was a major area for researchers. Customer relationship marketing became more refined in the 1990s and three sectors were leaders in CRM: leading-edge technology, financial services, and the telecommunications industries (Wright 2004, p. 117).

In the 2000s, IT had such an effect that mass marketing was quickly being replaced by mass customisation: marketing to individuals as individuals. Technological solutions offered the opportunity to sell directly. There was a lot of interest in the Internet for online B2B procurement; this left the B2B sector with new challenges, some of which were met by computer-assisted self-completion interviewing (CASI) approaches, using the Internet as a delivery conduit. Some of these aspects are summarised in Table 11.4.

Secondary data

In the B2B sector, there is a great deal of informal information gathering. This is sometimes not considered to be 'marketing research' because it does not follow the standardised procedures most often associated with sample survey research. Nevertheless, this activity is essential for the organisation and provides marketing intelligence.

Trade body estimates, company annual reports, and trade directories are particularly useful to estimate market sizes. Business research practitioners use two techniques to estimate market

Notable events for business to business

Years	Nature of the business infrastructure	Typical research needs and techniques
1950s	Basic production	Desk research, expert interviews
1960s	Agriculture Construction Office equipment (copiers, electric typewriters) Office consumables Licensing production	Desk research Use of consumer research techniques introduced Identification of distributors, dealers, etc. Estimates of market size and players, shares, etc.
1970s	Microchip production Assembly of components Franchises in service industries	Evaluation of distributors, dealers, etc. Quantitative
1980s	Services marketing	Service quality measures, TQM
1990s	Customer relationship marketing	Satisfaction monitors
2000s	Marketing to individuals B2B online transactions	Technological solutions CASI

sizes: the top-down approach and the bottom-up approach. The 'top-down' approach means identifying market size data that embraces the sector of interest, seeking known information from subsectors and then removing these to leave the sector of interest. In terms of the SIC coding system, this means identifying all relevant codes and then consulting directories for corresponding companies, then following these through to annual reports and other sources. The 'bottom-up' approach means amalgamating known information for areas (or subsectors of the SIC code) contained in the sector of interest. The market research exercise is usefully completed using 'expert interviews' with people involved directly or indirectly in the specific marketplace; they will confirm and give their views on the approximations created. Such reactions will often bring forth unexpected data, such as future developments, that can be of use to clients. Future trends can also be detected by analysis of longitudinal data, often provided by government departments. Delphi forecasting carried out among those same experts can give a full picture. One technique that has emerged in recent years is the 'network picture': key members of a DMU are asked to draw a map showing other members and to explain their roles and other details. See Ellis (2011) for more on this.

Qualitative research

Groups and depth interviews are used widely in B2B research. Group discussions are often overlooked due to the geographic dispersion of customers; however, they are possible at events such as trade shows. Additionally, we must bear in mind that several interviews at one

Research in focus
Network pictures

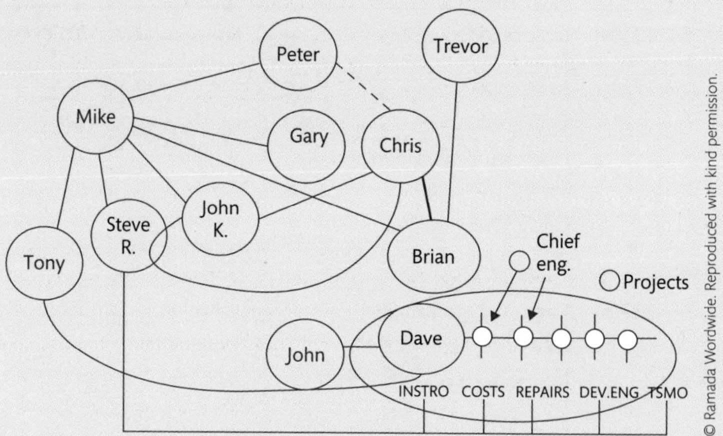

Research has traditionally examined processes inside the single firm. A study in 2009 shifted the level of analysis to the network. It was probably the first to explore 'the differences and similarities of network pictures developed by different actors from both sides of a single inter-firm relationship – the buyer and the supplier'.

Objective: Network pictures are visual representations that can show the relationships between people in the work environment. This study concerned customer–supplier relationships. The aim was to examine the boundaries of network pictures, the lines of communication, the perceived relationship atmosphere, and the impact of environmental factors.

Method: Two engineering firms were used. Company A was the supplier, outsourcing work to a customer, company B. The study spanned the first 18 months of the relationship. Five people were chosen because they were seen to be key to the relationship. Three people were from the supplier: Gary, Chris and John; and two people were from the customer: Tony and Mike.

Independently, all five were asked to draw a network picture to depict the key people, their role, influence, and bearing on the relationship. A researcher observed this, posed questions and recorded explanations. Over these 18 months a monthly self-completion questionnaire was completed by all five informants. Every three months, depth interviews of one hour's duration took place.

Results: Within the companies the individuals were found to have different network pictures that reflect their managerial level and function. The boundaries, communications, and perceptions may vary with their managerial level.

Compiled by Nigel Bradley 2012.

Source:

Leek, S. and Mason, K. (2009) Network pictures: Building an holistic representation of a dyadic business-to-business relationship. *Industrial Marketing Management* 38, pp. 599–607.

Questions

1 What are the advantages and benefits of creating network diagrams?

2 Should researchers amalgamate several diagrams from different firms?

3 What are the criticisms of using network diagrams?

company with different members of the DMU may be useful and these can be organised as a focus group, on the company premises or nearby. Clearly this requires a great deal of planning and a sympathetic contact; networking is extremely important. 'Employee research' often begins with qualitative focus groups, typically held at company premises. Designs vary, but it is useful to run groups by level: by excluding line managers, it is easier to encourage employees to articulate negativity, or to avoid using the sessions in a political way. In using qualitative approaches, there is a reduced likelihood of using some of the flamboyant projective techniques: some of these may erode credibility in the research.

Quantitative research

In employee research, when deciding on a quantitative primary research approach, a major decision needs to be made about whether to use sampling or whether to interview all staff. Selective sampling can alienate those not chosen, or may affect their acceptance of results, in spite of the fact that their views will be accounted for.

'Cold calls' are less acceptable for 'personal interviews' in a business context than for domestic populations. For this reason, the telephone, traditional letters sent by post, and email messages must be considered as a means of gaining access and agreement to interviews. Incentives can also be used strategically, but can be a source of problems. For example, there may be company policies that do not allow employees to receive gifts; there may be personal embarrassment at receiving a gift, or indeed an insult if one is not offered. Respondents may feel duty-bound to give 'the right' answers if receiving personal benefit. People in the professions, such as doctors, solicitors, and so forth, often expect the incentive to equate to the fee they charge; in brief, they expect to be recompensed for the time they spend. One major incentive that has been successful is a donation made to a charity chosen by the respondent. This can avoid problems with employers and avoid bias in answers.

Another important aspect for personal interviewing concerns hierarchies within organisations. Hierarchies may influence the decision to agree to an interview at the place of work, and this brings us to the physical space available. There is evidence to show a direct relationship between office space and responsibility within an organisation. A senior manager/director typically has a private office of 20–30 square metres, as opposed to a clerical worker with 7–9 square metres of space in an open-plan office or group room (van Meel 2000). Clearly, the confidentiality of interview is important and may affect the quality of response. Interviews in open-plan areas are particularly vulnerable in this respect.

Telephone interviews carried out during the day are usual at the workplace, unlike interviewing domestic respondents, where evening and weekend telephoning is the norm. There are, however, problems with 'gatekeepers', who might be switchboard operators or a personal assistant—this in spite of the fact that direct lines are now more common.

Postal research has other challenges. Given the amount of direct mail received by businesses, a postal questionnaire is easily buried, lost, or simply thrown away. In a business context, a paper questionnaire has a low priority and response rates can therefore suffer. The addressee is not always the person who will open mail and so the cover letter must be extremely persuasive; it may need to be written for several people in one organisation. Effective letters are addressed to named people rather than job functions and, given the fact that roles change within organisations, there is a good probability that the questionnaire will not go to

Common mistakes

Launching products inadvertently

Some research requires us to talk to customers about a new product that may be ready in the near future. In casual conversation, it is possible to give the impression that such a new product will definitely be launched, and, worse still, to imply that this will be soon. This is hot news in a small industry and word travels fast. It is perfectly possible for such information of the new product to appear in the next issue of a trade magazine. This alerts other customers to the new product and most decide to wait before replacing existing ones in use. Why replace now when a short wait will mean a more advanced version? As a result of the research, there may be a sales decline and the researcher will have put the client company in a dangerous position.

the correct recipient. There is one exception to this: employee research. An employee is more likely to see the value of completing the form and can complete it secure in the knowledge that their employer will not begrudge their spending time on it. Typical response rates for employee questionnaires in organisations will increase up the management hierarchy.

Online research is a viable option because there is now a good penetration of computers among employees. Where employees have access to a terminal, intranet and Internet systems make it easy to carry out employee research; those without a terminal can be invited to a room with a terminal provided. Customer lists, with email addresses, can facilitate online surveys of a more traditional nature.

Marketing researchers have refined techniques for all of the purposes of B2B research, whether these are to monitor satisfaction, employee performance, or image. Some of these are proprietary products: for example, one research institute (Harris Interactive 2000) has created the 'reputation quotient' (RQ) to calibrate attitudes to corporations.

Publication considerations in B2B research

Incentives in B2B research may involve publishing results: a project carried out by Critical, a UK research agency, said that 68 per cent of senior decision-makers surveyed would be more likely to participate in research if they were offered a summary of results (Mackenzie 2005); it is probable that this type of incentive would be unlikely to motivate respondents in the FMCG sector.

There are many advantages in conducting 'satisfaction' studies, whether they are among customers or employees. The process itself demonstrates that the corporation may be responsive to comments. There are, however, several problems. It is important to design a mechanism whereby feedback is made available properly. This may mean a series of face-to-face meetings with numerous personnel. There is a risk that such sessions can have a negative

Research in focus
Diesel engines

© istockphoto.com/Oleg Tokarev

We are all familiar with motor cars, taxis, and trucks that use diesel fuel. What is less obvious is the fact that another type of application exists, and that is the marine diesel engine: engines that power small and large craft that are used out at sea and on inland waterways. From the manufacturer's viewpoint this is a very different marketplace from the motor vehicle sector as it is smaller, boats are less likely to be branded, but branding of the engine is paramount, and the sector requires a different expertise. At other levels there are similarities: there is a nationwide set of dealers, there are end-users who can express a preference for model and brand, and there are different segments. Importantly, there is an industry where boats and craft are built and require marine diesel engines during that process.

Let us take a peek at a typical study that is carried out in this sector. The manufacturer of marine diesel engines has commissioned a research agency to carry out the study. We are using the United Kingdom as our example but the same study was adapted to many other countries of the world. The overall objective is *'to understand what buyers consider and expect when deciding to buy marine diesel engines'*. The study also forecasts the sales or purchases in the next five years.

In the UK we are interested in two end-user segments: leisure users and commercial users. The first segment includes owners and buyers of craft used by private individuals on inland waterways, lakes, and at sea. Marine commercial engines are found in workboats such as pilots, tug-boats, supply vessels, coast guards, and patrols. Both of these groups are served by dealers who supply spare parts and also repair engines. Initially diesel engines are purchased by boat builders, and this is also a group of interest.

To arrive at a feasible method the client has supplied lists of dealers and end-user segments. To conform to data protection legislation, the lists do not give names of individuals, simply company names, any individuals have been excluded, which means that the leisure user lists are low in numbers. The table shows the methods and sampling details. The questionnaire was identical for the different groups, where necessary filters and routes prevented inapplicable questions being posed. It covered such areas as spontaneous and prompted awareness of diesel engine brands; which makes had been bought, which were considered and which would be purchased today. Forecast questions asked the numbers of purchases in the last five years and whether these numbers would increase, decrease, or stay the same in the next five years. There were questions on after-sales service and satisfaction. Expectations of engines probed the importance of such things as fuel consumption, being green, noise levels, ease of installation, size, and working life.

Audience	Method	Sampling	Sample size
Leisure users	Face-to-face questionnaire	Snowball from owners and dealers	30
Commercial users	Face-to-face questionnaire	Client list, systematic random (1 in n) selection after alphabetical listing by postcode	30
Dealers (linked to client)	Face-to-face questionnaire	Client list, systematic random (1 in n) selection after alphabetical listing by postcode	30
Builders	Face-to-face questionnaire	Client list, systematic random (1 in n) selection after alphabetical listing by postcode	30
Marine journalists	Depth interviews	Details from trade journals	6
Total			126

Estimated populations for the different groups were estimated from information available so tables were weighted. The final sample of 120 allowed a total number to be compared with the results for individual groups.

The forecasts were created before interviewing the journalists who were asked their comments on these forecasts by way of confirmation. Personal presentations of results were made to client executives and a written report was produced. Results in the form of raw data were supplied so that the client company could mine the data further.

Compiled by Nigel Bradley 2012.

Source:
Based on real projects carried out by the author over several years. Methods have been disguised and company names have been excluded to respect client confidentiality.

Questions

1 What are the advantages and benefits of weighting the results to estimated populations?

2 Should researchers amalgamate several segments in results?

3 What are the criticisms of forecasting in this way, what risks are associated with sharing forecasts with journalists?

effect if findings are disputed or discussed in greater detail. Some staff will have been excluded from the research through natural sampling, but may feel that their views have been ignored. And this is why this type of research differs greatly from traditional marketing research: there does need to be a feedback mechanism and the results to employees are capable of bringing about real change that is outside the control of a management team. For example, the survey may take place, data may be collected with sensitivity and with professionalism, and there may be an expectation that some changes may result. If no changes occur, then employees may feel that the employer does not care. If changes take place, these may be popular with some employees, but not others. This may be interpreted as the employer using the survey to imply consultation.

The way to overcome dilemmas is to take as great care with the dissemination of results as with the collection of data. Experienced practitioners (for example, McNeil 1998, p. 950) advocate the involvement of as many employees as possible in setting up the research: a fully transparent exercise to assist cooperation and to assist in the dissemination of results and any action afterwards. A very full 'launch' of results may mean several presentations by location, by managerial level, or by specialism. However, the energy that is put towards such presentations may sometimes be seen as a poor allocation of company resources, thereby defeating the object of the exercise. It is useful to identify the fact that employees, customers, and other interested parties may not actually be able to make a meaningful contribution in this way.

Chapter summary

1 List the differences between FMCG research and B2B research

B2B research is more likely to use desk research, depth interviews, and online surveys. Daytime work is more likely. Business consumption is financed by the employer and is related to the employer's activities; this means that businesses have more gatekeepers than domestic buyers. Finally, segmentation is likely to be based on monetary metrics.

2 Explain the purposes of B2B research

B2B research looks at aspects of the relationship between the manufacturer and the retailer: satisfaction, quality, and image are all the focus of research. Competitive analysis is another activity that requires measures of market structure and size. Various aspects of the distribution relationship are measured and tested, for example, communications, promotions for the trade, brochures, rebates or discount policy, point of-sale (POS) effectiveness, usefulness of industrial or trade fairs and exhibitions. The use of customer relationship management (CRM) programmes requires research to monitor the service levels delivered to customers. Employee satisfaction studies or 'colleague opinion surveys' are one type of satisfaction study.

3 Describe the populations involved in B2B research

Respondents are selected on organisation size (employees, turnover, consumption), by SIC, and by job title and decision-making role. Decision-makers are: the user, the influencer, the decider, the buyer, and the gatekeeper. Respondents are board members, department heads, IT department managers, purchasing managers, executives, and administrative staff. In retail outlets there are owners, managers, buyers, after-sales service managers, and sales staff. Professionals include lawyers, solicitors, doctors, architects, and pharmacists. Opinion leaders are also researched.

4

Explain the procedures used in B2B research

In the B2B sector, there is a great deal of informal information gathering focused on secondary sources and expert interviews. Trade body estimates, company annual reports, and trade directories are particularly useful to estimate market sizes. Business research practitioners use two techniques to estimate market sizes: the top-down approach and the bottom-up approach. Delphi forecasting carried out among experts can give a full picture. Focus groups and depths are used. Personal interviewing relies heavily on the telephone and email as a means to gain access. Incentives can also be used. Online research is a viable option.

5

Show what must be considered at the publication stage of B2B research

B2B research may involve publishing results for respondents: a summary of results is sometimes used as an incentive. The process of conducting 'satisfaction' studies, whether they are among customers or employees, demonstrates that the corporation may be responsive to comments. However, it is important to design a mechanism whereby feedback is made available properly. This may mean a series of face-to-face meetings with numerous personnel. There is a risk that such sessions can have a negative effect if findings are disputed when discussed in greater detail. A very full 'launch' of results may mean several presentations by location or by managerial level.

Review questions

1. List the differences between B2B and B2C marketing.
2. Why is an understanding of the DMU important to the researcher?
3. What is the meaning of network pictures?
4. Researchers have been criticised for interviewing the same decision-makers again and again. Why might this happen and why are they criticised?
5. Define these terms using examples: SIC, DMU, newbuy, image, gatekeepers.

Discussion questions

1. If we were to invite managers from competing firms to attend a focus group as respondents, what problems would you anticipate?
2. Investigate the role of the Internet in B2B research.
3. Ask local shopkeepers about their suppliers and customers. Do they keep records and how might these records be useful to the researcher?
4. How can business research results mislead clients?
5. Plan a study to measure the market size for photocopy paper.

Further reading

- Block, M.P. and Block, T.S. (2005) *Business to Business Marketing Research*. Andover, Hants: Thomson Higher Education.

A specialist text that looks at B2B research, it covers standard techniques and gives a detailed and useful examination of Standard Classifications in operation.

- Ellis, N. (2011) *Business to Business Marketing Relationships, Networks and Strategies*. Oxford: Oxford University Press
  Recent thinking on business decision-making in academia by the IMP Group, a focus on networks rather than hierarchy.
- McNeil, R. (2005) *Business to Business Market Research: Understanding and Measuring Business Markets*. London: Kogan Page.
  The very latest research techniques used in this sector. A very useful account of differences between different countries and a comparison of different sectors.

Key web links

- Business Intelligence Group http://www.b2bresearch.org
- Buyer's Guide http://b2bresearch.org/search/
- IMP Research Group http://www.impgroup.org

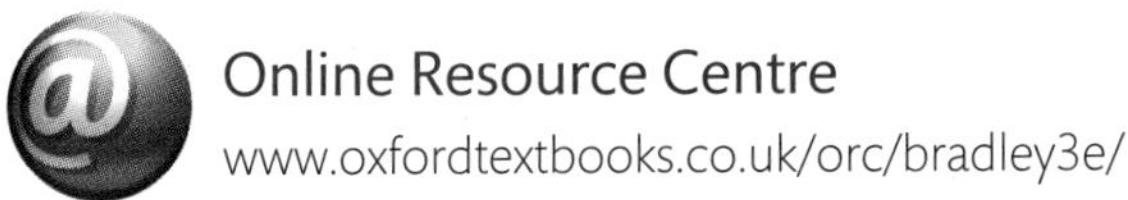

Visit the Online Resource Centre that accompanies this book to access more learning resources on this chapter topic.

References and sources

Block, M.P. and Block, T.S. (2005) *Business to Business Marketing Research*. Andover, Hants: Thomson Higher Education.

Bock, T. and Sergeant, J. (2002) Small sample market research, *International Journal of Market Research*, 44, pp. 235–244.

Bunn, M. (1993) Information search in industrial purchase decisions, *Journal of Business to Business Marketing*, 1, pp. 67–102.

Deming, W.E. (1960) *Sample Design in Business Research*. New York: John Wiley & Sons (reprinted Wiley Classics, 1990).

Ellis, N. (2011) *Business to Business Marketing Relationships, Networks and Strategies*. Oxford: Oxford University Press

Ghingold, M. and Wilson, D.T. (1998) Buying center research and business marketing practice: meeting the challenge of dynamic marketing, *Journal of Business and Industrial Marketing*, 13, pp. 96–108.

Grady, N.B., Fisher, D.L., and Fraser, B.J. (1996) Images of school through metaphor development and validation of a questionnaire, *Journal of Educational Administration*, 34, pp. 41–53.

Gray, E.R. and Balmer, J.M.T. (1998) Managing corporate image and corporate reputation, *Long Range Planning*, 31, pp. 695–702.

Harris Interactive (2000) *What is reputation quotient?*, http://www.harrisinteractive.com

Lulay, W. (1998) Business to business research, in McDonald, C. and MacFarlane, P. (eds.) *Handbook of Market and Opinion Research*, 4th edn. Amsterdam: ESOMAR, pp. 927–947.

Macfarlane, P. (2002) Structuring and measuring the size of business markets, *International Journal of Market Research*, 44, pp. 7–30.

Mackenzie, Y. (2005) B2B MR respondents 'want access to results summary', *Research*, August, p. 10.

McIntosh, A.R. and Davies, R.J. (1970) The sampling of non-domestic populations, reprinted in (1996) *Journal of the Market Research Society*, 38, p. 4.

McNeil, R. (1998) Employee research, in McDonald, C. and MacFarlane, P. (eds.) *Handbook of Market and Opinion Research*, 4th edn. Amsterdam: ESOMAR, pp. 949–955.

McNeil, R. (2005) *Business to Business Market Research Understanding and Measuring Business Markets*. London: Kogan Page.

Minett, S. (2002) *B2B Marketing: A Radically Different Approach for Business-to-business Marketers*. Harlow, Essex: Prentice Hall.

Siegel, P.H. and Sisaye, S. (1997) An analysis of the difference between organization, identification and professional commitment: a study of Certified Public Accountants, *Leadership & Organization Development Journal*, 18, pp. 149–165.

Smith, M.C., Kolassa, E.M., Perkins, G., and Siecker, B. (2002) *Pharmaceutical Marketing*. New York: Hawthorn Press Inc.

Spekman, R.E. (1996) A reflection on two decades of business-to-business marketing research, in Iacobucci, D. (ed.) *Networks in Marketing*. Thousand Oaks, CA: Sage Publications.

Talmage, P.A. (1988) *Dictionary of Market Research*. London: Market Research Society.

van Meel, J. (2000) The European Office: Office Design and National Context. Rotterdam: 010 Publishers, http://www. b-office.com/Documents/RevisitingOfficeSpaceStds.pdf

Wright, R. (2004) *Business to Business Marketing*. Harlow, Essex: Pearson Education.

12 International research

Contents

Chapter guide

Research in one country can be complex, so it is no surprise to learn that this complexity is exaggerated with each extra country we include in a project. This chapter looks at the specific challenges associated with conducting studies across different nations, languages, and cultures. We focus on the question of whether it is possible to apply equivalent techniques to different marketplaces. Differences have implications for desk research, sampling, and instrument design, whether the research is qualitative or quantitative in nature.

Learning outcomes

By the end of this chapter, you should be able to:

1. **List the differences between domestic research and international research**
2. **Explain the purposes of international research**
3. **Describe the populations involved in international research**
4. **Explain the procedures used in international research**
5. **Show what must be considered at the publication stage of international research**

Introduction

International marketing research takes the researcher into different languages, geographies, and cultures; it examines needs and requirements across different nations. It is an important part of research; trade association figures show that domestic clients commission about three-quarters of all research with agencies in their countries, which means that we can say 'non-domestic' clients account for about one-quarter of research expenditure (ESOMAR 2005, p. 16). There has been growth in this area, parallel to the globalisation of companies in general. One commentator noted that international research '*has been conducted since the middle 1950s, increased during the 1960s, grew considerably during the 1970s and experienced a boom in the 1980s, which has continued in the 1990s*' (Kelly 1998). From 2000 onwards, we could say that the Internet has continued the trend of growth, but blurred it somewhat, because cross-border research now takes place with little effort. It is interesting to compare the evolution of research with communication technology over corresponding decades: in the 1970s, telex machines were in use, soon to be replaced, in the 1980s, by facsimile machines. By the 1990s, video-conferencing, carried out in conjunction with telephone services, was a reality, breaking across national boundaries. Since the mid-1990s, the Internet has brought countries closer together, not least because of the ease of using electronic mail communications.

Differences between domestic and international research

International research may take place from a central point or it can be organised locally; it may be centralised or decentralised. Faced with coordination, an agency (or in-house researcher) is faced with following the procedures of regular agency selection, but these are multiplied linguistically and in terms of communications. To obtain three quotes or proposals from each country can be a challenging task.

The ESOMAR directory is useful in agency selection. Knowledge of market research bodies by country (e.g. Syntec in France) can help to identify specific agencies with expertise. There are agency differences that affect clients who commission research. As stated in Chapter 1, many operational roles, specifically interviewing, draw heavily on part-time workers—these are paid on an hourly and weekly basis. This has implications for international research, because there may well be a relationship between quality of research work and the commitment personnel have to an agency. Some countries rely more on part-time workers than others.

Once commissioned, an executive from the coordinating agency should ideally visit the countries to brief staff and field forces on the project, and then attend early interviews (whether these are qualitative or quantitative). This gives a reassurance that everything is understood, that the procedures are in place, and any problems are identified at the outset. An alternative is a video briefing, either live or recorded; briefings are extremely important. Close attention must be paid to the purpose, population, procedures, and publication.

Planning international research efficiently means that teams must be chosen carefully. If we consider team composition, each member of the research staff may be one of three things: multilingual, bilingual, or monolingual. These are important distinctions, and it is necessary to be aware of the fact that each member of the team brings unique benefits to any research project. Here are some examples in relation to questionnaire design. The multilingual researcher is able to look at three or more questionnaires in different languages and may detect differences (and similarities) that allow the research instruments to be consistent across the study. The bilingual researcher usually has a more focused view of two specific languages and is often better placed to identify idioms and areas that may need careful treatment.

The disadvantage of bilingual, trilingual, and multilingual researchers is the possibility that their knowledge of language may become confused. It is easy to 'invent' phrases or even words that are not used (or are used but rarely). This is easily overcome by asking monolingual researchers to check the research instrument. Such researchers do not have the necessary 'baggage' of conflicting vocabularies.

In qualitative research, two situations are worthy of consideration: one is where a local researcher visits a local respondent; the second is where a researcher travels from another country to visit a respondent.

On the face of it, we might recommend that it is most appropriate to use local researchers—they will know the norms and be best placed to probe in an appropriate way to

Table 12.1 Distinctions between domestic and international research

Domestic research	International research
Likely to be conducted in one language, familiar to the research team	Possible language obstacles
Sampling made easier by a reasonable knowledge of geography	Possible sampling obstacles
Data collection may be feasible with a small team	Possible obstacles related to a larger team and subcontracting
Reasonably straightforward to communicate results	Many ways to communicate results
Research likely to be concentrated within one nation	Research conducted across the globe

achieve the objectives of the study. They will also speak the right language and use the right vocabulary to elicit responses. The researcher from another country will not know the norms and this may lead to the respondent's tension, discomfort, or even flat refusal to answer questions.

However, the reality may not be as straightforward as this; there can be problems when the local researcher assumes, incorrectly, that the same norms are shared when, in reality, they are not. The outcome for the local researcher may therefore be the same: tension, discomfort, and refusal to answer. A researcher from abroad, perhaps with an interpreter, will clearly not share norms and adjustments may be made that reduce tension and discomfort, and which help in providing answers.

The researcher's best option is to gather as much information about the types of respondent and cultural norms as possible, and to be open to modifying the methodology in the light of advice (see Table 12.1).

The purposes of international research

At a strategic level, manufacturers have several options before establishing a presence in overseas markets. Market entry decisions may relate to exporting, so may concern finding distributors or deciding whether to establish wholly owned distribution. Joint ventures may be considered, in which case, background research becomes extremely important to help in the identification of partners, and to provide information for negotiations. International research therefore embraces both FMCG and B2B sectors. It may look at consumer behaviour or it may examine organisational buyer behaviour. The country of origin (COO) may impact on the success of a product or service, so this area is often the part or purpose of studies.

Once established in an overseas market, a firm makes tactical and operational decisions, and so research focuses on areas of the marketing mix such as the product, price, place, and promotions. At this point, new product development tests, pricing testing, and the fine-tuning of marketing communications become more relevant than distribution.

The populations involved in international research

To make sense of the 'players' or likely respondents in international studies, it is useful to take a broad view and look at the planet from a distance. Immediately, we can say that countries or nations can be divided into two: developed countries and developing countries. There are some specific measures that distinguish these. 'Developed' countries are sometimes known as the 'first world' or 'industrialised countries' or 'more economically developed countries' (MEDCs). Other terms for 'developing' nations are ' third-world countries' or ' non-industrialised countries'.

Developed countries differ from developing countries in terms of research. Developed countries are better equipped to carry out such studies. Residents in developed countries are aware of research techniques from **opinion polls** that are published widely. This, to some extent, makes them prepared to accept interviewing techniques and therefore more 'predisposed' towards cooperation. Table 12.2 gives an indication of which countries are agreed to be 'developed'. The second column shows countries that may be seen as developed, under certain circumstances. Countries not appearing on the table are those that are 'developing'.

Statistics about countries and country differences are extremely important to the researcher and marketing manager, so must be discovered at the outset from desk research. Such statistics include temperature and climates, and social networks, in addition to aspects of the infrastructure (transport, communication, energy, and electricity). There are different ways of doing business, which may relate to the population size, income, and other demographics. These features are important because there is a relationship between poverty and illiteracy. Purchasing powers are therefore affected: so PPP (purchasing power parity) is important. Table 12.3 shows example key indicators listed for an example country.

Culture

Having established the major features of nations, we must consider the populations and who is available for research. In most nations, there is a hierarchy of household members, which, in some cases, may mean that speech with strangers (researchers) is no more than polite interchange. The researcher must be aware of this. Sometimes, tradition or religion may mean that people will dress in a certain way; they may also expect visitors (interviewers) to respect this by reciprocating. The dress goes beyond clothing to the way hair is worn or hidden; it includes footwear and ornaments on display.

When dealing with people, we need to be aware of the fact that freedom of expression varies among members of different populations. It can be rude, or even unacceptable, to

Table 12.2 Developed countries

Developed countries	
Andorra	Liechtenstein
Australia	Luxembourg
Austria	Malta
Belgium	Monaco
Canada	Netherlands
Cyprus	New Zealand
Denmark	Norway
Finland	Portugal
France	San Marino
Germany	Spain
Greece	Sweden
Iceland	Switzerland
Ireland	United Kingdom
Israel	United States of America
Italy	Vatican City
Japan	
Countries where status is under debate	
Antigua	Oman
Bahamas	Poland
Bahrain	Qatar
Barbados	Saudi Arabia
Barbuda	Singapore
Brunei	Slovenia
Hong Kong	South Africa
Kuwait	South Korea
Latvia	Taiwan
Lithuania	Turkey
Macau	United Arab Emirates
Mexico	

Derived from accounts by the CIA, IMF, and the World Bank.

Table 12.3 Key indicators for countries: worked example for Latvia (see map of Latvia on p. 404)

Population	2.231 million
Surface area	64.6 thousand square km
Population density	34 people per square km
Gross national income (GNI)	$ 6,760 m
Gross domestic product (GDP) real growth rate	–5%
Life expectancy at birth	72 years
Adult literacy rate	99%
Internet penetration	47% of population
Currency	Latvian Lat
Inflation	10.5%
Average household size	2.5

Compiled by Nigel Bradley 2012.

Sources:

Sites accessed 17 April 2009

http://www.cia.gov http://www.internetworldstats.com/eu/lv.htm

World Bank Group (2009) World Development Indicators, http://www.worldbank.org

pose questions to some people in certain circumstances. Coulthard (1977) outlined several 'norms of interaction' in discourse analysis, which are valuable to us in international market research. He said: '*All communities have an underlying set of non-linguistic rules which governs when, how and how often speech occurs*'. His examples include reference to children, who, in some countries, in certain situations, are encouraged to be silent. In other countries, in similar circumstances, children are encouraged to talk.

Respondent selection

In creating a database for sampling purposes, the numbers of fields need to be studied very carefully to accommodate the naming systems in use. Similarly, the fieldwork must take account of these conventions. In Britain, we frequently meet people who have a Christian name and a family name; these may be called the 'first' and 'last' name. Another way of describing it is the 'forename' and 'surname'. We may be 'on first name terms' or we may make a more formal approach, prefixing the surname with Mr, Mrs, or Ms. After marriage, a wife generally adopts the husband's name and the maiden name is lost. Children take the father's name. This short description illustrates several conventions that exist in the UK; it is indicative of social stratification (by age, marriage, position), the historical prevalence of the Christian faith, and many other things. For international research, we cannot always assume that everyone has a surname, that everyone has a first name, and that the order of names is simple. For example, some people may use a surname first and the first name last (Chinese). The father's origin may come first, then the father's given name followed by the person's own name (Hindus in South India). A wife may not fully adopt the husband's name (Italians). The Sikh religion has a convention where 'Kaur' (meaning 'princess') is used as a middle name for the female and 'Singh' (meaning 'lion') is used as a middle name for the male. Some names can become extremely long (Spain), and in due course they may be abbreviated.

In some parts of the world, societal norms make it impossible to approach certain respondents directly. It is interesting to find that Dr Nimir C. Eid made several observations on doing market research with women in the Arab Gulf countries (1999). He said that snowballing is a common technique. He wrote: '*Each contact being made is asked for an introduction to some of her own acquaintances*'. Eid warns that a large number of interviews might come from a narrow circle of acquaintances and offers three solutions: set a cap of two acquaintances from each contact/respondent; after pursuing interviews with two 'levels' of acquaintance, move to a new neighbourhood; make contacts in diverse areas of any city. This is reinforced by an account of interviewing Saudi women (Havermans 2005), in which we find that participants are selected through referrals and taken to focus groups by a driver; research is carried out by a women-only Arab research team.

The term 'guanxi', which relates to the close networks that exist in China, is also relevant to the discussion (Merrilees and Miller 1999). An example that shows the usefulness of

Common mistakes
Making assumptions about respondents

There is sometimes a strong temptation to use stereotypes. Consider the example of a colleague in Canada. A respondent said: *'Your accent is different. May I ask where you are from?'*. The response was straightforward: *'I come from England'*. After a pause the questioner added: *'Where is England? Is it in the United States?'*. The English colleague gave a look of total disbelief which shocked the person into a very fast retraction: *'Is it in Asia?'*. And then a minor adjustment: *'... Somewhere near China ... or India?'*. Resisting the temptation to mock the young girl, my colleague politely explained that it was in Europe. This restraint was rewarded by the unlikely and unexpected solution to the mystery. It is hard to think that someone may never have heard of England, but further enquiry revealed that this young lady had grown up on an Indian reservation, a long way from any town or city. In such situations, for both qualitative and quantitative work, researchers need to avoid assumptions.

snowballing in international studies came from researchers based in Hong Kong (Selmer *et al.* 2002). It illustrates how a self-completion questionnaire can be used. The researchers were investigating perceptions of career management and wanted to contact Chinese mainland business expatriates (CMBEs). One of the researchers, himself a CMBE, *'made use of his guanxi (direct and particularistic ties between two or more individuals)'*. A number of questionnaires were sent to these contacts and they, in turn, forwarded the questionnaire to their peers and friends, who did the same. Four hundred questionnaires were distributed and 121 were returned. This raises an interesting question about whether awareness of hierarchy may be beneficial (or not) to cooperation, or indeed, whether it results in any sample biases.

Classification systems

Members of the population in any given country can be classified according to the well-known segmentation methods. In the UK, there are several established systems that are associated with government surveys: these include socioeconomic groupings (SEG), social class, and socioeconomic classes (SEC). Of particular note in the UK is 'social grade'—not actually a government classification. This divides the population into groups, denoted with letters and numbers: A, B, C1, C2, D, and E. In order to move towards a European equivalent of the UK social grade, the European Commission worked closely with ESOMAR to develop a system that could be applied across European member nations. The very large pan-European survey called 'Eurobarometer' has been used as the testing vehicle for such a classification. This is based on the age at which education ends (terminal education age or TEA), the occupation of the main income earner (MIE), and finally, ownership of ten consumer durables, which is a proxy for income and indicative of lifestyle aspects.

The European social grade therefore emerged and, in basis, is not dissimilar from the UK social grade (see ESOMAR 1997, Reif *et al.* 1991). One version appears as A, B, C1, C2, D, E1, E2, E3. The advantages of this system are that it is an agreed system, based on a fully

Table 12.4 Working definitions of the European social grade system

Grade	Description
A	Well-educated top managers and professionals
B	Middle managers
C1	Well-educated non-manual employees, skilled workers, and business owners
C2	Skilled workers and non-manual employees
D	Skilled and unskilled manual workers and poorly educated people in non-manual/managerial positions
E	Less well-educated skilled and unskilled manual workers, small business owners, and farmers/fishermen

Source: http://www.informationcommissioner.gov.uk

researched method, using known parameters. On the other hand, it has been criticised for having lengthy questions, and being extremely time-consuming at both the data collection and the analysis stages. Furthermore, the question that asks about ownership of specific, named consumer durables is criticised not least for the relevance of the items included. Working definitions are shown in Table 12.4.

From time to time, attempts have been made to create a fully global system that embraces all local systems. A recent one was proposed by Wicken *et al.* (2005). This was based on the **Target Group Index (TGI)** surveys worldwide and the authors say it can be used on ad hoc studies. Points are awarded to respondents out of a possible 100.

'Geodemographic classifications' were developed in the UK in the 1980s in the form of ACORN and MOSAIC and soon emerged elsewhere in other countries. MOSAIC is now available in most European countries.

In the USA, socioeconomic status (SES) score is used by the United States Bureau of the Census, alongside others. An American geodemographic system that has become well-known is called 'PRIZM'.

Procedures involved in international research

The cost of research changes from place to place: there are more expensive and less expensive countries. Similarly, response rates vary considerably across countries, which lead to some interesting methodological solutions that have cost implications.

The range of prices for research is made clear by a regular study carried out by ESOMAR. A recent version of this indicated high-cost countries to be Ireland, USA, and France; lower

Research in focus
European hotels

Founded in 1968, J.D. Power and Associates is one of the top 20 market research agencies in the USA. The continual success of the company must be attributed to tracking studies which guarantee a continuous income. Furthermore, many of these quality and satisfaction projects are carried out in several countries using the same methodology with millions of respondents; this means that the firm is constantly one of the top 25 market research agencies in the world.

The company is associated with cars but it has numerous other market specialities ranging from tracking opinion of airlines, airports, rental car companies, home improvement companies, consumer electronics, health and car insurance, mobile phones, major appliances, and hotels. All of these are substantial industries and on an international scale require a great deal of skill and careful coordination. J.D. Power ratings are based on the responses from consumers who are randomly selected or specifically targeted.

The company's surveys are carried out in local languages in India, Japan, China, the Philippines, Indonesia, Singapore, Thailand, Malaysia, South Africa, Canada, Mexico, Germany, France, Brazil, and many more nations.

Let us focus on Europe and the hotel sector. J.D. Power has conducted studies for this sector since 2003. The 2011 European Hotel Guest Satisfaction Index Study took place between May and September 2011 and related to hotel stays between April and September 2011. Results are based on 18,147 responses. The study examines overall satisfaction of European hotel guests at 45 hotel brands on seven measures: guest room, costs and fees, hotel facilities, check-in/check-out, food and beverage, hotel services, and reservation.

The overall message from the 2011 survey was that there was a decline in overall satisfaction levels after several years of improvement. It has been speculated that this is indirectly due to the global economic downturn which has left expectations mismatching reality. An interesting statement came from Stuart Greif, vice president of the hospitality practice at J.D. Power. Greif has observed that an increase in the frequency of guest interactions with hotel staff can help raise satisfaction and loyalty. He said that after check-in, each additional interaction with other employees such as housekeeper, manager, and concierge will increase satisfaction by an average of 28 points. The study also found that the availability of Internet service surpassed complimentary breakfast as the most important amenity: 47 per cent of guests said they used their hotel's Internet connection in 2011, compared with 17 per cent in 2005.

The results are divided by the different types of hotel, namely Upper Upscale Segment, Upscale Segment, Midscale Segment, and the Economy Segment. This means that hotels ranking at the top of each segment can communicate their success. For the record here are the top ranking names:

- Upper Upscale Segment—Steigenberger Hotels and Resorts
- Upscale Segment—Hilton Garden Inn
- Midscale Segment—Ramada Hotels
- Economy Segment—Premier Inn.

Ramada used these results on their website. They say '*We invite you to come and see for yourself why we were ranked "**Highest in Guest Satisfaction Among Midscale Hotel Chains**" in the J.D. Power and Associates 2011 European Guest Satisfaction StudySM*'.

Compiled by Nigel Bradley 2012.

© istockphoto.com/mattjeacock

Sources:

Baker, M.B. (2011) J.D. Power: European Hotel Guest Satisfaction Again Declines. Business Travel News October 28, http://www.businesstravelnews.com/Hotel-News/J-D-Power-European-Hotel-Guest-Satisfaction-Again-Declines/?a=trans

JD Power Corporate Site Pages at http://www.jdpower.com/library/index.htm?contentType=press-release http://businesscenter.jdpower.com/news/pressrelease.aspx?ID=2011174

PRNewswire (2011) D. Power and Associates Reports: Overall Satisfaction with Hotel Brands in Europe Declines across All Areas of the Guest Experience October 27 at http://www.prnewswire.co.uk/news-releases/jd-power-and-associates-reports-overall-satisfaction-with-hotel-brands-in-europe-declines-across-all-areas-of-the-guest-experience-144880455.html

PRNewswire (2011) Hilton Worldwide's upscale focused service hotel brand ranked highest within 2011 European Hotel Guest Satisfaction Index Study for first time in brand's 15-year history 3 November, http://www.prnewswire.com/news-releases/hilton-garden-inn-awarded-top-ranking-in-europe-by-jd-power-and-associates-133147883.html

Ramada Hotel Website, http://www.ramada.com/Ramada/control/special_offers_worldwide8?variant=uk&cid=RA_UK_JDPOWER

Questions

1. What are the advantages and drawbacks of using different languages for hotel satisfaction studies?
2. Sample sizes were too small to incorporate some hotels in some segment results. Indeed the 'luxury segment' was excluded completely from the results. Is this a reasonable step to take?
3. What are the criticisms of the methods used in the hotel study and what is missing from the methodological description?

costs were found in Pakistan, Macedonia, and Bulgaria. This is shown in Table 12.5. What is not obvious from the table is the fact that there are differences in cost by type of technique; this is in part due to the technical difficulties of operating with specific approaches—it is sometimes a reflection of the infrastructure that affects cooperation.

Postal systems differ in their delivery efficiency and we may suggest that developed countries are best suited to this form of research. Harzing (1998, 2000, 2009) examined response rates in international mail surveys across 22 countries and showed that return rates differ, not least because of cultural differences.

There are important issues to consider with the research instrument itself. In paper self-completion questionnaires, the respondent must leave a mark to indicate their answer to a question. There are two basic ways to do this. One is to write words, in which case the

Table 12.5 The cost of research in selected countries

High cost	Ireland, USA, France, UK, Belgium, Germany, Switzerland, Japan, Sweden, Finland
Low cost	Pakistan, Macedonia, Bulgaria, Guatemala, Panama, Egypt, Ukraine, Ecuador, Cyprus, Peru

Based on information from ESOMAR.

handwriting, which differs by nation, must be understood and the language also understood. The second way of 'making a mark' is to use the famous 'tick', commonly used by teachers to mark schoolwork—therefore, well-known to many; let us bear in mind that those same teachers use an 'X' to show an answer to be wrong. For most people, the act of producing the tick mark is accompanied by thoughts of satisfaction; perhaps that everything is in agreement—it is okay. Conversely, writing the X is accompanied by thoughts of disagreement, which in turn can affect the amount of cooperation in the research project.

The tick is used widely in some countries, but is less used in others. In the USA, the word 'check' is used rather than 'tick'. In fact, the 'V' shape of the tick often changes to a check mark in the form of a cross (X), depending on the country of interview. Finland is a good example of a country where there are conflicting signs in use. Here, teachers use a tick to indicate an *incorrect* answer (the correct answer resembles the per cent sign). For questionnaires, a cross is used. This clearly questions basic assumptions we might make when receiving questionnaires: what was really intended.

There is now good penetration of Internet connections in many countries and the use of CAWI seems to be replacing postal surveys. Interestingly, the split between female and male usership gives a good indication of countries that have reached 'maturity' in this sector.

The major problem with self-completion studies is that we may not know what was really intended by respondents, so there is still a role for interviewers. Face-to-face interviewing dominates in some places, but telephone interviews are more important in others. The USA is a case in point, where telephone interviews dominate: we can speculate that this is possibly due to a combination of vast distances, the speed offered, and the economy of this method. It is worthwhile to note that many countries offer omnibus services.

The greatest obstacle is language: there are 6000 languages spoken today and there are mixes of languages in each country. Of these languages, about 3000 are spoken by over 10,000 people (Ostler 2004). This gives a substantial number of people for whom market segments could be feasible. But clearly this would mean potentially creating 3000 different marketing mix variations. For the researcher, it may mean that a working knowledge of at least 3000 languages might be necessary for effective research to take place. There are also great differences between the spoken and the written language.

The issue is compounded because there are mixes of languages in each country. The European Commission (2005) found this to be the case in the Baltic States: 29 per cent of their interviewees in Latvia, 19 per cent of their interviewees in Estonia, and 8 per cent in Lithuania all indicated Russian as their mother tongue. This shows that there are people who live in nations where their mother tongue is a language other than one of the official languages.

Another more challenging aspect of language is that it is dynamic. It is always changing: every year, new words appear in our vocabularies; some existing words are used more frequently and other existing words fall into disuse; we find words are invented; some are outlawed or fall out of favour and have negative connotations. All of these developments may occur in a specific geographic region, or in a specific workplace, and they are unlikely to be documented in dictionaries until the changes are obvious.

Instrument design

Many companies that operate at a global level want to see comparable results. This may mean that a questionnaire is used in more than one country. Unfortunately, this is not a simple case of translating from one language to another. Very often, this may mean adapting the questionnaire itself: pre-codes for brands may need adapting; local behaviour may need to be embraced in the questions. Where translation is needed, the researcher can use two methods: 'back' translation and 'parallel' translation.

For quality control, these, respectively, mean that: the questionnaire can be translated back to the original language and compared with the original questionnaire; two or more translations can be created, which can be compared with using the best wording. The word equivalence is important here.

Projective techniques offer an alternative to direct questions, and allow us to open the respondent's mind to any topic in a very unique way. Projective techniques may be selected that will work internationally and with which there will be meaningful results. We have looked at projective techniques such as:

- Analogies
- Brand mapping
- Brand personalities
- Cartoon completion
- Collage
- Creative writing
- Gaming
- Guided dreams
- Image response
- Metaphors
- Photo sorts
- Picture completion
- Psychodrama
- Psychodrawing
- Role-play.

Cooper (1989, p. 517) says: '*All these techniques "travel" well. For example, picture completions, collages, psychodrawings, work as well in the US or the UK, or elsewhere in Europe. They also are demonstrably effective in other cultures—Japan, South East Asia, Africa, etc. Norms have now been developed for responses in a number of these countries. The importance of this is that international comparisons can be made. In many developing countries, the quality of moderators is low. The use of these techniques upgrades and standardises qualitative research*'.

Research in focus
Beauty in three nations

BuzzBack Market Research conducted a study examining beauty in three nations: China, USA, and the UK. This study gives a good indication of the value of cross-country comparison. The objectives were as follows:

- To explore women's practical and emotional relationships with beauty and beauty products, including colour cosmetics, skin care, and hair care products
- To understand category usage for these products
- To uncover the emotional perceptions and attitudes of women towards their personal appearance and self-image, and to show how these might influence their choice of beauty products.

The sample size in the USA was 1010 women aged 25–64, representative of US census on age, gender, and ethnicity. A smaller sample of 510 female UK respondents and 517 Chinese respondents were also recruited and included in the study. The Chinese respondents were largely recruited from Tier 1 and Tier 2 cities. The fieldwork period was 13–20 May 2010, using online questionnaires. A variety of tools were employed to explore the objectives.

The study used BuzzBack's proprietary eCollage™ tool, allowing the agency to identify new insights related to appearance, beauty, and personal emotions. These aspects sought to show how women approach their beauty regimes, put themselves together day-to-day, and present an image to the world. BuzzBack's eCollage™ allows respondents to create an online collage that expresses how they feel about a particular topic—in this case, their personal appearance. This patent-pending technology yields richer and deeper insights than those uncovered through standard online probing techniques.

The study also made use of Language and Behaviour (LAB) profiling, a linguistic technique used to identify frequently occurring language patterns in verbatim text. The technique is derived from the field of NLP (Neuro Linguistic Programming) and uses the language patterns in the profile to reveal how consumers think and behave in a specific context.

The results made it clear that the women in this study prioritise beauty in emotional terms, and want to be able to devote time and energy to improving their personal appearance, but their good intentions are often overtaken by other life factors and commitments jostling for precedence. As a result, they often feel stressed and overwhelmed by the demands on their time, and find it difficult to feel truly in control of their relationships with their own bodies.

Particularly in the US and UK, how a woman looks on the outside directly reflects how she feels on the inside. Beauty comes from within, and is not simply composed of external factors. In China, more attention is placed on honing the array of physical details to create a workable image or look that can appeal to others, as well as resonate with the woman herself.

Across all countries, women are looking for brands that perform well and reliably, and which they can trust. They are not expecting miracles, and would prefer to see small incremental improvements to their appearance than drastic changes, but they do want products that slot neatly into their often hectic lifestyles and that they can integrate into their already established routines. Convenience and efficacy are both key to product choice.

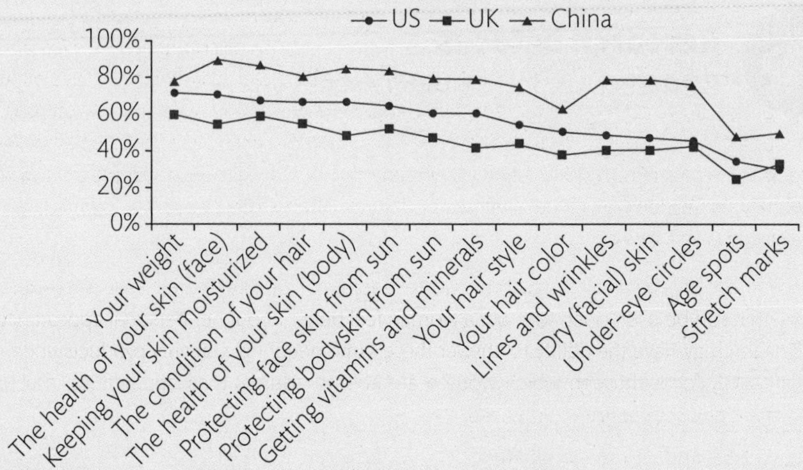

Figure 12.1 Beauty and health concerns. © BuzzBack LLC. Reproduced with kind permission.

Figure 12.2 China word cloud: desired personal appearance changes. © BuzzBack LLC. Reproduced with kind permission.

Figure 12.3 US word cloud: desired personal appearance changes. © BuzzBack LLC. Reproduced with kind permission.

The central function that brands must perform in order to correspond to what these women want is to make women feel better about themselves—to ease any discomfort with their personal appearance and reinforce their own feelings that they are beautiful, both internally and externally. Feeling better and looking better are interdependent for many women, so brands must endeavour to answer both these needs. In China, the picture complicates itself slightly; alongside an intensely personal, individualised, and holistic view of beauty, a desire to please and gratify others emerges. Brands must speak to this desire to simultaneously present an acceptable image to the outside world, and to nurture the inner life.

These central concepts may not be unique to traditional beauty products—it is possible that anything that can be positioned to make a woman feel better about her personal appearance and overall health may have the ability to answer these same needs—but beauty products undeniably represent a key focus through which women are able to address their appearance insecurities, and to refine their self-image accordingly.

Compiled by Martin Oxley and Nigel Bradley 2012.

Source:
BuzzBack Marketing Research (2010) *Exploring Beauty: her self-image, attitudes and beliefs. US, UK and China 2010*. Published by BuzzBack 40 pp.

Questions

1 Why are there differences between countries?

2 Should researchers amalgamate country results or simply comment on similarities and differences?

3 What are the advantages and disadvantages of using projective techniques in quantitative research?

Publication considerations in international research

Throughout the lifetime of the international research project, all parties must see the importance of progress reporting; when small problems emerge, they can often be eliminated or accommodated. Where there are findings available, a face-to-face debriefing is recommended. Face-to-face, the researcher and the client can identify issues of major concern and can focus on the decision-making areas. At the outset, the proposal should specify very clear reporting agreements. The client has an option of receiving synoptic or separate reports—in other words, the 'synoptic report' will bring all country results to one written document, with tables that clearly compare them. 'Separate reports' allow extra countries to be added after fieldwork has ended, building a body of knowledge about the specific marketplace. The client may be given the option of both modes of reporting, at which point there should be no doubt about the implications for timing and the massive amount of information that will need to be read. The use of bullet points may seem to be a good option for swift communication to a multilingual audience, but it can be extremely misleading.

From an organisational point of view, the lead researcher should coordinate report-writing by dictating the style, by giving headings to use; in qualitative research, the topic guide sections usually provide the framework. It is very usual to use PowerPoint, but for a coordinated international study, it can become rather complicated; an early decision is needed about how subcontractors will report back and whether they will be allowed to report back to client representatives local to them.

Problems at the publication stage of quantitative research that takes place simultaneously in several countries can stem from inconsistent coding of open-ended questions. It is essential to create common code frames and these are often provided by one country, called the 'lead country'. Certain percentages, if extremely high for that country, may mean that codes are structured around specific themes that are relevant for that nation; this then means that agencies elsewhere use the 'others' option too much. Ideally, code frames should be created simultaneously and then applied to a sample; they should then be inspected and, if necessary, readjusted if there are inconsistencies. It is important for tables to be valuable, and high percentages listed under 'others' cannot be used.

In qualitative research, transcripts are often created. A decision needs to be made whether they are then translated into other languages or simply used by the local research agency—and then, whether they should be provided to managers working with the client. We must stress that transcripts can be extremely misleading in their isolated state.

Chapter summary

1 List the differences between domestic research and international research

Domestic research has familiar geography, uncomplicated data collection, and reasonably straightforward sampling. International research may be centralised or decentralised. Selection and briefing can become a major task as problems arise from communications, not least linguistically. Domestic studies are likely to be conducted in one language, familiar to the research team. Although multilingual research staff bring unique benefits, there are some less obvious problems. The researcher is advised to gather as much information as possible about the type of respondent and cultural norms. The team must be open to modifying the methodology in the light of advice.

2 Explain the purposes of international research

International marketing research examines needs and requirements across different nations. Market entry decisions may relate to exporting and may concern finding distributors. Joint ventures may be considered, so background research becomes extremely important to identify partners, and to provide information for negotiations. It may look at consumer behaviour or it may examine organisational buyer behaviour. The country of origin (COO) may impact on the success of a product or service, so this area is often part or purpose of studies. Once established overseas, a firm makes tactical and operational decisions, and so research focuses on areas of the marketing mix.

3 Describe the populations involved in international research

Country profiles are important because there are relationships between demographics and purchasing power. Sampling must accommodate different conventions such as naming, hierarchies in households, tradition or religion, dress, appearance, and modes of expression. It is unacceptable to pose questions in certain circumstances. Population members can be classified according to many segmentations. These include SES (USA), SEG, and social grade (UK), the European social grade, and geodemographics (MOSAIC and PRIZM).

4 **Explain the procedures used in international research**

Research costs and cooperation levels vary by country, which affects methodological choices. Similarly infrastructures vary, postal systems differ in efficiency and Internet penetration differs by country. Many countries offer omnibus services. The greatest obstacle is language: there are 6000 languages spoken and there are mixes of languages in each country. The researcher must check translation quality. Projective techniques offer an alternative to direct questions.

5 **Show what must be considered at the publication stage of international research**

Progress reporting and face-to-face debriefing are preferred. Clients may want synoptic or separate reports. The lead researcher should dictate the style and give guidelines; in qualitative research, the topic guide sections usually provide the framework; transcripts must be treated with extra caution. In quantitative studies coding open-ended questions frames should be created simultaneously and adjusted. Tables must avoid high percentages under 'others'.

Review questions

1. What strategic decisions might be based on international research decisions?
2. In international research, an understanding of globalisation is important. Why?
3. In what circumstances might we decide to coordinate research from a central point?
4. Researchers have been criticised for placing too much emphasis on knowing the language and neglecting culture. Why?
5. Define these terms using examples: MEDC, COO, GDP, TEA, ABC1.

Discussion questions

1. Explain the likely outcome of using a researcher to moderate a focus group in a different country.
2. Investigate the contribution of Hofstede to international research.
3. Ask family and friends about countries they have visited. Ask them to explain the culture and how they felt about the people. Do this for numerous countries and explore how such experience is useful to the researcher.
4. How can international research be criticised? What are the good points about it?
5. Plan an international study to investigate the use of perfumes in five countries of your choice. Create a proposal, using objectives that concern the launch of a new product.

Further reading

- Kelly, J. (1998) International market research co-ordination, in McDonald, C. and Vangelder, P. (eds.) *Handbook of Market & Opinion Research*. Amsterdam: ESOMAR.
  An excellent summary of this area of research.

- Usunier, J.C. & Lee, J. (2012) *Marketing Across Cultures*. Harlow, Essex: Pearson Education.
  Examines cross-cultural market research and digs deeper into: translation equivalence, direct translation, back translation, and parallel translation. It distinguishes between organic and atomistic approaches to research.

Key web links

- CIA World Factbook http://www.cia.gov
- Anne-Wil Harzing's website http://www.harzing.com
- Hofstede™ Cultural Dimensions http://geert-hofstede.com

Online Resource Centre
www.oxfordtextbooks.co.uk/orc/bradley3e/

Visit the Online Resource Centre that accompanies this book to access more learning resources on this chapter topic.

References and sources

Barnard, P. (1982) Conducting and co-ordinating multi-country quantitative studies across Europe, *Journal of the Market Research Society*, 24, pp. 46–64.

Cooper, P. (1989) Qualitative research, *Journal of the Market Research Society*, 31, pp. 509–520.

Coulthard, M. (1977) *An Introduction to Discourse Analysis*. Harlow, Essex: Longman.

Eid, N.C. (1999) Market research with women in the Arab gulf countries, *Marketing and Research Today*, 28, pp. 52–57.

ESOMAR (1997) *Harmonisation of Socio-Demographics: The Development of the ESOMAR European Social Grade*. Amsterdam: ESOMAR.

ESOMAR (2005) *Annual Study of the Market Research Industry 2004*. Amsterdam: ESOMAR, 43 pp.

ESOMAR (2007) *Global Prices Study 2007*. Amsterdam: ESOMAR.

European Commission (2005) Europeans and Languages. Special Eurobarometer 237—Wave 63.4. TNS Opinion & Social, http://www.europa.eu.int/comm/public_opinion/archives/ebs/ebs_237.en.pdf

Gordon, W. (2000) *Goodthinking: A Guide to Qualitative Research*. London: ADMAP Publications.

Gordon, W. and Langmaid, R. (1988) *Qualitative Market Research: A Practitioner's and Buyer's Guide*. Aldershot, Hants: Gower.

Harzing, A.W. (1998) Response rates in international mail surveys: results of a 22-country study, *International Business Review*, 6, pp. 641–665.

Harzing, A.W. (2000) Cross-national mail surveys: why do response rates differ by countries?, *Industrial Marketing Management*, 29, pp. 243–254.

Harzing, A.W. *et al.* (2009) Rating versus ranking: what is the best way to reduce response and language bias in cross- national research?, *International Business Review*, 18(4), http://www.harzing.com/download/ranking.pdf

Havermans, J. (2005) Connecting with Saudi women: research in a vibrant environment, *Research World*, August, pp. 17–18.

Hofstede, G. (1980) *Culture's Consequences: International Differences in Work-related Values*. Beverly Hills, CA: Sage.

Hofstede, G. (1991) *Cultures and Organizations: Software of the Mind*. New York: McGraw-Hill.

Kelly, J. (1998) International market research co-ordination, in McDonald, C. and Vangelder, P. (eds.) *Handbook of Market & Opinion Research*. Amsterdam: ESOMAR.

Merrilees, B. and Miller, D. (1999) Direct selling in the West and East: the relative roles of product and relationship (Guanxi) drivers, *Journal of Business Research*, 45, pp. 267–273.

Moisander, J. and Valtonen, A. (2009) *Qualitative Marketing Research. A Cultural Approach*. Sage: London

Ostler, N. (2004) *Empires of the World: A Language History of the World*. London: Harper Collins.

Reif, K., Marbeau, Y., Quatresooz, J., and Vancraeynest, D. (1991) Eurodemographics! Almost there! *Progress report of the ESOMAR working party on 'harmonization of demographics'*, http://www.europa.eu.int/comm/public_opinion/archives/ebs/ebs_055_en.pdf

Selmer, J., Ebrahimi, B.P., and Mingtao, L. (2002) Career management of business expatriates from China, *International Business Review*, 11, pp. 17–33.

Usunier, J.C. & Lee, J. (2012) *Marketing Across Cultures*. Harlow, Essex: Pearson Education.

Wicken, G., van Staveren, M., and Dinning, A. (2005) Global socioeconomic levels: development of a global non-occupational classification system, *International Journal of Market Research*, 47, pp. 597–614.

World Bank Group (2012) World Development Indicators, http://www.worldbank.org

13 Audience and advertising research

Contents

Chapter guide

This chapter looks at audience and advertising research. A great deal of money is spent on advertising and consequently a great deal is also spent on research. Media measurement surveys dictate the amounts paid to buy advertising space; they also offer ready-made segmentation to marketing managers. This chapter addresses newspapers, magazines, radio, television, the Internet, outdoor, and cinema. For media owners, audience research offers guidance on what is of interest to readers, viewers, or listeners. Advertising effectiveness is a key issue and research is expected to give some indication of success. Various measures are used, including impact, emotional involvement, brand recall, image, comprehension, reactions, associations, recognition, appeal, and persuasiveness.

Business-to-business research

International research

Audience and advertising research

Web metrics

Learning outcomes

By the end of this chapter, you should be able to:

1. **Explain the purposes of audience and advertising research**
2. **Explain the procedures used in audience and advertising research**
3. **Show what must be considered at the publication stage**

Introduction

Promotion is an important part of the marketing mix: it is contained in the now-famous four Ps (Figure 13.1). We can break this 'promotional mix' down further into four elements (Figure 13.2). One division lists the elements as personal selling, public relations, sales promotion, and advertising. In this chapter, advertising is our central interest. Advertising is a promotional method that carries a clear cost; it is a message or a collection of messages that are paid for by an advertiser with a specific objective. Advertising is big business and, in turn, advertising research is big business.

Business objectives will give direction to a firm and will be translated into marketing objectives by the marketing managers (Figure 13.3). In turn, the promotional objectives (or the communications objectives or the advertising objectives) derive from the marketing objective. Once established, it is then a case of using creativity to create the right mood, impact, and idea to convey the appropriate messages.

Advertising can be carried by any one of these media:

- Print (newspaper, magazine)
- Radio
- TV

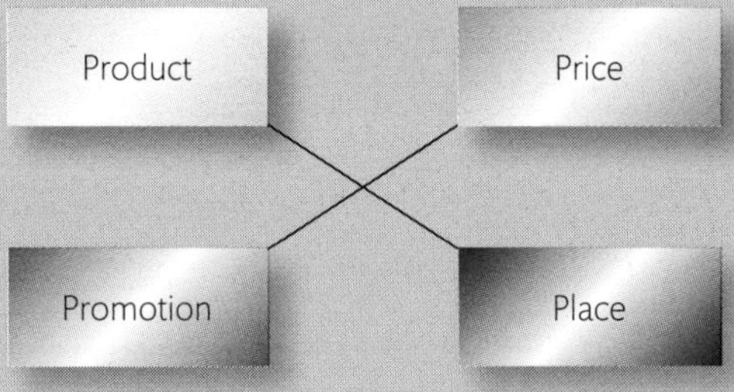

Figure 13.1 Marketing mix

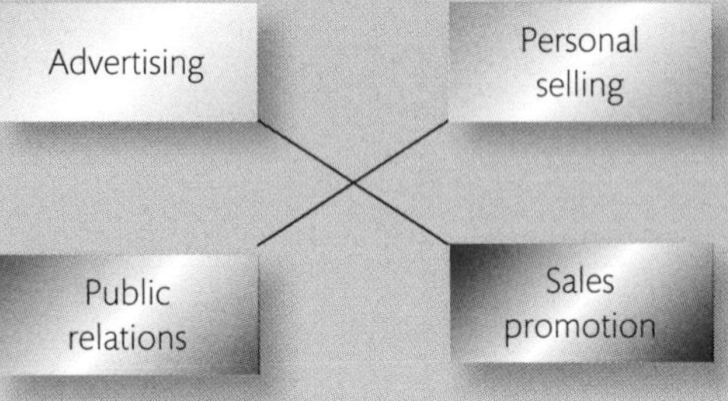

Figure 13.2 Promotional mix

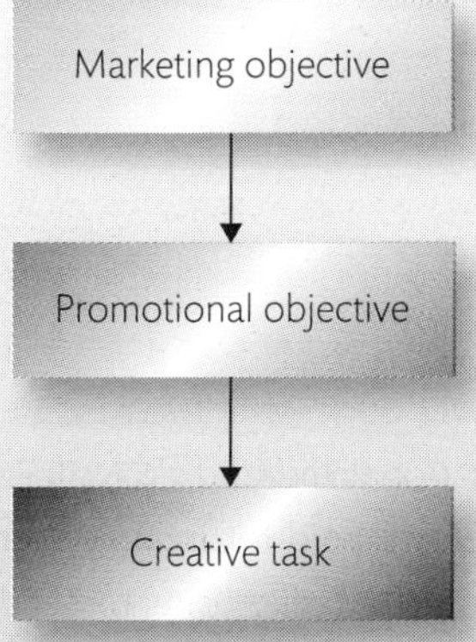

Figure 13.3 Marketing objective

- Outdoor (posters, taxi, bus, etc.)
- Online (websites, electronic communications).

These 'vehicles' can be used to communicate different messages, to reinforce the same messages, or to complement each other. These media have various points in common, and reach is one. 'Reach' is a measurement to show the number of prospects who are exposed, at least once, to an advertisement in a given time period. These media are also very different in many respects and creative personnel are fully aware of these differences when adverts are created.

Advertisers need to be fully aware that promotions follow a pattern in the mind of the audience, and this change occurs because of many variables. This is explained by models under the title of 'hierarchy of effects' (Figure 13.4). The basic 'hierarchy of effects'

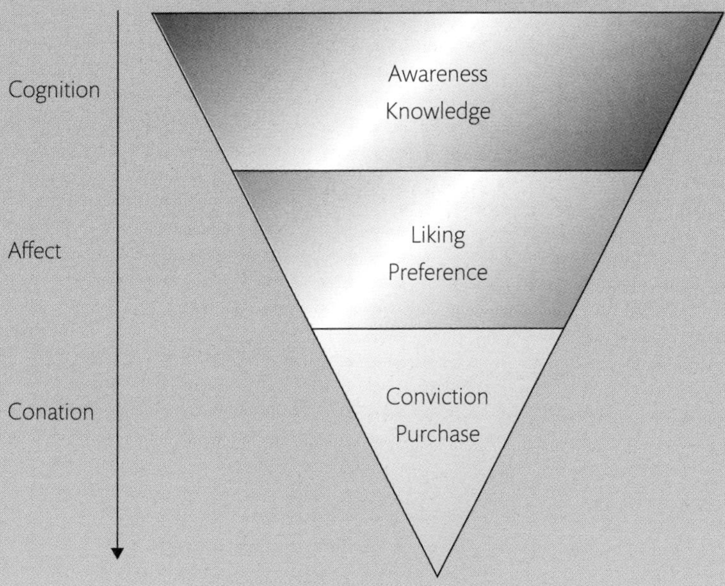

Figure 13.4 Hierarchy of effects

model is AIDA, which suggests that consumers pass through four stages before making a purchase: they will have their attention drawn to the offering; they will show an interest and a desire; they will then take action. So, the model is 'attention, interest, desire, and action'. More complex models have been developed using wider descriptions: cognition, affection, and conation (see Lipstein 1985 for more on this).

At the *cognition* stage, there will be recognition and recall of advertising. There will be a strength of belief that a product does what it claims to do and a basic awareness of the brand. At the *affect* stage, there will be some preference and attitude that can be discerned. There will be a process within the prospective user, which assesses the product with a view to seeing if it meets the needs or wants. At the *conation* stage, there will be a real intention to buy, an intention to try the product, and a real action of making a purchase. We will return to such models when establishing which procedures to use in advertising research.

Purposes of audience and advertising research

The purpose of audience research is to provide information on who and how many people have the opportunity to be reached using a specific medium, whether that be print, broadcast, or another. The classification of customers is important to marketing, so media studies take on the formal task of profiling them into groups. In turn, this information is used to decide the price that media owners set to sell advertising space; they decide the 'currency'. The information is also important because it is a ready-made segmentation, based on common demographics such as social grade, class, gender, age, and geodemographic type. Knowledge of audiences helps media owners to decide what content to offer.

Advertising research is quite different. Many descriptors are used to denote the methods; they include **copy testing**, pretesting, post-testing, and advertising tracking. We can distinguish two broad reasons for advertising research: the first is to provide ideas for advertising content; the second is to evaluate existing advertising—to investigate effectiveness. Some differences in the purposes have been outlined in Table 13.1. On the one hand, we might see 'idea generation', where an advertisement does not exist and as such is not required for the research to take place: research is largely exploratory and uncovers vocabulary used in the sector. In contrast, 'advert evaluation' might take place because an advert does exist: pretesting works within the boundaries of existing knowledge before messages are broadcast and may give an indication of effectiveness. Whereas idea generation studies may question existing knowledge and assumptions, post-testing evaluation studies are able to compare

Table 13.1 Three main purposes of advertising research compared

Idea generation	Pretesting advert evaluation	Post-testing advert evaluation
Advert not required	Advert not yet broadcast	Advert already broadcast
Exploratory	Within the boundaries of existing knowledge	Within the context of the marketplace
Uncovers vocabulary used in sector	Indicates likely impact and effectiveness	Indicates impact and effectiveness
May question existing knowledge and assumptions	Can only be a snapshot	May compare over time
Develops creative ideas appropriate to media types	Tests the execution only	Tests the execution and media
Tells what advertising should achieve	Tells what advertising might achieve	Tells what advertising has achieved

Common mistakes
Confusing readership with circulation

When faced with information about the readership of newspapers, the user of data will meet two distinct terms: 'readership' and 'circulation'. The newcomer to this sector often confuses the two. Readership is an indication of the number of people who read the newspaper in a given period. Circulation refers to the number of copies of a specific issue, which have been printed and distributed. In the situation where one copy of the publication is read by one person, the circulation and readership figures would be identical. Clearly, however, there may be two or more readers of one copy, so circulation may be lower than readership. Conversely, if there are some copies that are not read, the circulation will be greater than readership. Taken together, these two indicators give a new one known as 'readers per copy', usually abbreviated to RPC.

such things as awareness over a time period, in a longitudinal way. These divisions are not always clearly distinguishable because pretesting and post-testing may generate new ideas or may provide ideas for modifications and variations. Pretesting can test effectiveness before the advert is broadcast.

The tests to evaluate advertisements that already exist are the most numerous and complex. Such tests examine the mental processes of the consumer; they look at the 'hierarchy of effects'. The purposes of advertising research are thus to examine the recognition and awareness of advertising, attitudes towards the advertising, whether responses are positive or negative, and finally to examine the persuasiveness of the advertising. It may evaluate the choice of medium for the particular execution compared with another (TV versus radio) or the choice within a medium (*Daily Telegraph* versus *The Times*). The research will help to decide whether the communications encourage respondents to buy or commit themselves in some way.

Procedures for audience research

In the past, different methodological approaches have been used for each medium to be measured: we have seen one method for the press, another for radio, and another for television. Many of the procedures in the media measurement sector are moving towards mechanical observation. This is probably because the emphasis is on factual behaviour and the cost of technological solutions has fallen dramatically in recent years. This is not to say that opinion and attitude are unimportant in this area, but the major measurement studies are not primarily for this purpose. Technology is also now making it possible for all media to be 'captured' by single studies or indeed single devices. For example, GFK has developed MediaWatch, which claims to do precisely this job (see *Research in focus*).

Press

Publishers can gather internal secondary data about their own periodicals. They know how many copies were printed, how many were distributed, and how many returned. This basic information gives circulation figures. This is cheap, relatively easy, and can give a good indication of demand; advertisers can use circulation as an indicator of how many people their advert will reach. However, it can be manipulated by the unscrupulous publisher who can 'inflate' numbers in order to attract more advertising revenue. An independent body or 'auditor' can be used to verify that a publisher's declaration is indeed accurate. In the UK, the Audit Bureau of Circulation (ABC) is used by many publishers to carry out this work. Even with accurate circulation figures, however, audit data can never show who reads and what is read; this requires a readership study. In the UK, the National Readership Survey (NRS) uses personal interviews of about 60 minutes and uses computer-assisted personal interviewing (CAPI) to assess reading of over 250 publications. Details of the NRS have been provided in earlier chapters, in particular Chapter 10, *Snapshot*.

Radio

Also in the UK, for many years, radio listening has been monitored by RAJAR, which uses listening diaries that are delivered to households by interviewers, completed by respondents, and either collected or returned by post. Therefore, RAJAR's radio-listening survey uses pen-and-paper self-completion diaries, but electronic data capture devices are being developed and tested. Details of RAJAR have been provided earlier in this book, in particular Chapter 5, *Snapshot*, and Chapter 10, *Snapshot*.

Television

Mechanical devices are used to monitor television audiences. In the UK, audiences are measured by an industry organisation called BARB, and the study is subcontracted to research suppliers. The method makes full use of mechanical observation. In any household, there are numerous items of equipment related to the television, such as television sets, video cassette recorders, DVD players, and set-top box decoders. All of this television-receiving equipment is electronically monitored in a panel of households that has been carefully selected. The system automatically identifies and records the channel to which each television set is tuned when switched on and all viewing involving a VCR (recording, playback, viewing through the VCR, etc.). Details of BARB are provided in the *Research in focus: How to deliver data 24/7*.

Outdoor

In order to know how many people travel past a particular location, various procedures, called 'counts' are used. If people who are walking are to be monitored, these are called 'pedestrian counts'; if people are travelling in cars, buses, or trains, they are called 'vehicular' or 'traffic

Research in focus
Media watching

Technology is being applied to media studies and research suppliers are racing against time and each other to provide solutions that will satisfy their clients. We will briefly examine the case of Arbitron and GFK.

In the USA, a portable 'peoplemeter' system has been developed and tested by Arbitron. It resembles a pager and is carried by consumers. Inaudible codes that radio broadcasters embed in their programming are automatically detected. At the end of each day, the survey participants place the meters into base stations that recharge the devices and send the collected codes to Arbitron for tabulation.

In June 2004, GFK unveiled MediaWatch, a metering unit designed in the form of a wristwatch. This device measures any form of media with which the wearer has contact. It is described as the first device able to measure contact with radio, TV, newspapers, magazines, freesheets, and other printed matter, as well as cinema and outdoor advertising. To date, research has been media-specific, which means it specialises in measuring the use of one particular medium. Now, for the first time, it is possible to carry out research into media consumption, which is user-specific, and thereby record and analyse the complex multimedia mix to which people are exposed. The watch is described as 'a miracle of microtechnology'. A recording unit records and encodes audio and radio signals, three times a minute. The new MediaWatch is able to record data for up to four weeks before it has to be changed. Pilot projects are running in ten countries.

Compiled by Nigel Bradley 2012.

Sources:
Press info (14 June 2004), http://www.gfk.com
http://www.arbitron.com

counts'. Various means, both human and mechanical, are used to make these counts, for example:

- Interviewers may register numbers on a hand-held click-counter
- Infrared sensors may trigger a counter when beams are broken by someone walking or driving past
- Activity may be captured by video camera and the data processed by software
- Black rubber strips placed on a road may register the number of wheels passing that point
- Piezoelectric pressure mats have been used to count pedestrians and cyclists.

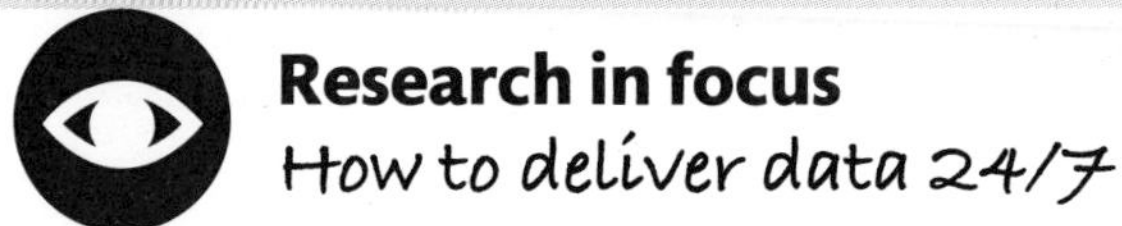

Research in focus
How to deliver data 24/7

Television, radio, and newspaper audience research surveys are truly continuous: data are collected every day of the year; some of the operations take place every single minute of each day. These three projects are also quantitative: they generate millions of numbers that can be manipulated in many ways. The projects are therefore useful in that they illustrate how complicated data sets can be delivered to hundreds of users.

BARB is the UK television viewing monitor. Detailed viewing data for all BARB-reported television channels and services are only available to subscribers. All subscribers pay an annual registration fee, currently £3850, plus a quarterly subscription fee, and there is an additional cost for the data itself. Some BARB-related services, usually for a particular one-off purpose, may be purchased from a data bureau, to be used strictly for internal purposes, in return for an ad hoc registration fee.

The computer bureaux registered with BARB are: AGB Nielsen Media Research Ltd; CCA (International) Ltd; David Graham & Associates Ltd; Donovan Data Systems Ltd; Guerillascope Ltd; Helen-Harrison & Company Ltd; KMR Software Ltd; Markdata Media Information Systems (UK) Ltd; Mediametrie (France); Nielsen Media Research Ltd; Peaktime UK Ltd; RSMB Television Research Ltd; Television Research Partnership Ltd; Thomson Intermedia PLC; and Xtreme Information Ltd.

The National Readership Survey (NRS) estimates readership of newspapers and magazines. Every year, over 35,000 individuals are interviewed. This data capture takes place every day throughout the year, organised as 12 monthly assignments. The funds for the project are provided by the three industry associations whose members are involved in buying and selling national press advertising space. These bodies are the Institute of Practitioners in Advertising (IPA), the Newspaper Publishers Association (NPA), and the Periodical Publishers Association (PPA). Anyone can see top-line information freely on the NRS website, but for more detail, advertising agencies subscribe via the IPA, magazine publishers subscribe via the PPA, and newspapers subscribe via the NPA. Anyone else must subscribe directly through NRS Ltd. The standard annual subscription in 2005 was £3280.

Subscribers may access NRS data in three ways: hard-copy reports, a password-protected part of the website, and through authorised computer bureaux. Hard-copy reports containing 260 data tables of readership and marketing information are published twice a year. Volume 1 covers the July–June fieldwork period and is available in August; Volume 2 covers the January–December fieldwork period and is available in February; Volume 3 gives specific data and is available in February. A monthly bulletin provides rolling updates of top-line readership data.

The full NRS database is updated quarterly and made available to subscribers via the authorised bureaux. These bureaux have their own software that enables users to carry out a range of different analyses of the data. The bureaux authorised by the NRS are divided into full service bureaux—Interactive Market Systems (UK) Ltd (IMS), KMR Software, Telmar Communications Ltd—and other bureaux—MediaTel and Claritas.

An NRS codebook, which costs £186 for four updated copies a year, is useful in deciding on special analyses.

NRS Ltd stresses that its information should not be misused, in particular in interpreting results obtained from small samples. All users are told that any published interpretation of the data, or the supply of data to third parties, is subject to NRS copyright rules.

RAJAR is a company specifically established to manage the UK's agreed system of radio audience measurement. It is jointly owned by the CRCA (on behalf of commercial radio companies) and by the BBC. Because hundreds of people use the data, reporting is rather complex.

The *Radio Analysis Book* contains an analysis of commercial stations' performance against a range of demographic variables; printed volumes are available every quarter. Other hard-copy publications include a *Quarterly Summary of Radio Listening* with top-line results for most UK radio stations. This is fondly known as the 'press release'. *The Radio Audience* is available to subscribers 10 days after the top-line results; these volumes contain station-by-station results, together with group, network, and regional information, analysed by standard demographics. A 'summary report' is issued with *The Radio Audience* published reports. It is also available, as a separate volume, to non-broadcast subscribers. This contains a condensed summary of each individual station's results. Two more items—the *Trend Analyser* and the *Station Ranker*—provide trend and competitive data. 'Standard results' for their own services are provided to each participating commercial radio station or group. These results are made available to stations early in the morning of the data release day. 'Full tables' are then produced for the stations and their authorised representatives. These provide extended analyses for all competing stations overlapping with the 'home' station's survey area. These tables are made available to stations about 10 days after the 'press release'.

In addition to the hard-copy format, most of these volumes are also available on the RAJAR website. RAJAR licensed bureaux provide analysis systems based on 'respondent level' data and other services based on data held at the 'aggregated' level. These systems can be accessed by participating stations and other RAJAR subscribers, subject to the payment of the appropriate access fees.

Radio stations like to talk about their RAJAR results to attract advertisers and to reassure existing advertisers that they are choosing wisely. Findings are therefore heard on broadcasts, as the spoken word; they appear on publicity material and in press releases from the radio station. This activity is called 'publication' and advice is given on this in a 'Publication Code'.

The guidelines are rather detailed and lengthy, but there are some extremely pertinent points. Clearly, the ability to manipulate raw data can lead to analyses that are meaningless; the basic idea of sampling is that a certain number of respondents must be involved for the data to make sense. Therefore, the RAJAR Publication Code gives precise indications on the minimum sample size that should be used. The same thing applies to comparisons, whether with competitors or with different time periods. There are strict guidelines on timing: for example, there is much at stake and so there is an embargo on publishing new results until 11am of the release day.

Compiled by Nigel Bradley 2012.

Sources:

http://www.barb.co.uk/about.cfm?report=computerBureaux&flag=about

http://www.nrs.co.uk/access.html

http://www.rajar.co.uk/content.php?page=about_process_publication

Questions

1 In what ways do results from the three surveys appear in hard copy?

2 Outline the ways in which results from the three surveys appear in electronic form.

3 Consider a frozen food company, which advertises on TV, the radio, and in newspapers. What results will be available to it on 15 March next year?

4 Why do publication rules exist for all of these bodies? Consider the question from the viewpoints of: media owners, the survey management, trade bodies, and buyers of advertising.

Various technology-driven solutions have been applied to outdoor advertising and are being developed. These include technologies such as a hand-held global positioning system (GPS) to acquire data that are able to provide audience demographics, geographic definitions, and audience estimates, such as reach, frequency, and gross rating points (GRPs).

In the UK, the best-known monitor providing estimates of audience for outdoor media such as posters is called POSTAR. This monitors some 100,000 roadside billboards. POSTAR merged local authority traffic counts for 10,000 panels with estimates for over 100,000 panels across the UK. Pedestrian information was measured from over 9000, 12-minute pedestrian counts, over 18 months, at poster sites across the country. This gives us audience figures: for example, the number of people who have an 'opportunity to see' (OTS) each advertising panel (see http://www.postar.co.uk/).

Online

To examine 'online behaviour', software can be installed onto PCs or terminals with the user's permission. Such software can monitor the behaviour of the user and the information can be sent back to a central point. Studies using this idea allow the most popular websites to be identified. Major providers were described in Chapter 3, *Competition and web activity analysis*.

Website server records (log files) provide detailed analysis of website activity. These are described in Chapter 14. Such metrics can cover length of visit, user hardware, software, and behaviour. Analysis can be carried out by the web page owner or by an external body. Examples of two external bodies are the Audit Bureau of Circulation (ABC, see http://www.abce.org.uk) and the BPA (see http://www.bpaww.com/). Both have conducted Internet audits since 1995 to give a common currency for media space sale.

The ABC international standards working party has developed a set of rules and definitions that act as a worldwide standard. Rules for the UK are controlled and developed by JICWEBS, the Joint Industry Committee for Web Standards. The Digital Analytics Association (DAA) has also created a set of standards. More information on website analytics can be found in Chapter 14.

Procedures for advertising research

One general rule is that advertising should be tested in the mode of transmission. For example, a radio advert is best tested by asking respondents to listen; press adverts are best tested by asking targets to read; web adverts are best tested on screen; television adverts are best tested on a television screen. There are modifications to this: for example, storyboards may be shown to focus group members to help in the development of television advertising.

Scientific instruments that measure the physical or physiological effects of advertising have been used with varied success. These include instruments to measure eye movement, pupil dilation, skin response, pulse rate, and so on. Memory has been tested by removing the logo or brand name from adverts; this masking might be extended to the descriptions, straplines, or even visuals (leaving sound). It might be tested at intervals after exposure: for example, the day after. Emotion has been tested with simple questions or by projective techniques that elicit a response.

Another aspect to consider with advertising is the issue of time. There may be both short-term and long-term benefits of advertising and these can have an influence on the 'effectiveness' of a given communication. Research may therefore test single and multiple exposures. Similarly, we see seasonality in every market sector and this aspect must be considered when designing procedures. Research before major festivals may give completely different results from research carried out afterwards. Similarly, unforeseen events can affect responses and indeed can make adverts more or less visible: newspaper sales increase during natural disasters, but readers focus on the main news stories. We might argue that there are times when 'good adverts may be buried'.

Various measures are used in testing advertising, including: impact, emotional involvement, brand recall, communication, image evoked, persuasiveness, and ability to change attitude (see Ambler and Goldstein 2003 for quantification of the principal ones in use). The important thing is to use those that are appropriate to the research objectives and the task in hand; there is little likelihood that 'off-the-shelf' methods will be applicable without adaptation.

Secondary data

Secondary data sources can be used to analyse 'conation' via customer transactions on databases. Such analyses can show trials, repurchases, and switching behaviour. When placed against known advertising campaigns, these can be a simple but efficient tool. Advertising by competitors is also available for most market sectors. This is found by inspecting the use of media, then making analyses by brand and amalgamating these to company level. This is done continuously by specialist companies. They monitor the media: press cuttings services have been available for many decades; similarly, there are companies that listen to broadcasts to measure advert length and note the topics. These evaluations are then set against advertising rate cards to create a likely expenditure by specific publication or channel. Detailed analyses are available by category and by time period. These are available for print, radio, television, posters, and new media. Simple correlation analyses, taking sales and advertising expenditure, can lead to some interesting observations. Semiotic analysis of existing advertising can provide information on competitive approaches and positioning.

Qualitative research

Qualitative research is particularly valuable at the 'idea generation' phase and focus groups have been used for this purpose for many years. Here, concepts can be proposed to respondents. Concepts may be spoken, written, or in the form of visuals. Respondents might be asked to propose their own solution to the marketing and communications objective. Concept boards might be used to try ideas and to gather reaction. Respondents may offer criticisms at any level or viewpoint: ethical, legal, technical, and social objections may exist to a particular approach. Depth interviews are used in conjunction with focus groups and tend to uncover different aspects: being on the respondent's 'home ground' it is likely that the advertising will be considered in a different way, one that is more directly linked to the respondent's personal circumstances. Qualitative research may give misleading indications of impact and memorability, so must be used cautiously for these two purposes. The major benefit of qualitative research is to examine 'affect'.

Quantitative research

Quantitative research can measure 'cognition', 'affect', and 'conation', making this an extremely powerful tool. Quantitative methods show the frequency of purchases. They also provide quantities used and number of users. Measures used include saliency, strength of branding, comprehension, reactions, associations, recognition, message appeal, and persuasiveness. Spontaneous awareness can be measured by careful probing. When stimulus materials are used, adverts can allow respondents to confirm their knowledge of advertising, allowing prompted awareness to be measured.

Telephone interviews are less able than personal interviews to use visual stimulus materials. However, audio can be used, which lends itself to radio advertisements and jingles. Both personal and telephone approaches can be used for 'day after recall' (DAR), which measures the impact of TV, radio, or press adverts within a 48-hour period after broadcast. DAR is usefully set against benchmark figures for similar market sectors; such figures will be kept by research information suppliers. DAR measures are indicative of impact, but also of how memorable is a given execution. It is particularly effective for television adverts that are broadcast in a specific region and often appear within programmes with maximum viewers (e.g. soap operas such as *Coronation Street* in the UK).

Postal research does have a role, but is less used for advertising research. In a real-life market situation, mail-order advertising can provide valuable information on response. Treatments can be changed in the covering letter—use of colour, return mechanism, etc. Here, multivariate analysis can play a useful role. Online research can bridge all methods and, where possible, can use multimedia to assess animated, moving adverts.

Hall tests, panels, and omnibus surveys are often seen as suitable vehicles for advertising tracking. Additionally, a choice of executions can be tested in these ways. Specifically, the panel and the omnibus surveys offer an economical way to gather longitudinal information, so can act as monitors to measure spontaneous and prompted awareness of brands and advertising recall. The omnibus is particularly useful in international advertising campaigns. One powerful feature is its ability to monitor awareness before a campaign actually begins. Often, this can identify likely sources of confusion in the minds of the target audience. Similar brand names or similar advertising can mean that audiences misattribute the advertising of competitor companies. When set against advertising expenditure and media use, such measures can offer some specific guidelines on effective executions.

Prompted awareness

If we reduce sales to an equation, we can say that sales are likely to be the result of many variables; advertising is just one. Sales are likely to be a function of PR activity (PR), sales force

(S), sales promotions (Sp), advertising (Ad), buyer needs (B), company image (I), media chosen (M), etc. So:

Sales = f (PR + S + Sp + Ad + B + I + M, etc.).

It would be a complex task to isolate and identify the weights and relationships between each of these different variables, but the study of 'econometrics' attempts to do precisely that. It takes empirical observations, advertising knowledge, and statistical theories, and uses these as inputs; it then provides outputs of predictions and associations between variables. Work in the 1970s by Corlett (1978), O Herlihy (1978), and others outlined exactly how this could be achieved, and with powerful data-mining software, this approach has recently seen a revival.

In assessing advertising effectiveness in the online environment, web pages offer a unique set of challenges to the researcher. It is firmly accepted that there is a relationship between good website design and effectiveness, therefore usability testing is important. E-marketing campaigns can be evaluated in several ways using web analytic tools (in Chapter 14). But, as with offline methods, research judges advertising according to communications objectives set by the company. Table 13.2 indicates how common objectives can be assessed.

Table 13.2 How common objectives can be assessed

Communication objective	Pretest	Post-test
To inform	Group and depth interviews	Spontaneous and prompted awareness (quant)
To generate interest	Group and depth interviews	Number of enquiries in secondary internal data
To remind	Group and depth interviews	Usage and attitude surveys, tracking studies
To change attitude	Group and depth interviews	Usage and attitude surveys, tracking studies
To sell product	Split test, experiment, hall test, cinema test	Database mining, coupon redemption, A/B website tests

Publication considerations in audience and advertising research

Media audience research can be confusing because the use of abbreviations and acronyms leads to a jargon that needs to be understood before figures can be used to make decisions. We must also bear in mind that the average audience survey generates hundreds of pages of tabulations, all of which can be misleading without full knowledge of their origin and significance. Typically, data are delivered electronically by media bureaux, which offer the advantage of easy analysis. However, electronic data reports take us further away from the tangible, physical quality associated with paper reports.

In order to be introduced to some of the language used in these sectors, let us consider some concepts that have been used. It is important to consider that terms and their meanings change frequently, particularly in the new media sector. For that reason, up-to-date definitions can usually be found on the websites of major surveys, usually under the title of 'glossary'.

Some 'glossary' definitions

AIR	average issue readership
Amount of viewing/ listening/reading	number of hours exposed to TV, radio, or press
Audience share	percentage of people viewing/listening/reading as a percentage of the total
CTR	measure of times an advert link is chosen from a web page
Cover or reach	how many people are 'reached' or 'covered'
Frequency	the average number of times people are counted as exposed to specified media outputs (for example, viewers of programmes or readers of magazines)
GRPs	gross rating points
HUTs	households using television
OTS	opportunities to see
PUTs	people using television
Rating	the average percentage of the population who view
RPC	readers per copy
TRPs	target rating points
TVRs	TV ratings

Different types of media data are reported at different intervals (daily, monthly, etc.) and as we have seen, each carries its own techniques and language. The major dilemma is whether reports should simply give figures or offer softer data such as appreciation scores of satisfaction with programmes or quality of articles.

A major problem with communicating the findings of advertising research concerns timing. There are usually many deadlines and overlapping activities related to advertising production, so the research is often needed before data collection has been completed. Typically, advertising agency personnel will take information from early focus groups and create a concept board for testing at the next few groups. Before a report is written, the team is likely to begin work on final executions. Another danger lies with the different people who have an interest in the results. Typically, we will see: an advertising agency with creative personnel who have created or will create the communication; an account team who will defend the ad agency's decisions; and client company personnel who want to satisfy their marketing objectives. These three groups of people will invest time and effort at different phases of a campaign. There will be points at which they want the results to show specific things and their expectations will not always coincide. None of them will abandon deep-seated ideas readily. The researcher is therefore faced with a potentially hostile audience before the study even begins. For this reason, the onus must be on the researcher to secure agreement about what is to be tested. If there is disagreement about what is being tested, there are certain to be problems.

In relation to quantitative data, the risk is one of being confused by a mass of awareness and transactional data, and therefore researchers must beware of creating too many documents for the client to read.

Chapter summary

1 Explain the purposes of audience and advertising research

Audience studies dictate the price media owners set to sell advertising space; they are a 'currency'. They also offer a ready-made segmentation, based on common demographics. Media content is guided by knowledge of audience profiles. The purpose of advertising research projects is to establish whether advertising is working; research should therefore measure adverts against the communications objectives. Studies provide ideas for advertising content and then evaluate existing advertising. Pretesting works within the boundaries of existing knowledge before messages are broadcast and may give an indication of effectiveness; post-testing evaluation studies are carried out after broadcast. The tests to evaluate advertisements that already exist examine the mental processes of the consumer: they look at the 'hierarchy of effects'. Advertising research therefore examines the recognition and awareness of advertising–attitudes towards the advertising and, finally, the persuasiveness of the advertising. It may evaluate the choice of medium for the particular execution compared with another or the choice within a medium. The research will help to decide whether the communications encourage respondents to buy or to commit themselves in some way.

Explain the procedures used in audience and advertising research

Different methodologies are used for each medium. In the UK, the main readership survey uses personal interviews; radio listening uses pen-and-paper self-completion diaries. Mechanical devices are used to monitor television, Internet, and outdoor audiences. Measurement is moving towards mechanical observation, and technology is now making it possible for all media to be 'captured' by single studies or single devices. Advertising research uses both qualitative and quantitative research to identify and measure impact, emotional involvement, brand recall, image, comprehension, reactions, associations, recognition, appeal, and persuasiveness. With powerful data-mining software, econometrics has seen a revival. It attempts to isolate and identify the weights and relationships between different variables.

Show what must be considered at the publication stage

Media audience research data is delivered electronically by media bureaux, which offer the advantage of easy analysis. Standard terms have been developed over time and an up-to-date knowledge of these is important. For advertising research, timing is crucial and safeguards must be taken to assure report quality in the time constraints. Interim written reports from the researcher should eliminate misunderstandings. In the case of quantitative data, one risk is that of having too many documents to read.

Review questions

1 Explain the different appeals of the press and television to advertisers.
2 Outline the main reasons for audience and advertising research.
3 What is social grade? And what other classifications can be used?
4 Why can media audience research be misleading?
5 Define these abbreviations and terms: CTR, BARB, RPC, AIR, TVR, econometrics, copy testing, advertising effectiveness, reach.

Discussion questions

1 Explore the reasons for looking at how an identical advert performs in different countries.
2 Investigate the reasons why the Audit Bureau of Circulation (ABC) is important.
3 Ask family and friends about adverts they see on TV and hear on the radio. Ask them to describe the adverts. Why do they remember these ads? What were the communications objectives? Were they achieved? How could you estimate the annual income from advertising?
4 How can qualitative research be used by the audience and advertising researcher?
5 Plan a study to describe the audience of a university magazine of your choice.

Further reading

- ADMAP archives, http://www.admapmagazine.com
  A monthly magazine published in the UK. It is written by practitioners for practitioners. It contains the most up-to-date knowledge in the area of advertising testing.
- Fill, C. (2002) *Marketing Communications*. Harlow, Essex: Prentice Hall.
  A solid account of marketing communications techniques and the corresponding research techniques are shown. A very good academic text.

Key web links

- The Media Research Group http://www.mrg.org.uk
- World Advertising Research Center http://www.warc.com
- Advertising Standards Authority http://www.asa.org.uk

Online Resource Centre
www.oxfordtextbooks.co.uk/orc/bradley3e/

Visit the Online Resource Centre that accompanies this book to access more learning resources on this chapter topic.

References and sources

Ambler, T. and Goldstein, S. (2003) *Copytesting: Practice & Best Practice*. Oxford: World Advertising Research Center.

Corlett, T. (1978) Anyone for Econometrics? *ADMAP*, August, pp. 376–383.

Feldwick, P. (2002) *What is Brand Equity Anyway?* Henley-on-Thames, Oxon: World Advertising Research Centre.

Fill, C. (2002) *Marketing Communications*. Harlow, Essex: Prentice Hall.

Flanders, V. (2002) *Son of Web Pages that Suck*. London: Sybex.

Gunter, B. (2000) *Media Research Methods*. London: Sage.

Havermans, J. (2004) Understanding the prosumer, *Research World*, 12(9), October, pp. 22–23.

Hedges A., Ford-Hutchinson S., and Stewart-Hunter, M. (1997) *Testing to Destruction*. London: IPA.

Lipstein, B. (1985) An historical retrospective of copy research, *Journal of Advertising Research*, 24, pp. 11–14.

McDonald, C. (2000) Monitoring advertising performance, *ADMAP monograph No. 4*. Henley-on-Thames, Oxon: WARC.

McDonald, C. (2000) Pre-testing advertising, *ADMAP monograph No. 5*. Henley-on-Thames, Oxon: WARC.

McDonald, C. (2000) Tracking advertising and monitoring brands, *ADMAP monograph No. 6*. Henley-on-Thames, Oxon: WARC.

McDonald, M. and Monkman, M. (eds.) (1995) *MRG Guide to Media Research*. London: MRG.

O Herlihy, C. (1978) Why econometrics can make advertising and marketing scientific, *ADMAP*, October, pp. 472–480.

Tellis, G. (2004) *Effective Advertising: Understanding When How and Why Advertising Works*. Thousand Oaks, CA: Sage Publications.

Twyman, T. (ed.) (2000) Special issue on media research, *International Journal of Market Research*, 42, pp. 365–493.

14 Web metrics

Contents

Chapter guide

This chapter on web metrics incorporates the two main threads of web analytics and social media monitoring. Web analytics measures official outputs BY companies, whereas social media monitoring measures unofficial outputs ABOUT companies. The sections are structured around the marketing research mix, so after introducing the topics and distinguishing between the two approaches we examine the purpose, population, procedure, and some aspects related to publication. Because of limitations of space the chapter excludes search engine optimisation (SEO) and email campaign monitoring. The content is intended to introduce knowledge of this important area, but also to provide practical help in using some of the principles, whether this is to enrich academic projects or application to active companies and brands.

Learning outcomes

By the end of this chapter, you should be able to:

1. **List the differences between web analytics and social media monitoring**
2. **Explain the purposes of web metrics**
3. **Describe the populations involved in web metrics**
4. **Explain the procedures used in the web metrics sector**
5. **Show what must be considered at the publication stage of web metrics research**

Introduction

With the arrival of the World Wide Web in 1990 we saw the creation of web pages, which collectively became websites. Whether large or small, all companies wanted a presence on the World Wide Web and low costs made this possible. As a result website design and creation was big business. What is fascinating is that silently an industry grew in the shadows, an industry designed to monitor the performance of these websites. This started in a basic way, using simple web page counters in 1990, then moved to logfile analysis in 1995. That industry grew and has become known as *web analytics*. Our definition is '*the capture and processing of data from software and hardware that produces performance indications (e-metrics). This is output by companies, rather than output about companies*.'

A next major advance was the arrival of 'social media' whereby Internet users created content; similarly energies have gone into facilitating the production of millions of conversations. Again, in the shadows, another industry grew to allow corporations to make sense of the content. This industry is known as social media monitoring (SMM) and the origins can be traced back to 2004 (Sponder 2012), Our definition for this is '*the use of techniques used to observe and register consumer generated comments, questions and conversations, usually concerning a specific brand or organisation or campaign.* This is output *about* companies, rather than output *by* companies' (Bradley 2012). Social media monitoring can take place even when there is no corporate website present, web analytics requires a website to be in place. These are therefore relatively recent developments yet the procedures can be extremely complex.

Corporate interest in web metrics

Within any organisation, it is true to say that different people have different interests in web metrics. Top management need to be aware of the overall trends, marketing managers and content creators need to monitor changes continually, this then allows the sales force to act and engage with the ultimate aim of concerting interest into transactions. Public relations personnel also need to act and engage but with the objective of rectifying misconceptions and ensuring the corporate reputation is intact. The webmaster looks at web metrics to understand the pressures on the site in terms of usage. Online marketing executives look at the flow to products to understand how to get users to specific content. Consumer insights executives and advertising executives look at the number of unique users, viral statistics, and social media statistics.

Companies have differed in their dedication to analysing the rich data feeds available online. In order to understand the different attitudes it is useful to refer to a model created by Stéphane Hamel (2009), he calls it 'the Online Analytics Maturity Model' or OAMM. The model has six areas of interest which are management, objectives, scope, team expertise, continuous improvement process, and tools technology. The degree of applicability for each of these areas is applied to a specific company on a five-point scale. The outcome is plotted on a diagram. The resulting visual can then show the organisational strength and weakness for their commitment to the use of online metrics. The model can show that organisations not using web analytics tools have a long way to go to reach competitive advantage. This is a useful starting point for an analyst wanting to understand the organisation before starting to use web metrics (see Hamel 2009 for the questions used to create the model structure).

A big issue that has been discussed in recent years is where the web analytic function should sit within a company. There are arguments for it to sit in a marketing role, others suggest the marketing research department, or the IT department. The situation becomes more complex when we consider that there can be numerous employees dedicated to these analytic functions. Avinash Kaushik (2009) describes centralised approaches, with one analytics team serving the whole organisation, compared with a decentralised approach; neither of which he finds acceptable, preferring an in-between approach. We do know that many companies use outside analytic consultants and systems. The 2012 Social Media Marketing Industry Report (Social Media Examiner 2012) survey mainly with respondents in the USA shows that 11 per cent of respondents outsource analytics and 7 per cent outsource monitoring.

Digital communication channels

Before entering into the detail of web analytics and SMM, it is important to understand the channels of communication, and indeed the channels of distribution that are involved, particularly in the digital world. The term 'channels of communication' is more commonly referred to as media. Corporate and social media are closely linked; they oppose each other but also complement each other. In recent years we have seen a distinction drawn between paid-for, owned and earned media, sometimes turned into the acronym POEM. This distinction can help us to understand why web metrics are important and how they operate across the different media. The POEM concept goes back to 2008 and was used at the company Nokia (Goodall 2009); Forrester (Corcoran 2009) then extended the idea and gave it a wider awareness, other works have followed to elaborate the model (Burcher 2012).

Let us, for one moment, forget the online world and apply POEM to traditional marketing. *Paid for media* includes advertising that we can buy, whether it be in the form of outdoor posters; ads in the press, television, or radio; it includes sponsorship that is paid-for whether this be an event or a physical entity such as a soccer ground. The idea of campaigns that use *paid-for media* is to drive buyers or prospects to *owned media*, and in a traditional sense we are talking about retail outlets which of course have signage, employee uniforms, point of sale displays, package designs, sales promotions, and many other opportunities for the company to communicate with their customers. Owned media, of course, will have its own impact; it could be the starting point of the customer journey whereby paid-for media reinforces any messages.

The third area is earned media, and this is least influenced by the marketer. Recognition and engagement with the customer can, however, be 'earned' through careful message content, timely and quality response in the specific medium. Here we are suggesting that company messages and other communications that surround the customer are absorbed and passed on to other people. This is by word-of-mouth, by letters pages in newspapers, private conversations, magazine reviews, and so on. It must be said that this could be positive or negative. The traditional marketer would use paid-for media in an attempt to keep opinions positive. This, of course, needed traditional questioning of respondents to identify underlying opinion and attitude.

Let us now turn to the online world, where the POEM model works extremely well and can be understood clearly, Table 14.1 summarises the situation. On line, paid-for media includes advertising that we can buy from media owners: their property includes banners,

Table 14.1 Distinctions between paid-for, owned, and earned media

Paid-for media	Owned media	Earned media
Traditional and online advertising space that can be purchased	In the full control and ownership of the advertiser	Media content is produced by 'others' but advertisers can influence by appropriate responses. Reputation is 'earned'
Media owner property, temporary	Corporate property, more permanent	Social media, less permanent
Display ads	Corporate web pages	WOM, Buzz, viral
Banners, pop-up ads	Corporate mobile pages	Clicks
Interstitial/superstitial	Corporate blog	Shares
SMS/SMM ads	Corporate twitter account	Likes
Third party apps	Corporate Facebook account	Contributions
Paid search	Own apps	Comments and reviews

pop-up ads, interstitials and superstitials, mobile phone campaigns through SMS or SMM ads or messages, we can even think of third party apps that can be free to the user. Another big area is the purchase of keywords the so called *paid search* which can buy advantage in search engine result listings. Let us reiterate that one reason to use *paid-for media* is to drive prospects to *owned media*. In the online world, owned media is the property of the organisation so it will include corporate web pages and any microsites, it will include mobile pages, the corporate blog, it will even extend to company twitter and Facebook accounts if they have been created. Like traditional owned media, the online versions have their own abilities to attract traffic first. The third area is earned media, this is by word of mouth, but online this is email forwarding, retweets on twitter, sharing links and information, exclaiming a like for something.

Let us use an example to illustrate this: Yeo Valley Organic is based in Somerset, England. The company has been producing organic yoghurts since 1993. In 2010 the company allocated £5 million to a campaign. The objective was to drive demand to a broader, more mainstream audience. A two minute television advert in the form of a song was used in the commercial break for X-Factor, this is paid-for media. This was then made available on YouTube (with the corporate channel called YeoTube)—this is owned media. Users of Facebook and twitter then took the brand to an even wider public and here is an example of earned media. Public attention was moved from paid and owned media to earned media. Research played a role, focus groups were used to pretest the advert, web analytics were used to track the journey of website visitors and SMM was used. Additionally sales audit figures gave a tangible number of increased sales. We are told *'there were 1.6 million YouTube views, 20,000 entries into a campaign-related competition, a 400% increase in site traffic and the sale of 12,000 iTunes downloads of the song'* (Utalkmarketing 2011).

Differences between web analytics and social media monitoring

The features that are at the centre of web analytics fall into the category of *owned and paid-for media* as defined above. This is output produced by companies and their brands rather than created by competitors, customers, or other stakeholders. So we are considering these areas: websites, non-corporate websites (used for promotion and advertising campaigns), online newspapers, corporate blogs, social media presence, mobile websites, and mobile apps. This relationship is shown in Figure 14.1.

The aspects covered by SMM fall into the category of *earned media* as defined above. This is output *about* companies and their brands rather than created by them. Therefore, these are the media involved: customer websites, personal blogs, microblogs (such as twitter), social networks, forums, groups and chat rooms, public emails and messages, consumer reviews, Q & A sites and comments, video, podcasts, wikis, photo sharing sites, and video-sharing site along with the comments, podcasts.

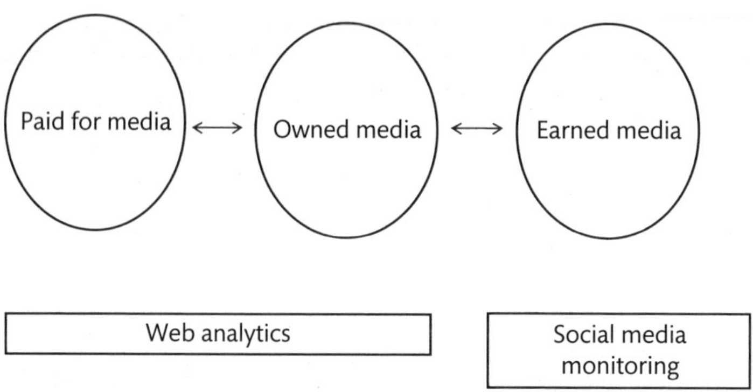

Figure 14.1 The relationship between POEM and analytics

Table 14.2 summarises differences between the two approaches using the framework of the marketing research mix: purpose, population, procedure, and publication. Web analytics has a slightly longer history. Started around 1990 with web counters, 1995 introduced logfile analysis, and then JavaScript tags in 2000. SMM has a very recent history; we can say it started around 2004 with early work by Collective Intellect and Brandwatch. Listening platforms operate in a similar way to search engines and search directories.

Finally let us say that there are many names being used for these two approaches. Web analytics is also known as website analytics or web traffic analysis, and on site visitor reporting tools. Social media monitoring is also known as social media metrics, social media measurement, text analytics, social media listening, social media tracking, social media analytics, social analytics, social marketing analytics, and off site visitor reporting tools.

Purposes of web metrics

Both web analytics and SMM can help improve the effectiveness of marketing by understanding web traffic and the motivations held by web users. They both examine product, promotion, place, and price decisions. Both tools can (and should) be used to optimise the user experience when visitors are on the website, so they do not just concern visitor acquisition.

Brian Clifton (2012) suggested a useful acronym to describe the purposes of web analytics, it is AMAT and means **A**cquisition of visitors - **M**easurement of performance - **A**nalysis of trends - **T**esting to improve. Specifically, the purposes of web analytics are to measure and improve the effective design of web pages and other platforms, they help to make the website the best it can be, or in the language of web analysts, they optimise the website. They also make it possible to understand the relationship between offline and online campaigns. This then allows us to evaluate customer satisfaction and involvement, customer insights are provided, ultimately providing financial guidance on the return on marketing investment (ROMI). Action is taken in the form of redesigning or modifying web pages or specific details of campaigns.

The purposes of SMM are similar but using a different data set and a different audience. On a broad scale this approach allows the tracking of the volume of consumer comment

Table 14.2 Distinctions between web analytics and social media monitoring

Web analytics	Social media monitoring
PURPOSE	
Based on corporate-generated media, mainly investigating *paid-for and owned* media	Based on user-generated media mainly investigating earned media
Analysis will reveal patterns and trends without hypotheses	Hypotheses are valuable, search terms to be monitored must be carefully created
POPULATION	
Output is limited to visitors and audiences to channels of the organisation	Output is large, the size of the Internet user population, channels can be chosen
Audience is made up of website visitors (suspects, prospects, customers, etc.) Does not include competitors	Audience is made up of opinion leaders, influencers and detractors, includes competitors
Segmentation relatively easy	Segmentation less easy as identities are harder to verify online
PROCEDURE	
Can only take place if the company has a website	Can take place without a corporate website
The use of web counters, logfile analysis and JavaScript tags. Packet-sniffing solutions have been used. However, counts are made of cookies and IP addresses, not real visitors	Listening platforms operate in a similar way to search engines and search directories. They are supplemented with data feeds
Data capture and analysis is automated. Results generally delivered directly to clients	Data capture often automated but needs human intervention for analysis. Results reach clients via third parties
Analysis by statistics (numbers)	Analysis by text analytics (words)
Limited number of vendors	Numerous vendors
PUBLICATION	
Organisation has full control over communications visible to the public	Internet users have most control over communications visible to the public
Web users are blind to web analytic results	If web users view conversations, opinions may change
The organisation is less likely to interact with the website visitor	The organisation goes beyond research and will interact individually or collectively

on a market sector, then moving to more specific company names, brands, and promotions. Several key metrics can be seen over time to show engagement, positive and negative sentiment, and other important aspects for specific organisations. Action is taken in the form of responding to individual comments or at a group level. It may also involve modifying the focus of campaigns.

Populations involved in web metrics

The populations measured by **web analysts** include suspects, prospects, customers and non-customers, website visitors, search robots, and affiliate networks.

Suspects, prospects, customers, and non-customers are of interest because they represent the way income will be generated. *Suspects* are people we think may be potential customers but need to be investigated. Attracting them to web pages, addressing any interests they may have, allowing them to interact with our products or personnel can quickly transform them into prospects. *Prospects* need more attention in the form of free samples or trials with the product in order to turn them into customers. *Customers* clearly need to be continually reassured that their choice of company was correct, they need to remain satisfied and we want to keep them loyal, they may need product support. *Non-customers* are using competitor products and services, so they are an important group to attract to the website. Similarly, potential employees and shareholders need information and reassurance.

Website visitors may fall into any of the customer categories described above; once segmented by type and source, using the tools of web analytics, we can further understand their motives for visiting the website.

Search robots visit web pages and are helpful when search results place the site towards the top of lists, so it is important that the site is designed in an optimum way to facilitate this.

Affiliate networks may be associated with the company or web pages, not least because they may direct traffic to the main web pages, therefore this group is important in web analytics.

The populations measured by SMM include customers and non-customers, opinion leaders, influencers, detractors, and stakeholders.

Customers and non-customers, when 'in the wild' will make honest, unguarded comments about the suppliers of their products, which may give us ideas of how to modify the product, promotion, price, or method of distribution.

Opinion leaders, influencers, and detractors can be identified in various ways, and they have a clear impact on brands and reputation. Opinion leaders do not need to be customers to have an effect on the corporation, this applies equally to influencers and detractors. Social media marketing relies on amplifying positive word of mouth and attempting to silence negative word of mouth.

Stakeholders include a vast number of groups ranging from employees, shareholders, suppliers, the surrounding community, trade unions, and even government can be a stakeholder. Again, the social media conversations, once categorised, can show positive, negative, and neutral stances to any initiatives or simply to the company itself.

Procedures involved in the web metrics sector

Web analytics in theory

The procedures of web analytics can be seen in the following steps

1. Decide the objectives
2. Evaluate software available and select data capture method
3. Identify key performance indicators (KPIs) suitable for the objectives
4. Decide dashboard and reporting formats
5. Capture data
6. Analyse results
7. Take action
8. Continue data capture, analysis, and reporting to continually improve.

Websites are monitored in several ways. We will briefly mention a few things of use to the web analyst; these are visitor counters, log files, page tagging, and cookies.

Visitor counters are simply part of a web page that gives a count of the number of visits to the page, they are usually displayed and are visible to any user, and, although they have limited usefulness, they do represent a simple way to monitor web page traffic. Although less popular now, because other means provide richer data, they are still used—YouTube videos all display these numbers and give an indication of popularity.

Logfiles are held in web servers, which are computers that hold and 'serve' websites. The web server reliably records every action each web page makes in order to ensure correct functioning. This information is held in logfiles and, with purpose-built programmes, can be analysed to provide useful data. After several years of use, various disadvantages became apparent with logfile analysis. The limitations of using logfiles were becoming clear as the numbers of visitors was either overestimated or underestimated, this was due to such things as page caches carried out by Internet service providers (to avoid pressure on networks), by the activity of robots, and other issues. A method called tagging emerged as a way to overcome some of the logfile shortfalls. Nevertheless logfiles provide information not available by tagging, so larger organisations will use both for a full picture.

JavaScript tags are a few lines of code that are added to each web page. When a page loads, these tags cause data to be sent to a data collection server (not the web server). This means that the analysis usually shifts from inside the company to a web analysis software provider. Google revolutionised this field in late 2005 by offering a service based on page tagging called Google Analytics. This product was no more remarkable than other services except for one fact—it became the most used software because it was made available free of charge when other suppliers charged by visit volume. See http://www.google.com/analytics

The *'cookie'* is a text file with an identifier that is unique to the user; when a website is visited, a cookie may be placed in the browser. Visits to different pages lead the cookie to send information back to the server. This tracks the movements it observes, mechanically. Cookies are associated with browsers rather than users; therefore, the user's behaviour may not be observed. Cookies have been criticised as being an invasion of privacy to the respondent; however, they are necessary for web pages to function efficiently and they are an important ingredient for web analytic services. It is worthwhile mentioning that cookies are stored on the visitor's machine so users have complete control over viewing and deleting them—either directly or via their browser settings. Therefore, this can lead to inaccuracies in counts. Table 14.3 shows a selection of web analytic services or tools available.

Key performance indicators are measurements that allow managers to assess whether objectives will be met. They are usually quantifiable and will vary from organisation to organisation. Let us look briefly at a few metrics that you will come across in web analytics.

First of all the term *visit* is a measure of the number of sessions an individual user spends on a website or page. We also refer to *visit duration*, which is the number of minutes an individual user spends on a website or page; of course a *visitor* is an individual user who spends time on a web page. *Pageviews* are the number of times a web page was displayed to a user.

Impressions are the number of opportunities people have to see a web page and are important because they form part of the definition for *clickthroughs*, which is the number of times a mouse click was made on a page to reach another page or advert, as a formula:

$$\text{Clickthroughs (N)} = \text{Clickthrough rate (\%)} \times \text{Impressions (N)}.$$

The reaction of a web visitor to an ad or page design is evident in the *clickthrough rate* (CTR), as this is the number of clickthroughs divided by the total number of times the page in question has been served (the number of page impressions).

$$\text{Clickthrough rate \%} = \text{Clickthroughs(N)/Impressions (N)}.$$

If we have a clickthrough rate of 70%, the page may be more popular than another with just 30%. Another measure of the quality of a web page is the *bounce rate*. This is a percentage of visits in which users leave a website from the page they entered. Effectively, there is little of interest and so it is visited once and left immediately. Finally, the *conversion rate* is a percentage

Table 14.3 Website analytics solutions

Type	Description	Example
Visitor counters	Device which counts the number of page hits or visitors, usually displayed on the page	http://www.digits.com http://www.free-counters.co.uk http://www.webcounter.com
Logfile analysis software	Analysis of logfiles from web server transactions	http://www.analog.cx http://awstats.sourceforge.net http://www.mrunix.net/webalizer
Web-tagging	Analysis of web activity where JavaScript tags are added to each page. When a page loads, data are sent to a data collection server	http://www.google.com/analytics http://web.analytics.yahoo.com http://www.omniture.com/en/products/online_analytics http://www.webtrends.com

created by dividing the total number of visitors to a site by the number who carry out some act (such as placing an order or requesting information).

At this point let us mention A/B testing. This is very simple, and direct mail marketers will be familiar with the idea. If we have two executions of a web page, we simply call the first 'A' and the second 'B'. These two pages are created and the server is told to alternate the viewing: so A goes to the first visitor, B to the second, A to the third, and so on. Then a conversion funnel is created for both options and we can see the difference. This is simple but effective experimentation and can be extended to offers communicated. An extension of this test is known as MVA, which means multivariate analysis, it goes beyond testing two versions (bivariate analysis) and tests several versions.

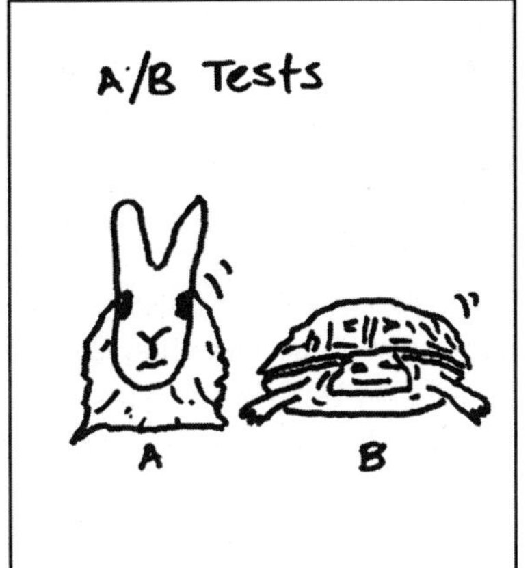

Web analytics in practice

It is a challenge to gain experience without being employed by an organisation and without having access to logfiles and web pages; however, it is not impossible. A first step is to refer to the Website Evaluation Form in the Market Researcher's Toolbox. Use this on two or more websites of your choice, this gives a basic appreciation of what is important in website design before going further into technical details.

Our suggestion as a next stage is to concentrate on page tagging. Logfile analysis requires greater technical expertise, for example the page tagging service manages the process of assigning cookies to visitors; whereas with logfile analysis, the server has to be configured to do this. For these reasons, we will focus on page tagging. A feasible task is to create a blog and to attach tags to each page. Once you have built your confidence doing this contact The Analysis Exchange and offer your time. This is what they say 'we are creating an entirely new way to teach digital measurement best practices by connecting great causes with experienced mentors and motivated students'. The idea is that simple, non-profit organisations are provided with your services, guided by a mentor, all free of charge. The organisations gain rich data, you gain experience, and the mentor has a feeling of altruism. See a full description at http://www.webanalyticsdemystified.com/ae/index.asp

It is suggested that you use Google Analytics because at present this is the most popular method and it is free. There are several steps involved in this

1. To visit Google Analytics at http://www.google.com/analytics
2. Click Sign Up Now (you will need a Gmail account)
3. Follow the instructions and seek any Tutorial Help throughout your learning
4. Google offer an easy-to-use blog service at http://www.blogger.com Of course, you need to create some content, and promote the blog to your colleagues to create some traffic
5. There will come a point where you are instructed to copy some text (Java tracking code) and to paste this into the HTML of your web page. Tracking code will work anywhere on the page but for various reasons it is best placed at the end of the page (right above </body>)

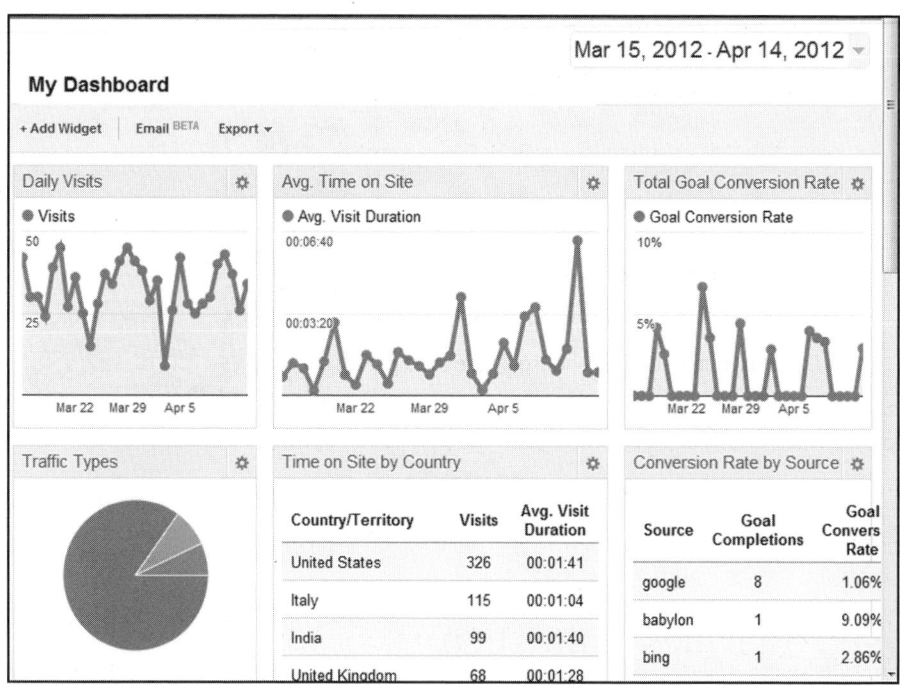

Figure 14.2 Google Analytics standard dashboard

6. Google will automatically create a dashboard for you, and later on you can adapt it to your needs
7. You will need to wait for a few days (48 hours is typical) for traffic to register and be visible on the dashboard. An example is shown in Figure 14.2.

All websites have a purpose, and usually it is to persuade the visitor to carry out some action. It might be to read the content, to sign up to a newsletter, to request a brochure, to make contact or to place an order. The metrics that appear on the dashboard help us to achieve those goals.

Beyond the free tools such as Google and Yahoo Analytics, many services can be accessed. It is worth noting that a series of mergers and name changes has transformed the early pioneers; such consolidation is likely to continue as the sector matures. The following list is in order of market importance and is provided to understand the current offerings: Google Analytics, Adobe Omniture, IBM SPSS, Coremetrics and Unica, Webtrends, Quantcast, Comscore, Yahoo Analytics, and Datanautix. In all cases these and other commercial tools must be evaluated for their appropriateness for the tasks in hand, this can be done by comparing their features: cost, speed, and ease of use. There are audience panel operators under the names of Compete, Comscore, Experian Hitwise, and Nielsen. These companies are able to detect web traffic by knowing which sites their panels visit, usually this is a program installed in the panellist's computer. More traditional and familiar questionnaire formats are used in the so-called Voice of Customer (VOC) services. Protaganists in this area include ForeSee, iPerceptions, Kampyle, and OpinionLabs.

Social media monitoring in theory

The process of SMM can be seen in the following steps

1. Decide the objectives and the reasons for needing data
2. Choose media categories to cover
3. Decide geographic regions and languages to be covered
4. Choose suitable data capture methods
   a. Decide whether to listen in real time or by examining past data
   b. Decide whether to do in-house or use third parties
5. Capture these for analysis
6. Search for keywords on the brand or company and competition
7. Analyse data by categorising conversations
8. Take action—converse and engage with individuals and groups
9. Monitor changes over time.

The methods used for capturing social media data fall into many categories (see Table 14.4), as shown in Figure 14.3 we find an entire reselling sector exists to connect original sources of data with end-users, it matches supply with demand and prices are negotiated accordingly. Therefore, we see that there are aggregators, who combine multiple sources and sell this information on, or there are resellers of single products, for example the entire datastream of twitter is called the 'twitter Firehose' and Gnip was the first company to offer this on behalf of twitter. There are many enterprises involved in this complex area. Sometimes the information physically moves from one place to another, other times it is hosted with one of the intermediaries and therefore updated and interrogated in situ. The public face of SMM are the free and paid-for listening and monitoring services such as Klout and Radian6. These services work behind the scenes buying

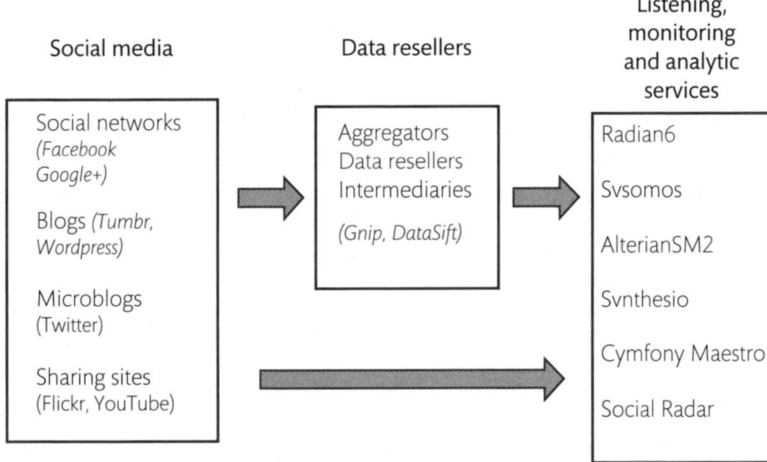

Figure 14.3 Social media data are sold directly and indirectly to analytics firms

Table 14.4 Social media data capture methods

Type	Description	Example
Web crawlers	Have crawlers to create massive data sets that are 'searched' by users of search engines. Simple searching will give results for brand mentions on social medias channels, similarly alerts can be sent to your mailbox	http://www.google.com/alerts http://alerts.yahoo.com/ http://www.google.com/trends/ http://rbl.botslist.ca
Web-scraping software	Extracts information from user-generated content for further scrutiny. This can be automated or done manually. It is more selective than web crawling activity, which copies most material visited. Scraped data are then stored in local databases	http://www.commentful.com/ http://co.comments.com/
RSS and other feeds, firehoses etc.	*Data feeds* need special software readers to understand the information. There are many feeds, some not intended for the public	http://www.radian6.com/crawler/ http://gnip.com/
Human cutting and pasting	Sometimes even the best web-scraping technology cannot replace a human's manual examination and copy and paste, and sometimes this may be the only workable solution when the websites for scraping explicitly set up barriers to prevent machine automation	Crowdsourcing sometimes used to speed up the work http://www.abbottandcox.com/services_crowdsourcing_datamining.shtml
Panels	May give a toolbar to panellists or place software on one or more of the panellist's computers to track visiting behaviour	http://www.alexa.com/ http://www.compete.com/us/about/our-data/ http://www.comscore.com/About_comScore/Methodology http://www.hitwise.com/uk/about-us/how-we-do-it http://www.nielsen-online.com
MROCs	Market Research Online Communities, created especially for the topic under investigation. Community members consent to their comments being used	http://blog.vovici.com/blog/bid/33769/Online-Research-Communities-by-Type
Netnography	Human observation of online communities by participation. This is covert so community members are unaware of any research activity until asked for permission	See Chapter 7 for explanation

and renting media streams to supply a service that looks complete to the user. We will return to free and paid-for services in the section (Social media monitoring in practice).

Let it be said that only information on public sites is subject to resale and use in analysis, Terms of Use (ToU) of most social media sources do not allow the copying and further dissemination of private conversations. Another point worth making is that there is a great deal of spam available on these public sites, and it is essential that software activates some type of spam filter to avoid such 'noise'.

Here we will briefly consider web crawlers, web-scraping software, data feeds (RSS and other feeds, firehoses etc.), human cutting and pasting, panels, MROCs, Netnography, and text analytics.

Web crawlers are software, also known as spiders, robots or bots, which fetch copies of content from the World Wide Web and bring it to local data centres for storage and further manipulation. Regular search engines operate in this way and queries are run against the cached copy, when a result is chosen the link is then reactivated back to the original source on the World Wide Web.

Web-scraping software extracts information from user-generated content for further scrutiny. This can be automated or done manually. It is more selective than web crawling activity, which copies most material visited. Scraped data are then stored in local databases for further interrogation.

Data feeds are sometimes available to the public, and special software readers are needed to understand the information, so with an RSS feed, an RSS reader is needed. There are many other feeds, some not intended for the public, therefore we have the full data set from twitter known as the twitter Firehose, and various parts of it: the halfhose (50% of tweets), the decahose (10% of tweets), the mentionhose (retweets and replies). There are similar services available from providers of blogs, message boards, sharing sites and so on. This is a very efficient way to 'capture' data as the format is known, all that is necessary is to analyse. It should be stated that in some cases the data remain with the seller until required.

Cutting and pasting carried out by a human being is not an efficient method of capturing social media data, but for small companies it may be a feasible way to move data from one place to another for further scrutiny. Certainly to create word clouds and to examine for sentiment it can be a low-cost alternative to subscription to listening services.

Panels in the context of the online world are evident, with companies such as Alexa who have successfully equipped millions of people with their toolbar, this then monitors their online behaviour, permitting the creation of traffic rankings, trends of interest, and social media participation. Other companies take a similar approach Compete (2 million), Hitwise (25 million), Comscore (2 million) and Nielsen Online panel (500,000). The important thing here is to decide which have been carefully calibrated to be representative.

Market Research Online Communities (MROCs) are a recent idea proposed by the market research industry to overcome the idea that social network or forum members have not given permission for their conversations to be used for research purposes. The MROC membership understands the research element from the outset permission is granted, indeed the conversations are driven by research questions. Market Research Online Communities are formed around the topic of interest; they may be temporary or they may outlive an initial research project. Qualitative MROCs typically have 150–200 members and those used for both qual and quant research may be between 300 and 1500.

Netnography is human observation of online communities by participation. This is covert so community members are unaware of any research activity until asked for permission. This is controversial in that privacy can easily become an issue. See Chapter 7 for a fuller explanation.

Key performance indicators are measurements that allow managers to assess whether objectives will be met. They are usually quantifiable and will vary from organisation to organisation. Let us look briefly at a few metrics that you will come across in SMM.

The term *conversation* is used in this area because it is the most frequently used form of communication between people using social media. Conversations come in many forms, and component parts include complaints, compliments, questions, problems and referrals, some of these are negative, some positive and some neutral. Conversations or comments may be forwarded and repeated (as retweets etc.) and this goes to make up a so-called *amplification rate*. This can be measured by detecting the number of times social media buttons were used to share content, so on a blog amplification is the number of share clicks per post.

A related metric is the *applause rate*, which is simply the number of 'Likes' expressed as a number. On Facebook: this is the number of likes per post, on Google Plus it is the number of '+1s' per post.

Engagement is a difficult concept to define but we can agree that it represents the idea that someone's mind is fully occupied and not distracted; therefore we can measure this in terms of the amount or time of interaction, perhaps by looking at the percentage of users who 'interact with a page' out of the total number of 'fans'. This is also called the conversation rate.

Here are three more important metrics:

Share of voice (%) = Brand mentions (N)/Overall conversations (N)

Share of mind (%) = Influencers who mention the brand at least once (N)/Influencers of that community (N)

Share of conversation (%) = Brand mentions of specific topic(N)/Conversations of a topic (N)

Sentiment is a common metric that has commonly been scaled into three: positive, negative, and neutral. This can be extended to five or seven points for greater precision.

Social media monitoring in practice

We must say, as we did for web analytics, that it is a challenge to gain experience in SMM without being employed by an organisation and without having access to vendor databases that can be interrogated; however, it is not impossible. Our suggestion at this stage is to concentrate on services that are freely available. Then move to some solus solutions, once you are familiar with these services go to the websites of paid-for services, familiarise yourself with their offerings and read their case studies and white papers.

It is suggested that you use Google services and alerts because at present these are the most popular methods. There are several steps to follow:

1. First of all decide on a company and brand to investigate, for example we will use Dove soap from Unilever
2. Visit Google at http://www.google.co.uk/intl/en/options/ Here you will see several things of interest: Alerts, Blog Search, Google Trends, Videos

Figure 14.4 Topic cloud of comments about concern for the rainforest, the orangutan, and the trees. Triggered by the keyword Dove

3. Search for your company and brand for each of these, set up an alert
4. At the videos look at one or two videos not produced by your chosen company
5. Look at the comments made by other people. Cut and paste these. We found a GreenPeace video opposed to Dove and extracted the comments
6. Using a word cloud generator at http://www.abcya.com/word_clouds.htm the summary in Figure 14.4 was created, we see that areas of concern are the rainforest, the orang-utan, and the trees.

Choosing a SMM vendor is not an easy task, there are numerous services available. Furthermore, this is a sector where new entrants appear regularly, there are mergers and takeovers, and new product development are rife. Therefore, the offerings by any one company are quickly subject to change. In an attempt to simplify the offerings, Luke Brynley-Jones offers three types (see Table 14.5), to this we have added solus listening platforms.

The following is approximately in order of market importance and is provided to help understand the current marketplace: Alterian SM2, Radian6, Synthesio, Sysomos, Cision, Vocus, Brandchats, Hootsuite, UberVU, Scoutlabs, Filtrbox (Jive), Telligent, Social Radar. A full list can be found at http://www.socialmediamonitoring.ca/monitoring_tools_directory.html

In all cases these and other commercial tools must be evaluated for their appropriateness for the tasks in hand, this can be done by comparing their features: cost, speed, and ease of use.

Table 14.5 Social media monitoring solutions adapted from Brynley-Jones (2011)

Type	Description	Example
Social media listening platforms	Have crawlers to gather data and monitor patterns. These tools have less features than others but more sources and a longer retained history	Nielsen Buzzmetrics http://us.linkfluence.net/ www.brandwatch.com
Monitoring and reporting tools	The most popular monitoring tools focus on real-time monitoring, primarily for PR purposes, so they offer more user-friendly features for tracking conversations and producing reports. Many now offer customer engagement and social CRM features. But they do not retain a long history of data and have been criticised for their data quality and range of sources	http://synthesio.com/corporate/ http://www.radian6.com/ http://buzz.meltwater.com/
Monitoring and engagement tools	Some tools focus on engagement so Community Managers can listen and respond to social media issues in real time. With an emphasis on the dashboard and team-working features, these solutions do not offer many sources but are user-friendly	http://hootsuite.com http://marketmesuite.com www.conversocial.com
Solus listening platforms	Crawl and gather data from single channels such as twitter, blogs etc.	http://www.twitscoop.com/ http://twitterfall.com/ http://www.tweetdeck.com/ http://www.google.com/blogsearch http://openfacebooksearch.com/

Publication considerations in web metrics research

Ethical issues

Guidelines for Social Media Research have been created by various industry bodies such as ESOMAR, for those created by CASRO, see http://www.casro.org/pdfs/1011/Social_Media_Research_Guidelines.pdf These guidelines offer advice on how to protect identities and to respect Terms of Use of the services offered on the web.

Some mechanism must be used to protect the anonymity of people having conversations. We are fully aware of this from traditional qualitative analysis of depths and groups. Online it

Research in focus
Computer software for qualitative analysis

The quiet world of the qualitative researcher was shocked by the arrival of software packages that purported to replace some of the work carried out by the human being. Life would apparently not be the same, and very soon several offerings came to the marketplace such as Nvivo and XSight.

Credit: NVivo and XSight are designed and developed by QSR International Pty Ltd. NVivo and XSight are trademarks or registered trademarks of QSR International. Patent pending. www.qsrinternational.com

The sales description for XSight illustrates some benefits of this approach to the analysis of qualitative data. It says that its product allows the user to import project artefacts and mark up transcripts. There is flexibility in that detailed or brief summaries of data can be entered. Once entered, it is possible to manipulate the data with queries, filtering, and refining. Because images can be imported, it is possible to include these. For content analysis, the software can make instant tallies by using simple frequency counts. Finally, it is easy to create reports and presentations that can be exported to MS Word or MS PowerPoint. In terms of secondary data, the software allows key elements of a project to be stored together and subsequently leads to the development of a cumulative knowledge base.

In Surrey, the CAQDAS Networking Project has no commercial links to software developers, but is funded by the UK Economic and Social Research Council (ESRC). This small entity provides training and information in the use of a range of software programs that have been designed to assist qualitative data analysis. Demonstration versions can be found at the website http://caqdas.soc.surrey.ac.uk

Compiled by Nigel Bradley 2012.

Sources:
http://caqdas.soc.surrey.ac.uk/
http://www.qsrinternational.com/products/productoverview/XSight.htm

Questions

1 What can qualitative software do that other methods cannot?

2 How can software assist in desk research of secondary data?

3 What are the disadvantages of using software?

Common mistakes
Dashboard difficulties

Few (2006) identifies common mistakes with dashboards. They include: going beyond a single screen, giving too much detail, arranging data badly, misuse of colour, cluttering, and using inappropriate displays. See http://www.enterprise-dashboard.com for a dashboard collection.

has been given the name 'masking'—a way to disguise comments or images from computer users so that their identity can be protected in a research context. Here is an example of a comment found in the 'wild' and the same comment which has been masked.

ORIGINAL COMMENT

> 'I live next door to the grocer shop at the front of Old Trafford soccer ground and sometimes the noise is unbearable, I have complained to Councillor Davies but he has no sympathy whatsoever. I don't know what to do next.'
>
> – Alison Hood

MASKED COMMENT

> 'I live near a famous soccer ground in Manchester and sometimes the noise is unbearable, I have complained to a Councillor but he has no sympathy whatsoever. I don't know what to do next.'
>
> – Female user

All social networks and services provided on the World Wide Web have a set of terms of use. Sometimes these state that the information cannot be used outside the service itself, other times there is strong encouragement to share the information, and buttons are often provided. There is also a concept called 'walled gardens', whereby a number of services are selected by providers for their customers, and kept within a secure area only accessible to subscribers. Within these types of areas there may be a rich picking of conversations, reviews, and so on. The social analyst must respect these regulations and where in doubt refuse to monitor conversations.

An example of what happens when a forum is used without permission came in May 2010. Nielsen Buzzmetrics work on behalf of major pharmaceutical companies to investigate and alert them to any negative conversations about their brands. We know that they collect data from 130 million blogs, 8000 message boards, twitter and social networks, but we are unaware of exactly where they focus their listening except for one forum, which did not take kindly to covert subscribers. PatientsLikeMe.com have a discussion board where members exchange personal experiences about emotional disorders. The team at the board detected that a new member of the site was 'scraping' every message from the forum. The news hit the media and it can be argued that the reputation of Nielsen suffered: 'It was a bad legacy practice that we don't do anymore', says Dave Hudson, who took over in June as chief executive of the Nielsen

Research in focus
Dataviewing centres

Nokia, Gatorade, KLM, Volkswagen, and Dell have all got something in common. Each company has created a dedicated space in their offices to view social media in real time. Employees may wish to monitor unfolding stories by day and night, every day of the year.

Gatorade has six large monitors with five seats for viewers in its Chicago office, Dell has ten monitors to track the 22,000 daily topic posts related to the company. The VW room is called the Socialsphere and has 22" touchscreens. The applications pull real-time social data from twitter, Foursquare, and Flickr. Here are some of the names used for this idea:

- Social Media Intelligence Command Centre
- Mission Control Centre
- Ground Control Centre
- Mission Control
- Data Visualisation Centre
- Flight Control Centre
- Social Media Listening Command Centre
- Social Media Listening Post

Compiled by Nigel Bradley 2012.

Sources:

Myatt L. (2010) Dell launches social media ground control. *ContentVox*, 15 December, http://www.contentvox.com/news/dell-launches-social-media-ground-control

Ostrow, A. (2010) Inside Gatorade's Social Media Command Center. *Mashable*, 15 June, http://mashable.com/2010/06/15/gatorade-social-media-mission-control/

van Roekel, E. (2011) Social Media Tools & Listening Centers 2011. *Conversation Management*, 21 July http://www.theconversationmanager.com/2011/07/21/social-media-tools-listening-centers-2011/

Saul, D.J. (2011) "That's cool, but it's 'small' compared to the room we built for VW in Germany" Comment online 24 June, http://www.istrategylabs.com/2011/06/the-socialsphere-data-visualization-in-the-motor-city-of-germany/

Tarran, B. (2012) Nokia puts insights into HQs with visualisers. *Research*, 13 February, http://www.research-live.com/4006873.article

Thompson, B. (2011) The Next-Generation Voice of Customer Command Center: Tool Time for Chief Customer Officers. *Customerthink*. 22 July, http://www.customerthink.com/article/next_generation_voice_of_customer_command_center_tool_time_for_chief_customer_officers

Questions

1 What are the advantages and disadvantages of such accessible rooms for the company?

2 How could and how should a company organise itself to ensure such rooms are constantly monitored?

3 What are the benefits and disadvantages of command centres for customers?

unit that scraped PatientsLikeMe in May. *'It's something that we decided is not acceptable, and we stopped'* (Angwin and Stecklow 2010).

The episode certainly opened a debate and some research agencies decided to create their own MROCS, where members know that their information will be used for research.

Chapter summary

1 List the differences between web analytics and social media monitoring

Web analytics deals with what a company says about itself, looking at owned and paid-for media, rather than output by other people and so called earned media. Web analytics has a slightly longer history as it started around 1990, SMM started around 2004. In the former output is limited to visitors and audiences to channels of the organisation in SMM. Output is as large as the size of the Internet user population. Web analysts use logfile analysis and JavaScript tags to analyse by numbers, whereas listening platforms operate in a similar way to search engines and manipulate words.

2 Explain the purposes of web metrics

Web analytics improves the design of web pages; making it possible to understand the relationship between offline and online campaigns. This then allows us to evaluate customer satisfaction and involvement, ultimately providing the return on marketing investment (ROMI). Action is taken in the form of redesigning or modifying web pages or specific details of campaigns. Social media monitoring tracks consumer comment for market sectors, company names, brands, and promotions. Key metrics show engagement and sentiment. Action is taken in the form of responding to individuals. It may also involve modifying the focus of campaigns. The two approaches improve the effectiveness of marketing by examining product, promotion, place, and price decisions.

3 Describe the populations involved in web metrics

Web analysts examine suspects, prospects, customers, and non-customers because they represent the way income will be generated. Search robots are helpful in optimising search. Affiliate networks are important as they may direct traffic to the website. The populations examined in social media include customers, non-customers, opinion leaders, influencers, and detractors. Stakeholders include employees, shareholders, suppliers, the community, trade unions; even government. For all these groups social media conversations can show positive, negative, and neutral stances.

4 Explain the procedures used in the web metrics sector

The procedures of both web analytics and SMM can be seen in a series of steps beginning with setting objectives, deciding the best way to capture data, which vendors services to use, then how to analyse, and what action to take. Websites are monitored with logfiles and page tagging, whereas social media data capture uses web crawlers, web-scraping software and data feeds. There are various key performance indicators (KPIs) associated with each approach: web analysts use visitors, visits, visit duration, pageviews, impressions, clickthrough, bounce, and conversion rate. In SMM, KPIs include the amplification rate, the applause rate, engagement , share of voice, share of mind, share of conversation, and finally sentiment commonly scaled as positive, negative, and neutral.

5 Show what must be considered at the publication stage of web metrics research

Ethical issues are important and several industry bodies have developed guidelines for social media research. These guidelines contain such things as 'masking'—a way to disguise comments so that identities can be protected. All social networks have terms of use, sometimes these prohibit the use of comments outside the service and the social analyst must respect this. Some research agencies decided to create their own Market Research Online Communities (MROCs), where members know that their information will be used for research, effectively circumventing restrictions posed by existing forums.

Review questions

1 What are the similarities between web analytics and social media monitoring?

2 Why is an understanding of the objectives of web analytics and social media monitoring important to top management, marketing managers, and the personnel implementing web analytics and social media monitoring?

3 In which circumstances might we decide to use web analytics rather than social media monitoring?

4 Web analysts and social media monitoring researchers have been criticised for publishing results based on dubious foundations. Why are they criticised and why might this happen?

5 Define these terms using examples: bounce rate, tonality, scraping.

Discussion questions

1 Apply the POEM model to a campaign you have seen recently. You may need to investigate parts of the campaign that you are unaware of, therefore search YouTube, the social networks, and blog search engines. What have you learnt from this?

2 Investigate the role of social media monitoring for the business-to-business sector.

3 How would small businesses differ from large corporations in the use of web analytics and social media monitoring?

4 How can dashboards mislead users of research results?

5 Create a draft analytics plan for a company selling a well-known chocolate bar. Your plan should propose using Google Analytics and one of the free twitter monitoring tools.

Further reading

- Clifton, B. (2012) *Advanced web metrics with Google analytics*. 3rd edition. Indianapolis, John Wiley & Sons.
  An excellent book with everything necessary on the subject of Google Analytics and web analytics in general.
- Lovett J. (2011) *Social Media Metrics Secrets!* Indianapolis: Wiley.
  The author has a vast knowledge of Social Media research. A thorough book on this subject.

Key web links

- The Digital Analytics Association (DAA) http://www.digitalanalyticsassociation.org
- Social Media Advertising Consortium (SMAC) http://www.smac.org
- Google Analytics Website http://www.google.com/analytics/

Online Resource Centre
www.oxfordtextbooks.co.uk/orc/bradley/3e

Visit the Online Resource Centre that accompanies this book to access more learning resources on this chapter topic.

References and sources

Angwin, J. and Stecklow, S. (2010) Scrapers' Dig Deep for Data on Web, *Wall Street Journal*, 11 October, http://online.wsj.com/article/SB10001424052748703358504575544381288117888.html

Arikan, A. (2008) *Multichannel marketing: metrics and methods for on and offline success*. Indianapolis: John Wiley & Sons.

Brown, E. (2010) *Working the Crowd: Social Media Marketing for Business*. Swindon, UK: British Informatics Society Ltd.

Brynley-Jones, L. (2011) *The 3 types of social media monitoring tools*. 21 July, blog at http://www.monitoring-social-media.com/the-3-types-of-social-media-monitoring-tools.

Burcher, N. (2012) *Paid, Owned, Earned: Maximising Marketing Returns in a Socially Connected World*, London: Kogan Page.

Clifton, B. (2012) *Advanced web metrics with Google analytics*. 3rd edition. Indianapolis: John Wiley & Sons.

Corcoran, S. (2009) *Defining Earned, Owned And Paid Media*. 16 December 16, http://blogs.forrester.com/interactive_marketing/2009/12/defining-earned-owned-and-paid-media.html

Evans, D. (2010) *Social media marketing: an hour a day*. Indianapolis: Wiley Publishing.

Goodall, D. (2009) *Owned, Bought and Earned Media*. 2 March 2, http://danielgoodall.com/2009/03/02/owned-bought-and-earned-media/

Hamel, S. (2009) *The web analytics maturity model. A strategic approach based on business maturity* and critical success factors, https://docs.google.com/viewer?url=http%3A%2F%2Fwww.cardinalpath.com%2Fcpwp%2Fwp-content%2Fuploads%2FWAMM_ShortPaper_091017.pdf (See http://www.cardinalpath.com/oamm/assessment/ to create a live assessment for any company you know.)

Kaushik, A. (2007) *Web analytics: an hour a day*. Indianapolis: John Wiley & Sons.

Kaushik, A. (2010) *Web Analytics 2.0*. Sybex, Wiley.

Kaushik, A. (2009) *Who Owns Web Analytics? A Framework For Critical Thinking*. 9 December, http://www.kaushik.net/avinash/owns-web-analytics-framework-critical-thinking/

Kozinets, R. V., De Valck, K., Wojnicki, A. C., and Wilner, S. J. S. (2010). Networked Narratives: Understanding Word-of-Mouth Marketing in Online Communities. *Journal of Marketing* 74(2), pp. 71–89.

Kutcher, A. and Solis, B. (2011) *Engage: The Complete Guide for Brands and Businesses to Build, Cultivate, and Measure Success in the New Web*, New Jersey: John Wiley & Sons.

Lovett J. (2011) *Social Media Metrics Secrets!* Indianapolis: Wiley Publishing.

Miller, J. (2011) New Survey Results: Nearly Half of SMBs Utilize Social Media Marketing. *Zoomerang Blog* 8 September, http://www.zoomerang.com/

blog/2011/09/08/new-survey-results-nearly half-smbs-utilize-social-media-marketing

Nakatani, K. and Chuang, T-T (2011) A web analytics tool selection method: an analytical hierarchy process approach. *Internet Research*, 21(2), pp. 171–186.

Peterson, E. T. (2004) *Web analytics demystified: a marketer's guide to understanding how your web site affects your business.* USA: Celilo Group Media.

Peterson, E. T. (2005) *Web site measurement hacks.* O Reilly & Associates.

Peterson, E. T. (2006) *The Big Book of Key Performance Indicators*, Self Published.

Powell, G.R., Groves, S. W. and Domos, G. (2011) *ROI of Social Media. How to improve the return on your social marketing investment.* Singapore: John Wiley.

Social Media Examiner (2012) *The 2012 Social Media Marketing Industry report*, http://www.socialmediaexaminer.com/social-media-marketing-industry-report-2012/

Sponder, M. (2012) *Social Media Analytics: Effective Tools for Building, Interpreting and Using Metrics.* Whitby, ON, USA: McGraw Hill Ryerson.

Sterne, J. (2002) *Web Metrics. Proven methods for measuring web site success*, New Jersey: Wiley.

Sterne, J. (2010) *Social Media Metrics. How to measure and optimise your marketing investment*, New Jersey: Wiley.

Utalkmarketing (2011) *How Yeo Valley used rap to make organic food accessible*, 14 February, http://www.utalkmarketing.com/Pages/Article.aspx?ArticleID=20333&Title=How_Yeo_Valley_used_rap_to_make_organic_food_accessible

Market Researcher's Toolbox

Contents

Checklist for audit of MR activities

Does the organisation carry out any of the following?

	Yes	No
Purpose		
New product development research	☐	☐
Product tests	☐	☐
Package tests	☐	☐
Brand tracking research	☐	☐
Brand research	☐	☐
Place/outlet research	☐	☐
Price research	☐	☐
Sale promotion research	☐	☐
Pre-advertising research	☐	☐
Post-advertising research	☐	☐
Media research	☐	☐
Public relations research	☐	☐
Sales force research	☐	☐
Satisfaction research	☐	☐
Usage and attitude studies	☐	☐
Competitive research	☐	☐
Population		
New customer research	☐	☐
Lapsed customer research	☐	☐
Potential customer research	☐	☐
Existing customer research	☐	☐
Competitor research	☐	☐
Employee research	☐	☐
Shareholder research	☐	☐
Journalist research	☐	☐
Retailer research	☐	☐
Wholesaler research	☐	☐
Channel/intermediary research	☐	☐
Procedure		
Continuous research	☐	☐
Snapshot research	☐	☐
Secondary internal data research	☐	☐
Secondary external data research	☐	☐

Semiotic research	☐	☐
Ethnographic research	☐	☐
Website usability research	☐	☐
Social media monitoring	☐	☐
Web analytics research	☐	☐
Panel research	☐	☐
Qualitative research	☐	☐
Quantitative research	☐	☐
Mystery shopping	☐	☐
Retail audits	☐	☐
Omnibus research	☐	☐

Publication

Strategic decision-maker reporting in place	☐	☐
Operational decision-maker reporting in place	☐	☐
Tactical decision-maker reporting in place	☐	☐
Frequent reporting	☐	☐
Dashboard reporting	☐	☐
Hard copy reports	☐	☐
Presentations	☐	☐

Checklist for objective verbs

Does the research lend itself to using these verbs in the objectives?

	Yes	No
Qualitative objectives		
To ascertain	☐	☐
To assess	☐	☐
To choose	☐	☐
To compare	☐	☐
To define	☐	☐
To describe	☐	☐
To determine	☐	☐
To establish	☐	☐
To examine	☐	☐
To explore	☐	☐
To generate	☐	☐
To identify	☐	☐
To investigate	☐	☐
To obtain	☐	☐

To select	☐	☐
To uncover	☐	☐

Quantitative

To audit	☐	☐
To benchmark	☐	☐
To compare	☐	☐
To consider	☐	☐
To evaluate	☐	☐
To measure	☐	☐
To monitor	☐	☐
To prioritize	☐	☐
To profile	☐	☐
To select	☐	☐
To test	☐	☐
To track	☐	☐

Marketing metrics checklist: boardroom

Do your objectives require any of the following metrics to be built into the research design?

	Yes	No
Average acquisition cost	☐	☐
Average retention cost	☐	☐
Brand development index	☐	☐
Brand penetration	☐	☐
Category development index	☐	☐
Customer lifetime value	☐	☐
Customer profit	☐	☐
Economic profit (EVA)	☐	☐
Internal rate of return (IRR)	☐	☐
Market penetration	☐	☐
Market share	☐	☐
Net present value (NPV)	☐	☐
Net profit	☐	☐
Payback	☐	☐
Penetration share	☐	☐
Prospect lifetime value	☐	☐
Relative market share	☐	☐
Retention rate	☐	☐

	Yes	No
Return on investment (ROI)	☐	☐
Return on marketing investment (ROMI); revenue	☐	☐
Return on sales (ROS)	☐	☐
Unit share	☐	☐

Marketing metrics checklist: product

Do your objectives require any of the following metrics to be built into the research design?

	Yes	No
Average price per unit	☐	☐
Brand equity	☐	☐
Cannibalization rate	☐	☐
Conjoint utilities and consumer preferences	☐	☐
Conjoint utilities and volume projections	☐	☐
Contribution margin (%)	☐	☐
Contribution per unit	☐	☐
Growth (CAGR)	☐	☐
Growth (percentage)	☐	☐
Margin (%)	☐	☐
Penetration	☐	☐
Price per statistical unit	☐	☐
Repeat volume	☐	☐
Segment utilities	☐	☐
Target revenues	☐	☐
Target volume	☐	☐
Unit margin	☐	☐
Variable and fixed costs	☐	☐
Volume projections	☐	☐

Marketing metrics checklist: promotion

Do your objectives require any of the following metrics to be built into the research design?

	Yes	No
Ad awareness	☐	☐
Average frequency	☐	☐
Brand knowledge	☐	☐
Cost per thousand impressions (CPM)	☐	☐
Customer satisfaction	☐	☐

Effective frequency	☐	☐
Effective reach	☐	☐
Frequency response	☐	☐
Gross rating points (GRPs)	☐	☐
Impressions	☐	☐
Intentions	☐	☐
Likeability	☐	☐
Loyalty	☐	☐
Net reach	☐	☐
Prompted awareness	☐	☐
Purchase habits	☐	☐
Spontaneous awareness	☐	☐
Top of mind	☐	☐
Willingness to recommend	☐	☐
Willingness to search	☐	☐

Marketing metrics checklist: place

Do your objectives require any of the following metrics to be built into the research design?

	Yes	No
All-commodity volume (ACV)	☐	☐
Channel margins	☐	☐
Direct product profitability (DPP)	☐	☐
Facings	☐	☐
Gross margin return on inventory investment (GMROII)	☐	☐
Inventories	☐	☐
Markdowns	☐	☐
Numeric distribution (%)	☐	☐
Out of stock (%)	☐	☐
Product category volume (PCV)	☐	☐
Total distribution (%)	☐	☐

Marketing metrics checklist: price

Do your objectives require any of the following metrics to be built into the research design?

	Yes	No
Optimal price	☐	☐
Percent good value	☐	☐

Price elasticity of demand	☐	☐
Price premium	☐	☐
Reservation price	☐	☐
Residual elasticity	☐	☐

Marketing metrics checklist: sales force

Do your objectives require any of the following metrics to be built into the research design?

	Yes	No
Average deal depth	☐	☐
Baseline sales	☐	☐
Compensation	☐	☐
Costs for coupons and rebates	☐	☐
Incremental sales/promotion lift	☐	☐
Pass-through	☐	☐
Percent sales on deal	☐	☐
Percent time on deal	☐	☐
Percentage sales with coupon	☐	☐
Price waterfall	☐	☐
Redemption rates	☐	☐

Marketing metrics checklist: web metrics

Do your objectives require any of the following metrics to be built into the research design?

	Yes	No
Abandonment rate	☐	☐
Amplification rate	☐	☐
Applause rate	☐	☐
Bounce rate	☐	☐
Click-through rate	☐	☐
Conversion rate	☐	☐
Cost per click	☐	☐
Cost per customer acquired	☐	☐
Cost per order	☐	☐
Engagement	☐	☐
Impressions	☐	☐
Page views	☐	☐
Sentiment tone	☐	☐

Share of conversation	☐	☐
Share of mind	☐	☐
Share of voice	☐	☐
Visit duration	☐	☐
Visitors	☐	☐
Visits	☐	☐

Questions to ask about secondary data

Purpose

- Why was it done?
- Who paid for it?
- What was the problem to be solved?

Population

- Who are the players in the sector?
- Who was interviewed? How many?
- What was the source of names?

Procedure

- What data capture method was used?
- What quality control was there?
- Does the method make sense? What is wrong?

- Is it valid and reliable?

Publication

- Why was it distributed?
- Who are the likely readers?
- What decisions may have been made on the basis of this project?

Options for primary data capture

Pre-notification to respondent

By advert	☐	By post	☐
By fax	☐	By leaflet drop	☐
By phone	☐	By email	☐
In person	☐	By word of mouth	☐

Questionnaire delivery

By phone	☐	In person	☐
By post	☐	By fax	☐
By email	☐	By web	☐
Other	☐		

Questionnaire retrieval

By phone	☐	In person	☐
By post	☐	By fax	☐
By email	☐	By web	☐
Other	☐		

Reminder options

Reminder delivery

By phone	☐	In person	☐
By post	☐	By fax	☐
By email	☐	By web	☐
Other	☐		

Number of reminders

☐ One ☐ Two
☐ Three ☐ More

Nature of reminders

☐ Individual ☐ Mass
☐ Mass with appearance of customized

Timing of reminders

☐ When replies stop ☐ After a specified time
☐ When replies slow ☐ Other

Checklist for focus groups

Purpose

	Yes	No
Are the objectives agreed with the client?	☐	☐
Is the topic guide agreed with the client?	☐	☐

Population

	Yes	No
Are invitations organised?	☐	☐
Will respondents talk?	☐	☐
Do respondents have things in common?	☐	☐
Will there be respondent harmony?	☐	☐

Number of respondents

2 3 4 5 6 7 8 9 10 11 +

Procedure

	Yes	No
Is the moderator trained?	☐	☐
Has the moderator been briefed on this study?	☐	☐
Has the moderator learnt the technical aspects of this sector?	☐	☐
Has the moderator learnt the brand names in this sector?	☐	☐
Has the moderator agreed projective techniques?	☐	☐

Group type

Face to face	☐	Video conference	☐		
Telephone conference	☐	Online	☐		

Duration

30 minutes	☐	45 minutes	☐	1 hour	☐
1.5 hours	☐	2 hours	☐	3 hours	☐

Venue

House	☐	Office	☐	Hotel	☐
Agency	☐	Pub	☐	Studio	☐

Observation

None	☐	Mirror	☐		
In-room	☐	Remote viewing	☐		

Stimulus material

None	☐	Visual	☐	Sound	☐
Smell	☐	Taste	☐	Texture	☐

Incentives

None	☐	Money	☐	Gift	☐
Food	☐	Other	☐ ______		

Ease of travel for respondents

Railway station	☐	Airport	☐	Taxis	☐
Parking	☐	Other	☐ ______		

Data capture

None	☐	Video	☐		
Audio	☐	Other	☐ ______		

Seat layout (see diagrams)

Round ☐

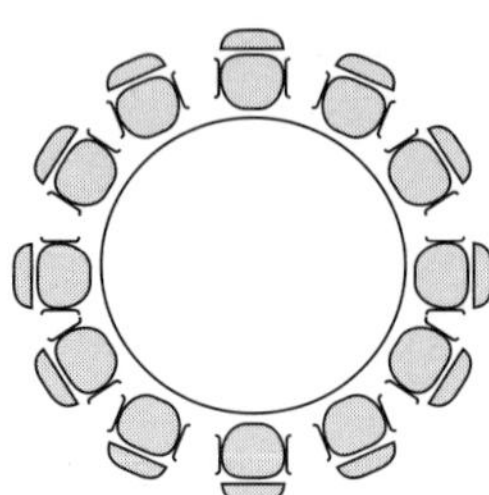

Horseshoe ☐

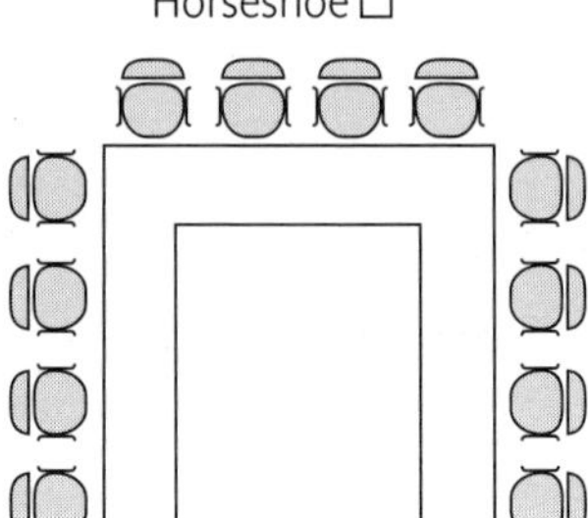

Oval ☐

Theatre ☐

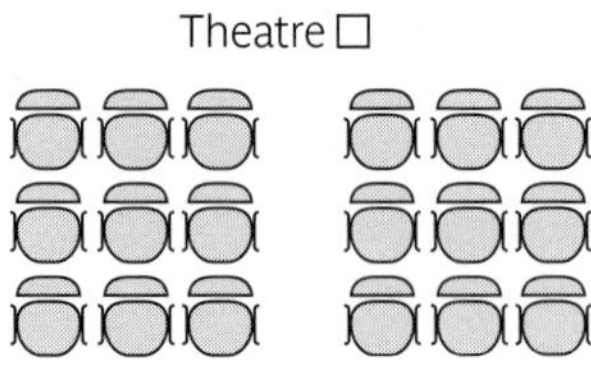

(Hollow) Square ☐

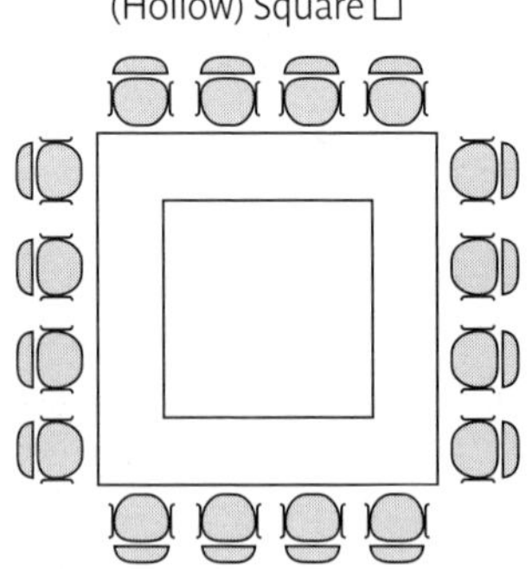

Classroom ☐

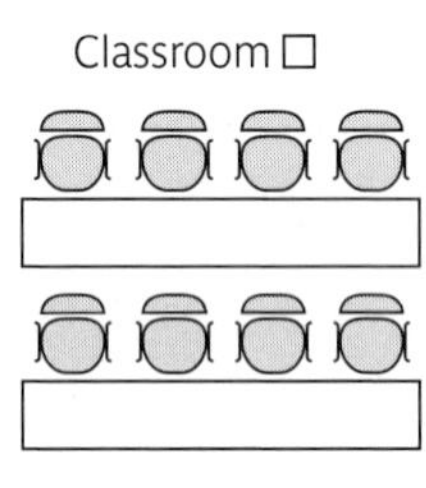

Website evaluation form

1 URL ______________________ Time evaluation started ____________________

2 Effective use of visuals

Strongly agree 1 2 3 4 5 6 Strongly disagree

Comments: ____

3 Consistent look and feel throughout site

Strongly agree 1 2 3 4 5 6 Strongly disagree

Comments: ____

4 Professional use of wording

Strongly agree 1 2 3 4 5 6 Strongly disagree

Comments: ______________________

5 Site easy to navigate

Strongly agree 1 2 3 4 5 6 Strongly disagree

Comments: ______________________

6 Site features good FAQs

Strongly agree 1 2 3 4 5 6 Strongly disagree

Comments: ______________________

7 Site contents are appealing

Strongly agree 1 2 3 4 5 6 Strongly disagree

Comments: ______________________

8 Site appears to be up to date

Strongly agree 1 2 3 4 5 6 Strongly disagree

Comments: ______________________

9 Overall evaluation of site

Excellent 1 2 3 4 5 6 Poor

Comments: ______________________

10 Would you recommend this site to other people? (Please tick as appropriate.)

Yes ☐ No ☐ Don't know ☐

Date ______________ Time evaluation ended ______________________

© Nigel Bradley 2012. This observation form is duplicated and completed for several sites. An average for each feature can be calculated and comparisons made with individual sites. Based on various ideas, including some from Misic, M.M. and Johnson, K.L. (1999) Benchmarking: a tool for website evaluation and improvement, *Internet Research: Electronic Networking Applications and Policy*, **9**(5), 383–92.

Common screener questions

Introductory remarks and screener questions help to establish whether a person is eligible for the interview; this means that they are designed in conjunction with the sampling procedure. Some questions in the classification section (see later) may need to come forward to this part of the interview.

This is a crucial time because a negative word, remark, or tone of voice can lead to refusal or bias in subsequent responses. The general rule is to minimize the time (and words). Therefore the interviewer must have a script but must know what can be left unsaid; the word 'optional' indicates what can be left out. Codes of conduct say that the average interview length must be specified. This can be determined by pilots and changed during fieldwork, looking at real averages of earlier interviews.

S1 Hello, my name is ____________ calling from _____.

S2a Please may I speak to ____________? or

S2b Please may I speak to the person in your household/company responsible for__?

S3 We are conducting a survey about _____ and would like to know your views and opinions.

S4 Would you mind spending __ minutes helping us by answering a few questions?

S5 (OPTIONAL) Please be assured that any comments you make will be kept confidential to the research team. Final results will be added together.

An 'exclusion screener' is a question posed to determine if the informant, or their family or friends, work in specific occupations. If the answer is 'Yes', then the interview will not take place. Other occupations related to the topic under study may be added to this list. The idea behind this is to avoid news of this project reaching competitors and also to avoid answers that might not be typical of the target audience.

Ex. 1 Do you, or any members of your family, or close friends, work in any of the following industries?

Market research .... ☐

Advertising or marketing .... ☐

Journalism .... ☐

An organisation involved with_____ .... ☐

(If 'yes', close.)

Common rating scales

Simple itemized rating scales in common use

Excellent	Good	Fair	Poor	
Very interested	Somewhat interested	Not very interested		
Very good	Fairly good	Neither	Not very good	Not good at all
Very true	Somewhat true	Not very true	Not at all true	
Very important	Fairly important	Neutral	Not so important	Not at all important
Definitely yes	Probably yes	Probably no	Definitely no	
Very important	Fairly important	Neither	Not very important	Not at all important
Very different	Somewhat different	Slightly different	Not at all different	
Extremely unique	Very unique	Somewhat unique	Slightly unique	Not at all unique

Likert scales

Strongly disagree	1	2	3	4	5	6	7	Strongly agree
Strongly disagree	☐	☐	☐	☐	☐	☐	☐	Strongly agree

Strongly disagree   Somewhat disagree   Undecided   Somewhat agree   Strongly agree

Strongly agree   Agree   Undecided   Disagree   Strongly disagree

Strongly agree   Agree   Neither   Disagree   Strongly disagree

Strongly agree   Tend to agree   Neither   Tend to disagree   Strongly disagree

Simple satisfaction rating scales in common use

How satisfied are you with ________?

1 Very dissatisfied
2 Somewhat dissatisfied
3 Neither satisfied nor dissatisfied
4 Somewhat satisfied
5 Very satisfied

Recommendation to a friend

How likely would you be to recommend _______ to a friend?

1 Very likely
2 Somewhat likely
3 Neither likely nor unlikely
4 Somewhat unlikely
5 Very unlikely

Common classification questions

These questions have been derived from commercial and government studies. Therefore they allow results to be compared with widely published population data. It is unlikely that you would use all the questions in a single project, and they would normally appear at the end of a questionnaire. Question numbers help to identify items of interest. For details of UK government question harmonization, see http://surveynet.ac.uk/sqb/harmonisation/ons.asp

Q1 Sex   Male ☐   Female ☐

Q2a Respondent working status (tick appropriate box below)

Q2b Chief income earner (CIE), working status (tick appropriate box below)

	Q2a	Q2b
Working full-time (30 hours or more per week)	☐	☐
Working part-time (8–29 hours per week)	☐	☐

Working part-time (less than 8 hours per week)	☐	☐
Full-time student	☐	☐
Retired from full-time job	☐	☐
Other/not working	☐	☐

Q3 Exact age last birthday: ____________years

(Record age and code below. If respondent refuses exact age ask: 'Which age group applies to you?')

15–17	☐
18–24	☐
25–29	☐
30–34	☐
35–39	☐
40–44	☐
45–49	☐
50–54	☐
55–59	☐
60–64	☐
65+	☐

Q4a Occupation details of CIE

Occupation ______________________________

Industry ______________________________

Qualifications/apprenticeships ______________________________

Number of people responsible for ______________________________

Number in establishment ______________________________

Q4b Occupation details of respondent

Occupation ______________________________

Industry ______________________________

Qualifications/apprenticeships ______________________________

Number of people responsible for ______________________________

Number in establishment ______________________________

Q5a Household social grade*

A	☐	B	☐	C1	☐
C2	☐	D	☐	E	☐

Q5b Individual social grade*

A	☐	B	☐	C1	☐
C2	☐	D	☐	E	☐

**Q4 allows researcher to determine the grade; see also MRS Dictionary*

Q6 Marital status

Single	☐
Married/civil partner/living as married	☐
Widowed	☐
Divorced	☐
Separated	☐

Q7 Are you responsible, or mainly responsible, for the household shopping?

Yes ☐

No ☐

Q8a What is the total number of people in your household, including yourself and any children?

1 2 3 4 5 6 7 8 9+

Q8b How many people aged 15+ are there in your household (including yourself)?

1 2 3 4 5 6 7 8 9+

Q9 At what age did you finish your full-time education? (*i.e. terminal education age (TEA)*)

15 or under ☐

16 ☐

17–18 ☐

19+ ☐

Still at school/full-time student ☐

Q10 How many children are there in your household aged:

0–4 __________

5–9 __________

10–14 ________

Q11 Which, if any, of these items are there in your household?

Television set(s) ☐

Satellite TV (requiring a satellite dish) ☐

Cable TV ☐

Telephone ☐

Video recorder ☐

Mobile phone ☐

Personal computer* ☐

Video games console (NOT home computer) ☐

None ☐

**PC, PCTV, desktop, laptop, or other type of home computer*

Q12 Which of these applies to your home? (*i.e. tenure*)

It is being bought on a mortgage ☐

It is owned outright ☐

It is rented from the local authority ☐

It is rented from a private landlord ☐

It belongs to a housing association ☐

Other ☐

Q13 Income showcard

Which of these ranges comes closest to the total annual income of the whole of your household, before anything is deducted for tax, National Insurance, pension schemes, etc.?

Please indicate which letter applies to you.

(The card shows the letters A to L with ranges of income; the respondent simply answers with a letter so that no one can hear an amount. Often the letters are mixed up so that L is not the highest.)

Q14 Does your household have the use of a car for private motoring?

Yes ☐
No ☐
If 'yes': How many?

Q15 What is your ethnic group?

A. White
English/Welsh/Scottish ☐
Northern Irish/British ☐
Irish ☐
Gypsy or Irish Traveller ☐
Other ☐

B. Mixed
White and Black Caribbean ☐
White and Black African ☐
White and Asian ☐
Other ☐

C. Asian or Asian British
Indian ☐
Pakistani ☐
Bangladeshi ☐
Chinese ☐
Other ☐

D. Black or Black British
Caribbean ☐
African ☐
Other ☐

E. Other ethnic group
Arab ☐
Other ☐

Q16 What is your religion?

None ☐
Christian* ☐
Buddhist ☐
Hindu ☐
Muslim ☐
Sikh ☐
Other ☐

**(includes Church of England, Catholic, Protestant, and all other Christian denominations)*

Q17 Respondent details

First name ______________________ Surname ______________________
Informant telephone numbers (home, work, mobile) ______________________

Informant address ______________________________
Street ______________________________
Town ______________________________
Postcode ______________________________

Q18 Thank you very much for taking part in this survey.
Would you be willing to take part in similar surveys in the future?

Yes ☐
No ☐

Interviewer declaration: I declare that the informant was unknown to me until the interview took place; and that this questionnaire has been conducted according to the manual and the MRS code of conduct, and has been checked.

Signed ______________________________
Date ______________________________
Length of interview in minutes ______________________________

Checklist for sampling

Purpose

	Yes	No
Is the sample representative?	☐	☐
Will the required precision be achieved?	☐	☐

Population

	Yes	No
Has the population size been established?	☐	☐
Is the population articulate?	☐	☐
Is a suitable sampling frame available?	☐	☐
Is the sampling frame easy to use?	☐	☐
Is the sampling frame complete?	☐	☐
Have duplicates already been removed?	☐	☐
Is screening efficient?	☐	☐
Will exclusion screeners affect sampling?	☐	☐
Is sample size correct?	☐	☐

Procedure

	Yes	No
Is field piloting planned?	☐	☐
Will sampling happen in the field?	☐	☐
Are there good instructions for fieldworkers?	☐	☐
Is the fieldworker workload reasonable?	☐	☐
Are quota controls efficient?	☐	☐
Will sampling happen in the office?	☐	☐

Publication

	Yes	No
Do screener questions match sampling?	☐	☐
Is the recording method efficient?	☐	☐
Is personal data kept secure?	☐	☐
Is the Data Protection Act respected?	☐	☐
Is the MRS Code respected?	☐	☐

Checklist for online surveys

Purpose

	Yes	No
Is anything missing?	☐	☐
Does it match the objectives?	☐	☐

Population

	Yes	No
Can the respondent navigate easily?	☐	☐
Is it multilingual?	☐	☐
Can the respondent stop and resume later?	☐	☐
Is DOB asked? (to exclude minors/multiple forms)	☐	☐
Are minors screened out?	☐	☐
Can non-technical respondents use it?	☐	☐
Will all browser types see it in the same way?	☐	☐

Procedure

	Yes	No
Does it follow 'best practice' guidelines?	☐	☐
Does it follow data protection laws?	☐	☐
Are radio button pre-settings disabled?	☐	☐
Is the software set to refuse multiple attempts?	☐	☐
Is routing documented for other researchers/clients?	☐	☐
Is the postcode asked for? (to check for multiple submissions)	☐	☐
Is the software set to stop entries after fieldwork ends?	☐	☐

Publication

	Yes	No
Do extra windows carry other questions?	☐	☐
Is there a 'progress bar'?	☐	☐

Is there a link to your organisation's website?	☐	☐
Does your email address appear?	☐	☐
Can the respondent link to your privacy statement?	☐	☐
Is emphasis used (italics, bold type, etc.)?	☐	☐
Are there regular summaries?	☐	☐
Are there a variety of visuals?	☐	☐
Is the font size large enough?	☐	☐
Is everything visible without scrolling?	☐	☐
Are there less than 50 words per CAWI screen?	☐	☐
Are there less than 25 words per CAMI screen?	☐	☐
Are grids used sensibly?	☐	☐

Checklist of projective techniques

Is this technique suitable for your chosen respondent group?

	Yes	No
Association		
Image response	☐	☐
Picture association	☐	☐
Word association	☐	☐
Completion tasks		
Cartoon completion	☐	☐
Picture completion	☐	☐
Picture frustration test	☐	☐
Picture interpretation	☐	☐
Sentence completion	☐	☐
Story completion	☐	☐
Thematic apperception test	☐	☐
Analogy		
Analogy/symbolic analogy	☐	☐
Brand personalities	☐	☐
Indirect questions	☐	☐
Metaphor	☐	☐
Obituary	☐	☐
Personification	☐	☐
Role-playing	☐	☐
Third-person test	☐	☐

Techniques that require respondent effort

Brand mapping	☐	☐
Collage	☐	☐
Construction tasks	☐	☐
Creative writing	☐	☐
Fantasy	☐	☐
Friendly Martian	☐	☐
Future scenario	☐	☐
Gaming	☐	☐
Network pictures	☐	☐
Photo and tale method/photosorts	☐	☐
Pictured aspirations technique	☐	☐
Postcard writing	☐	☐
Protocol analysis	☐	☐
Psychodrama	☐	☐
Psychodrawing	☐	☐
Role-playing	☐	☐
Shopping lists	☐	☐
Storytelling	☐	☐

Checklist for questionnaires

Purpose

	Yes	No
Do the questions cover the objectives?	☐	☐
Does the intro explain the purpose?	☐	☐
Is commercial sensitivity protected?	☐	☐
Does the intro avoid 'priming' the respondent?	☐	☐
Is the client identified directly or indirectly?	☐	☐
Does the intro give the length of interview?	☐	☐
Is the code of conduct fully considered?	☐	☐
Is it complete?	☐	☐

Population

	Yes	No
Are there assurances (of confidentiality, privacy)?	☐	☐
Does the screener match sampling?	☐	☐

Is screening efficient?	☐	☐
Is an exclusion screener used?	☐	☐
Is the respondent able to answer?	☐	☐
Is the respondent willing to answer?	☐	☐
Is the respondent's workload reasonable?	☐	☐
Are there good instructions for respondents?	☐	☐
Does it ask for age, sex, and occupation?	☐	☐
Are other classification questions asked?	☐	☐
Are there any sleeper (integrity) questions?	☐	☐

Procedure

	Yes	No
Will other researchers check it before use?	☐	☐
Is field piloting planned?	☐	☐
Are there good instructions for fieldworkers?	☐	☐
Is the interviewer's workload reasonable?	☐	☐

Publication

	Yes	No
Is the recording method efficient?	☐	☐
Is the wording clear?	☐	☐
Is the question sequence logical?	☐	☐
Are there a variety of techniques?	☐	☐
Is there good use of showcards/stimuli?	☐	☐
Are filters used properly?	☐	☐
Is any wording ambiguous?	☐	☐
Are double-barrelled questions avoided?	☐	☐
Are leading questions avoided?	☐	☐
Are there any cheater (integrity) questions?	☐	☐

Checklist for report-writing

Purpose

	Yes	No
Do the sections cover the objectives?	☐	☐
Is everything there?	☐	☐
Do the subheadings/titles give key facts?	☐	☐

Population

	Yes	No
Can the reader scan and skim-read easily?	☐	☐
Will the reader be interested?	☐	☐
Are the paragraphs of a reasonable length?	☐	☐
Has the client had sight of the findings?	☐	☐

Procedure

	Yes	No
Is reporting in line with the ESOMAR/MRS code?	☐	☐
Are sample sizes shown properly?	☐	☐
Is jargon used properly?	☐	☐
Is emphasis used correctly (italics, bold type)?	☐	☐
Will all reader types like the report?	☐	☐

Publication

	Yes	No
Is the inverted pyramid/Wall Street approach used?	☐	☐
Are there regular summaries?	☐	☐
Are respondent identities masked?	☐	☐
Are there a variety of visual displays?	☐	☐
Is it suitable for display on both screen and printed paper?	☐	☐

Checklist for presentations

Purpose

	Yes	No
Do you know the purpose?	☐	☐
Have you satisfied the objectives?	☐	☐
Will attendees know the purpose?	☐	☐
Is the correct message communicated?	☐	☐
Is anything missing?	☐	☐

Population

	Yes	No
Do you know the audience size?	☐	☐
Do you know who will attend?	☐	☐
Will listeners be interested?	☐	☐
Will they find results acceptable?	☐	☐

Procedure

	Yes	No
Is the style appropriate?	☐	☐
Do you know the room size? (i.e. small, medium, large)	☐	☐
Do you understand the acoustics?	☐	☐
Has the client seen the findings?	☐	☐
Do the visuals give key facts?	☐	☐
Is anything too long? (i.e. text, speeches)	☐	☐
Is jargon used appropriately?	☐	☐
Are there a variety of visual displays?	☐	☐
Is the 'mood' of the meeting positive?	☐	☐

Publication

	Yes	No
Will a handout be given before the session?	☐	☐
Has a handout been prepared?	☐	☐
Have all likely questions been predicted?	☐	☐
Have 'emergency slides' been prepared?	☐	☐
Will non-attendees receive something?	☐	☐
Was anything extra promised?	☐	☐
Was it your best presentation?	☐	☐

Five reflective research questions

1 Are the results a surprise?
2 If you were to repeat the study, would you get the same results?
3 Does the headline match the data?
4 Are you baffled?
5 What is missing?

Are the results a surprise?

If the answer is 'yes', there may be something wrong. Check how the study was set up: look at the research tools; look at the competence of the researchers; look at the objectives; look at everything. If there are surprises, there may be methodological reasons. Either way, you can say that you checked.

If you were to repeat the study, would you get the same results?

Here, we are looking at reliability. Without repeating a study, we can make a simple judgement. Ask the people who produced the data, or work with quantitative data using simple subtraction: remove respondents one by one. When do the results start to look odd?

Does the headline match the data?

Sometimes, people write what they expect their bosses want to hear. Here, you are looking to see that the points made by the commentator (in a memo, report, or whatever) are supported by the raw data, by close inspection of the detail or by asking the people involved.

Are you baffled?

If the research uses jargon, has very long sentences (45 words is long), or is grammatically complex, you should suspect that something may be wrong. Such techniques confuse the reader and may misrepresent the research.

What is missing?

Here, you need to think laterally and summon up all the knowledge you have about the topic. To evaluate the information, think about what was not collected. Why was it missed? Why was a specific question not posed to respondents? You also need to consider what was collected but not reported. Researchers need to be selective, but sometimes brevity can be misleading.

These simple questions can help your organisation to make the most of the resources available and, more importantly, they can help you as an employee. They help you to maintain your integrity and credibility.

Example of a market research brief

Market research brief

To: Research agencies chosen to submit a proposal
From: John Peterson, Market Research Manager, J.W. Farina Ltd
Date: 13 April 2015

I am pleased to invite you to propose for a major study we will be conducting. While the enclosed brief gives clear guidelines, we are open to fresh thoughts. We have provided information that we think is relevant to your response.

The study is important to Farina and we hope that it will give a valuable insight into oil purchase decision-making.

I look forward to receiving your response.

Yours sincerely

John Peterson

Background

J.W. Farina Ltd was established in Italy in 1888 and has become a market leader in the supply of Italian wines and oils to countries outside Italy. It is particularly strong in France, Austria, and the UK. For more information, please refer to our enclosed annual report, promotional brochures, and websites.

Olive oil has been used in many applications in recent years. Olive oil is protective to the digestive tract. Externally, it soothes dry skin. It helps to keep the heart healthy, and regular use is shown to prevent a build-up of cholesterol in the arteries. Olive oil can be used in salads or sauces. It stores well and will keep for up to a year in the right conditions.

Project rationale

In the UK, Farina supplies its oil to restaurants but not to the general public. This is not the case in France and Austria, where Farina has been selling to the mass market for several years. Farina is now considering the possibility of offering the same quality olive oil that it currently supplies to restaurants to the general public in the UK. The working name for this oil is 'Domestoil'. The company now wishes to commission research to help decision-making.

Objectives

We feel that it is necessary to investigate customers' attitudes towards the oils and brands in this sector. This research should aim to gain a clear understanding of customers' perceptions and experiences. Their attitudes should be measured against relevant indicators. We suspect that the name 'Domestoil' may be confused with a bleach that has a similar name, and we would like that aspect to be investigated. After numerous internal discussions, we have agreed that the overall objective is *'to examine attitudes to the use of olive oil in the home'*.

This has been broken down into the following sub-objectives:

- to examine how oils are used in domestic settings
- to gather reactions to Domestoil
- to determine promotional platforms that can be used to launch Domestoil.

Possible methodology

The agency chosen for the research must have experience with foodstuffs. Furthermore, we require both qualitative and quantitative capabilities because we expect to use both approaches.

Please consider existing olive oil users, rather than non-users, because that is our immediate target audience.

Data will be provided on all restaurants we serve directly and also on wholesalers we supply. This will include the restaurant or wholesaler name, address, and telephone number; we do not wish to supply the names of individuals to avoid any possible complications with the Data Protection Act.

If it is useful, we will also give access to our sales force. We have 50 full-time sales support staff, ten in each of our five UK regions. This number includes five regional sales managers and five deputy field managers. Their work will be extended somewhat because they will also take on domestic oils when launched. They are often very busy individuals and they travel extensively for work, so we would be pleased to set up meetings if that is helpful; many come together for monthly sales meetings at our head office. We will provide any support that may be required in contacting them.

Reporting and presentational requirements

Following this brief, a research proposal will be required. We would be pleased to have a meeting to discuss this written brief; alternatively, please use email or the telephone to clarify any issues. A brief email describing your thinking would be most welcome.

When the project is underway, we would like regular progress reports. At a suitable point during fieldwork, we would like an interim report and meeting. A formal presentation of the research findings to the board of directors will be required, supported by a final written report.

Timing

The project timeframe must respect the needs of the product launch and the availability of sales staff involved. Important signpost dates include:

15 May 2015	Proposal deadlines
1 June 2015	Go-ahead given
End October 2015	Expected presentation date
November 2015	Annual sales conference (we would like you to repeat the presentation at this)
May 2016	'Domestoil' launch expected.

Budget

There is a set budget of £20,000 for this project, which cannot be exceeded. We expect the proposal to show a breakdown of direct costs and staff time. Please separate the distinct elements of your proposal in the event that budget constraints do not allow us to commission your entire solution.

John Peterson
Market Research Manager
J.W. Farina Ltd
Tel: 0909 765543
Email: peterson@farina.oil.com

Example of a market research proposal

Project Purple

Research to prepare for Domestoil launch in the UK

A research proposal
May 2015
Prepared for: J.W. Farina Ltd
Prepared by:
Research for Success
PO Box 205
Harrow HA1 1ZU
United Kingdom

Contact: Nigel Bradley
A response to a brief from John Peterson

Contents

1 INTRODUCTION

J.W. Farina Ltd was established in Italy in 1888 and has become a market leader in the supply of Italian wines and oils to countries outside Italy. The company is particularly strong in France, Austria, and the UK. Olive oil is valuable to the human body, both inside and out. It eases dry skin and helps to keep the heart healthy. Major competitors are butter and margarines; the advantage of olive oil is that it has a shelf life of up to a year. There are many advantages that can be probed in the research.

In the UK, Farina supplies the oil to restaurants, but not to the general public. Farina is now considering the possibility of offering to the UK general public the same quality olive oil that it currently supplies to restaurants. The working name for this oil is 'Domestoil'. The company has experience of this market segment in Austria and France, which may be useful for this research.

Research for Success has been approached and a meeting took place in mid-April this year. This meeting involved a discussion of a written brief prepared by J.W. Farina Ltd. Subsequent telephone conversations clarified outstanding issues and the following proposal has been prepared.

2 OBJECTIVES

The overall objective is '*to examine attitudes to the use of olive oil in the home*'. This has been broken down into the following sub-objectives.

1. To examine how oils are used in domestic settings.
2. To identify attitudes to Domestoil and competing brands.
3. To determine promotional platforms that can be used to launch Domestoil.

We have detailed further areas beneath each objective.

1. **To examine how oils are used in domestic settings** This objective would seek to follow the oil from arrival in the home until it is consumed or disposed of in some other way. It will establish how many households keep olive oil in the home and what kinds of olive oil are usually kept. It will look at what olive oil is currently used for and, perhaps most importantly, it will attempt to identify what should constitute the target audience.
2. **To identify attitudes to Domestoil and competing brands** You will note that we have modified your original objective slightly. This objective would seek to go beyond the practical uses. It will need to introduce the product and discover which groups of people are most likely to make use of this high-quality olive oil. This should give indications of the quantities they are likely to buy and whether they would be prepared to pay more for Domestoil. It will establish what other kinds of olive oil householders are aware of. It will look at both spontaneous and prompted awareness.
3. **To determine promotional platforms that can be used to launch Domestoil** This objective is far more exploratory and will help to discover what appeals to the most promising segments for the brand. The proposed research will have three stages. The first stage will be to inspect existing sources to uncover usage figures and any useful information. The second stage will involve qualitative research to provide in-depth information on oil usage in the home, attitudes to oils, and the possibilities for the use of olive oil. This will help to design the questionnaire to be used in the third stage.

3 DESK RESEARCH

3.1 Purpose

Our search of secondary sources will be carried out to refine the objectives and provide lines of enquiry for the next stages. Specifically, the desk research phase will gather information on national usage of oils over the last 10 years. This trend data should give a useful indication about the status of the marketplace. At this point, we must also generate a list of brand names and uncover any pertinent information on competing brands that may be useful in the next parts of the research.

The desk research will attempt to establish the following.

- How many households keep olive oil in the home?
- What kinds of olive oil are usually kept?
- What is olive oil currently used for?
- What prices are charged?
- What bottle sizes are used?
- What promotions are currently used?
- Who should be the target audience?

3.2 Procedure

The search will begin internally with Farina; we would ask you to allow us to consult personnel who may have access to records. We would brief them on the requirements of the research and we would expect to hold three meetings for this purpose. The sales team mentioned in the brief may be part of this. We would expect access to (possibly indirectly) internal reports on the domestic marketplace, information on distribution to restaurants, correspondence with customers, regional buying patterns, and any complaints. These will all be indicative of the likely domestic marketplace, and will indicate strengths and weaknesses that will help in segmentation.

An external search will also take place. We will obtain and analyse existing market assessments by companies such as Mintel or Keynote. We will contact relevant trade associations. We will inspect published research (the NRS, TGI, etc.) for any indications of oil use. We intend to create a portfolio of advertising and promotional materials used by your competition. This will give materials that will allow us to explore likely promotional platforms.

4 QUALITATIVE RESEARCH

4.1 Purpose

Given the exploratory nature of some aspects of the objectives, we will provide you with detailed qualitative information. Focused research will be used to explore and understand the attitudes of potential customers towards the new brand, and subsequent quantitative research will be used to measure how widespread these attitudes are.

The qualitative phase will probe the following.

- How and where olive oil is stored in the home.
- The kinds of olive oil that are usually kept.
- Olive oils of which householders are aware.
- What olive oil is currently used for.
- Which groups of people are most likely to make use of this high-quality olive oil.
- The quantities they are likely to buy.
- Whether they would be prepared to pay more for Domestoil.
- Whether the brand name Domestoil is confused with the brand name of a household bleach.

4.2 Population and sampling

We propose four groups with the following profiles:

Group 1	Group 2	Group 3	Group 4
North ABC1	North C2DE	East C2DE	West ABC1

These will include:

- light users and heavy users
- mix of males and females.

4.3 Procedure

We will need to introduce the product and, because we have the opportunity to do so, we intend to describe, and then show, the product along with the likely competitors. One issue here is that of packaging, which could be an important variable. The skilled moderator will ensure that this does not become a distraction; we might use the packaging used in your other markets (Austria or France).

5 QUANTITATIVE RESEARCH

We propose to carry out a telephone study using a questionnaire on CATI. This has been chosen as a cost-effective way of contacting relevant respondents. Personal interviewing would go outside your budget. We have not proposed a postal study or online approach because we feel that the telephone gives us the opportunity to select people accurately and swiftly. This gives an assurance of achieving the desired number and type of respondents.

5.1 Purpose

The aim of this stage is to quantify how many households keep olive oil in the home and the kinds of olive oil that are usually kept. It will also give percentages of olive oil brand names of which householders are aware. We will provide percentages for both spontaneous and prompted awareness. By establishing classification data, we will know what type of olive oil people buy and use, and the prices they are prepared to pay. We do not think that the negative name association will need to be probed at this phase, but we can add a question on that as well.

5.2 Population and sampling

We have made the decision to carry out 200 interviews in households of different sizes. This will give a spread of responses and the opportunity to identify interesting differences. The interview will be with 'the person mainly responsible for the household shopping'.

We have set interlocking quotas as follows.

Household size	**Male**	**Female**	**Total sample**
1	25	25	50
2	25	25	50
3	25	25	50
4+	25	25	50
Total	100	100	200

5.3 Procedure

The questionnaire will be developed by Research for Success and sent to Farina for approval. It will probe the following.

- What kinds of olive oil are usually kept?
- What other kinds of olive oil are householders aware of?
- What is olive oil currently used for?
- Which groups of people are most likely to make use of high-quality olive oil?
- What quantities are they likely to buy?
- Would they be prepared to pay more for Domestoil?

Where possible, questions will be pre-coded, but for costing purposes we have assumed five open-ended questions and a maximum duration of 10 minutes. In the case of the open-ended questions, code frames will be prepared based on the response of the first 10 per cent.

The analysis will involve computer tabulations, in the form of frequency distributions. Subsequent requirements for statistical analysis will be discussed once the initial data is evaluated. We intend to weight the data to bring it in line with national figures from the latest census.

6. REPORTING

Following the qualitative section of the research, an interim presentation report will be submitted. This will be followed by a meeting with Farina to discuss the quantitative stage of the research. A PowerPoint presentation will be created for a formal presentation of all findings. This presentation will include visual displays (pie charts, word clouds, etc.). We have planned for three copies of a report which will summarise all phases of the research. Three sets of tabulations will also be provided. It is not our normal practice to provide transcripts of the interviews, but these can be provided at extra cost (available on request).

7. TIMING

The table below indicates our suggested timeframe for the project. This meets the deadlines set out in the brief. When the project is under way, we will send weekly progress reports in the form of emails at 12 noon every Friday. This allows us to summarise the week's work and gives us the opportunity of the weekend to put into place any modifications you might suggest. Please note that there are overlapping periods; these have been carefully studied to ensure that your deadlines are respected. Timing is tight; therefore if we are to conduct the research to match the deadlines you provided, we would require sign-off within the next two weeks. If your own launch date changes, our timetable can be applied to the new requirements.

Week	Activity
1–4	Desk research
4–6	Qualitative fieldwork
7	Qualitative/desk research report available
8	Questionnaire development
9	Pilot ($n = 15$)
10	Pilot debriefing
11–12	Quantitative stage ($n = 200$)
12–13	Coding and data preparation
14	Analysis
16	Presentation
19	Final report available

8. FEES

The fees quoted below are exclusive of VAT and are subject to the standard terms and conditions, which are appended. The fees are subject to the assumptions contained in these proposals and we reserve the right to make adjustments should any assumptions prove to be incorrect.

Phase	**Description**	**Fee**
Desk research	15 hours senior executive	£4250
	30 hours junior executive	
	£1000 to purchase/access relevant reports	
Qualitative research	Four focus groups	£9000
Quantitative research	200 CATI interviews	£12,000
Total fee		£25,250

9. CREDENTIALS

The project will be carried out by the Consumer Research Division of Research for Success Ltd under its director, Nigel Bradley, who has worked for many years in the market research field. He has specialized in the application of research techniques to the food industry and, before founding the company in 2005, spent many years with leading international research agencies. He has worked and studied in the UK, France, and Italy.

Chloe Green will have day-to-day responsibility for the project. Chloe is an associate director. She joined the company in 2013 after working with two other leading agencies. Since she arrived, she has managed a variety of ad hoc projects, several of them in this sector.

For further credentials, please see our web pages at www.researchforsuccess.com

Quality control

All interviewers are trained and supervised. We check 10 per cent of interviews in one of three ways: in person, by telephone, or by post. All fieldwork meets the industry standards laid down by our professional bodies, the MRS and ESOMAR.

Contract details

A copy of our contract and standard terms of business is provided in the appendix.

Example of a topic guide

Topic guide for a life insurance study

Key questions

(a) How and why people buy life insurance.

(b) Why people choose specific policies.

1. Introduction

Respondent gender, age, occupation, marital status, TEA, qualifications, family situation, children, pastimes, interests.

2. Perceptions

(a) Definition

- What does life insurance mean to you?
- Why do people take out life insurance?

(b) Companies

- Spontaneous awareness (prompted awareness later in interview): Prudential, Standard Life, Axa-Sun Life, Equitable Life, Aviva (Norwich Union, Commercial Union, and General Accident), Legal & General, Allied Dunbar, Scottish Equitable, Scottish Widows, Friends Provident.

(c) Life insurance

- Advantages and disadvantages.
- A good or bad thing.
- Honest–dishonest.
- Expensive–cheap.
- Selfish or not.
- Ir/responsible.
- For other people—who?
- Practical.
- Complicated/easy.
- Good value for money.
- For progressive people or for traditional people.
- Exciting/boring.
- For in/secure people.

(d) Products

- Spontaneous awareness of any brand names.
- Spontaneous awareness of product types, and what they mean.
- Whole of life vs term assurance vs endowment mortgage vs unit-linked endowment vs with-profits endowment vs personal pension plans (PPPs).
- If no answer, ask for words/vocabulary used, and probe each to build up/recall the respondent's knowledge.

(e) Source of knowledge

- Where has this knowledge come from? (*Probe*: experience, friends, family, employer, agent, broker, IFA, insurance company, TV, radio, newspapers, financial press, trade association?)

3. Respondent policy

(a) Characteristics

- Company, product type, brand?
- When started/finished.
- Joint with partner?
- How much coverage?
- Did you pay lump sum or make regular payments?

(b) Decision

- Why did you take out this insurance? (*Probe*: change in family, job, outlook, etc.)
- Did you bother searching? How?
- How did you evaluate different products?
- Why did you choose a particular provider? (*Influences*: experience, family, friends, salesperson, providers of existing insurance (car/house), news articles, direct mail, bank.)
- Was it part of/tied to another package (e.g. essential part of loan/mortgage/ partnership loan)?

(c) Satisfaction

- Are you pleased with it?
- Who will benefit?
- Advantages/disadvantages
- Are you satisfied that the coverage you have purchased is adequate?
- How do you judge whether you have made the right decision (word of mouth, financial press, etc.)? Or is it of no concern?
- Do you feel that maybe you could have searched a little bit more?

(d) Decision process

- Attempt to draw decision flowchart:
  - buy phases (need, specification, search, evaluation, decision, contact, contract, go/no-go);
  - include involvement of people/resources at each stage.

(e) Influences

- Have you influenced others to take/not to take out life insurance?
- Would you say that life insurance:
  - is a low or high priority for you?
  - is confusing or easy to understand?
  - requires a lot of trust in the providers?

4. Closing

- Can we please summarise the key areas?
- Is there anything not covered?
- Thank you for your time and participation.

Example of operational instructions

Helicopter Ambulance Project

(This supports the questionnaire at the end of Chapter 6.)

Memo

To: Sue Jacobs, Postal Survey Administration Dept, Research for Success

From: Nigel Bradley, Research Director, Research for Success

Re: Postal Questionnaire Operational Guidelines

The following operational guidelines are designed to explain the study and ensure efficient mailing and preparation of questionnaires for analysis. The document is to be used by personnel at Research for Success.

Background

The East Anglian Air Ambulance (EAAA) is a 365 days a year life-saving charity that serves Bedfordshire, Cambridgeshire, Norfolk, and Suffolk. It depends on fund-raising and contributions to keep two helicopters flying and provide advanced medical equipment. They are reviewing their website and Research for Success is helping.

Objectives

The study will answer the following objectives:

1. To establish if supporters have access to a computer and the internet.
2. To establish if supporters know of the EAAA website and the information it contains.
3. To identify why the supporters access the EAAA site and the frequency.
4. To identify how more supporters can be encouraged to access the website.
5. To establish supporter opinion of the website.
6. To identify how the EAAA website compares with the competition.

Selection process

The EAAA will supply Research for Success with a database of over 20,000 of their supporters. Our sampling technique will be used to gain representation of supporters from all over East Anglia. The database is divided by the four counties of interest; it identifies the type of supporter segment along with postal address, postcode, name, and title (Mr, Mrs, etc.).

The first step is to ensure that these fields are complete. If there are any duplicates, they should be identified and removed from the database; there may be a problem if the named person appears in more than one of the supporter segments. Please analyse the list carefully before extracting the sample for the survey and if necessary we will adjust the instructions below. The database must be 'cleaned' as far as possible, since we do not want to waste money or respondent time unnecessarily.

After cleaning the database we will extract 1200 addresses with the aim of receiving completed questionnaires from at least 400; this assumes a 33 per cent response rate. We would like to exceed 50 per cent, and therefore reminders will be sent. We have decided on stratified random sampling; systematic sampling will take place within these strata. The addresses within each cell should be selected randomly as follows: you will select '1 in *n*' (which is a systematic random sample).

For example, there are 1345 volunteers in the Bedfordshire cell, and we require 75 questionnaires to be mailed. Dividing 1345 by 75 gives 17.93. This is nearly 18, so choose a number at random between 1 and 18 and assign it to the first respondent, count 17 more people and choose the 18th, the next 18, and so on, until 75 are made available. There are 2437 volunteers in the Cambridgeshire cell, and we require 75 questionnaires to be mailed. Dividing 2437 divided by 75 gives 32.49. This is near to 32, so choose a number at random between 1 and 32 and assign it to the first respondent, count 32 more people and choose the 32nd, the next 32, and so on, until 75 are made available.

Sampling frame

Supporter type	Norfolk	Suffolk	Cambridgeshire	Bedfordshire	Total
Time volunteer	476	609	2437	1345	4867
Occasional donations	3098	3023	2450	3750	12,321
Corporate sponsor	277	207	312	104	900
Lottery member	375	488	897	1340	3100
Total	4226	4327	6096	6539	21,188

Extracted sample

Supporter type	Norfolk	Suffolk	Cambridgeshire	Bedfordshire	Total
Time volunteer	75	75	75	75	300
Occasional donations	75	75	75	75	300
Corporate sponsor	75	75	75	75	300
Lottery member	75	75	75	75	300
Total	300	300	300	300	1200

Expected end sample

Supporter type	Norfolk	Suffolk	Cambridgeshire	Bedfordshire	Total
Time volunteer	25	25	25	25	100
Occasional donations	25	25	25	25	100
Corporate sponsor	25	25	25	25	100
Lottery member	25	25	25	25	100
Total	100	100	100	100	400

The number of expected responders identified in each segment is not proportional to the total number of supporters in that segment. For example, most supporters are based in Bedfordshire. Also bear in mind that we do not know the extent of overlap. Such differences and issues will be corrected at the analysis stage, when we will weight and gross data to our estimated total numbers for the total supporter population in the four counties. Population figures are being calculated by researchers.

Preparing for mailing

Reminders will be sent, and so all questionnaires, cover letters, and envelopes will carry a serial number. This serial number will be created as follows.

Extracted sample

Supporter type	Norfolk	Suffolk	Cambridgeshire	Bedfordshire
Time volunteer	NT01–NT75	ST01–ST75	CT01–CT75	BT01–BT75
Occasional donations	ND01–ND75	SD01–SD75	ND01–ND75	ND01–ND75
Corporate sponsor	NC01–NC75	SC01–SC75	NC01–NC75	NC01–NC75
Lottery member	NL01–NL75	SL01–SL75	NL01–NL75	NL01–NL75

The greater the response rates, the better the quality of results. Therefore, please follow these guidelines.

Cover letter

The cover letter must contain the name of the person in the database. It is being sent by us on behalf of our client, Viv Winders, and her name is at the bottom of the letter. All letters must carry a good reproduction of her signature (we know that no signature loses cooperation). If a reminder letter is sent, again this must include a signature and a replacement questionnaire.

Postage

A pre-paid addressed envelope will accompany the questionnaire. The pre-paid return envelope will have a real postage stamp, rather than a freepost or pre-paid printed logo. We know that real stamps help cooperation levels, as respondents are reluctant to throw money in the bin (and a postage stamp is regarded as 'near-money'). The stamp should be first-class.

Structure and colour

The structure of the questionnaire is intended to be easy to follow and in a logical order. It is deliberately friendly, using short sentences. It relies on the 'feel-good factor' of helping a charity. It has been tested on several respondents as part of a pilot.

The questionnaire is intended to be eye-catching—thus the reason for the logo and helicopter photo. It will be instantly recognizable as being a communication from the EAAA. The colour should be a very light yellow; we know that this colour makes the questionnaire obvious in a pile of post that is mostly white.

The letter and questionnaire must contain the name of the person in the database. Use a plain white envelope for mail out and return. The outgoing letter should not use the company franking machine; it should have a real postage stamp. The respondent's name and address should be printed directly onto the envelope front, along with their unique serial number. On the rear of the envelope should be the following words.

In case of non-delivery please return unopened to:

Research for Success, PO Box 205, HARROW HA1 1ZU

This allows us to monitor the number of 'invalid' addresses.

On receipt, please monitor and provide a daily progress report as follows:

Postal Dept Analysis

Serial number	**Date original sent**	**Date reminder 1 sent**	**Date reminder 2 sent**	**Date qre returned**	**Outcome: enter code**
NT01					
NT02					
Etc.					

Outcome codes: REF, refused; INV, invalid address (returned by post office); NAA, not at address; REP, requested results report; COM, completed questionnaire received; INELIG, not a supporter.

Daily progress report content: each cell should contain the number of completed questionnaires received, and each final column and row should contain a percentage

Supporter type	**Norfolk**	**Suffolk**	**Cambs**	**Beds**	**Total**	**% response**
Time volunteer	0/75	0/75	0/75	0/75	0/300	0
Occasional donations	0/75	0/75	0/75	0/75	0/300	0
Corporate sponsor	0/75	0/75	0/75	0/75	0/300	0
Lottery member	0/75	0/75	0/75	0/75	0/300	0
Total	0/300	0/300	0/300	0/300	0/1200	0
% response	0	0	0	0	0	0

Abbreviations

ABC	Audit Bureau of Circulations (UK)
ACORN	A Classification of Residential Neighbourhoods
AMA	American Marketing Association (USA)
AMSO	Association of Market Research Survey Organisations
ARS	Audience response systems
ASP	Active Server Page
ASR	automated speech recognition
CAMI	computer-assisted mobile interviewing
CAPI	computer-assisted personal interviewing
CASI	computer-assisted self-completion interviewing
CASOC	Computer-Aided Standard Occupational Classification
CATI	computer-assisted telephone interviewing
CAWI	computer-assisted web interviewing
CGM	consumer-generated media
CIM	Chartered Institute of Marketing (UK)
CRM	cause-related marketing or customer relationship marketing
CTR	clickthrough rate
DAA	Digital Analytics Association
DMU	decision-making unit
DOB	date of birth
DOI	day of interview
EPOS	electronic point of sale or electronic processing of sales
GHQ	General Health Questionnaire
HOH	head of household
HTML	hypertext markup language
http	hypertext transfer protocol
ICT	information and communication technology
ISCO	International Standard Classification of Occupations
IT	information technology
KPI	key performance indicators
MDSS	marketing decision support system
MIS	management information system
MKIS	marketing information system
MMRA	Mobile Marketing Research Association

MMS	Multimedia Messaging Service
MOI	month of interview
MROC	Market Research Online Community
MRS	Market Research Society (UK)
NA	not applicable
NACE	Nomenclature statistique des activités économiques dans la Communauté Européenne (Statistical Classification of Economic Activities in the European Community)
NRS	National Readership Survey
ONS	Office for National Statistics
PLC	product lifecycle
POD	point of display
POP	point of purchase
POS	point of sale
RGSC	Registrar General's Social Classification
SEG	socioeconomic group
SIC	Standard Industrial Classification
SMA	Social Media Analysis
SMS	short message service
SOC	Standard Occupational Classification
TBA	to be agreed
TEA	terminal education age
TGI	Target Group Index
TQM	total quality management
U&A	usage and attitude study
URL	uniform (or universal) resource locator
USP	unique selling proposition
VOC	Voice of Customer
WAP	web application protocol or wireless application protocol
WiFi	wireless fidelity
WML	wireless markup language
WWW	World Wide Web
XML	extensible markup language

Glossary of marketing research terms

acquiescence response bias A respondent agrees rather than disagrees with a proposition that is posed in the research. This may be done to please the researcher or to conclude the research quickly and it may mask the true answer.

ad hoc research Studies that are designed specifically for a client's need, i.e. customised or bespoke.

aggregator An amalgamation of a specific set of data files, e.g. Google uses automated software to trawl 4500 news sources and organises the results at Google News. This can then be read.

aided recall The use of stimulus material to assist the memory to recall details, usually of brands.

alternative hypothesis A carefully constructed proposition that is likely to be accepted.

attitude The definition of attitude is the subject of much debate by psychologists. It is generally accepted to describe the way in which a person judges an object, situation, concept, company, product, or other item (cf. *belief* and *opinion*).

automated speech recognition (ASR) A method of recording data, by capturing the human voice in a digital form, and converting it to another medium such as the written word.

belief An acceptance of a suggestion, concept, explanation, or way of thinking. Beliefs generally have an emotional component (cf. *attitude* and *opinion*).

benchmarking Comparing the performance of products or services.

bracketing Putting aside (in 'brackets') the knowledge that a researcher may have of a problem, in order to probe for other information.

brand equity The measured value of a brand which often embraces the financial value to shareholders but also customer attitude, belief, and perception.

causality Investigations into the reason, or cause, of certain behaviour or observed effects.

central location test See *hall test*, *clinic*, and *mall intercept surveys*.

cheater questions Questions used to detect interviewers who are not following the required procedures.

cinema tests See *theatre tests*.

classification questions Questions identifying demographics or 'classifiers' needed for analysis. These include age, sex, social grade, family size, income, and specifics to the topic under study. Usually asked at the end of an interview.

client surreptitious sampling Using a list of customers who have not agreed to their names being used for research purposes.

clinic A variation of the *hall test*. A quantitative approach where respondents are taken to a location to view product concepts or prototypes; they are observed and interviewed. The clinic is often associated with cars (the 'car clinic'), but the idea has been extended to other vehicles and products.

closed questions Questions for which answers are pre-coded. These answers may be disclosed to informants or may not.

comments cards Small cards distributed by service organisations to monitor satisfaction.

computer-assisted mobile phone interviewing (CAMI) A type of interviewing that may be interviewer-assisted, and therefore *CATI*, or self-completion, therefore *CASI*. In the

CASI mode, it may be by SMS, MMS, or WAP. In SMS, the respondent is sent a text message with questions to be answered by text. The questions are visible to the respondent on the handset and answers are input using the telephone keys. The WAP mode is similar to *CAWI*.

computer-assisted personal interviewing (CAPI) A respondent is interviewed face-to-face and questions are asked. The questions are read from a screen and answers are input using a keyboard.

computer-assisted self-completion interviewing (CASI) A respondent answers a questionnaire that is visible on a computer screen or other medium. The answers are recorded by a keyboard, touch screen, or even automatic speech recognition methods. No interviewer is involved.

computer-assisted telephone interviewing (CATI) Questions are asked of a respondent over the telephone. The questions are read from a screen and answers are input by an interviewer using a keyboard.

computer-assisted web interviewing (CAWI) A variation of *CASI*, which uses the Internet to deliver the questionnaire. Respondents will answer using a keyboard, a mouse, or voice recognition software.

concept tests An early stage of new product or new service development. An idea or concept is communicated to potential users or customers.

consumer-generated media (CGM) Information left by individuals online; for example, blogs or personal websites. These can be used in marketing research.

copy tests A study that evaluates the effectiveness of an advertisement, slogan, or other form of communication.

cover letters and cover emails A form of introduction and way to persuade respondents to cooperate.

crowdsourcing The extraction and use of information or resources from a large number of undefined people, effectively this is outsourcing as a result of an open call.

dashboard A single computer screen containing visual displays of performance information, usually from several sources, a type of portal.

database A collection of data held on individuals or organisations that is structured in such a way that data can be reorganised to provide meaningful information.

data dredging An approach used to analyse data when hypotheses have not been created. Each variable is cross-analysed against other variables in the study. The researcher looks for patterns.

data mart A collection of subject areas based on the needs of a given department.

data mining The procedure that selects and manipulates large amounts of data to uncover previously unknown relationships and patterns.

data warehouse An extremely large database with a store of transactional data that allows the researcher to make useful analyses.

decision-making unit (DMU) The group of people involved in a buying decision process.

demographics The classification information collected during a survey. Standard demographics include age, sex, and social grade. Non-standard demographics are common to all studies, but less used, and may include TEA, nationality, and income. Other demographics are specific to the topic under study, e.g. lapsed users, number of years subscribing. Demographics are the first process in segmenting the market.

descriptive research Studies that portray the market situation, attitudes, beliefs, or opinions. Such studies aim to describe rather than to explain causes.

diary An autobiographical record, which is usually intended for the writer's own reference. In marketing, it can be used in both qualitative and quantitative research. It is a unique account of personal reflection.

discussion guide See *topic guide*.

dogfooding Testing new products by inviting employees to use them.

drop-and-collect Method of distributing questionnaires for self-completion then collection at a later time.

dugging Database building under the guise of research.

Earned Media This is media space that is not owned by an advertiser, nor can promotional space be bought. Media content is produced by third parties but the advertiser can have an influence by providing information and appropriate responses to messages. Therefore the reputation can be 'earned'. Offline this includes published letters and word of mouth; online it includes consumer blogs and social networks. Advertising space is not purchased but it can be influenced.

electronic point (or processing) of sale (EPOS) The use of technology, particularly the bar-code, to allow swift transactions to take place in retail outlets. The records are a powerful form of internal secondary data. In research terms, this is mechanical observation.

ethnography An extreme form of participant observation whereby the researcher spends time with the subjects who are under investigation.

exclusion screener A question to determine if the informant, or their family or friends, work in occupations that risk news of the project reaching competitors or to avoid atypical answers.

experimentation Conditions or procedures that are arranged in a deliberate way. This manipulation of variables allows a hypothesis to be tested. There are many experimental designs.

exploratory research Studies that attempt to provide information where very little is available. This preliminary data collection can help to define a research objective and to understand the problem in hand.

focus group The group comprises several people who have been invited to a location. They are asked to focus their attention on a specific issue and then to articulate their opinions, attitudes, and beliefs.

forecasting Estimating a future set of conditions. Typically in marketing, this is a forecast on demand, based on the information available. Many techniques can be used in forecasting.

form A structured document, often on paper, but can also be onscreen. The form has a set of words that will instruct or direct the user to consider specific issues. The most common types are known as questionnaires and observation records.

FRAC profiles Profiles of the frequency of use, the recency of use, the amount of use, and the category of product being used.

frugging Fund-raising under the guise of research.

gatekeepers In a decision-making unit, these are the people who control the dissemination of information to other people in the unit.

Gallup poll Polls originally named after G.H. Gallup, a pioneer in political opinion research. The term has entered everyday language to mean a questionnaire administered across a national sample.

geodemographics Demographic information (sex, age, etc.) cross-analysed by geographic location (postcode, province, region, etc.), popularised as computer analyses of census data became commercially available. In the UK, the most well-known geodemographic classifications are ACORN, Pinpoint, Mosaic, and super profiles.

grid Several questions for one respondent, which are similar, but which will result in different answers, are put together into a grid (or battery).

hall tests Hall tests typically test packaging, new products, and advertising in a quantitative way. Respondents are recruited and taken to a specified location, usually a church hall, village hall, or hotel. Materials are presented to respondents and a questionnaire is administered.

incentive A device used to encourage respondents to cooperate with the researcher. Examples are money, entry to a prize draw, a charity donation, or a gift (summary of results, pen, food, or drink).

Infographic A visual representation of knowledge, identifiable for the numerous messages that are communicated by both words and pictures, often called a pictogram.

insight management Proactive management of knowledge rather than reaction to events; insight managers are constantly 'data-mining'.

instrument A research instrument is something used to collect data. It may be a tangible item, such as a photographic camera, or recording device, or a document, such as a questionnaire or topic guide. The term also covers supporting materials such as fieldwork instructions, showcards, etc.

instrumentation effect The measuring device (questionnaire, camera, or other instrument) may have an effect on the respondent's response; this is due to learning. This may be detected if we repeat the procedure and there is a difference in outcome.

integrity questions Sometimes known as cheater or sleeper questions. These check consistency of both respondent and fieldworker.

interview schedule See *topic guide*.

interviewer instructions (or manual) A set of guidelines for the fieldworker with instructions on how to select respondents and how to conduct the interviewing.

JavaScript tags A few lines of code added to each web page. When a page loads, these tags cause data to be sent to a data collection server. An important tool in web analytics.

key performance indicators (KPIs) Measurements that allow managers to assess whether objectives will be met. They are usually quantifiable and will vary from organisation to organisation.

Likert scale A rating scale used to measure the strength of agreement towards one or more clearly worded statements.

logfile A record of the download activity of a specific set of web pages. Logfile analysers are used to make sense of the data. Useful to create online measures for marketing.

mall intercept surveys The North American name for the *hall test*. These are concentrated in purpose-built shopping centres. Respondents are recruited and taken to a facility within the mall. Materials are presented to respondents and a questionnaire is administered.

market research Research that looks at specific marketplaces; it describes users in those markets and how much product they may use—an examination of *marketing metrics*. Term often used interchangeably with *marketing research*.

market research agencies Agencies offering three types of information service. These services are industrial, trade, and consumer.

market share The amount of the market that can be attributed to each supplier. Usually expressed as a percentage.

market size The potential for a product or service expressed by a quantitative measure. This may be the number of users, the number of buyers, the monetary value, etc.

marketing *'The management process responsible for identifying, anticipating and satisfying customer requirements profitably'* (Chartered Institute of Marketing).

marketing decision support system (MDSS) A system that gives users reports that are appropriate, and relevant, to their specific needs.

marketing information system (MKIS) A set of procedures that have been linked to deliver information from different sources to decision-makers.

marketing metric A measurement taken from the marketplace that may be indicative of financial performance; for example, market share and perceived product quality.

marketing research Inquiry into the topic of marketing; it looks at the different aspects that must be considered when satisfying requirements. It is the process of providing information to assist in marketing decisions. Term often used interchangeably with *market research*.

masking A way to disguise comments or images from computer users so that their identity can be protected in a research context.

media Print (newspapers, periodicals); broadcast (radio, television); outdoor (posters, moving media, signage).

mere measurement effect The simple act of taking a measure of attitudes creates an attitude or changes existing attitudes.

metaphor A projective technique.

metrics Measurements that indicate the status of different activities.

multiclient studies Studies that are paid for by two or more clients. Also known as *syndicated studies*.

mystery shopping Researchers assume the role of a potential or actual customer. Certain aspects of the process are observed and noted by the researcher.

network pictures Visual maps of DMU members and their role in business-to-business buying.

non-domestic markets Also known as 'industrial markets' and 'business-to-business markets'.

non-sampling error An error due to the way observations are made.

null hypothesis A proposition that is the least likely, so it is usually intended to be rejected.

observation A method of primary data collection that involves seeing, tracking, or sensing behaviour or actions in some way.

observation forms A device with which to make a record of observations. It is similar to the self-completion questionnaire, but designed to be answered by a researcher rather than a respondent.

omnibus A general-purpose survey vehicle, which covers a wide range of survey topics, usually shared by many clients.

opendata Data that can be republished without fear of copyright restrictions.

open-ended questions Questions for which the researcher may not be able to anticipate the type of response that will be received, from an informant. Respondents reply using their own words.

opinion A point of view that can be expressed. An opinion is based on some facts or information rather than emotions (cf. *beliefs*) and has a more narrow definition than an attitude.

opinion poll A survey of opinions, usually taking the form of a quantitative sample survey using a structured questionnaire.

order effect When respondents answer with early statements on any list. Also known as *position bias*.

Osgood scale See *semantic differential scale*.

owned media. This is media space that is in the full control and ownership of the advertiser. Offline this includes trucks, premises signage; online it includes websites and corporate blogs. Promotional communication takes place but advertising space is not purchased.

paid (or bought) media. This is traditional and online advertising space that can be purchased.

panel The panel is a set of individuals who are questioned or observed or who report over a period of time. Any changes can therefore be identified and if necessary, investigated.

personification A projective technique.

perception A process that a person uses to understand the environment. Perception depends on such factors as attention, motivation, prior knowledge, etc.

pictured aspirations technique (PAT) Several photographs are shown to the informant, and these are sorted to communicate aspirations.

placement tests Tests where respondents are asked to try out products in the normal way in which the product would be used, usually in private, mostly at home.

POEM paid, owned, earned media. See individual entries.

portal A workspace, often a web page, that offers the user a starting point to analyse, organise, and share information. The *dashboard* is a type of portal.

position bias When respondents answer with early statements on any list. Also known as order effect.

primary data Information that is collected for a specific purpose. The same information has not been available before.

priming effect When respondents are led to react in a certain way, this may be a result of introducing them to a certain environment or exposing them to stimuli that naturally lead them to a given reaction.

probing A technique used to clarify unclear or incomplete answers. Probing attempts to motivate the informant to communicate more information without introducing bias into the questions or answers. Common probes are: a repeated question, a pause to motivate the respondent to speak, a repeat of the respondent's answer or last word, standard (neutral) probe questions.

projective techniques Projective techniques enable the subject (informant or respondent) to communicate things to the researcher. For this reason, they are sometimes known as 'enabling' techniques. They offer an alternative to direct questions, and allow us to open the respondent's mind to any topic in a very unique way.

prompts Stimulus material used to assist respondents when being interviewed. They may be words, photos, pictures, jingles, sounds, etc. They will help to 'prompt' recall.

protocol analysis A projective technique.

qualitative research Studies that do not aim to quantify markets in any way. They aim to describe the depth and breadth of attitude, belief, or opinion. Typical tools are focus groups, depth interviews, and observation.

quantitative research Studies designed to describe the quantity of some feature of a marketplace. That quantity may describe market size and market share. Typical tools are structured questionnaires and mechanical measuring devices.

quota sampling A method of non-probability sampling whereby a certain number of informants are required that meet certain criteria. Quotas may be interlocking or non-interlocking.

quota sheet A document issued to interviewers in order to keep a record of sampling progress and to assist in identifying appropriate respondents to complete the assignment.

reach The number (or percentage) of individuals who are exposed to a campaign.

recruitment questionnaire A few essential questions to ensure that the correct person is recruited.

refusal Occurs when a respondent does not cooperate in the research.

response rate The number of complete responses obtained compared with the number of eligible individuals. The response rate is always expressed as a percentage.

return envelope Included with postal questionnaires to increase response rates.

river sampling Online technique that avoids using databases by intercepting users by popups, banners, and other devices. Also known as real-time sampling.

rotation A method used either to measure or to diminish the effect of *order bias*.

sample A number of people selected from a population for questioning or study. The data collected are expected to assist understanding of the entire population.

sampling The process of selecting parts from a defined population in order to examine these parts, usually with the aim of making judgements about the parts of the population that have not been investigated.

sampling error The difference between the sample value and the true value in the population.

sampling frame The basis by which respondents are selected; respondents are sampled from a frame. It can be a tangible list, such as a phone directory, or it might be a set of instructions.

satisficing Occurs when a 'sufficient' answer is given, although a better one may have been available.

scale A device used on questionnaires that measures attitudes. The scale commonly uses words or numbers. There are hundreds, among which are the *Likert scale* and the *semantic differential scale*.

schedule A set of instructions, written for the researcher. A schedule is designed to give an interview or a research session some direction and structure.

screener questions A mechanism to select the correct informant. All instruments should have some form of filtering or screening at the start. This avoids interviewing respondents who are not needed.

search agents These allow users to search for information taking the user's specific needs into account; an intelligent search engine.

search engines Provide users with a way of locating and retrieving information from documents located on the Internet. Search engines can search all media whether text, sound, or images.

secondary data Information that has been collected previously, probably for a specific purpose. Secondary data may be internal or external to the organisation.

segmentation The process of subdividing a market into several groups of people or users or other group. This subdivision may be done on the basis of demographics, lifestyle, geography, or other variables that are shared and are appropriate to the product area in question.

semantic differential scale A scale designed to measure the 'semantic space' of interpersonal experience. Respondents do not make an evaluation using numbers; they identify the 'position' of their answer on a line, or space between two descriptions.

semiotics Study of communication through careful analysis of signs.

significance testing Sampling does not collect findings from all members of a population; significance tests are a way to show how 'accurate' those results may be.

sleeper questions Questions used to determine whether a respondent is giving correct answers.

social class Divisions of society. Traditionally, these are lower class, middle class, and upper class; there are many related classifications such as SEG, SEC, and *social grade*.

social grade Six-category classification system used in the UK; appears as A, B, C1, C2, D, E.

social mèdia monitoring The use of techniques used to observe and register consumer-generated comments, questions, and conversations, usually concerning a specific brand or organisation or campaign. This is output *about* companies, rather than output *by* companies.

spreadsheet A worksheet with cells that can be filled with numbers to perform simple calculations.

suggestion cards Small cards distributed by service organisations to monitor satisfaction.

sugging Selling under the guise of research.

survey Another word for the term 'study'; it may be a census survey, a sample survey, or a desk research survey. Many surveys use questionnaires, so the term is sometimes used, incorrectly, instead of the word 'questionnaire'.

syndicated studies Syndicated studies are financially supported by two or more companies. These companies have a common interest in the subject area or in the target market. Also known as *multiclient studies*.

Target Group Index (TGI) A study conducted by BMRB in the UK. This study collects information on the profiles of people who use (or do not use) a vast number of products.

telescoping effect Involves remembering an event as occurring more recently than it actually did.

tertiary data Information that has been collected before and has been classified in some way. Examples of tertiary data are index pages in books, abstracts, citations, search engine results.

test marketing A procedure whereby a new product is evaluated in a real or simulated market setting.

theatre tests A cinema is hired and a film or television programme is shown, along with advertisements. Any (or all) of these three may be tested using a self-completion questionnaire.

topic guide A short document used to agree the areas for discussion containing carefully chosen areas in qualitative research. Also known as a discussion guide or an *interview schedule*.

total quality management (TQM) A management idea that tries to ensure employees are all aware of the need for high quality.

transcripts A written record of spoken words, utterances, and other events during fieldwork.

trellis chart Several visual displays with similar axes placed together for easy comparison.

triangulation The process of examining a problem from three or more viewpoints.

usage and attitude studies (U&A studies) Quantitative method of examining the amount of product used and attitudes towards it and competing brands. Commonly found in the FMCG sector.

van test A variation of the *hall test*. A caravan or motorised caravan is parked in a suitable area and respondents are recruited, then invited inside the 'mobile' facility to view products and answer questions.

verbatim A term used to describe the answers to open-ended questions that are captured, word for word, from a respondent.

vox pop Small sound or vision clips of an individual making a specific point. The vox pop gives a qualitative indication of public opinion.

Wall Street approach A summary of research results is reported immediately; the details follow. This allows a presentation to end at any point.

web analytics The capture and processing of data from software and hardware that produces performance indications (e-metrics). This is output *by* companies, rather than output *about* companies.

word cloud Visual representations of the vocabulary used, with greater prominence given to important content.

Index

C

D

Q